Rome:
The Augustan Age

Rome

The Augustan Age

A Source Book

Part 1 edited by
KITTY CHISHOLM and JOHN FERGUSON

Part 2 edited by
KITTY CHISHOLM

Oxford University Press
in association with
The Open University Press
1981

Oxford University Press, Walton Street, Oxford OX2 6DP

London Glasgow New York Toronto
Delhi Bombay Calcutta Madras Karachi
Kuala Lumpur Singapore Hong Kong Tokyo
Nairobi Dar es Salaam Cape Town
Melbourne Auckland
and associate companies in
Beirut Berlin Ibadan Mexico City

Published in the United States by
Oxford University Press, New York

British Library Cataloguing in Publication Data

Rome, the Augustan age.
    1. Rome – History – Augustus, 30 B.C.-14 A.D.
    I. Chisholm, Kitty   II. Ferguson, John, 1921-
937'.07   DG231
    ISBN 0-19-872108-0
    ISBN 0-19-872109-9 Pbk

Set by Hope Services, Abingdon
and printed in Great Britain
by Richard Clay Ltd., Bungay

PREFACE

This anthology has been compiled as a source book for an Open University course, A293 Rome: The Augustan Age. The texts, chosen from a wide range of literary and epigraphic sources, cover Roman politics, administration, art, religion, social history, literature, and philosophy. We have arranged the material in two parts, each fulfilling a different purpose. Part 1 (§§ A–F) contains the sources necessary for a detailed study in depth of Augustus from his rise to power in 44 BC to his death in AD 14. These texts have been carefully chosen to provide primary evidence for a comprehensive study of this whole period from a variety of aspects, as well as for the detailed study of particular topics. The material in Part 2 (§§ G–O) is arranged thematically and includes texts set for detailed study in the course. Part 2 provides the primary sources for the study of the intellectual and social context of the Age of Augustus, the development of the Principate under his successors, and the development of Rome as a city. We have also included sources for case studies of four Roman provinces. The themes in Part 2, raised and partly covered by material in Part 1, extend well beyond the chronological period 44 BC–AD 14. The A293 Course Team has been closely involved in the choice of passages, especially for Part 2. We hope that this collection will also fill a gap for those students, beyond the Open University, who are studying Roman history and civilization without extensive knowledge of Latin and Greek.

Many passages have been translated especially for this anthology. We have also used out-of-copyright translations in some cases where more modern ones exist, in order to limit the cost. We are indebted to those who have published selective collections of sources for Roman history and have drawn gratefully from: V. Ehrenberg and A. H. M. Jones *Documents Illustrating the Reigns of Augustus and Tiberius* (Oxford 1970); N. Lewis and M. Reinhold *Roman Civilization* volumes 1 and 2 (Columbia University Press 1951, 1955); A. H. M. Jones *A History of Rome through the Fifth Century* volume 2 (Walker & Company, Inc. 1969 and Macmillan 1970); The publications of the London Association of Classical Teachers (LACTOR); N. Lewis *The Roman Principate* (Hakkert 1974); R. K. Sherk *Roman Documents from the Greek East* (Johns Hopkins 1969); H. Dessau *Inscriptiones Latinae Selectae* (3 volumes Berlin 1892–1916) and others.

The introductions are limited to setting passages in their context and to brief explanations of obscure or difficult points. We have tried to provide cross-references and a limited bibliography to help those students who wish to follow up a particular passage or theme. We hope the sources will speak for themselves, in all their variety, and that both students and the general reader may gain a first-hand knowledge of Augustan Rome.

Our thanks are due to the Arts Faculty of the Open University for their help in the preparation of this book, and to the Publishing Division for their advice and patience. We are especially grateful to those members of the A293 Course Team who helped with the introductory material and offered helpful comments: Beryl Bowen, Colin Cunningham, Chris Emlyn-Jones (Course Team Chairman), Lorna Hardwick (Course Team Chairman, Planning Stage), Tony Lentin, Jennifer Potter, Peter Salway, E. Mary Smallwood, Colin Wells and Edith Wightman. Our particular thanks to John Carter (Course Assessor) and Joyce Reynolds for their help with translations. For the typing and retyping of individual passages and the preparation of the typescript, we owe thanks to Tara Reddy, Wendy Clarke, and Gillian Turner.

K. CHISHOLM AND J. FERGUSON

CONTENTS

List of Plates		xxi
Acknowledgements		xxii
Abbreviations		xxiv

PART 1

A   Documentary   3

A 1	*Res Gestae*	3
A 2	The *Fasti*	11
A 3	The Calendars	16

B   Politics and power   21

B 1	The Octavians	22
B 2	Caesar's will	23
B 3	A brief outline of Augustus' life	23
B 4	Funds for Octavian	24
B 5	Conflict with Antony	25
B 6	Cicero and Octavian	26
B 7	Cicero praises Octavian	29
B 8	Octavian's position legitimized	29
B 9	Antony on Octavian	30
B10	Private armies	31
B11	Octavian defers to the Senate	32
B12	A *coup d'état*	32
B13	The triumvirate	33
B14	The proscription edict	35
B15	The death of Cicero	36
B16	Octavian's brutality	37
B17	Cleopatra and Antony	39
B18	Reconciliation of Octavian and Antony	40
B19	Soldiers' rewards	41
B20	Riots in Rome	43
B21	Pact of Tarentum	44

CONTENTS

B22	Octavian returns from war	45
B23	The Donations of Alexandria	46
B24	Antony delays war	47
B25	Actium	48
B26	The spoils of victory	50
B27	Peace	50
B28	Dio's account of the settlement of 27 BC	52
B29	Augustus' intentions	56
B30	The settlement of 23 BC	56
B31	Census and *Lectio*	56
B32	Law on Vespasian's *imperium*	58
B33	Dio's account of events after 23 BC	59
B34	Further grants of power in 19 BC	61
B35	An analysis of Augustus' rule	62
B36	Pliny on Augustus	68
B37	Philo on Augustus	69
B38	Augustus' later reputation	70
B39	*Lassa crudelitas*	71
B40	Augustus' eyes	73
B41	Anecdotes	73
B42	Augustus and Timagenes	76
B43	Augustus and Vedius Pollio	77
B44	Augustus joins a private *consilium*	77
B45	Expressions of affection and regard for Augustus	78
B46	Conspiracies against Augustus	79
B47	Freedom of speech	80
B48	Augustus' personality	81
B49	Literary pursuits	82
B50	Virgil *Eclogues* 1	83
B51	A plea for Augustus' return	86
B52	Ovid flatters Augustus	88
B53	Death of Augustus	89
B54	Honours granted to Augustus after his death	91
B55	The family and the succession	92
B56	Augustus' will	94
B57	Agrippa	94
B58	Livia	94
B59	The death of Drusus	96

B60	Livia and her grandchildren	97
B61	The Julias	97
B62	The *Consolation* to Livia	99
B63	Resolution on the coming of age of Gaius Caesar	100
B64	Gaius given command in the East	100
B65	Resolutions of the town council of Pisa on the deaths of Augustus' grandsons	101
B66	Augustus plans to recall Postumus	104
B67	Letters to Tiberius	104
B68	Tiberius victorious	105
B69	Germanicus	105

C Administration 107

C 1	The reorganization of government	108
C 2	Access to the Princeps	111
C 3	The army	112
C 4	Edict of Octavian on the privileges of veterans	115
C 5	Senatorial careers under Augustus	115
C 6	Equestrian careers under Augustus	117
C 7	Sepulchral inscriptions	118
C 8	Declaration of surety	119
C 9	The provinces	119
C10	Provinces and client kingdoms	120
C11	Rome and Italy	121
C12	Alpine roads	122
C13	Client states	123
C14	*Tropaea Augusti*	123
C15	Administration of Spain under Augustus	124
C16	An exceptional province	125
C17	The first prefect of Egypt	126
C18	The prefect of Egypt	127
C19	Egyptian mines	127
C20	The Cyrene edicts	128
C21	Dedication of the Augustan market of Lepcis Magna	132
C22	A decree of 27 BC	132
C23	Treaty with Mytilene	133
C24	Letter of Agrippa to the Gerusia of Argos	134
C25	Letter of a proconsul to Chios	134

C26	Letter to Chios	135
C27	Grant of privileges to the Admiral Seleucos	135
C28	Letter to Mylasa	138
C29	Letter of the proconsul and decrees of the provincial assembly of Asia	139
C30	Paphlagonian oath of allegiance	140
C31	Excesses in provincial government	141
C32	Augustus' dispositions in Armenia	141
C33	Public works	142
C34	The Golden Milestone	142
C35	Rome's water supply	143
C36	Augustus repairs the aqueducts	147
C37	Trade	148

D	**The new traditions**	**149**
D 1	Augustus' revival of ancient religious customs	149
D 2	The Ludi Saeculares	150
D 3	The Robigalia	157
D 4	The Lemuria	158
D 5	Military Festivals	159
D 6	Prodigies and portents	160
D 7	The religion of the countryside	160
D 8	Superstitions and beliefs	163
D 9	Foreign rites	163
D10	Emperor worship	164
D11	Religious honours to Augustus	165
D12	Dedications to Augustus	166
D13	Religious administration	167
D14	Honours to Augustus' family	168
D15	Administration of justice and new laws	168
D16	Luxury	169
D17	Sumptuary laws	170
D18	The importance of citizenship	171
D19	Condemnation of Roman customs	171
D20	Lex Aelia Sentia	172
D21	Lex Fufia Caninia on manumission	175
D22	Lex Julia on violence and embezzlement	176
D23	Leges Juliae on treason and adultery	176

D24	The need for social legislation	177
D25	Augustus admonishes Livia	177
D26	Poetic evidence	178
D27	Marriage legislation	179
D28	Lex Julia on adultery	180
D29	*Lex Julia de maritandis ordinibus*	180
D30	Lex Papia Poppaea on the succession of freemen	181
D31	Provisions of the Lex Julia and Papia Poppaea for guardians, testaments, and legacies	183
D32	Laws on inheritance	185
E	**Art and architecture**	**187**
E 1	Augustus beautifies Rome	187
E 2	Rome before the Augustan building programme	189
E 3	Splendours of Rome	190
E 4	The Campus Martius	190
E 5	Forum of Augustus	191
E 6	The temple of Mars the Avenger	192
E 7	The Temple of Caesar	193
E 8	Octavian commemorates the victory of Actium	193
E 9	The restoration of the temple of Jupiter Feretrius	194
E10	The temple of Apollo	195
E11	The Mausoleum of Augustus	198
E12	The Pantheon	198
E13	The Basilica Pauli	199
E14	The Ara Pacis of Augustus	200
E15	The Lupercal	201
E16	The Volcanal	201
E17	The closing of the temple of Janus	202
E18	The house of Augustus on the Palatine	203
E19	Livia as builder	204
E20	Dedication and display of paintings	204
E21	Wall paintings	205
E22	Sculpture	206
E23	Statue of Marsyas	208
E24	Portraiture	208
E25	Mosaic	210
E26	Gem-collecting	210

E27	A collector	211
E28	An art gallery	211
E29	Augustus' seal	211
F	**Augustan poetry**	**213**
F 1	The *Life* of Virgil	213
F 2	The *Messianic Eclogue*	217
F 3	The *Georgics*	219
F 4	The *Aeneid*	221
F 5	A letter	225
F 6	*Aeneid* Book 6	225
F 7	*Life* of Horace	247
F 8	*Satires* 1. 6	249
F 9	*Epistles* 1. 13	250
F10	*Epistles* 2. 1	251
F11	*Odes* 1. 1	252
F12	*Odes* 1. 4	253
F13	*Odes* 1. 5	254
F14	*Odes* 1. 9	255
F15	*Odes* 1. 14	255
F16	*Odes* 1. 27	256
F17	*Odes* 1. 37	257
F18	*Odes* 2. 1	258
F19	*Odes* 2. 7	260
F20	*Odes* 2. 15	261
F21	*Odes* 2. 16	261
F22	*Odes* 3. 5	262
F23	*Odes* 3. 9	264
F24	*Odes* 3. 29	265
F25	*Odes* 3. 30	267
F26	*Odes* 4. 4	267
F27	*Odes* 4. 7	270
F28	Ovid's life: *Tristia* 4. 10	270
F29	Ovid *Tristia* 2. 353–370	274
F30	Ovid *Metamorphoses* 15. 745–879	274
F31	*Ars Amatoria*	279
F32	*Amores* 1. 1	282
F33	*Amores* 1. 2	284

F34	*Amores* 1. 4	285
F35	*Amores* 1. 5	287
F36	*Amores* 1. 11	288
F37	*Amores* 1. 13	290
F38	*Amores* 2. 5	291
F39	*Amores* 2. 7	293
F40	*Amores* 2. 10	295
F41	*Amores* 3. 2	296
F42	*Amores* 3. 11	298
F43	*Amores* 3. 14	300

PART 2

G	**Cicero *De Officiis* Book 3**		305
	G 1	Two verdicts on Cicero	306
	G 2	Conflict and values in the late Republic	307
	G 3	Standing for public office	308
	G 4	Cicero on writing philosophy	309
	G 5	Cicero justifies turning to philosophy	311
	G 6	The subject of *De Officiis*	312
	G 7	The distinction between *medium officium* and *perfectum officium*	313
	G 8	A defence of Scepticism	314
	G 9	The derivation of moral obligation	315
	G10	Examples from Book 2	316
	G11	Rejection of the 'Social Contract'	320
	G12	The distinction between human and civic obligations	321
	G13	Cicero *De Officiis* Book 3	322
H	**Lucretius *On the Nature of Universe***		350
	H 1	Invocation to Venus	350
	H 2	The nature of matter	352
	H 3	Introduction to Book 2	356
	H 4	The swerve	357
	H 5	Philosophy in verse	358
	H 6	Sensation	359
	H 7	Optical illusions and knowledge	360
	H 8	Death is nothing to us	362

CONTENTS

H 9	The mortality of the soul	363
H10	The Epicurean attitude to death	364
H11	The gods	367
H12	The origins of civilization	369
H13	Cicero on Lucretius	374
H14	St. Jerome on Lucretius	374
H15	Cicero on Epicureanism	375
H16	Differing views on the gods	376
H17	Cicero's criticism of the Epicurean view of the gods	376
H18	Diodorus Siculus on the creation of man	377

I   The Roman outlook   **379**

I 1	Propertius' Rome	379
I 2	Contrasting attitudes to the empire	382
I 3	The religious traditions	383
I 4	The laws of war	384
I 5	Cicero on religious law	385
I 6	The Roman gods	385
I 7	Polybius on Roman religion	386
I 8	Augury	387
I 9	Roman traditional piety	388
I10	Augustus' religious policy	389
I11	Benefactor cult	390
I12	The Sibylline oracle	391
I13	Letter of the consuls concerning Bacchic associations	392
I14	The cult of Aesculapius	393
I15	The cult of Isis and Serapis	394
I16	Juvenal on foreign rites	395
I17	Augustus' treatment of the Jews in Rome	398
I18	A decree of Augustus about the rights of the Jews (AD 2/3)	398
I19	The case against Greek influence	399
I20	Cicero acknowledges Greek influence	400
I21	Cicero emphasizes the moral role of literature	402
I22	A need for Roman historiography	402
I23	Hellenic values	403
I24	Changes in the function and characteristics of oratory	404
I25	Art collecting or plunder	406
I26	The cost of luxury	407

127	The increase of luxury (AD 22)	407
128	Trade	408
129	Travel and trade by sea	409
130	Wheat from the provinces	410
131	Claudius' dispositions in the provinces	410
132	Armenia	411
133	Prosecution of a provincial governor	412
134	The importance of farming	413
135	The elder Cato on agriculture	414
136	Varro on agriculture	415
137	Columella on running a farm	417
138	An agricultural calendar	418
139	Civil war and the land problem	420
140	A poetic contrast	421
141	The younger Pliny's villa	423
142	The younger Pliny's wife	423
143	Metal for tools and agricultural implements	424
144	The grain supply	425
145	Games	426
146	Election notices	427
147	A show of violence	428
148	A triumph	428
149	Duty under bad rule	430
150	The trial of Marcus Scribonius Libo Drusus (AD 16)	430
151	The condemnation of Silius	431
152	The prosecution of Cremutius Cordus	432
153	Tiberius' fear of political conspiracy	433
154	Claudius' history	433
155	Accusation against Publius Suillius Rufus	434
156	The death of Thrasea Paetus	434
157	Fear of associations	439
158	A burial society	440
159	Honours from the city of Veii to a freedman of Augustus	441
160	Dedicatory inscriptions	442
161	Claudius rules on the protection of sick slaves	443
162	The murder of the city prefect	443
163	A potential danger	444
164	Seneca on slaves	444

CONTENTS

J   On architecture   446

   J 1   Dedicatory inscriptions ✗   446

   J 2   Aqueducts   448

   J 3   The great fire   449

   J 4   The Golden House   450

   J 5   The Capitol   452

   J 6   1 Preface: Vitruvius' dedication to Augustus   452

   J 7   1. 1. 1-11: On the training of architects   454

   J 8   1. 2. 1-9: Of what things architecture consists   457

   J 9   1. 3. 1-2: On the parts of architecture   459

   J10   1. 5. 1-5: On the foundations of walls and the establishment
           of towns   459

   J11   1. 6. 1-3; 6-8: Respecting the division of works inside the walls   460

   J12   1. 7. 1-5: On the sites of public buildings   462

   J13   2. 1. 1-5: The origin of building   462

   J14   2. 3. 1-4: On bricks   463

   J15   2. 4. 1-3: On sand   464

   J16   2. 6. 1-6: On *pozzolana*   465

   J17   2. 7. 1-5: On stone   467

   J18   2. 8. 1-20: On walling   468

   J19   5. 1. 1-10: On the forum and basilica   470

   J20   5. 3. 3-5: On the site of the theatre   472

   J21   5. 9. 1-9: On colonnades and passages behind the scenes   473

   J22   5. 10. 1-5: On baths   474

   J23   5. 12. 1-7: On harbours and shipyards   475

   J24   6. 3. 1-11: On the plan of a house   477

   J25   6. 5. 1-3: On building suitably for different ranks of society   479

   J26   6. 8. 1-10: On the stability of buildings   480

   J27   7. 3. 1-8: On stucco   482

   J28   7. 4. 4-5: On stucco in damp places   484

   J29   7. 5. 1-4: On wall painting   484

   J30   7. 6. 1: On the use of marble   485

   J31   7. 9. 1-4: On the preparation of vermilion   486

   J32   8. 6. 1-10: On aqueducts, leaden and earthen pipes   487

K   The succession   489

   K 1   Tacitus on the writing of history   489

   K 2   Tiberius' early career   490

K 3	Augustus' opinion of Tiberius	493
K 4	Tiberius' appearance	494
K 5	The accession of Tiberius	495
K 6	Germanicus and the mutiny on the Rhine	500
K 7	Favourable assessments of the early years of Tiberius' principate	505
K 8	Trials under Tiberius	509
K 9	Popular agitation	512
K10	Tiberius rejects honours from Spain	513
K11	Sejanus	514
K12	Tiberius leaves Rome	519
K13	The fall of Sejanus	520
K14	The end of Tiberius' rule	525
K15	The beginning of Gaius' principate	528
K16	An oath of allegiance	530
K17	Gaius receives the embassy of Alexandrian Jews	530
K18	The death of Gaius	532
K19	Claudius	533
K20	Early career	535
K21	The accession of Claudius	535
K22	The letter to the Alexandrians	539
K23	Senators from Gaul	542
K24	The freedmen	545
K25	Messalina	546
K26	The death of Claudius	547

L–O The provinces 549

L   Rome and the Northern Gauls 550

L 1	The division of Gaul	550
L 2	The social structure of the Gauls	550
L 3	Rome against the Helvetii	552
L 4	Julius Caesar's policy	553
L 5	Augustus' reorganization of Gaul	553
L 6	Licinus' maladministration	555
L 7	A funerary inscription	556
L 8	Gaul under Tiberius	557
L 9	The revolt of Florus and Sacrovir	559
L10	Gaius' rule in Gaul	560

L11	The rule of Claudius	561
L12	Gallic wealth	562

M Germany — 563

M 1	Augustus' foreign policy	563
M 2	The Roman view of the Germans	563
M 3	Tacitus' description of the Germans	568
M 4	The defeat of Lollius	570
M 5	The new army regulations of 13 BC	571
M 6	The campaigns of Drusus	572
M 7	Tiberius' campaigns in Germany	573
M 8	The Varian disaster	576
M 9	The mutiny on the Rhine (AD 14)	580
M10	The further campaigns of Germanicus	581

N Britain — 591

N 1	Caesar and Britain	591
N 2	Cicero's brother Quintus a senior officer serving with Caesar	593
N 3	Suetonius on Caesar's expeditions	593
N 4	A British view?	594
N 5	The panegyric of Constantius	594
N 6	Roman knowledge of Britain: literary sources	595
N 7	Religion	598
N 8	Augustus and Britain	599
N 9	Augustus' intentions	600
N10	Strabo's assessment of the worth of Britain	601
N11	Relations with Britain under Tiberius and Gaius	602
N12	Claudius and Britain	603
N13	Claudius' celebration of victory	605
N14	Extraordinary revivals of old customs	607
N15	Two inscriptions relating to the conquest	607
N16	Persistence of Claudius' reputation	608
N17	The part played by Vespasian in Britain under Claudius	609
N18	A summary of events in Britain in the period from Claudius to Nero	609
N19	The Claudian conquest in poetry	610
N20	The second governor: Ostorius Scapula	611
N21	The defeat of Caratacus and the magnanimity of Claudius	612

N22	Events after Caratacus' defeat	613
N23	The rebellion of Boudicca	614
N24	The spread of the rebellion	615
N25	Dio's version of the outbreak of the rebellion	616
N26	The fall of London and Verulamium	617
N27	Britain after the defeat in battle of Boudicca and her allies	617
N28	The Emperor Nero's attitude to Britain	618
N29	The fall of the client kingdoms	618
N30	Britain after Nero	619

O   Judaea 621

O 1	Herod's interview with Octavian after Actium	621
O 2	Antonia	622
O 3	Herod's three towers at the north-west angle of the city and his palace	622
O 4	Masada	623
O 5	Herod's new port of Caesarea	625
O 6	Herod's benefactions to places outside his kingdom	626
O 7	Herod's attempt at Hellenization in Jerusalem	627
O 8	Herod's new Temple in Jerusalem	628
O 9	The Balustrade inscription	630
O10	Herod's loss of Augustus' favour	630
O11	The Pharisees' opposition to Herod's increasingly secular rule	632
O12	Further opposition to Herod, 5 BC	632
O13	Herod's last will	633
O14	Archelaus' conduct immediately after Herod's death early in 4 BC	633
O15	Negotiations in Rome about Herod's kingdom	634
O16	The reign of Archelaus, 4 BC–AD 6	635
O17	Philip's reign and his death in AD 33/4	636
O18	The foundation of Tiberias	637
O19	The consequences of Antipas' second marriage	637
O20	Antipas' proudest hour	638
O21	The start of Roman rule over the province of Judaea, AD 6	639
O22	An inscription of Pontius Pilate	641
O23	Pilate and the military standards	641
O24	Pilate and the aqueduct	642
O25	Pilate and the votive shields	642
O26	The end of Pilate's governorship	643

CONTENTS

O27   Gaius' attempt to desecrate the Temple   644
O28   Agrippa I's appeal to Gaius   647
O29   The deposition of Antipas and Aggripa I's acquisition of his
        territory, AD 40   648
O30   Agrippa I as king of the whole of Palestine (AD 41-4)   649
O31   Agrippa I's new north wall of Jerusalem   650
O32   Agrippa I's Hellenism and his conference of Eastern client
        kings   650
O33   The death of Agrippa I, AD 44   651
O34   The reconstitution of the province of Judaea, AD 44   652
O35   The question of the High Priest's vestments and Claudius'
        decree, AD 45   652
O36   The first pseudo-messiah, between AD 44 and 46   654
O37   The procuratorship of Ventidius Cumanus, AD 48-52   654
O38   The Sicarii   656
O39   Pseudo-messiahs during the procuratorship of Felix,
        AD 52-58/9   657
O40   The execution of James, bishop of Jerusalem   658
O41   The corrupt administration of Lucceius Albinus, AD 62-4   659
O42   Josephus' indictment of the last procurator   659
O43   The 'Sermon on the Mount' from the Gospel according to
        St. Matthew   660
O44   Excerpts from the Gospel according to St. Luke   664
O45   An Excerpt from the Gospel according to St. John   681
O46   Excerpts from the Acts of the Apostles   682
O47   Excerpts from Paul's letter to the Church in Rome   697
O48   Two excerpts from letters to the Church at Corinth   698
O49   Pliny on the Christians   699

Index of Sources   701

LIST OF PLATES

(between pp. 358 and 359)

1   Bronze bust of Augustus

2a Detail from the inscription of the *Res Gestae*

2b Inscription from the Mausoleum of Augustus in Rome: epitaphs of Marcellus and Octavia

3a Bust of Marcus Tullius Cicero

3b The Augustan *rostra* in the Forum in Rome

4   Statue of Augustus in armour from the villa of Livia at Prima Porta

5a Coin showing the Arch of Augustus

5b Copy of the *Clupeus Virtutis* of Augustus found in Arles

6   The Forum of Augustus, Rome

7a Arch at Rimini commemorating the restoration of the major roads of Italy by Augustus

7b Fortified gate in Turin

8a Commemorative arch erected in honour of Augustus in Susa

8b Monument of La Turbie, Alpes Maritimes

9a The Maison Carrée at Nîmes

9b The aqueduct of Nîmes, known as the Pont du Gard

10 The theatre at Orange

11 The Augustan market at Lepcis Magna

12 Detail from the Ara Pacis, depicting the sacrifice by Aeneas of the white sow

13 Group from the south frieze of the Ara Pacis, probably members of the Imperial family

14a Bust of Tiberius

14b Green basanite portrait bust of a Julio-Claudian prince, probably Germanicus

15a Onyx cameo of Claudius and his family

15b A sardonyx cameo known as the 'Gemma Augustea'

16 The Julio-Claudians illustrated by coins. The coins are not shown to the same scale

The authors and publishers would like to thank the following who have given permission for the photographs to be reproduced:

Arles, Musée Lapidaire d'Art Paien, photo: Michel Lacanaud, 5b; Ashmolean Museum, 16; Trustees of the British Museum, 1, 14a, 14b; Deutsches Archäologisches Institut, Rome, 2a, 12; Fototeca Unione, Rome, 2b, 3b, 5a, 6, 7a, 7b, 8a, 9b; French Government Tourist Office, 8b; Giraudon, 10; Kunsthistorisches Museum, Vienna, 15a, 15b; Lauros–Giraudon, 9a; Mansell/Alinari, 4, 13; Victoria and Albert Museum, 3a; Roger Wood, London, 11.

ACKNOWLEDGMENTS

Acknowledgement is made to the following for permission to reprint translations in copyright:

E. J. Brill (Leiden) for extracts from Philo *Legatio ad Gaium*, translated by E. M. Smallwood (2nd edition) 1970.

Cambridge University Press for extracts from Cicero *Letters to Atticus*, translated by D. R. Shakleton-Bailey (1968); Justinian *Digest*, translated by C. H. Monro (1904); and for extracts from *New English Bible*.

Jonathan Cape Ltd., and the Executors of the Estate of C. Day Lewis for extracts from Virgil *Georgics* (1940), and *Eclogues* (1963), translated by C. Day Lewis.

Centaur Press Ltd., for extracts from *The Poems of Sextus Propertius*, translated by A. E. Watts (1965).

Chatto & Windus Ltd., the translators, Russel Sharp and David R. Godine Publ. Inc., for extracts from Julius Caesar *The Battle for Gaul* translated by Anne & Peter Wiseman. © 1980 David R. Godine.

Columbia University Press, for extracts from *Roman Civilization*, 2 vols., edited by N. Lewis and M. Reinhold (1951–55).

J. M. Dent & Sons Ltd., for extracts from Horace *Epodes* 9, translated by M. Oakley (Everyman's Library Series, 1967).

David Higham Associates Ltd., for extracts from Horace *Odes*, translated by James Michie (Granada, 1965).

Hogarth Press Ltd., **Literistic Ltd.**, and the Executors of the Estate of C. Day Lewis for extracts from Virgil *Aeneid*, translated by C. Day Lewis. Copyright © 1952 C. Day Lewis.

Indiana University Press, for extracts from Ovid *Art of Love*, translated by R. Humphries (1957).

LACT Publications, for extracts from LACTOR 3: *A Short Guide to Electioneering*, translated by D. W. Taylor and J. Nunell; LACTOR 4: *Some Inscriptions from Roman Britain*, edited by M. C. Greenstock; LACTOR 11: *Literary Sources for Roman Britain*, edited by J. C. Mann and R. G. Penman.

Loeb Classical Library (Harvard University: William Heinemann) for extracts from the following: Cato *On Agriculture*, translated by W. D. Hooper and H. B. Ash (1935); Cicero *De Divinatione*, translated by W. A. Falconer (1923); Cicero *De Finibus*, translated by H. Rackham (1931); Cicero *De Natura Deorum*, translated by H. Rackham (1933); Cicero *De Officiis*, translated by W. Miller (1913); Cicero *Laws*, translated by C. W. Keyes (1928); Cicero *Philippics*, translated by W. C. A. Ker (1926); Cicero *Pro Archia Poeta*, translated by N. H. Watts (1923); Cicero *Pro*

Sestio, translated by R. Gardiner (1958); extracts from Dio Cassius *Roman History*, translated by E. Cary (1914-27); Dionysius of Halicarnassus *Roman Antiquities*, translated by E. Cary (1937-50); Josephus *Antiquitates Judaicae*, Books 15-17, translated by R. Marcus and A. Wikgren (1963), and Books 18-22 translated by L. H. Feldman (1965); Ovid *Metamorphoses*, translated by F. J. Miller (1916); Ovid *Tristia*, translated by A. L. Wheeler (1924); Pliny *Natural History*, translated by H. Rackham (1940-52); Plutarch *Cicero* (*Lives* v.9), translated by B. Perrin (1920); Plutarch *Moralia*, translated by W. C. Helmbold; Polybius *Histories* (Bks. 5-7) translated by W. R. Paton (1923); Seneca *Apocolocyntosis*, translated by W. H. D. Rouse (1936); Seneca *Moral Essays*, translated by J. W. Basore (1931, 1935); Strabo *Geography*, translated by H. L. Jones (1917-32); Suetonius *Works*, translated by J. C. Rolfe (1914); St. Augustine *City of God*, translated by W. M. Green; Tacitus *Agricola* and *Germania*, translated by M. Hutton (1969); Tacitus *Annals*, translated by J. Jackson (1931); Velleius Paterculus *Res gestae Divi Augusti*, translated by F. W. Shipley (1924); Vitruvius *On Architecture*, translated by F. Granger (1931-4).

John Murray (Publishers) Ltd., and **Viking Penguin Inc.**, for extracts from Ovid *Amores*, translated by Guy Lee. Copyright (translation © 1968 by Guy Lee).

New American Library, Inc. (New York) for extracts from *The Annals of Tacitus*, translated by Donald R. Dudley. Copyright © 1966 by Donald R. Dudley.

The Open University for extracts from A291 Unit 12, translations from Tacitus by Peter Salway. Copyright © 1974 The Open University Press.

Penguin Books Ltd., for extracts from the following: Caesar: *The Conquest of Gaul*, translated by S. A. Handford (1970); Horace *Epistles and Satires*, translated by P. Green (1970); Lucretius *On the Nature of the Universe*, translated by R. E. Latham (1970); Plutarch *Antony*, translated by I. Scott-Kilvert; Plutarch *Cicero*, translated by Rex Warner (1970); Tacitus *Annals*, translated by M. Grant (1971); Josephus *The Jewish War*, translated by G. Williamson (1970).

A. D. Peters & Co. Ltd., and the author for translations by Donald R. Dudley from *Urbs Roma* (Phaidon, 1967).

Professor J. J. Pollitt for translations from *The Art of Rome* (Prentice-Hall, 1966).

Walker & Company, Inc., for extracts from *A History of Rome Through the Fifth Century*, translated by A. H. M. Jones. Copyright © 1970 A. H. M. Jones.

A. P. Watt Ltd., for extracts from *Suetonius: The Twelve Caesars*, translated by Robert Graves, and published by Penguin Books (2nd. ed., 1979).

Translations by Kitty Chisholm, John Ferguson and Tony Lentin are published for the first time in this anthology and are the copyright of the translators.

All possible care has been taken to trace ownership of the selections included and to make appropriate acknowledgement, but if any errors or omissions are noticed the publishers will be glad to hear of them and to correct the list when practicable.

ABBREVIATIONS

The following abbreviations have been used for periodicals, collections of documents, works of reference, and for the most frequently cited translations.

AJA   *American Journal of Archaeology*
AJP   *American Journal of Philology*
Acts of the Arval Brethren   *acta Arvalium,*   CIL 1, p. 214
Abdy and Walker   J.T. Abdy and B. Walker edd. and tr. *The Commentaries of Gaius and Rules of Ulpian* (Cambridge 1876)
BGU   *Berliner griechische Urkunden* (Ägyptische Urkunden aus den Kgl. Museen zu Berlin 1895–1934)
CAH   *Cambridge Ancient History*
CIL   *Corpus Inscriptionum Latinarum* (Berlin 1862–   )
CRAI   *Comptes rendus de l'Académie des Inscriptions*
Caesar *BG*   Caesar *Bellum Gallicum*
Dryden, rev. A.H. Clough   Plutarch *Lives* translated by Dryden, revised A.H. Clough
Dudley *Urbs Roma*   D.R. Dudley *Urbs Roma* (Phaidon 1967)
Ehrenberg and Jones   V. Ehrenberg and A.H.M. Jones *Documents illustrating the reigns of Augustus and Tiberius* (Oxford 1970)
FIRA   S. Riccobono and others *Fontes Iuris Romani Anteiustiniani* (2nd edn. 3 vols. Florence 1940–43)
Foster (Jones)   H.B. Foster *Dio's Rome, a Historical Narrative Composed in Greek and Now Presented in English* (Troy 1905) adapted in A.H.M. Jones *A History of Rome Through the Fifth Century* vol. 2. *The Empire* (Macmillan 1970)
HSCP   *Harvard Studies in Classical Philology*
HTR   *Harvard Theological Review*
IG   *Inscriptiones Graecae* (Berlin 1873–   )
IGRR   *Inscriptiones Graecae ad Res Romanas Pertinentes* (Paris 1906–27) ed. R. Cagnat and others
ILS   *Inscriptiones Latinae Selectae* ed. H. Dessau (Berlin 1892–1916)
ILTG   *Inscriptions Latines des Trois Gaules*
IRT   *The Inscriptions of Roman Tripolitania* J.M. Reynolds and J.B. Ward-Perkins.
Johnson et al.   *Ancient Roman Statutes* A.C. Johnson, P.R. Coleman-Norton and F.C. Bourne *Ancient Roman Statutes* (University of Texas Press 1961)
Jones *History of Rome*   A.H.M. Jones *A History of Rome Through the Fifth Century* Vol. 2. *The Empire* (Macmillan 1970)
Josephus *AJ*   *Antiquitates Judaicae*
Josephus *BJ*   *Bellum Judaicum*
JRS   *Journal of Roman Studies*
LACT *Literary Sources*   LACT *Literary Sources for Roman Britain* edd. J.C. Mann and R.G. Penman (LACTOR 11, 1977)
— *Some Inscriptions*   *Some Inscriptions from Roman Britain* ed. M.C. Greenstock (LACTOR 4, 1971)
Lewis *Roman Principate*   N. Lewis *The Roman Principate* (Hakkert, Toronto 1974)

Lewis and Reinhold   N. Lewis and M. Reinhold *Roman Civilization* (2 vols. Macmillan 1951, 1955)

Loeb   Loeb Classical Library, Heinemann

Millar *The Emperor*   Fergus Millar *The Emperor in the Roman World* (Duckworth 1977)

OGIS   *Orientis Graecae Inscriptiones Selectae* ed. G. Dittenberger

P. Oslo.   *Papyri Osloenses* vols. 1 and 2, The Academy of Science and Letters of Oslo

Pollitt *The Art of Rome*   J. J. Pollitt *The Art of Rome* (Prentice Hall 1966)

REA   *Revue des Études Anciennes*

RIB   *The Roman Inscriptions of Britain* ed. R. G. Collingwood and R. P. Wright (Oxford 1965)

RG   *Res Gestae Divi Augusti*

Salway *Roman Britain and the Early Empire*   P. Salway, Unit 12 *Roman Britain and the Early Empire* (Open University Press 1974)

Sherk *Roman Documents*   R. G. Sherk *Roman Documents from the Greek East* (Senatus Consulta *and* Epistulae *to the Age of Augustus*) (Johns Hopkins 1969)

SIG   *Sylloge Inscriptionum Graecarum* ed. G. Dittenberger

Syme *RR*   R. Syme *The Roman Revolution* (Oxford 1960)

Williamson rev. Smallwood   Josephus *BJ* tr. G. A. Williamson, revised E. M. Smallwood (Penguin 1981)

Wiseman, Anne and Peter   (translators) Julius Caesar *The Battle for Gaul* (Chatto & Windus 1980)

Part 1

A DOCUMENTARY

The epigraphic sources for the period of Augustus' rule are abundant and varied. In this section we include those inscriptions which provide a chronological framework for the period, the *Fasti* and the Calendars, as well as the *Res Gestae*, Augustus' own account of his rule.

The *Fasti* and the Calendars have their origins in the records kept in early Rome for religious and cult purposes. They began as records of days when public business (such as trials, elections, assemblies) was allowed–*dies fasti*–and of days when it was forbidden–*dies nefasti*. These were gradually expended to include lists of magistrates, of triumphs, and notes of events of both secular and religious importance.

The *Fasti* are taken from the *Fasti consulares*, official lists of the holders of the higher magistracies. These were published annually at Rome, and some Italian municipalities and priestly colleges also kept such records. The Calendars are the *Fasti anni Iuliani*; calendars which note the days of the week, their nature (*fasti* or *nefasti*), religious festivals, and important events arranged according to the Julian year. Such calendars were also published in many towns.

These lists are useful aids for dating other inscriptions and historical accounts; they also provide a record of the fluctuations of political power: certain family names occur in the list of consuls again and again, others are missing or excised, while others disappear.

Augustus intended the *Res Gestae* to be inscribed in front of his mausoleum at Rome. It is not a complete account of his life but a record of the achievements of Augustus' public career.

A1 The *Res Gestae*

This inscription is perhaps the single most important document for Roman Imperial history. It is Augustus' own account of his achievements, which he intended to be engraved on two bronze pillars in front of his mausoleum (Suetonius Augustus 101). The original has perished, but it has been possible to reconstitute the text from copies set up in provincial cities; the best preserved is that from the temple of Rome and Augustus at Ancyra (modern Ankara in Turkey) with a Greek translation.

The Res Gestae *was not intended as a complete record of Augustus' rule; rather an account of those events and deeds by which he wanted to be remembered. Even so it is often as informative in its omissions as in the language and style of its presentation. Note the frequent references to traditional Republican practice; note also the absence of the names of any of Augustus' opponents. The text is in Ehrenberg and Jones. P. A. Brunt and J. M. Moore* The Achievements of the Divine Augustus *(Oxford 1967) provide a detailed commentary.*

Below is a copy of the achievements of the deified Augustus, whereby he brought the whole world under the rule of the Roman people, and of the sums which he expended on the Republic and people of Rome. The original is at Rome, engraved on two bronze pillars.

1   At the age of nineteen, on my own initiative and at my own expense, I raised an army, with which I liberated the Republic from the tyranny of a faction by which it was oppressed, and restored it to freedom.

In acknowledgement of this the Senate, with honorific decrees, made me a member of its order in the consulship of Gaius Pansa and Aulus Hirtius, [43 BC] giving me the right to vote among the consulars; it also granted me *imperium*. It ordered me as propraetor to take steps together with the consuls to see that the Republic should come to no harm.

In the same year, moreover, both consuls having fallen in battle, the people made me a consul and appointed me as one of the triumvirs for the settlement of public affairs.

2   Those who murdered my father I drove into exile, avenging their crime by due process of law, and later, when they waged war on the Republic, I twice defeated them in the field.

3   I undertook many wars, civil and foreign, by land and sea, in every part of the world; and as victor I pardoned all citizens who sought mercy. Foreign peoples who could safely be pardoned, I preferred to spare rather than put to the sword.

Some 500,000 Roman citizens swore the oath of military allegiance to me. Of these I settled in colonies or sent back to their own municipalities after their period of service, just over 300,000, and to all of these I gave lands or cash bounties as rewards for their service.

I captured 600 ships, excluding vessels smaller than triremes.

4   I twice celebrated an ovation and three times I enjoyed a curule triumph; and I was hailed as *imperator* on twenty-one occasions.

Although the Senate decreed further triumphs for me, I declined them all. I deposited in the Capitol the laurel symbolizing my victorious command, having fulfilled in each of my wars the vows which I had made. For successes on land and sea brought about by me or by my legates under my auspices, the Senate decreed on fifty-five occasions that prayers be offered to the immortal gods. The number of days on which by decree of the Senate such prayers were held, was 890.

In my triumphs nine kings, or children of kings, were led in front of my chariot.

I have been consul thirteen times at the time of writing, and am in the 37th year of my tribunician power. [AD 14]

5   The dictatorship offered to me both in my absence and in my presence both by the people and the Senate in the consulship of Marcus Marcellus and Lucius Arruntius [22 BC] I refused to accept.

I did not refuse, at a time of severe food shortage, official responsibility for the corn supply, which I so administered that within a few days I relieved the entire city from the fear and danger in which it stood, at my own expense and by my own efforts.

The consulship, which was also offered to me at that time on an annual basis for life, I refused to accept.

6   In the consulship of Marcus Vinicius and Quintus Lucretius [19 BC] and again in the consulship of Publius Lentulus and Gnaeus Lentulus [18 BC] and a third time in the consulship of Paullus Fabius Maximus and Quintus Tubero [11 BC], though the Senate and people of Rome agreed that I should be made sole Guardian of laws and morals with full powers, I declined to accept the offer of any office not in accordance with tradition and precedent.

The particular measures that the Senate wished me to carry out at that time, I carried out by virtue of my tribunician power; and on five occasions, of my own accord, I asked for and received from the Senate a colleague to share that power.

7   I was for ten successive years a member of the triumvirate for the settlement of the Republic.

Up to the time of writing I have been *princeps senatus* for forty years.

I have been *pontifex maximus*, augur, one of the fifteen commissioners for sacred rites, one of the seven commissioners for religious feasts, one of the Arval fraternity, a member of the Titian society, and a *fetialis*.

8   In my 5th consulship [29 BC] I increased the number of patricians by order of the people and Senate.

I revised the senatorial roll three times and in my 6th consulship [28 BC] with Marcus Agrippa as my colleague, I carried out a census of the people. I held a *lustrum* after an interval of forty-two years. At this *lustrum*, 4,063,000 Roman citizens were registered. I performed a second *lustrum* in the consulship of Gaius Censorinus and Gaius Asinius [8 BC] acting alone, by virtue of consular *imperium*. At this *lustrum* 4,233,000 Roman citizens were registered. I held a third *lustrum*, by virtue of a consular *imperium* and with my son, Tiberius Caesar, as my colleague, in the consulship of Sextus Pompeius and Sextus Appuleius [AD 14]. At this *lustrum* 4,937,000 Roman citizens were registered.

By the passing of new laws at my instigation, I restored numerous traditional ways that were falling into abeyance and I personally set numerous precedents for imitation by posterity.

9   The Senate decreed that vows for my health should be offered by the consuls and priests every five years. In accordance with these vows, games have frequently been held in my honour during my lifetime, sometimes by the four principal colleges of priests, sometimes by the consuls. Moreover, the whole body of citizens, both privately and as municipalities, have with one accord continually offered sacrifices for my health at all the shrines.

10   My name, by decree of the Senate, was included in the Salian hymn; and it was enacted by law that I should enjoy permanent sacrosanctity and should hold tribunician power for life.

I refused to become *pontifex maximus* in place of my colleague during his lifetime, though the people offered me that priestly office which my father had held. I did accept it some years later, in the consulship of Publius Sulpicius and Gaius Valgius [12 BC] on the death of the previous occupant, who had secured it at a time of civil commotion—such a multitude congregating at Rome for my election from the whole of Italy as had never before been recorded.

11 In honour of my homecoming, the Senate consecrated an altar to Fortune the Homebringer at the Porta Capena in front of the temple of Honour and Virtue, where it ordered the pontiffs and Vestal virgins to perform a yearly sacrifice on the anniversary of my return to Rome from Syria in the consulship of Quintus Lucretius and Marcus Vinicius [19 BC] and called the day 'Augustalia' after my title.

12 By authority of the Senate, some of the praetors and tribunes of the people, together with the consul Quintus Lucretius, and leading men of state, were sent to Campania to meet me, an honour which to this day has been decreed to no one except myself.

On my return to Rome from Spain and Gaul, in the consulship of Tiberius Nero and Publius Quintilius [13 BC], after the successful conclusion of affairs in those provinces, the Senate in honour of my return decreed that an altar to the Peace of Augustus should be consecrated on the Campus Martius, where it commanded the magistrates and priests and the Vestal virgins to perform an annual sacrifice.

13 The temple of Janus Quirinus, which our ancestors resolved should be closed whenever peace with victory was secured throughout the empire of the Roman people by land and sea, and which before my birth according to tradition has been closed only twice in all since the foundation of Rome, was ordered by the Senate to be closed three times during my principate.

14 My sons, Gaius and Lucius Caesar, whom fortune snatched from me in their youth, were made consuls designate in my honour by the Senate and people of Rome in their fifteenth year, so that they might enter upon that office after five years. The Senate also decreed that from the day on which they were ceremonially led into the forum, they should attend its public debates. Furthermore, the whole body of Roman *equites* named each of them as *princeps iuventutis* and bestowed upon them silver shields and spears.

15 To every man of the common people of Rome I paid 300 sesterces in accordance with my father's will; and in my own name I gave 400 sesterces from the spoils of war in my 5th consulship [29 BC]; again in my 10th consulship [24 BC] I gave every man a gratuity of 400 sesterces from my own patrimony; and in my 11th consulship [23 BC] I made twelve distributions of corn from grain purchased at my own expense; and in the 12th year of my tribunician power [11 BC] for the third time I gave every man 400 sesterces. These gratuities of mine reached never fewer than 250,000 persons. In the 18th year of my tribunician power and my 12th consulship [5 BC] I gave to 320,000 of the common people of Rome 60 denarii apiece. In my 5th consulship [29 BC] I also gave to each of my soldiers in the military colonies 1,000 sesterces from the spoils of war; this triumphal largesse was received by about 120,000 persons in the colonies. In my 13th consulship [2 BC] I gave

60 denarii to each of the common people then in receipt of the corn-dole, namely slightly over 200,000 persons.

16 I reimbursed the municipalities for lands which I assigned to my soldiers in my 4th consulship [30 BC] and later, in the consulship of Marcus Crassus and Gnaeus Lentulus Augur [14 BC], I paid approximately 6,000,000 sesterces for estates in Italy and approximately 260,000,000 sesterces for land in the provinces. I was the first and only person on record to do so of all those who founded military colonies in Italy or the provinces up to my time. And later, in the consulship of Tiberius Nero and Gnaeus Piso [7 BC] and likewise in the consulships of Gaius Antistius and Decimus Laelius [6 BC] and of Gaius Calvisius and Lucius Pasienus [4 BC] and of Lucius Lentulus and Marcus Messalla [3 BC] and of Lucius Caninius and Quintus Fabricius [2 BC], I bestowed cash bounties on the soldiers whom, on the completion of their service, I sent back to their own municipalities, contributing some 400,000,000 sesterces to this end.

17 On four occasions I assisted the treasury with my own funds, paying over 150,000,000 sesterces to those in charge of the treasury. And in the consulship of Marcus Lepidus and Lucius Arruntius [AD 6] I transferred 170,000,000 sesterces from my own patrimony into the military treasury set up on my advice to provide bonuses for soldiers who had served for twenty years or more.

18 Starting in the year when Gnaeus and Publius Lentulus were consuls [18 BC], whenever the revenues fell short, I made up the deficit in grain or cash from my own estates and patrimony, sometimes on behalf of 100,000 persons, sometimes many more.

19 I built the Senate house and the Chalcidicum adjoining it, and the temple of Apollo on the Palatine with its porticoes, the temple of the deified Julius, the Lupercal, the portico at the Circus Flaminius, which I allowed to be called the Octavian portico after the man who built a previous one on the same site, a ceremonial box at the Circus Maximus, the temples of Jupiter Feretrius and Jupiter the Thunderer on the Capitol, the temple of Quirinus, the temples of Minerva and Queen Juno and Jupiter Libertas on the Aventine, the temple of the Lares at the top of the Via Sacra, the temple of the Penates in the Velia, the temple of Youth, and the temple of the Great Mother on the Palatine.

20 I restored the Capitol and the theatre of Pompey, both at great expense, without any inscription of my name on them. I repaired the conduits of the aqueducts, which in a great many places were falling into disrepair through lapse of time: and in the case of the aqueduct known as the Marcian aqueduct, I doubled its supply by diverting a new spring into it.

The Forum Julium and the basilica which used to stand between the temple of Castor and the temple of Saturn, works begun and almost finished by my father, I completed: and when the same basilica was destroyed by fire, I commenced its rebuilding on an enlarged site in the name of my sons, and gave orders that if I did not live to complete it, my heirs should do so.

In my 6th consulship [28 BC] by authority of the Senate, I repaired eighty-two temples of the gods in Rome, omitting none then in need of repair.

In my 7th consulship [27 BC] I rebuilt the Via Flaminia from Rome to Ariminum and all the bridges except the Mulvian and the Minucian.

21   On my own land I built the temple of Mars the Avenger and the Forum of Augustus from the spoils of war.

I built the theatre next to the temple of Apollo on a site largely purchased from private owners, to be named after my son-in-law Marcus Marcellus.

I consecrated gifts from the spoils of war, to the value of approximately 100,000,000 sesterces, in the Capitol and in the temple of the deified Julius and the temple of Apollo and the temple of Vesta and the temple of Mars the Avenger.

In my 5th consulship [29 BC] I sent back 35,000 lb. of gold designated for crowns which the municipalities and colonies of Italy contributed towards my triumphs; afterwards, too, whenever I was hailed as *imperator*, I refused to accept the gold which the municipalities and colonies decreed as generously as before.

22   Three times I held a gladiatorial spectacle in my own name and five times in the name of my sons or grandsons; in which spectacles some 10,000 men took part in combat.

Twice in my own name and a third time in the name of my grandson, I provided a public display by athletes summoned from all parts.

I held games four times in my own name and twenty-three times on behalf of other magistrates.

On behalf of the College of Fifteen, as master of the college, with Marcus Agrippa as my colleague, I held the Secular Games in the consulship of Gaius Furnius and Gaius Silanus [17 BC].

In my 13th consulship [2 BC] I was the first to hold the Games of Mars, which since then the consuls have held in each succeeding year by decree of the Senate and by law.

I have provided public spectacles of the hunting of wild beasts from Africa twenty-six times in my own name or that of my sons and grandsons, in the circus or the forum or the amphitheatres, in which some 3,500 beasts have been slaughtered.

23   I provided the public spectacle of a naval battle on the other side of the Tiber, on the present site of the Grove of the Caesars, having excavated an area 1,800 feet long by 1,200 feet wide, where thirty beaked ships, triremes or biremes, and many other smaller vessels, joined in battle. In these fleets some 3,000 men, apart from the oarsmen, took part in the combats.

24   After my victory, I restored to the temples of all the cities of the province of Asia the ornaments which my opponent in war, having despoiled the temples, had appropriated to his own use.

Silver statues of myself, on foot, on horseback, or in a chariot, of which some eighty stood in Rome, I removed, and spent the money from them on gold offerings which I placed in the temple of Apollo in my name and in the names of those who had honoured me with the statues.

25   I brought peace to the seas by freeing them from pirates. In that war I restored to their masters for punishment nearly 30,000 slaves who had fled from their masters and had taken up arms against the Republic.

The whole of Italy of its own accord took an oath of allegiance to me and demanded that I should be its leader in the war which I won at Actium. The same oath was taken by the provinces of Gaul and Spain, and by Africa, Sicily, and Sardinia.

Of those who fought at that time under my standards, more than 700 were senators. Eighty-three of these have become consuls, whether earlier or later, up to the time of writing; and approximately 170 became priests.

26 I extended the frontiers of all the provinces of the Roman people where the neighbouring peoples were not subject to our rule.

I pacified the provinces of Gaul and Spain, and likewise Germany— the whole area bounded by the Ocean from Gades to the mouth of the River Elbe.

I pacified the Alps from the region next to the Adriatic sea to the Tuscan sea, without waging war unjustly on any people.

My fleet navigated the Ocean from the mouth of the Rhine eastward as far as the lands of the Cimbri, where no Roman had ever previously penetrated either by land or sea; and the Cimbri and the Charydes and the Semnones and other German peoples of the same region through their envoys sought my friendship and that of the Roman people.

On my order and under my auspices, two armies were led, at almost the same time, into Ethiopia and into that part of Arabia which is called Felix, and large numbers of enemy forces of both peoples were killed in battle and numerous towns were captured. In Ethiopia, the town of Nabata was reached, close to Meroe. In Arabia the army penetrated to the town of Mariba in the territory of the Sabaeans.

27 I added Egypt to the empire of the Roman people.

Greater Armenia, which, on the murder of its King Artaxes, I could have made a province, I preferred, following the example of our ancestors, to bestow as a kingdom on Tigranes, son of King Artavasdes and grandson of King Tigranes, acting through Tiberius Nero, who was then my step-son. And when that same nation later rose up and rebelled and was then subdued by my son Gaius, I bestowed it on King Ariobarzanes, son of Artabazus, king of the Medes, to rule over, and after his death, to his son Artavasdes. When he was killed, I sent Tigranes, who was descended from the royal family of Armenia, to rule the kingdom.

I regained all the Eastern provinces beyond the Adriatic, and also Cyrene, most of which were in the possession of foreign kings. I had already recovered Sicily and Sardinia, which had been seized during the slave war.

28 I established military colonies in Africa, Sicily, Macedonia, in both provinces of Spain, in Achaea, Asia, Syria, Gallia Narbonensis, and Pisidia.

Moreover Italy possesses twenty-eight colonies established under my authority, which in my own lifetime have become very populous and flourishing.

29 Numerous military standards, lost by other commanders, I recovered, after completely defeating the enemy, from Spain and Gaul and from the Dalmatians.

I compelled the Parthians to restore to me the spoils and standards of three Roman armies and to seek the friendship of the Roman people as suppliants; and I placed these standards in the inner shrine in the temple of Mars the Avenger.

30   The peoples of Pannonia, where no army of the Roman people had ever been before my principate, I completely defeated through Tiberius Nero, who was then my step-son and legate, and brought them under the rule of the Roman people; and I extended the frontiers of Illyricum to the bank of the River Danube. An army of Dacians which crossed to this side was defeated and totally destroyed under my auspices; and later my own army crossed the Danube and compelled the peoples of Dacia to submit to the orders of the Roman people.

31   Royal embassies were frequently sent to me from India, a sight never before seen in the camp of any Roman general.

Our friendship was sought through ambassadors by the Bastarnae and the Scythians and the kings of the Sarmatians on this side of the River Don and of those beyond, and by the kings of the Albani, the Iberi, and the Medes.

32   The following kings fled to me as suppliants: Tiridates, king of the Parthians, and later Phraates, son of King Phraates; Artavasdes, king of the Medes; Artaxares of the Adiabeni, Dumnobellaunus and Tincommius of the Britons; Maelo of the Sugambri and . . .rus of the Marcomannian Suebi.

Phraates, king of the Parthians, the son of Orodes, sent all his sons and grandsons to me in Italy, not through defeat in war, but sending his own children in token of his desire for our friendship.

Numerous other peoples, with whom hitherto there had been no exchange of embassies or friendship with the Roman people, also enjoyed the good faith of the Roman people during my principate.

33   The peoples of Parthia and Media, through envoys consisting of their leading men, sought and accepted kings at my hands: the Parthians—Vonones, the son of King Phraates, grandson of King Orodes, the Medes—Ariobarzanes, the son of King Artavasdes, grandson of King Ariobarzanes.

34   In my 6th and 7th consulships [28–27 BC], after I had put an end to the civil wars, having by universal consent acquired control of all affairs, I transferred government from my own authority to the discretion of the Senate and people of Rome.

For this service of mine, by decree of the Senate I received the name Augustus, and the doorposts of my house were publicly decked with laurels, a civic crown was fixed above my door, and a golden shield was set up in the Julian Senate house, the inscription to which testifies that it was given to me by the Senate and people of Rome in honour of my fortitude, clemency, justice, and piety.

Henceforth, I exceeded all men in authority, but I had no greater power than those who were my colleagues in any given magistracy.

35   During my 13th consulship [2 BC] the Senate, the Equestrian order, and the entire Roman people gave me the title Father of his Country, and decreed that this be inscribed in the entrance-hall to my house and in the Senate house and in the Forum of Augustus beneath the chariot erected in my honour by decree of the Senate.

At the time of writing, I am in my seventy-sixth year.

tr. A. Lentin

A2 The *Fasti*

Most of the surviving fragments of the Fasti *date from the first century BC and the first century AD and are therefore a valuable record for our period. Two important compilations, known in modern times as the* Fasti Capitolini *and* Fasti Triumphales *were made under Augustus. The following list of consuls is taken from the conflation by Ehrenberg and Jones from all the epigraphic* Fasti *(published by A. Degrassi in* Inscriptiones Italiae *vol. 13 fasc. 1, Rome 1947). The notation follows Ehrenberg and Jones: square brackets indicate lost portions of names, round brackets indicate names found from other sources and not appearing in the* Fasti; *'no suffects' is added under any year in which the* Fasti *normally including suffects do not record any for that year; the numbers of years of* tribunicia potestas *for Augustus, Agrippa, and Tiberius have been added in round brackets.*

43 BC   Gaius Vibius Pansa (Caetronianus), son of Gaius
         Aulus Hirtius, son of Aulus
         suffects: Gaius Julius Caesar, son of Gaius
                 Quintus Pedius, son of Quintus
                 Gaius Carrinas, son of Gaius
                 Publius Ventidius, son of Publius

42 BC   Marcus Aemilius Lepidus, son of Marcus, 2nd consulship,
         Lucius Munatius (Plancus), son of Lucius
         no suffects

41 BC   Lucius Antonius (Pietas), son of Marcus
         Publius Servilius (Vatia Isauricus), son of Publius, 2nd consulship
         no suffects

40 BC   Gnaeus Domitius Calvinus, son of Marcus, 2nd consulship
         Gaius Asinius (Pollio), son of Gnaeus
         suffects: Lucius Cornelius (Balbus), son of Lucius
                 Publius Canidius (Crassus), son of Publius

39 BC   Lucius Marcius (Censorinus, son of Lucius)
         Gaius Calvisius (Sabinus, son of Gaius)
         suffects: Gaius Cocceius (Balbus)
                 Publius Alfenus (Varus, son of Publius)

38 BC   Appius Claudius (Pulcher, son of Gaius)
         Gaius Norbanus (Flaccus, son of Gaius)
         suffects: Lucius Cornelius (Lentulus)
                 Lucius Marcius (Philippus, son of Lucius)

37 BC   Marcus Agrippa, son of Lucius
         Lucius Ca[niniu]s (Gallus, son of Lucius)
         suffect: Titus Statilius (Taurus, son of Titus)

36 BC   Lucius Gellius, son of Lucius (Poplicola)
         Marcus Cocceiu[s] (Nerva)
         suffects: Lucius Nonius (Asprenas), son of Lucius
                 [? . . M]arcius

11

35 BC   Sextus Pomp(eius son of Sextus)
             Lucius Cornifi(cius son of Lucius)
             suffects: Publius Cornelius (Scipio, son of Publius)
                     Titus Peducaeus

34 BC   Marcus Anton(ius, son of Marcus), 2nd consulship
             Lucius Scribonius (Libo, son of Lucius)
             suffects: Lucius Sempronius (Atratinus, son of Lucius)
                     Paul(lus) Aemilius (Lepidus, son of Lucius)
                     Gaius Memmius (son of Gaius)
                     Marcus Herennius

33 BC   Imperator Caesar (son of the divine (Julius); 2nd consulship
             Lucius Volcacius (Tullus, son of Lucius)
             suffects: Lucius Autronius (Paetus, son of Publius)
                     Lucius Flavius
                     Gaius Fonteius (Capito, son of Gaius)
                     Marcus Acilius (Glabrio)
                     Lucius Vinicius (son of Marcus)
                     Quintus Laronius

32 BC   Gnaeus Domitius (Ahenobarbus, son of Lucius)
             Gaius Sossius (son of Gaius)
              suffects: Lucius Cornelius (Cinna?)
                     Marcus Valerius Messal(la)

31 BC   Imperator Caesar son of the divine (Julius); 3rd consulship
             Marcus Valerius Messal(la) Corvinus (son of Marcus)
             suffects: Marcus Titus, son of Lucius
                     Gnaeus Pompeius, son of Quintus

30 BC   Imperator Caesar (son of the divine (Julius); 4th consulship
             Marcus Licinius Crassus (son of Marcus)
             suffects: Gaius Antistius Vetus (son of Gaius)
                     Marcus Tullius Cicero (son of Marcus)
                     Lucius Saenius, son of Lucius

29 BC   Imperator Caesar (son of the divine (Julius), 5th consulship
             Sextus Appuleius (son of Sextus)
             suffect: Potit(us) Valeri(us) (Messalla, son of Marcus)

28 BC   Imperator Caesar (son of the divine (Julius), 6th consulship
             Marcus Agrippa, (son of Lucius), second consulship
             no suffects

27 BC   Imperator Caesar (son of the divine (Julius), 7th consulship
             Marcus Agrippa (son of Lucius), third consulship
             no suffects

26 BC   Imperator Caesar (son of the divine (Julius), 8th consulship
             Titus Statilius Taurus, son of Titus, second consulship
             no suffects

25 BC   Imperator Caesar (son of the divine (Julius), 9th consulship
         Marcus Iunius Silanus (son of Marcus)
         no suffects

24 BC   Imperator Caesar (son of the divine (Julius), 10th consulship
         Gaius Norbanus Flaccus (son of Gaius)
         no suffects

23 BC   (Augustus' tribunician year 1) Imperator Caesar Augustus, son of the
         divine (Julius), grandson of Gaius, consul for the eleventh time,
         resigned the consulship. In his place, [Lucius Sestius, son of
         Publius, grandson of Lucius], Quirin(alis) [Albinus?] was made
         consul.
         Aulus T[erentius Var]ro Murena [son of Aulus, grandson of ?]
         In his place [Gnaeus Calpurn]ius Piso, son of Gnaeus, grandson of
         Gnaeus, was made consul.
         [Imperator Caesar, both of the divine (Julius), grandson of Gaius,
         accepted tribunician power after resigning the consulship]

22 BC   (tribunician year 2) Marcus Claudius Mar[cellus] (Aeserninus), son of
         Marcus.
         Lucius Arruntius, son of Lucius
         no suffects

21 BC   (tribunician year 3) Quintus Aemilius Lepid(us) (son of Manius)
         Marcus Lolliu[s] (son of Marcus)
         no suffects

20 BC   (tribunician year 4) Marcus Appuleius, son of Sextus
         Publius Silius (Nerva, son of Publius)
         no suffects

19 BC   (tribunician year 5) Gaius Sentius Saturn[inus] (son of Gaius)
         Quintus Lucreti(us Vespillo, son of Quintus)
         suffects: Marcus Vinicius, son of Publius

18 BC   (Augustus' year 6, Agrippa's 1). Publius Cornelius (Lentulus
         Marcellinus) son of Publius
         Gnaeus C[ornelius] Lentul[us, (son of Lucius)
         no suffects

17 BC   (Augustus' year 7, Agrippa's 2). Gaius Furnius, son of Gaius
         Gaius Iun[ius] Silanus (son of Gaius)
         no suffects

16 BC   (Augustus' year 8, Agrippa's 3). Lucius Domitius (Ahenobarbus) son
         of Gnaeus
         Publius Corne[lius] Scipio, (son of Publius)
         suffect: Lucius Tarius (Rufus)

15 BC   (Augustus' year 9, Agrippa's 4). Marcus (Livius) Drusus (Libo), son
         of Lucius
         Lucius (Calpurnius) Piso (Frugi), (son of Lucius)
         no suffects

14 BC   (Augustus' year 10, Agrippa's 5). Marcus Licinius (Crassus Frugi) son
of Marcus
Gnaeus (Cornelius Lentulus) Augu[r], (son of Gnaeus)

13 BC   (Augustus' year 11, Agrippa's 6). Tiberius Claudius (Nero), son of Tiberius
Publius Quinctil(ius Varus, son of Sextus)
no suffects

12 BC   (Augustus' year 12). Marcus Valerius (Messalla Barbatus) Appian(us), son
of Marcus
Publius Sulpic(ius Quirinius, son of Publius)
suffects: Gaius Valgius Ruf(us), son of Gaius
          Gaius Caninius Rebil(us), (son of Gaius)
          Lucius Volusius Sa[turninus], (son of Quintus)

11 BC   (Augustus' year 13). (Paulus) [Fa]bi[us] (Maximus, son of Quintus)
(Quintus) Aelius (Tubero, son of Quintus)
no suffects

10 BC   (Augustus' year 14). (Iullus Antonius, son of Marcus)
(Africanus) [F]ab(ius Maximus, son of Quintus)
no suffects

 9 BC   (Augustus' year 15). (Nero Claudius Drusus, son of Tiberius)
(Titus Quinctius Crispinus, son of Titus)
no suffects

 8 BC   (Augustus' year 16). (Gaius Marcius Censorinus, son of Lucius)
(Gaius Asinius Gallus, son of Gaius)
no suffects

 7 BC   (Augustus' year 17). Tiberius Claudius Nero, son of Tiberius
for the second time: Gnaeus Calpurnius Piso, (son of Gnaeus)
no suffects

 6 BC   (Augustus' year 18, Tiberius' 1). Gaius Antistius (Vetus, son of Gaius)
Decimus Laelius (Balbus, son of Decimus)
no suffects

 5 BC   (Augustus' year 19, Tiberius' 2). Imperator Caesar August(us) (son of
the divine (Julius), consul for the twelfth time.
Lucius (Cornelius) Sulla, (son of Publius)
suffects: Lucius Vinicius, son of Lucius
          Quintus Haterius
          Gaius Sulpicius Galba, son of Gaius

 4 BC   (Augustus' year 20, Tiberius' 3). Gaius Calvisius Sabinus, son of Gaius
Lucius Passien(us Rufus)
suffects: Gaius Caelius
          Galus Sulpic(ius)

 3 BC   (Augustus' year 21, Tiberius' 4). Lucius (Cornelius) Lentulus, (son of
Lucius)
Marcus (Valerius) Messal(la Messallinus), (son of Marcus)
no suffects

2 BC   (Augustus' year 22, Tiberius' 5). Imperator Caesar (Augustus, son of
       the divine (Julius), consul for the thirteenth time
       Marcus Plaut(ius) (Silvanus, son of Marcus)
       suffects: Lucius Caninius (Gallus, son of Lucius)
                  Gaius Fufius (Geminus)
                  Quintus Fabricius
1 BC   (Augustus' year 23). Cossus Cornelius (Lentulus, son of Gnaeus)
       Lucius (Calpurnius) Piso, (son of Gnaeus)
       suffects: Aulus Plautius
                  Aulus Caecina (Severus)
AD 1   (Augustus' year 24). Gaius Caesar, son of Augustus
       Lucius (Aemilius) Paullus, (son of Paullus)
       suffect: Marcus Herennius Picens, son of Marcus
AD 2   (Augustus' year 25). Publius Vinicius, son of Marcus
       Publius Alfenus Varus, son of Publius
       suffects: Publius Cornelius (Lentulus) Scipio, son of Gnaeus
                  Titus Quinctius [Crispi]nus Val[erianus], son of Titus
AD 3   (Augustus' year 26). Lucius Aelius Lamia, son of Lucius
       Marcus Servilius, (son of Marcus)
       suffects: Publius Silius, son of Publius
                  Lucius Volusius [Saturni]n(us), son of Lucius
AD 4   (Augustus' year 27, Tiberius' 6). Sextus Aelius Catus, son of Quintus
       Gaius Sentius Saturn(inus), (son of Gaius)
       suffects: Gnaeus Sentius Saturnin(us), son of Gaius
                  Gaius Clodius Licinus, son of Gaius
AD 5   (Augustus' year 28, Tiberius' 7). Lucius Valerius Messalla Volesus, son
       of Potitus
       Gnaeus Cornelius Cinna Mag(nus), son of Lucius
       suffects: Gaius Vibius Postumus, son of Gaius
                  Gaius Ateius Capito, son of Lucius
AD 6   (Augustus' year 29, Tiberius' 8). Marcus Aemilius Lepidus, son of Paullus
       Lucius Arruntius, son of Lucius
       suffect: Lucius Nonius Asprenas, son of Lucius
AD 7   (Augustus' year 30, Tiberius' 9). Quintus Caecilius Metellus Creticus
       Silan(us), son of Quintus
       Aulus Licinius Nerva Silianus, son of Aulus
AD 8   (Augustus' year 31, Tiberius' 10). Marcus Furius Camill(us), son of Publius
       Sextus Nonius Quinctilian(us), son of Lucius
       suffects: Lucius Apronius, son of Gaius
                  Aulus Vibius Habitus, son of Gaius
AD 9   (Augustus' year 32, Tiberius' 11). Gaius Poppaeus Sabinus, son of Quintus
       Quintus Sulpicius Camerinus, son of Quintus
       suffects: Marcus Papius Mutilus, son of Marcus
                  Quintus Poppaeus Secund(us), son of Quintus

AD 10   (Augustus' year 33, Tiberius' 12). Publius Cornelius Dolabella, son of Publius

Gaius Iunius Silanus, son of Gaius, *flamen* of Mars

suffects: Servius Cornelius Lentulus Malug(inensis), son of Gnaeus, *flamen* of Jupiter

Quintus Iunius Blaesus

AD 11   (Augustus' year 34, Tiberius' 13). Manius Aemilius Lepidus, son of Quintus

Titus Statilius Taurus, son of Titus

suffect: Lucius Cassius Longinus, son of Lucius

AD 12   (Augustus' year 35, Tiberius' 14). Germanicus Caesar, son of Tiberius

Gaius Fonteius Capito, son of Gaius

suffect: Gaius Visellius Varro, son of Gaius

AD 13   (Augustus' year 36, Tiberius' 15). Gaius Silius Caecina Largus, son of Publius

Lucius Munatius Plancus, son of Lucius

AD 14   (Augustus' year 37, Tiberius' 16). Sextus Pompeius (son of Sextus)

Sextus Appuleius (son of Sextus)

no suffects

tr. K. Chisholm

A3 The Calendars

Fragments of Augustan calendars survive from some eighteen cities. The following entries have been selected from the conflation in Ehrenberg and Jones.

43 BC 7 Jan.

  Cumae   on this day Caesar first took office. Thanksgiving to eternal Jupiter.

  Praeneste   Imperator Caesar Augustus first took office in the consulship of Hirtius and Pansa.

AD 13 8 Jan.

  Praeneste   in the consulship of Plancus and Silius a statue of the Justice of Augustus was dedicated.

29 BC 11 Jan.

  Praeneste   Imperator Caesar Augustus ended war and closed the temple of Janus for the third time since Romulus, in his 5th consulship with Appuleius as colleague.

27 BC 13 Jan.

  Praeneste   the Senate decreed that an oak-leaf garland be placed above the door of the house of Imperator Caesar Augustus because he restored the Republic to the people of Rome.

82 BC 14 Jan.
  Verulae   an unfavourable day, by Senatorial decree; Antony's birthday.
  Oppianum   unfavourable [day].
27 BC 16 Jan.
  Cumae   on this day Caesar was named Augustus. Thanksgiving to Augustus.
  Praeneste   Imperator Caesar was named Augustus in his 7th consulship with
              Agrippa, in his 3rd, as colleague.
AD 10 16 Jan.
  Verulae   a day of festival by Senatorial decree as on this day the temple of
              Concord in the forum was dedicated.
  Praeneste   the temple of The Concord of Augustus was dedicated in the con-
              sulship of Publius Dolabella and Gaius Silanus.
38 BC 17 Jan.
  Verulae   a day of festival by Senatorial decree as on this day Augusta
              married the divine Augustus.
AD 6 27 Jan.
  Praeneste   the temple of Castor and Pollux was dedicated.
9 BC 30 Jan.
  Cumae   on this day the altar of the Peace of Augustus was dedicated.
              Thanksgiving to the *imperium* of Augustus Caesar guardian of
              Roman citizens and of the world.
  Caere   day of festival by Senatorial decree as on this day the altar of the
              Peace of Augustus was dedicated.
  Praeneste   day of festival by Senatorial decree as on this day the altar of the
              Peace of Augustus in the Field of Mars was dedicated in the con-
              sulship of Drusus and Crispinus.
2 BC 5 Feb.
  Praeneste   holiday by Senatorial decree as on this day Imperator Caesar
              Augustus, *pontifex maximus*, in the 21st year of his tribunician
              power, in his 13th consulship, was called Father of the Country
              by the Senate and people of Rome.
12 BC 6 Mar.
  Maffeiani   on this day Caesar was made *pontifex maximus*.
  Cumae   on this day Caesar was elected *pontifex maximus*. Thanksgiving to
              Vesta and to the State *Penates* of the people of Rome, the Quirites.
  Praeneste   holiday by Senatorial decree as on this day Imperator Caesar
              Augustus was made *pontifex maximus* in the consulship of
              Quirinius and Valgius; the *duoviri* sacrifice for this event and the
              people, donning wreaths, celebrates a holiday.
43 BC 14 Apr.
  Cumae   on this day Caesar was victorious for the first time. Thanksgiving
              for the Victory of Augustus.
43 BC 16 Apr.
  Cumae   on this day Caesar was first acclaimed *imperator*. Thanksgiving to
              the Good Fortune of his *imperium*.

12 BC 28 Apr.

    Caere — holiday, as on this day the statue of Vesta in the Palatine house was dedicated.

    Praeneste — holiday by Senatorial decree, as on this day the chapel and altar of Vesta in the house of Imperator Caesar Augustus, *pontifex maximus*, was dedicated, in the consulship of Quirinius and Valgius.

from 19 BC annually on 12 May

    Cumae — on this day the temple of Mars was dedicated. Thanksgiving to the Might of Mars.

    Maffeiani — the games of Mars in the Circus.

    Philocalus — day of Martian games.

AD 4 26 or 27 June

    Amiternum — holiday by Senatorial decree, as on this day Imperator Augustus adopted Tiberius Caesar as his son in the consulship of Aelius and Sentius.

13 BC 4 July

    Amiternum — holiday by Senatorial decree as on this day the altar of the Peace of Augustus was set up on the Field of Mars in the consulship of Nero and Varus.

    Antium — the altar of the Peace of Augustus was set up.

30 BC 1 Aug.

    Praeneste — Egypt brought under the power of the people of Rome. Offering to Victory the Virgin on the Palatine and to Hope in the vegetable market; holiday by Senatorial decree as on this day Imperator Caesar Augustus saved the Republic from the gravest peril.

    Acts of the Arval Brethren — to Hope in the vegetable market; holiday by Senatorial decree as on this day Imperator Caesar saved the Republic from the gravest peril.

    Amiternum — holiday by Senatorial decree as on this day Imperator Caesar, son of a god, saved the Republic from the gravest peril.

    Antium — Festival of Hope. Augustus regained Alexandria.

AD 7 10 Aug.

    Vallenses — holiday; the altars of Plenty and Ceres in the Jugarian quarter were set up.

    Amiternum — holiday as on this day altars were erected to Mother Ceres and the Plenty of Augustus in fulfilment of a vow, in the consulship of Creticus and Longius.

    Antium — holiday in honour of Ceres and the Plenty of Augustus.

29 BC 13–15 Aug.

    Antium — Augustus celebrated a triumph.

43 BC 19 Aug.

    Cumae — on this day Caesar entered upon his first consulship. Thanksgiving.

AD 14 19 Aug.

    Amiternum — day of deepest mourning.

    Antium — Augustus died.

31 BC 2 Sept.

Acts of the Arval Brethren	holiday by Senatorial decree in honour of Imperator Caesar as on this day he was victorious at Actium.
Amiternum	holiday by Senatorial decree as on this day Imperator Caesar Augustus, son of the divine (Julius) was victorious at Actium; he and Titus were the consuls.
Antium	Augustus was victorious at Actium.

36 BC 3 Sept.

Acts of the Arval Brethren	day of festival and thanksgiving ceremonies at all the couches of the gods as on this day Augustus Caesar was victorious in Sicily.
Amiternum	day of festival and thanksgiving ceremonies at all the couches of the gods as on this day Caesar, son of the divine (Julius) was victorious in Sicily, in the consulship of Censorinus and Calvisius (*wrong date*).

AD 14 17 Sept.

Oppiani	holiday by Senatorial decree as on this day divine honours were voted by the Senate to divine Augustus in the consulship of Pompeius and Appuleius.
Amiternum	holiday by Senatorial decree as on this day divine honours were voted to divine Augustus by the Senate in the consulship of Sextus Appuleius and Sextus Pompeius.
Antium	divine honours voted to Augustus.

63 BC 23 and 24 Sept.

Acts of the Arval Brethren	holiday by Senatorial decree as on this day Augustus Caesar, *pontifex maximus*, was born; sacrifice to Neptune in the Campus Martius and to Apollo by the theatre of Marcellus.
Acts of the Arval Brethren	... on the birthday of divine Augustus, ... sacrificed a bull to divine Augustus.
Maffeiani	Augustus' birthday, games in the circus.

AD 14 annually on 5 Oct.

Amiternum	games held in honour of divine Augustus and Fortune the Home-bringer.

28 BC 9 Oct.

Acts of the Arval Brethren	in honour of the public Genius, Good Luck, Victorious Venus on the Capitol, Apollo on the Palatine.
Amiternum	games in honour of the public Genius, Good Luck, Victorious Venus on the Capitol, and Apollo on the Palatine.
Antium	games. Augustus dedicated the temple of Apollo.

19 BC 12 Oct.

Amiternum	holiday by Senatorial decree as on this day Imperator Caesar entered the city from provinces overseas and the altar to Fortune the Homebringer was established.
Oppiani	holiday by Senatorial decree, divine Augustus returned from the provinces overseas and dedicated the altar to Fortune the Home-bringer.

Philocalus   the Augustalia. Games of 24 heats.
c. *48 BC* 18 or 19 Oct.
Cumae   on this day Caesar assumed the *toga virilis*; thanksgiving to Hope
              and Youth.
Antium   divine Augustus assumed the *toga virilis*.
42 BC 23 Oct.
Praeneste   Imperator Caesar Augustus was victor at Philippi, Brutus being
              killed in the second battle.
19 BC 15 Dec.
Cumae   on this day was dedicated the altar of Fortune the Homebringer
              who brought back Caesar Augustus from the provinces overseas.
              Thanksgiving to Fortune the Homebringer.
Amiternum   (16 Dec.) the altar of Fortune the Homebringer was dedicated.

tr. K. Chisholm

B POLITICS AND POWER

The rise of Octavian from the relative obscurity of holding no official position (B2–8), through the triumvirate (B13–24), to a position of the greatest authority in Rome was startling in its rapidity. Mark Antony (B5, 17, 24), a successful and popular general, seemed set to assume the mantle of Julius Caesar's *auctoritas* (a word combining our sense of authority with respect, responsibility, and capacity for leadership) along with the leadership of the Caesarian 'faction'–the group of people who favoured Caesar and whose careers or fortunes were bound closely to his. It was, however, the nineteen-year-old Octavian, adopted in Caesar's will (B2) and thus inheritor of his name (B9) who succeeded in taking over the authority, power, respect, and legions.

Octavian was backed against Antony by Cicero and the Senate (B6–8), but he used them to establish his own position and then changed sides.

It is easier to trace through the sources the sequence of events of Octavian's rise to power than it is to understand how and why he succeeded. The evidence we possess is often from historians writing very much later than our period, who can see Octavian only from the viewpoint of the established Principate; another problem is that, as Augustus, he was in power long enough for most of the opposition to be suppressed or won over. An analysis of the events of Octavian's rise to power is further complicated by the way ancient authors interpret the effects of character and personality; for them character tends to be fixed–good or bad–and actions which are incompatible with that fixed assessment are seen as arising from guile or subterfuge. We must beware of taking even contemporary accounts of Augustus' character too literally (B36 ff.). The young Octavian, ruthless in his search for power, presents a contrast with the benevolent, wise Augustus, that was often ignored by the ancient authorities.

We need to examine vigorously what he did, and in what conditions and circumstances: as Fergus Millar aptly puts it (*The Emperor in The Roman World* p. 6) 'the Emperor was what the Emperor did.'

Augustus' achievements were considerable: he established a stable form of government at a time when the political structure of the Republic, the rule of an aristocracy by consent, was in chaos. He established a system of administration, using Republican structures, effective not only in Rome and Italy but also in the provinces. His attempt to establish a hereditary succession (B55) was notoriously less successful than the forms of government and administration.

B1 The Octavians

The Life *of the Divine Augustus is a detailed, anecdotal biography—one of the* Lives *of the Twelve Caesars by Gaius Suetonius Tranquillus (AD c.69–c.150). Suetonius served as secretary to Hadrian and thus probably had access to the state archives. In the* Lives *Suetonius seems to have used his sources uncritically so that valuable information is included with much gossipy and unreliable material. For the Octavian family see further R. M. Geer in* AJP *55 (1934) 337 ff; D. C. Earl in* Latomus *19 (1966) 657 ff.*

1.   The Octavians, by all accounts, were famous in ancient Velitrae. An 'Octavian Street' runs through the busiest part of the city, and an altar is shown there consecrated by one Octavius, a local commander. Apparently news of an attack by a neighbouring city reached him while he was sacrificing a victim to Mars; snatching the intestines from the fire, he offered them only half-burned, and hurried away to win the battle. The Velitraean records include a decree that all future offerings to Mars must be made in the same fashion, the carcase of every victim becoming a perquisite of the Octavians.

2   King Tarquinius Priscus admitted the Octavians, among other plebeian families, to the Roman Senate, and though Servius Tullius awarded them patrician privileges, they later reverted to plebeian rank until eventually Julius Caesar made them patricians once more. . . .

3   I cannot believe that Gaius Octavius, the father, was also a money-changer who distributed bribes among the voters in the Campus and undertook other electioneering services. He was certainly born rich enough to achieve office without having to engage in such practices; and proved a capable administrator. After his praetorship, he became governor of Macedonia, and the Senate commissioned him to pass through Thurii on his way there and disperse a group of outlawed slaves who, having fought under Spartacus and Catiline, were now terrorizing the district. He governed Macedonia courageously and justly, winning a big battle in Thrace, mainly against the Bessians; and letters survive from Cicero reproaching his brother Quintus, then proconsular governor of Asia, for inefficiency, and advising him to make Octavius his model in all diplomatic dealings with allies.

4   Gaius died suddenly on his return to Rome, before he could stand as a candidate for the Consulship. He left three children: Octavia the Elder, Octavia the Younger, and Augustus. The mother of Octavia the Elder was Ancharia; the other two were his children by Atia, daughter of Marcus Atius Balbus and Julius Caesar's sister Julia. Balbus's family originated in Aricia, and could boast of many ancestral busts of senators; his mother was also closely related to Pompey the Great. Balbus served first as praetor, and then with a Commission of Twenty appointed under the Julian Law to divide estates in Campania among the commons. Mark Antony likewise tried to belittle Augustus's maternal line by alleging that his great-grandfather Balbus had been born in Africa, and kept first a perfumery and then a bakehouse at Aricia. Cassius of Parma similarly sneers at Augustus as the

grandson of a baker and a money-changer, writing in one of his letters: 'Your mother's flour came from a miserable Arician bakery, and the coin-stained hands of a Nerulian money-changer kneaded it.'

Suetonius *Augustus* 1–2; 3–4
tr. R. Graves (Penguin 1957)

B2 Caesar's will

We do not know what Caesar saw in Octavian, but there is no reason to doubt that he genuinely adopted him, though presumably conditionally on Calpurnia's not bearing a posthumous child. For allegations of chicanery see W. Schmidthenner Octavian und das Testament Cäsars, Zetemata Monographien zur klassischen Alter-tumswissenschaft *(Munich 1973); for a defence of Suetonius' evidence, G. E. F. Chilver in* JRS *44 (1954) 126 ff.*

In his most recent will he appointed three heirs, his sister's grandsons, Gaius Octavius to take three-quarters, and Lucius Pinarius and Quintus Pedius a quarter between them; right at the end of the document he adopted Gaius Octavius into his family, with his family name. He named several of his assassins among the guardians of his son if one should be born to him, and Decimus Brutus among the heirs of the second degree as well.

Suetonius *Julius Caesar* 83
tr. J. Ferguson

B3 A brief outline of Augustus' life

On his return to Italy Octavian accepted his inheritance, and as Caesar's adopted son the name C. Julius Caesar (Octavianus) (cf. B9).

At the age of four Augustus lost his father. At twelve he delivered a funeral oration in honour of his grandmother Julia, Julius Caesar's sister. At sixteen, having now come of age, he was awarded military decorations when Caesar celebrated his African triumph, though he had been too young for overseas service. Caesar then went to fight Pompey's sons in Spain; Augustus followed with a very small escort, along roads held by the enemy, after a shipwreck, too, and in a state of semi-convalescence from a serious illness. This energetic action delighted Caesar, who soon formed a high estimate of Augustus's character.

Having recovered possession of Spain, Caesar planned a war against the Dacians and Parthians, and sent Augustus ahead to Apollonia, in Illyria, where he spent his spare time studying Greek literature. News then came that Caesar had been assassinated, after naming him his heir, and Augustus was tempted, for a while, to put himself under the protection of the troops quartered nearby. However, deciding that this would be rash and injudicious, he returned to Rome and there entered upon his inheritance, despite his mother's doubts and the active opposition of his stepfather, Marcius Philippus the ex-Consul. Augustus now took command of the Army, and governed the Empire: first with Mark Antony and Lepidus as his colleagues; next, for nearly twelve years, with Antony alone; finally by himself for another forty-four years.

Suetonius *Augustus* 8
tr. R. Graves (Penguin 1957)

B4 Funds for Octavian

On arrival at Brundisium in April 44 BC Octavian learnt he was Caesar's heir. By June 44 he had raised an army of 3,000 loyal veterans. The source of Octavian's funds has not been definitely traced but these passages give some indication that he might have appropriated state money—the tax from Asia; see Syme RR p. 131 and note.

(a) *Nicolaus of Damascus (born c. 64 BC) was friend and chronicler to Herod of Judaea who took him to Rome and introduced him to Augustus. Nicolaus' Life of Augustus (only surviving in parts) is very detailed, strongly favours Augustus, and is a valuable source for his stay in Apollonia and the events surrounding the death of Caesar.*

This was the beginning of good both for himself and all mankind, but especially for the state and the entire Roman people. He sent immediately to Asia for the money and means that Caesar had previously despatched for the Parthian war, and when he received it along with a year's tribute from the people of Asia, contenting himself with the portion that had belonged to Caesar he turned the public property over to the state treasury.

Nicolaus of Damascus *Life of Augustus* 18
tr. C. M. Hall, Smith College Classical Studies (Northampton, Mass. 1923)

(b) *Appian is less detailed.*

Directly multitudes of men from all sides flocked to him as Caesar's son, some from friendship to Caesar, others his freedmen and slaves, and with them soldiers besides, who were either engaged in conveying supplies and money to the army in Macedonia, or bringing other money and tribute from other countries to Brundisium.

Appian *Civil Wars* 3. 2. 11
tr. H. White (Loeb 1913; 1979 edn.)

(c) *Dio gives no indication as to the source of the funds, but confirms that Octavian was in control of large sums of money.*

When, however, he had crossed to Brundisium and had been informed about Caesar's will and the people's second thoughts, he made no delay, particularly as he had large sums of money and numerous soldiers who had been sent ahead under his charge, but immediately assumed the name of Caesar, succeeded to his estate, and began to busy himself with public affairs.

Dio Cassius 45. 3. 2
tr. E. Cary (Loeb 1969)

B5 Conflict with Antony

Plutarch (AD c. 46– c. 126) wrote his Life of Antony *largely from sources hostile to his protagonist, but it remains a useful source for the period between the death of Caesar and Actium (44–31 BC.) This passage relates the early conflict between Antony and the young Octavian, Caesar's heir; (cf. Dio 45. 5. 3 and Appian* Civil Wars *3. 14. 48 ff. on Antony's attitude to the ratification of Caesar's will). For a penetrating analysis of this conflict see Syme* RR *pp. 112–22.*

16   While matters went thus in Rome, the young Caesar, Caesar's niece's son and by testament his heir, arrived at Rome from Apollonia, where he was when his uncle was killed. The first thing he did was to visit Antony, as his father's friend. He spoke to him concerning the money that was in his hands, and reminded him of the legacy Caesar had made of seventy-five drachmas to every Roman citizen. Antony, at first laughing at such words from so young a man, told him he lacked good sense and that he needed good counsel and friends to tell him how difficult was the burden of being Caesar's executor. He would not take this for an answer, but persisted in demanding the property. Antony went on injuring him both in word and deed, opposed him when he stood for the tribune's office, and, when he was taking steps for the dedication of his adoptive father's golden chair, as had been enacted, he threatened to send him to prison if he did not stop cultivating the people. This made the young Caesar attach himself to Cicero and all those that hated Antony; by them he was recommended to the senate, while he himself courted the people and drew together the soldiers from the colonies, till Antony

got alarmed and arranged a meeting with him in the Capitol where, after some words, they came to an accommodation.

That night Antony had a very unlucky dream, fancying that his right hand was hit by a thunderbolt. And, a few days later, he was informed that Caesar was plotting to take his life. Caesar made explanations, but was not believed, so that the breach was now very wide. Each of them hurried through Italy to engage, by great offers, the old soldiers that were scattered in their colonies, and to be the first to secure the troops that still remained undischarged.

17   Cicero was at this time the man of greatest influence in Rome. He made use of all his art to turn the people against Antony, and at length persuaded the senate to declare him a public enemy, to send Caesar the rods and axes and other marks of honor usually given to praetors, and to issue orders to Hirtius and Pansa, who were the consuls, to drive Antony out of Italy. The armies met in battle near Mutina, and Caesar himself was present and took part in it. Antony was defeated, but both the consuls were slain. Antony in his flight was overtaken by hardships of every kind, and the worst of them all was famine. But it was his habit in calamities to be better than at any other time... Antony, on this occasion, was a wonderful example to his soldiers. He, who had just left so much luxury and sumptuous living, made no fuss about drinking foul water and feeding on wild fruits and roots. It is related they ate the bark of trees and, in passing over the Alps, lived upon creatures that no one before had ever been willing to touch.

> Plutarch *Antony* 16–17 (abridged)
> tr. Dryden, rev. A. H. Clough

B6 Cicero and Octavian

Cicero (106–43 BC) was an orator, philosopher, and statesman with great prestige and significant political influence (cf. §G) He saw Antony as the greatest threat to the re-establishment of Senatorial authority and power, and attacked him in several speeches (known as the Philippics,*—see B7 and 8). Cicero tried to use Octavian against Antony, but Octavian used him and the Senate to strengthen his own position and then joined Antony. The following passages are taken from Cicero's voluminous correspondence, of which over 900 letters survive. Atticus was the nickname of Titus Pomponius, a wealthy Equestrian and a friend of Cicero's from their school-days; the public games ((e) below) were those organized for 20–30 July 44 BC in honour of Julius Caesar; Matius and Rabirius Postumus were supporters of Caesar.*

(a)
I should like news of Octavius' arrival. Was there a popular demonstration in his favour? Was there a suspicion of a *coup d'état*?

> Cicero *To Atticus* 14.5 (11 Apr. 44 BC, from Astura)

(b)

The news of Octavius is neither here nor there.

Ibid. 14.6 (12 Apr. from Fundi)

(c)

Octavius reached Naples on 18 Apr. Balbus met him there the following morning; he joined me later that day in my house at Cumae with the news that Octavius would accept the inheritance.

Ibid. 14.10 (19 Apr. from Cumae)

(d)

Octavius is here with us, and is showing us the highest respect and friendliness. His own people have begun to address him as Caesar. Philippus doesn't; neither do I; I regard it as impossible for a loyal citizen to do so. There are many people around who are threatening the lives of our friends, saying that the whole thing is insupportable. What do you think will happen when the lad gets to Rome, when our liberators cannot feel safe there?

Ibid. 14.12 (22 Apr. from Puteoli)

(e)

I have the same views as yours about Octavian's speech, and do not like his preparations for public games or his use of Matius and Postumus to represent him.

Ibid. 15.2 (18 May from Vescia)

(f)

A letter from Octavian on the evening of the first. He's got a big job on hand. He's won over the veterans at Casilinum and Calatia to his point of view. Not surprising at 500 denarii a head. He's thinking of visiting the other colonies. He's obviously got his eye on war against Antony with himself as commander; so I see that it won't be long before we're in arms. But under whose command? Look at his name; then look at his age. He's asking me, before anything else, to meet for secret talks at or near Capua. It's childish to suppose it can be done secretly. I've written to say that it is neither possible nor necessary. He sent a friend of his from Volaterra named Caecina, who brought the news that Antony is making for Rome with the Alauda legion, levying tolls on the towns, and marching with the legion under arms. He asked my advice about starting for Rome with 3,000 veterans, or holding Capua and blocking Antony's approach, or going to the three Macedonian legions which are on their way to the northern Adriatic and which he expects to be on his side. They refused Antony's bribes (so he says), threw abuse at him, and went away while he was addressing them. As you can guess he is offering himself as our leader,

27

and thinks we ought not to let him down. My advice was to make for Rome. I think he should have the urban rabble with him and the patriots too if he can win their confidence.

Ibid. 16.8 (2 Nov. from Puteoli)

(g)
Two letters in one day from Octavian; he now wants me to make straight for Rome; he wants to take action through the Senate. I told him I didn't see how the Senate could meet before 1 January, and that was an honest opinion. He goes on 'with your advice'. In other words he is pressing and I am hedging. I've no confidence in his age, and I've no knowledge of his mind.

Ibid. 16.9 (4 Nov. from Puteoli)

(h)
I haven't buried myself in the house at Pompeii as I originally wrote partly because of the weather which has been ghastly, and partly because of daily letters from Octavian: I must do something; I must come to Capua; I must save the Republic a second time; anyway I must go straight to Rome.

Ashamed to hold back and yet afraid to grasp
(Homer *Iliad* 7.93)

However he's been taking vigorous action; he still is. He'll come to Rome with a large army—but he's only a boy. He's thinking of an immediate Senate. Who will come? If anyone does come, who's going to offend Antony in all this uncertainty? Perhaps on 1 Jan. he'll act as bodyguard—or perhaps the battle will be over by then. The towns strongly support the boy. On his way to Samnium he reached Cales and stopped at Teanum. What a welcome! What a mass of people! Would you have thought it?

Ibid. 16.11 (5 Nov. from Puteoli)

(i)
Young Caesar has incredible natural qualities. I only hope that once he achieves position and influence we shall be able to direct and control him as easily as we have done so far! That's a harder job, but I don't despair. The young man's convinced—I have played some part in that—that our salvation depends on him.

To M. Brutus 1.3 (21 Apr. 43 from Rome)

(j) BRUTUS TO ATTICUS
... Octavius may call Cicero 'father', consult him about everything, praise him, thank him, but it will become clear that his actions run counter to his words.

To M. Brutus 1.17 (May 43)

(k) D. BRUTUS TO M. CICERO

Labeo Segulius, a totally reliable man, tells me he has been with Caesar and that they talked a good deal about you. He said that Caesar had no real complaints about you except for your epigram 'He is a young man to be praised, honoured, and removed'; he has no intention of putting himself in a position to be removed.

To Friends 11.20 (24 May from Eporedia)

tr. J. Ferguson

B7 Cicero praises Octavian

Cicero charges Antony with his attacks on Octavian. Nobility is a technical term meaning the possession of consular ancestors. M. Gelzer, The Roman Nobility *(Blackwell 1969) p. 32, specifically discusses this passage.*

How insulting, how uncivilized, how crude he appears in his edicts! He has heaped on Caesar filthy charges drawn from the memory of his own immoral behaviour. The young man is the perfection of purity and decorum; we have no more brilliant example of traditional piety among our youth. It is his accuser who is an exemplification of unchastity. He taunts C. Caesar's son with lack of nobility, though his natural father too would have become consul had he lived. 'His mother came from Aricia.' You might think he was referring to a woman from Tralles or Ephesus!

Cicero *Philippics* 3.6.15

tr. J. Ferguson

B8 Octavian's position legitimized

Cicero made this proposal on 1 January 43.

I come to Caius Caesar, Conscript Fathers; and if he had not lived, who of us could have been alive now? There was flying to the city from Brundisium a man of most ungovernable temper, burning with hatred, with a mind hostile to all loyal men, a man with an army—in short, Antonius. What could have been opposed to this man's audacity and iniquity? As yet we had no commanders, no forces; there was no council of State, no liberty; our necks were at the mercy of his lawless cruelty; we were all looking to flight, and flight itself afforded no escape. What God at that time presented to us, to the Roman people, this Heaven-sent young man, who, when every avenue to our destruction lay open for that pestilent citizen, suddenly, beyond the hope of all, arose and got together an army to oppose to the frenzy of Marcus Antonius before anyone suspected any such intention of his? . . . But Caesar has armed veterans now desirous of rest; he has embraced the cause that would be most grateful to the Senate, to the people, to all Italy, and to Gods and men. . . .

Let us therefore give Caesar the command, without which no military affairs can be administered, no army held together, no war waged; let him be pro-praetor with the fullest power of a regular appointment. That honour is a great one at his age, but it serves to assist the measures necessary to be taken, not merely to enhance his dignity. Therefore let us ask for that, which is as much as we shall gain to-day.

But I do hope that both we and the Roman people shall often be enabled to distinguish and honour this young man. However, at this time I propose that the following should be our decree:

'Whereas Caius Caesar, the son of Caius, Pontifex, pro-praetor, at a serious crisis of the State has exhorted the veteran soldiers to defend the liberty of the Roman people, and has enrolled them; and whereas the Martian legion and the Fourth, with the utmost zeal, and the most admirable unanimity in serving the State, under the command and authority of Caius Caesar, are defending, and have defended, the State and the liberty of the Roman people; and whereas Caius Caesar, pro-praetor, has with an army set out for the relief of the province of Gaul, has brought within his own obedience and that of the Roman people cavalry, archers, and elephants, and has, at a most difficult crisis of the State, come to the assistance of the lives and dignity of the Roman people—therefore for these reasons it is the pleasure of the Senate that Caius Caesar, the son of Caius, Pontifex, pro-praetor, be a senator, and express his opinion on the praetorian benches; and that, whatever be the office he shall seek, the same account be taken of his candidature as would be legally permissive if he had been quaestor the preceding year.'

Cicero *Philippics* 5.16–17 (abridged)
tr. W. C. Ker (Loeb 1969)

B9 Antony on Octavian

These words of Antony were quoted by Cicero in the Senate in April 43. The name is of course Caesar, which Octavian (then Octavius (see B3)) took on his adoption, and there was some truth in Antony's gibe.

You, boy, owe everything to your name.

Cicero *Philippics* 13. 11. 24–5
tr. J. Ferguson

B10 Private armies

Appian of Alexandria (AD c. 95–165) wrote a History of Rome *which concentrates mainly on military history. It is, however, a useful source for the first century BC especially for the period after the death of Julius Caesar. Private armies played a major role in Roman affairs from the civil wars of Marius and Sulla. Octavian had to pay Caesar's veterans considerable sums to raise his own army (cf. RG 1 and B19); note that the troops' faith in future victory (with its accompanying rewards of land and money) was perhaps not always enough to ensure loyalty to a particular commander.*

(a)

Presently news was brought to Octavian by his secret emissaries that the army at Brundisium and the colonized soldiers were incensed against Antony for neglecting to avenge the murder of Caesar, and that they would assist him (Octavian) to do so if they could. For this reason Antony departed to Brundisium. As Octavian feared lest Antony, returning with the army, should catch him unprotected, he went to Campania with money to enlist the veterans who had been settled in those towns by his father. He first brought over those of Calatia and next those of Casilinum, two towns situated on either side of Capua, giving 500 drachmas to each man. He collected about 10,000 men, not fully armed and not mustered in regular cohorts, but serving merely as body-guard under one banner.

Appian *Civil Wars* 3. 6. 40
tr. H. White (Loeb 1913)

(b)

Antony was angry at their silence. He did not keep his temper, but charged them with ingratitude in that they had expressed no thanks for being transferred from the Parthian expedition to Italy. He blamed them [his troops] because they had not arrested and delivered to him the emissaries of a rash boy (for so he called Octavian) who had been sent among them to stir up discord. Those men he would find out himself, he said; but the army he would lead to the province voted to him, the prosperous Gallic country, and would give 100 drachmas to each man present. They laughed at his parsimony, and when he became angry they broke out in tumult and went away.

Appian *Civil Wars* 3. 7. 43
tr. H. White (Loeb 1913)

B POLITICS AND POWER

B11 Octavian defers to the Senate

An early example (from 44 BC) of Octavian's adherence to conventional Republican forms, in spite of the Senate's lack of power.

Octavian had two legions equally efficient, those which had deserted from Antony to him, also one legion of new levies, and two of veterans, not complete in numbers or in arms, but these also filled up with new recruits. He brought them all to Alba and there communicated with the Senate, which congratulated him in such a way that now one would have been at a loss to know who were those who had lately ranged themselves with Antony; but it regretted that the legions had not come over to the Senate itself instead of to him. It praised them and Octavian nevertheless, and said that it would vote them whatever was needful as soon as the new magistrates should enter upon their duties. It was plain that the Senate would use these forces against Antony; but having no army of its own anywhere, and being unable to levy one without consuls, it adjourned all business until the new consuls should come in.

The soldiers of Octavian furnished him lictors provided with fasces and urged him to assume the title of propraetor, carrying on war and acting as their leader, since they were always marshalled under magistrates. He thanked them for the honour, but referred the matter to the Senate. When they wanted to go before the Senate *en masse* he prevented them and would not even allow them to send messengers, believing that the Senate would vote these things to him voluntarily; 'and all the more,' he said, 'if they know of your zeal and my hesitation.'

Appian *Civil Wars* 3. 7. 47–8
tr. H. White (Loeb 1913)

B12 A *coup-d'état*

These events occurred in July 43 BC. Octavian demanded one of the consulships left vacant by Hirtius and Pansa, and backed up his demand with his army. Pompey the Great was first made consul in 70 BC, six years below the minimum age, and without going through the necessary preliminary offices of quaestor and praetor; P. Cornelius Dolabella was nominated by Caesar for the consulship of 44 BC; Caesar himself was first elected consul in 60 BC, but, in fact, had just reached the minimum legal age of forty-three when he took up office at the beginning of 59.

'I see only one path of safety now for both of us: if I should obtain the consulship by your help. In that case all my father's gifts to you will be confirmed, the colonies that are still due to you will be forthcoming, and all your rewards will be paid in

32

full; and I should bring the murderers to punishment and release you from any more wars.'

At these words the army cheered heartily, and forthwith sent their centurions to ask the consulship for Octavian. When the Senate began to make talk about his youth, the centurions replied, as they had been instructed, that in the olden times Corvinus had held the office and at a later period the Scipios, both the elder and the younger, before the legal age, and that the country profited much from the youth of each. They instanced, as recent examples, Pompey the Great and Dolabella and said that it had been granted to Caesar himself to stand for the consulship ten years before the legal age. While the centurions were arguing with much boldness, some of the senators, who could not endure that centurions should use such freedom of speech, rebuked them for exceeding the bounds of military discipline. When the army heard of this, they were still more exasperated and demanded to be led immediately to the city, saying that they would hold a special election and raise Octavian to the consulship because he was Caesar's son.

Appian *Civil Wars* 3. 12. 87–8
tr. H. White (Loeb 1913)

B13 The triumvirate

The triumvirate was formed in November 43 after Octavian had become consul and could deal with Antony from a position of strength.

(a)

Octavian and Antony composed their differences on a small depressed islet in the river Lavinius, near the city of Mutina. Each had five legions of soldiers whom they stationed opposite each other, after which each proceeded with 300 men to the bridges over the river. Lepidus by himself went before them, searched the island, and waved his military cloak as a signal to them to come. Then each left his three hundred in charge of friends on the bridges and advanced to the middle of the island in plain sight, and there the three sat together in council, Octavian in the centre because he was consul. They were in conference from morning till night for two days, and came to these decisions: that Octavian should resign the consulship and that Ventidius should take it for the remainder of the year; that a new magistracy for quieting the civil dissensions should be created by law, which Lepidus, Antony, and Octavian should hold for five years with consular power (for this name seemed preferable to that of dictator, perhaps because of Antony's decree abolishing the dictatorship); that these three should at once designate the yearly magistrates of the city for the five years; that a distribution of the provinces should be made, giving Antony the whole of Gaul except the part bordering the Pyrenees

Mountains, which was called Old Gaul; this, together with Spain, was assigned to Lepidus; while Octavian was to have Africa, Sardinia and Sicily, and the other islands in the vicinity thereof.

Appian *Civil Wars* 4. 1. 2
tr. H. White (Loeb 1913)

(b) *This passage emphasizes the financial aspect of the proscriptions. Syme (*RR *p. 195) calls them a peculiar levy on capital. The victory at Philippi enhanced Antony's popularity. Compare this account with that of B16 where Augustus is shown as victor.*

21   This triumvirate was hateful to the Romans, and Antony most of all bore the blame, because he was older than Caesar, and had greater authority than Lepidus, and also because he had no sooner settled his affairs than he turned to his luxurious and dissolute way of living. Besides the bad reputation he gained by his general behaviour, it was a considerable disadvantage for him to be living in the house of Pompey the Great, who had been much admired for his temperance and his sober, citizen-like habits of life, and for having triumphed three times. It made them angry to see the doors of that house shut against magistrates, officers, and envoys, who were shamefully refused admittance, while it was filled inside with players, jugglers, and drunken flatterers, upon whom were spent the greatest part of the wealth which violence and cruelty procured. For they did not limit themselves to the sale of the estates of those who were proscribed, defrauding the widows and families, nor were they content to levy every possible kind of tax and imposition; but hearing that sums of money were deposited, both by strangers and citizens of Rome, in the hands of the Vestal Virgins, they went and took the money away by force. When it was clear that nothing would ever be enough for Antony, Caesar at last called for a division of property. The army was also divided between them, when they marched into Macedonia to make war on Brutus and Cassius, Lepidus being left with the command of the city.

22   However, after they had crossed the sea and engaged in warlike operations and camped near the enemy, Antony opposite Cassius, and Octavius Caesar opposite Brutus, Caesar did nothing worth relating, and the success and victory were Antony's. In the first battle, Caesar was completely routed by Brutus, his camp taken, he himself very narrowly escaping by flight. As he himself writes in his Memoirs, he retired before the battle, on account of a dream which one of his friends had. But Antony, on the other hand, defeated Cassius; though some have written that he was not actually present in the engagement, and only joined afterwards in the pursuit. Cassius was killed, at his own entreaty and order, by one of his most trusted freedmen, Pindar, not being aware of Brutus's victory. After a few days' interval, they fought another battle, in which Brutus lost the day, and slew himself; and Caesar being sick, Antony had almost all the honor of the victory.

Plutarch *Antony* 21–2
tr. Dryden, rev. A. H. Clough

B14 The proscription edict

The proscription edict was in the following words: 'Marcus Lepidus, Marcus Antonius, and Octavius Caesar, chosen by the people to set in order and regulate the Republic, declare as follows:

'Had not perfidious traitors begged for mercy and when they had obtained it become the enemies of their benefactors and conspired against them, neither would Gaius Caesar have been slain by those whom he saved by his clemency after capturing them in war, whom he admitted to his friendship, and upon whom he heaped offices, honors, and gifts, nor should we have been compelled to use this widespread severity against those who have insulted us and declared us public enemies. Now, seeing that the malice of those who have conspired against us and by whose hands Gaius Caesar perished cannot be mollified by kindness, we prefer to anticipate our enemies rather than suffer at their hands. Let no one who sees what both Caesar and we ourselves have suffered consider our action unjust, cruel, or immoderate. Although Caesar was clothed with supreme power, although he was *pontifex maximus*, although he had overthrown and added to our sway the nations most formidable to the Romans, although he was the first man to attempt the untried sea beyond the Pillars of Hercules and was the discoverer of a country hitherto unknown to the Romans, this man was slain in the middle of the senate house, which is designated as sacred, under the eyes of the gods, with twenty-three dastardly wounds, by men whom he had taken prisoner in war and had spared, while some of them he had named co-heirs of his wealth. After this execrable crime, instead of arresting the guilty wretches, the rest sent them forth as commanders and governors, in which capacity they seized upon the public money, with which they are collecting an army against us and are seeking reinforcements from barbarians ever hostile to Roman rule. Cities subject to Rome that would not obey them they have burned, ravaged, or levelled to the ground; other cities they have forced by terror to bear arms against the country and against us.

'Some of them we have punished already; and by the aid of divine providence you shall presently see the rest punished. Although the chief part of this work has been finished by us or is well under control, namely the settlement of Spain and Gaul as well as matters here in Italy, one task still remains, and that is to march against Caesar's assassins beyond the sea. On the eve of undertaking this foreign war for you, we do not consider it safe, either for you or for us, to leave other enemies behind to take advantage of our absence and watch for opportunities during the war; nor again do we think that in such great urgency we should delay on their account, but that we ought rather to sweep them out of our pathway once and for all, seeing that they began the war against us when they voted us and the armies under us public enemies.

'What vast numbers of citizens have they, on their part, doomed to destruction with us, disregarding the vengeance of the gods and the reprobation of mankind! We shall not deal harshly with any multitude of men, nor shall we count as enemies all who have opposed or plotted against us, or those distinguished for their riches merely, their abundance or their high position, or as many as another man slew who held the supreme power before us when he too was regulating the common-wealth in civil convulsions, and whom you named the Fortunate on account of his success; and yet necessarily three persons will have more enemies than one. We shall take vengeance only on the worst and most guilty. This we shall do for your interest no less than for our own, for while we keep up our conflicts you will all be involved necessarily in great dangers, and it is necessary for us also to do some-thing to quiet the army, which has been insulted, irritated, and decreed a public enemy by our common foes. Although we might arrest on the spot whomsoever we had determined on, we prefer to proscribe rather than seize them unawares—and this too on your account, so that it may not be in the power of enraged soldiers to exceed their orders against persons not responsible, but that they may be restricted to a certain number designated by name and spare the others according to order.

'So be it then! Let no one harbor anyone of those whose names are appended to this edict, or conceal them, or send them away anywhere, or be corrupted by their money. Whoever shall be detected in saving, aiding, or conniving with them we will put on the list of the proscribed without allowing any excuse or pardon. Let those who kill the proscribed bring us their heads and receive the following rewards: to a free man 25,000 Attic drachmas per head, to a slave his freedom and 10,000 Attic drachmas and his master's right of citizenship. Informers shall receive the same rewards. In order that they may remain unknown the names of those who receive the rewards shall not be inscribed in our records.' Such was the language of the proscription edict of the triumvirs as nearly as it can be rendered from Latin into Greek. . . .

Appian *Civil Wars* 4. 2. 8–11
tr. H. White (Loeb 1913) abridged. Lewis and Reinhold vol. 1

B15 The death of Cicero

(a)
But after Antony had been defeated and, both consuls having died after the battle, the forces had united under Caesar, the senate became afraid of a young man who had enjoyed such brilliant good fortune, and endeavoured by honours and gifts to call his troops away from him and to circumscribe his power, on the ground that there was no need of defensive armies now that Antony had taken to flight. Under these circumstances Caesar took alarm and secretly sent messengers to Cicero begging and urging him to obtain the consulship for them both, but to manage affairs as he himself thought best, after assuming the office, and to direct in all things a youthful colleague who only craved name and fame. And Caesar himself admitted afterwards that it was the fear of having his troops disbanded and the danger of finding himself left alone which led him to make use in an emergency

of Cicero's love of power, by inducing him to sue for the consulship with his co-operation and assistance in the canvass.

Here, indeed, more than at any other time, Cicero was led on and cheated, an old man by a young man. He assisted Caesar in his canvass and induced the senate to favour him. For this he was blamed by his friends at the time, and shortly afterwards he perceived that he had ruined himself and betrayed the liberty of the people. For after the young man had waxed strong and obtained the consulship, he gave Cicero the go-by, and after making friends with Antony and Lepidus and uniting his forces with theirs, he divided the sovereignty with them, like any other piece of property. And a list was made out by them of men who must be put to death, more than two hundred in number. The proscription of Cicero, however, caused most strife in their debates, Antony consenting to no terms unless Cicero should be the first man to be put to death, Lepidus siding with Antony, and Caesar holding out against them both. They held secret meetings by themselves near the city of Bononia for three days, coming together in a place at some distance from the camps and surrounded by a river. It is said that for the first two days Caesar kept up his struggle to save Cicero, but yielded on the third and gave him up. The terms of their mutual concessions were as follows. Caesar was to abandon Cicero, Lepidus his brother Paulus, and Antony Lucius Caesar, who was his uncle on the mother's side. So far did anger and fury lead them to renounce their human sentiments, or rather, they showed that no wild beast is more savage than man when his passion is supplemented by power.

Plutarch *Cicero* 45. 4–46. 4
tr. B. Perrin (Loeb 1919)

(b)   *Augustus' opinion of Cicero*

A long time afterwards, so I have been told, Caesar was visiting the son of one of his daughters. The boy had a book of Cicero's in his hands and, terrified of his grandfather, tried to hide it under his cloak. Caesar noticed this and, after taking the book from him, stood there and read a great part of it. He then handed it back to the young man with the words: 'A learned man, my child, a learned man and a lover of his country.'

Plutarch *Cicero* 49
tr. Rex Warner (Penguin 1958)

B16 Octavian's brutality

(a)

12   However, when Augustus heard that Mark Antony had been taken under Lepidus' protection and that the other military commanders, supported by their

troops, were coming to terms with these two, he at once deserted the aristocratic party. His excuse was that some of them had contemptuously called him 'the boy', while others had not concealed their view that, once publicly honoured, he should be done away with—to avoid having to pay his veterans and himself what they expected. Augustus showed regret for this temporary defection from the popular cause by imposing a heavier fine on the Nursians than they could possibly meet, and then exiling them from their city; they had offended him by erecting a monument to fellow-citizens killed at Mutina, with the inscription: 'Fallen in the cause of freedom!'

13   As member of a triumvirate consisting of Antony, Lepidus, and himself, Augustus defeated Brutus and Cassius at Philippi, though in ill-health at the time. In the first of the two battles fought he was driven out of his camp, and escaped with some difficulty to Antony's command. After the second and decisive one he showed no clemency to his beaten enemies, but sent Brutus's head to Rome for throwing at the feet of Caesar's divine image; and insulted the more distinguished of his prisoners. When one of these humbly asked for the right of decent burial, he got the cold answer: 'That must be settled with the carrion-birds.' And when a father and his son pleaded for their lives, Augustus, it is said, told them to decide which of the two should be spared, by casting lots. The father sacrificed his life for the son, and was executed; the son then committed suicide; Augustus watched them both die. His conduct so disgusted the remainder of the prisoners, including Marcus Favonius, a well-known disciple of Cato's, that while being led off in chains they courteously saluted Antony as their conqueror, but abused Augustus to his face with the most obscene epithets.

(b)   *The city is Perusia, which fell to Octavian in 41 BC. It may be that Aeneas' sacrifice of Trojan prisoners (Virgil Aeneid 11. 81 ff.) reflects these events.*

15   After the fall of the city Augustus took vengeance on crowds of prisoners and returned the same answers to all who sued for pardon or tried to explain their presence among the rebels. It was simply: 'You must die!' According to some historians, he chose 300 prisoners of equestrian or senatorial rank, and offered them on the Ides of March at the altar of the God Julius, as human sacrifices. Augustus fought, it is said, because he wished to offer his secret enemies, and those whom fear rather than affection kept with his party, a chance to declare themselves by joining Lucius Antonius; he would then crush them, confiscate their estates, and thus manage to pay off his veterans.

Suetonius *Augustus* 12–13; 15
tr. R. Graves (Penguin 1957)

B17 Cleopatra and Antony

(a) *This meeting took place at Tarsus in 41 BC. Ruler-worship was an established Eastern custom—indeed Roman governors had been worshipped before; Antony's acceptance of the role of Dionysus was perhaps part of a policy to conciliate as well as consolidate the Eastern provinces. The true relationship between Antony and Cleopatra has been clouded by the propaganda of the victor of Actium: politically it helped Antony's position in the East, but was fatal in Rome and Italy.*

She received several letters, both from Antony and from his friends, summoning her, but she took no account of these orders; and at last, as if in mockery of them, she came sailing up the river Cydnus, in a barge with gilded stern and outspread sails of purple, while oars of silver beat time to the music of flutes and pipes and lutes. She herself lay under a canopy of cloth of gold, dressed as Venus in a picture, and beautiful young boys, like Cupids in paintings, stood on each side to fan her. Her maids were dressed like Nereïds and Graces, some steering the rudder, some working the ropes. The perfumes spread from the vessel to the shore, which was covered with multitudes, part following the galley up the river on either bank, part running out of the city to see the sight. The market place emptied, and Antony at last was left alone sitting upon the tribunal; while the word went through all the multitude, that Venus had come to feast with Bacchus, for the common good of Asia.

On her arrival, Antony sent and invited her to supper. She thought it more fitting that he should come to her; so, willing to show his good humour and courtesy, he complied and went. He found the preparations to receive him magnificent beyond expression, but nothing so admirable as the great number of lights; for all of a sudden there was let down altogether a great number of branches with lights in them so ingeniously disposed, some in squares and some in circles, that the whole thing was a spectacle that has seldom been equalled for beauty.

Plutarch *Antony* 26
tr. Dryden, rev. A. H. Clough

(b) *Cleopatra was a woman of consummate ability, ambitious to rule the world. In this prophecy, she had a vision that she would cast Rome down from heaven to earth, then raise her from earth to heaven, inaugurate a golden age for Asia and Europe alike, and end feud, war, and bloodshed. See W. W. Tarn in* JRS *22 (1932) 135-60.*

> Tranquil peace shall journey to the land of Asia.
> Europe shall then be blessed, the atmosphere be fruitful,
> lasting, sturdy, free from storm or hail,
> bearing all creatures of the world, winged and earthbound.
> Blessed above all the man or woman who shall see that day . . .

> For from the starry sky, in its fullness the rule of law
> and righteousness will descend upon man, and with it
> the saving grace of concord, cherished beyond all else by mortals,
> love, trust, friendship with the stranger. Far from man
> poverty will flee, compulsion will flee,
> and lawlessness, carping, envy, anger, folly,
> murder and deadly strife and bitter conflict,
> robbery by night and every evil—in those days.

Sibylline Oracles 3. 367–80
tr. J. Ferguson

B18 Reconciliation of Octavian and Antony

This passage refers to the pact of Brundisium of 40 BC (cf. Dio Cassius 48. 28. 3–29. 1). Virgil's fourth Eclogue, *written in 40 BC reflects the hopes of peace (F2).*

When Octavian's soldiers learned these facts they chose deputies and sent the same ones to both commanders. They took no notice of accusations because they had been chosen, not to decide a controversy, but to restore peace. Cocceius was added to their number as a friend of both, together with Pollio from Antony's party and Maecenas from that of Octavian. It was determined that there should be amnesty between Antony and Octavian for the past and friendship for the future. Moreover, as Marcellus, the husband of Octavian's sister Octavia, had recently died, the umpires decided that her brother should betroth her to Antony, which he did immediately. Then Antony and Octavian embraced each other. Thereupon shouts went up from the soldiers and congratulations were offered to each of the generals, without intermission, through the entire day and night.

Now Octavian and Antony made a fresh partition of the whole Roman empire between themselves, the boundary line being Scodra, a city of Illyria which was supposed to be situated about midway up the Adriatic gulf. All provinces and islands east of this place, as far as the river Euphrates, were to belong to Antony and all west of it to the ocean to Octavian. Lepidus was to govern Africa, inasmuch as Octavian had given it to him. Octavian was to make war against Pompeius unless they should come to some agreement, and Antony was to make war against the Parthians to avenge their treachery toward Crassus. Octavian was to make the same agreement with Ahenobarbus that Antony had already made. Both of them might freely enlist soldiers in Italy in equal numbers.

These were the last conditions of peace between Octavian and Antony.

Appian *Civil Wars* 5. 7. 64–5
tr. H. White (Loeb 1913)

B19 Soldiers' rewards

The power conferred by the loyalty of the legions meant that their interests were put first; for a powerful expression of feeling against dispossession see B50. Mark Antony's wife Fulvia and his brother Lucius saw the dangerous influence and power gained by Octavian as the one leader dispensing grants of land and, in trying to obstruct him, sparked off war in Italy of which Antony was probably entirely ignorant. They were defeated finally at Perusia. Antony was reconciled to Octavian at Brundisium in 40 BC (see B16 and 18).

The task of assigning the soldiers to their colonies and dividing the land was one of exceeding difficulty. For the soldiers demanded the cities which had been selected for them before the war as prizes for their valour, and the cities demanded that the whole of Italy should share the burden or that the cities should cast lots with the other cities, and that those who gave the land should be paid the value of it; and there was no money. They came to Rome in crowds, young and old, women and children, to the forum and the temples uttering lamentations, saying that they had done no wrong for which they, Italians, should be driven from their fields and their hearth-stones, like people conquered in war. The Romans mourned and wept with them, especially when they reflected that the war had been waged, and the rewards of victory given, not on behalf of the commonwealth, but against themselves and for a change of the form of government; that the colonies were established to the end that democracy should never again lift its head,—colonies composed of hirelings settled there by the rulers to be in readiness for whatever purpose they might be wanted.

13   Octavian explained to the cities the necessity of the case, but he knew that it would not satisfy them; and it did not. The soldiers encroached upon their neighbours in an insolent manner, seizing more than had been given to them and choosing the best lands; nor did they cease even when Octavian rebuked them and made them numerous other presents, since they needed them to confirm their power, for the five years' term of the triumvirate was passing away, and army and rulers needed the services of each other for mutual security. The chiefs depended on the soldiers for the continuance of their government, while, for the possession of what they had received, the soldiers depended on the permanence of the government of those who had given it. Believing that they could not keep a firm hold unless the givers had a strong government, they fought for them, from necessity, with good-will. Octavian made many other gifts to the indigent soldiers, borrowing from the temples for that purpose, for which reason the affections of the army were turned toward him, and the greater thanks were bestowed upon him both as the giver of the land, the cities, the money, and the houses, and as the object of denunciation on the part of the despoiled and as one who bore this contumely for the army's sake.

14   Observing this, Lucius Antonius, the brother of Antony, who was then consul, and Fulvia, the wife of Antony, and Manius, his procurator during his absence, resorted to artifices to delay the settlement of the colonies till Antony

should return home, in order that it might not seem to be wholly the work of Octavian, and that he might not reap the thanks alone, and Antony be bereft of the favour of the soldiers. As this evidently could not be done, on account of the haste of the soldiers, they asked that Octavian should take the colony leaders of Antony's legions from Antony's own friends, although the agreement with Antony yielded the selection to Octavian exclusively; they made it a matter of complaint that Antony was not present. They themselves brought Fulvia and Antony's children before the soldiers, and, in terms such as would cause ill feeling, besought them not to forget Antony or allow him to be deprived of the glory or the gratitude due to his service to them. The fame of Antony was then at its height, not only among the soldiers, but among all others. The victory of Philippi was considered wholly due to him, on account of Octavian's illness. Although Octavian was not ignorant that it was a violation of the agreement, he yielded as a matter of favour to Antony, and appointed friends of the latter as colony leaders for Antony's legions. These leaders, in order that they might appear more favourable to the soldiers than Octavian was, allowed them to commit still greater outrages. So there was another multitude from another group of communities, neighbours of the dispossessed ones, suffering many injuries at the hands of the soldiers, and crying out against Octavian, saying that the colonisation was worse than the proscription, since the latter was directed against foes, while the former was against unoffending persons.

15 Octavian knew that these citizens were suffering injustice, but he was without means to prevent it, for there was no money to pay the value of the land to the cultivators, nor could the rewards to the soldiers be postponed, on account of the enemies who were still on foot. Pompeius ruled the sea and was reducing the city to famine by cutting off supplies: Ahenobarbus and Murcus were collecting a new fleet and army: the soldiers would be less zealous in the future if they were not paid for their former service. It was a matter of much importance that the five years' term of office was running out, and that the good-will of the soldiers was needed to renew it, for which reason he was willing to overlook for the time being their insolence and arrogance. Once in the theatre when he was present, a soldier not finding his own seat, went and took one in the place reserved for the knights. The people pointed him out and Octavian had him removed. The soldiers were angry. They gathered around Octavian as he was going away from the theatre and demanded their comrade, for, as they did not see him, they thought that he had been put to death. When he was produced before them they supposed that he had been brought from prison, but he denied that he had been imprisoned and related what had taken place. They said that he had been instructed to tell a lie and reproached him for betraying their common interests. Such was the example of their insolence in the theatre.

Appian *Civil Wars* 5. 2. 12–15
tr. H. White (Loeb 1913)

B20 Riots in Rome

These events occurred in late 40 BC. Note that at this time Octavian's resources and popularity were at a low ebb, his need of Antony's support and of a victory against Sextus Pompeius considerable.

Now famine fell upon Rome, since the merchants of the Orient could not put to sea for fear of Pompeius, who controlled Sicily, and those of the west were deterred by Sardinia and Corsica, which the lieutenants of Pompeius held, while those of Africa opposite were prevented by the same hostile fleets, which infested both shores. Thus there was a great rise in cost of provisions, and the people considered the cause of it to be the strife between the chiefs and cried out against them and urged them to make peace with Pompeius. As Octavian would by no means yield, Antony advised him to hasten the war on account of the scarcity. As there was no money for this purpose, an edict was published that the owners of slaves should pay a tax for each one, equal to one-half of the twenty-five drachmas that had been ordained for the war against Brutus and Cassius, and that those who acquired property by legacies should contribute a share thereof. The people tore down the edict with fury. They were exasperated that, after exhausting the public treasury, stripping the provinces, burdening Italy itself with contributions, taxes, and confiscations, not for foreign war, not for extending the empire but for private enmities and to add to their own power (for which reason the proscriptions and murders and this terrible famine had come about), the triumvirs should deprive them of the remainder of their property.

They banded together, with loud cries, and stoned those who did not join them, and threatened to plunder and burn their houses until the whole populace was aroused, and Octavian with his friends and a few attendants came into the forum intending to intercede with the people and to show the unreasonableness of their complaints. As soon as he made his appearance they stoned him unmercifully, and they were not ashamed when they saw him enduring this treatment patiently, and offering himself to it, and even bleeding from wounds. When Antony learned what was going on he came with haste to his assistance. When the people saw him coming down the Via Sacra they did not throw stones at him, since he was in favour of a treaty with Pompeius, but they told him to go away. When he refused to do so they stoned him also. He called in a larger force of troops, who were outside the walls. As the people would not allow him even so to pass through, the soldiers divided right and left on either side of the street and the forum, and made their attack from the narrow lane, striking down those whom they met. The people could no longer find ready escape on account of the crowd, nor was there any way out of the forum. There was a scene of slaughter and wounds while shrieks and groans sounded from the housetops. Antony made his way into the forum with difficulty, and snatched Octavian from the most manifest danger, in which he then was, and brought him safe to his house. The mob having been dispersed, the corpses were thrown into the river in order to avoid their gruesome appearance. It was a fresh cause of lamentation to see them floating down the stream, and the soldiers stripping them, and certain miscreants, as well as the soldiers, carrying off the clothing of the better class as their own property.

Appian <i>Civil Wars</i> 5. 8. 67–8
tr. H. White (Loeb 1913)

B21 Pact of Tarentum

The treaty of Misenum (39 BC) between Antony, Octavian, and Sextus Pompeius was short-lived. Appian gives a vivid description of the war between Octavian and Pompeius which rapidly followed (Civil Wars 5.9.81–13.122). Initially Octavian suffered repeated defeats, partly due to fierce storms, and in the spring of 37 he came to an arrangement with Antony, the pact of Tarentum; Octavian's final victory was largely due to Agrippa's skill at sea. Octavia's role might be exaggerated in the interests of propaganda (cf. M. A. Levi Ottaviano Capoparte (Florence 1933) pp. 11, 71) but Appian's account of Antony's position seems less biased than those of Dio Cassius (48.54.1 ff.) and Plutarch (Antony 35).

92 Less than half of Octavian's ships were saved, and these badly damaged. He left certain officers in charge of them and proceeded to Campania much cast down, for he had no other ships and he needed many; nor did he have time to build them, pressed as he was by the famine and by the people, who were again harassing him about a new treaty and mocking at the war as being in violation of the old one. He needed money, but had none. The Romans were not paying the taxes, nor would they allow the use of the revenues that he had devised. But he was always clever at discovering what was for his advantage. He sent Maecenas to Antony to change the mind of the latter representing the things about which they had lately had some bickering, and to bring him to an alliance. If Maecenas should not succeed, he intended to embark his infantry on merchant vessels, cross over to Sicily, abandon the sea, and wage war on land. While in this state of dejection the news reached him that Antony had agreed to the alliance, and he heard of a splendid victory over the Gauls of Aquitania, gained under the leadership of Agrippa. . . His friends and certain cities also promised him ships, and built them.

Accordingly, Octavian cast off his despondency, and made more formidable preparations than his previous ones.

93 At the beginning of spring, Antony set sail from Athens to Tarentum with 300 ships to assist Octavian as he had promised. But the latter had changed his mind and postponed his movement until his own ships should be finished. When called upon again and told that Antony's forces were ready and sufficient, he advanced other reasons for delay. It was evident that he was again offended with Antony about something, or that he disdained his assistance because his own resources were abundant. Antony was vexed, but he remained, nevertheless, and

communicated with Octavian again, because the expense of his fleet was burdensome. Moreover, he needed Italian soldiers for his war against the Parthians, and he contemplated exchanging his fleet for a part of Octavian's army; for, although it was provided in their treaty that each of them might recruit soldiers in Italy, it would be difficult for him to do so when Italy had fallen to the lot of Octavian. Accordingly, Octavia betook herself to her brother to act as mediator between them. Octavian complained that he had been abandoned by Antony when he was overtaken by danger in the straits; she replied that that had been explained through Maecenas. Octavian said that Antony had sent his freedman Callias to Lepidus in Africa to induce the latter to make an alliance against him; she replied that she knew that Callias had been sent to make arrangements about a marriage, because Antony desired, before setting out on his Parthian expedition, to marry his daughter to the son of Lepidus, as had been agreed. After Octavia had made this statement Antony sent Callias to Octavian with permission to put him to the question. Octavian would not receive him, but he said that he would go and have an interview with Antony between Metapontum and Tarentum, at a place where there is the river whence the town is named between them.

94   They both chanced to reach the river at the same time. Antony sprang down from his chariot and leaped alone into one of the skiffs moored near by, and rowed toward Octavian, showing confidence in him as a friend. When Octavian saw this he followed the example. So they met in the stream and contended with each other which of them should disembark on the other's bank. Octavian prevailed because he was going to make a visit to Octavia at Tarentum. He took a seat with Antony in the latter's chariot, and proceeded to his lodgings at Tarentum unprotected, and passed the night there without guards. On the following day Antony made the same exhibition of trust. Thus they were continually changing from suspicion born of rivalry to confidence due to their mutual needs.

Appian *Civil Wars* 5. 10. 92–4
tr. H. White (Loeb 1913)

B22 Octavian returns from war

This passage refers to the aftermath of the war against Sextus Pompeius. Octavian's position was now very strong, and it was strengthened further by his successful campaign in Illyria. Appian is mistaken in the conferring of the office of tribune for life. Octavian received only the sacrosanctity of a tribune at this stage (36 BC) according to Dio Cassius (49. 15. 5); he was granted tribunician power for life in 23 BC (see B30). The 'placing amongst tutelary gods' is also controversial as Octavian was deified after his death (as Augustus). This passage could refer perhaps to prayers of thanksgiving offered to him, or to statues of him put up by Italian municipalities in their temples (Syme RR p. 233).

This seemed to be the end of the civil dissensions. Octavian was now twenty-eight years of age. Cities joined in placing him among their tutelary gods. At this time Italy and Rome itself were openly infested with bands of robbers, whose doings were more like barefaced plunder than secret theft. Sabinus was chosen by Octavian to correct this disorder. He executed many of the captured brigands, and within one year brought about a condition of absolute security. At that time, they say, originated the custom and system of cohorts of night watchmen still in force. Octavian excited astonishment by putting an end to this evil with such unexampled rapidity. He allowed the yearly magistrates to administer public affairs, in many particulars, according to the customs of the country. He burned the writings which contained evidence concerning the civil strife, and said that he would restore the constitution entirely when Antony should return from the Parthian war, for he was persuaded that Antony, too, would be willing to lay down the government, the civil wars being at an end. Thereupon he was chosen tribune for life by acclamation, the people urging him, by offer of this perpetual magistracy, to give up his former one. This he accepted, and at the same time he wrote privately to Antony in refer- ence to the government. Antony gave instructions to Bibulus, who was going away from him, to confer with Octavian. He sent governors to take charge of his provinces in like manner as Octavian had done, and he had thoughts of joining the latter in his expedition against the Illyrians.

Appian *Civil Wars* 5. 13. 132
tr. H. White (Loeb 1913)

B23 The Donations of Alexandria

After disastrous defeats in Parthia in 36 BC Antony subdued Armenia in 34 BC but celebrated his triumph in Alexandria. This was followed by the granting of territory to Cleopatra and her children at an opulent ceremony (Caesarion's legitimacy was also proclaimed). Plutarch's account shows the effect of Octavian's propaganda, successful in identifying Antony with an Eastern, foreign, threat and casting him in the role of aggressor.

54   Antony also aroused great resentment because of the division of his inherit- ance which he carried out in Alexandria in favour of his children. People regarded this as an arrogant and theatrical gesture which seemed to indicate a hatred for his own country. Nevertheless, he assembled a great multitude in the athletic arena there, and had two thrones of gold, one for himself and one for Cleopatra, placed on a dais of silver, with smaller thrones for his children. First, he proclaimed Cleopatra Queen of Egypt, Cyprus, Libya, and Coele Syria and named Caesarion as her consort. This youth was believed to be a son of Julius Caesar, who had left Cleopatra pregnant. Next he proclaimed his own sons by Cleopatra to be Kings of

Kings. To Alexander he gave Armenia, Media, and Parthia, as soon as he should have conquered it, and to Ptolemy Phoenicia, Syria, and Cilicia. At the same time he presented his sons to the people, Alexander in a Median costume which was crowned by a tiara, and Ptolemy in boots, a short cloak, and a broad-brimmed hat encircled by a diadem. The latter wore Macedonian dress like the kings who succeeded Alexander the Great, and the former the dress of the Medes and Armenians. After the children had embraced their parents, the one was given a guard of honour of Armenians and the other of Macedonians. Cleopatra not only on this but on other public occasions wore a robe which is sacred to Isis, and she was addressed as the New Isis.

55 Octavius Caesar reported these actions to the Senate, and by repeatedly denouncing Antony in public he did his utmost to rouse the Roman people's anger against him. Antony for his part made a number of counter-accusations against Octavius. The most important of these were, first that after capturing Sicily from Sextus Pompeius he had not given Antony any share of the island; secondly, that after borrowing some of Antony's ships for this campaign he kept them for his own use; thirdly, that after removing his colleague Lepidus from his position as triumvir and degrading him, he took possession himself of the troops, the territories, and the revenues which had been assigned to Lepidus, and, finally, that he had distributed almost all the available land in Italy to his own soldiers and left nothing for Antony's. Octavius Caesar's retort to these charges was that he had deprived Lepidus of his authority because he was misusing it, and that as for his conquests in war he was willing to divide these with Antony as soon as Antony offered to share Armenia with him. He added that Antony's soldiers had no claim upon any lands in Italy. Their rewards lay in Media and Parthia which they had added to the Roman empire by their gallant campaigns under their Imperator.

Plutarch *Antony* 54–5
tr. I. Scott-Kilvert (Penguin 1965)

B24 Antony delays war

This passage refers to the summer of 32 BC.

The speed and extent of Antony's preparations alarmed Caesar, who feared he might be forced to fight the decisive battle that summer. For he lacked many necessaries, and the people hated to pay the taxes; citizens were called upon to pay a fourth of their income, and freedmen an eighth of their property, so that there were loud outcries against him, and disturbances throughout all Italy. And it is looked upon as one of the greatest of Antony's mistakes that he did not then press the war. For he allowed time for Caesar to make his preparations and for the commotions to pass. For while people were having their money called for, they were mutinous and violent; but, having paid it, they held their peace.

Plutarch *Antony* 58
tr. Dryden, rev. A. H. Clough

B25 Actium

On Actium see J. M. Carter The Battle of Actium: The Rise and Triumph of Augustus Caesar *(London 1970) which provides a clear account; cf. also Horace* Odes *1. 37 (F17).*

(a)

Then, in the consulship of Caesar and Messala Corvinus, the decisive battle took place at Actium. The victory of the Caesarian party was a certainty long before the battle. On this side commander and soldiers alike were full of ardor, on the other was general dejection; on the one side the rowers were strong and sturdy, on the other weakened by privations; on the one side ships of moderate size, not too large for speed, on the other vessels of a size that made them formidable in appearance only; no one was deserting from Caesar to Antony, while from Antony to Caesar someone or other deserted daily. . . .

Then came the day of the great conflict, on which Caesar and Antony led out their fleets and fought, the one for the safety of the world, the other for its ruin. . . . When the conflict began, on the one side was everything—commander, rowers, and soldiers; on the other, soldiers alone. Cleopatra took the initiative in the flight; Antony chose to be the companion of the fleeing queen rather than of his fighting soldiers, and the commander, whose duty it would have been to deal severely with deserters, now became a deserter from his own army. Even without their chief his men long continued to fight bravely, and despairing of victory they fought to the death. Caesar, desiring to win over by words those whom he might have slain with the sword, kept shouting and pointing out to them that Antony had fled, and kept asking them for whom and with whom they were fighting. But they, after fighting long for their truant commander, reluctantly surrendered their arms and yielded the victory, Caesar having promised them pardon and their lives before they could bring themselves to sue for these. . . .

The following year Caesar followed Cleopatra and Antony to Alexandria and there put the finishing touch to the civil wars. Antony promptly ended his life, thus by his death redeeming himself from the many charges of lack of manliness. As for Cleopatra, eluding the vigilance of her guards she caused an asp to be smuggled in to her, and ended her life by its venomous sting. . . .

Velleius Paterculus 2. 84-7
tr. F. W. Shipley (Loeb 1924) abridged Lewis and Reinhold vol. 1

(b)

Oh, when shall I, in joy at Caesar's victory,
    Drink Caecuban put by for feasts,
With you, my favoured friend, Maecenas, just as Jove
    Would wish, within your lofty hall,
While piping flutes and lyre combine their melodies,
    One Dorian, one Phrygian?
So drank we, not so long ago, when *Neptune's son*,
    Who'd sworn to put on Rome the chains
He'd taken from the faithless slaves he'd made his friends,
    Fled overseas, his ships all burned.
Now Roman soldiers—lies, you'll say in later times—
    Made over to a woman, bear
Weapons and stakes for her, can bring themselves to do
    Whatever wrinkled eunuchs bid.
While, reared among our battle-standards—shameful sight!—
    The sun can see mosquito-nets.
With snorting steeds, two thousand Gauls desert to us,
    With 'Caesar!' as their battle-cry;
And, backing water, ships among the foeman's fleet
    Lie skulking in the harbour walls.
Hail, triumph god! Do you keep back your golden car,
    Your oxen none has ever yoked?
Hail, triumph god! Not even from Jugurtha's war
    Brought you a captain like to this,
Nor Scipio, to whom, where Carthage lies forlorn,
    Valour has built a monument.
Conquered by land and sea, the enemy has changed
    His scarlet cloak for one of gloom;
Either he means, despite the adverse winds, to sail
    To Crete, that boasts a hundred towns,
Or to the Syrtes quicksands, stirred by southern gales,
    Or drifts haphazard on the sea.
Bring hither, boy, some cups that hold more wine than these,
    Some Chian, too, or Lesbian,
Or—that will do to keep our wambling stomachs still—
    Measure us out some Caecuban.
It's good to wash away in sweet, releasing wine
    Our anxious fears for Caesar's life.

Horace *Epodes* 9
tr. M. Oakley (Everyman 1967)

B26 The spoils of victory

A great deal of money came into circulation after the conquest of Egypt. This passage refers to the summer of 29 BC, when Octavian celebrated his triple triumph: for his Illyrian wars, for Actium, and for Egypt. It is interesting to note how quickly the vanquished at Actium had become identified with a foreign enemy.

After this Caesar bestowed eulogies and honours upon his lieutenants, as was customary, and to Agrippa he further granted, among other distinctions, a dark blue flag in honour of his naval victory, and he gave gifts to the soldiers; to the people he distributed four hundred sesterces apiece, first to the men who were adults, and afterwards to the children because of his cousin Marcellus. In view of all this, and because he would not accept from the cities of Italy the gold required for the crowns they had voted him, and because, furthermore, he not only paid all the debts he himself owed to others, as has been stated, but also did not insist on the payment of others' debts to him, the Romans forgot all their unpleasant experiences and viewed his triumph with pleasure, quite as if the vanquished had all been foreigners. So vast an amount of money, in fact, circulated through all parts of the city alike, that the price of goods rose and loans for which the borrower had been glad to pay twelve per cent. could now be had for one third of that rate.

Dio Cassius 51. 21. 2-5
tr. E. Cary (Loeb 1917)

B27 Peace

Velleius Paterculus (c.19 BC–after AD 30) wrote a Compendium of Roman History *which contains a full account of the principates of Augustus and Tiberius; it is a valuable, though partisan, source for this period, rather biographical in style. Velleius served in Germany and Pannonia under Tiberius, was quaestor in AD 7 and praetor in AD 15; he praised Tiberius, his family, and Sejanus lavishly (see K5 and 11b) and may have been personally affected by Sejanus' fall from power. This passage reflects the official propaganda on the restoration of the Republic (cf. RG 34), but also indicates a reason for its success: the genuine feeling of relief at the end of civil war in both Rome and Italy. Velleius unfortunately does not give details of constitutional changes and the two extra praetors he mentions were not introduced until 23 BC.*

(a)
The acclaim which greeted Augustus on his return to Italy and Rome, the welcome which he received from men of every calling, age, and rank, the magnificence of his triumphs and public shows could not fittingly be described even within the scope of an authoritative history, and certainly not in a limited work of this kind. There is

no boon that men can desire of the gods or gods grant to mankind, no conceivable wish or blessing which Augustus, on his return to Rome, did not bestow on the Republic, the Roman people, and the world.

Twenty years of civil war came to an end and abroad all hostilities ceased. Peace was re-established and the madness of armed conflict was assuaged in every quarter. Law and order were restored: the courts and the Senate once more enjoyed authority and prestige. The legal power of the magistrates was reinstated on its former footing (except that two additional praetors were appointed to supplement the customary eight). Thus the traditional time-honoured constitution of the Republic was restored. Agriculture revived, and with it religious observance and security of life and property. There was useful law reform and beneficial legislation. Appointments to the Senate were made dispassionately but not uncritically. Eminent men and those who had earned triumphs and the principal honours of state were invited by the Princeps to grace Rome with their presence. True, Augustus was unable to avoid holding the consulship eleven times in succession, despite his frequently expressed and deeply felt reluctance; for he was as adamant in refusing a dictatorship as the people was persistent in offering him one.

As for the wars waged under his command, his successful pacification of the world and his numerous achievements at home and abroad, to cover these would exhaust a writer prepared to spend a lifetime on the subject. My professed intention has simply been to give a general picture of his principate.

> Velleius Paterculus, 2. 89 (Teubner with Madvig's emendations)
> tr. A. Lentin

(b) *Augustus' 6th consulship was in 28 BC.*

And in as much as he had put into effect very many illegal and unjust regulations during the factional strife and the wars, especially in the period of his joint rule with Antony and Lepidus, he abolished them all by a single decree, setting the end of his sixth consulship as the time for their expiration.

> Dio Cassius 53. 1. 5
> tr. E. Cary (Loeb 1917)

(c) *On the temple of Janus see further E17.*
For Augustus' conquests see RG 25–30 and C3b.

The gates of the Temple of Janus on the Quirinal, which had been closed no more than twice since the foundation of Rome, he closed three times during a far shorter period, as a sign that the Empire was at peace on land and at sea. He enjoyed a triumphal ovation after Philippi, and again after his Sicilian successes—and celebrated three full triumphs for his victories won in Dalmatia, off Actium, and at Alexandria.

> Suetonius *Augustus* 22
> tr. R. Graves (Penguin 1957)

B28 Dio's account of the settlement of 27 BC

Dio Cassius, from Nicaea in Bithynia, wrote a history of Rome from the beginnings to AD 229; writing two centuries after the settlement of 27 BC, he is perhaps too inclined to present the constitutional changes as a sufficient legal framework from which Augustus could emerge as a fully formed autocrat. However, according to Strabo (18. 3. 24–5) Augustus did accept 'the leadership of the Empire' at that time. It is interesting to compare Augustus' own statement in RG 34 and the precedents cited in the Lex de Imperio *of Vespasian as dating back to him (B32). Modern scholars conflict in their interpretation of Augustus' motives in 'restoring the Republic'; see L. Mitteis* Römisches Privatrecht *(Leipzig 1908) p. 352; O. Hirschfeld* Die kaiserlichen Verwaltungsbeamten *(Berlin 1905, 1963 edn.) p. 470; Syme* RR *passim; E. T. Salmon 'The Evolution of the Augustan Principate'* Historia *5 (1956) 456–78. Note also B29.*

While Caesar was engaged in setting his decision before them, varied feelings filled the minds of the senators. A few of them knew his real intention and as a result kept applauding him enthusiastically. Of the rest some were suspicious of what was said and others believed in it, and were therefore both equally amazed, the one class at his great subtlety and the other at the decision that he had reached. One side was displeased at his involved scheming and the other at his change of mind. For already there were some who detested the republican constitution as a source of factional difficulties, were pleased at the change of government, and took delight in Caesar. Consequently, though the announcement affected different persons differently, their views in regard to it were in each case the same. As for those who believed his sentiments to be genuine, any who wished it could not rejoice because of fear, nor the others lament because of hope. And as many as disbelieved it did not venture to accuse him and confute him, some because they were afraid, and others because they did not care to do so. Hence they all either were compelled or pretended to believe him. As for praising him, some did not have the courage and others were unwilling. Even in the midst of his reading there were frequent shouts and afterward many more. The senators begged that a monarchy be established, and directed all their remarks to that end until they forced him to assume the reins of government. At once they saw to it that twice as much pay was voted to the men who were to compose his bodyguard as to the rest of the soldiers, that this might incite the men to keep a careful watch on him. Then he began to show a real interest in setting up a monarchy.

In this way he had his headship ratified by the senate and the people. As he wished even so to appear to be republican in principle, he accepted all the care and superintendence of public business on the ground that it required expert attention, but said that he would not personally govern all the provinces and those that he did govern he would not keep in his charge perpetually. The weaker ones, because (as he said) they were peaceful and free from war, he gave over to the senate. But the more powerful he held in possession because they were unsettled and dangerous and either had enemies in adjoining territory or on their own account were able to cause a great uprising. His pretext was that the senate should fearlessly gather the fruits of the finest portion of the empire, while he himself had the labors and dangers; his real purpose was that by this plan the senators be unarmed and unprepared for battle, while he alone had arms and kept soldiers. Africa and Numidia, Asia and Greece with Epirus, the Dalmatian and Macedonian territories, Sicily, Crete, and Libya adjacent to Cyrene, Bithynia with the adjoining Pontus, Sardinia, and Baetica, were consequently held to belong to the people and the senate. Caesar's were the remainder of Spain, the neighborhood of Tarraco and Lusitania, all the Gauls (the Narbonensian and the Lugdunensian, the Aquitani and the Belgae), both themselves and the aliens settled among them. Some of the Celts whom we call Germans had occupied all the Belgic territory near the Rhine and caused it to be called Germania, the upper part extending to the sources of the river and the lower part reaching to the Ocean of Britain. These provinces, then, and the so-called Hollow Syria, Phoenicia and Cilicia, Cyprus and the Egyptians, fell at that time to Caesar's share. Later he gave Cyprus and Gaul adjacent to Narbo back to the people, and he himself took Dalmatia instead. This was also done subsequently in the case of other provinces, as the progress of my narrative will show. I have enumerated these in such detail because now each one of them is ruled separately, whereas in old times and for a long period the provinces were governed two and three together. The others I have not mentioned because some of them were acquired later, and the rest, even if they had been already subdued, were not being governed by the Romans, but either were left to enjoy their own laws or had been turned over to some kingdom or other. All of them that after this came into the Roman empire were attached to the possessions of the emperor then ruling. This then was the division of the provinces.

Wishing to lead the Romans still further away from the idea that he looked upon himself as absolute monarch, Caesar undertook the government of the regions given him for ten years. In the course of this time he promised to reduce them to quiet and he carried his hypocrisy to the point of saying that if they should be sooner pacified, he would deliver them sooner to the senate. Thereupon he first appointed the senators themselves to govern both classes of provinces except Egypt. This land, alone, for the reasons mentioned, he assigned to the *eques* previously named. Next he ordained that the rulers of senatorial provinces should be annual magistrates, selected by lot, unless any one had the special privilege accorded to a large number of children or to marriage. They were to be sent out by the general assembly of the senate, with no sword at their side and not wearing the military garb. The name proconsul was to belong not only to the two ex-consuls but also to the rest who had served as praetors or who at least held the rank of ex-praetors. Both classes were to employ as many lictors as were usual in the capital. He ordered further that they were to put on the insignia of their office immediately on leaving the *pomerium* and were to wear them continually until they should return. The heads of imperial provinces, on the other hand, were to be chosen by himself and be his agents, and they were to be named propraetors even if they were from the ranks of the ex-consuls. Of these two names which had for long been prevalent under the republic he gave that of praetor to the class chosen by him because from very early times war had been their care, and he called them also propraetors: the name of consul he gave to the others, because their duties were more peaceful, and called them in addition proconsuls. These particular names of praetor and consul he continued in Italy, and spoke of all officials outside as governing as their representatives. He caused the class of his own choosing to employ the title of propraetor and to hold office for as much longer than a year as should please him, wearing the military costume and having a sword with which they are empowered to punish soldiers. No one else, proconsul or propraetor or procurator, who is not empowered to kill a soldier, has been given the privilege of wearing a sword. It is permitted not only to senators but also to *equites* who have this function. This is the condition of the case. All the propraetors alike employ six lictors: as many of them as do not belong to the number of ex-consuls hold a title derived from this very number. Both classes alike assume the decorations of their position of authority when they enter their appointed district and lay them aside immediately upon finishing their term.

It is thus and on these conditions that governors from among the ex-praetors and ex-consuls have customarily been sent to both kinds of provinces. The emperor would send one of them on his mission wherever and whenever he wished. Many while acting as praetors and consuls secured the presidency of provinces, as sometimes happens at the present day. In the case of the senate he specially gave Africa and Asia to the ex-consuls and all the other districts to the ex-praetors. He publicly forbade senators to cast lots for a province until five years after such a candidate had held office in the city. For a short time all persons that fulfilled these requirements, even if they were more numerous than the provinces, drew lots for them. Later, as some of them did not govern well, this appointment too reverted to the emperor. Thus they also in a sense receive their position from him, and he ordains that only a number equal to the number of provinces shall draw lots, and that they shall be whatever men he pleases. Some emperors have sent men of their own choosing there also, and have allowed certain of them to hold office for more than a year: some have assigned certain provinces to *equites* instead of to senators.

These were the customs thus established at that time in regard to those senators that were authorized to execute the death penalty upon their subjects. Some who have not this authority are sent out to the provinces called 'provinces of the senate and the people'—namely, such quaestors as the lot may designate and men who are assessors to those who hold the actual authority. This would be the correct way to speak of these associates, with reference not to their ordinary name but to their duties: others call these also *presbeutai*, using the Greek term; about this title enough has been said in the foregoing narrative. Each separate official chooses his own assessors, the ex-praetors selecting one from either their peers or their inferiors, and the ex-consuls three from among those of equal length, subject to the approval of the emperor. There were certain innovations made also in regard to these men, but since they soon lapsed this is sufficient to say here.

This is the method followed in regard to the provinces of the people. To the others, called provinces of the emperor, which have more than one citizen-legion, lieutenants are sent chosen by the ruler himself, generally from the ex-praetors but in some instances from the ex-quaestors or those who had held some office between the two. Those positions, then, appertain to the senators.

From among the *equites* the emperor himself despatches the military tribunes, both the prospective senators and the remainder, concerning whose difference in rank I have previously spoken in the narrative, the former to the legions only, the latter also to the auxiliary units according to the custom then instituted by Caesar. The procurators (a name that we give to the men who collect the public revenues and spend what is ordered) he sends to all the provinces alike, his own and the people's, and some of these officers belong to the *equites*, others to the freedmen. By way of exception, the proconsuls levy the tribute upon the people they govern. The emperor gives certain mandates to the procurators, the proconsuls, and the propraetors, in order that they may proceed to their place of office on fixed conditions. Both this practice and the giving of salaries to them and to the remaining employees of the government were made the custom at this period. In old times contractors from the public treasury furnished them with everything needed for their office. It was only in the days of Caesar that they themselves began to receive a definite sum. This salary was not assigned to all of them in equal amounts, but as need demanded. The procurators get their very titles of rank from the amount of money which they receive. The following laws were laid down for all alike, that they should not conscript troops or levy money beyond the amount appointed, unless the senate should so vote or the emperor so order: also that when their successors should arrive, they were immediately to leave the province and not to delay on their return, but be back within three months.

These matters were so ordained at that time—or at least one might say so. In reality Caesar himself was destined to hold absolute control of all of them for all time, because he commanded the soldiers and was master of the money; nominally the public funds had been separated from his own, but in fact he spent the former also as he saw fit.

When this decade had come to an end, there was voted him another five years, then five more, after that ten, and again another ten, and a like number the fifth time, so that by a succession of ten-year periods he continued monarch for life. . . .

When he had really completed the details of administration, the name Augustus was finally bestowed upon him by the senate and by the people. They wanted to call him by some name of their own, and some proposed this, while others chose that. Caesar was exceedingly anxious to be called Romulus, but when he perceived that this caused him to be suspected of desiring the kingship, he no longer insisted on it but took the title of Augustus, signifying that he was more than human. All most precious and sacred objects are termed *augusta*. Therefore they saluted him also in Greek as *sebastos*, meaning an august person, from the verb *sebazesthai*.

In this way all the power of the people and the senate reverted to Augustus, and from his time there was a genuine monarchy.

Dio Cassius 53. 11-16. 4; 16. 6-17. 1
tr. Foster (Jones vol. 2)

B29 Augustus' intentions

With hindsight Suetonius sees Augustus as retaining the government in his own hands but at the time the author of the Laudatio Turiae *could say 'the Republic having been restored'; the* Fasti Praenestini *refer to the 'Republic restored to the people of Rome'; Ovid (*Fasti *1. 589) could refer to all provinces being returned to our people'. (See also B30 and RG 34).*

Twice Augustus seriously thought of restoring the Republican Constitution: immediately after the fall of Antony, when he remembered that Antony had often accused him of being the one obstacle to such a change; and again when he could not shake off an exhausting illness. He then actually summoned the chief Officers of State, with the rest of the Senate, to the Palace and gave them a faithful account of the military and financial state of the Empire. On reconsideration, however, he decided that to divide the responsibilities of government among several hands would be to jeopardize not only his own life, but national security; so he did nothing. The results were almost as good as his intentions, which he expressed from time to time and even published in an edict: 'May I be privileged to build firm and lasting foundations for the Government of Rome. May I also achieve the reward to which I aspire: that of being known as the author of the best possible Constitution, and of carrying with me, when I die, the hope that these foundations will abide secure.' And, indeed, he achieved this success, having taken great trouble to prevent his political system from causing any individual distress.

Suetonius *Augustus* 28
tr. R. Graves (Penguin 1957)

B30 The settlement of 23 BC

This passage is the only account of the changes in Augustus' constitutional position, known as the settlement of 23 BC. There was unrest and dissatisfaction at Rome. The trial of Marcus Primus, governor of Macedonia, threw into prominence the position of Marcellus as intended heir; the conspiracy of Fannius Caepio and Varro Murena was directed at Augustus himself. Feeling perhaps that the troubles arose from his holding the consulship every year since 31 and thereby limiting the availability of the highest magistracies, Augustus resigned from the consulship of 23. He received instead, from the Senate, the tribunicia potestas *(tribunician authority) for life, the right to bring matters to the Senate at any time, the right to retain his proconsular* imperium *even within the* pomerium *(the sacred boundary of the city) and he received a greater* imperium *for all provinces than that of any proconsul.*
This last conferred the most effective power and authority and Augustus chose

to play it down in official documents and lists of his titles. He emphasized instead his tribunician power, dating his reign by it, perhaps because it had favourable connotations as the authority of the traditional champion of the people. Dio's account of the greater proconsular imperium has often been questioned in the past but the Cyrene edicts (first published in 1927, see C20) are now generally held to be a confirmation of it.

Besides doing this Augustus appointed ten praetors, feeling that he did not require any more. This number remained constant for several years. The rest were intended to fulfill the same duties as before and two of them to have charge of the administration of the finances each year. Having settled these details he resigned the consulship and went to Albanum. He himself, ever since the constitution had been arranged, had held office for the entire year, as had most of his colleagues, and he wished now to interrupt this custom again, in order that as many as possible might be consuls. His resignation took place outside the city, to prevent his being hindered in his purpose.

For this act he received praise, as also because he chose to take his place Lucius Sestius, who had always been an enthusiastic follower of Brutus, had campaigned with the latter in all his wars, and even at this time spoke of him, kept his images, and delivered eulogies upon him. So far from disliking the friendly and faithful qualities of the man, the emperor even honored him.

The senate consequently voted that Augustus be tribune for life and that he might bring forward at each meeting of the senate any business he liked concerning any one matter, even if he should not be consul at the time, and allowed him to hold the office of proconsul once and for all perpetually, so that he had neither to lay it down on entering the *pomerium* nor to take it up again outside. The senate also granted him more power in subject territory than the several governors possessed. As a result both he and subsequent emperors gained a certain legal right to use of the tribunician authority, in addition to their other powers. But the actual name of tribune neither Augustus nor any other emperor has held.

Dio Cassius 53. 32
tr. Foster (Jones vol. 2)

B31 Census and *Lectio*

In the Res Gestae *Augustus states that he three times refused a* cura legum et morum *with supreme power but acted on the wishes of the Senate in this sphere by virtue of his tribunician power and did not accept any office contrary to the* mos maiorum; *in RG 8 he mentions three 'reviews' of the Senate and three census without specifying the powers under which he acted. Suetonius, in this passage, seems to contradict Augustus' account. Dio Cassius (52. 42; 54. 13-14, 26, 35; 55. 13; 53. 1) is consistent with the* Fasti *of Venusia (*ILS *1623) which states that the census of 28 BC was carried out by Augustus, with Agrippa as colleague, by virtue of a grant of* censoria potestas, *a power not mentioned in* RG. *For a full discussion see A. H. M. Jones* Studies in Roman Government and Law *(Blackwell 1968).*

The commons awarded Augustus life-long tribunician power, and once or twice he chose a colleague to share it with him for a five-year period. The Senate also voted him the task of supervising public morals and scrutinizing the laws—another lifelong appointment. Thus, although he did not adopt the title of Censor, he was privileged to hold a public census, and did so three times, assisted by a colleague on the first and third occasions, though not the second.

Suetonius *Augustus* 27
tr. R. Graves (Penguin 1957)

B32 Law on Vespasian's *imperium*

This enactment of AD 70 is probably a law of the people which embodies a Senatorial decree. It quotes earlier grants of power to Augustus, Tiberius, and Claudius as precedents. It was probably by such a law of imperium *that the powers given to Augustus in 23 BC were ratified by the people (see B30).*

... that he shall have the right, just as the deified Augustus and Tiberius Julius Caesar Augustus and Tiberius Claudius Caesar Augustus Germanicus had, to conclude treaties with whomever he wishes;

And that he shall have the right, just as the deified Augustus and Tiberius Julius Caesar Augustus and Tiberius Claudius Caesar Augustus Germanicus had, to convene the senate, to put and refer proposals to it, and to cause decrees of the senate to be enacted by proposal and division of the house;

And that when the senate is convened [in special session] pursuant to his wish, authorization, order, or command, or in his presence, all matters transacted shall be considered and observed as fully binding as if the meeting of the senate had been regularly convoked and held;

And that at all elections especial consideration shall be given to those candidates for a magistracy, authority, *imperium*, or any post whom he has recommended to the Roman senate and people or to whom he has given and promised his vote;

And that he shall have the right, just as Tiberius Claudius Caesar Augustus Germanicus had, to extend and advance the boundaries of the *pomerium* whenever he deems it to be in the interest of the state;

And that he shall have the right and power, just as the deified Augustus and Tiberius Julius Caesar Augustus and Tiberius Claudius Caesar Augustus Germanicus had, to transact and do whatever things divine, human, public, and private he deems to serve the advantage and the overriding interest of the state;

And that the Emperor Caesar Vespasian shall not be bound by those laws and plebiscites which were declared not binding upon the deified Augustus or Tiberius Julius Caesar Augustus or Tiberius Claudius Caesar Augustus Germanicus, and the Emperor Caesar Vespasian Augustus shall have the right to do whatsoever it was proper for the deified Augustus or Tiberius Julius Caesar Augustus or Tiberius Claudius Caesar Augustus Germanicus to do by virtue of any law or enactment;

And that whatever was done, executed, decreed, or ordered before the enactment of this law by the Emperor Caesar Vespasian Augustus, or by anyone at his order or command, shall be as fully binding and valid as if they had been done by order of the people or plebs.

Sanction

If anyone in consequence of this law has or shall have acted contrary to laws, enactments, plebiscites, or decrees of the senate, or if he shall have failed to do in consequence of this law anything that it is incumbent on him to do in accordance with a law, enactment, plebiscite, or decree of the senate, it shall be with impunity, nor shall he on that account have to pay any penalty to the people, nor shall anyone have the right to institute suit or judicial inquiry concerning such matter, nor shall any [authority] permit proceedings before him on such matter.

CIL 6.930
tr. Lewis and Reinhold vol. 2

B33 Dio's account of events after 23 BC

Augustus took up the reins of government firmly after the settlement of 23 BC. On Murena's conspiracy see M. Swan HSCP 71 (1966).

The following year, during which Marcus Marcellus and Lucius Arruntius were the consuls [22 BC], the river caused another flood which submerged the city, and many objects were struck by thunderbolts, among them the statues in the Pantheon; and the spear even fell from the hand of Augustus. The pestilence raged throughout Italy so that no one tilled the land, and I think that the same was the case in foreign parts. The Romans, therefore, reduced to dire straits by disease and by famine, thought that this had happened to them for no other reason than they did not have Augustus for consul at this time also. They accordingly wished to elect him as dictator, and shutting the senate up in its hall they forced it to vote this measure by threatening to burn down the building. Next they took the twenty-four rods and accosted Augustus, begging him both to be named dictator and to become commissioner of grain, as Pompey had once been. He accepted the latter duty under compulsion and ordered two men from among those who had served as praetors five years or more previously to be chosen annually to attend to the distribution of grain. As for the dictatorship, however, he would not hear of it and went so far as to rend his clothing when he found himself unable to restrain them in any other way, either by reasoning or by prayer. As he already had authority and honor even beyond that of dictators he did right to guard against the jealousy and hatred which the title would arouse. His course was the same when they wished to elect him censor for life. Without entering upon the office himself he immediately designated others as censors, namely Paulus Aemilius Lepidus and Lucius Munatius Plancus, the latter a brother of that Plancus who had been proscribed and the former a person who at that time had himself been under sentence of death. These were the last private citizens to hold the appointment, as was at once made manifest by the men themselves. The platform on which they were intended to perform the ceremonies pertaining to their position fell to the ground in pieces when they had ascended it on the first day of their office. After that there were no other censors appointed together, as they had been. Even at this time Augustus in spite of their having been chosen took care of many matters which properly belonged to them. Of the public banquets he abolished some altogether and reformed others so that greater temperance prevailed. He committed the charge of all the festivals to the praetors, commanding that an appropriation be given them from the public treasury. Moreover he forbade any of them to spend from their own means on these occasions more than the others, or to give gladiatorial shows unless the senate should so decree, and even then there were to be not more than two such contests in each year and they should consist of not more than one hundred and twenty men. To the curule aediles he entrusted the fire service, for which purpose he granted them six hundred slave assistants. And since *equites* and women of note had thus early appeared on the stage, he forbade not only the children of senators, to whom the prohibition had even previously extended, but also their grandchildren, who naturally found a place in the equestrian class, to do anything of the sort again.

In these ordinances he let both the substance and the name of the lawgiver and emperor be seen. In other matters he was more moderate and even came to the aid of some of his friends when their conduct was subjected to official scrutiny. But a certain Marcus Primus was accused of having made war upon the Odrysae, while he was governor of Macedonia, who said at one time that he had done it with the approval of Augustus, and again with that of Marcellus. The emperor thereupon came of his own accord into the court and, when interrogated by the praetor as to whether he had instructed the man to make war, entered a denial. The advocate of Primus, Licinius Murena, in the course of some rather disrespectful remarks that he made to him, enquired: 'What are you doing here?' and 'Who summoned you?' To this Augustus only replied: 'The public good.' For this he received praise from sensible persons and was even given the right to convene the senate as often as he pleased. Some of the others looked down upon him. Indeed, not a few voted for the acquittal of Primus and others united to form a plot against Caesar. Fannius Caepio was at the head of it, though others had a share. Murena also was said, whether truly or by way of calumny, to have been one of the conspirators, since he was insatiate and unsparing in his outspokenness to all alike. These men did not appear for trial in court but were convicted by default on the supposition that they intended to flee; shortly after, however, they were put to death. Murena found neither his brother Proculeius nor Maecenas, his sister's husband, of any avail, though they were the recipients of distinguished honors from Augustus. And as some of the jurymen actually voted to acquit these conspirators, the emperor made a law that votes should not be cast secretly in cases by default and that the persons on trial must receive a unanimous conviction. That he authorized these provisions not in anger but as really conducive to the public good he gave overwhelming evidence. Caepio's father liberated one of his slaves who had accompanied his son on his flight, because he had wished to defend the younger man when he met his death; but a second slave who had betrayed him the father led through the middle of the Forum with an inscription making known the reason why he should be killed, and after that crucified him: yet at all this the emperor showed no indignation. He would have allayed all the criticism of those not pleased with the course of events had he not allowed sacrifices, as for some victory, to be both voted and offered.

It was at this period that he restored both Cyprus and Gallia Narbonensis to the people as provinces no longer needing military protection. Thus proconsuls began to be sent to these places also.

> Dio Cassius 54. 1-4
> tr. Foster (Jones vol. 2)

B34 Further grants of power in 19 BC

The winter of 23 had brought flood, famine, and rioting; Augustus, pressed by the people of Rome to accept a dictatorship, perpetual consulship, or the censorship, declined (cf. RG 5) but took a cura annonae *(charge of the corn supply). He then went to the East (22-19 BC) and in his absence the people tried to elect him consul for 21, and then again for 19; rioting followed when a certain Egnatius Rufus presented himself as an alternative candidate. The Senate gave Augustus a rapturous welcome (cf. RG 11-15) and seem to have given him a consular* imperium *for life, though this has been frequently disputed.*

The consul that year [19 BC] was Gaius Sentius. When it was found necessary that a colleague be appointed to hold office with him, for Augustus again refused to accept the place which was being saved for him, an uprising once more broke out in Rome and assassinations occurred, so that the senators voted Sentius a guard. When he expressed himself as opposed to using it, they sent envoys to Augustus, each with two lictors. As soon as the emperor learned this and felt assured that nothing but evil would come of it, he did not adopt an attitude like his former one toward them but appointed a consul from among the envoys themselves, Quintus Lucretius, though this man's name had been posted among the proscribed, and hastened to Rome himself. For this and his other actions while absent from the city many honors of all sorts were voted, none of which he would accept, save the founding of an altar to Fortuna Redux (this being the name they applied to her), and that the day on which he arrived should be numbered among the thanksgiving days and be called Augustalia. Since even then the magistrates and the rest made preparations to go out to meet him, he entered the city by night; and on the following day he gave Tiberius the rank of ex-praetor and allowed Drusus to become a candidate for offices five years earlier than custom allowed. The quarrelsome behavior of the people during his absence did not accord at all with their conduct, influenced by fear, when he was present; he was accordingly invited and elected to be commissioner of morals for five years, and to hold the authority of the censors for the same length of time and that of the consuls for life, being allowed to use the twelve rods always and everywhere and to sit in the chair of office between the consuls of each year. After voting these measures they begged him to set right all these matters and to enact what laws he liked. And whatever ordinances might be composed by him they called from that time *leges Augustae* and desired to take an oath that they would abide by them. He accepted their principal propositions, believing them to be necessary, but absolved them from the requirement of an oath.

Dio Cassius 54. 10
tr. Foster (Jones vol. 2)

B35 An analysis of Augustus' rule

Tacitus (c. AD 55–after 117), a serious historian whose vivid style often reveals his own strong opinions and prejudices, begins the Annals *proper with the reign of Tiberius, the section on Augustus is only introductory. In these chapters he is examining Augustus as the first of a line of autocrats and conveys some sense of inevitability about the principate, an approach which does not reveal the opportunistic nature of Augustus' early career. See R. Syme* Tacitus *(Oxford 1958) for a magisterial account.*

1   The city of Rome was at first ruled by kings. Republican institutions and the consulship were established by Lucius Brutus. Dictatorships were assumed for an emergency: the powers of the Decemviri lasted no more than two years: those of the military tribunes were also short-lived. Neither Cinna nor Sulla held long supremacy. The ascendancy of Pompey and Crassus soon passed to Caesar, as did the forces of Lepidus and Antony to Augustus. A world exhausted by civil war passed into his control, under the name of the principate.

Eminent historians have recounted the story of the old Republic in triumph and disaster. The times of Augustus, too, did not lack distinguished writers, until they were deterred by the mounting tide of adulation. The history of Tiberius, Gaius, Claudius, and Nero was, in their own lifetime, depicted in false colors through fear:

after their deaths, raging hatred distorted the accounts. My purpose, then, is to deal briefly with Augustus, especially the end of his reign, and then to pass on to the principate of Tiberius and his successors. This I shall do without prejudice or partisanship, having no motives for either.

2   After Brutus and Cassius were killed there were no more armies of the Republic. Sextus Pompeius was crushed in Sicily. Lepidus was deprived of his powers. Even Caesar's party had no leader save Octavian. He discarded the name of triumvir, bore himself as consul, and said that a tribune's powers were enough for him to protect the common people.

But when he had seduced the army by gifts, the common people by the provision of cheap food, and everyone by the blandishments of peace, then little by little he began to enlarge his powers, to encroach on the proper functions of the Senate, the magistrates, and the laws. No one opposed him. Men of spirit had died on the battle-field, or in the proscriptions. The remainder of the aristocracy were rewarded by wealth and position in proportion to their readiness to accept servitude. Having done well out of the revolution, they naturally preferred the existing security to the dangers and uncertainties of the old regime. The provinces showed no hostility to the new system. The rivalries of the contestants for power, the greed of republican governors, had made them distrustful of the rule of the Senate and people. They had derived no help from the laws, which were nullified by violence, intrigue, and, above all, by corruption.

3   As a support for his supremacy, Augustus made his sister's son, Claudius Marcellus, high priest and aedile, despite his tender years. He also dignified Marcus Agrippa, of plebeian origin, but a fine general and his ally in victory, with two successive consulships. When Marcellus died, he took Agrippa as his son-in-law. His stepsons Tiberius Nero and Claudius Drusus were honored as victorious generals: this was when his own house was still intact. For he adopted Agrippa's sons, Gaius and Lucius, into the imperial family; even before they had ceased to be minors he was avid for them to receive the title of Princes of Youth, and to have consulships marked out for them, although he put on a show of reluctance. But Agrippa died; premature death or the intrigues of their stepmother Livia overtook Lucius as he was setting out for service in Spain, and then Gaius as he was returning, seriously wounded, from Armenia. Drusus was long dead. Tiberius was the only surviving stepson, and on him everything converged. He was made Augustus' son, shared his military command and tribunician powers, and was formally presented to all the armies. This was no longer, as before, the result of his mother's secret intrigues; it was done at her open request. She had so prevailed on the aging Augustus that he banished his only living grandson, Agrippa Postumus, to the island of Planasia. That young man was, it is true, void of any honorable accomplishment and of a brutish physique, but he had not been involved in any open scandal. But it was Germanicus, son of Drusus, whom the Emperor placed in command of the eight legions on the Rhine, and whose adoption by Tiberius he engineered. There was at this time a grown son of Tiberius (Drusus), but Augustus wished to buttress himself with all the support possible.

This was a period with no wars on hand except that against the Germans—a war undertaken not so much to extend the imperial frontiers nor for any worthwhile advantage, as to wipe out the disgrace of the army lost under Quintilius Varus. At home there was tranquillity. The magistrates retained their titles. The young men had been born since the battle of Actium, most of the older generation during the civil wars. How many were left who could ever have seen the Republic?

4   So the state had been transformed, and the old free Roman character no longer existed. Equality among citizens had gone by the board: all awaited the Emperor's commands. There was no immediate danger, so long as Augustus retained his physical powers, and could support himself, the imperial house, and peace. But when he became advanced in age, and impaired by weakness, his approaching end brought hope of a change.

There was, in some circles, an idle discussion of freedom: most people dreaded war, though a few hoped for it. The great majority exchanged gossip, slanted this way and that, about the candidates for empire. Agrippa was a lout, embittered by his disgrace: neither in years nor in experience was he qualified for so gigantic an office. Tiberius was of mature age, and had proved himself in war. But he had all the ancestral haughtiness of the Claudian house, and had given many signs of a cruel disposition, though he tried to conceal them. Moreover, from his earliest years he had been reared in an imperial household: as a young man he had been loaded with triumphs and consulships; even those years in Rhodes—exile under the guise of retirement—had really been devoted to hatreds, dissimulation, and secret vice. Then there was his mother, with all her feminine excesses—'We shall be the slaves of a woman,' men complained, 'and of two youths, who will first burden down the state and then tear it in two between them!'

5   Amid these discussions, Augustus grew worse, and some suspected foul play by his wife. Indeed, there was a prevalent rumor that, only a few months earlier, Augustus, after taking a few people into his confidence, had gone with Fabius Maximus as his sole attendant to Planasia to see Agrippa. There had been a reconciliation, and so many tears on both sides that it seemed highly probable that Agrippa would be restored to favor in his grandfather's house. Maximus had told this to his wife Marcia; she had passed it on to Livia. This had come to Augustus' knowledge: when, soon after, Maximus died (suicide was never established), Marcia was heard to lament at the funeral that she had caused her husband's death. However that may be, Tiberius had only just reached Illyricum when he was recalled by a letter from his mother. It is uncertain whether he found Augustus alive or dead when he got to Nola. The house and all the streets had been placed under strict guard by Livia. Hopeful bulletins were released, until the precautions dictated by the position had been taken. Then a single announcement proclaimed that Augustus had died, and that Tiberius now ruled.

6   The first crime of the new reign was the murder of Agrippa Postumus. The soldier in charge was determined, Agrippa unarmed and unprepared, but the deed was performed with difficulty. Tiberius made no reference to it in the Senate. He gave it out that it had been done on his father's orders: that the officer left in charge

had been given standing instructions not to delay over the murder of Agrippa, once Augustus was dead. There is no doubt that Augustus had complained loudly, and often about the young man's character, and had induced the Senate to ratify his exile. But he had never steeled himself to murder any member of his house, nor was it credible that he should order the death of a grandson for the advantage of a stepson. A more likely reason would be that Tiberius, through fear, and Livia, with a stepmother's hatred, had hastened the end of the young man, whom they suspected and feared. The centurion announced, as soldiers do, that he had carried out his orders; Tiberius replied that he had given no orders, and that the matter must be answered for in the Senate.

When Sallustius Crispus, who had been privy to the plot and had sent instructions to the military tribune, learned of this, he was afraid that he would be produced as the person accused. If so, he would run an equal risk from truth or falsehood. He therefore warned Livia that the secrets of the palace, the advice of the Emperor's friends, and the faithful services of soldiers, were no matters for publicity. Tiberius must not undermine the principate by constant reference of business to the Senate. The essence of autocracy was that accounts would only balance if they had a single auditor.

7   But, in Rome, the consuls, the Senate, the knights, rushed headlong into servitude. The more illustrious, the more eager and hypocritical they were. To display joy at the death of an Emperor, or gloom at the succession of another, was equally untimely; countenances were carefully composed in a judicious blend of tears and relief, of grief and flattery. Sextus Pompeius and Sextus Appuleius, as consuls, were the first to take the oath of allegiance to Tiberius. Then, in their presence, it was taken by Seius Strabo, commander of the Guard, and Gaius Turranius, in charge of the grain supply: next, the Senate, army, and people. Tiberius always acted through the consuls, as though it were still the era of the Republic, and he himself uncertain whether to rule or not. Even in the edict which called the senators together he only made use of his tribunician powers, which he had received from Augustus. Its terms were brief, and notably modest, announcing that he proposed to arrange for his parent's honors, that he would not leave the body, and that this was the sole public duty he meant to assume.

Yet, at the death of Augustus, Tiberius had issued the watchword to the Guard as its commander. He had bodyguards, armed attendants, and all the features of a court. Soldiers accompanied him to the Forum and to the Senate House. He sent dispatches to the army as though already in power. Only when addressing the Senate did he display hesitation. This was chiefly due to the fear that Germanicus, who had so many legions, besides a huge force of auxiliaries under his command, and was unanimously popular with the people, might prefer to possess himself of the throne rather than to wait for it. Besides, Tiberius deferred to public opinion far enough to prefer to seem the candidate chosen and summoned by the Senate, rather than the usurper smuggled to power by a dotard's adoption and the ambitions of his wife. Later, it was realized that his reluctance was assumed in order to expose the inclinations of the leaders of the state. What men said, how they looked, was distorted to some criminal significance—and stored for future use.

8   On the first day of the Senate's session he allowed no business except the funeral of Augustus. The vestal virgins brought in the Emperor's will. It named Tiberius and Livia as his heirs, and adopted Livia into the Julian house. The grand-children and great-grandchildren were all heirs of the second order, followed by the leaders of the state. Many of them he had hated, but here was an ostentatious claim for future glory. His legacies were not beyond the scale of a private citizen, save a bequest of 43½ million sesterces to the state and to the people of Rome, 1,000 a head to soldiers in the Guard, 500 each to soldiers serving in Rome, 300 each to Roman citizens serving in the legions or auxiliary regiments.

There followed a debate on his funeral arrangements. The most noteworthy speeches were those of Gallus Asinius, proposing that the funeral procession should pass through a triumphal arch, and of Lucius Arruntius, who wanted it to be pre-ceded by the titles of the laws he had passed and the names of the peoples he had conquered. Messala Valerius further proposed that the oath of allegiance to Tiberius should be renewed every year. Tiberius asked him whether he himself had prompted this suggestion; Messala replied that it was his own idea, and that in matters of public interest he intended to use his own judgment and nobody else's, even if he risked causing offense. This was the only kind of flattery still left open. Then senators exclaimed that the body of Augustus should be borne to the funeral pyre on their shoulders. Tiberius, with haughty condescension, refused. He also issued an edict warning the public against the same excessive enthusiasm that they had displayed at the funeral of Julius Caesar, lest they should insist that Augustus be cremated in the Forum rather than the Campus Martius, his appointed resting place.

On the day of the funeral, troops were posted as though for security. This drew mockery from those who had witnessed or had heard from their parents of that occasion when slavery was in its salad days and there was an unsuccessful attempt to recover freedom. Then the attempted assassination of Caesar had seemed a fearful deed to some, but a glorious achievement to others. But now here was this aged princeps, after his long tenure of power, and with his heirs amply provided with resources against the state, and yet he needed a military guard to ensure a seemly burial!

9   Then followed much talk about the character of Augustus. Most people concentrated on such idle topics as the fact that the day when he first took up the sovereignty coincided with that of his death, that he died at Nola, in the same house and the same bedroom as his father Octavius. Attention was drawn to the number of his consulships—equal to those of Valerius Corvus and Gaius Marius put together—to the thirty-seven consecutive years during which he had held tribunician power, to his twenty-one salutes as victorious general, and to other aspects of his honors, whether repeated or novel.

Among the intelligent there was praise or criticism of his life in varying degree. Some maintained that filial duty and a national emergency which left no part for the laws to play had driven him to civil war—and this no decent method can ever begin or maintain. To avenge his father's murderers, he had had to make many concessions to Lepidus and to Antony. But when Lepidus grew indolent, and

Antony deteriorated in debauchery, the rule of a single man was the only possible remedy for a country in turmoil. Even so, the regime set up was neither a monarchy nor a dictatorship, but a principate. The Empire was protected by the ocean, or by distant rivers: legions, fleets, provinces formed a single system. There was the rule of law for Roman citizens, decent treatment for the provincials. Rome itself had been splendidly adorned. If a few instances of force could be cited, it was to provide tranquillity for the majority.

10   Against this it was urged that piety toward his father and the necessities of the state had only been put forward as pretexts. Lust for power had led him to muster the veterans by bribes, to raise a private army—though a mere boy—to seduce the consuls' armies from their allegiance, and to feign support for Sextus Pompeius. Then a senatorial decree enabled him to assume the powers and rights of a praetor. Hirtius and Pansa had been killed, whether by the enemy, or perhaps, in the case of Pansa, by infecting his wound with poison, in that of Hirtius, by his own troops at the instigation of Octavian. He had then taken over their troops: forced the Senate, against their will, to make him consul: turned against the state the forces he had been given to use against Antony. His proscriptions and reassignments of lands had not even won the praise of those who carried them out. Brutus and Cassius had, admittedly, met their deaths because of a feud he had inherited from Caesar. Even so, private vendettas must yield to the needs of the commonwealth. But he had deceived Sextus Pompeius by a false peace, Lepidus by a false friendship. Antony had been trapped by the treaties of Tarentum and Brundisium, and by marriage with his sister: this treacherous relationship had cost him his life. Peace had followed, certainly, but it was a bloody one—the disasters of Lollius and Varus, the murders of Varro, Egnatius, Iullus.

Nor did criticism spare his private life. He had stolen Nero's wife, then insulted the pontiffs by asking them whether it was in order to marry her when she was pregnant. There had been the gross extravagance of Vedius Pollio. Finally, Livia had been a national disaster as a mother, a calamity to the house of Caesar as a stepmother. There was no scope for the worship of the gods, when Augustus wished to foster his own cult through temples, divine effigies, and the service of flamens and priests. Even the selection of Tiberius as his successor had not been prompted by affection or regard for the state. Once Augustus had grasped his arrogance and cruelty, he sought glory for himself by the worst of possible comparisons. And indeed, a few years earlier, when Augustus had asked the Senate to renew Tiberius' powers as tribune, he had made certain references to his dress, deportment, and habits. Outwardly these were excuses; in reality, they were criticisms.

Augustus' funeral was duly held, and he was endowed by decree with a temple and divine worship.

Tacitus *Annals* 1–10
tr. D. R. Dudley (Mentor 1966)

B36 Pliny on Augustus

Gaius Plinius Secundus (Pliny the Elder, AD 23–79) had a distinguished public career and was a close associate of Vespasian. This view of Augustus is taken from the Natural History, *a fascinating compilation of scientific, social, political, and economic knowledge about the Roman world. Pliny's account is a valuable counterbalance to the adulation of Velleius Paterculus (B27) as it provides some evidence that Augustus' rise to power was not always smooth, and gives additional support to the 'conspiracy theory' for the banishment of Julia (see B61). For Agrippa Postumus (here called Postumius) see also B66 and K5c.*

Also in the case of his late Majesty Augustus, whom the whole of mankind enrols in the list of happy men, if all the facts were carefully weighed, great revolutions of man's lot could be discovered: his failure with his uncle in regard to the office of Master of the Horse, when the candidate opposing him, Lepidus, was preferred; the hatred caused by the proscription; his association in the triumvirate with the wickedest citizens, and that not with an equal share of power but with Antony predominant; his flight in the battle of Philippi when he was suffering from disease, and his three days' hiding in a marsh, in spite of his illness and his swollen dropsical condition (as stated by Agrippa and Maecenas); his shipwreck off Sicily, and there also another period of hiding in a cave; his entreaties to Proculeius to kill him, in the naval rout when a detachment of the enemy was already pressing close at hand; the anxiety of the struggle at Perugia, the alarm of the Battle of Actium, his fall from a tower in the Pannonian Wars; and all the mutinies in his troops, all his critical illnesses, his suspicion of Marcellus' ambitions, the disgrace of Agrippa's banishment, the many plots against his life, the charge of causing the death of his children; and his sorrows that were not due solely to bereavement, his daughter's adultery and the disclosure of her plots against her father's life, the insolent withdrawal of his stepson Nero, another adultery, that of his grand-daughter; then the long series of misfortunes—lack of army funds, rebellion of Illyria, enlistment of slaves, shortage of man-power, plague at Rome, famine in Italy, resolve on suicide and death more than half achieved by four days' starvation; next the disaster of Varus and the foul slur upon his dignity; the disowning of Postumius Agrippa after his adoption as heir, and the sense of loss that followed his banishment; then his suspicion in regard to Fabius and the betrayal of secrets; afterwards the intrigues of his wife and Tiberius that tormented his latest days. In fine, this god—whether deified more by his own action or by his merits I know not—departed from life leaving his enemy's son his heir.

Pliny *Natural History* 7. 147–50
tr. H. Rackham (Loeb 1942)

B37 Philo on Augustus

Philo's estimate of Augustus, given in the context of the attack made on the Jews of Alexandria in AD 38, when the Greeks desecrated their synagogues by putting statues of the Emperor Gaius in them. His point is that Augustus was much more deserving of worship than Gaius, and yet the Alexandrian Greeks had refrained from honouring him by infringing Jewish religious liberty.

Then again: What about the Emperor whose every virtue outshone human nature, who through the greatness of his imperial rule and of his valour alike became the first to bear the name 'Augustus', who did not receive the title by inheritance from his family as part of a legacy, but was himself the source of the reverence paid to his successors also? What about the man who pitted himself against the general confusion and chaos as soon as he took charge of public affairs? For islands were struggling for supremacy against the continents and continents against islands, with the Romans of the greatest distinction in public life as their generals and leaders. Again, large parts of the world were battling for the mastery of the empire. Asia against Europe and Europe against Asia; European and Asian nations from ends of the earth had risen up and were engaged in grim warfare, fighting with armies and fleets on every land and sea, so that almost the whole human race would have been destroyed in internecine conflicts and disappeared completely, had it not been for one man, one *princeps*, Augustus, who deserves the title of 'Averter of evil'. This is the Caesar who lulled the storms which were crashing everywhere, who healed the sickness common to Greeks and barbarians alike, which descended from the South and East and swept across to the West and North, sowing misery in the lands and seas between. This is he who not merely loosened but broke the fetters which had confined and oppressed the world. This is he who ended both the wars which were before everyone's eyes and those which were going on out of sight as a result of the attacks of pirates. This is he who cleared the sea of pirate-ships and filled it with merchant-ships. This is he who set every city again at liberty, who reduced disorder to order, who civilized all the unfriendly, savage tribes and brought them into harmony with each other, who enlarged Greece with many other Greek lands, and who Hellenized the most important parts of the barbarian world. This is he who safeguarded peace, gave each man his due, distributed his favours widely without stint, and never in his whole life kept any blessing or advantage back.

During the forty-three years of this wonderful benefactor's rule over Egypt, the Alexandrians neglected him and did not make a single dedication on his behalf in the synagogues—neither a statue nor a wooden image nor a painting. Yet if new and exceptional honours should have been voted to anyone, it was appropriate in his case. This was not merely because he founded and originated the Augustan dynasty, nor because he was the first and greatest universal benefactor, who ended the rule of many by handing the ship of state over to a single helmsman, namely himself, with his remarkable grasp of the science of government, to steer. (The saying 'the rule of many is not good' is very true, since a multitude of votes causes manifold evils.) It was because the whole world voted him honours equal to those of the Olympians. Temples, gateways, vestibules, and colonnades bear witness to this, so that the imposing buildings erected in any city, new or old, are surpassed by the beauty and size of the temples of Caesar, especially in our own Alexandria. There is no other precinct like our so-called 'Augusteum', the temple of Caesar, the protector of sailors. It is situated high up, opposite the sheltered harbours, and is very large and conspicuous; it is filled with dedications on a unique scale, and objects of gold and silver. The extensive precinct is furnished with colonnades, libraries, banqueting-halls, groves, gateways, open spaces, unroofed enclosures, and everything that makes for lavish decoration. It gives hope of safety to sailors when they set out to sea and when they return.

Philo, *Legatio ad Gaium* 143–51
tr. E. M. Smallwood (E. J. Brill, 2nd edn. 1970)

B38 Augustus' later reputation

(a) *Written early in Tiberius' reign.*

The Romans and their allies have never enjoyed such peace and prosperity as that provided by Caesar Augustus from the point when he acquired absolute dominion, and is now being provided by his son and heir Tiberius, who takes Augustus as the norm of his own administration and enactments, as do Tiberius' sons and associates, Germanicus and Drusus.

Strabo 6. 4. 2 (end)
tr. J. Ferguson

(b) *Crispus Passienus was a respected orator, consul in AD 42, and Nero's stepfather.*

Crispus Passienus used often to say that from some men he would rather have their esteem than their bounty, and that from others he would rather have their bounty than their esteem; and he would add examples. 'In the case of the deified Augustus,' he would say, 'I prefer his esteem, in the case of Claudius, his bounty.'

Seneca *On Benefits* 1. 15. 5
tr. J. W. Basore (Loeb 1935)

(c) *Part of a prayer for a new Emperor, written by the historian Eutropius, whose* Account of Roman History *is partly based on the* Epitome *of Livy*

May he be even luckier than Augustus, even better than Trajan.

Eutropius 8.5
tr. J. Ferguson

(d) *Sextus Aurelius Victor wrote in the fourth century AD and probably used an abridged version of the lost books of Livy.*

He had the manner of a civil, pleasant man, his sensuality was passionate and unrestrained, as was his love of gaming, and he overslept excessively.

Aurelius Victor 1. 4
tr. K. Chisholm

B39 *Lassa crudelitas*

Seneca is extolling before Nero (aged eighteen in AD 55) the virtue of clementia, *the failure to use the absolute power you possess. Seneca is under no illusions about the young Augustus (cf. B15a and 16); the key is at the end: Augustus' clemency was* lassa crudelitas, *weariness of cruelty. For the other conspiracies see Suetonius* Augustus 19 (B46); 66; Dio Cassius 48. 33; *for this one 55. 14. 22. Dio places the episode in Rome in AD 4 and (rightly) calls him Cn. Cinna. L. Cinna was the latter's father, himself son-in-law to Pompey.*

By an example from your own family I wish to remind you how true this is. The deified Augustus was a mild prince if one should undertake to judge him from the time of his principate; but when he shared the state with others, he wielded the sword. When he was at your present age, having just passed his eighteenth year, he had already buried his dagger in the bosom of friends; he had already in stealth aimed a blow at the side of the consul, Mark Antony; he had already been a partner in proscription. But when he had passed his fortieth year and was staying in Gaul, the information was brought to him that Lucius Cinna, a dull-witted man, was concocting a plot against him. He was told where and when and how he meant to attack him: one of the accomplices gave the information. Augustus resolved to revenge himself upon the fellow, and ordered a council of his friends to be called. He spent a restless night, reflecting that it was a young man of noble birth, blameless but for this act, the grandson of Gnaeus Pompeius, who was to be condemned. He could not now bear to kill one man, he to whom Mark Antony had dictated the edict of proscription while they dined. He moaned, and now and then would burst forth into fitful and inconsistent speech: 'What then? shall I let my murderer walk about in unconcern while I am filled with fear? . . . What end will there be of punishments, and of bloodshed? I am the obvious victim for whom young men of noble birth should whet their swords. If so many must perish in order that I may not, my life is not worth the price.' At length Livia, his wife, broke in and said: 'Will you take a woman's advice? Follow the practice of physicians, who when the usual remedies do not work try just the opposite. So far you have accomplished nothing by severity. Salvidienus was followed by Lepidus, Lepidus by Murena, Murena by Caepio, Caepio by Egnatius, to say nothing of the others whose monstrous daring

71

makes one ashamed. Try now how mercy will work: pardon Lucius Cinna. . . .'
[*Augustus summons Cinna and tries to discover his reasons*]

'What is your purpose in this? Is it that you yourself may become the prince? On my word, the Roman people are hard put to it if nothing stands in the way of your ruling except me. You cannot guard your own house; just lately the influence of a mere freedman defeated you in a private suit; plainly, nothing can be easier for you than to take action against Caesar! Tell me, if I alone block your hopes, will Paulus and Fabius Maximus and the Cossi and the Servilii and the great line of nobles, who are not the representatives of empty names, but add distinction to their pedigree—will these put up with you?'

Not to fill up a great part of my book in repeating all his words—for he is known to have talked more than two hours, lengthening out this ordeal with which alone he intended to be content—at last he said: 'Cinna, a second time I grant you your life; the first time you were an open enemy, now, a plotter and a parricide. From this day let there be a beginning of friendship between us; let us put to the test which one of us acts in better faith—I in granting you your life, or you in owing it to me.' Later he, unsolicited, bestowed upon him the consulship, chiding him because he did not boldly stand for the office. He found Cinna most friendly and loyal, and became his sole heir. No one plotted against him further.

Your great-great-grandfather spared the vanquished; for if he had not spared them, whom would he have had to rule? Sallustius and a Cocceius and a Deillius and the whole inner circle of his court he recruited from the camp of his opponents; and now it was his own mercifulness that gave him a Domitius, a Messala, an Asinius, a Cicero, and all the flower of the state. What a long time was granted even Lepidus to die! For many years he suffered him to retain the insignia of a ruler, and only after the other's death did he permit the office of chief pontiff to be transferred to himself; for he preferred to have it called an honour rather than a spoil. This mercifulness led him on to safety and security, this made him popular and beloved, although the necks of the Roman people had not yet been humbled when he laid hand upon them; and to-day this preserves for him a reputation which is scarcely within the power of rulers even while they live. A god we believe him to be, but not because we are bidden; that Augustus was a good prince, that he well deserved the name of father, this we confess for no other reason than because he did not avenge with cruelty even the personal insults which usually sting a prince more than wrongs, because when he was the victim of lampoons he smiled, because he seemed to suffer punishment when he was exacting it, because he was so far from killing the various men whom he had convicted of intriguing with his daughter that he banished them for their greater safety, and gave them their credentials. Not merely to grant deliverance, but to guarantee it, when you know that there will be many to take up your quarrel and do you the favour of shedding an enemy's blood—this is really to forgive.

Such was Augustus when he was old, or just upon the verge of old age. In youth he was hot-headed, flared up with anger, and did many things which he looked back upon with regret. To compare the mildness of the deified Augustus with yours no one will dare, even if the years of youth shall be brought into competition with an old age that was more than ripe. Granted that he was restrained and merciful—yes, to be sure, but it was after Actium's waters had been stained with Roman blood, after his own and an enemy's fleet had been wrecked off Sicily, after the holocaust of Perusia and the proscriptions. I, surely, do not call weariness of cruelty mercy.

Seneca *On Mercy* 1.9.1–1.11.2 (abridged)
tr. J. W. Basore (Loeb 1928)

B40 Augustus' eyes

According to Suetonius (Augustus 79) Augustus liked to believe that his eyes were too dazzling to be looked at for a long time.

The divine Augustus had grey eyes like those of horses, the whites being larger than normal in a human being; for this reason he grew angry if anyone stared too intently at him.

Pliny *Natural History* 11.54.143
tr. J. Ferguson

B41 Anecdotes

Macrobius' (fl. c. AD 400) Saturnalia, a work knitting many topics onto the main theme of a discussion at a banquet, is a valuable source of philological, historical, and antiquarian lore. Macrobius drew on Varro, Gellius, and Plutarch amongst others. Most of the anecdotes explain themselves. No. 11, though recorded in Latin, must have been in Greek, where it is a pun; it refers to the Jewish food-laws; no. 18 is of serious import.

1   Avienus went on 'Caesar Augustus liked jokes provided that they did not detract from his dignity and honour and he did not fall into scurrility.'

2   He had written a tragedy called *Ajax*, and later, dissatisfied with it, destroyed it. Subsequently L. Varius, a writer of tragedies, asked him what had happened to his *Ajax*. He replied 'Committed suicide with a sponge.'

3   Augustus again when a nervous petitioner kept advancing and then withdrawing the hand with the petition said 'Do you think you are giving a penny to an elephant?'

4   Again, when Pacuvius Taurus asked him for a present and said that people everywhere were speaking about the large sum he'd received from him, said 'Well, you don't believe what they say.'

73

5 A cavalry officer wanting to resign was asking for retirement pay and said 'I'm not asking it for myself because I care about money; I'd like it to be seen that I'd resigned after receiving material signs of your approval.' The Emperor retorted: 'Just tell everyone you've received them; I won't deny it.' . . .

11 When he learned that among the two-year-olds or younger whom Herod, king of the Jews, had ordered to be executed, the king's own son had died, he said 'I'd rather be Herod's swine than his son.'

12 Again, knowing that his close friend Maecenas had a careless, affected, effeminate style, Augustus would often put on the same style in his letters to Maecenas, and, contrary to the usual critical style he observed in letter-writing, in a personal letter to Maecenas he allowed himself an amusing expansiveness. 'Goodbye, my ebony of Medullia, my ivory of Etruria, my aromatic spice of Arretium, my diamond of the Adriatic, my pearl of the Tiber, my emerald of the Cilnii, my jasper of Iguvium, my beryl of Porsenna, my carbuncle of Italy, *enfin mon coussin* of whores.'

13 He was once entertained to a very ordinary light meal: he hardly ever refused an invitation. After such a poor unelaborate dinner as he was saying goodbye on leaving he murmured 'I'd no idea I was such a close friend of yours.'

14 He had had some Tyrian purple bought and complained it was too dark. The shopkeeper said 'Hold it up and look at it from underneath.' His witty reply was 'What? To show the people of Rome that I'm properly dressed, have I got to walk on a terrace?' . . .

17 He was told of a huge debt—over 20,000,000 sesterces—contracted by a Roman *eques* during his lifetime without anyone knowing. He ordered his pillow to be purchased at the auction for his personal use. There were some raised eyebrows, but he explained 'The pillow on which he could sleep with all those debts must be specially conducive to sleep.'

18 I must not omit the words he spoke in honour of Cato. He happened to enter Cato's old house. Strabo criticized Cato's pigheadedness in order to flatter Caesar. 'Anyone who does not want the political status quo to be changed' he said 'is a true patriot.' There was a serious point in his praise of Cato, self-protection against revolution.

19 I have more admiration for Augustus' acceptance of the jokes at his own expense than the ones he produced himself. Patience is more commendable than skill with words, especially in the cheerful tolerance of words which go beyond the limits of pleasantry.

20 There is a record of a bitter joke by a man from the provinces. He came to Rome. He looked very like Caesar and attracted everyone's attention. Augustus ordered the man to be brought into his presence, had a look at him, and asked 'Tell me, young man, was your mother ever in Rome?' 'No' he said, but could not resist adding 'But my father often was.'

21 At the time of the triumvirs Augustus wrote some coarse verses attacking Pollio. Pollio said 'I'm saying nothing. It's not easy to inscribe lines against a man who can proscribe.'

22 Curtius, a Roman *eques* of luxurious habits, was dining with Caesar and was

served with a rather skinny thrush. He asked if he could let it go. The Emperor said 'Why not?' So he threw it out of the window.

23   Augustus without being asked paid the debts of a senator he liked, to the extent of 4,000,000 sesterces. The other wrote to thank him with the words: 'And nothing for myself.'

24   His freedman Licinius used to advance large sums to his patron at the beginning of an operation. In this way he made him a written promise of 10,000,000 sesterces, but the part of the stroke placed over the figure was prolonged so that there was an empty space underneath. Caesar seized his opportunity and wrote in a second 10,000,000 in his own hand, being careful to fill the space and imitate Licinius's script, and received the double amount. Licinius pretended not to notice, but when there was a new operation on hand, he gently confronted Caesar with his action by offering him a note of hand 'Sir, for the expenses of your new undertaking, I make available to you the figure you decide on.'

25   Augustus' patience in the office of censor was most commendable. A Roman *eques* was charged by the Emperor with wastage of his resources. He proved that he had increased them. Subsequently he charged the same man with ignoring the marriage laws. He said he had a wife and three children, then added 'In future, Caesar, use honest agents to inquire about honest men.'

26   With one soldier he tolerated freedom which passed over into temerity. In a country house his nights were disturbed by an owl hooting continually. He ordered the owl to be trapped. A soldier, who was expert at trapping birds, brought him the owl in the hope of a substantial reward. The Emperor complimented him and presented him with a hundred sesterces. He had the impudence to say 'I'd rather the bird lived' and let it go. It is amazing that Caesar took no offence and let the soldier go despite his insolence.

27   A veteran soldier was in danger of losing his case and approached Caesar publicly asking him to give him his support. He chose a lawyer from his court immediately with his recommendation. The veteran shouted at the top of his voice: 'Caesar, when you were in danger at Actium I did not find a delegate; I fought for you myself' and uncovered the scars on his body. Caesar blushed, and acted as his counsel, fearing to seem proud or ungrateful. . . .

29   He returned to Rome with all the glory of the victory at Actium. Among those congratulating him was a man carrying a raven which he had taught to say 'Hail, Caesar, victor, commander!' Caesar was amazed by this patriotic bird, and paid 20,000 sesterces for it. A friend of this operator who had received no part of the gift told Caesar that the man had a second raven and asked him to insist on its production. The bird was brought and spoke the words it had learned 'Hail, victor, commander, Antony!' Caesar was not angry, but was content to order the man to divide the gift with his partner.

30   He was greeted in like manner by a parrot, and ordered its purchase; so too with a magpie. This example persuaded a poor cobbler to train a raven to a similar greeting. Ruined by the expense when the bird refused to reply he would say 'I've wasted my money and my effort.' Eventually the bird began to speak the prescribed

greeting. Augustus, passing by, heard this and said 'I've enough claqueurs at home already.' The raven's memory was good enough to add the words it had repeatedly heard its owner grumbling 'I've wasted my money and my effort.' At this Caesar roared with laughter and ordered the bird to be purchased at a higher price than any of the others.

31   When Caesar was coming down from the Palatine there was a poor Greek who would offer an epigram in his honour. He did this several times without success. Augustus saw that he was going to repeat the performance, and himself hastily scratched a Greek epigram in his own hand on a piece of paper, and gave it to the man. The Greek read it, approved it, and showed his approval in his looks and words; he came to the throne, plunged his hand into a worn purse, and produced a few pence which he gave to the Emperor with the words 'By your Fortune, Augustus, if I had more I'd have given you more.' Everyone burst out laughing and Caesar called his steward and ordered him to pay the poor Greek 100,000 sesterces.

Macrobius *Saturnalia* 2.4 (abridged)
tr. J. Ferguson

B42   Augustus and Timagenes

Timagenes, an Alexandrian Greek brought to Rome as a slave in 55 BC, taught rhetoric until Augustus became his patron. He was possibly commissioned to write a history of Augustus' early life, and his writings may have been used by Strabo. Note the incidental reference to the recitationes *or public readings instituted by Pollio.*

The divine Augustus produced plenty of memorable actions and sayings, demonstrating that he was not governed by anger. The historian Timagenes had made some adverse comments on his wife and family; they were remembered, for daring witticisms are the more likely to circulate widely. Caesar often warned him to keep closer control of his tongue; when he did not listen Augustus debarred him from his house. Timagenes subsequently lived to a ripe old age in Asinius Pollio's home, lionized throughout Rome. Caesar's exclusion closed no other door to him. He gave public readings of the histories he subsequently wrote; the books containing the record of Caesar Augustus he put in the fire and burned. He remained hostile to Caesar, but no one was afraid to be friendly with him or avoided him as the victim of lightning; despite his fall from the heights there was always someone to welcome him. As I remarked, Caesar tolerated all this; he was not even stirred by the attack on his fame and his achievements; he had no quarrel with his enemy's host, merely saying to Asinius Pollio 'You like a wild animal for a pet.' Pollio began to make excuses but he broke in, 'Enjoy yourself, my dear Pollio, enjoy yourself.' Pollio rejoined 'If you instruct me, Caesar, I will debar him from my house without demur.' Augustus replied 'Do you really think I would do that, when I was responsible for bringing you together again?' Pollio had in fact previously quarrelled with Timagenes, and his only reason for ending the quarrel was the beginning of Caesar's.

Seneca *On Anger* 3. 23. 4–8
tr. J. Ferguson

B43 Augustus and Vedius Pollio

An anecdote showing the politic humanity of Augustus contrasted with one of his counsellors. The story was a famous one: see also Dio Cassius 54. 25; Seneca On Clemency *1. 18; Pliny* Natural History *9. 23. 39; 9. 53. 78; Tacitus* Annals *1. 10; 12. 60.*

To rebuke a man when he is in a temper and to lose your temper with him besides is only an encouragement to him. You will do better to change your approach and use gentleness—unless you happen to be a person of sufficient importance to check his temper, as the divine Augustus did when at dinner with Vedius Pollio. One of the slaves had broken a crystal cup. Vedius ordered his arrest and condemned him to a novel death, to be thrown to the gigantic lampreys he kept in his fishpond. Who would not imagine that he did this for an extravagant demonstration! It was cruelty. The lad slipped out of their hands and took refuge at Caesar's feet with the single request that his execution take some other form than being eaten. Caesar was shocked at this innovation in brutality and ordered his release, the destruction in his presence of the remaining crystal ware and the filling up of the pond. Caesar could rebuke one of his associates in this way; he made good use of his authority: 'Do you give orders for human beings to be torn away from a dinner-party, and to be lacerated by punishments of your own invention? Just because a cup of yours has been smashed, is a human being to be disembowelled? Are you going to be so self-important that you order an execution in the actual presence of Caesar?'

Seneca *On Anger* 3. 40. 1–4
tr. J. Ferguson

B44 Augustus joins a private *consilium*

L. Rufus Tarius was a man of obscure origins who came to wealth and power. This passage shows Augustus' tact and his concern for at least the outward show of traditional procedures. The dangers in an autocracy, where a ruler may be tempted by his subjects' wealth, are clear.

I will now use this very case to show you an example of a good prince with whom you may compare the good father. When Tarius was ready to open the inquiry on his son, he invited Augustus Caesar to attend the council; Augustus came to the hearth of a private citizen, sat beside him, and took part in the deliberation of another household. He did not say, 'Rather, let the man come to my house'; for, if he had, the inquiry would have been conducted by Caesar and not by the father. When the case had been heard and all the evidence had been sifted—what the young fellow said in his defence, and what was brought up in accusation against him—Caesar requested each man to give his verdict in writing, lest all should vote according to his lead. Then, before the tablets were opened, he solemnly declared that he would accept no bequest from Tarius, who was a rich man. Some will say, 'He showed weakness in fearing that he might seem to be trying to clear the field for his own prospects by sentencing the son.' I think differently; any one of us might well have had enough faith in his own good conscience to withstand hostile criticism, but princes are bound to give much heed even to report. He solemnly declared that he would not accept a bequest. Tarius did indeed on one and the same day lose a second heir also, but Caesar saved the integrity of his vote; and after he had proved that his severity was disinterested—for a prince should always have regard for this—he said that the son ought to be banished to whatever place the father should decide. His sentence was not the sack, nor serpents, nor prison, since his thought was not of the man on whom he was passing sentence, but of him for whom he was acting as counsellor. He said that the mildest sort of punishment ought to satisfy a father in the case of a son who was very youthful and had been moved to commit this crime, but, in committing it had shown himself faint-hearted—which was next door to being innocent; therefore the son should be banished from the city and from his father's sight. How worthy he was of being asked by parents to share their counsels! how worthy of being recorded a co-heir with the children who were innocent!

Seneca *On Mercy* 1.15.3–1.16.1
tr. J. W. Basore (Loeb 1928)

B45 Expressions of affection and regard for Augustus

57 The degree of affection that Augustus won by such behaviour can easily be gauged. The grateful Senatorial decrees may, of course, be discounted as to a certain extent inspired by a sense of obligation. But the Equestrian Order voluntarily and unanimously decided to celebrate his birthday, spreading the festivities over two days; and once a year men of all classes would visit the Curtian Lake, into which they threw the coins previously vowed for his continued well-being. They would also climb to the Capitol on New Year's Day with money presents, even if he happened to be out of town. With the sum that thus accrued Augustus bought

valuable images of the gods, which he set up in each of the City wards: among them the Apollo of Sandal Street, and Juppiter of the Tragedians.

When his Palace on the Palatine Hill burned down, a fund for its rebuilding was started by the veterans, the guilds of minor officials and the City tribes; to which people of every sort made further individual contributions according to their means. Augustus, to show his gratitude for the gift, took a token coin from each heap, but no more than a single silver piece. His homecomings after tours of the Empire were always acclaimed with respectful good wishes and songs of joy as well; and it became a custom to cancel all punishments on the day he set foot in Rome.

58   In a universal movement to confer on Augustus the title 'Father of his Country', the first approach was made by the commons, who sent a deputation to him at Antium; when he declined this honour a huge crowd met him outside the Theatre with laurel wreaths, and repeated the request. Finally, the Senate followed suit but, instead of issuing a decree or acclaiming him with shouts, chose Valerius Messala to speak for them all when Augustus entered the House. Messala's words were:

'Caesar Augustus, I am instructed to wish you and your family good fortune and divine blessings; which amounts to wishing that our entire City will be fortunate and our country prosperous. The Senate agree with the People of Rome in saluting you as Father of your Country.'

With tears in his eyes, Augustus answered—again I quote his exact words: 'Fathers of the Senate, I have at last achieved my highest ambition. What more can I ask of the immortal gods than that they may permit me to enjoy your approval until my dying day?'

Suetonius *Augustus* 57–8
tr. R. Graves (Penguin 1957)

B46   Conspiracies against Augustus

This passage gives the impression of a continuous series of conspiracies against Augustus, difficult to reconcile with the image of the beloved 'Father of his Country' (cf. B45); but cf. also B36 and see Suetonius Tiberius 8.

Next, he suppressed a series of sporadic riots and revolts; besides certain conspiracies, all of them detected before they became dangerous. The leaders of the conspiracies were, in historical sequence: Lepidus the Younger; Varro Murena, and Fannius Caepio; Marcus Egnatius; Plautius Rufus and Lucius Paulus (the husband of Augustus's grand-daughter), aided by Lucius Aridasius, a feeble old man who had been indicted for forgery. Then came Audasius and Epicadus, whose plan had been to rescue Augustus' daughter Julia and his grandson Agrippa Postumus from the prison islands where they were confined, and forcibly take them to the legions abroad. But attempts against Augustus's life were made by men from even the lowest walks of life; so I must not forget one Telephus, a slave, whose task it had been to remind a noble mistress of her engagements; he nursed a delusion that he was fated to become emperor, and planned an armed attack on the Senate as well. Then an Illyrian camp-orderly, who had managed to sneak into the Palace without being noticed by the porters, was caught one night near the Imperial bedroom, brandishing a hunting-knife; but since no statement could be extracted from him by torture it is doubtful whether he was really insane or merely pretending to be.

Suetonius *Augustus* 19
tr. R. Graves (Penguin 1957)

B47 Freedom of speech

The Rufus of this anecdote is not certainly known: there was a Plautius Rufus who conspired against Augustus. The bulls and calves are, of course, the sacrificial victims. Augustus could be ruthless, but he knew the value of a politic generosity.

Under the deified Augustus, it was not yet true that a man's utterances endangered his life, but they did cause him trouble. Rufus, a man of senatorial rank, once at a dinner expressed the hope that Caesar would not return safe from the journey that he was planning; and he added that all the bulls and the calves wished the same thing. Some of those who were present carefully noted these words. At the break of day, the slave who had stood at his feet when he was dining told him what he had said at dinner while he was drunk, and urged him to be the first to get Caesar's ear and volunteer charges against himself. Following this advice, Rufus met Caesar as he was going down to the forum, and, having sworn that he had been out of his mind the night before, expressed the hope that his words might recoil upon his own head and the head of his children, and begged Caesar to pardon him and restore him to favour. When Caesar had consented to do so, he said: 'No one will believe that you have restored me to favour unless you bestow upon me a gift,' and he asked for a sum that no favourite need have scorned, and actually obtained it. 'For my own sake,' said Caesar, 'I shall take pains never to be angry with you!' Caesar acted nobly in pardoning him and in adding to his forgiveness liberality. Every one who hears of this incident must necessarily praise Caesar, but the first to be praised will be the slave. You need not wait for me to tell you that the slave who had done this was set free. Yet it was not a gratuitous act—Caesar had paid the price of his liberty!

Seneca *On Benefits* 3. 27. 1–4
tr. J. W. Basore (Loeb 1935)

B48 Augustus' personality

Augustus appears from Suetonius' account to have had the gift of the right gesture when it came to 'public relations'; taken in conjunction with his presentation of his constitutional position this might indicate how important he believed a good public image to be, and how well considered and planned his image was. For modern estimates of his personality see also A. H. M. Jones Augustus *(London 1970) pp. 163 ff.; D. C. Earl* The Age of Augustus *(Elek 1968) pp. 191 ff.; and F. E. Adcock in* CAH² *vol. 10 pp. 590 ff.*

(a)

Although the voting of temples to popular proconsuls was a commonplace, he would not accept any such honour, even in the provinces, unless his name were coupled with that of Rome. He even more vigorously opposed the dedication of a temple to himself at home, and went so far as to melt down the silver statues previously erected, and to spend the silver coined from them on golden tripods for Palatine Apollo.

Suetonius *Augustus* 52
tr. R. Graves (Penguin 1957)

(b)

He had a habit of watching the Games from the upper rooms of houses overlooking the Circus, which belonged to his friends or freedmen; but occasionally he used the Imperial Box, and even took his wife and children there with him. Sometimes he did not appear until the show had been running for several hours, or even for a day or more; but always excused his absences and appointed a substitute president. Once in his seat, however, he watched the proceedings intently; either to avoid the bad reputation earned by Julius Caesar for reading letters or petitions, and answering them, during such performances, or just to enjoy the fun, as he frankly admitted doing. This enjoyment led him to offer special prizes at Games provided by others, or give the victors valuable presents from the Privy Purse; and he never failed to reward, according to their merits, the competitors in any Greek theatrical contests that he attended. His chief delight was to watch boxing, particularly when the fighters were Italians—and not merely professional bouts, in which he often used to pit Italians against Greeks, but slogging matches between untrained roughs in narrow City alleys.

To be brief: Augustus honoured all sorts of professional entertainers by his friendly interest in them; maintained, and even increased, the privileges enjoyed by athletes; banned gladiatorial contests if the defeated fighter were forbidden to plead for mercy; and amended an ancient law empowering magistrates to punish stage-players wherever and whenever they pleased—so that they were now competent to deal only with misdemeanours committed at games or theatrical performances. Nevertheless, he insisted on a meticulous observance of regulations during

81

wrestling matches and gladiatorial contests; and was exceedingly strict in checking the licentious behaviour of stage-players. When he heard that Stephanio, a Roman actor, went about attended by a page-boy who was really a married woman with her hair cropped, he had him flogged through all the three theatres—those of Pompey, Balbus, and Marcellus—and then exiled. Acting on a praetor's complaint, he had a comedian named Hylas publicly scourged in the hall of his own residence; and expelled Pylades not only from Rome, but from Italy too, because when a spectator started to hiss, he called the attention of the whole audience to him with an obscene movement of his middle finger.

Suetonius *Augustus* 45
tr. R. Graves (Penguin 1957)

(c)
75 Augustus spared no expense when celebrating national holidays and behaved very light-heartedly on occasion. At the Saturnalia, for instance, or whenever else the fancy took him, he whimsically varied the value of his gifts. They might consist of rich clothing and gold or silver plate; or every sort of coin, including specimens from the days of the early monarchy, and foreign pieces; or merely lengths of goat-hair cloth, or sponges, or pokers, or tongs—all given in return for tokens inscribed with misleading descriptions of the objects concerned.

At some dinner parties he would also auction tickets for prizes of most unequal value, and paintings with their faces turned to the wall, for which every guest present was expected to bid blindly, taking his chance like the rest: he might either pick up most satisfactory bargains, or throw away his money.

76   In this character sketch I need not omit his eating habits. He was frugal and, as a rule, preferred the food of the common people, especially the coarser sort of bread, whitebait, fresh hand-pressed cheese, and green figs of the second crop; and would not wait for dinner, if he felt hungry, but ate anywhere.

Suetonius *Augustus* 75–6
tr. R. Graves (Penguin 1957)

B49 Literary pursuits

Augustus was fortunate in having the friendship and support of Maecenas, a rich aristocrat of Etruscan descent. Augustus' patronage of Virgil and Horace, due to the discerning taste and influence of Maecenas, created an environment favourable to the rise of a new literature celebrating a new order. The following passages give some indication of Augustus' own taste in literature. For his relationship with the poets see §F and note especially the letters in F5 and 7.

(a)

85 Augustus wrote numerous prose works on a variety of subjects, some of which he read aloud to a group of his closer friends as though in a lecture-hall: the *Reply to Brutus's Eulogy of Cato*, for instance. In this case, however, he tired just before the end—being then already an old man—and handed the last roll to Tiberius, who finished it for him. Among his other works were *An Encouragement to the Study of Philosophy* and thirteen books of *My Autobiography*, which took the story only up to the time of the Cantabrian War. He made occasional attempts at verse composition; including *Sicily*, a short poem in hexameters, and an equally short collection of *Epigrams*, most of them composed at the Baths. Both these books survive; but growing dissatisfied with the style of his tragedy, *Ajax*, which he had begun in great excitement, he destroyed it. When friends asked: 'Well, what has Ajax been doing lately?' he answered: 'Ajax has not fallen on his sword, but wiped himself out on my sponge.'

86 He cultivated a simple and easy oratorical style, avoiding purple passages, artfully contrived prose-rhythms, and 'the stink of far-fetched phrases', as he called it; his main object being to say what he meant as plainly as possible. . . .

89 . . . Augustus gave all possible encouragement to intellectuals; he would politely and patiently attend readings not only of their poems and historical works, but of their speeches and dialogues; yet objected to being made the theme of any work unless the author were known as a serious and reputable writer, and often warned the praetors not to let his name be vulgarized by its constant occurrence in prize orations.

Suetonius *Augustus* 85-6; 89 (abridged)
tr. R. Graves (Penguin 1957)

(b) *Augustus censors Julius Caesar's writings.*

There are records of writings from his youth and adolescence, *The Praises of Hercules*, *Oedipus* (a tragedy), and *Collected Sayings*. Augustus in a brief, straightforward letter to his chief librarian, Pompeius Macer, gave instructions that none of these trivia was to be published.

Suetonius *Julius Caesar* 56.7
tr. J. Ferguson

B50 Virgil *Eclogues* 1

The Eclogues *(the name means, in Greek, 'extract' or 'excerpt'—the poems were more generally known as the* Bucolics*) are Virgil's earliest poems, pastoral in nature, taking their inspiration from the Greek poet, Theocritus. The first* Eclogue *(although*

one of the latest composed) takes its inspiration from the poet's successful inter-
cession with Octavian in Rome when threatened with the loss of his family estates
in the land confiscation for the veterans of the triumviral armies. The poet owed his
success to the mediation of powerful friends, C. Asinius Pollio, the dedicatee, and
L. Alfenus Varus, but the impression made on Virgil by Octavian in this poem is
clearly expressed. The poem is usually assigned to 41–39 BC, but it may be later.
The land settlement of veterans began in 42 BC but continued throughout the 30s BC.
(cf. B19, 139a and b). For further discussion of the historical background see H. J.
Rose The Eclogues of Vergil *(University of California 1942);* Vergil Eclogues *ed.*
R. Coleman (Cambridge 1977).

MELIBOEUS

Tityrus, here you loll, your slim reed-pipe serenading
The woodland spirit beneath a spread of sheltering beech,
While I must leave my home place, the fields so dear to me.
I'm driven from my home place: but you can take it easy
In shade and teach the woods to repeat 'Fair Amaryllis'.

TITYRUS

O Meliboeus, a god has given me this ease—
One who will always be a god to me, whose altar
I'll steep with the blood of many a tender lamb from my sheep-folds
It's by his grace, you see, that my cattle browse and I
Can play whatever tunes I like on this country reed-pipe.   10

MELIBOEUS

Well, I don't grudge you that: but it does amaze me, when
Such a pack of troubles worry us countrymen everywhere.
On and on, sick-hearted, I drive my goats: look, this one
Can hardly move—in that hazel thicket she dropped her twin kids,
The hope of my flock, but she has to leave them upon bare flint.
Times enough, I know it, I was forwarned of this.
When lightning struck the oaks—my wits must have been addled.
But tell me about that god of yours, my friend: who is he?

TITYRUS

The city men call Rome—in my ignorance I used to
Imagine it like the market town to which we shepherds   20
Have so often herded the weanlings of our flocks.
Thus I came to know how dogs resemble puppies.
Goats their kids, and by that scale to compare large things with small.
But Rome carries her head as high above other cities
As cypresses tower over the tough wayfaring tree.

MELIBOEUS

What was the grand cause of your setting eyes on Rome, then?

TITYRUS

Freedom gave me a look—oh, long-delayed it was.

And I apathetic; my beard fell whiter now as I clipped it—
Still, she gave me that look and late in the day she came.
After my Galatea had left me, when Amaryllis   30
Possessed my heart. Believe me, while Galatea reigned
I had no chance of freedom, no attention to spare for savings:
Many a fatted beast I took to sell in the temple,
Many the rich cheeses I pressed for ungrateful townsfolk.
Yet never did I get home with much money in my pocket.

MELIBOEUS

I used to wonder why Amaryllis called so sadly
Upon the gods, and let her apple crop go hang.
Tityrus was not there. The very springs and pine-trees
Called out, these very orchards were crying for you, my friend.

TITYRUS

What was I to do? There was no way out from my slavery,   40
Nowhere else could I find a divine one ready to help me.
At Rome, Meliboeus, I saw that young prince in whose honour
My altar shall smoke twelve times a year. At Rome I made
My petition to him, and he granted it readily, saying, 'My lads,
Pasture your cattle, breed from your bulls, as you did of old.'

MELIBOEUS

Fortunate old man!—so your acres will be yours still.
They're broad enough for you. Never mind if it's stony soil
Or the marsh films over your pastureland with mud and rushes.
At least no queer vegetation will tempt your breeding ewes,
And there's no risk of their catching disease from a neighbour's flock.   50
Ah, fortunate old man, here among hallowed springs
And familiar streams you'll enjoy the longed-for shade, the cool shade.
Here, as of old, where your neighbour's land marches with yours,
The sally hedge, with bees of Hybla sipping its blossom,
Shall often hum you gently to sleep. On the other side
Vine-dressers will sing to the breezes at the crag's foot;
And all the time your favourites, the husky-voiced wood pigeons
Shall coo away, and turtle doves make moan in the elm tops.

TITYRUS

Sooner shall lightfoot stags go grazing on thin air,
Or the sea contract, leaving its fishes high and dry;   60
Sooner the Germans and the Parthians, migrating
Across each other's frontiers, drink of each other's broad
Rivers, than I'll forget the look that young prince gave me.

MELIBOEUS

But the rest of us must go from here and be dispersed—
To Scythia, bone-dry Africa, the chalky spate of the Oxus,
Even to Britain—that place cut off at the very world's end.

Ah, when shall I see my native land again? after long years,
Or never?—see the turf-dressed roof of my simple cottage,
And wondering gaze at the ears of corn that were all my kingdom?
To think of some godless soldier owning my well-farmed fallow,   70
A foreigner reaping these crops! To such a pass has civil
Dissension brought us: for people like these we have sown our fields.
Well, graft your pears, Meliboeus, and set your vines in rows.
Move onward, little she-goats, onward, once-happy flock!
No more shall I, stretched out in some green dingle here,
Watch you poised far off on the bushy brows of a hillside.
No more singing for me, no taking you to browse,
My little goats, on bitter willow and clover flower.
TITYRUS
Yet surely you could rest with me tonight and sleep
On a bed of green leaves here? You're welcome to taste my mellow   80
Apples, my floury chestnuts, my ample stock of cheese.
Look over there—smoke rises already from the rooftops
And longer fall the shadows cast by the mountain heights.

Virgil Eclogues 1
tr. C. Day Lewis (Oxford 1966)

B51 A plea for Augustus' return

Horace published the fourth book of the Odes *in 13 BC or later, after he had been commissioned to compose a hymn for* the Ludi Saeculares *(D2). Many of the* Odes *had political themes (cf. F17, and 26) but Horace was no court poet, writing to order.*

Great guardian of the race of Romulus
Born when the gods were being good to us,
    You have been absent now
    Too long. You pledged your word
    (The august Fathers heard)
To swift home-coming. Honour, then, that vow.

Restore, kind leader, to your countrymen
The light they lack. For, like the sunshine when
    It's springtime, where your face
    Lights on the people, there
    The weather turns to fair
And the day travels with a happier pace.

Picture a mother whose young son, detained
Beyond the sailing months by a cross-grained
    Southerly gale that sweeps
    The miles of Cretan foam,
    Winters away from home,
Sweet home; she calls for him, she keeps

Consulting omens, worrying the skies
With orisons and promises, her eyes
    Fixed on the curving shore.
    So does the motherland
    Keep loyal look-out and
Still miss the loved one she is waiting for.

When Caesar's here the ox plods safe and sound;
Ceres and gentle Plenty feed the ground
    With fruitfulness; across
    The uninfested seas
    Men speed with bird-like ease;
Honesty is afraid of its own loss;

No immoralities contaminate
Domestic faith, for custom and the State
    Have purged the taint of sin;
    Proud wives in children trace
    The true inherited face;
Crime hears the tread of Justice closing in.

Who fears the swarms that Germany brings forth
From her rough loins? Let Scythians in the north,
    Or Parthians rearm,
    Or the wild tribes of Spain
    Rally to war again,
We sleep as long as Caesar's safe from harm.

The husbandman on his own hillside sees
The day to bed, and gives his lonely trees
    In marriage to the vine.
    To supper thence he goes
    Cheerfully, at the close
Of the first course inviting your divine

Assistance at his table. Wooed with prayers
And bowls of unmixed wine, your godhead shares
    His worship with the Lar
    That guards familial peace.
    Rome bows to you, as Greece
Did to great Hercules or Castor's star.

'Dear Emperor, long may you live to bless
Our Italy with holiday happiness!'
  Daily we raise the cry—
  At dawn before we've wet
  Our throats, and when the set
Sun's hidden in the sea and we're less dry.

Horace *Odes* 4. 5
tr. J. Michie (Penguin 1967 rev. 1978)

B52 Ovid flatters Augustus

(a) *Ovid praises Augustus by contrasting him with an unflattering image of Romulus. This 'debunking' of a revered Roman tradition contrasts with Horace's approach (B51) and indeed with Augustus' own attitude to traditional Roman values (cf. §§ D and I). For Ovid's complex relationship with Augustus, see further (§F.)*

Holy Father of your country! Commons and Nobles give you the name.
  So do we knights.
The actuality came first; the title came too late.
  You've long been father of the world.
You've the name on earth which Jupiter holds in heaven—
  father, he of gods, you of men.
Make way, Romulus. He's guarded your walls and made them great;
  you let Remus jump them.
You knew Tatius, Caenina, poor little Cures;
  he's made both sides of the sun Roman.
You held a particle of conquered land;
  he holds the whole earth.
You're a rapist; his authority makes wives chaste.
  You fostered, he blocked blasphemy.
You loved war; Caesar's a man of peace.
  Your title was Lord, his First Citizen.
Remus arraigns you; he forgives his foes.
  Your father brought you, he his father to heaven.

Ovid *Fasti* 2. 127-44
tr. J. Ferguson

(b) *This is more conventional praise.*

> To Caesar's numberless titles (which does he rank highest?)
>   has been added High Priest.
> Over the undying fires the undying divinity of Caesar presides;
>   you see the joint symbols of empire.
> O gods of ancient Troy, prize worthy of its rescuer,
>   you who saved Aeneas,
> One of Aeneas's line is the priest to touch your power.
>   Vesta, guard your kinsman
> Fed by his hand, the flames are alive.
>   Live on, fire; live on, leader!

Ovid *Fasti* 3. 419-28
tr. J. Ferguson

B53 Death of Augustus

The death of Augustus does not seem to have caused chaos at Rome: the transfer of power to Tiberius went smoothly (see further §K).

(a)

100 Augustus died in the same room as his father Octavius. That was 19 August 14 A.D., at about 3 p.m., the Consuls of the year being Sextus Pompey and Sextus Appuleius. Before the close of the following month he would have attained the age of seventy-six. Senators from the neighbouring municipalities and veteran colonies bore the body, in stages, all the way from Nola to Bovillae—but at night, owing to the hot weather—laying it in the town hall or principal temple of every halting place. From Bovillae, a party of Roman knights carried it to the vestibule of the Palace at Rome.

The senators vied with one another in proposing posthumous honours for Augustus. Among the motions introduced were the following: that his funeral procession should pass through the Triumphal Gate preceded by the image of Victory from the Senate House, and that boys and girls of the nobility should sing his dirge; that on the day of his cremation iron rings should be worn instead of gold ones; that his ashes should be gathered by priests of the leading Colleges; that the name 'August' should be transferred to September, because Augustus had been born in September but had died in the month now called August; and that the period between his birth and death should be officially entered in the Calendar as 'the Augustan Age'.

Though the House as a whole decided not to pay him such excessive honours, he was given two funeral eulogies—by Tiberius from the forecourt of Julius Caesar's

Temple, and by Tiberius's son Drusus from the original Rostrum—after which a party of Senators shouldered the body and took it to a pyre on the Campus Martius, where it was burned; and an ex-praetor actually swore that he had seen Augustus's spirit soaring up to Heaven through the flames. Leading knights, barefoot, and wearing unbelted tunics, then collected his ashes and placed them in the family Mausoleum. He had built this himself forty-two years previously, during his sixth consulship, between the Flaminian Way and the Tiber; at the same time converting the neighbourhood into a public park.

101   Augustus's will, composed on 3 April of the previous year, while Lucius Plancus and Gaius Silius were Consuls, occupied two note-books, written partly in his own hand, partly in those of his freedmen Polybius and Hilarion. The Vestal Virgins to whose safe-keeping he had entrusted these documents now produced them, as well as three rolls, also sealed by him. All were opened and read in the House. It proved that he had appointed Tiberius and Livia heirs to the bulk of his estate, directing that Tiberius should take two-thirds and adopt the name 'Augustus', while Livia took the remaining third and adopted the name 'Augusta'. If either of these two beneficiaries could not, or would not, inherit, the heirs in the second degree were to be Tiberius's son Drusus, entitled to one-third of the reversion; and Augustus's great-grandson Germanicus, with his three sons, jointly entitled to the remainder. Many of Augustus's relatives and friends figured among the heirs in the third degree. He also left a bequest of 400,000 gold pieces to the Roman commons in general; 35,000 to the two tribes with which he had family connexions; ten to every Praetorian guard; five to every member of the City companies; three to every legionary soldier. These legacies were to be paid on the nail, because he had always kept enough cash for the purpose. There were other minor bequests, some as large as 200 gold pieces, which were not to be settled until a year after his death because:

'...my estate is not large; indeed, my heirs will not receive more than 1,500,000 gold pieces; for, although my friends have bequeathed me some 14,000,000 in the last twenty years, nearly the whole of this sum, besides what came to me from my father, from my adoptive father, and from others, has been used to buttress the national economy.'

He had given orders that 'should anything happen' to his daughter Julia, or his grand-daughter of the same name, their bodies must be excluded from the Mausoleum. One of the three sealed rolls contained directions for his own funeral; another, a record of his reign, which he wished to have engraved on bronze and posted at the entrance to the Mausoleum; the third, a statement of how many serving troops were stationed in different parts of the Empire, what money reserves were held by the Public Treasury and the Privy Purse, and what revenues were due for collection. He also supplied the names of freedmen and slave-secretaries who could furnish details, under all these heads, on demand.

Suetonius *Augustus* 100–1
tr. R. Graves (Penguin 1957)

(b)   *For Livia see also B58 and 60.*

Finally he kissed his wife with 'Goodbye Livia: never forget whose wife you have been'.

Suetonius *Augustus* 99. 1
tr. R. Graves (Penguin 1957)

B54 Honours granted to Augustus after his death

On ruler cult see L. R. Taylor The Divinity of the Roman Emperor *(Middletown 1931); see also D10-14.*

Now these rumours began to be current at a later date. At the time they declared Augustus immortal, assigned to him priests and sacred rites, and made Livia, who was already called Julia and Augusta, his priestess; they also permitted her to employ a lictor when she exercised her sacred office. On her part, she bestowed a million sesterces upon a certain Numerius Atticus, a senator and ex-praetor, because he swore that he had seen Augustus ascending to heaven after the manner of which tradition tells concerning Proculus and Romulus. A shrine voted by the senate and built by Livia and Tiberius was erected to the dead emperor in Rome, and others in many different places, some of the communities voluntarily building them and others unwillingly. Also the house at Nola where he passed away was dedicated to him as a precinct. While his shrine was being erected in Rome, they placed a golden image of him on a couch in the temple of Mars, and to this they paid all the honours that they were afterwards to give to his statue. Other votes in regard to him were, that his image should not be borne in procession at anybody's funeral, that the consuls should celebrate his birthday with games like the Ludi Martiales, and that the tribunes, as being sacrosanct, were to have charge of the Augustalia. These officials conducted everything in the customary manner—even wearing the triumphal garb at the horse-race—except that they did not ride in the chariot. Besides this, Livia held a private festival in his honour for three days in the palace, and this ceremony is still continued down to the present day by whoever is emperor.

Such were the decrees passed in memory of Augustus, nominally by the senate, but actually by Tiberius and Livia. For when some men proposed one thing and some another, the senate decreed that Tiberius should receive suggestions in writing from its members and then select whichever he chose. I have added the name of Livia because she, too, took a share in the proceedings, as if she possessed full powers.

Dio Cassius 56. 46. 1–47. 1
tr. E. Cary (Loeb 1924)

B55 The family and the succession

The question of the succession first arose in 23 BC when Augustus was seriously ill. According to Dio Cassius (53. 30. 1 ff.) everyone expected M. Marcellus, his nephew and husband of his daughter Julia, to be the chosen successor, but Augustus handed his signet ring to M. Agrippa. It is far from certain that at that stage the position of the Princeps was seen as one which could be inherited. After Marcellus' death, Julia was married to M. Agrippa (21 BC); their sons, Gaius and Lucius, were adopted by Augustus in 17 BC (Dio Cassius 54. 18. 2) and their education and subsequent careers indicate that Augustus hoped they would eventually succeed him. Agrippa died in 12 BC and in the following year Julia was married to Tiberius, Augustus' step-son. Augustus' adopted sons, Gaius and Lucius, died within two years of each other (AD 2 and AD 4) and Augustus made Tiberius his heir, adopting him together with Agrippa Postumus, the third son of Julia and Agrippa (Dio Cassius 55. 13. 1a). On the question of the succession see Syme RR chs. 23, 27, and 28; see also §K.

(a)

63   Scribonia bore him a daughter, Julia; but to his great disappointment the marriage with Livia proved childless, apart from a premature birth. Julia was betrothed first to Mark Antony's son and then to Cotiso, King of the Getans, whose daughter Augustus himself proposed to marry in exchange; or so Antony writes. But Julia's first husband was Marcellus, his sister Octavia's son, then hardly more than a child; and, when he died, Augustus persuaded Octavia to let her become Marcus Agrippa's wife—though Agrippa was now married to one of Marcellus's two sisters, and had fathered children on her. At Agrippa's death, Augustus cast about for a new son-in-law, even if he were only a knight, eventually choosing Tiberius, his step-son; this meant, however, that Tiberius must divorce his wife, who had already given him an heir.

64   Julia bore Agrippa three sons—Gaius, Lucius, and Agrippa Postumus; and two daughters—Julia the Younger, and Agrippina the Elder. Augustus married this Julia to Lucius Paulus whose father, of the same name, was Censor; and Agrippina to Germanicus—the son of Octavia's daughter Antonia by Tiberius's younger brother Drusus. He then adopted Gaius and Lucius, and brought them up at the Palace; after buying them from Agrippa at a token sale—touching the scales three times with a bronze coin in the presence of the City praetor. He trained his new sons in the business of government while they were still young, sending them as commanders-in-chief to the provinces when only consuls-elect. The education of his daughter and grand-daughters included even spinning and weaving; they were forbidden to say or do anything, either publicly or in private, that could not decently figure in the imperial day-book. He took severe measures to prevent them forming friendships without his consent, and once wrote to Lucius Vinicius, a young man of good family and conduct: 'You were very ill-mannered to visit my daughter at Baiae.' Augustus gave Gaius and Lucius reading, swimming and other simple lessons, for the most part acting as their tutor himself; and was at pains to make them model

their handwriting on his own. Whenever they dined in his company he had them sit at his feet on the so-called lowest couch; and, while accompanying him on his travels, they rode either ahead of his carriage, or one on each side of it.

65 His satisfaction with the success of this family training was, however, suddenly dashed. He found out, to his misfortune, that the Elder and the Younger Julia had both been indulging in every sort of vice; and banished them. When Gaius then died in Lycia, and Lucius eighteen months later at Marseilles, Augustus publicly adopted his remaining grandchild, Agrippa Postumus and, at the same time, his step-son Tiberius; a special bill to legalize this act was passed by a people's court, consisting of thirty lictors under the Chief Pontiff. Yet he soon disinherited Postumus, whose behaviour had lately been vulgar and brutal, and packed him off to Sorrento in disgrace.

Suetonius *Augustus* 63–5
tr. R. Graves (Penguin 1957)

(b)

Some three years before the plot of Egnatius was exposed, about the time of the conspiracy of Murena and Caepio, fifty years from the present date, Marcus Marcellus died, the son of Octavia, sister of Augustus, after giving a magnificent spectacle to commemorate his aedileship and while still quite a youth. People thought that, if anything should happen to Caesar, Marcellus would be his successor in power, at the same time believing, however, that this would not fall to his lot without opposition from Marcus Agrippa. He was, we are told, a young man of noble qualities, cheerful in mind and disposition, and equal to the station for which he was being reared. After his death Agrippa, who had set out for Asia on the pretext of commissions from the emperor, but who, according to current gossip, had withdrawn, for the time being, on account of his secret animosity for Marcellus, now returned from Asia and married Julia the daughter of Caesar, who had been the wife of Marcellus, a woman whose many children were to be blessings neither to herself nor to the state.

Velleius Paterculus 2. 93
tr. F. W. Shipley (Loeb 1924)

(c)

The deified Augustus, when he had lost his children, and his grandchildren, and the supply of Caesars had been exhausted, bolstered his depleted house by adoption; nevertheless, he bore his lot with the bravery of one who was already counting it a personal affair and his deepest concern that no man should make complaint of the gods.

Seneca *To Marcia on Consolation* 15. 2
tr. J. W. Basore (Loeb 1932)

93

B56 Augustus' will

*The accounts of Dio Cassius (in Xiphilinus' epitome 56. 32) and Tacitus (*Annals *1. 8) do not mention these disparaging words.* Suetonius Augustus *101 (B53) gives a more detailed version of Augustus' dispositions.*

The preamble to the will ran as follows: 'Since fate has cruelly carried off my sons Gaius and Lucius, Tiberius must inherit two-thirds of my property...' This ungracious wording strengthened the suspicion that Augustus had nominated Tiberius as his successor only for want of any better choice.

Suetonius *Tiberius* 23
tr. R. Graves (Penguin 1957)

B57 Agrippa

Marcus Vipsanius Agrippa was a close friend and colleague of Augustus. An excellent naval tactician, he was responsible for victories at Mylae (Velleius Paterculus 2. 84), Naulochus, and, significantly, at Actium (Velleius Paterculus 2. 85). Augustus, seriously ill in 23 BC, handed his signet ring to Agrippa, presumably to indicate him as his successor. Agrippa was closely associated with Augustus in public works (Dio Cassius 53. 26. 5–27. 1) and in 21 BC took over the administration of the city (Dio Cassius 54. 6. 1–5). In 18 BC he received the tribunician power and the proconsular imperium *over all the Imperial provinces, possibly also the* maius imperium *(see M. Reinhold* Marcus Agrippa *(Geneva, N.Y. 1933) pp. 167 ff.), and these were renewed in 13 BC. The text is Ehrenberg and Jones no. 366.*

Tribunician power was granted to you for five years by Senatorial decree in the consulship of the Lentuli, and again for another five years in the consulship of Tiberius Nero and Quintilius Varus your sons-in-law. Furthermore, it was ratified by law that in whatever provinces you might be drawn by the public business of Rome (to act), no one should have greater authority than yourself . . .of height and our. . .to the private. . .of all men. . .

P. Colon inv. no. 4701
tr. K. Chisholm

B58 Livia

Tacitus portrays Livia as a powerful influence on both Augustus and Tiberius.

(a)

In the following year, when Gaius Fufius Geminus and Lucius Rubellius Geminus were consuls, the aged Augusta died. By her own Claudian family, and her adoption into the Livii and Julii, she was of the highest nobility. Her first husband, and the father of her children, had been Tiberius Claudius Nero, who, after emigrating in the Perusian war, returned to Rome when peace was concluded between Sextus Pompeius and the Triumvirate. The future Augustus, fascinated by her beauty, removed her from him—with or without her encouragement—and hastily conducted her to his own home even before the baby she was expecting (the future Nero Drusus) was born. That was her last child. But her connection with Augustus through the marriage of her grandson Germanicus to his granddaughter Agrippina gave them great-grandchildren in common. Her private life was of traditional strictness. But her graciousness exceeded old-fashioned standards. She was a compliant wife, but an overbearing mother. Neither her husband's diplomacy nor her son's insincerity could outmanoeuvre her.

The implementation of her will was long delayed. At her modest funeral, the obituary speech was pronounced by her great-grandson Gaius, soon to be emperor. Tiberius did not interrupt his own self-indulgences for his mother's last rites, but wrote excusing himself and pleading important business. Moreover, when the senate decreed extensive honours to her memory, he curtailed them in the name of moderation, conceding only a few. Tiberius added that she was not to be deified—she herself had not wished it.

The same letter contained strictures on 'female friendships'. This was an implied criticism of the consul Gaius Fufius Geminus, whom the Augusta's patronage had elevated. Fufius could attract women. Moreover, his sharp tongue had often ridiculed Tiberius with sarcastic jokes such as autocrats long remember.

Now began a time of sheer crushing tyranny. While the Augusta lived there was still a moderating influence, for Tiberius had retained a deep-rooted deference for his mother. Sejanus, too, had not ventured to outbid her parental authority. Now, however, the reins were thrown off, and they pressed ahead. A letter was sent to Rome denouncing Agrippina and Nero Caesar. It was read so soon after the Augusta's death that people believed it had arrived earlier and been suppressed by her.

Tacitus *Annals* 5. 1–2
tr. M. Grant (Penguin 1973)

(b)

Among the many excellent utterances of [Livia's] that are reported are the following. Once, when some naked men met her and were to be put to death in consequence, she saved their lives by saying that to chaste women such men are no whit different from statues. When someone asked her how and by what course of action she had obtained such a commanding influence over Augustus, she answered that it was by being scrupulously chaste herself, doing gladly whatever pleased him, not meddling with any of his affairs, and, in particular, by pretending neither to hear of nor to notice the favourites that were the objects of his passion. Such was the character of Livia.

Dio Cassius 58. 2. 4–5
tr. E. Cary (Loeb 1924)

(c) *Phaedrus, a poet who flourished under Tiberius, explicitly claimed to use animal fables for political and social satire. The fable of the she-goats' beards is supposed to refer to Livia, who (to vary the metaphor) wore the trousers in the Imperial house.*

> The she-goats won a grant of beards from Jove.
> Sore were the he-goats, murmuring loud that shes
> Should reach the level of their dignity
> The God replied: 'Leave them for idle boast
> The trappings and insignia of your state,
> If rivals of your strength they may not be.'

Phaedrus 4. 16
tr. J. P. Postgate *Translation and Translations* (London 1922)

B59 The death of Drusus

Julia Augusta is Livia, Augustus' wife: the reference is to the death of her younger son Drusus (by her first marriage) in 9 BC. Drusus was popular and believed to be something of a Republican. Areus or Areius was a Stoic philosopher who was a kind of philosophical chaplain at Augustus' court. According to one story Augustus said that he spared Alexandria for the sake of Areus (Themistius Orations 8. 108 b), and according to another that he valued Areus as highly as Agrippa (Themistius Orations 10. 130 b). On Areus as an example of the influence of personal attendants of the Emperor see F. Millar The Emperor in the Roman World *p. 85.*

I doubt not that the example of Julia Augusta, whom you regarded as an intimate friend, will seem more to your taste than the other; she summons you to follow her. She, during the first passion of grief, when its victims are most unsubmissive and most violent, made herself accessible to the philosopher Areus, the friend of her husband, and later confessed that she had gained much help from that source— more than from the Roman people, whom she was unwilling to sadden with this sadness of hers; more than from Augustus, who was staggering under the loss of one of his main supports, and was in no condition to be further bowed down by the grief of his dear ones; more than from her son Tiberius, whose devotion at that untimely funeral that made the nations weep kept her from feeling that she had suffered any loss except in the number of her sons.

Seneca to *Marcia on Consolation* 4. 1–4
tr. J. W. Basore (Loeb 1932)

B60 Livia and her grandchildren

(a) *Gaius' shame at his plebeian origins*

He called his great-grandmother Livia Augusta a 'she-Ulysses', and in a letter to the Senate dared describe her as of low birth—'her maternal grandfather Aufidius Lurco having been a mere army sergeant from Fundi'—although the public records showed Lurco to have held high office at Rome.

Suetonius *Gaius* 23. 2
tr. R. Graves (Penguin 1957)

(b) *Julia, daughter of Agrippa and Augustus' daughter, died in AD 28.*

This was about the time when Julia died. Convicted of adultery, she had been condemned by her grandfather Augustus to banishment on the island of Trimerum off the Apulian coast. There she had endured exile for twenty years. The Augusta had helped her: after secretly ruining her step-daughter's family when they prospered, she openly showed pity for them in their ruin.

Tacitus *Annals* 4. 71
tr. M. Grant (Penguin 1973)

B61 The Julias

Julia, Augustus' daughter by his first wife Scribonia, was accused of adultery and banished in 2 BC. It is probable that this charge covers up a conspiracy: the list of her lovers forms a powerful aristocratic faction. Amongst them was Iullus Antonius, son of Mark Antony, who could well have coveted Augustus' position. For the political implications see Syme RR pp. 426 ff.

(a) *Augustus did not in fact report the matter to the Senate in person, but left it to the quaestor (cf. Suetonius Augustus 25).*

97

The deified Augustus banished his daughter, who was shameless beyond the indict-ment of shamelessness, and made public the scandals of the imperial house—that she had been accessible to scores of paramours, that in nocturnal revels she had roamed about the city, that the very forum and the rostrum, from which her father had proposed a law against adultery, had been chosen by the daughter for her debaucheries, that she had daily resorted to the statue of Marsyas, and, laying aside the role of adulteress, there sold her favours, and sought the right to every indul-gence with even an unknown paramour.

Carried away by his anger, he divulged all these crimes, which, as emperor, he ought to have punished, and equally to have kept secret, because the foulness of some deeds recoils upon him who punishes them. Afterwards, when with the lapse of time shame took the place of anger, he lamented that he had not veiled with silence matters that he had not known until it was disgraceful to mention them, and often exclaimed: 'If either Agrippa or Maecenas had lived, none of this would have happened to me!' So difficult was it for one who had so many thousands of men to repair the loss of two! When his legions were slaughtered, others were at once enrolled; when his fleet was wrecked, within a few days a new one was afloat; when public buildings were swept away by fire, finer ones than those destroyed rose in their place. But the place of Agrippa and Maecenas remained empty all the rest of his life. What! Am I to suppose that there were no more like them who could take their place, or that it was the fault of Augustus himself, because he chose rather to sorrow than to search for others? There is no reason for us to suppose that Agrippa and Maecenas were in the habit of speaking the truth to him; they would have been among the dissemblers if they had lived. It is a characteristic of the kingly mind to praise what has been lost to the detriment of what is present, and to credit those with the virtue of telling the truth from whom there is no longer any danger of hearing it.

Seneca *On Benefits* 6. 32. 1–4
tr. J. W. Basore (Loeb 1935)

(b) *Julia's daughter, also called Julia, was accused of immorality and banished in AD 8. This may well have covered as political an offence as the elder Julia's. On Augustus' moral legislation see D23 ff.*

The Emperor Augustus had been notably fortunate in all his public dealings, but his private life was calamitous because of the immorality of his daughter and grand-child. He expelled them both from Rome; their lovers were visited with banishment or death. Misbehavior between men and women—an everyday offense—he described by the high-sounding terms of sacrilege and treason. This led him far from the toler-ance our ancestors had displayed, and even that embodied in his own legislation.

Tacitus *Annals* 3. 24
tr. D. R. Dudley (Mentor 1966)

(c)   *Aemilius Paulus was involved in a conspiracy against Augustus (cf. Suetonius Augustus 19. 1) in which Julia may well have been involved.*

He is referring to Augustus' grand-daughter Julia. She was married to Aemilius Paulus. He was executed on a charge of treason. She was banished by her grand-father, subsequently recalled, exposed herself to charges of immorality, and was condemned to lifelong exile. Her brother Agrippa was banished to Sicily by Augustus on account of his vicious character.

Scholiast to Juvenal 6. 158
tr. J. Ferguson

B62 The *Consolation to Livia*

The Consolation to Livia *was attributed to Ovid in the fifteenth-century MSS, but was probably written considerably later in imitation of his style.*

> He buries Agrippa in your tomb, Marcellus,
>   the resting-place of two sons-in-law.
> The door of the grave was scarcely closed on Agrippa
>   when his sister received the rites of death.
> Three funerals and now a new loss: Drusus is the fourth
>   to draw tears from Caesar.
> Fates, shut that tomb—it has been too often unsealed.
>   Shut it; that house has been unfairly open.

Consolation to Livia 67–74
tr. J. Ferguson

B63 Resolution on the coming of age of Gaius Caesar

Gaius Caesar assumed the toga virilis *in 5 BC and was designated to be consul in five years (i.e. 1 BC). Sardis celebrated this occasion by making the day of Gaius' coming of age into an annual holiday. An embassy was sent to Augustus with a copy of this decree, and it was preserved, together with Augustus' reply, on a stele erected in honour of one of the members of that embassy, Menogenes son of Isidorus. This inscription was published in 1914 in* AJA *18 by W. H. Buckler and D. M. Robinson; also by the same authors, with plate, in* Sardis *7. 1 (Leiden 1932) no. 8.*

99

On motion of the *strategi* Metrodorus son of Conon, Clinius, Musaeus, and Dionysius—

Whereas Gaius Julius Caesar, the eldest of the sons of Augustus has—as has been
fervently prayed for—assumed in all its splendor the pure-white toga (of manhood)
in place of the purple-bordered toga (of youth), and all men rejoice to see the
prayers for his sons rising together to Augustus;

And whereas our city in view of so happy an event has decided to keep the day
which raised him from a boy to a man as a holy day, on which annually all shall
wear wreaths and festal garb, and the annual *strategi* shall offer sacrifices to the
gods and render prayers through the sacred heralds for his preservation; to unite
in consecrating an image of him set up in his father's temple; also on the day on
which the city received the good news and the decree was ratified, to wear wreaths
and perform most sumptuous sacrifices to the gods; and to send an embassy concerning these matters to go to Rome to congratulate him and Augustus;

Therefore it was resolved by the council and the people to dispatch envoys chosen
from the most distinguished men for the purpose of bringing greetings from the city,
of delivering to him the copy of this decree sealed with the public seal, and of discussing with Augustus the common interests of the province of Asia and of the city . . .

The Emperor Caesar Augustus, son of a god, *pontifex maximus*, holding the
tribunician power for the nineteenth year, to the chief magistrates and council of
Sardis, greeting. Your envoys, Iollas son of Metrodorus and Menogenes son of
Isidorus, grandson of Menogenes, had an audience with me in Rome and presented
me with the decree sent by you in which you make known your resolutions concerning yourselves and express your joy on the coming to manhood of the elder of
my sons. I commend you, therefore, for your earnest endeavor to demonstrate your
gratitude to me and all my house for the benefits you receive from me. Farewell.

IGRR 4. 1756 lines 6–27
tr. Lewis and Reinhold vol. 2

B64 Gaius given command in the East

*In 1 BC Gaius Caesar was sent to re-establish Roman influence over Armenia; he
negotiated an agreement with Phraataces the new king of Parthia (cf. Dio Cassius
55. 10. 18 ff.).*

Caesar is now preparing to fill the gap in his conquests:
    East, you'll be ours!
Parthian, now for the penalty. Rejoice, buried Crassi;
    rejoice, standards in alien hands
An avenger is living and sending a general in the first flush of youth,
    a boy with a man's task.

Timid ones, don't try to reckon the birthdays of gods: the Caesars
are men before their day.

Ovid *Ars Amatoria* 1. 177–84
tr. J. Ferguson

B65   Resolutions of the town council of Pisa on the deaths of Augustus' grandsons

*In 17 BC Augustus adopted Gaius and Lucius Caesar, the sons of his daughter Julia
and Agrippa, and named them his heirs (Dio Cassius, 54. 18. 1–2). The whole empire
mourned their untimely deaths. These decrees came from Pisa and record the
resolutions passed in AD 2 on the death of Lucius Caesar, and in AD 4 on the death
of Gaius Caesar. The text is Ehrenberg and Jones no. 68.*

(a)
19 September, at Pisa in the Augusteum in the forum; present when the record was
made were: Quintus Petillius, son of Quintus, Publius Rasinius Bassus, son of Lucius,
Marcus Puppius, son of Marcus, Quintus Sertorius Pica, son of Quintus, Gnaeus
Octavius Rufus, son of Gnaeus, Aulus Albius Gutta, son of Aulus.

Whereas Gaius Canius Saturninus, son of Gaius, the *duovir*, made a resolution to
offer greater funerary honours to Lucius Caesar, augur, consul designate, leader of
the youth, patron of our colony, son of Augustus Caesar father of the country,
pontifex maximus, in the 25th year of his tribunician power, the town council
decreed as follows:

Whereas the Senate of the people of Rome [decre]ed amongst all the other
great honours to Lucius Caesar, augur and consul designate, son of Augustus
Caesar the father of his country, *pontifex maximus*, in the 25th year of his tribunician power, by the agreement of all the classes zealously . . . [3 lines missing]
. . . Gaius Canius Saturninus, *duovir*, and the *decemviri* (*leading members of the
town council*) were given the task of inspecting and selecting which of their two
sites appears the most suitable for a monument, ⟨and of⟩ buying with public funds
from the private owners that site which they would have approved as the better
one; (it was also decided) that every year on 20 August sacrifices shall be made
at that altar to his departed spirit at public expense by the magistrates or those in
charge of judicial administration there, clothed in mourning togas, (those amongst
them who have the right to wear these garments on that day); a black ox and a
black ram adorned with dark fillets shall be sacrificed to his departed spirit and
these ⟨ ⟩ victims shall be burned in the same place, and over them shall be poured
libations consisting of one urn each of milk, honey, and oil; when this has been
done by the city, any private person who wishes to sacrifice to the departed spirit
on his own behalf (provided that he) does not offer more than one taper or torch

101

or crown, and that those who sacrifice are girdled in the Gabian manner (with the toga tucked up) as they kindle the pyre and in the same manner as they make use of it; (it was also decided) that the ground before the altar, on which the wood for the pyre is to be collected and heaped up, shall be 40 feet square, and be enclosed by oak stakes, and that every year a pile of wood shall be set up there for that purpose; (further that) this decree, as well as the previous decrees concerned with honours paid to him (Lucius Caesar) should be inscribed or incised on a large memorial stone fastened alongside the altar.

As for other ceremonies, from which they had resolved and now resolve to abstain on that day, the procedure as decreed by the Senate and people of Rome should be followed.

(It was also decided) that, at the first opportunity, ambassadors from our order should approach Imperator Caesar Augustus, father of his country, *pontifex maximus*, in the 25th year of his tribunician power, and request that he allow the Julian colonists of the colony of Julia Obsequens Pisa to carry out and execute all the provisions of this decree.

Dessau *ILS* 139
tr. K. Chisholm

(b) *The introduction of this resolution has been omitted.*

Whereas observations were made that the actions recorded below were taken when there were no magistrates in our colony on account of the election campaign—

Since on April 2 the news reached us that Gaius Caesar, son of Augustus (father of his country, *pontifex maximus*, guardian of the Roman Empire and protector of the whole world), grandson of a god—after the consulship which he had auspiciously completed by waging war beyond the farthest dominions of the Roman people and after he had administered the state well and had conquered or received under our protection most warlike and mighty peoples—had been wounded defending the state and had as a result of this mischance been snatched by cruel fates from the Roman people when he had already been designated *princeps* most just and most like his father in virtues, and sole protector of our colony; and since this event, coming when the mourning had not yet subsided which the entire colony had undertaken as a result of the death of his brother Lucius Caesar, consul designate, augur, our patron, leader of the youth, has renewed and increased the grief of all, individually and collectively;

For these reasons, all the decurions and colonists (since at the time of this misfortune there were in the colony no duovirs or prefects or anyone in charge of the administration of justice) agreed, in consideration of the magnitude of so great and unexpected a calamity, that from the day on which his death was announced to the day on which his bones are brought back and buried and the due rites are performed to his departed spirit all should wear mourning, keep the temples of the immortal gods, the public baths, and all shops closed, and abstain from festivity, and the matrons in our colony should make public lamentation; that the day on which Gaius Caesar died, viz., February 21, should go down in history and be observed at the present time by order and wish of all as a day of mourning like that of the Allia, and that it should be expressly forbidden to hold, plan, or announce for or on that day, viz., February 21, any public sacrifice, thanksgivings, weddings, or public banquets or to hold or view on that day any theatrical performances or circus games; that every year on that day solemn public sacrifice shall be offered to his departed spirit by the magistrates or by those who are in charge of the administration of justice at Pisa in the same place and in the same manner as the solemn sacrifice established in honor of Lucius Caesar; that an arch adorned with the spoils of the peoples conquered or received under our protection by him shall be erected in a much-frequented place in our colony, and that upon it shall be placed a statue of him standing in his triumphal attire and, flanking this, two gilded equestrian statues of Gaius and Lucius Caesar; that, as soon as we can lawfully elect and have duovirs for the colony, the first duovirs elected shall submit this decision of the decurions and all the colonists to the [body of] decurions so that it may be legally enacted by the exercise of their public authority and entered by their authorization in the public records; and that meanwhile Titus Statulenus Juncus, flamen of Augustus, *pontifex minor* of the public worship of the Roman people, shall be requested to go with envoys, explain the present unavoidable circumstances of the colony, and report this proper public action and disposition of all by delivering a notification to the Emperor Caesar Augustus, father of his country, *pontifex maximus*, holding the tribunician power for the twenty-sixth year (and this Titus Statulenus Juncus, leader of our colony, flamen of Augustus, *pontifex minor* of the public worship of the Roman people, has done, delivering the notification, as stated above, to the Emperor Caesar Augustus, *pontifex maximus*, holding the tribunician power for the twenty-sixth year, father of his country).

It is hereby decreed by the decurions that all that was done, enacted, and decided by the unanimous agreement of all classes on April 2 in the consulship of Sextus Aelius Catus and Gaius Sentius Saturninus, shall be so done, carried out, conducted, and observed by Lucius Titius son of Aulus and by Titus Allius Rufus son of Titus, the duovirs, and by whoever hereafter shall be duovirs, prefect, or any other magistrates in our colony, and that all these things shall be done, carried out, conducted, and observed in perpetuity; and that Lucius Titius son of Aulus and Titus Allius Rufus son of Titus, the duovirs, shall see to it that everything recorded above shall in accordance with our decree be in the presence of the proquaestors entered by the town clerk in the public records at the earliest opportunity. Adopted.

Dessau *ILS* 140
tr. Lewis and Reinhold vol. 2

B66 Augustus plans to recall Postumus

A variation of the story in Tacitus Annals *1. 5 (see B35). Postumius is Agrippa Postumus, son of Augustus' daughter Julia and Agrippa, who was banished to the island of Planasia (AD 7) because of his violence and depravity. He was killed immediately after Augustus' death, perhaps by order of Augustus, perhaps by Tiberius as a possible rival.*

But Fulvius, the friend of Caesar Augustus, heard the emperor, now an old man, lamenting the desolation of his house: two of his grandsons were dead, and Postumius, the only one surviving, was in exile because of some false accusation, and thus he was forced to import his wife's son into the imperial succession; yet he pitied his grandson and was planning to recall him from abroad. Fulvius divulged what he had heard to his own wife, and she to Livia; and Livia bitterly rebuked Caesar: if he had formed this design long ago, why did he not send for his grandson, instead of making her an object of enmity and strife to the successor to the empire. Accordingly, when Fulvius came to him in the morning, as was his custom, and said, 'Hail, Caesar', Caesar replied, 'Farewell, Fulvius'. And Fulvius took his meaning and went away; going home at once, he sent for his wife. 'Caesar has found out', he said, 'that I have not kept his secret, and therefore I intend to kill myself'. 'It is right that you should', said his wife, 'since, after living with me for so long a time, you have not learned to guard against my incontinent tongue. But let me die first'. And, taking the sword, she dispatched herself before her husband.

Plutarch *Moralia* 508 A–B
tr. W. C. Helmbold (Loeb 1939)

B67 Letters to Tiberius

These letters reveal more of Augustus' own character than they do of his relationship with Tiberius.

My dear Tiberius,
. . . we had the same company for dinner, except that Vinicius and the elder Silius were also invited; and we gambled like old men all through the meal, and until yesterday turned into to-day. Anyone who threw the Dog—two aces—or a six, put a silver piece in the pool for each of the dice; and anyone who threw Venus—when each of the dice shows a different number—scooped the lot.

My dear Tiberius,
We spent the five-day festival of Minerva very pleasantly keeping the gaming table warm by playing all day long. Your brother Drusus made fearful complaints

about his luck, yet in the long run was not much out of pocket. He went down heavily at first, but we were surprised to see him slowly recouping most of his losses. I lost two hundred gold pieces; however, that was because, as usual, I behaved with excessive sportsmanship. If I had dunned every player who had forfeited his stakes to me, or not handed over my legitimate winnings when dunned myself, I should have been at least five hundred to the good. Well, that is how I like it: my generosity will gain me immortal glory, you may be sure!

My dear Tiberius,

Not even a Jew fasts so scrupulously on his sabbaths, as I have done to-day. Not until dusk had fallen did I touch a thing; and that was at the baths, before I had my oil rub, when I swallowed two mouthfuls of bread.

Suetonius *Augustus* 71; 76
tr. R. Graves (Penguin 1957)

B68 Tiberius victorious

Crinagoras, a poet from Mytilene in Greece, took part in an embassy to Augustus in 26/5 BC. Tiberius' victories were not often honoured by triumphs (cf. K2). His full name was Tiberius Claudius Nero.

> Sunrise, sunset—the world's limits. Nero's exploits
> rang through the ends of the earth.
> The sun rising saw him conquer Armenia,
> setting, Germany.
> Honour the double victory. Araxes and Rhine know it:
> slaves drink their waters now.

Crinagoras (*Greek Anthology* 16.61)
tr. J. Ferguson

B69 Germanicus

Germanicus Caesar (to whom this poem is addressed) was the son of Tiberius' brother Drusus. He won the triumphal insignia for the campaign he and Tiberius fought against the Dalmati in AD 9: the celebration was postponed because of the defeat of Varus (see also M8). Ovid was in exile in the Crimea.

Thanks, Fame, you've helped me to see the spectacle of triumph
    in my Crimean jail.
Your evidence has told me that lately countless people
    gathered to see the general,
and Rome, which takes a worldwide circuit within its walls
    could hardly contain her guests.
You told me how, for many days before, the clouds from the South
    poured ceaseless showers,
then came the sun, calm and bright in heavenly splendour,
    smiling to match the people.
The conquered praised the heroes in a clear voice, and gave them
    the honours of war.
He was ready to put on the robes with their glorious embroidery,
    but first offered incense,
honouring with due solemnity the justice of his father
    enshrined in his heart.
Wherever he went, cheering greeted him with favouring omen,
    the street was red with roses.
Before him were carried silver models of the cities conquered
    with models of the men,
rivers too and mountains, and battles in the forests,
    weapons in profusion.
The trophies were of gold, the sun set them on fire,
    the roofs seemed aflame.
Chieftains in such numbers bore chains upon their shoulders—
    enough for an army.
The greater part among them received pardon and life,
    including the ring-leader Bato.
How can I think that the divine anger is permanently against me
    when the gods spare their enemies?

Ovid *From Pontus* 2.1.19–48
tr. J. Ferguson

C ADMINISTRATION

Dio Cassius' accounts of the constitutional settlements of 27 and 23 BC (B28 and 30) give the structural basis for administration during the Principate. Augustus carefully avoided titles, honours, and positions which might have connotations of autocratic rule. He used existing institutions and worked with and through the Senate (C1–5); his personal power was unique and was subject to none of the checks and balances of a conventional magistracy yet he administered the state using the Republican forms (C1a) which he expanded rather than radically altered (C1b). He opened the business of government to the *equites* and made permanent posts out of some duties of annual magistrates. He used members of his family, his friends, and also members of his household, following the Republican tradition of a member of a great family holding high office.

We are fortunate in possessing a vast number of inscriptions dealing in detail with administrative procedure under Augustus; these were the official public records of the day and included letters on government business (C25, 26, 28) as well as laws, edicts, procedures to be followed, records of events or works of public importance, in short, covering all 'affairs of state'. These contemporary documents taken with the less detailed narrative accounts of Dio Cassius and Suetonius give us vivid descriptions of what Augustus actually did, what occupied his attention during a working day. A great number of inscriptions deal with affairs of Greek cities (C23–9)–a disproportionate number if we consider the relative importance of Greece under the Romans (for the influence of Greece on Rome see I 19–23), problems of citizenship, rewards for loyalty (C27), organization of public services in Rome, Italy (C34, 35) and the provinces (C33), all important and even many trivial matters appear to have required Augustus' personal attention.

Augustus had supreme power 'for making peace and war' and apparently an *imperium maius*, the power to overrule all provincial governors; in other words he determined all foreign policy. The Senate continued to receive some foreign embassies and presumably retained some interest in foreign affairs.

The amount of detail in some of the inscriptions may be surprising; on the other hand we have an example (C27) of a series of inscriptions beginning with an edict issued at Rome to provincial governors, then from governor to individual cities, and in this process we see relevance determining the amount of information. Some edicts or letters may have been translated by Augustus' own secretarial staff, and some may have been drafted by them.

Authoritative treatments of the administration will be found in *CAH* vol. 10, ch. 7; P. Sattler *Augustus und der Senat* (Göttingen 1960); Syme *RR*; A. H. M. Jones *Studies in Roman Government and Law* (Blackwell 1968).

C1 The reorganization of government

After the settlements of 27 BC and 23 BC (see B28, 30) Augustus held the govern-ment firmly on a basis of tribunicia potestas, *a proconsular* imperium *superior to any individual proconsul, and control of the provinces with the greater number of legions. His administration adhered broadly to a Republican framework. He still used the Senate as a legislative and judicial body, and instituted six-monthly con-sultative committees, using a smaller number of Senators as a* consilium *to formu-late proposals which would then be put before the Senate as a whole.*

(a)
Augustus attended to all the business of the empire with more zeal than before, as if he had received it as a free gift from all the Romans, and in particular he enacted many laws. ... He did not, however, enact all these laws on his sole responsibility, but some of them he brought before the public assembly in advance, in order that, if any features caused displeasure, he might learn it in time and correct them; for he encouraged everybody whatsoever to give him advice, in case any one thought of any possible improvement in them, and he accorded them complete liberty of speech, and actually changed some provisions of the proposed laws. Most important of all, he took as advisers for periods of six months the consuls (or the other consul, when he himself also held the office), one of each of the other kinds of officials, and fifteen men chosen by lot from the remainder of the senatorial body, with the result that all legislation proposed by the emperors is usually communicated after a fashion through this body to all the other senators; for although he brought certain matters before the whole senate, yet he generally followed this plan, considering it better to take under preliminary advisement most matters and the most important ones in consultation with a few; and sometimes he even sat with these men in the trial of cases. The senate as a body, it is true, continued to sit in judgment as before, and in certain cases transacted business with embassies and heralds, from both peoples and kings; and the people and the plebs, moreover, continued to meet for the elections; but nothing was done that did not please Caesar. It was he, at any rate, who selected and placed in nomination some of the men who were to hold office, and though in the case of others he adhered to the ancient custom and left them under the control of the people and the plebs, yet he took care that none should be appointed who were unfit or as the result of partisan cliques or bribery.
It was in this way, broadly speaking, that he administered the empire.

Dio Cassius 53 .21. 1–22. 1 (abridged)
tr. E. Cary (Loeb 1917)

(b) *In this passage Suetonius gives some idea of the extent and variety of Augustus' reforms. The 'acts of enrolment' refer to the* lectio *of 28 BC (see also* RG 8*); sons of Senators were now expected to do military service, and a Senatorial career was open to young men of Equestrian rank through the tribunate. The frequent inspec-tions were probably official revisions of the Equestrian roll by Augustus as censor or with censorial* potestas.

35   The Senatorial Order now numbered more than 1,000 persons, some of whom were popularly known as the 'Orcus Men'. This was really a name for ex-slaves freed in the masters' wills, but had come to describe senators who had bribed or otherwise influenced Mark Antony to enrol them in the Order on a pretence that Julius Caesar, before he died, had chosen them for this honour. The sight of this sad rabble, wholly unworthy of office, decided Augustus to restore the Order to its former size and repute by two new acts of enrolment. First, each member was allowed to nominate one other; then Augustus and Agrippa together reviewed the list and announced their own choice. When Augustus presided on this second occasion he is said to have worn a sword and a steel corselet beneath his tunic, with ten burly senatorial friends crowding around him. According to Cremutius Cordus, the senators were not even then permitted to approach Augustus's chair, except singly and after the folds of their robes had been carefully searched. Though shaming some of them into resignation, he did not deny them the right to wear senatorial dress, or to watch the Games from the Orchestra seats, or to attend the Order's public banquets. He then encouraged those selected for service to a more conscientious (and less inconvenient) discharge of their duties, by ruling that each member should offer incense and wine at the altar of whatever temple had been selected for a meeting; that such meetings should not be held more than twice a month—at the beginning and in the middle—and that, during September and October, no member need attend apart from the few whose names were drawn by lot to provide a quorum for the passing of decrees. He also arranged that privy councillors should be chosen by lot every six months, their duty being to study the drafts of bills which would later be laid before the House as a whole. During debates of critical importance Augustus shelved the custom of calling on members in order of seniority, and instead singled out speakers arbitrarily; this was intended to make all present take an alert interest in proceedings and feel responsible for constructive thought, instead of merely rising to remark: 'I agree with the last speakers.'

36   Among Augustus' other innovations were: a ban on the publication of *Proceedings of the Senate*; a statutory interval between the conclusion of City magistracies and their holders' departure to appointments abroad; a fixed mule-and-tent allowance to provincial governors, replacing the system by which they contracted for these necessities and charged them to the Public Treasury; the trans-ference of the Treasury from the control of City quaestors to that of ex-praetors or praetors; and the ruling that a Board of Ten, instead of the ex-quaestors, should convoke the so-called Centumviral Court—an ancient tribunal, now consisting of 180 members, that met in the Julian Basilica.

37   To give more men some experience of governmental duties he created new offices dealing with the upkeep of public buildings, roads and aqueducts; the clear-ing of the Tiber channel; and the distribution of grain to the people—also a Board of Three for choosing new senators, and another for inspecting the troops of knights, whenever this was needed. He also revived the long obsolete custom of appointing Censors; increased the number of praetors; and requested not one colleague but two whenever he held a consulship. The Senate, however, refused this last plea:

everyone shouting that it was sufficient detraction from his supreme dignity to acknowledge even a single colleague.

38   Augustus showed equal generosity in recognizing strategic skill, by letting full triumphs be voted to more than thirty of his generals, and triumphal regalia to an even larger number.

Senators' sons were now encouraged to familiarize themselves with the administration; they might wear purple-striped gowns immediately upon coming of age and attend meetings of the House. When their military careers began, they were not merely given colonelcies in regular legions, but the command of cavalry squadrons; and Augustus usually appointed two to the command of each squadron, thus ensuring that no senior officer lacked experience in this arm of the service.

He frequently inspected the troops of knights, and revived the long-forgotten custom of making them ride in procession; yet he withdrew the spectators' right of challenging knights to dismount while the parade was in progress; and those who were so old or infirm that they would look ridiculous, if they took part, might now send their riderless mounts to the starting point and report to Augustus on foot. Later, all knights over thirty-five years of age who did not wish to retain their chargers, were excused the embarrassment of publicly surrendering them.

39   With the assistance of ten senators, Augustus cross-examined every knight on his personal affairs. Some, whose lives proved to have been scandalous, were punished; others were degraded; but in most cases he was content to reprimand culprits with greater or less severity. The luckiest were those whom he obliged merely to take the tablets handed them, and read his censure in silence where they stood. Knights who had borrowed money at a low rate of interest, in order to invest it at a higher, earned Augustus's particular displeasure.

40   If insufficient candidates of the required senatorial rank presented themselves for election as tribunes of the people, Augustus nominated knights to fill the vacancies; but allowed them, when their term of office had expired, either to remain members of the Equestrian Order or to become senators, whichever they preferred. Since many knights had lost so much money during the Civil Wars that they no longer possessed the property qualification of their rank, and therefore refrained from taking their seats in the fourteen rows reserved for the Order at the Circus, he announced that they were not liable to punishment under the law governing theatres—which protected anyone who had once been a knight, or who was a knight's son.

Augustus revised the roll of citizens, ward by ward; and tried to obviate the frequent interruptions of their trades or businesses which the public grain-distribution entailed, by handing out tickets, three times a year, valid for a four months' supply; but was implored to resume the former custom of monthly distributions, and consented. He also revived the traditional privilege of electing all the City magistrates, not merely half of them (he himself had been nominating the remainder), and attempted to suppress bribery by the imposition of various penalties; besides distributing on Election Day a bounty of ten gold pieces from the Privy Purse to every member both of the Fabian tribe—the Octavian family were Fabians—and of the

Scaptian tribe, which included the Julians. His object was to protect the candidates against demands for further emoluments.

Suetonius *Augustus* 35–40
tr. R. Graves (Penguin 1957)

(c) *Dio Cassius attributes this change in procedure to AD 13.*

He also asked for twenty annual counsellors because of his age, which did not permit him to go to the senate-house any longer except on rare occasions; previously, it seems, he had associated with himself fifteen advisers for six months at a time. It was also voted that any measure should be valid, as being satisfactory to the whole senate, which should be resolved upon by him in deliberation with Tiberius and with these counsellors, as well as the consuls of the year and the consuls designate, together with his grandchildren (the adopted ones, I mean) and such others as he might at any time call on for advice. Having gained by this decree these privileges, which in reality he had possessed in any case, he continued to transact most of the public business, though he sometimes reclined while doing so.

Dio Cassius 56. 28. 2–3
tr. E. Cary (Loeb 1924)

C2 Access to the Princeps

The amici principis *were not so much personal friends as those of the Senators or Equestrians who attended the Princeps as members of his* consilium *as advisors or those admitted to his* salutatio. *It is likely that Augustus had a number of friends who were regularly part of his* consilia *but it is not certain whether this was as formalized a structure as under Claudius (who gave a ring to those who had unchecked access to his presence; Pliny* Natural History *33. 3. 41). For a discussion of the* amici *and the* consilia *of Augustus see J. Crook* Consilium Principis *(Cambridge 1955) pp. 23; 31–6.*

Your great-grandfather spared the vanquished; for over whom would he have ruled if he had not done so?

It was from the camp of his enemies that he recruited Sallustius and men like Cocceius and Deillius and the whole company of men admitted to his presence first (on the occasions when he received visitors).

Seneca *On Mercy* 1. 10. 1
tr. K. Chisholm

111

C3 The army

Augustus had some sixty legions under his control after Actium—by 13 BC these had been reduced to twenty-eight, deployed mainly on the frontiers. Dio Cassius (54. 25. 5—M5) records for this year legislation regulating length of service and discharge payments for both praetorians and legionaries; in AD 5 both the period of service and the amounts paid on discharge were increased. A new treasury, the aerarium militare, *was set up in the next year for paying the soldiers; taxes on inheritance and sales were paid into this fund and the Princeps no longer provided for veterans out of his own private resources (Dio Cassius 55. 24. 9—25. 6). This was a movement towards a professional standing army. See further Graham Webster* The Roman Imperial Army *(London² 1979); H. M. D. Parker* The Roman Legions *(Oxford 1928); R. Syme 'Some notes on the legions under Augustus' JRS 23 (1934) 14-33.*

(a)

24   Augustus introduced many reforms into the Army, besides reviving certain obsolete practices, and exacted the strictest discipline. He grudged even his generals home-leave, and granted this only during the winter. When a Roman knight cut off the thumbs of his two young sons to incapacitate them for Army service, Augustus had him and his property publicly auctioned; but, realizing that a group of tax-collectors were bidding for the man, knocked him down to an imperial freedman—with instructions that he should be sent away and allowed a free existence in some country place. He gave the entire Tenth Legion an ignominious discharge because of their insolent behaviour, and when some other legions also demanded their discharge in a similarly riotous manner, he disbanded them, withholding the bounty which they would have earned had they continued loyal. If a company broke in battle, Augustus ordered the survivors to draw lots, then executed every tenth man, and fed the remainder on barley bread instead of the customary wheat ration. Company commanders found absent from their posts were sentenced to death, like other ranks, and any lesser dereliction of duty earned them one of several degrading punishments—such as being made to stand all day long in front of general headquarters, sometimes wearing tunics without sword-belts, sometimes carrying ten-foot poles, or even sods of turf—as though they had been private soldiers whose task it was to measure out and build the camp ramparts.

25   When the Civil Wars were over, Augustus no longer addressed the troops as 'Comrades', but as 'Men'; and had his sons and step-sons follow suit. He thought 'Comrades' too flattering a term: consonant neither with military discipline, nor with peacetime service, nor with the respect due to himself and his family. Apart from the City fire-brigades, and militia companies raised to keep order during food shortages, he enlisted freedmen in the Army only on two occasions. The first was when the veteran colonies on the borders of Illyricum needed protection; the second, when the Roman bank of the Rhine had to be held in force. These soldiers were recruited, as slaves, from the households of well-to-do men and women, and

then immediately freed; but he kept them segregated in their original companies, not allowing them either to mess with men of free birth or to carry arms of standard pattern.

Most of the decorations with which Augustus rewarded distinguished conduct in the field were valuable silver and gold medallions or collars, rather than mural crowns—so-called because traditionally earned by the first man who scaled an enemy wall. These crowns he awarded as rarely as possible and with due regard to merit; private soldiers sometimes won them. Marcus Agrippa earned the right to fly a blue ensign in recognition of his naval victory off Sicily. The only fighting men whom Augustus held ineligible for decorations were generals who had already celebrated triumphs, even though they might have fought beside him and shared in his victories; he explained that they themselves had the right to confer such awards at their discretion. The two faults which he condemned most strongly in a military commander were haste and recklessness, and he constantly quoted such Greek proverbs as 'More haste, less speed,' and 'Give me a safe commander, not a rash one,' and the Latin tag: 'Well done is quickly done.' It was a principle of his that no campaign or battle should ever be fought unless more could clearly be gained by victory than lost by defeat; and he would compare those who took great risks in the hope of gaining some small advantage to a man who fishes with a golden hook, though aware that nothing he can catch will be valuable enough to justify its loss.

Suetonius *Augustus* 24-5
tr. R. Graves (Penguin 1957)

(b)   *For Augustus' foreign policy see also* §§ *L-O*

20   Augustus commanded armies in only two foreign wars: against the Dalmatians while he was still in his 'teens, and against the Cantabrians after defeating Antony. In one of the Dalmatian battles his right knee was bruised by a sling-stone; in another, he had one leg and both arms severely crushed when a bridge collapsed. The remainder of his foreign wars were conducted by his lieutenants; though during some of the Pannonian and German campaigns he either visited the front or kept in close touch with general headquarters by moving up to Ravenna, Milan, or Aquileia.

21   Either as a local commander, or as a commander-in-chief at Rome, Augustus conquered Cantabria, Aquitania, Pannonia, Dalmatia, and the whole of Illyricum, besides Raetia and the Alpine tribes known as Vindelicians and Salassians. He also checked the raids of the Dacians, inflicting heavy casualties on them—three of their generals fell in action; drove all the Germans back across the Elbe, except the Suebians and Sigambrians, who surrendered and agreed to settle in Gallic territory near the Rhine; and pacified other tribes who gave trouble.

Yet Augustus never wantonly invaded any country, and felt no temptation to increase the boundaries of Empire or enhance his military glory; indeed, he made certain barbarian chieftains swear in the Temple of Avenging Mars that they would faithfully keep the peace for which they sued. In some instances he tried to bind them to their oaths by demanding an unusual kind of hostage, namely women; well aware that barbarians do not feel bound to respect treaties secured only by male hostages. But he let them send acceptable substitutes as often as they pleased. Even when tribes rebelled frequently or showed particular ill-faith, Augustus's most severe punishment was to sell as slaves the prisoners he took, ordering them to be kept at some distance from their own country and not to be freed until thirty years had elapsed. Such was his reputation for courage and clemency that the very Indians and Scythians—nations of whom we then knew by hearsay alone—voluntarily sent ambassadors to Rome, pleading for his friendship and that of his people. The Parthians also were ready to grant Augustus's claims on Armenia and, when he demanded the surrender of the Eagles captured from Crassus and Mark Antony's lieutenants, not only returned them but offered hostages into the bargain; and once, because several rival princes were claiming the Parthian throne, announced that they would elect whichever candidate he chose.

Suetonius *Augustus* 20-1
tr. R. Graves (Penguin 1957)

(c)

His military dispositions were as follows. The legions and their auxiliaries were distributed among the various provinces; one fleet being stationed at Misenum, and another at Ravenna, to command respectively the Western and Eastern Mediterranean. The rest of his armed forces served partly as City police, partly as palace-guards; for after Antony's defeat he had disbanded a company of Calagurritanian Gauls, from near Lyons, and a company of Germans after the Varus disaster—both of which had served in his personal bodyguard. However, he never kept more than three companies on duty at Rome, and even these had no permanent camp but were billeted in various City lodging houses; the remainder he stationed in near-by towns, changing them regularly from summer to winter quarters. Augustus also standardized the pay and allowances of the entire Army—at the same time fixing the period of service and the bounty due on its completion—according to military rank; this would discourage them from revolting, when back in civil life, on the excuse that they were either too old or had insufficient capital to earn an honest living. In order to have sufficient funds always in hand for the upkeep of his military establishment and for pensioning off veterans, he formed an Army Treasury maintained by additional taxation. At the beginning of his reign he kept in close touch with provincial affairs by relays of runners strung out at short intervals along the highways; later, he organized a chariot service, based on posting stations—which has proved the more satisfactory arrangement, because post-boys can be cross-examined on the situation as well as delivering written messages.

Suetonius *Augustus* 49
tr. R. Graves (Penguin 1957)

C4 Edict of Octavian on the privileges of veterans

This edict dates from 31 BC and seems to be cited by a veteran who was being drafted against his will for a second term as a collector of taxes. See A. C. Johnson, P. R. Coleman-Norton, and F. C. Bourne Ancient Roman Statutes *(University of Texas 1961) p. 112.*

Imperator Caesar, son of a god, triumvir for the second time for the settlement of the commonwealth, declares: I have decided to decree that all veterans be granted exemption from tribute . . . to grant to them, their parents and children, and the wives they have or shall have, exemption of all their property from taxation; and to the end that they may be Roman citizens with fullest legal right, they shall be exempt from taxation, exempt from military service, and exempt from the performance of compulsory public services. Likewise, the aforementioned shall have the right to cast their votes and be enrolled in the census in any tribe they wish; and if they wish to be enrolled *in absentia*, it shall be permitted, both to the aforementioned themselves and to their parents, wives, and children. Likewise, just as I desired the veterans to be privileged in the said respects, I grant permission that they possess, use, and enjoy also whatever priesthoods, offices, prerogatives, privileges, and emoluments they possessed. Neither the other magistrates nor a legate nor a procurator nor a farmer of the tribute shall be in their homes for the purpose of lodging or wintering, nor shall anyone be conducted to winter quarters therein aginst their will.

Berlin Papyrus no. 628 (*FIRA* 1. 56)
tr. Lewis and Reinhold vol. 1

C5 Senatorial careers under Augustus

(a) *Lucius Munatius Plancus was a* novus homo *from a respectable family from Tibur. He served with Julius Caesar in Gaul and Spain, then fought with Antony in the Civil war but went over to Octavian in 32 BC. Cicero (*Letters to his friends *10. 3. 3) knew him as one who was 'too much at the service of the times'. The texts of (a) and (b) are in Ehrenberg and Jones.*

Lucius Munatius Plancus, son of Lucius, grandson of Lucius, great-grandson of Lucius, consul, censor, acclaimed *imperator* for the second time, member of the priestly college supervising sacrifices, he celebrated a triumph over the Raeti, built a temple to Saturn with money from spoils of the war, allocated land in Italy at Beneventum, and founded veteran colonies in Gaul at Lugdunum and Raurica.

ILS 886
tr. K. Chisholm

(b) *Publius Cornelius Dolabella, of an ancient and noble family, was consul in AD 10; he was legate in Dalmatia at the time of Augustus' death and went on to become proconsul of Africa under Tiberius. This inscription is from Epidaurus in Dalmatia.*

In honour of Publius Cornelius Dolabella, consul, member of the priestly college supervising sacrifices, member of the Titiensine fraternity, legate of the divine Augustus and of Tiberius Caesar Augustus, with propraetorian authority, the tribes of the province of upper Illyria [dedicate this].

ILS 938

tr. K. Chisholm

(c) *Leading families from Italian towns had provided Senators at Rome in some considerable numbers since Julius Caesar; this inscription shows that for some areas (the Paeligni were a tribe of central Italy) participation in the higher levels of government at Rome was only achieved under Augustus. Ovid, also a Paelignian, had withdrawn from a Senatorial career (cf. F28).*

In honour of Quintus Varius Geminus, son of Quintus, legate of the divine Augustus on two occasions, proconsul, praetor, tribune of the people, quaestor, *quaesitor* (judicial examiner), prefect for distribution of corn in Rome, member of the tribunal for deciding cases of citizenship and liberty, superintendent for maintenance of public temples and sacred monuments in Rome. He was the first of all the Paelignians to become a Senator and to hold all these public positions. The people of Superaequum (set this up) to their patron at public expense.

ILS 932

tr. K. Chisholm

C6 Equestrian careers under Augustus

(a) *'Chief of engineers' is a translation of* praefectus fabrum *by now an honorary post equivalent to staff officer. For Quirinius see also O 21.*

Quintus Aemilius, son of Quintus, Secundus, of the Palatine tribe. I received decorations in the camp of the deified Augustus under Publius Sulpicius Quirinius, legate of Caesar of Syria, and was prefect of the First Augustan Cohort and the Second Naval Cohort. I also by order of Quirinius held the census of the city of Apamea, 117,000 citizens. I also was sent by Quirinius against the Itureans of Mount Lebanon and took one of their forts. And before my military service I was entered at the treasury as chief of engineers by two consuls, and was quaestor, twice aedile, and twice *duumvir*, and *pontifex* in my colony. My son Quintus Aemilius, son of Quintus, Secundus, of the Palatine tribe, and my freedwoman Aemilia Chia are buried here. This tomb does not go to my further heirs.

ILS 2683
tr. Jones *History of Rome* vol. 2

(b) *The 18th legion was one of those destroyed under Varus (see further M8). The text is Ehrenberg and Jones no. 240.*

Gaius Pompeius Proculus, son of Gaius, of the tribe Teretina, military tribune of legion 18, prefect of engineers, one of the six commanders of the troops of *equites*, lies buried here.

ILS 1314
tr. K. Chisholm

(c) *Mount Berenice was a mining area in Egypt.*

Marcus Artorius Priscillus Vicasius Sabidianus son of Marcus of the tribe Palatina, tribune of the 15th cohort of volunteer Roman citizens, tribune of legion 7 Claudia, the dutiful and loyal, commander of the first Pannonian cavalry troop, prefect in charge of Mount Berenice, priest of the divine Augustus, patron of the colony, and in charge of the district of the Thebaid, (dedicated) this in fulfilment of a vow.

ILS 1. 2700
tr. K. Chisholm

(d) *The Lucius Pinarius Natta mentioned here may be the same as the 'client of Sejanus' in Tacitus Annals 4. 34 who prosecuted Aulus Cremutius Cordus in AD 25.*

To Lucius Pinarius Natta, son of Lucius, of the tribe Galeria, aedile and *duovir* of the city (*town magistracies*) quaestor, military tribune of legion 3, prefect in charge of Benices (*Mount Berenice*), Marcus Bivellius, son of Gaius, of the tribe Galeria, (dedicated this).

ILS 2698
tr. K. Chisholm

C7 Sepulchral inscriptions

A series of funerary inscriptions found at the site of Pisidian Antioch, or Antioch Caesarea, in Phrygia. This Hellenistic town was refounded as a Roman colony c.25

BC and was linked by military roads to other colonies founded by Augustus as part of his plan for subduing the area. In (f) there is a common pun between vivo, *I live,* and bibo, *I drink.*

(a)
Titus Cissonius, son of Servius, of the tribe Sergia, veteran of legion 7.

CIL 3.6826

(b)
Lucius Coelius, son of Lucius, of the tribe Aniensis, soldier of legion 7. (This was set up by) Faustus (his) freedman in accordance with the provisions of (Coelius') will.

CIL 3.6827

(c)
Marcus Tiberius, son of Marcus, of the tribe Sergia, veteran of legion 5 Gallica.

CIL 3.6828

(d)
Statius Pescennius, son of Lucius, of the tribe Sergia, acting for Drusus when Drusus was *duovir* in the 2nd year of Drusus' duovirate (*town magistracy*), high priest and five-yearly *duovir* for taking the census.

CIL 3.6843
tr. K. Chisholm

(e)
Titus Campusius, son of Gaius, of the tribe Sergia, veteran of legion 5 Gallica.

ILS 2237

(f)
Titus Cissonius, son of Quintus, of the tribe Sergia, veteran of legion 5 Gallica.

While I lived, cheerfully I drank—
drink! you who still live.

Publius Cissonius, son of Quintus, of the tribe Sergia, his brother, erected (this tomb).

ILS 2238
tr. K. Chisholm

C8 Declaration of surety

This document, interesting for the Egyptian name of the centurion, dates from 20 BC (cf. CAH vol. 10 p. 286).

Petesuchos son of Petesuchos to the centurion Anchoriphis from Sendrypaei. I agree to stand surety for Taphamounis from the same village and I will present her whenever you choose or (pay) 8½ artabae of good wheat measured by the standard of the village, pure and uncontaminated, which I will measure in the village of Sendrypaei. When I have measured it out, I must recover the [?aforementioned] note of surety and be absolutely clear of all obligation.

In the 10th year of Caesar,
on the twenty-fifth day of Epephis.

Papyri Osloenses (Academy of Science and Letters of Oslo 1925-31) 30
tr. K. Chisholm

C9 The provinces

According to Strabo, Augustus was given a 'power of war and peace for life' in 27 BC not restricted to his own provinces and the client kingdoms. The list of 'public' provinces includes Gallia Narbonensis and Cyprus, added in 23 BC; not all were totally without military forces: Africa, for example, had one legion. For the special arrangements for Egypt see C16. For detailed treatment of Gaul, Germany, Britain, and Judaea see §§ L–O.
On the provinces generally see T. Mommsen The Provinces of the Roman Empire *(2 vols. ET London 1886), which will be superseded by the series* The History of the Provinces of the Roman Empire *of which S. S. Frere's* Britannia *and J. J. Wilkes's* Dalmatia *have been the first two volumes. There is also some useful material in the relevant volumes of CAH.*

Of all this territory which is subject to the Romans, some is ruled by kings, and they themselves hold the rest under the name of 'provinces' sending out governors and collectors of taxes. There are also free cities, some which originally joined them in friendly relations, and others which have been freed by the Romans themselves as an honor. There are also various dynasts and tribal chiefs and priests. These live under their own ancestral laws. The provinces have been divided up in various ways at different times, but at present they are as Caesar Augustus laid down. For when his native country entrusted him with the leadership of the empire and he was given the power of war and peace for life, he divided all Roman territory into two and assigned one part to himself and the other to the people. To himself he gave whatever required a military garrison, that is the barbarian area which is near the tribes which have not yet been subdued, or is rugged and unsuited to agriculture, so that for lack of other resources and having plenty of strongholds the population is restive and disobedient; to the people the rest which is peaceful and easy to govern without military force. He divided each section into a number of provinces, some called Caesar's, the others those of the people. Caesar sends out governors and administrators to Caesar's provinces, dividing the territory up in various ways from time to time, making arrangements suitable to the occasion. The people send out ex-praetors or ex-consuls to the public provinces: they, too, are distributed in various ways as convenience dictates. But at the beginning he made two provinces consular, Africa (the part under Roman rule, excluding the area ruled first by Juba and now by his son Ptolemy) and Asia within the Halys and the Taurus, excluding the Galatians and other tribes under Amyntas and Bithynia and Propontis, and ten praetorian: in Europe and the adjacent islands, the so-called Further Spain on the rivers Baetis and Anas and Narbonensis of the Celtic area; third, Sardinia and Corsica; fourth, Sicily; fifth and sixth, the part of Illyricum next Epirus and Macedonia; seventh, Achaea, including Thessaly and Aetolia and Acarnania and the tribes of Epirus adjacent to Macedonia; eighth, Crete with Cyrenaica; ninth, Cyprus; tenth, Bithynia with Propontis and some parts of Pontus. Caesar has the other provinces and sends consuls to look after some of them, and praetors to some, and equestrians to some. And kings and dynasts and decarchies are in his portion and always were.

Strabo 17. 3. 24–5
tr. Jones *History of Rome* vol. 2

C10 Provinces and client kingdoms

Suetonius' general account of Augustus' policy omits any mention of the army. 'Vigorous' provinces were those where legions were stationed; their administration by Imperial legates involved control of most of the legions (cf. B28) Augustus confirmed or set up client kings where it suited Rome to do so, and loyal rulers were sometimes rewarded with grants of additional territory. Royal children brought up at Rome could be used as hostages as well as to ensure that future rulers were brought up sympathetic to Rome and the Roman way of life.

47   Augustus kept for himself all the more vigorous provinces—those that could not be safely administered by an annual governor—and nominated his own imperial procurators; the remainder went to proconsuls chosen by lot. Yet, as occasion arose, he would change the status of provinces from imperial to senatorial, or contrariwise, and paid frequent visits to either sort. Finding that certain city-states which had treaties of alliance with Rome were ruining themselves through political irresponsibility, he took away their independence; but also granted subsidies to others crippled by public debts, rebuilt some cities which had been devastated by earthquakes, and

even awarded full citizenship to states that could show a record of faithful service in the Roman cause. So far as I know, Augustus inspected every province of the Empire, except Sardinia and North Africa, and would have toured these, too, after his defeat of Sextus Pompey in Sicily, had not a sequence of gales prevented him from sailing; later, he had no particular reason, nor any opportunity, for visiting either province.

48   He nearly always restored the kingdoms which he had conquered to their defeated dynasties, rarely combined them with others, and followed a policy of linking together his royal allies by mutual ties of friendship or intermarriage, which he was never slow to propose. Nor did he treat them otherwise than as imperial functionaries, showing them all consideration and finding guardians for those who were not yet old enough to rule, until they came of age—and for those who suffered from mental illness, until they recovered. He also brought up many of their children with his own, and gave them the same education.

> Suetonius *Augustus* 47–8
> tr. R. Graves (Penguin 1957)

C11   Rome and Italy

Improvements and reorganization at Rome concerned building works, the supply of water and corn, and the gradual, piecemeal creation of an urban administration by establishing permanent or long-term posts (such as the praefectura vigilum *and* praefectura annonae) *for municipal affairs. The building works did not stop at Rome (see further C33) and a regular* cura viarum *was created. In* RG *16 Augustus states that he paid for the land on which he settled his veterans; there is no confirmation, however, that the system of voting at a distance described here by Suetonius was ever in use.*

After thus improving and reorganizing Rome, Augustus increased the population of Italy by personally founding twenty-eight veteran colonies. He also supplied country towns with municipal buildings and revenues; and even gave them, to some degree at least, privileges and honours equalling those enjoyed by the City of Rome. This was done by granting the members of each local senate the right to vote for candidates in the City Elections; their ballots were to be placed in sealed containers and counted at Rome on polling day. To maintain the number of knights he allowed any township to nominate men capable of taking up such senior Army commands as were reserved for the Equestrian Order; and, to encourage the birth-rate of the Roman commons, offered a bounty of ten gold pieces for every legitimate son or daughter whom a citizen could produce, on his tours of the [regions of Italy].

> Suetonius *Augustus* 46
> tr. R. Graves (Penguin 1957)

C12 Alpine roads

Augustus extended the road system throughout Italy, an important step towards better administration and unification.

Towards the other parts (I mean the parts which slope towards Italy) of the aforesaid mountainous country dwell both the Taurini, a Ligurian tribe, and other Ligures; to these latter belongs what is called the land of Donnus and Cottius. And after these peoples and the Padus come the Salassi; and above them, on the mountain-crests, the Ceutrones, Catoriges, Varagri, Nantuates, Lake Lemenna (through which the Rhodanus courses), and the source of the Rhodanus. And not far from these are also the sources of the Rhenus, and Mount Adula, whence flows not only, towards the north, the Rhenus, but also, in the opposite direction, the Addua, emptying into Lake Larius, which is near Comum. And beyond Comum, which is situated near the base of the Alps, lie, on the one side, with its slope towards the east, the land of the Rhaeti and the Vennones, and on the other, the land of the Lepontii, Tridentini, Stoni, and several other small tribes, brigandish and resourceless, which in former times held the upper hand in Italy; but as it is, some of the tribes have been wholly destroyed, while the others have been so completely subdued that the passes which lead through their territory over the mountain, though formerly few and hard to get through, are now numerous, and safe from harm on the part of the people, and easily passable—so far as human device can make them so. For in addition to his putting down the brigands Augustus Caesar built up the roads as much as he possibly could; for it was not everywhere possible to overcome nature by forcing a way through masses of rock and enormous beetling cliffs, which sometimes lay above the road and sometimes fell away beneath it, and consequently, if one made even a slight misstep out of the road, the peril was one from which there was no escape, since the fall reached to chasms abysmal. And at some places the road there is so narrow that it brings dizziness to all who travel it afoot—not only to men, but also to all beasts of burden that are unfamiliar with it; the native beasts, however, carry the burdens with sureness of foot. Accordingly, these places are beyond remedy; and so are the layers of ice that slide down from above—enormous layers, capable of intercepting a whole caravan or of thrusting them all together into the chasms that yawn below; for there are numerous layers resting one upon another, because there are congelations upon congelations of snow that have become ice-like, and the congelations that are on the surface are from time to time easily released from those beneath before they are completely dissolved in the rays of the sun.

Strabo 4. 6. 6
tr. H. L. Jones (Loeb 1923)

C13 Client states

M. Julius Cottius ruled as praefectus *over a number of tribes in the Cottian Alps apparently combining the role of client king and representative of Augustus. This inscription from Segusio in the Cottian Alps dates from 9/8 BC.*

(Dedicated) to the Emperor Caesar Augustus, son of a god, *pontifex maximus*, holding the tribunician power for the fifteenth year, acclaimed *imperator* thirteen times, by Marcus Julius Cottius, son of King Donnus, prefect of the following tribes—the Segovii, Segusini, Belacori, Caturiges, Medulli, Tebavii, Adanates, Savincates, Ecdinii, Veaminii, Venisami, Iemerii, Vesubianii, and Quadiates—and by the tribes which are under his command.

CIL 5. 7231
tr. Lewis and Reinhold vol. 2

C14 *Tropaea Augusti*

Pliny records the inscription from the monument in La Turbie, which commemorates Augustus' conquest of the Alpine tribes.

It seems not out of place to append here the inscription from the triumphal arch erected in the Alps, which runs as follows:

> To the Emperor Augustus, son of the late lamented
> Caesar, Supreme Pontiff, in his fourteenth year of
> office as Commander-in-chief and seventeenth year of
> Tribunicial Authority—erected by the Senate and
> People of Rome, to commemorate that under his
> leadership and auspices all the Alpine races
> stretching from the Adriatic Sea to the Mediterranean
> were brought under the dominion of the Roman people.
> Alpine races conquered—the Triumpilini, Camunni,
> Venostes, Vennonetes, Isarchi, Breuni, Genaunes,
> Focunates, four tribes of the Vindelici, the
> Cosuanetes, Rucinates, Licates, Catenates, Ambisontes,
> Rugusci, Suanetes, Calucones, Brixentes, Leponti, Uberi,
> Nantuates, Seduni, Varagri, Salassi, Acitavones, Medulli,
> Ucenni, Caturiges, Brigiani, Sobionti, Brodionti, Nemaloni,
> Edenates, Vesubiani, Veamini, Galli taetri, Ullati, Ecdini,
> Vergunni, Egui, Turi, Nematuri, Oratelli, Nerusi, Velauni,
> Suetri.

This list does not include the fifteen states of the Cottiani which had not shown hostility, nor those that were placed by the law of Pompeius under the jurisdiction of the municipal towns.

Pliny *Natural History* 3. 136–8
tr. H. Rackham (Loeb 1942)

C15 Administration of Spain under Augustus

The provinces under Augustus' imperium, known as the Imperial provinces, were governed by legati Augusti pro praetore, *delegates of Augustus with praetorian imperium (who could be ex-consuls as well as ex-praetors). These were primarily military commanders assisted by* legati legionis, *military tribunes and prefects; they also had judicial and administrative power (in Spain the* legatus Augusti *had a legate to assist him with judicial functions). Finances were in the charge of Equestrian procurators, whereas in Senatorial provinces they were concerned only with the property of the Princeps and a quaestor was in charge of public finance.*

But now, the provinces having been allotted, some to the people and the senate, some to the leader of the Romans, Baetica belongs to the people, and a praetor is sent to it with a quaestor and a legate; they have fixed its boundary to the east near Castulo. The rest is Caesar's, and he sends out two legates, a praetorian and a consular. The praetorian, with a legate with him, administers justice to the Lusitanians, who live next to Baetica and extend to the river Durius and its mouth; that is the name they now give to this area. Here there is Augusta Emerita. The rest, the greater part of Spain, is under the consular governor, with a considerable army of three legions and three legates. One of these keeps guard with two legions over all the country beyond the Durius to the north, what used to be called Lusitania and dubbed Callaecia; the northern mountains with the Astures and the Cantabri join on to it. The river Melsus runs through the Astures and a little further on is the city of Noega. Nearby is the turn of the ocean which divides the Astures from the Cantabri. The adjacent coast as far as the Pyrenees is guarded by the second legate with the other legion, and the third oversees the inland area. It contains the already mentioned peaceful peoples who have adopted civilized Italian manners and wear the toga, the Celtiberians and those that live on either side of the Iberus down to the maritime area. The governor himself winters in the maritime area, especially in Carthago and Tarraco, administering justice. And in the summer he goes on circuit, inspecting anything that needs reform: and there are equestrian procurators of Caesar who pay out money for the maintenance of the troops.

Strabo 3. 4. 20
tr. Jones *History of Rome* vol. 2

C16 An exceptional province

Egypt was governed by equestrians—*senators had to apply for special permission even to enter the province. The prefect had unrestricted independent jurisdiction; under him the* juridicus, *also a Roman equestrian directly appointed by the Princeps, had judicial power extending over the whole of Egypt. The* archidicastes *(chief judge) was not a chief justice, but an official connected with Alexandria, usually a Roman citizen drawn from one of the leading families there, who had authority over debt collecting and the Public Record Office as well as specifically Alexandrian affairs.*

The idiologus *was a financial officer in charge of the* idios logos *('special account') and was usually a Roman citizen. This account included all irregular or sporadic sources of income such as fines and confiscations. For a comprehensive list of such funds see BGU 5 1210 which is late but based on Augustan precedents.*

Egypt is now a Province; and it not only pays considerable tribute, but also is governed by prudent men—the praefects who are sent there from time to time. Now he who is sent has the rank of the king; and subordinate to him is the administrator of justice, who has supreme authority over most of the law-suits; and another is the official called Idiologus, who inquires into all properties that are without owners and that ought to fall to Caesar; and these are attended by freedmen of Caesar, as also by stewards, who are entrusted with affairs of more or less importance. There are also three legions of soldiers, one of which is stationed in the city and the others in the country; and apart from these there are nine Roman cohorts, three in the city, three on the borders of Aethiopia in Syene, as a guard for that region, and three in the rest of the country. And there are also three bodies of cavalry, which likewise are assigned to the various critical points. Of the native officials in the city, one is the Interpreter, who is clad in purple, has hereditary prerogatives, and has charge of the interests of the city; and another the Recorder; and another the Chief Judge; and the fourth the Night Commander. Now these officers existed also in the time of the kings, but, since the kings were carrying on a bad government, the prosperity of the city was also vanishing on account of the prevailing lawlessness. At any rate, Polybius, who had visited the city, is disgusted with the state of things then existing; and he says that three classes inhabited the city: first, the Aegyptian or native stock of people, who were quick-tempered and not inclined to civic life; and, secondly, the mercenary class, who were severe and numerous and intractable (for by an ancient custom they would maintain foreign men-at-arms, who had been trained to rule rather than to be ruled, on account of the worthlessness of the kings); and, third, the tribe of the Alexandrians, who also were not distinctly inclined to civil life, and for the same reasons, but still they were better than those others, for even though they were a mixed people, still they were Greeks by origin and mindful of the customs common to the Greeks. But after this mass of people had also been blotted out, chiefly by Euergetes Physcon, in whose time Polybius went to Alexandria (for, being opposed by factions, Physcon more often sent the masses against the soldiers and thus caused their destruction)—

such being the state of affairs in the city, Polybius says, in very truth there remained for one, in the words of the poet, merely

> 'to go to Aegypt, a long and painful journey.'

Such, then, if not worse, was the state of affairs under the later kings also; but the Romans have, to the best of their ability, I might say, set most things right, having organised the city as I have said, and having appointed throughout the country officials called Epistrategi and Nomarchs and Ethnarchs, who were thought worthy to superintend affairs of no great importance. Among the happy advantages of the city, the greatest is the fact that this is the only place in all Aegypt which is by nature well situated with reference to both things—both to commerce by sea, on account of the good harbours, and to commerce by land, because the river easily conveys and brings together everything into a place so situated—the greatest emporium in the inhabited world.

Strabo 17. 1. 12-13
tr. H. L. Jones (Loeb 1932)

C17 The first prefect of Egypt

This inscription from Philae in Egypt was erected in 29 BC by Cornelius Gallus to celebrate his suppression of an uprising in the Thebaid. He was a poet as well as a politician and a friend of Augustus, but his vanity caused his disgrace and he committed suicide in 26 BC (see also Dio Cassius 53. 23). The text is Ehrenberg and Jones no. 21.

Gaius Cornelius Gallus son of Gnaeus, Roman *eques*, first prefect of Alexandria and Egypt after the overthrow of the kings by Caesar, son of a god—having been victorious in two pitched battles in the fifteen days within which he suppressed the revolt of the Thebaid, capturing five cities—Boresis, Coptus, Ceramice, Diospolis Magna, and Ophieum—and seizing the leaders of these revolts; having led his army beyond the Nile cataract, a region into which arms had not previously been carried either by the Roman people or by the kings of Egypt; having subjugated the Thebaid, the common terror of all the kings; and having given audience at Philae to envoys of the king of the Ethiopians, received that king under (Roman) protection and installed a prince over the Triacontaschoenus, a district of Ethiopia—dedicated this thank offering to his ancestral gods and to the Nile his helpmate.

CIL 3. 14147
tr. Lewis and Reinhold vol. 2

C18 The prefect of Egypt

The prefect of Egypt was exceptional in that he held full judicial powers, unlike Imperial procurators who were in effect the private agents of the Princeps.

The prefect of Egypt does not divest himself of the prefectship, or the right of *imperium* given him by statute under Augustus on the model of the proconsulship, until his successor has actually entered Alexandria, even though the latter should have arrived at the province; this is set down in the prefect's instructions.

Justinian *Digest* 1. 17 (from Ulpian *On the Edict* 15)
tr. C. H. Munro (Cambridge 1904)

C19 Egyptian mines

This inscription, from Mons Claudianus in Egypt, gives some idea of the administrative structure at a local level. The text is Ehrenberg and Jones no. 232.

In the 40th year of Caesar, the first day of Payn (*Egyptian month*) good fortune be with us; when Publius Iuventius Rufus, tribune of legion 3, was in command at Berenice and chief supervisor of mines at Smaragdus, Bazius and Margaritus, and of all Egyptian mines, a temple was dedicated at Ophiatis to the great god Pan; Publius Iuventius Agathopous, his freedman, was overseer, supervisor and patron of all Egyptian mines; this is the offering of Ptolemy, curator of the cohort of Florus and century of Bassas, who erected this.

CRAI 1910
tr. K. Chisholm

C20 The Cyrene edicts

The five edicts are followed by a decree of the Senate. They were discovered and published in 1927, and have produced considerable discussion. The first four date from 7/6 BC and the fifth, which includes a Senatorial decree, from 4 BC. All five are important for their individual subjects: a revision of the judiciary system, a case of maiestas, *dual citizenship and public services, the composition of the jury in Cyrene and a new system for speeding up cases of extortion. The whole series is also important in that it seems to provide evidence that Augustus had some form of* maius imperium *(cf. B30 and 34); Crete and Cyrene were a Senatorial province yet these are edicts from the Princeps, tactfully phrased (see (i) below) but implying an authority superior to that of the provincial governor. They were first published in G. Oliverio* Notiziario archeologio del Ministero delle Colonie *4 (Milan-*

Rome 1927) 15-67; see also J. Stroux and L. Wenger, Abhandlungen der Bayeris-
chen Akademie der Wissenschaften, Phil. hist. Klasse, *34. 2 (Vienna 1928) 1-145;
F. de Visscher* Les Édicts d'Auguste découverts à Cyrène *(Louvain-Paris 1940);
P. A. Brunt 'Charges of Provincial Maladministration under the Early Principate'*
Historia *10 (1961); P. Romanelli,* La Cirenaica Romana *(Verbania 1943) pp. 80-7.
For a useful summary see G. W. Bowersock* Augustus and the Greek World *(Oxford
1965) pp. 88-9.*

i

The Emperor Caesar Augustus, pontifex maximus, in his seventeenth tribunician
power, acclaimed imperator fourteen times, declares:

Since I find that there are all told in the provincial territory of Cyrene 215
Romans of all ages with a census rating of 2,500 *denarii* or more, from whom the
jurors are chosen; and since embassies from the cities of the province have complained bitterly that among these same Romans there exist certain conspiracies to
oppress the Greeks in trials on capital charges, the same individuals acting in turn
as accusers and as witnesses for one another; and since I myself have ascertained
that some innocent people have in this way been oppressed and carried off to the
supreme penalty, it is my view that, until the senate makes a decision on this
matter or I myself find some better solution, it will be the right and proper procedure for those governing the province of Crete and Cyrene to impanel in the
provincial territory of Cyrene the same number of Greek jurors from the highest
census rating as of Romans—no Greek or Roman to be less than twenty-five years
of age; and none to have a census rating and property of less than 7,500 *denarii*,
if there is a sufficient number of such persons, or, if the full number of jurors who
need to be impaneled cannot be made up on this basis, they shall impanel men
possessing half this census rating, but not less, as jurors in trials of Greeks on
capital charges.

A Greek under indictment shall be given the right to decide, the day before the
prosecution opens its case, whether he wants his jurors to be all Romans or half
Greeks; and if he chooses half Greeks, then the balls shall be checked for equal
weight and the names shall be written on them, and from one urn the names of
the Romans and from the other those of the Greeks shall be drawn until a total of
twenty-five is obtained in each group. Of these the prosecutor may, if he wishes,
dismiss one from each group, and the accused three out of the total, provided he
does not dismiss either all Romans or all Greeks. Then all the others [after hearing
the case] shall separate for the balloting, the Romans casting their votes separately
in one box, the Greeks separately in a second; then a separate count shall be made
of the votes on either side, and the governor shall pronounce in open court the
verdict of the majority of all the jurors.

Furthermore, since the kinsmen of murdered persons generally do not leave
unjustifiable deaths unavenged and it can be expected that those responsible will
not lack Greek prosecutors to demand justice on behalf of their slain relatives or
fellow citizens, it is my view that all who in the future govern Crete and Cyrene

will act rightly and fittingly if in the provincial territory of Cyrene they do not permit a Roman to act as prosecutor of a Greek for the murder of a Greek man or woman, except where someone who has been honored with Roman citizenship takes action concerning the death of one of his relatives or fellow citizens.

ii

The Emperor Caesar Augustus, pontifex maximus, in his seventeenth tribunician power, declares:

Publius Sextius Scaeva does not merit reproach or censure for ordering Aulus Stlaccius Maximus son of Lucius, Lucius Stlaccius Macedo son of Lucius, and Publius Lacutanius Phileros, freedman of Publius, to be sent on to me from the province of Cyrene under guard because they had said that they had knowledge concerning my security and the commonwealth and wished to declare it. In so doing Sextius performed his duty conscientiously. However, since they have no information that concerns me or the commonwealth but have declared and convinced me that they had misrepresented and lied about this in the province, I have set them free and am releasing them from custody. But as for Aulus Stlaccius Maximus, whom the envoys of the Cyreneans accuse of having removed statues from public places, among them even the one on the base of which the city inscribed my name, I forbid him to depart without my order until I have investigated this matter.

iii

The Emperor Caesar Augustus, pontifex maximus, in his seventeenth tribunician power, declares:

Persons from the province of Cyrene who have been honored with [Roman] citizenship I order nonetheless to perform in their turn the personal compulsory public services of the Greeks. Excepted are those to whom, by decree of my father or myself in accordance with a law or a decree of the senate, exemption was granted together with citizenship. And even for those to whom such exemption was granted, it is my pleasure that they shall be exempt only as to the property they possessed at the time, but for all subsequent acquisitions they shall be subject to the usual charges.

iv

The Emperor Caesar Augustus, pontifex maximus, in his seventeenth tribunician power, declares:

Regarding disputes which occur henceforth between Greeks within the province of Cyrene, excluding indictments for capital crimes, where the governor of the province must himself conduct the inquiry and render a decision or else set up a panel of jurors—for all other cases it is my pleasure that Greek jurors shall be assigned unless some defendant or accused desires to have Roman citizens as jurors; and for those to whom in accordance with this decree of mine Greek jurors are assigned, it is my pleasure that no juror shall be assigned from the city from which either the plaintiff or the accuser or the defendant or the accused comes.

129

V

The Emperor Caesar Augustus, pontifex maximus, in his nineteenth tribunician power, declares:

A decree of the senate was passed in the consulship of Gaius Calvisius and Lucius Passienus, with me as one of those present at the writing. Since it affects the welfare of the allies of the Roman people, I have decided to send it into the provinces, appended to this my prefatory edict, so that it may be known to all who are under our care. From this it will be evident to all the inhabitants of the provinces how much both I and the senate are concerned that none of our subjects should suffer any improper treatment or any extortion.

Decree of the Senate

Whereas the consuls Gaius Calvisius Sabinus and Lucius Passienus Rufus spoke 'Concerning matters affecting the security of the allies of the Roman people which the Emperor Caesar Augustus, our *princeps*, following the recommendation of the council which he had drawn by lot from among the senate, desired to be brought before the senate by us,' the senate passed the following decree:

Whereas our ancestors established legal process for extortion so that the allies might more easily be able to take action for any wrongs done them and recover moneys extorted from them, and whereas this type of process is sometimes very expensive and troublesome for those in whose interest the law was enacted, because poor people or persons weak with illness or age are dragged from far-distant provinces as witnesses, the senate decrees as follows:

If after the passage of this decree of the senate any of the allies, desiring to recover extorted moneys, public or private, appear and so depose before one of the magistrates who is authorized to convene the senate, the magistrate—except where the extorter faces a capital charge—shall bring them before the senate as soon as possible and shall assign them any advocate they themselves request to speak in their behalf before the senate; but no one who has in accordance with the laws been excused from this duty shall be required to serve as advocate against his will.

In order that the cases of those bringing such charges in the senate may be heard, the magistrate who grants them access to the senate shall the same day in the presence of the senate, with not less than two hundred [members] on hand, choose by lot four from all those of consular rank who are in Rome itself or within twenty miles of the city; likewise three from all those of praetorian rank who are in Rome itself or within twenty miles of the city; likewise two from all the other senators and those possessing the right to voice opinion in the senate who are then either in Rome or less than twenty miles from the city. But he shall not choose anyone who is seventy years of age or over, or is the incumbent of a magistracy or an authority, or presiding officer of a law court, or commissioner of grain distribution; or anyone prevented by illness from performing this duty, who excuses himself on oath before the senate and presents three members of the senate to attest this on oath; or anyone who is so closely related by family or marriage to the accused that he may not, in accordance with the Julian Judiciary Law, be compelled to give evidence in a public action against his will; or anyone who the accused swears before the senate is hostile to him (but he shall not by such oath eliminate more than three). From the nine selected in this manner, the magistrate who does the drawing shall see to it that within two days those claiming the money and the one from whom they claim it make rejections in turn until five are left. If any of these judges dies before the case is decided, or some other cause prevents him from rendering his decision and his excuse is approved by the sworn statement of five members of the senate, then the magistrate, in the presence of the judges and of those claiming the money and the man from whom they claim it, shall again choose by lot from those members who are of the same rank or have held the same magistracies as the man who is being replaced, provided he does not thus choose a member who may not by this decree of the senate be chosen to try the accused.

The judges chosen shall hear and inquire into only those cases in which a man is accused of having appropriated money from a community or from private parties; and, rendering their decision within thirty days, they shall order him to restore such sum of money, public or private, as the accusers prove was taken from them. Those whose duty it is to inquire into and pronounce judgment in these cases shall, until they complete the inquiry and pronounce their judgment, be exempted from all public duties except public worship.

The senate decrees also that the magistrate who does the drawing of the judges —or, if he cannot, the ranking consul—shall preside over the proceedings and shall grant permission to summon those witnesses who are in Italy, with the proviso that he shall allow a man making a private claim to summon not more than five, and those pressing public claims not more than ten.

The senate likewise decrees that the judges who are selected in accordance with this decree of the senate shall pronounce in open court each his several finding, and what the majority pronounces shall be the verdict.

SEG 9.8
tr. Lewis *Roman Principate*

C21 Dedication of the Augustan Market at Lepcis Magna

Lepcis Magna was an important trading city in Tripolitanian Africa. This inscription dates from 9/8 BC. The text is Ehrenberg and Jones no. 105 b.

[Imperator Caesar Augustus, son of the divine (Julius)], consul eleven times, acclaimed *imperator* fourteen times, in the 15th year of his tribunician power, *pontifex maximus*. Marcus Licinius Crassus Frugi son of Marcus, augur, patron (of the colony) was the proconsul; Iddibal son of Aris and [Ammicar] son of Annobal were the priests of Augustus; M[uttun son of Hanno and . . .] were the sufets (*chief magistrates of the town*).

Annobal Tapapius Rufus, son of Himilcho, sufet, priest, and prefect in charge of the rites undertook this building at his own expense and also dedicated it.

J. M. Reynolds and J. B. Ward-Perkins *The Inscriptions of Roman Tripolitania*
no. 319
tr. K. Chisholm

C22 A Decree of 27 BC

This important inscription, from Cyme in Asia Minor, is firmly datable to 27 BC; the association of Agrippa with Augustus dates it to 28/7; the title Augustus was granted only on 16 Jan. 27. It falls into three parts. The first is a decree in Greek; the second a letter in Latin from the proconsul of Asia, which it is reasonable to refer to the substance of the decree; the third is a Greek translation of this last. Our version closely follows Pleket. A few letters are missing: we have not indicated probable or certain restorations. The final sentence of the proconsul's letter is however uncertain. Liber Pater is Dionysus, independently attested at Cyme.

Imperator Caesar, son of a god, Augustus . . . and Marcus Agrippa, son of Lucius, consuls, have appointed as follows: If there are any public or holy places either within the cities or within the territory of each city of the province, and if there are now or will be in the future any dedicated offerings in these places, no one is to remove, purchase, or accept them as a gift from any. It is the duty of the governor of the province to see to it that any object removed from these places, purchased or presented as a gift are restored to the said public or holy place within the city, and to take no legal action over any object restored immediately.

L. Vinicius, proconsul, offers greeting to the authorities at Cyme. Apollonides, son of Lucius, Noraceus, your fellow-citizen, has approached me and has proved that the Temple of Liber Pater is by virtue of a monetary transaction a possession of Lysias, son of Diogenes, Tucalleus, your fellow-citizen, and when the worshippers wished to restore the sacred property to the god, as instructed by Augustus Caesar, after payment of the price inscribed on the Temple of Liber Pater they were [prevented] by Lysias. I wish you to see to it, if this is true, that Lysias repays the price paid for the Temple and restores the Temple to the god, and that an inscription is set on it: RESTORED BY IMPERATOR CAESAR AUGUSTUS, SON OF A DIVINITY. But if Lysias objects to the claim made by Apollonides, Lysias is to promise bail to him, with a guarantee to present himself where I shall be.

H. W. Pleket *The Greek Inscriptions in the 'Rijksmuseum van Oudheden' at Leiden*
(Leiden 1958) no. 57
tr. J. Ferguson

C23 Treaty with Mytilene

Mytilene was the principal city of the island of Lesbos. The inscription, which dates from 25 BC, also contained the record of agreement with Mytilene accepted by Julius Caesar.

Decree of the senate concerning the treaty. In the consulship of Imperator Caesar Augustus for the ninth time and Marcus Silanus . . . by command of Marcus Silanus pursuant to a decree of the senate . . . in the Julian senate house. Present at the writing were Paulus Aemilius Lepidus, son of Lucius, of the Palatine tribe; Gaius Asinius Pollio, son of Gaius . . . Lucius Sempronius Atratinus, son of Lucius, of the Falernian tribe; Marcus Terentius Varro, son of Marcus, of the Papirian tribe; Gaius Iunius Silanus . . .; Quintus Acutius . . . son of Quintus. . . .

Whereas Marcus Silanus declared that a letter had been sent to and answered by his co-consul Imperator Caesar Augustus, so that, if it pleased the senate that there be a treaty with Mytilene, the charge of this matter be turned over to him, Silanus, concerning this matter it was decreed that the consul Marcus Silanus at his discretion see to it that there be a treaty with Mytilene such as he shall deem to be in keeping with the public interest and his own good faith. Decreed.

[Terms of the treaty] . . . the people of Mytilene shall not by public decision allow the enemies of the Roman people to pass through their dominion to make war on the Roman people or on those under their rule or on the allies of the Roman people, and shall not aid them with arms, money or ships. The Roman people shall not by public decision allow the enemies of the people of Mytilene to pass through their land or dominion to make war on the people of Mytilene or on those under their rule or on the allies of the people of Mytilene, and shall not aid them with arms, money or ships. If anyone attacks the people of Mytilene or the Roman people or the allies of the Roman people, the Roman people shall come to the aid of the people of Mytilene and the people of Mytilene to the aid of the Roman people and the allies of the Roman people, [and each] shall be a loyal [ally]. There shall be peace [between them] in perpetuity.

IGRR 4. 33
tr. Lewis *Roman Principate*

C24 Letter of Agrippa to the Gerusia of Argos

The Gerusia, or council of elders, existed in many Greek cities, sometimes as a survival of the aristocratic councils of the eighth or seventh century BC. The Romans fostered and maintained them, indeed may even have re-established some where necessary (J. H. Oliver 'The Sacred Gerusia' Hesperia suppl. 6 (Baltimore 1941)) probably in order that they might organize the local Imperial cult, fulfilling a similar role to that of the Augustales (J. H. Oliver 'Gerusiae and Augustales'

Historia *7 (1958)). This letter was written by Agrippa some time in the period between 17 and 13 BC. Found inscribed on a stele at Argos, it was published in* Mnemosyne *47(1919) by W. Vollgraff. The text is in Ehrenberg and Jones no. 308.*

Property of the Gerontes: Agrippa greets the Gerontes of Argos, descendants of Danaus and Hypermestra. I am aware from the information with which I have been provided of the reason for the continuation of your system and the preservation of your ancient honours, and I have restored many of your rights which had lapsed and for the future I am able to provide and care for you . . . think . . .

tr. K. Chisholm

C25 Letter of a Proconsul to Chios

This inscription, datable to between AD 5 and AD 14, relates to the important Greek island of Chios. The final clause subjecting Roman citizens in Chios to local decisions apparently without appeal is more unusual. Augustus' 8th consulship was 26 BC.

. . . to the envoys of Chios, reading a letter of the eminent proconsul before me, Antistius Vetus. Pursuant to my general policy of observing the ordinances of the proconsuls before me, I judged it fair to confirm also the letter of Vetus adduced in behalf of them. Next I heard both sides pleading their claims in confrontation and in keeping with my customary practice I asked both sides to submit detailed written memoranda. Taking these and giving them due attention, I discovered in time a sealed copy of a very old decree passed by the senate in the second consul-ship of Lucius Sulla, in which the senate guaranteed the Chians, in response to their representations as to all they had done in loyal support of the Romans against Mithridates and had suffered at his hands, that they might continue to employ the laws, customs and legal procedures which they observed when they entered the friendship of the Romans, that they not be subject to any writ whatever of (Roman) magistrates or pro-magistrates, and that (even) the Romans residing among them be subject to the laws of Chios. Imperator Augustus, son of the deified (Caesar), wrote a letter to Chios in his eighth consulship . . .

SIG 785
tr. Lewis *Roman Principate*

C26 Letter to Cnidos

This letter, written in 6 BC, was found in a private house at Astypalaea. It is in reply to an appeal by the Cnidians in a case seemingly without political implications and an example of the detail with which the Princeps' secretariat, if not the Princeps himself, had to deal.

Imperator Caesar Augustus, son of the deified (Julius), pontifex maximus, consul designate for a twelfth time, in his eighteenth tribunician power, to the chief magistrates, council and people of Knidos, greeting. Dionysios II and Dionysios II son of Dionysios appealed to me in Rome and, giving me your decree, charged Euboulos son of Anaxandrides, now deceased, and his surviving wife Tryphera, with the death of Euboulos son of Chrysippos. I ordered my friend Asinius Gallus to question under torture those of the slaves involved in the charge. I learned that Philinos son of Chrysippos had three nights in a row violently attacked the house of Euboulos and Tryphera, besieging them as it were. On the third night he brought with him his brother Euboulos. The owners of the house, Euboulos and Tryphera, as they were unable to enjoy safety in their own house either by negotiating with Philinos or by barricading themselves against his attacks, ordered one of their slaves, not to kill him outright (as one might be impelled in justifiable anger), but to drive him off by emptying their chamber pots. But the slave, whether intentionally or not (he persists in denial), let go the pot as well, with the result that Euboulos fell struck, though he would have deserved to be spared more than his brother. Enclosed are the depositions themselves. I should have been at a loss to understand why the defendants were so fearful of your questioning their slaves, if you had not given them strong evidence of being hard and hostile to opposition, angry not at those deserving to suffer any and every punishment for thrice launching a nocturnal attack with force and violence against another's house and (thereby) threatening the common safety of you all, but at those who did no wrong but suffered misfortune even when they tried to defend themselves. Now, you would do well, in my view, by seeing to it that the records in your public archives conform to my judgment in this matter. Farewell.

IGRR 4.1031b
tr. Lewis *Roman Principate*

C27 Grant of privileges to the Admiral Seleucos

*This important series of documents found at Rhosus in Syria and published by P. Roussel (*Syria *15 (1934) 33–74) dates from the period between 42 and 30 BC, and is an excellent example of procedure in provincial administration.*

The letter (no. 1) introducing the edict seems to imply that the following document is an extract, not a copy, of the original published at Rome. Thus the provincial magistrates might only have received that part of the law or edict which was directly relevant to them. The original could have had a wider application, and was perhaps a grant of citizenship to a group of veterans of the wars against Sextus

Pompeius. For the text with a discussion of the problems raised by the documents and a comprehensive bibliography, see Sherk Roman Documents *no. 58 pp. 294 ff.*

1

    Year . . . , . . . of the month Apellaios
    Imperator Caesar, son of divine Julius, [acclaimed]
imperator for the fourth time, consul for the second time and designated for the third time, to the chief magistrates, council and people of the worshipful, inviolate, independent city of Rhosus, greetings. If you are well, good; I too, together with my army, am in good health. I ask you to enter in your public records the following, which was copied from a monument on the Capitol at Rome; also to send a copy of this to the council and people of Tarsus, the council and people of Antioch, and the council and people of [Seleucia?] that they too may enter it in their records.

2

Imperator Caesar, one of the triumvirs in charge of ordering the Republic gave citizenship and immunity from all property tax, according to the Munatian-Aemilian law, in these words:

    Whereas Seleucos the Rhosian, son of Theodotus, campaigned with us in [. . . . . . .] under our command, suffered a great deal of hardship and danger on our behalf heedless of the terrors he had to endure, gave the Republic all his loyalty and good-will, bound his own advantage to my safety, and endured all harm for the sake of the Republic of the people of Rome, he became a good and useful friend to us, both in our presence and in our absence.

    1   We grant citizenship and immunity from taxation on property to him and his parents, his children, and his wife for the present on the same terms as those who are citizens in full and legal right and untaxed; and let them be released from military service and from all public services.

    2   Let the above-mentioned (Seleucos), his parents, children and descendants be enrolled in the Cornelian tribe and let them vote therein and be entitled [to vote, and be counted at the census?]; and if they wish to be counted in absence at the census . . . . . Italy . . . . .

    3   In so far as the above-mentioned, his wife, parents, children, and descendants, before he became a tax-exempt Roman citizen [enjoyed privileges?] he may also after having become a tax-exempt Roman citizen, according to the law, [enjoy?] if he wishes, and make use of the privileges, honours, priestly offices [and rights he already has and?] enjoy their benefits exactly as someone who does so by full and legal right.

(4–7 badly mutilated)

    8   If anyone wishes to prosecute a case against them or accuse them of a crime, or seek judgement against them, or bring them to court, they are then in all these

cases to have the choice as to whether they wish to be tried at home, under their own laws or in any free city, or under Roman magistrates or pro-magistrates ... nor is anyone to act otherwise than is written here above or to judge or pass sentence on them in any other way. And if a trial is held against these terms it is not to be valid.

9   If anyone wishes to accept an accusation or make a preliminary judgement on a capital charge against the above-mentioned, his parents, wife, children, or descendants ... it is decreed that the above-mentioned have the right to appear before the Senate, magistrates, and pro-magistrates as envoys or to send envoys concerning their private affairs. Whichever city or whichever magistrate or whatever [authorities have a duty under this edict and do not perform it, or act contrary?] to these provisions, or give a preferential decision or take security from them, or with criminal intent prevent them from being able to enjoy any of these decreed privileges, then they are to be liable to a fine of 100,000 sesterces to the Roman people, and anyone who so chooses has the right to ask for and exact it, whether he wishes to do so in the province before the Roman magistrates or pro-magistrates, or in Rome; and it is resolved that a case concerning these matters is to be heard when sufficient securities have been given. The Roman magistrates and pro-magistrates who are charged with the administration of justice there will determine and ensure that these above-mentioned matters occur according to this edict.

3
Year ... on the fifteenth of Dustrus, Imperator Caesar, son of a god, *imperator* for the sixth time, consul for the third time, and designated for the fourth time, to the magistrates, council, and people of the worshipful, inviolate, independent city of Rhosus, greeting. If you are well, good. I too, together with my army, am in good health. The ambassadors you sent to me, Seleucos my admiral, Heras, Kalli...eros, Symmachos—all noble men from a good loyal allied state—having arrived in Ephesos spoke to me on matters about which they had orders. I, for my part, on receiving the embassy, found them patriotic and honourable men and accepted the honours and the crown. I will try to come to your city and play my part in bringing you some benefit, and to preserve your privileges—indeed I will do this with all the more pleasure because of my admiral Seleucos, who campaigned with me throughout the war, excelled in all fields, and gave me every proof of goodwill and loyalty—and did not lose any opportunity to petition me on your behalf and is bringing all zeal and eagerness to bear for your advantage.
   Farewell.

4
      Year ... on the ninth of Apellaios.
Imperator Caesar, son of a god, acclaimed *imperator* for the sixth time, consul for the fourth time, to the magistrates, council, and people of the worshipful, inviolate, and independent state of Rhosus. If you are well, good. I too, together with my army, am in good health. Seleucos your fellow-citizen and my admiral who campaigned

with me throughout the wars, and gave me many proofs of his goodwill, loyalty, and bravery, as was proper for those bearing arms with me and distinguishing themselves in battle, is honoured with privileges, exemption from taxation, and citizenship. I recommend him to you, for men of this stamp increase my desire to show goodwill towards their own countries. Being confident that I will be more inclined, for Seleucos' sake to do whatever I can for you, send to me for what you want.

Farewell.

L. Jalabert and R. Mouterde *Inscriptions grecques et latines de la Syrie* 3. 1
(1950) no. 718
tr. J. Carter

C28 Letter to Mylasa

This inscription, from 31 BC, was found on two fragments of a stone in Mylasa, and is now in the Louvre. The events to which it refers occurred in 40, when the citizens of Mylasa, having been persuaded (cf. Strabo 14. 2. 24) to resist Labienus, a Roman refugee in Parthia (sent there originally by Brutus and Cassius), were defeated by him. Augustus' letter was written after Actium, probably from his winter quarters at Samos (E. Malcovati Imperatoris Augusti Operum Fragmenta *(Turin[4] 1962) p. 40). The text is Ehrenberg and Jones no. 303.*

(a)
Imperator Caesar, son of the divine Julius, appointed consul for the third time, greets the magistrates, council, and people of Mylasa; if you are in good state that is well; I too, together with my army am in good health. You have already sent a deputation to me about the fate which has befallen you and now, your ambassadors having come before me . . . Ouliades . . .

(b)
. . . . of the enemy you came to grief, your city was sold, you lost many citizens as prisoners-of-war; many were murdered, some burnt to death in the conflagration (that destroyed) the city, as the savagery of the enemy did not spare either the temples or most holy sanctuaries. They informed me about the devastation of the countryside and burning of the farms, which have resulted in utter misery for you. In addition to all this I am conscious that in these sufferings of yours, your attitude to the Romans has made you worthy of all honour and gratitude.

tr. K. Chisholm

C29 Letter of the proconsul and decrees of the provincial assembly of Asia

*The assembly (*koinon*) of the provincial cities of Asia had been in existence from the beginning of the first century BC (see Sherk* Roman Documents *p. 334). Such assemblies met annually and were used by the Roman government as a vehicle for official communications with all the sections of a province. They were concerned with maintaining the cults of Rome and the Emperor, reviews of provincial admin- istration, and appeals to the Emperor from the province as a whole—in effect they helped to create closer ties with Rome and the Emperor.*

The following inscriptions (from Greek originals) consist of a letter from Paulus Fabius Maximus, proconsul of Asia, to the assembly of the cities of Asia (a), and the decree passed in reply (b). Paulus' letter is interesting for its high-flown, poetic praise of Augustus, compared by Sherk to Virgil's fourth Eclogue *(F2). He calls Augustus 'most divine' which is not out of place in a letter written to Eastern Greek cities, but which could be an addition by a Greek secretary, rather than Paulus' own words, as it is not found in the Latin copy (fragments of which have been found in Apameia and Dorylaion).*

(a) . . . whether the birthday of the divine Caesar has brought more joy or blessing, a day which we would rightly account equal to the beginning of the world, if not by nature, at least in practical usefulness, since at a time when everything was falling apart and turning out disastrously, he restored it, and gave the whole world a new look, the world which might have welcomed dissolution if Caesar had not been born as a common blessing to all. The fact of his birth was an end and bound to misery, and we may rightly account it the beginning of real life. Since no one could enter on any enterprise whether for public or private gain under better auspices than on the day which has proved a blessing to all mankind, and since entry upon public office happens to come at about the same time in all the cities of the prov- ince of Asia (evidently a predetermined ordinance of the divine will to be a source of honour to Augustus), and since it is not easy to give thanks commensurate with his beneficent actions without designing some new expression of gratitude suited to all his good deeds, and since men will be the more willing to celebrate the birth- day as a general festival if it is associated with the particular pleasure of the inaug- uration of new officials, it is my proposal that the citizens of all the cities adopt a single universal beginning to the new year in Caesar's birthday, and that this shall be the day for entering office, that is 23 September, so that that day may receive external marks of respect and greater acknowledgement, and may be universally familiar, a day which I regard as likely to confer exceptional blessing on the exer- cise of office. This decree will have to be formally recorded by the Commonwealth of Asia together with a catalogue of his virtues, so that our intention with regard to doing honour to Augustus may remain in perpetuity. I shall give orders for the decree to be inscribed on a pillar and set up in the temple, having given previous instructions about the detailed enunciations.

(b) Decree of the Greeks in Asia, on a proposal from the High Priest Apollonius, Menophilus' son, from Azanoi. Since the Providence which has controlled the whole of our life, bringing with it an active concern and sense of honour, has added the coping-stone to our life in presenting us with Augustus, whom Providence filled with virtue so that he might bring benefactions to men, sending him to us and our successors as a Saviour to put an end to war and set all in order, and since Caesar, having become manifest has fulfilled the hopes of earlier generations ... not only outstripping all benefactors who preceded him but leaving no hope of outstripping him in time to come, and since the god's birthday has been the beginning of good news brought through his agency for the whole world ... therefore the Greeks in the province of Asia decreed with Fortune's blessing for their own well-being that the new year should begin for all the cities on 23 September, the same being Caesar's birthday ...

OGIS 458
tr. J. Ferguson

C30 Paphlagonian oath of allegiance

*This oath was taken in 3 BC, when Paphlagonia was annexed to the province of Galatia. It is an oath of loyalty and allegiance personal to Augustus and his family — no indication is given that in this he represents Rome. A. H. M. Jones (*History of Rome *vol. 2 p. 43) sees this oath as having the same form as the* coniuratio Italiae, *the oath of allegiance sworn to Augustus by all Italy before Actium.*

In the third year after the twelfth consulship of *Imperator* Caesar, son of the god, Augustus, on the day before the nones of March at Gangra in the market place, this oath was sworn by the inhabitants of Paphlagonia and the Romans who do business in the country.

I swear by Zeus, Hera, the Sun, and all the gods and goddesses, and Augustus himself, that I will be loyal to Caesar Augustus and his children and descendants all the time of my life by word and deed and thought, holding as friends whomsoever they so hold, and considering as enemies whomsoever they so judge, and for their interests I will spare neither body nor soul nor life nor children, but will endure every peril for their cause. If I see or hear anything being said or planned or done against them, I will lay information and I will be the enemy of such sayer or planner or doer; whomsoever they themselves judge to be their enemies, them I will pursue and resist by land and by sea, with arms and with iron. If I do anything contrary to this oath or not according as I have sworn, I invoke death and destruction upon myself and my body and soul and children and all my race and interests to the last generation of my children's children, and may neither the earth nor the sea receive the bodies of my family and my descendants, nor bear crops for them.

The same oath was sworn by all the rural population at the shrines of Augustus in the districts beside the altars of Augustus, and similarly the Phazimonites, who inhabit what is now called the New City, all swore in the shrine of Augustus beside the altar of Augustus.

OGIS 532
tr. Jones *History of Rome* vol. 2

C31 Excesses in provincial government

Lucius Valerius Messalla Volesus was consul in AD 5.

Not long ago, Volesus, proconsul of Asia under the divine Augustus, had 300 people executed in a single day, and paraded himself haughtily among the dead bodies, as if he had been responsible for an act of conspicuous glory, calling out in Greek 'the act of a king!'.

Seneca *On Anger* 2.5.5
tr. J. Ferguson

C32 Augustus' dispositions in Armenia

Armenia was a buffer state between Asia and Parthia. This passage from Tacitus gives some idea of the complexity of Armenian internal politics which Rome constantly tried to manipulate, often unsuccessfully.

3   But the treachery of his kinsfolk caused the death of Artaxias, after which Augustus gave Tigranes as king to the Armenians, and Tiberius Nero conducted him to his kingdom. The reign of Tigranes did not last long, nor did that of his children, although following the oriental custom they were united in matrimony as well as power.
4   After this, and at the command of Augustus, another Artavasdes was set up, only to be ejected, with some misfortunes to our arms. Then Gaius Caesar was appointed to settle affairs in Armenia. He crowned Ariobarzanes, a Median by birth, but acceptable to the Armenians because of his physical beauty and high intelligence. When Ariobarzanes met an accidental death they would have nothing to do with his descendants. For a while they sampled the rule of a queen, Erato, but that did not last long. Finally, irresolute, disorganized, and masterless rather than enjoying freedom, the Armenians placed the refugee Vonones on the throne. But Artabanus became a menace: Vonones could command little support from the

141

Armenians, and help from us would mean a Parthian war. So the governor of Syria, Creticus, sent for him and kept him under guard, allowing him the title and full royal state. How Vonones intrigued to escape from this degrading position I shall recount in its proper place.

Tacitus *Annals* 3-4
tr. D. R. Dudley (Mentor 1966)

C33 Public works

Under the Republic wealthy citizens had a tradition of paying for public works, such as aqueducts, arches, streets, etc. Augustus took over this tradition and with the help of his friends and colleagues (especially Agrippa) established a reputation for munificence on an Imperial scale. He did not limit his generosity to Rome, but as the following inscriptions show, was responsible for improvements throughout Italy and the provinces. (Cf. the edicts on the water supply at Rome—C35—and RG 20.) The texts are in Ehrenberg and Jones.

(a) *An inscription from Alexandria, AD 10-11*

Schedia was a town of lower Egypt. The river is named after the Emperor: Sebastos *means Augustus.*

Imperator Caesar Augustus, son of the divine (Julius), *pontifex maximus*, brought in the Sebastos river from Schedia 25 miles away, so that it flowed through all the town, when Gaius Julius Aquila was prefect of Egypt in the 40th year of Caesar.

ILS 9370

(b) *This dates from 27 BC.*

The Senate and people [of Rome set this up in honour of Imperator Caesar Augustus, son of the divine (Julius), acclaimed *imperator* seven times], consul for the seventh time, consul designate for the eighth time because by his good counsel [and at his ex]pense the [Via Flamin]ia [and the rest] of the busiest roads in Italy were repaired.

ILS 84

(c) *Another inscription from Italy, from a milestone*

Imperator Caesar Augustus, *pontifex maximus*, consul thirteen times, in the 22nd year of his tribunician power, undertook the repair of the Via Aemilia from Ariminum to the River Trebia. 79 miles.

ILS 9371

(d)   *This inscription from Baetica in Spain dates from 2 BC; from a milestone.*

Imperator Caesar Augustus, son of the divine (Julius), consul thirteen times, in the 21st year of his tribunician power, *pontifex maximus*, (built the road) from Baetis and the Arch of Augustus to the Ocean. 63 miles.

ILS 102

(e)   *This dates from 6 BC from Pisidia.*

Imperator Caesar Augustus, son of the divine (Julius), *pontifex ma*[*x*]*imus*, consul eleven times, consul designate for the twelfth time, acclaimed *imperator* fifteen times, in the 28th year of his tribunician power, [b]uilt the Via Sebaste, under the supervision of Cornutus Aquila, [his] legate with propraetorian authority.

ILS 5828
tr. K. Chisholm

C34 The Golden Milestone

The time is 20 BC; Augustus took the cura viarum *himself but also set up a board of Senatorial* curatores *for the maintenance of roads which continued to function under his successors. Augustus occasionally paid for roads himself (ILS 9371) or contributed to the* aerarium *for that purpose.*

At this time, Augustus was appointed commissioner for all roads in the neighbourhood of Rome. As such, he set up the Golden Milestone, as it is called, and also appointed ex-praetors, each attended by two lictors, to see to their actual maintenance.

Dio Cassius 54.8.4
tr. Dudley *Urbs Roma*

C35 Rome's water supply

Augustus' reorganization of the water supply at Rome has been fortunately preserved in the works of Sextus Julius Frontinus (c. AD 30–104), appointed curator aquarum *by Nerva in AD 97. Agrippa had administered the water supply from 33 BC to his death in 12 BC, when Augustus took over the charge as well as the company of slaves trained by Agrippa to maintain the aqueducts. The following edict and Senatorial decrees all date from 11 BC. The Lex Quinctia, proposed by T. Quinctius Crispinus, was passed two years later. On Rome's water supply see T. Ashby* Aqueducts of Ancient Rome *(Oxford 1935); E. B. van Denman* The Building of the Roman Aqueduct *(1934).*

(a)

'The consuls, Quintus Aelius Tubero and Paulus Fabius Maximus, having made a report relating to the duties and privileges of the water-commissioners appointed with the approval of the Senate by Caesar Augustus, and inquiring of the Senate what it would please to order upon the subject, it has been RESOLVED that it is the sense of this body: That those who have the care of the administration of the public waters, when they go outside the City in the discharge of their duties, shall have two lictors, three public servants, and an architect for each of them, and the same number of secretaries, clerks, assistants, and criers as those have who distribute wheat among the people; and when they have business inside the City on the same duties, they shall make use of all the same attendants, omitting the lictors; and, further, that the list of attendants granted to the water-commissioner by this resolution of the Senate shall be by them presented to the public treasurer within ten days from its promulgation, and to those whose names shall be thus reported the praetors of the treasury shall grant and give, as compensation, food by the year, as much as the food-commissioners are wont to give and allot, and they shall be authorized to take money for that purpose without prejudice to themselves. Further, there shall be furnished to the commissioners tablets, paper, and everything else necessary for the exercise of their functions. To this effect, the consuls, Quintus Aelius and Paulus Fabius, are ordered, both or either one, as may seem best to them, to consult with the praetors of the treasury in contracting for these supplies.

'Furthermore, inasmuch as the superintendents of streets and those in charge of the distribution of grain occupy a fourth part of the year in fulfilling their State duties, the water-commissioners likewise shall adjudicate (for a like period) in private and State causes.'

(b)

'The consuls, Quintus Aelius Tubero and Paulus Fabius Maximus, having made a report upon the number of public fountains established by Marcus Agrippa in the City and within structures adjacent to the City, and having inquired of the Senate what it would please to order upon the subject, it has been RESOLVED that it is the sense of this body: That the number of public fountains which exist at present, according to the report of those who were ordered by the Senate to examine the public aqueducts and to inventory the number of public fountains, shall be neither increased nor diminished. Further, that the water-commissioners, who have been appointed by Caesar Augustus, with the endorsement of the Senate, shall take pains that the public fountains may deliver water as continuously as possible for the use of the people day and night.'

(c)

'The consuls, Quintus Aelius Tubero and Paulus Fabius Maximus, having made a report that some private parties take water directly from the public conduits, and having inquired of the Senate what it would please to order upon the subject, it has been RESOLVED that it is the sense of this body: That it shall not be permitted to any private party to draw water from the public conduits; and all those to whom the right to draw water has been granted shall draw it from the reservoirs, the water-commissioners to direct at what points, within the City, private parties may suitably erect reservoirs for the purpose of drawing from them the water which they had received at the hands of the water-commissioner from some public reservoir; and no one of those to whom a right to draw water from the public conduits has been granted shall have the right to use a larger pipe than a *quinaria* for a space of fifty feet from the reservoir out of which he is to draw the water.'

(d)

'The consuls, Quintus Aelius Tubero and Paulus Fabius Maximus, having made a report upon the necessity of determining in accordance with what law those persons, to whom water had been granted, should draw water inside and outside the City, and having inquired of the Senate what it would please to order upon the subject, it has been RESOLVED that it is the sense of this body: That a grant of water, with the exception of those supplies which have been granted for the use of bathing establishments, or in the name of Augustus, shall remain in force as long as the same proprietors continue to hold the ground for which they received the grant of the water.'

(e)

'The consuls, Quintus Aelius Tubero and Paulus Fabius Maximus, having made a report relating to the restoration of the canals, conduits, and arches of Julia, Marcia, Appia, Tepula, and Anio, and having inquired of the Senate what it would please to order upon the subject, it has been RESOLVED: That when those canals, conduits, and arches, which Augustus Caesar promised the Senate to repair at his own cost, shall be repaired, the earth, clay, stone, potsherds, sand, wood, etc., which are necessary for the work in hand, shall be granted, removed, taken, and brought from the lands of private parties, their value to be appraised by some honest man, and each of these to be taken from whatever source it may most conveniently and, without injury to private parties, be removed, taken, and brought; and that thorough-fares and roads through the lands of private parties shall, without injury to them, remain open and their use be permitted, as often as it is necessary for the transportation of all these things for the purposes of repairing these works.'

(f)

'The consuls, Quintus Aelius Tubero and Paulus Fabius Maximus, having made a report that the routes of the aqueducts coming to the city are being encumbered with tombs and edifices and planted with trees, and having inquired of the Senate what it would please to order upon the subject, it has been RESOLVED: That since, for the purpose of repairing the channels and conduits (obstructions must be removed) by which public structures are damaged, it is decreed that there shall be kept clear a space of fifteen feet on each side of the springs, arches, and walls; and that about the subterranean conduits and channels, inside the City, and inside buildings adjoining the City, there shall be left a vacant space of five feet on each side; and it shall not be permitted to erect a tomb at these places after this time, nor any structures, nor to plant trees. If there be any trees within this space at the present time they shall be taken out by the roots except when they are connected with country seats or enclosed in buildings. Whoever shall contravene these provisions, shall pay as penalty, for each contravention, 10,000 *sestertii*, of which one-half shall be given as a reward to the accuser whose efforts have been chiefly responsible for the conviction of the violator of this vote of the Senate. The other half shall be paid into the public treasury. About these matters the water-commissioners shall judge and take cognizance.'

(g)

'The consul Titus Quinctius Crispinus duly put the question to the people, and the people duly passed a vote in the Forum, before the Rostra of the temple of the Deified Julius on the thirtieth day of June. The Sergian tribe was to vote first. On their behalf, Sextus Varro, the son of Lucius, cast the first vote for the following measure: Whoever, after the passage of this law, shall maliciously and intentionally pierce, break, or countenance the attempt to pierce or break, the channels, conduits, arches, pipes, tubes, reservoirs, or basins of the public waters which are brought into the City, or who shall do damage with intent to prevent water-courses, or any portions of them from going, falling, flowing, reaching, or being conducted into the City of Rome; or so as to prevent the issue, distribution, allotment, or discharge into reservoirs or basins of any water at Rome or in those places or buildings which are now or shall hereafter be adjacent to the City, or in the gardens, properties, or estates of those owners or proprietors to whom the water is now or in future shall be given or granted, he shall be condemned to pay a fine of 100,000 *sestertii* to the Roman people; and in addition, whoever shall maliciously do any of these things shall be condemned to repair, restore, re-establish, reconstruct, replace what he has damaged, and quickly demolish what he has built—all in good faith and in such manner (as the commissioners may determine). Further, whoever is or shall be water-commissioner, or in default of such officer, that praetor who is charged with judging between the citizens and strangers, is authorized to fine, bind over by bail, or restrain the offender. For that purpose, the right and power to compel, restrain, fine, and bind over, shall belong to every water-commissioner, or if there be none, to the praetor. If a slave shall do any such damage, his master shall be condemned to pay 100,000 *sestertii* to the Roman people. If any enclosure has been made or shall be made near the channels, conduits, arches, pipes, tubes, reservoirs, or basins of the public waters, which now are or in future shall be conducted into the City of Rome, no one shall, after the passage of this law, put in the way, construct, enclose, plant, establish, set up, place, plough, sow anything, or admit anything in that space unless for the purpose of doing those things and making those repairs which shall be lawful and obligatory under this law. If any one contravenes these provisions, against him shall apply the same statutes, the same law, and the same procedure in every particular as could apply and ought to apply against him who in contravention of this statute has broken into or pierced the channel or conduit of an aqueduct. Nothing of this law shall revoke the privilege of pasturing cattle, cutting grass or hay, or gathering brambles in this place. The water-commissioners, present or future, in any place which is now enclosed about any springs, arches, walls, channels, or conduits, are authorized to have removed, pulled out, dug up, or uprooted, any trees, vines, briars, brambles, banks, fences, willow-thickets, or beds of reeds, so far as they are ready to proceed with justice; and to that end they shall possess the right to bind over, to impose fines, or to restrain the offender; and it shall be their privilege, right, and power to do the same without prejudice. As for the vines and trees inside the enclosures of country-houses, structures or fences; as to the fences, which the commissioners after due process have exempted their owners from tearing down, and on which have been inscribed or carved the names of the commissioners who gave the permission—as to all these, nothing in this enactment prevents their remaining. Nor shall anything in this law revoke the permits that have been given by the water-commissioners to any one to take or draw water from springs, channels, conduits, or arches, and besides that to use wheel, *calix*, or machine, provided that no well be dug, and that no new tap be made.'

Frontinus *The Water Supply of Rome* 100, 104, 106, 108, 125, 127, 129
tr. C. E. Bennett (Loeb 1925)

C36 Augustus repairs the aqueducts

This inscription dates from 5/4 BC, and was found on the Marcia aqueduct at Rome. The text is Ehrenberg and Jones no. 281.

The Imperator Augustus, son of the divine Julius, *pontifex maximus*, consul twelve times, in the 19th year of his tribunician power, acclaimed *imperator* fourteen times repaired the channels of all the aqueducts.

CIL 6. 1244
tr. K. Chisholm

C37 Trade

(a) *For the elimination of piracy cf.* RG *25. 1; see also H. J. Ormerod* Piracy in the Ancient World *(Liverpool 1924).*

But all the foreign trade of the country is carried on with Italy and Rome, since the voyage as far as the Pillars is good, except, perhaps, for a certain difficulty in passing the strait, and also the voyage on the high seas of Our Sea. For the sea-routes all pass through a zone of fair weather, particularly if the sailor keeps to the high seas; and this fact is advantageous to the merchant-freighters. And further, the winds on the high seas are regular. Added to that, too, is the present peace, because all piracy has been broken up, and hence the sailors feel wholly at ease.

Strabo 3. 2. 5
tr. H. L. Jones (Loeb 1923)

(b) *Roman imports exceeded exports*

The exports at Alexandria exceed the imports. Anyone can tell this if he stands in either Alexandria or Puteoli watching the merchantmen at their arrival and departure, comparing their loads in the two directions.

Strabo 17. 1. 7
tr. J. Ferguson

D THE NEW TRADITIONS

With his rule firmly based on Republican precedents (cf. *RG passim* and B29, 30, 33) Augustus further reaffirmed and strengthened respect for the *mos maiorum*, the ancestral traditions, by his attention to cult and ritual (D1-10), the building and restoration of temples (§ E) and his moral legislation (D16 ff.). This respect is strongly reflected in both literature (§ F) and the visual arts.

The expansion of empire as the reason for the decay of Rome's ruling classes had become almost a literary commonplace (D17, 19), but after the chaos of the civil wars (cf. B4–26) the stability of Augustus' rule seemed like a new golden age. The person of the Princeps became the focus for a new kind of tradition to suit the new Romans, citizens from Italian municipalities who were taking a greater part in administration and government. This new age was celebrated by the Secular Games (D2), an example of how Augustus used Republican precedents to enhance the public image of his rule. Gratitude for peace and stability was often given religious expression, for Roman official religion was primarily concerned with cult observances to ensure the safety and well-being of the state, and this gratitude was often directed towards Augustus personally, although he never accepted divine honours in his own right (D11, 12). His moral legislation seems to have been concerned to restore the ruling classes of Rome and Italy, depleted after the ravages of civil war (cf. D28 ff.). It is often extremely difficult to disentangle specifically Augustan legislation from the compilations of the sixth century AD which form the bulk of the legal source material. Much of the evidence has to be gleaned indirectly, from contemporary sources which indicate the concerns and problems prevalent at that time, rather than any specific measures taken to remedy them.

D1 Augustus' revival of ancient religious customs

See in general J. Ferguson Greek and Roman Religion: A Source Book *(Park Ridge 1980) and* Religions of the Roman Empire *(London 1970).*

Salus, the old Roman goddess of Safety (later often identified with Hygieia, the Greek goddess of Health) was frequently linked with Augustus in prayers. The augurium salutis *was an annual ritual enquiry, taken on a day free of war, into whether prayers for the* salus *of the Roman people could be held. This had fallen into disuse during the civil wars. The* Flamen Dialis *was the most senior of priests; his person was sacrosanct and his behaviour rigidly controlled by an elaborate system of tabu. For the Ludi Saeculares see D2; the Lupercalia, a festival held on 15 February, is described by Dionysius of Halicarnassus (1. 80. 1).*

He also revived certain obsolescent rites and appointments: the augury of the Goddess Safety, the office of Flamen Dialis (a priesthood of Juppiter), the Lupercalian Festival, the Saecular Games, and the Cross-Roads Festival. But at the Lupercalia he forbade any boys to run who had not yet shaved off their first beards; and at the Saecular Games no young people might attend a night performance unless accompanied by an adult relative. The images of the Cross-Road gods were to be crowned twice a year, with wreaths of spring and summer flowers.

Suetonius *Augustus* 31
tr. R. Graves (Penguin 1957)

D2 Ludi Saeculares

In 17 BC Augustus held a celebration of the Ludi Saeculares, the Festival of the Century, a ritual of purification and rebirth, supposed to take place once in the lifetime of the longest-lived citizen. The festival is well documented. We have the text of the Sibylline Oracle *enjoining the celebration (a) below. The place of celebration by the Tiber, called Tarentum, was believed to be an entry to the Underworld. Hence the black victim and the offering by night. The Moirae (Fates) and Ilithyiae (Powers of Childbirth) are Greek goddesses. Jupiter (Zeus) and Juno (Hera) have white offerings on a high altar by day. Phoebus Apollo was Augustus' patron god; his shrine at Actium overlooked the site of the Princeps' decisive victory; he was a god of youth, culture, and the arts of peace, appropriate to the image of the new regime; his temple on the Palatine was Augustus' greatest foundation (cf. E10). We also have a long, repetitive inscription (b) recording the proceedings, the first part of which is too fragmentary to reconstruct. The* sellisternium *is a kind of banquet for the gods; the* atalla *is unknown. In addition we have Horace's carefully scripted and skilfully composed hymn, working in references to Virgil's* Aeneid, *to many of the ceremonies, to the figure of the Sun crowning Apollo's temple, to Augustus' moral reforms (c). The hymn seems to have been sung twice, once before the temple of Jupiter on the Capitol, by a chorus of boys and girls. See further W. Warde Fowler* Roman Essays and Interpretations *(Oxford 1920) pp. 111 ff.*

(a)

But when the longest span of life for men
has passed, journeying through a hundred-and-ten-year cycle,
remember, Roman, and if you should forget,
remember all this. To the immortal gods
make offering in the meadow by the copious flow of Tiber,
at the narrowest point, when night has come on the earth,
and the sun has hidden his beams. There sacrifice

to the Moirae, source of all being, lambs and goats
dark in colour, and for the Ilithyiae, placate
the protectors of birth with offerings in due ritual. To Earth
let a black sow be consecrated, pregnant with her farrow.
Let spotless white bulls be led to Zeus's altar,
by day not night. To the gods of heaven
sacrifice is made by day. So likewise make
your offering. Hera's temple must receive from your hands
a fine white cow. Phoebus Apollo too,
who bears the name of the Sun, must receive the same
offering, being Leto's son. Hymns sung in Latin
by boys and girls must echo round the temples
of the gods. The girls must have their own separate choir,
the boys' male-voice chorus be separate, but all
have their parents alive, their family tree in flower.
On that day the matrons yoked in marriage
must bow the knee by Hera's sacred altar
and invoke the goddess. Give expiatory offerings to all,
men and women, especially the women.
All must bring from home appropriate gifts
for mortals to bring from the first-fruits of their possessions,
gifts for the powers of the underworld and the blessed
gods of heaven. All these should lie in a pile
until the men and women duly seated
are ready to receive them. By day
and night without interruption, on seats fit for a god,
let all the people keep festival. Let merriment mix with solemnity.
Keep this firmly fixed in your mind:
so shall all the land of Italy, all the land of Latium
be always subject to your rod.

> *Sibylline Oracle* in Zosimus 2.6
> tr. J. Ferguson

(b) *The first part of this inscription is fragmentary; lines 50-63 record two decrees of the Senate; lines 64 ff. are a record of the games.*

May 23, in the Julian Voting Hall. ... Present at the writing were ... Aemilius Lepidus, Lucius Cestius, and Lucius Petronius Rufus. ...

Whereas the consul Gaius Silanus reported that after a lapse of many years the Secular Games would be celebrated in the present year under the direction of the Emperor Caesar Augustus and Marcus Agrippa, holders of the tribunician power, and that, because as many as possible ought to view these games out of religious duty and also because no one will attend such a spectacle again, it seemed proper to permit ... those who were not yet married to be present with impunity on the days of these games; and whereas he asked the senate what it was pleased to do in the matter, concerning this matter the senate decreed as follows: Since these games have been ordained for religious purposes and since it is not granted to any mortal to view them more than once ... those who are liable under the Law on Classes Permitted to Marry shall be permitted to view with impunity the games which the masters of the board of fifteen for performing sacrifices will present.

And on the same day in the same place, the same were present at the writing, and the following decree of the senate was passed.

Whereas the consul Gaius Silanus declared that it was appropriate for the preservation of the memory of this great benevolence of the gods that a record of the Secular Games be inscribed on a bronze and on a marble column, both to be erected for the future remembrance of the event in the place where the games would be held, and asked the senate what it was pleased to do in the matter, concerning this matter the senate decreed as follows: The consuls, one or both, for the future remembrance of the event shall erect in that place a column of bronze and a second of marble on which a record of these games has been inscribed, and they shall likewise contract for this work and shall order the praetors who are in charge of the treasury to pay to the contractors the sum for which they have contracted.

CIL 6. 32323 lines 50–63
tr. Lewis and Reinhold vol. 2

On the following night in the meadow by the Tiber the Emperor Caesar Augustus sacrificed to the Moirae nine ewe-lambs, to be wholly offered, according to the Greek ritual, and nine-she-goats according to the same ritual, with the following prayer:

'O Moirae, as is written in the Great Books for you that in every respect everything may prosper for the citizens, the people of Rome, you should receive a sacrifice of nine ewe-lambs and nine she-goats. I pray and beseech you to increase the power and authority of the citizens, the people of Rome, in war and peace, protect for ever the name of Latium, grant for all time safety, victory, and might to the citizens, the people of Rome, look favourably upon the citizens, the people of Rome, and the armies of the citizens, the people of Rome, and keep safe the state of the citizens, the people of Rome; that you may look with kindly grace on the citizens, the people of Rome, on the College of Fifteen, on me, my family and household, and that you may receive this sacrifice of nine ewe-lambs and nine she-goats duly offered. For this reason accept the sacrifice of this ewe-lamb and look with kindly grace on the citizens, the people of Rome, and on me, my family and household.'

On the completion of the sacrifice performances were held by night on a stage with no auditorium attached and no seats for spectators; 110 wives of free citizens, in a script presented by the Fifteen, held a *sellisternium*, with two seats provided for Juno and Diana.

On 1 June on the Capitol the Emperor Caesar Augustus offered a bull in perfect condition to Jupiter the Best and Greatest, and M. Agrippa offered a second at the same place. They used the following prayer:

'Jupiter, Best and Greatest, as is written in the Great Books for you that in every respect everything may prosper for the citizens, the people of Rome, you should receive a sacrifice of this noble bull. I pray and beseech you'—the rest as previously.

At the *atalla* were Caesar, Agrippa, Scaevola, Sentius, Lollius, Asinius Gallus, Rebilus.

Next performances were given in Latin in a theatre constructed of wood in the meadow by the Tiber, and the wives of free men gave presentations of a *sellisternium* in the same manner. The mighty performances previously presented were continued without break. A proclamation was made:

'From the Fifteen.

Since according to excellent precedent frequently exemplified in the past, in that there has been a fit occasion for public rejoicing, the resolution has been passed to reduce the period of mourning for the wives of free citizens, and since at the time of the sacred performance of traditional ritual it has been decided that the restoration of and meticulous attention to this practice is appropriate to the worship of the gods and the observance of the cult, we give notice that it is our public duty to decree a reduction in the period of mourning for women.'

In addition by night the Emperor Caesar Augustus made a sacrifice of nine flat cakes, nine pastry-cakes, and nine cup-cakes to the divinities Illithyiae by the Tiber, using the following prayer:

'Ilithyia, as is written in the Great Books for you, that in every respect everything may prosper for the citizens, the people of Rome, you should receive a sacrifice of nine flat cakes, nine pastry-cakes and nine cup-cakes, I pray and beseech you'—the rest as previously.

On 2 June on the Capitol the Emperor Augustus sacrificed a cow to Juno the Queen, and M. Agrippa offered a second at the same place, using the following prayer:

'Juno Queen, as is written in the Great Books for you, that in every respect everything may prosper for the citizens, the people of Rome, you should receive a sacrifice of a noble cow, I pray and beseech you'—the rest as previously.

Then 110 married wives of free men, duly instructed . . . he spoke for them as follows:

'Juno Queen, the prosperity of the citizens, the people of Rome . . . we, the married wives of free men, on bended knee, pray you to . . . and to increase the authority of the citizens, the people of Rome, in war and peace, to protect forever the name of Latium, grant for all time safety, victory, and might to the citizens, the people of Rome, look favourably upon the citizens, the people of Rome, and the armies of the citizens, the people of Rome, and keep safe the state of the citizens, the people of Rome, that you may look with kindly grace on the citizens, the people of Rome, on the College of Fifteen, and on us . . . So we, 110 wives of free men of the citizens, the people of Rome, on bended knee, pray and beseech you.'

At the *atalla* were M. Agrippa . . .

153

Performances were given as on the previous day . . .

In addition by night the Emperor Caesar Augustus made a sacrifice of a pregnant sow to Mother Earth by the Tiber, using the following prayer:

'Mother Earth, as is written in the Great Books for you, that in every respect everything may prosper for the citizens, the people of Rome, you should receive the sacrifice of a pregnant sow in perfect condition. I pray and beseech you'—the rest as previously.

The wives of free men presented a *sellisternium* as on the previous day.

On 3 June on the Palatine, the Emperor Caesar Augustus and M. Agrippa made a sacrifice of nine flat cakes, nine pastry-cakes, and nine cup-cakes to Apollo and Diana, using the following prayer:

'Apollo, as is written in the Great Books for you, that in every respect everything may prosper for the citizens, the people of Rome, you should receive the sacrifice of nine flat cakes, nine pastry-cakes, and nine cup-cakes, I pray and beseech you'—the rest as previously.

'Apollo, I have presented you with these flat cakes, and prayed in due form, so to this end receive the offering of these pastry-cakes, and look down with kindly favour.'

So for the cup-cakes.

With the same words for Diana.

On the completion of the sacrifice a hymn was sung by twenty-seven boys, on whom the duty was laid, all with both parents living, and the same number of girls. This was repeated on the Capitol. Q. Horatius Flaccus composed the hymn.

The following members of the Fifteen were present: Caesar, M. Agrippa, Q. Lepidus, Potitus Messalla, C. Stolo, C. Scaevola, C. Sosius, C. Norbanus, M. Cocceius, M. Lollius, C. Sentius, M. Strigo, L. Arruntius, C. Asinius, M. Marcellus, D. Laelius, Q. Tubero, C. Rebilus, Messala Messallinus.

At the conclusion of the dramatic performances . . . close to the place where sacrifice was offered on the previous nights, an auditorium and stage were constructed, turning-posts were set up and the starting-signal given for a race for four-horse chariots. Potitus Messalla gave the signal for acrobatic riders. A proclamation was made:

'From the Fifteen.

We present seven days of performances in Latin in addition to the prescribed festival, in the wooden theatre by the Tiber, beginning on 5 June, Greek musical shows in Pompey's theatre at 9 a.m., Greek stage plays in the theatre in the Circus Flaminius at 10 a.m.'

On 10 June a proclamation was made in the following terms: 'From the Fifteen. On 12 June we shall present a hunt in . . . and circus performances . . .'

On 12 June there was a preliminary procession. Boys . . .

M. Agrippa presented chariot-racing.

For the whole celebration the Fifteen was the Emperor Caesar Augustus, M.
Agrippa . . . Cn. Pompeius, C. Stolo, C. Scaevola . . . M. Marcellus . . .

CIL 6. 32323 lines 64-end
tr. J. Ferguson

(c) *The Centennial Hymn*

> Diana, queen of forests, and Apollo,
> O honoured and for ever to be honoured
> Twin glories of the firmament, accord us
>   All we beseech today —
>
> Day of devotion, when the Sibyl's verses
> Enjoin the chaste, the chosen youths and maidens
> To chant their hymns of worship to the patron
>   Gods of our seven hills.
>
> Kind sun, bright charioteer, bringer and hider
> Of light, newborn each morning yet each morning
> Unaltered, may thou never view a city
>   Greater on earth than Rome.
>
> Moon, gentle midwife, punctual in thy office,
> Lucina, Ilithyia, Genitalis —
> Be called whichever title is most pleasing —
>   Care for our mothers' health.
>
> Goddess, make strong our youth and bless the Senate's
> Decrees rewarding parenthood and marriage,
> That from the new laws Rome may reap a lavish
>   Harvest of boys and girls
>
> So that the destined cycle of eleven
> Decades may bring again great throngs to witness
> The games and singing: three bright days and three long
>   Nights of the people's joy.
>
> And you, O Fates, who have proved truthful prophets,
> Your promise stands — and may time's sacred landmarks
> Guard it immovably: to our accomplished
>   Destiny add fresh strength.
>
> May Mother Earth, fruitful in crops and cattle,
> Crown Ceres' forehead with a wreath of wheat-ears,
> And dews and rains and breezes, God's good agents,
>   Nourish whatever grows.

Sun-god, put by thy bow and deign to listen
Mildly and gently to the boys' entreaties.
Moon, crescent sovereign of the constellations,
    Answer the virgins' prayers.

Rome is your handiwork; in your safe-keeping
The Trojan band reached an Etruscan haven,
That remnant which, at your command, abandoned
    City and hearth to make

The auspicious voyage, those for whom pure-hearted
Aeneas, the last pillar of royal manhood
Left standing in burnt Troy, paved paths to greater
    Fame than they left behind.

Gods, by these tokens make our young quick pupils
Of virtue, give the aged peace and quiet,
Rain on the race of Romulus wealth, offspring,
    Honours of every kind;

And when, tonight, with blood of milk-white oxen
The glorious son of Venus and Anchises
Invokes you, grant his prayers. Long may Augustus
    Conquer but spare the foe.

Now Parthia fears the fist of Rome, the fasces
Potent on land and sea; now the once haughty
Ambassadors from the Caspian and the Indus
    Sue for a soft reply.

Now Faith and Peace and Honour and old-fashioned
Conscience and unremembered Virtue venture
To walk again, and with them blessed Plenty,
    Pouring her brimming horn.

Apollo, augur, bright-bowed archer, well-loved
Music-master of the nine Muses, healer
Whose skill in medicine can ease the body's
    Ills and infirmities,

By thy affection for the Palatine altars
Prolong, we pray, the Roman State and Latium's
Prosperity into future cycles, nobler
    Eras, for evermore.

Diana, keeper of the sacred hilltops
Of Aventine and Algidus, be gracious

To the prayers of the Fifteen Guardians, to the children
    Bend an attentive ear.

That Jove and all the gods approve these wishes
We, the trained chorus, singers of the praises
Of Phoebus and Diana, carry homewards
    Happy, unshaken hope.

tr. J. Michie
(Penguin 1967, repr. 1978)

D3 The Robigalia

Ovid gives an account of the festival in April in honour of Robigus or Robigo, the power of rust, a disease of wheat. The sacrifice of a reddish-brown dog is suggestive of the colour of the disease.

When I was returning to Rome from Nomentum that day,
    a white-robed crowd blocked my path.
A priest was passing to the grave of ancient Robigo
    to offer on the altar entrails of dog and sheep.
I went straight to him, wishing to understand the rite.
    Quirinus's priest spoke:
'Cruel Rust, spare the springing corn,
    let the ear wave unblemished above ground.
Let the crops, nourished by favourable weather, grow
    till fit for the sickle.
Your power is strong; when you set your mark on corn,
    the farmer grieves its loss.
Winds and rains and frost burning white
    do not harm wheat
as much as the sun when he bakes dank stalks;
    then, awesome goddess, is the time of your wrath.
Be merciful, I pray, take your scabby hands off the harvest.
    Do no harm; be content with the power.
Set your grasp on hard iron not on pliant crops;
    destroy the destroyer.
You'll have better results from swords and lethal weapons;
    no need for them, the world's at peace.
Now let the farmer's tools, rakes, hoe, and curving share,
    shine, and arms rust,
so that any who tries to draw sword from scabbard, feels
    it stick with long disuse.

Do not rape the corn-goddess, be absent when the farmer
    pays you his vows.'
He finished. On his right arm was a loose-woven cloth;
    he'd a bowl of wine and jar of incense.
He laid on the hearth incense, wine, sheep's gut, dog's inwards—
    we saw it with our eyes.
Then 'Did you ask why the unusual victim?' (I had)
    'Here's the answer' he said.
'There's a Dog-Star, called Icarus's Dog, when it rises,
    the earth thirsts, the crop ripens early.
This dog is laid on the altar instead of the dog in the sky,
    killed for his name.'

Ovid *Fasti* 4. 905–42
tr. J. Ferguson

D4 The Lemuria

*The Lemuria was a festival on 9 May when the dead came back to life. The year
once began in March (September means the seventh month) so the* februa *(expiations
appropriate to February) had not been introduced. Ovid derives May from* maiores
*(ancestors). The ritual contains familiar magic. Knots bind and are dangerous. The
apotropaic gesture of thumb between the first two fingers is still used; beans are
phallic in shape and black for the dead; bronze, not new-fangled iron, is used.*

When from the Nones the Evening Star has three times shown his lovely face,
    three times Phoebus routed the stars,
there will be by night an ancient religious ritual, the Lemuria,
    bringing gifts to the silent shades.
The year was once shorter, they knew no religious expiations,
    two-headed Janus did not lead the months.
Even then they brought offerings to the ashes of the dead,
    descendant honouring ancestor.
The month was May, named from the Great Majority;
    it keeps part of the tradition.
When midnight comes, bending silence to sleep,
    and dogs and birds are hushed,
the man who honours traditional religion and fears the gods,
    rises, no knots near his feet,
and makes a sign, thumb between knuckles
    to avert silent encounter with a ghost.

He cleanses his hands with water from a spring,
  turns, takes black beans,
faces away, and throws them down saying 'These are my offerings;
  with these beans I redeem me and mine.'
Nine times he says it without looking back. It is thought that the ghost
  follows unseen and gathers them.
Again he touches water and clangs Temesan bronze,
  asking the shade to leave his house.
Nine times he says 'Spirits of my fathers, be gone,'
  then looks back in the knowledge of ritual fulfilled.

Ovid *Fasti* 5. 419-44
tr. J. Ferguson

D5 Military festivals

This calendar of military festivals, dating from the first half of the third century AD was found in Dura–Europos on the Euphrates. Many have to do with honouring recent Emperors but some go back further. The Five-Day Festival (19 March) is the Quinquatrus to Minerva. The festival on 17 December is the Saturnalia. For the crowning of the standards see A. S. Hoey 'Rosaliae Signorum' HTR 30 (1937) 15-35, and in general R. O. Finck, A. S. Hoey, W. F. Snyder 'The Feriale Duranum' Yale Classical Studies 7 (1940) 1-222; A. D. Nock 'The Roman Army and the Roman Religious Year' HTR 45 (1952) 186-252.

9 Jan. — In view of the honourable discharge of those returning in full enjoyment of privileges and of the calculation of military pay, an ox to Jupiter Best and Greatest, a cow to Juno, a cow to Minerva, a cow to Wellbeing, a bull to Mars the Father . . .

1 Mar. — For the birthday celebrations of Mars, Father and Victor, a bull to Mars, Father and Victor.

19 Mar. — For the first day of the Five-Day Festival, an act of prayer; the same acts of prayer to be repeated for the 23rd.

21 Apr. — For the birthday of Rome the Eternal City a cow to Rome the Eternal City.

10 May — For the crowning of the standards with roses, an act of prayer.

12 May — For the Games in honour of Mars, a bull to Mars, Father and Avenger.

31 May — For the crowning of the standards with roses, an act of prayer.

12 July — For the Birthday of the Divine Julius an ox to the Divine Julius.

23 Sept. — For the birthday of the Divine Augustus an ox to the Divine Augustus.

17 Dec. — . . . an act of prayer; the same acts of prayer to be repeated for the 23rd.

Feriale Duranum
tr. J. Ferguson

D6 Prodigies and portents

The transactions were allocations of land and towns in Italy for the veterans and the proscriptions arranged by the triumvirs as soon as their position was legalized (cf. B14, 19).

While these transactions were taking place many fearful prodigies were observed at Rome. Dogs howled continuously like wolves—a fearful sign. Wolves darted through the forum—an animal unused to the city. Cattle uttered a human voice. A newly born infant spoke. Sweat issued from statues; some even sweated blood. Loud voices of men were heard and the clashing of arms and the tramp of horses where none could be seen. Many fearful signs were observed around the sun, there were showers of stones, and continuous lightning fell upon the sacred temples and images; and in consequence of these things the Senate sent for diviners and soothsayers from Etruria. The oldest of them said that the kingly rule of former times was coming back, and that they would all be slaves except only himself, whereupon he closed his mouth and held his breath till he was dead.

Appian *Civil Wars* 4. 4. 4
tr. H. White (Loeb 1913)

D7 The religion of the countryside

We have a number of attractive pictures of the religion of the countryside. Here paganism was to prove most durable; indeed 'pagan' simply means 'rustic' (though other explanations have been given). The first passage is from M. Terentius Varro (116-27 BC), an antiquarian. Robigus is the numen of a disease of wheat (D3), Flora of flowers, Lympha of water. The other passages are from poets. Tibullus (c.48-19 BC) gives a charming picture of the Ambarvalia, the Purification of the Fields; there is a stress on purity, cleanness, white; a holy day and a holiday; a ritual procession around the farm-boundary; a sacrifice. Ovid has left us a number of accounts of festivals. The Terminalia, in honour of Terminus, the numen of the boundary-stone, was held on 23 February.

(a)
They tell us that the gods help those who call on their names. I shall therefore invoke them, not, like Homer and Ennius, calling on the Muses, but on the twelve Gods of the Council, and at that not the gods of the city whose gilded statues stand in the forum, six gods and six goddesses but the Twelve Gods who give guidance to farmers. First, I call on Jupiter and Tellus who hold in heaven and earth all the fruits of agriculture; they are known as our Almighty Parents, Jupiter is our Father, Tellus is Mother Earth. Secondly, I call on the Sun and Moon whose seasons give

the signal for sowing and reaping. Thirdly, I call on Ceres and Liber, because their produce is essential to life; through their agency food and drink emerge from the farm. Fourthly, I call on Robigus and Flora: if they show favour rust will not damage the crops or trees, and there will be no premature flowering: this is why the public festival of the Robigalia has been established in honour of Robigus and the Floralia celebrated for Flora. Similarly, I worship Minerva and Venus, who protect the olive-groves and the garden; the country Vinalia was instituted in the name of Venus. In addition I invoke Lympha and Good Issue, since without water all agriculture is parched and poor, and without success and good issue there is no cultivation, only frustration.

Varro *On Agriculture* 1. 1. 4–6

(b)

Silence, all present. This is a purification of land and crops
in the traditional rites.
Be with us, Bacchus, with delicious grapes hanging from your horns,
and Ceres crowned with corn.
On this holy day the soil is to rest, the ploughmen to rest,
the plough to cease work.
Unfasten the yokes. Today the oxen shall stand,
garlanded, by full mangers.
Everything must be done for the god. No woman must dare
to spin wool.
Move to a distance, away from the altars, all you
who last night made love.
The powers above require purity. Come with clean clothes,
with hands clean from the spring.
Watch how the consecrated lamb moves to the blazing altar,
followed by the white procession.
Gods of our ancestors, we are cleansing the farms, the farmers,
drive evil from our fences.
Do not let the harvest mock us with tares among the wheat,
our lambs fear the wolves.
Afterwards the comfortable countryman, confident in his teeming
fields, will pile logs on the fire,
while a crowd of young slaves, signs of a farmer's prosperity,
play with the twigs.
My prayers are fulfilled. Look how the marks on the liver
announce the gods' favour.

Tibullus 2. 1. 1–26

(c)

> Once night has passed, give due honour to the god
>   who marks the limits of the fields.
> Terminus, be you a stone or a post in the ground,
>   you have been worshipped for ages past.
> The two owners on opposite sides crown your head,
>   bringing two garlands, two cakes.
> They build an altar. On a broken sherd the farmer's wife brings
>   fire from the warm hearth.
> The old man chops logs, piles them up with neat skill,
>   tries to stick branches in the firm earth,
> then fosters the first flames with dry bark.
>   A boy stands by with a wide basket.
> From this he throws grain three times into the middle of the fire
>   A little girl offers sliced honeycomb.
> Some hold jars of wine; there's a libation from each on the flames.
>   The congregation watch silently in white.
> Terminus, lord of both lands, is aspersed with the blood of a lamb,
>   and does not refuse a sucking-pig,
> The countryside join in a feast, with simple taste,
>   and hymn you, holy Terminus.
> You mark the bounds of peoples, cities, great empires.
>   Without you every field would mean a lawsuit.
> You are not to be bribed or corrupted with gold;
>   you guard your lands with the integrity of law.

Ovid *Fasti* 2. 639–62
tr. J. Ferguson

D8 Superstitions and beliefs

90   As for Augustus's superstitions: he is recorded to have been scared of thunder and lightning, against which he always carried a piece of seal-skin as an amulet, and to have taken refuge in an underground vault whenever a heavy storm threatened —because, as I have already mentioned, he had once narrowly escaped being struck on a night march.

91   Warnings conveyed in dreams, either his own or those dreamed by others, were not lost on him: for example, before the Battle of Philippi, when so ill that he decided not to leave his tent, he changed his mind on account of a friend's dream— most fortunately, too, as it proved. The camp was captured and a party of the enemy, breaking into the tent, plunged their swords through and through his camp-bed under the impression that he was still in it, tearing the bed-clothes to

ribbons. Every spring he had a series of ugly dreams, but none of the horrid visions seen in them came true; whereas what he occasionally dreamed at other seasons tended to be reliable. One day, after he had paid frequent visits to the Temple of Juppiter the Thunderer, founded by himself on the Capitoline Hill, Capitoline Juppiter approached him in a dream with a complaint that the newcomer was stealing his worshippers. He replied: 'I put the Thunderer so close to your Temple because I had decided to give you a janitor. When Augustus awoke, he hung a set of bells from the gable of the new building to make it look like a front door. Because of another dream he used to sit in a public place once a year holding out his hand for the people to give him coppers, as though he were a beggar.

92 Augustus had absolute faith in certain premonitory signs: considering it bad luck to thrust his right foot into the left shoe as he got out of bed, but good luck to start a long journey or voyage during a drizzle of rain, which would ensure success and a speedy return. Prodigies made a particularly strong impression on him. Once, when a palm tree pushed its way between the paving stones in front of the Palace he had it transplanted to the inner court beside his family gods, and lavished care on it. When he visited Capri, the drooping branches of a moribund old oak suddenly regained their vigour, which so delighted him that he arranged to buy the island from the City of Naples in exchange for Ischia. He also had a superstition against starting a journey on the day after a market-day, or undertaking any important task on the Nones of a month—although, in this case, as he explained to Tiberius in a letter, it was merely the unlucky *non*-sound of the word that affected him.

Suetonius *Augustus* 90–2
tr. R. Graves (Penguin 1957)

D9 Foreign rites

This passage indicates that Cicero felt the Eleusinian mysteries to be important in a Roman context; on Augustus' attitude cf. Suetonius Augustus *93 (I 10b).*

Atticus: I imagine you make an exception of those Mysteries in which we were initiated ourselves.

Marcus: I will surely do so. Your Athens has plainly made many outstanding contributions to human life, gifts from heaven, but none better than those Mysteries. They educated us out of a life of barbarous rusticity into civilization. The ceremonies are called initiations, and we recognize in them the first principles of living. We have gained from them the way of living in happiness and dying with a better hope.

Cicero *Laws* 2. 14. 36
tr. J. Ferguson

D10 Emperor worship

Ruler worship had been common in the East for centuries and Roman proconsuls stepped naturally into that role; probably not all rulers were thought to be gods, they just possessed some divine attributes to which homage was due. In Rome Julius Caesar was deified only after his death.

(a) *Valerius Maximus, a historian writing under Tiberius, dedicated a handbook of rhetorical examples to him.*

The rest we have received from tradition as gods, the Caesars we have created.

Valerius Maximus *Preface*
tr. J. Ferguson

(b) *On the deification of Julius Caesar see also F30.*

Julius died at the age of fifty-five and was added to the number of the gods alike by formal proclamation and popular belief. At the original games which Augustus, his successor, presented in honour of his deification, a comet shone for seven consecutive nights, appearing about an hour before sunset, and was believed to be the soul of Caesar after his arrival in heaven. This is why a star has been placed upon his forehead on his statue.

Suetonius *Julius Caesar* 88
tr. J. Ferguson

D11 Religious honours to Augustus

It was Augustus with his extraordinary political flair who set the pattern for Emperor-worship at Rome. His deification of Julius Caesar allowed him to call himself 'son of the divine Julius', and brought him, so to speak, half-way to deification. But, except in Egypt, he would not allow himself to be accorded divine honours in his lifetime; his name must be coupled with Roma or the Lares or Poseidon; a libation might be poured to his Genius, honour paid to his Peace or his Concord or his Well-being. But the mood of reverence was clear (cf. C29). The texts are in Ehrenberg and Jones.

For ruler worship see L. R. Taylor The Divinity of the Roman Emperor *(Middletown 1931); J. Ferguson* Religions of the Roman Empire *(London 1970) ch. 6; L. Cerfaux and J. Tondriau* Le Culte des souverains dans la civilisation greco-romaine *(Paris 1957); M. P. Charlesworth 'Some Observations on Ruler-Cult' HTR 28 (1935) 8 ff.*

An inscription from an altar erected in honour of Augustus at Narbonne
The first part dates from AD 11 and the second from AD 12/13.

i

In the consulship of Titus Statilius Taurus and Lucius Cassius Longinus, September 22. Vow taken to the divine spirit of Augustus by the populace of the Narbonensians in perpetuity: 'May it be good, favorable, and auspicious to the Emperor Caesar Augustus, son of a god, father of his country, *pontifex maximus*, holding the tribunician power for the thirty-fourth year; to his wife, children, and house; to the Roman senate and people; and to the colonists and residents of the Colonia Julia Paterna of Narbo Martius, who have bound themselves to worship his divine spirit in perpetuity!'

The populace of the Narbonensians has erected in the forum at Narbo an altar at which every year on September 23—the day on which the good fortune of the age bore him to be ruler of the world—three Roman *equites* from the populace and three freedmen shall sacrifice one animal each and shall at their own expense on that day provide the colonists and residents with incense and wine for supplication to his divine spirit. And on September 24 they shall likewise provide incense and wine for the colonists and residents. Also on January 1 they shall provide incense and wine for the colonists and residents. Also on January 7, the day on which he first entered upon the command of the world, they shall make supplication with incense and wine, and shall sacrifice one animal each, and shall provide incense and wine for the colonists and residents on that day. And on May 31, because on that day in the consulship of Titus Statilius Taurus and Manius Aemilius Lepidus he reconciled the populace to the decurions, they shall sacrifice one animal each and shall provide the colonists and residents with incense and wine for supplication to his divine spirit. And of these three Roman *equites* and three freedmen one. . . .
[*The rest of this inscription is lost.*]

ii

The populace of Narbo has dedicated the altar of the divine spirit of Augustus . . . under the regulations recorded below.

'O divine spirit of Caesar Augustus, father of his country! When this day I give and dedicate this altar to you, I shall give and dedicate it under such regulations and such rules as I shall here this day publicly declare to be the groundwork both of this altar and of its inscriptions: If anyone wishes to clean, decorate, or repair it as a voluntary service, it shall be lawful and permissible. If anyone sacrifices an animal without making the customary additional offering, it shall nevertheless be accounted properly done. If anyone wishes to donate a gift to this altar or honor it, he shall be permitted, and the same regulation as applies to the altar shall apply to such gift. The other regulations for this altar and its inscriptions shall be the same as those for the altar of Diana on the Aventine Hill. Under these regulations and these rules, just as I have stated, on behalf of the Emperor Caesar Augustus, father of his country, *pontifex maximus*, holding the tribunician power for the thirty-fifth year; of his wife, children, and house; of the Roman senate and people; and of the colonists and residents of the Colonia Julia Paterna of Narbo Martius, who have bound themselves to worship his divine spirit in perpetuity, I give and dedicate this altar to you that you may be favorably and kindly disposed.'

CIL 12. 4333
tr. Lewis and Reinhold vol. 2

D12 Dedications to Augustus

(a) *An inscription from AD 1 found at Tentyra in Egypt (Ehrenberg and Jones no. 116)*

In honour of Imperator Caesar Zeus Eleutherios Augustus, son of the divine (Julius), when Publius Octavius was prefect of Egypt, Marcus Claudius Postumus was in charge of the district, and Tryphon of the nome, the gateway for the great goddess Isis and the gods worshipped in her temple, (was built) by the inhabitants of the nome and its capital, in the 31st year of Caesar, sixth day of Thoth (*Egyptian month*) sacred to Augustus.

OGIS 659
tr. K. Chisholm

(b) *An inscription from Lepcis Magna, AD 11–12*

In honour of the divine spirit of Imperator Caesar Augustus, son of the divine (Julius), *pontifex maximus*, acclaimed imperator twenty times, consul thirteen times, in the 34th year of his tribunician power, the porch, portico, gate, and road (was dedicated) by the priestly College of Fifteen (*a local priesthood*).

IRT 324a
tr. K. Chisholm

D13 Religious administration

Nysa was a Greek city in Asia Minor. This inscription, dating from 1 BC, relates to the privileges granted to the temple of Pluto and Kore and its sacred cave, the Charonium (described by Strabo 14. 1. 44). Note that there was a priest not only for Augustus, but also for Tiberius Claudius Nero, the future Emperor Tiberius. Mastaura is a town of Caria. The texts are in Ehrenberg and Jones.

When Heracleides, son of Heracleides, of Mastaura was the priest of Rome and of Imperator Caesar Augustus and Diomedes, son of Athenagoras son of Diomedes, the priest for life of Capitoline Juppiter, was the crown-bearer (*magistrate who gave* his name to the year); on the nineteenth day of Gorpiaeus (*local month name*), the twelfth of August, in the consulship of Cossus Cornelius Lentulus and Lucius Piso, the secretary of the assembly being Heliodorus son of Maeandrius, son of Theodotus, priest for life of Tiberius Claudius Nero; Artemidorus Papas, son of Demetrius, one of the generals in charge of the city (*civic magistracies with police duties*) being in charge, deposited in the archive the sacred documents concerning the gods, their inviolable sanctuary, the right to receive suppliants, and the exemption of the temple from tax, after he had reported to Gnaeus Lentulus Augur the proconsul and delivered the letter written here below:

On the seventeenth day of the month Daisius (*local month name*), in the year of Diomedes son of Athenagoras, Gnaeus Lentulus Augur, proconsul, to the magistrates of Nysa. Artemidorus Papas, son of Demetrius inquired if it is necessary...

SIG 781
tr. K. Chisholm

(b) *An association for Imperial cult*

This papyrus dates from 6 BC.

In the 25th year of Caesar, on the twenty-second day of Hathyr (*Egyptian month*), at the meeting held in the Paratomus (*a square in Alexandria*) the August Association in honour of the divine Imperator Caesar (decided as follows); the president was Primus slave of Caesar, the priest Jucundus slave of Caesar, the gymnasiarch Alexander; a majority of members was present:

Whereas we had instructed the above-mentioned priest Jucundus to pay to [?]isus slave of Caesar, on behalf of Syntrophus Caesar's attendant, from the funds of the association which he (Jucundus) is entitled to receive, the sum of 120 silver Ptolemaic drachmae which (Syntrophus) owes him, at some time during the current year, it was agreed by common consent on the one hand that Jucundus should pay out the 120 silver drachmae on behalf of Syntrophus without interest within the month of Hathyr (*Egyptian month*), on the other that the members of the association should accept that sum as part payment of the total which Jucundus owes the association, Jucundus not being liable for it and nobody having a right to bring an action for its payment against him or to [?] such [. .] but confirm the [note] written below in the copies [. . .] of which on [. . .] and the other [. . .

Wilcken *Chrestomathie* 112
tr. K. Chisholm

D14 Honours to Augustus' family

This inscription, from the Greek island of Thasos, provides an example of the kind of honours that were paid not only to Augustus but also to his family in the Eastern provinces.

167

The people (of Thasos set up a statue of) Livia Drusilla, wife of Augustus Caesar, divine benefactress.

The people (of Thasos set up a statue) of Julia, daughter of Augustus Caesar, our benefactress following the tradition of her family.

Statue of Julia, daughter of Marcus Agrippa (set up by) the people (of Thasos).

ILS 8784
tr. K. Chisholm

D15 Administration of justice and new laws

Most of our knowledge of Augustan social legislation comes from secondary sources, compilations of jurists such as Gaius (2nd cent. AD) and Ulpian (early 3rd cent. AD). The Corpus Iuris Civilis, the sixth-century modification of Roman law by the Emperor Justinian, draws heavily on the work of the jurists. It is often very difficult to disentangle laws passed under Augustus from later accretions. Laws proposed by Augustus himself were known as 'leges Juliae' (laws were usually known by the name of their proposer) but some of these are difficult to distinguish from laws proposed by Julius Caesar or Tiberius. For a useful modern survey see H. F. Jolowicz Historical Introduction to the study of Roman Law *(Cambridge 1939, rev. edn.). W. W. Buckland* A Text-Book of Roman Law from Augustus to Justinian *(1963³ ed. P. G. Stein) is detailed and comprehensive.*

33 Augustus proved assiduous in his administration of justice, often remaining in Court until nightfall; and, if he happened to be unwell, would have his litter carried up to the tribunal. Sometimes he even judged cases from his sick-bed in the Palace. As a judge he was both conscientious and lenient. . . . Every year he referred to the City Praetor cases in which Roman citizens had exercised their right of appeal; foreigners' appeals would be handled by particular ex-Consuls whom he had appointed to protect nationals of the province concerned.

34 The existing laws that Augustus revised, and the new ones that he enacted, dealt, among other matters, with extravagance, adultery, unchastity, bribery, and the encouragement of marriage in the Senatorial and Equestrian Orders. His marriage law being more rigorously framed than the others, he found himself unable to make it effective because of an open revolt against several of its clauses. He was therefore obliged to withdraw or amend certain penalties exacted for a failure to marry; to increase the rewards he offered for large families; and to allow a widow, or widower, three years' grace before having to marry again. Even this did not satisfy the knights, who demonstrated against the law at a public entertainment, demanding its repeal. . . . When he then discovered that bachelors were getting betrothed to little girls, which meant postponing the responsibilities of fatherhood, and that married men were frequently changing their wives, he dealt with these evasions of the law by shorten-

ing the permissible period between betrothal and marriage, and by limiting the number of lawful divorces.

Suetonius <i>Augustus</i> 33–4 (abridged)
tr. R. Graves (Penguin 1957)

D16 Luxury

See also I 25–27.

(a) *The origins of luxury*

It was the conquest of Asia that first introduced luxury into Italy, inasmuch as Lucius Scipio carried in procession at his triumph 1400 lbs of chased silverware and vessels of gold weighing 1500 lbs: this was in the 565th year from the foundation of the city of Rome [189 B.C.]. But receiving Asia also as a gift dealt a much more serious blow to our morals, and the bequest of it that came to us on the death of King Attalus was more disadvantageous than the victory of Scipio. For on that occasion all scruples entirely disappeared in regard to buying these articles at the auctions of the king's effects at Rome—the date was the 622nd year of the city [132 B.C.], and in the interval of 57 years our community had learnt not merely to admire but also to covet foreign opulence; an impetus having also been given to manners by the enormous shock of the conquest of Achaia [sack of Corinth by Mummius, 146 B.C.], that victory itself also having during this interval of time introduced the statues and pictures won in the 608th year of the city.

Pliny <i>Natural History</i> 33. 148–9
tr. H. Rackham (Loeb 1952)

(b) *This passage occurs in the context of a crisis in 348 BC.*

The records say that ten legions were enlisted, each of 4,200 infantry and 300 cavalry; the recruits were drawn from all sides, city and country. The present strength of the people of Rome would not easily produce a fresh force of comparable size to combat external aggression even if solidly united, though the whole world can hardly contain it. Our growth has been confined to the objects of our energy, riches and luxury.

Livy 7. 25. 8–9
tr. J. Ferguson

(c) *Luxury as sophistication*

> Leave the past to others; I'm glad I was born now.
> The age suits my temperament.

It's not the mining of gold,
   the shellfish from abroad,
the marble quarried from the mountains,
   the jetties holding the sea back.
It's civilization. Thank God our grandfathers' simple life
   hasn't come down to us.

Ovid *Ars Amatoria* 3. 121–8
tr. J. Ferguson

D17 Sumptuary laws

In the first century BC a vast amount of wealth was concentrated 'into the hands of a few men' (Cicero against Verres 5. 48. 126) at Rome. Sumptuary laws were passed to curb excessive spending on display and luxuries but they did not prove effective.

The Attic Nights *of Aulus Gellius (AD c.123–69) covers a wide variety of topics and contains passages and quotations from many works now lost to us.*

The Lex Julia came before the people when Caesar Augustus was Emperor. This set an upper limit of expenditure on a dinner at 200 sesterces on working days, 300 on the Kalends, Ides, Nones, and some other holidays, 1,000 for weddings and wedding-feasts.

Ateius Capito records another edict—but I do not quite recall whether it belongs to the divine Augustus or to Tiberius Caesar—permitting expenditure on dinner at various festivals to increase from 300 sesterces to 2,000, so that the rising tide of extravagance might at least be confined within those limits.

Aulus Gellius 2. 24. 13–14
tr. J. Ferguson

D18 The importance of citizenship

For an interesting analysis of Roman attitudes to foreigners and slaves, see J. P. V. D. Balsdon Romans and Aliens *(Duckworth 1979).*

Augustus thought it most important not to let the native Roman stock be tainted with foreign or servile blood, and was therefore very unwilling to create new Roman citizens, or to permit the manumission of more than a limited number of slaves. Once, when Tiberius requested that a Greek dependent of his should be granted the citizenship, Augustus wrote back that he could not assent unless the man put in a personal appearance and convinced him that he was worthy of the honour. When Livia made the same request for a Gaul from a tributary province, Augustus turned it down, saying that he would do no more than exempt the fellow from tribute—'I would far rather forfeit whatever he may owe the Privy Purse than cheapen the value of the Roman citizenship.' Not only did he make it extremely difficult for slaves to be freed, and still more difficult for them to attain full independence, by strictly regulating the number, condition, and status of freedmen; but he ruled that no slave who had ever been in irons or subjected to torture could become a citizen, even after the most honourable form of manumission.

Augustus set himself to revive the ancient Roman dress and once, on seeing a group of men in dark cloaks among the crowd, quoted Virgil indignantly:

'Behold them, conquerors of the world, all clad in Roman gowns!'

and instructed the aediles that no one should ever again be admitted to the Forum, or its environs, unless he wore a gown and no cloak.

Suetonius *Augustus* 40. 3
tr. R. Graves (Penguin 1957)

D19 Condemnation of Roman customs

Dionysius of Halicarnassus, a Greek orator, historian, and literary critic came to Rome in c.30 BC. His Roman Antiquities, *a history covering a period from the foundation of Rome to the first Punic war, was scholarly but rather verbose and not always accurate; it was written primarily for a Greek audience and on the whole favourable to Rome.*

This, however, is not the case in our day, but things have come to such a state of confusion and the noble traditions of the Roman commonwealth have become so debased and sullied, that some who have made a fortune by robbery, housebreaking, prostitution and every other base means, purchase their freedom with the money so acquired and straightway are Romans. Others, who have been confidants and accomplices of their masters in poisonings, murders and in crimes against the gods or the state, receive from them this favour as their reward. Some are freed in order that, when they have received the monthly allowance of corn given by the public or some other largesse distributed by the men in power to the poor among the citizens, they may bring it to those who granted them their freedom. And others owe their freedom to the levity of their masters and to their vain thirst for popularity. I, at any rate, know of some who have allowed all their slaves to be freed after their death, in order that they might be called good men when they were dead and that many people might follow their biers wearing their liberty-caps; indeed, some of those taking part in these processions, as one might have heard from those who knew, have been malefactors just out of jail, who had committed crimes deserving of a thousand deaths. Most people, nevertheless, as they look upon these stains that can scarce be washed away from the city, are grieved and condemn the custom, looking upon it as unseemly that a dominant city which aspires to rule the whole world should make such men citizens.

One might justly condemn many other customs also which were wisely devised by the ancients but are shamefully abused by the men of to-day. Yet, for my part, I do not believe that this law ought to be abolished, lest as a result some greater evil should break out to the detriment of the public; but I do say that it ought to be amended, as far as possible, and that great reproaches and disgraces hard to be wiped out should not be permitted entrance into the body politic. And I could wish that the censors, preferably, or, if that may not be, then the consuls, would take upon themselves the care of this matter, since it requires the control of some important magistracy, and that they would make inquiries about the persons who are freed each year—who they are and for what reason they have been freed and how—just as they inquire into the lives of the knights and senators; after which they should enroll in the tribes such of them as they find worthy to be citizens and allow them to remain in the city, but should expel from the city the foul and corrupt herd under the specious pretence of sending them out as a colony. These are the things, then, which, as the subject required it, I thought it both necessary and just to say to those who censure the customs of the Romans.

Dionysius of Halicarnassus 4. 24. 4-6
tr. E. Cary (Loeb 1937)

D20 Lex Aelia Sentia

The Lex Aelia Sentia dates from AD 4 when the consuls were Sextus Aelius Catus and C. Sentius Saturninus, and was designed to make it more difficult for slaves with criminal records to acquire Roman citizenship if freed. Under Hadrian, the clause in (d) forbidding manumission to defraud creditors, was extended to aliens. Vindicta (b) was the staff or rod with which a slave was touched in the ceremony of manumission: it then came to mean the ceremony itself.

(a)

The law Aelia Sentia enacts that slaves who have been punished by their proprietors with chains or have been branded, or have been examined with torture on a criminal charge, and have been convicted, or have been delivered to fight with men or beasts, or have been committed to gladiatorial school or a public prison, if subsequently manumitted by the same or by another proprietor, shall acquire by manumission the status of enemies surrendered at discretion.

(b)

The requisition of a certain age of the slave was introduced by the lex Aelia Sentia, by the terms of which law, unless he is thirty years old, a slave cannot on manumission become a citizen of Rome, unless the mode of manumission is by the form of *vindicta*, preceded by proof of adequate motive before the council.

There is an adequate motive of manumission if, for instance, a natural child or natural brother or sister or foster child of the manumitter's or a teacher of the manumitter's child, or a male slave intended to be employed as an agent in business, or a female slave about to become the manumitter's wife, is presented to the council for manumission.

The council is composed in the city of Rome of five senators and five Roman knights above the age of puberty; in the provinces of twenty recuperators, who must be Roman citizens, and who hold their session on the last day of the assize. At Rome the council holds its session on certain days appointed for the purpose. A slave above the age of thirty can be manumitted at any time, and even in the streets, when the praetor or pro-consul is on his way to the bath or theatre.

(c)

Latins have many avenues to the Roman citizenship.

For instance, the lex Aelia Sentia enacts that when a slave below the age of thirty becomes by manumission a Latin, if he takes to himself as wife a citizen of Rome, or a Latin colonist, or a freedwoman of his own condition, and thereof procure attestation by not less than seven witnesses, citizens of Rome above the age of puberty, and begets a son, on the latter attaining the age of a year he is entitled to apply to the praetor, or, if he resides in a province, to the president of the province, and to prove that he has married a wife in accordance with the lex Aelia Sentia, and has had by her a son who has completed the first year of his age: and thereupon if the magistrate to whom the proof is submitted pronounce the truth of the declaration, that Latin and his wife, if she is of the same condition, and their son, are declared by the statute to be Roman citizens.

(d)

Not every owner who is so disposed is permitted to manumit.

An owner who would defraud his creditors or his own patron by an intended manumission, attempts in vain to manumit, because the lex Aelia Sentia prevents the manumission.

Again, by a disposition of the same statute, before attaining twenty years of age, the only process by which an owner can manumit is fictitious vindication, preceded by proof of adequate notice before the council.

It is an adequate motive of manumission, if the father for instance, or mother or teacher or foster-brother of the manumitter, is the slave to be manumitted. In addition to these, the motives recently specified respecting the slave under thirty years of age may be alleged when the manumitting owner is under twenty, and, reciprocally, the motives valid when the manumitting owner is under twenty are admissible when the manumitted slave is under thirty.

As, then, the lex Aelia Sentia imposes a certain restriction on manumission for owners under the age of twenty, it follows that, though a person who has completed his fourteenth year is competent to make a will, and therein to institute an heir and make bequests; yet, if he has not attained the age of twenty, he cannot therein enfranchise a slave.

And even to confer the Latin status, if he is under the age of twenty, the owner must satisfy the council of the adequacy of his motive before he manumits a slave in the presence of witnesses.

Gaius Institutes 1. 13; 18-20; 28-9; 36-41
tr. E. Poste (Oxford[4] 1904)

(e)

Latins are freedmen who have not been manumitted in regular form, those for instance manumitted privately, and in contravention of no regulation: and these in olden time the Praetor merely used to protect in the semblance of liberty; for in strict law they remained slaves. But at the present day they are free by strict law on account of the Lex Junia, by which *lex* those manumitted in the presence of our friends were styled Junian Latins.

Those are in the category of *dediticii* who have been put in chains by their masters as a punishment, or who have been branded, or who have been tortured for a misdeed and found guilty, or who have been delivered over to fight with the sword or against wild beasts, or cast into a gladiatorial school or into a prison for the like cause, and have afterwards been manumitted by any form. And these rules the Lex Aelia Sentia establishes.

By the same lex it was provided that a slave under thirty years of age when manumitted by *vindicta* should not become a Roman citizen, unless cause for manumission had been proved before the council; that is, it lays down that a slave of that age manumitted without application to the council remains a slave still: but when he is manumitted by testament it directs him to be regarded as though he were holding his freedom at his master's will, and therefore he becomes a Latin. The same lex prohibits a master under twenty years of age from manumitting a slave unless he have proved cause before the council. The council consists at Rome of five senators and five Roman knights, but in the provinces of twenty *recuperatores*, Roman citizens.

A slave ordered to be free and instituted heir in a testament by an insolvent master, although he be under thirty years of age, or so circumstanced that he ought to become a *dediticius*, yet becomes a Roman citizen and heir: provided only no one else be heir under that testament. But if two or more be ordered to become free and heirs, the one first named becomes free and heir: and this too the Lex Aelia Sentia enacts. The same *lex* forbids manumissions in fraud of creditors or patron.

Ulpian Epitome 1. 10-5
tr. Abdy and Walker

D21 Lex Fufia Caninia on manumission

This law was passed under Augustus (cf. Suetonius Augustus 40 no. D18) and was finally abrogated by Justinian. In some books it is wrongly called Lex Furia Caninia. cf. J. E. Allison and J. D. Cloud in Latomus *21 (1962) 711-31; A. E. Astin in* Latomus *23 (1964) 421-45.*

(a)

Moreover, by the lex Fufia Caninia a certain limit is fixed to the number of slaves who can receive testamentary manumission.

An owner who has more than two slaves and not more than ten is allowed to manumit as many as half that number; he who has more than ten and not more than thirty is allowed to manumit a third of that number; he who has more than thirty and not more than a hundred is allowed to manumit a fourth; lastly, he who has more than a hundred and not more than five hundred is allowed to manumit a fifth: and, however many a man possesses, he is never allowed to manumit more than this number, for the law prescribes that no one shall manumit more than a hundred. On the other hand, if a man has only one or two, the law is not applicable, and the owner has unrestricted power of manumission.

Nor does the statute apply to any but testamentary manumission, so that by the form of *vindicta* or inscription on the censor's register, or by attestation of friends, a proprietor of slaves may manumit his whole household, provided that there is no other let or hindrance to prevent their manumission.

If a testator manumits in excess of the permitted number, and arranges their names in a circle, as no order of manumission can be discovered, none of them can obtain their freedom, as both the lex Fufia Caninia itself and certain subsequent decrees of the Senate declare null and void all dispositions contrived for the purpose of eluding the statute.

(b)

Freedom cannot be bequeathed to an uncertain person, becuase the lex Fufia Caninia requires slaves to be enfranchised by name.

Gaius *Institutes* 1. 42-6; 2. 239
tr. E. Poste (Oxford[4] 1904)

D22 Leges Juliae on violence and embezzlement

The Lex Julia *on violence embraces two laws, one on public, and one on private violence. Embezzlement (*peculatus*) covered misappropriation of state property or public funds. The fuller title of the law was* lex Julia de peculatu et de sacrilegiis et de residuis. *The penalty was banishment and perhaps a fine four times the value of the property; but sacrilege, the appropriation of sacred things, carried the death* *penalty.* Residua *were moneys given for one purpose and applied to another. The* lex Julia de ambitu *dated from 18 BC allowing deportation for dishonest election practices; the* lex Julia de annona, *controlling the corn trade, was of the same date, but the Lex Julia on extortion went back to 59 BC.*

The *lex Julia* on violence, public or private, operates against those who use violence, whether armed or unarmed. If armed violence be proven the penalty established by the Julian law on public violence is deportation; for violence without arms, it is confiscation of a third of the criminal's property. But if the rape of virgins, widows and religious and others be perpetrated, then not only the ravishers themselves but all accomplices in the crime suffer capital punishment as provided by our constitution, a reading of which will reveal all on this matter. The *lex Julia* on embezzlement (*peculatus*) punishes those who appropriate public money or property or that used for the purposes of religion. Now, if judges, during their period of office, embezzle public money or property, they suffer capital punishment as also do those who are their accomplices therein, or who accept money which they know to be the fruits of such embezzlement; but others who contravene this statute suffer deportation ... There are, in addition, the *lex Julia* on bribery (*ambitus*) and the *lex Julia* on extortion (*repetundae*), the *lex Julia* on corn prices (*annona*) and that on arrears of public money (*residua*); they treat of particular offences and do not involve capital punishment but subject to other penalties those who contravene their provisions.

Justinian *Institutes* 4. 18. 8–11
tr. J. A. C. Thomas (Cape Town 1975)

D23 Leges Juliae on treason and adultery

The lex Julia maiestatis *embraces two laws, one passed by Julius Caesar in 46 BC and one by Augustus in 8 BC. The offence which had in the late Republic replaced* perduellio *and* proditio *embraced treason, sedition, desertion, and attacks on a magistrate. Under the Empire it was extended to embrace offences against the Princeps and his house. Intention was sufficient; see further J. E. Allison and J. D. Claud 'The Lex Julia Maiestatis' Latomus 21 (1962). The* lex Julia de adulteriis *of 18 BC was a law of Augustus introducing a statutory penalty for adultery and embracing other sexual offences.*

Public prosecutions are as follows. The *lex Julia* on treason (*maiestas*) directs its rigours against those who set in train any harm to the Emperor or the state; its penalty is death, and, even after the culprit's death, his memory is damned. Then the *lex Julia* for the suppression of adultery (*de adulteriis coercendis*) punishes with death not only those who dishonour the marriage-bed of another but also those who indulge their ineffable lust with males. The same *lex Julia* also punishes the offence of seduction when a person, without the use of force, deflowers a virgin or seduces a respectable widow. The penalty invoked by the statute against offenders is confiscation of half their estate if they be of respectable standing, corporal punishment and relegation in the case of baser persons.

Justinian *Institutes* 4. 18. 2-3
tr. J. A. C. Thomas (Cape Town 1975)

D24 The need for social legislation

This later condemnation of the preoccupations of the Roman ruling class may well reflect the kind of problem for which Augustus was trying to find a solution.

But later generations have been positively handicapped by the expansion of the world and by our multiplicity of resources. After senators began to be selected and judges appointed on the score of wealth, and wealth became the sole adornment of magistrate and military commander, after lack of children to succeed one began to occupy the place of highest influence and power, and legacy-hunting ranked as the most profitable profession, and the only delights consisted in ownership, the true prizes of life went to ruin, and all the arts that derived their name 'liberal' from liberty, the supreme good, fell into the opposite class, and servility began to be the sole means of advancement. This deity was worshipped by different men in different manners and in different matters, although every man's prayer was directed to the same end and to hopes of possessing; indeed even men of high character everywhere preferred to cultivate the vices of others rather than the good gifts that were their own. The consequence is, I protest, that pleasure has begun to live and life itself has ceased.

Pliny *Natural History* 14. 1. 5-6
tr. H. Rackham (Loeb 1945)

D25 Augustus admonishes Livia

Meanwhile a clamor arose in the senate over the disorderly conduct of the women and of the young men, this being alleged as a reason for their reluctance to enter into the marriage relation; and when they urged him to remedy this abuse also, with ironical allusions to his own intimacy with many women, he at first replied that the most necessary restrictions had been laid down and that anything further could not possibly be regulated by decree in similar fashion. Then, when he was driven into a corner, he said: 'You yourselves ought to admonish and command your wives as you wish; that is what I do.' When they heard that, they plied him with questions all the more, wishing to learn what the admonitions were which he professed to give Livia. He accordingly, though with reluctance, made a few remarks about women's dress and their other adornment, about their going out and their modest behaviour, not in the least concerned that his actions did not lend credence to his words.

Dio Cassius 54. 16. 3–5
tr. E. Cary (Loeb 1917)

D26 Poetic evidence

The detailed story of Augustus' marriage legislation is a matter of controversy. This poem of Propertius, certainly before 23 BC, is evidence that legislation was mooted early, though (despite the arguments of P. Jörs Die Ehegesetze des Augustus *pp. 4–28) probably not carried. By 23 May 17 BC the* lex *Julia de maritandis ordinibus had been enacted, and it and other legislation may be connected with the Ludi Saeculares and the inauguration of a new age. The aim of the legislation was to encourage marriage and penalize bachelordom, and the sort of free relations Propertius had with Cynthia. The meaning of lines 8 and 15 is uncertain. Propertius' rejection of militarism is noteworthy; see J. P. Sullivan* Propertius: a Critical Introduction *(Cambridge 1976) pp. 63–4.*

> Cynthia was delighted at the abrogation of the law
>   which brought us both long tears
> at the thought of parting—though Jupiter himself could not
>   separate two lovers against their will.
> 'But Caesar has the power.' Caesar's power lies in arms.
>   The conquest of tribes has no force in love.
> I'd sooner let my head be severed from my body
>   than quench our fires at a bride's whim
> or pass your shut door as a husband—I!—
>   glancing with tearful eyes at what I had betrayed.
> What sleep would my wedding-pipe sound for you.
>   It would be gloomier than a dead march!
> How should I get children for national victories?
>   No soldier will spring from me!
> But if I were attached to my girl's camp, the only real camp,
>   then Castor's war-horse wouldn't be strong enough.
> It was that camp which won my glory its repute,
>   a glory which has reached the Russians.

You are my only joy, Cynthia; let me be yours alone.
Our love will count far more than fatherhood.

Propertius 2. 7
tr. J. Ferguson

D27 Marriage legislation

Special privileges were granted to the parents of three children: ius trium liberorum.
*Penalties were attached to bachelors. But exceptions were made: (c) below. The
Lex Voconia dated from 169 BC (see further J. A. C. Thomas* Textbook of Roman
Law *(North-Holland 1976) p. 481 and note; p. 505 and note).*

(a) *This relates to 27 BC. The complete passage is B28.*

Next he decreed that the senatorial governors should be appointed annually by lot
except where legal precedence was granted by reason of marriage or number of
children.

Dio Cassius 53. 13. 2-3

(b) *18 BC*

He imposed heavier penalties on unmarried men and women, and at the same time
offered privileges for marriage and the production of children. And since there were
many more men than women among the freeborn, he allowed any who wished,
senators apart, to marry freedwomen, ruling that their children should be counted
legitimate.

Dio Cassius 54. 16. 1-2

(c) *9 BC*

Drusus died young. Livia was voted statues as a consolation and enrolled among
the mothers of three children. For when heaven has not granted that number of
births the law, through the senate originally and later the emperor, permitted
individuals, men or women, to receive the privileges appropriate to the parents of
three children.

Dio Cassius 55. 2. 5-6

(d) *AD 9*

Later he increased the privileges of those who had children; among the others he drew a distinction in the penalties attaching to the married and the unmarried; he granted a year's remission to both groups to amend their ways and avoid the penalties. Some women were allowed inheritances contrary to the Lex Voconia which permitted no woman an inheritance in excess of 100,000 sesterces. He granted the Vestal virgins all the privileges to which mothers were entitled. Later the Lex Papia Poppaea was proposed by M. Papius Mutilus and Q. Poppaeus Secundus, consuls for part of the year. It happened that neither had a child—or wife; which made the need for the legislation obvious.

Dio Cassius 56. 10
tr. J. Ferguson

D28 Lex Julia on adultery

The lex Julia de adulteriis coercendis *made adultery a public crime (cf. D23).*

But, to come to the provisions of the *Lex Julia* for punishing adultery, a man who confesses that he has committed that offence has no right to ask for a remission of the penalty on the ground that he was under age; nor, as I have added, will any remission be given where he commits any of those offences which the statute punishes in the same way as adultery; as, for example, where he marries a woman who was convicted of adultery, he knowing the fact, or where his own wife was detected in adultery, and he declines to dismiss her, or where he makes a profit of her adultery, or accepts a bribe to conceal illicit intercourse which he detected or lends his house for the commission of adultery or illicit intercourse therein; youth, as I said, is no excuse in the face of plain enactments in the case of a man who, though he appeals to the law, himself transgresses the law.

Justinian *Digest* 4. 4. 37 (from Tryphoninus *Disputations* 371)
tr. C. H. Monro (Cambridge 1904)

D29 Lex Julia de maritandis ordinibus

This law recognized marriages between free-born men and freedwomen, except for men of the Senatorial class.

By the Lex Julia senators and their descendants are forbidden to marry freedwomen, or women who have themselves followed the profession of the stage, or whose father or mother has done so; other freeborn persons are forbidden to marry a common prostitute, or a procuress, or a woman manumitted by a procurer or procuress, or a woman caught in adultery, or one condemned in a public action, or one who has followed the profession of the stage . . .

The Lex Julia allows women a respite from its requirements for one year after the death of a husband, and for six months after a divorce: but the Lex Papia allows a respite for two years after the death of a husband and for a year and six months after a divorce.

Ulpian *Epitome* 13-14
tr. Abdy and Walker

D30 Lex Papia Poppaea on the succession of freedmen

The Lex Papia Poppaea of AD 9 completed the lex Julia de maritandis ordinibus; *see J. A. Field, jnr. 'The Purpose of the lex Julia et Papia Poppaea'* Classical Journal *40 (1944/5) 398-416.*

(a)

At a still later period the lex Papia Poppaea augmented the rights of the patron against the estate of more opulent freedmen. For by the provisions of this statute whenever a freedman leaves property of the value of a hundred thousand sesterces and upwards, and not so many as three children, whether he dies testate or intestate, a portion equal to that of a single child is due to the patron. Accordingly, if a single son or daughter survives, half the estate is claimable by the patron, just as if the freedman had died childless; if two children inherit, a third of the property belongs to the patron; if three children survive, the patron is excluded.

In respect of the property of freedwomen no wrong could possibly be done to the patron under the ancient law: for, as the patron was statutory guardian of the freedwoman, her will was not valid without his sanction, so that, if he sanctioned a will, he either would be therein instituted heir, or, if not, had only himself to blame: for if he did not sanction a will and consequently the freedwoman died intestate, he was assured of the inheritance, for she could leave no *heres* or *bonorum possessor* who could bar the claim of the patron.

But when at a subsequent period, by the enactment of the lex Papia, four children were made a ground for releasing a freedwoman from the guardianship of her patron, so that his sanction ceased to be necessary to the validity of her will, it was provided by that law that the patron should have a claim to a portion of her estate equal to that of each single child she might have at the time of her death. So if a freedwoman left four children, a fifth part of her property went to her patron, but if she survived all her children, the patron on her decease took her whole property.

What has been said of the patron applies to a son of the patron, a grandson by a son, a great-grandson by a grandson by a son.

Although a daughter of a patron, a granddaughter by a son, a great-granddaughter by a grandson by a son have under the statute of the Twelve Tablets identical rights with the patron, the praetorian edict only calls the male issue to the succession: but the lex Papia gives a daughter of the patron a contra-testamentary or intestate claim against an adoptive child, or a wife, or a son's wife to a moiety of the inheritance on account of the privilege of being mother of three children; a daughter not so privileged has no claim.

In the succession to a testate freedwoman, mother of four children, a patron's daughter, though mother of three children, is not, as some think, entitled to the portion of a child: but, if the freedwoman die intestate, the letter of the lex Papia gives her the portion of a child; if the freedwoman die testate, the patron's daughter has the same title to contra-tabular possession as she would have against the will of a freedman, that is, as the praetorian edict confers on a patron and his sons in respect of the property of a freedman, (viz. a claim to half against all but natural children) though this portion of the law is carelessly written.

It is thus apparent that the external heirs of a patron are entirely excluded from the rights which the law confers on the patron himself, whether a freedman die intestate or it is a question of the freedman's will being set aside by the praetor in favour of the patron.

Before the lex Papia was passed, patronesses had only the same rights in the property of their freedmen as patrons enjoyed under the statute of the Twelve Tables: for neither did the praetor intervene to give them a moiety of the inheritance by contra-tabular possession against a will of an ungrateful freedman, nor by making a grant of possession against the intestate claim of an adoptive child or a wife or a son's wife, as he did in the case of the patron and the patron's son.

But subsequently by the lex Papia two children entitle a freeborn patroness, three children a patroness who is a freedwoman, to nearly the same rights as the praetor's edict confers on a patron; and it also provided that three children entitle a freeborn patroness to the same rights which the statute itself conferred on a patron: but the statute does not grant these latter rights to a patroness who is a freedwoman.

As to the successions of freedwomen who die intestate, no new right is conferred on a patroness through the title of children by the lex Papia; accordingly, if neither the patroness nor the freedwoman has undergone a *capitis deminutio*, the law of the Twelve Tables transmits the inheritance to the patroness, and excludes the freedwoman's children, even when the patroness is childless; for a woman, as before remarked, can never have a self-successor: but if either of them has undergone a *capitis deminutio*, the children of the freed woman exclude the patroness, because her statutory title having been obliterated by *capitis deminutio*, the children of the freedwoman are admitted by right of kinship in preference to her.

When a freedwoman dies testate, a patroness not entitled by children has no right of contra-tabular possession: but a patroness entitled by children has conferred upon her by the lex Papia the same right to a moiety by contra-tabular possession as the praetorian edict confers on the patron to the inheritance of a freedman.

By the same law a patroness's son privileged by having children has almost the rights of a patron (patroness?) but in this case one son or daughter is sufficient to give him the privilege.

This summary indication of the rules of succession to freedmen and freedwomen who are Roman citizens may suffice for the present occasion: a more detailed exposition is to be found in my separate treatise on this branch of the law.

Gaius *Institutes* 3. 42–54
tr. E. Poste (Oxford[4] 1904)

(b)

The Lex Papia Poppaea afterwards exempted freedwomen from the tutelage of patrons, by prerogative of four children, and having established the rule that they could henceforth make testaments without the patron's authorization, it provided that a proportionate share of the freedwoman's property should be due to the patron, dependent on the number of her surviving children. The male descendants of a patron have the same rights over the goods of the freedmen of their ascendants as the patron himself has. Under the law of the Twelve Tables female descendants have just as much right as male descendants of patrons, but *bonorum possessio* does not appertain to them either in opposition to the testamentary directions of a freedman, or on his intestacy as against those *sui heredes* who are not such by blood; yet if they have obtained the prerogative of three children, they acquire these rights also by virtue of the Lex Papia Poppaea.

Patronesses used to have only such rights over their freedmen's property as the law of the Twelve Tables established; the Lex Papia Poppaea, however, afterwards gave to a patroness of free-birth enjoying the privilege of two children, and to a freedwoman enjoying that of three, the same rights that the patron has under the Edict. So too the same *lex* gave to a woman of free-birth enjoying the privilege of three children all the rights which it conferred upon the patron himself.

Ulpian *Epitome* 29. 3–7
tr. Abdy and Walker

D31 Provisions of the lex Julia and Papia Poppaea for guardians, testaments, and legacies

(a)

Accordingly, when a brother and sister have a testamentary guardian, on attaining the age of puberty the brother ceases to be a ward, but the sister continues, for it is only under the lex Julia and Papia Poppaea and by title of maternity that women are emancipated from tutelage; except in the case of vestal virgins, for these, even in our ancestors' opinion, are entitled by their sacerdotal function to be free from control, and so the law of the Twelve Tables enacted.

Gaius *Institutes* 1. 145

(b)
Guardianship terminates for a freeborn woman by title of maternity of three children, for a freedwoman under statutory guardianship by maternity of four children: those who have other kinds of guardians, Atilian, for instance, or fiduciary, are released from ward-ship by title of three children.

Gaius *Institutes* 1. 194

(c)
A subsequent will duly executed is a revocation of a prior will, and it makes no difference whether a successor ever actually takes under it or no; the only question is whether one might. Accordingly, whether the successor instituted in a subsequent will duly executed declines to be successor, or dies in the lifetime of the testator, or after his death before accepting the succession, or is excluded by the expiration, or by failure of the condition under which he was instituted, or by celibacy as the lex Julia provides; in all these cases the testator dies intestate, for the earlier will is revoked by the later one, and the later one is inoperative, as it creates no actual successor.

Gaius *Institutes* 2. 144

(d)
The statement that a lapsed portion in legacy by condemnation falls to the heir, and in legacy by vindication accrues to the colegatee, be it observed, gives the rule of the civil law before the lex Papia; but since the lex Papia, a lapsed portion becomes caducous, and belongs to the devisees who have children.

And although the first title to a caducous legacy is that of heirs with children, and the second, if the heirs are childless, of legatees with children, yet the lex Papia itself declares that in joint bequest a legatee with children is to be preferred to heirs with children.

And it is generally agreed that as to the rights which the lex Papia gives to joint legatees, it makes no difference whether the bequest is by vindication or by condemnation.

Gaius *Institutes* 2. 206–8
tr. E. Poste (Oxford[4] 1904)

D32 Laws on inheritance

On the Lex Voconia see also D27d.

(a)

This led to the enactment of the lex Furia, whereby, excepting certain specified classes, a thousand asses was made the maximum that a legatee or donee in contemplation of death was permitted to take. This law, however, failed to accomplish its purpose, for a testator with an estate of, say, five thousand asses, might leave to five legatees a thousand asses apiece, and strip the heir of the whole.

This occasioned the enactment of the lex Voconia, providing that no legatee or donee in contemplation of death should take more than the heir. By this law, some portion at all events was secured to the heir, but like the former, it could be defeated, for the multitude of legatees between whom a man distributed his estate might leave so little to the heir as to make it not worth his while to undertake the whole burden of succession.

At last, the lex Falcidia was enacted, prohibiting to bequeath away more than three fourths of an estate, in other words, securing for the heir one fourth of the inheritance, and this is the rule of law now in force.

> Gaius *Institutes* 2. 225–7
> tr. E. Poste (Oxford[4] 1904)

(b) *Presumably this case was not covered by existing laws.*

Gaius Tettius had been disinherited by his father when an infant, although Petronia, his mother, was retained by his father as his legal wife as long as he lived. The divine Augustus ordered by decree that he should take possession of the father's property, and in this acted in the true spirit of a father of his country seeing that the elder Tettius had most unjustly renounced the name of father to a son born under his roof.

> Valerius Maximus 7. 7. 3
> tr. K. Chisholm

(c) *Restrictions on inheritance also strengthened the marriage laws.*

Sometimes husband and wife can receive, one from the other, the entire inheritance, for instance if both or either of them be not yet of the age at which the *lex* insists on children, i.e. if either the husband be under 25, or the wife under 20 years of age; also if both of them have, whilst their marriage subsists, exceeded the ages limited by the Lex Papia, i.e. the husband 60, the wife 50; likewise, if relations within the sixth degree have married, or if the husband be absent on public business, both whilst he is still absent and within a year after he has ceased to be absent.

There is also complete *testamenti factio* between them, if they have obtained from the emperor the privileges attaching to children, or if they have a son or daughter from their union, or have lost a son of the age of fourteen or a daughter of the age of twelve: or have lost two children of the age of three years, or three after their naming days, provided nevertheless that even one child lost at any age under puberty gives them the right of receiving the whole estate within a period of one year and six months from the death. Likewise if the wife within ten months after her husband's death bear a child by him, she takes the whole of his goods.

Sometimes they cannot take anything one from the other, i.e. when they have contracted a marriage contrary to the Lex Julia et Papia Poppaea, when for instance any freeborn man has married a woman of abandoned character, or when a senator has married a freedwoman.

A man who has conformed to neither *lex* within his sixtieth year, or a woman who has not done so within her fiftieth, although after such age exempt from compliance according to the rules of the *leges* themselves, yet will be liable to their standing penalties by reason of the *senatus-consultum Pegasianum.*

Ulpian *Epitome* 16. 1–3
tr. Abdy and Walker

(d)
Celibates also, whom the lex Julia disqualifies for taking successions or legacies, and childless persons whom the lex Papia prohibits from taking more than half a succession or legacy are exempt from these incapacities under the will of a soldier.

(e)
Unmarried persons, who are disabled by the lex Julia from taking inheritances and legacies, were formerly deemed capable of taking the benefit of a trust. And childless persons, who forfeit by the lex Papia, on account of not having children, half their inheritances and legacies, were formerly deemed capable of taking in full as beneficiaries of a trust.

Gaius *Institutes* 2. 111; 286
tr. E. Poste (Oxford[4] 1904)

E ART AND ARCHITECTURE

Augustus' claim to have found a Rome of brick and left one of marble was no vain boast (E1). The building programme carried out during his rule was on a vast scale, not only new buildings but restorations; not only temples and altars but roads, aqueducts, and new cities (cf. C33-6; J1). Vitruvius, whose detailed study of architecture is the only work on this subject surviving from antiquity, dedicated it to Augustus (cf. § J).

The programme of reconstruction and renovation in Rome began with the establishing of peace after the civil wars (E1). Apart from their functional purpose, many buildings served as visual expressions of the best qualities of the new regime (cf. E10, 14): victorious, peaceful, favoured by the gods. A favourable political climate allowed the arts to flourish and they provide evidence for a society enjoying prosperity and stability (E4, 17). The reliefs of the Ara Pacis (E14) seem to embody the essence of Augustan Rome; adherence to traditions, piety, dignity, and authority all expressed in workmanship of the highest quality.

From the second century BC onwards, large numbers of Greek works of art were imported into Rome and placed in private collections and in public places. Augustus and his family continued this tradition and examples of Greek art from the sixth century BC may be found among their dedications. Many of the artists working in Rome under Augustus were also Greek. We do, however, know of some Roman artists, particularly wall-painters (interior decorators). Easel-painting seems to have been considered a respectable, if eccentric, hobby for the upper classes; the professional easel-painters and wall-painters would be of lower social standing (cf. E21). Under Augustus the use of Hellenistic forms adapted to Roman symbolism continued. A specific 'Augustan' style, easily identified in architecture, sculpture and painting, does not exist. There is rather a more deliberate reflection of Roman traditions and ideals.

Our critical appreciation of the art of this period is limited by what has survived— either accidently, as in Pompeii, or by the choice of successive generations. Contemporary sources, such as Pliny and Vitruvius help to fill in some of the gaps.

E1 Augustus beautifies Rome

Three chapters of RG (19-21) list building works of Augustus: his personal taste seems to have been modest (see E18) but the public buildings at Rome undertaken during his rule were on a magnificent scale.

28   Aware that the City was architecturally unworthy of her position as capital of the Roman Empire, besides being vulnerable to fire and river floods, Augustus so improved her appearance that he could justifiably boast: 'I found Rome built of sun-dried bricks; I leave her clothed in marble.' He also used as much foresight as could have been expected in guarding against future disasters.

29   Among his larger public works three must be singled out for mention: the Forum dominated by the Temple of Avenging Mars; the Palatine Temple of Apollo; and the Temple of Juppiter the Thunderer on the Capitoline Hill. He built his Forum because the two already in existence could not deal with the recent great increase in the number of law-suits caused by a corresponding increase in population; which was why he hurriedly opened it even before the Temple of Mars had been completed. Public prosecutions and the casting of lots for jury service took place in this Forum. Augustus had vowed to build the Temple of Mars during the Philippi campaign of vengeance against Julius Caesar's assassins. He therefore decreed that the Senate should meet here whenever declarations of war or claims for triumphs were considered; and that this should be both the starting point for military governors, when escorted to their provinces, and the repository of all triumphal tokens when they returned victorious. The Temple of Apollo was erected in the part of his Palace to which, the soothsayers said, the God had drawn attention by having it struck with lightning. The colonnades running out from it housed Latin and Greek libraries; and in his declining years Augustus frequently held meetings of the Senate in the nave, or revised jury lists there. A lucky escape on a night march in Cantabria prompted him to build the Temple of Juppiter the Thunderer: a flash of lightning had scorched his litter and killed the slave who was going ahead with a torch.

Some of Augustus's public works were undertaken in the names of relatives: such as the colonnade and basilica of his grandsons Gaius and Lucius; the colonnades of his wife Livia and his sister Octavia; the theatre of his nephew Marcellus. He also often urged leading citizens to embellish the City with new public monuments or to restore and improve ancient ones, according to their means. Many responded: thus the Temple of Hercules and the Muses was raised by Marcius Philippus; that of Diana by Lucius Cornificius; the Hall of Liberty by Asinius Pollio; the Temple of Saturn by Munatius Plancus; a theatre by Cornelius Balbus; an amphitheatre by Statilius Taurus; and a variety of magnificent buildings by Marcus Agrippa.

30   Augustus divided the City into districts and wards; placing the districts under the control of magistrates annually chosen by lot, and the wards under supervisors locally elected. He organized stations of night-watchmen to alarm the fire brigades; and, as a precaution against floods, cleared the Tiber channel which had been choked with an accumulation of rubbish and narrowed by projecting houses. Also, he improved the approaches to the City: repaving the Flaminian Way as far as Ariminium, at his own expense, and calling upon men who had won triumphs to spend their prize money on putting the other main roads into good condition.

Furthermore, he restored ruined or burned temples, beautifying these and others with the most lavish gifts: for instance, a single donation to Capitoline Juppiter of

16,000 lb of gold, besides pearls and precious stones to the value of 500,000 gold pieces.

Suetonius *Augustus* 28–30
tr. R. Graves (Penguin 1957)

E2 Rome before the Augustan building programme

Rome was not lacking in fine and impressive buildings, as the following passages show. It was the scale of Augustus' building programme that overshadowed what went before.

(a) *Marius*

Gaius Marius, son of Gaius. Consul seven times, Praetor, tribune.... As Victor he dedicated a Temple to Honour and Valour from the spoils of the Cimbri and Teutones and (entered the Senate?) in triumphal costume and wearing patrician shoes ....

CIL 1^2. 32 (abridged)
tr. Dudley *Urbs Roma*

(b) *The theatre of Pompey*

At Mitylene ... Pompey was delighted with the theatre, and had sketches and plans of it made, so that he could build one like it at Rome, but larger and more magnificent.

When Pompey was building the large and splendid theatre which bears his name, he built close to it—like a small boat towed by a ship—a finer house than he had before. Even this was not so large as to provoke envy: when the next owner entered it, he asked in surprise, 'But where did Pompey the Great eat his dinner?'

Plutarch *Pompey* 42; 50. 5
tr. Dudley *Urbs Roma*

(c) *The theatre of Marcellus*

Julius Caesar was always undertaking great new works to embellish Rome.... His two first projects were for a temple of Mars, to be the biggest in the world, (for which he would have had to fill in and pave the lake where the *naumachiae* were held) and for a huge theatre, built into the side of the Tarpeian rock.

Suetonius *Julius Caesar* 44

When Augustus opened the Games at the dedication of the Theatre of Marcellus, his chair collapsed and sent him sprawling backwards. At a special performance in the Theatre in honour of Gaius and Lucius Caesar, there was a panic among the audience, who thought the walls were going to collapse. Augustus tried in vain to pacify them, but in the end left his private box and sat down in what seemed the most dangerous part.

Suetonius *Augustus* 43
tr. Dudley *Urbs Roma*

E3 Splendours of Rome

Should we not record among our splendid buildings the Basilica Pauli, with its superb columns from Phrygia, the Forum of Augustus, the Temple of Peace built by his Imperial Majesty the Emperor Vespasian? Those are the most beautiful buildings the world has ever seen.

Pliny *Natural History* 36. 102
tr. Dudley *Urbs Roma*

E4 The Campus Martius

The Campus Martius was used for army musters and voting by the comitia centuriata *as it was outside the* pomerium, *the sacred city boundary. Under Augustus a great number of buildings were added to the already extensive republican works—the largest of these being the theatre of Pompey built in 52 BC. The Mausoleum of Augustus was in the Campus Martius, as were the Pantheon and the Ara Pacis.*

In a word, the early Romans made but little account of the beauty of Rome, because they were occupied with other, greater and more necessary, matters; whereas the later Romans, and particularly those of to-day and in my time, have not fallen short in this respect either—indeed, they have filled the city with many beautiful structures. In fact, Pompey, the Deified Caesar, Augustus, his sons and friends, and wife and sister, have outdone all others in their zeal for buildings and in the expense incurred. The Campus Martius contains most of these, and thus, in addition to its natural beauty, it has received still further adornment as the result of foresight. Indeed, the size of the Campus is remarkable, since it affords space at the same time and without interference, not only for the chariot-races and every other equestrian exercise, but also for all that multitude of people who exercise themselves by ball-playing, hoop trundling and wrestling; and the works of art situated around the Campus Martius, and the ground, which is covered with grass throughout the year, and the crowns of those hills that are above the river and extend as far as its bed, which present to the eye the appearance of a stage-painting—all this, I say, affords a spectacle that one can hardly draw away from.

Strabo 5. 236
tr. H. L. Jones (Loeb 1942)

E5 Forum of Augustus

The Forum of Augustus was begun in 37 BC and the temple of Mars Ultor, the Avenger, was dedicated in 2 BC. The temple was surrounded by colonnades containing, in niches, statues of famous men (including generals who had triumphed) each with a list of achievements; cf. M1; RG 4 p. 4; Ovid Fasti 5. 551-3; 563-6.

(a)
Augustus' new Forum is so narrow because he could not bring himself to evict the owners of the houses which would have been demolished had his original plan been carried out.

(b)
Among his larger public works three must be singled out for mention: the Forum dominated by the Temple of Avenging Mars; the Palatine Temple of Apollo; and the Temple of Juppiter the Thunderer on the Capitoline Hill. He built his Forum because the two already in existence could not deal with the recent great increase in the number of law-suits caused by a corresponding increase in population; which was why he hurriedly opened it even before the Temple of Mars had been completed. Public prosecutions and the casting of lots for jury service took place only in this Forum. Augustus had vowed to build the Temple of Mars during the Philippi campaign of vengeance against Julius Caesar's assassins. He therefore decreed that the Senate should meet here whenever declarations of war or claims for triumphs were considered; and that this should be both the starting point for military governors, when escorted to their provinces, and the repository of all triumphal tokens when they returned victorious.

Suetonius *Augustus* 56; 29
tr. R. Graves (Penguin 1957)

E6 The temple of Mars the Avenger

Ovid celebrates the temple of Mars Ultor, dedicated on 12 May, 19 BC (see the Calendars A3), a round temple which housed for a time the standards retrieved from the Parthians; (cf. RG 20, 21).

> Am I wrong, or was there a sound of arms? I am right; there was!
>   Mars is coming with the sign of war.
> The Avenger comes down from heaven to receive his due honours,
>   to see his temple in Augustus's Forum.
> Colossal the god, the building to match. So Mars should live
>   in his son's city.
> The shrine is worthy of trophies won from the Giants.
>   The Marching God can march from here,
> whether some godless enemy attacks from the east,
>   or there's a westerner to beat.
> Strong in war he looks out on the towering roof with approval
>   that the heights are for the unconquered gods.
> On the doors he examines weaponry of different kinds,
>   arms conquered by his own soldiers.
> On one side he sees Aeneas with his beloved burden
>   and many progenitors of the Julians.
> On another he sees Romulus bearing on his back the arms of a commander,
>   and statues with a catalogue of heroism.
> He sees too the name of Augustus on the front of the temple
>   which is enhanced by Caesar's name.
> Augustus promised it in his youth, when he took up arms in duty's name,
>   augurs of the First Citizen.
> He stood in prayer, loyal troops on one side,
>   conspirators on the other, and said:
> 'If my father, priest of Vesta, is my *casus belli*,
>   avenging both godheads,
> Mars, be with me, glut the sword with criminal blood,
>   favour the right,
> and you shall win a temple, and, with my victory, the title Avenger.'
>   He promised—and was victorious.
> He was not content with making Mars the Avenger once only.
>   He went in pursuit of the Parthians' standards,
> a nation protected by plains, cavalry, archery,
>   and the barrier of rivers.
> The death of Crassus had fanned their pride,
>   when we lost army, standards, commander.
> The Parthians kept the Romans' standard, a mark of victory,
>   and every bearer hoisted the eagle of Rome!

That disgrace would still be with us, if Italy's riches
    were not defended by Caesar's army.
He removed the old long-standing disgrace;
    the standards knew their rightful owners.
What was the use of your familiar firing in retreat,
    your deserts, your galloping horses,
you Parthians? You surrender the eagles—and your conquered bows.
    You have no record of our shame.
So the temple and title are rightly the god's who twice avenged,
    the honour fulfils the promise.
Citizens of Rome, celebrate in the Circus the solemn Festival;
    the theatre is too small for the god of courage.

Ovid *Fasti* 5. 549–98
tr. J. Ferguson

E7 The temple of Caesar

Augustus dedicated the temple of Divus Julius on 18 August 29 BC (RG 19, 21).
The painting was famous, by Apelles (the fourth-century Greek artist) previously
in the temple of Aesculapius in Cos. Augustus obtained it by remitting 100 talents
from the Coan tribute (Strabo 14. 657).

The divine Augustus dedicated the painting of Venus rising from the sea, which is
called the Anadyomene, in the temple of his father Caesar.

Pliny *Natural History* 35. 91
tr. K. Chisholm

E8 Octavian commemorates the victory of Actium

Temples and spoils were visible reminders and indeed evidence of victory that any
Roman, or foreigner, could see and understand.

When he completed this [triumphal celebration] he dedicated the temple of Minerva
called the Chalcidicum and the Curia Julia, which was set up in honour of his father.
In this last building he set up the image of Victory which still exists, indicating, as
seems likely, that through her help he had gotten control of the empire. The Victory
belonged to the Tarentines, and after being taken from Tarentum to Rome, was set
up in the council chamber and decorated with spoils from Egypt. This was also the

case with the shrine of Julius Caesar which was consecrated at that time. For many of the spoils were also set up in this shrine, and likewise others were offered to Jupiter Capitolinus and to Juno and to Minerva; on the other hand, all the objects which either seemed to have been once set up there as votives or which were still actually in place were by decree taken down at this time on the grounds that they were polluted. And thus Cleopatra, even though she had been defeated and captured, was accorded glory, because her personal ornaments now lie in our temples and a golden statue of her may be seen in the temple of Venus.

Dio Cassius 51. 22. 1–3
tr. Pollitt *The Art of Rome*

E9 The restoration of the temple of Jupiter Feretrius

Cornelius Nepos (c.99–c.24 BC) wrote biographies of famous men; Atticus, Cicero's friend, was an Epicurean. He died in 32 BC which gives to the restoration a terminus ad quem. *Livy testifies to Octavian's personal interest.*

(a)
When the shrine of Jupiter Feretrius on the Capitol, a foundation of Romulus, was roofless and collapsing with age and neglect, it was on a suggestion from Atticus that Caesar saw to its restoration.

Cornelius Nepos *Atticus* 20
tr. J. Ferguson

(b) *Marcus Licinius Crassus, Octavian's colleague in the consulship of 30 BC, awarded a triumph for victories over the Thracians and Getae in 21 BC, claimed the right to dedicate the* spolia opima *for killing the leader of the enemy. This honour had only ever been granted to three Romans—Romulus, Cossus, and M. Claudius Marcellus—and Crassus claimed Cossus as precedent for being only a military tribune at the time (437 BC) and not fighting under his own auspices. During the restoration of the temple of Jupiter, however, the spoils of Cossus were found, with a convenient dedication showing him to have been consul at the time. This discovery allowed Octavian to deny Crassus the* spolia opima *(Dio Cassius 51. 24. 4); on the connection between this passage and Crassus, see Dessau Hermes 41 (1906) 142 ff. The relevance of this incident to a re-examination of Octavian's own position is discussed by E. Groag P-W 13. 283 ff.*

I actually heard Augustus Caesar, the founder or restorer of all our temples, say that he went into the shrine of Jupiter Feretrius, when it was collapsing with age and he restored it, and personally read the inscription on the linen breastplate; so

I thought it almost blasphemous to deprive Cossus of the testimony to his spoils provided by Caesar in his restoration of that temple.

Livy 4. 20. 7
tr. J. Ferguson

E10 The temple of Apollo

This was dedicated in 28 BC and was one of the most splendid temples in Rome. First to be built of the brilliant white marble from Carrara, it was elaborately decorated, and extravagantly praised (see also Virgil Aeneid 8. 720–2 (F4(b) and Servius on Aeneid 8. 720).

(a)

Asked by my lady why I came in so late,
I pleaded in excuse a call of state:
A tribute that our Prince to Phoebus paid,
Opening the sun-god's golden colonnade.
Spectacular it stood, and finely spaced
With Punic piers, and in between were placed
The girls whom Danaus in his lengthy span
Had fathered—in themselves a female clan.
High in the midst the marble shrine shone bright,
Dearer than Delos in Apollo's sight;
And over all the sun-gods' chariots lent
Their crowning glory to each pediment.
On double doors, of noblest ivory, grown
In Libya, was the graver's mastery shown:
Here Niobe's bereavements, there the plight
Of Gauls was pictured, hurled from Delphi's height.
Phoebus, stole-clad, in act of song, between
His mother and sister, next was seen,
In marble beauty seeming to eclipse
His living self, though mute and lyre and lips;
And round the altar Myron's cattle stood:
Four sculptured beasts, in lifelike attitude.

Propertius 2. 31
tr. A. E. Watts (Penguin[2] 1966)

(b)

Finally, on assuming the office of Chief Pontiff vacated by the death of Marcus Lepidus—he could not bring himself to divest his former colleague of it, even though he were an exile—Augustus collected all the copies of Greek and Latin prophetic verse then current, the work of either anonymous or little-known authors, and burned more than two thousand. He kept the Sibylline Books, and edited even these before depositing them in two gilded cases under the pedestal of Palatine Apollo's image.

Suetonius *Augustus* 31
tr. R. Graves (Penguin 1957)

(c) *Apollo was the god most closely associated with the victory at Actium and seen as Augustus' protecting deity. Propertius, celebrated as a love poet, had Maecenas as a patron (cf. Propertius 2. 1; 3. 9) and wrote poems rich in Roman traditional myths and cults.*

> The priest performs rites: let there be silence during the rites.
> Let the heifer be struck and fall before my altar.
> Now may a Roman wreath and Philetan clusters hang side
> By side; and the urn give up its Cyrenean waters.
> Give me the fragrance of costos, the tribute of sweet incense;
> Have the fillet of wool wound three times around the altar!
> Sprinkle my head with pure water. And, on new shrines, let
> The ivory flute pour forth its song from Phrygian
> Jars. Opportunists, walk behind at a distance! Scatter your poisons
> In another air. The new road is strewn with sacred laurel.
> We shall restore, O Muse, the temple of Palatine Apollo:
> An enterprise, Calliope, exalted enough for your
> Patronage. These songs are made for Caesar. You, Jupiter,
> I pray, attend while Caesar is celebrated!
>
> A wide water, Actium's memorial of Caesar's war fleet,
> Recedes toward the Athamanan shores of Phoebus' port—
> Where a bay shuts out the murmur of Ionia's sea—
> And, in response to sailors' prayers, forms a ready harbor.
> Here the leaders of the world met. Their fleets, equally great,
> Stood unequally favored by the omens. One,
> Unworthily commanded by a woman, was fated for
> Destruction at the hands of the Trojan Quirinus, great Caesar.
>
> Under full sail the Augustan flagship advanced. Its
> Protector was Jove. Its standard had been taught victory
> For Rome. Nereus manoeuvred the ships into twin crescents;
> Gaudy waters quivered under the sheen of arms.
> One fleet, mobile, contended with a strong south wind:
> And Phoebus, forsaking Delos (once floating, now fixed by him)
> Came and stood over Augustus' stern. A strange fire shone:
> Flashed three times in oblique manifestation.

196

Phoebus was not wearing his hair loose on his shoulders.
He came without his tortoise-shell lyre's unmartial music.
His aspect was such as when he gazed on Agamemnon, and
Decimated the Doric camps: or as when
He destroyed the Python, resting in its coils—
Serpent-terror of goddesses too timid to combat it.
He spoke. 'O native of Alba Longa, world redeemer,
Augustus, known as greater than your Trojan forbears—
Win now at sea! Already the land is yours. My bow militates
In your favor. All the arrows in my quiver are yours.
Relieve the homeland's fear. Confident, with you for
Protector, the public has pinned its hope to your prow.
Unless you win, Romulus will have been wrong in his augury
For Rome: he will have misinterpreted the Palatine birds.
See, the enemy approaches too close—disgrace to Latins,
You being only *princeps*, any sea should suffer *royal* sails!

'Fear not, if the other fleet moves with a hundred winged
Oars to each ship. It labors in a stormy element.
No matter how many prows bear Centaurian rock throwers,
You'll find the ships hollow, their terrors, painted imitations.
It's the cause that makes or breaks a soldier's courage:
The cause unjust, troops lay down their arms. This
Is zero hour. Engage your fleet. I, who fix the hour,
Shall lead the Julian curved-beak prow with my laurelbearing
Hand.' He spoke. And shot his quiverful into the enemy.
The next attack was Caesar's. And—for Phoebus kept his word—
Rome won. The woman paid.

Broken scepters floated in Ionian waters.
But Father Caesar, from his Idalian comet, said:
'I am a god. Victory proves you of our blood.'
Then followed Triton with his trumpet-blast. All the ocean
Goddesses, around freedom's standards, clapped applause.
In shameful flight, *she* (at the mercy of her ship) sought
Nile. Her one triumph—death, by her own appointment!
The gods knew best! What kind of triumph would one woman
Have made: led through streets Jugurtha traversed before her?

And Phoebus acquired a shrine in Actium. His every arrow,
Aimed to hit, had accounted for ten ships.

And that is enough of war. Apollo, victor, now wants
The cithara. He would exchange arms for a music
Restful to the ear. So, let whiterobed guests come into
The grove. Place wreaths of roses about my neck. Let

197

Falernian wines flow freely. Drench
My hair with saffron of Cilicia. And, O Muse, inspire
Your imbibing poets! (You, Bacchus, are ever a stimulus
To Apollo whom you love).

One will tell of conquered Sygambri, in their marshes;
Another, of Ethiopian Meroe, and sunless kingdoms—
Not forgetting the late Parthian treaty, defeat's confession:
'Let him return Remus' standards. Soon he'll give his own.
Or, should Augustus spare something of the East from conquest,
Let him reserve this trophy for his sons.
Rejoice, Crassus, if, in black sands, you can rejoice:
By way of the Euphrates one can now reach your grave.'

And so, with libation bowl, and song, night will pass:
Until daylight tosses its beans into my wine glass.

Propertius 4. 6
tr. F. Fletcher in L. R. Lind (ed.) *Latin Poetry in Verse Translation*
(Boston 1892, repr. 1957)

E11 The Mausoleum of Augustus

Augustus completed the Mausoleum by 28 BC. There are inscriptions for Marcellus,
Octavia, Tiberius (now lost), and Agrippa, but Augustus' own niche is empty and
no inscription has been discovered. The two Julias had been forbidden a place in
the family tomb; cf. Suetonius Augustus 100–101 (B53); Consolation to Livia (B62).

Marcellus son of Gaius	Octavia daughter of Gaius
son-in-law	sister
of Augustus Caesar	of Augustus Caesar

L'Année épigraphique 1928 no. 2
tr. K. Chisholm

E12 The Pantheon

Agrippa began his programme of embellishing Rome after 27 BC. The Pantheon
was finished in 25 BC, but the present building dates from Hadrian. Agrippa's
Pantheon was destroyed by fire in AD 80. It is not certain that the domed roof
mentioned by Dio was similar in conception to the rotunda and dome of the later
building.

(a)

Also he [Agrippa] completed the building called the Pantheon. It has this name perhaps because it received among the images which decorated it the statues of many gods, including Mars and Venus; but my own opinion of the name is that, because of its vaulted roof, it resembles the heavens. Agrippa, for his part, wished to place a statue of Augustus there also and to bestow upon him the honour of having the structure named after him; but when the emperor would not accept either honour, he placed in the temple itself a statue of the former Caesar and in the ante-room statues of Augustus and himself.

Dio Cassius 53. 27. 2–3
tr. E. Cary (Loeb 1917)

(b)

The Pantheon of Agrippa was embellished by Diogenes of Athens: his Caryatids, among the columns of the Temple, are works of the highest quality: so too are the other groups on the gable, though less well-known owing to their lofty position.

Pliny *Natural History* 36. 38
tr. Dudley *Urbs Roma*

(c)

The capitals on the columns in the Pantheon built by Marcus Agrippa are of Syracusan bronze.

Pliny *Natural History* 34. 13

(d)   *The inscription over the entrance of the Pantheon reads:*

Marcus Agrippa son of Lucius built this in his third consulship.

E13 The Basilica Pauli

The basilica is a Roman architectural form, consisting of a rectangular roofed hall, with or without exedrae, usually associated with a forum. The Basilica Pauli was one of the buildings circling the temple of Divus Julius, and when rebuilt had a long portico ending in a chapel dedicated to Gaius and Lucius Caesar.

(a)   *These events occurred in 14 BC.*

The next year . . . the Basilica Pauli caught fire. The flames spread to the Temple of Vesta, and the sacred objects were carried out to the Palatine by the Vestal Virgins (all except the eldest who was blind), and were placed in the house of the priest of

199

Jupiter. The Basilica was rebuilt, under the name of Aemilius, as being in the family of the original builder, but in fact the costs were met by Augustus and the friends of Paulus.

Dio Cassius 54. 24
tr. Dudley *Urbs Roma*

(b) *The superb columns from Phrygia mentioned by Pliny (see E3) may have been part of this redecoration in AD 22.*

At this time M. Lepidus came forward to ask the Senate to allow him to decorate the Basilica Pauli, a monument of the house of the Aemilii, at his own expense. The custom of public munificence was still maintained: Augustus had not forbidden a Taurus, a Philippus, and a Balbus from using the spoils of war or their overflowing wealth to the embellishment of the city and the glory of posterity. On these precedents Lepidus, though a man of moderate wealth, restored the noble memorial of his family.

Tacitus *Annals* 3. 72
tr. Dudley *Urbs Roma*

E14 The Ara Pacis of Augustus

The Ara Pacis, or Altar of Peace, has been called the supreme example of Augustan art. It was dedicated in 9 BC, but was set up in honour of Augustus' return from Spain and Gaul in 13 BC (see RG 12; Fasti Amiterni for 4 July 13 BC). There was a decorated precinct wall around the altar; the two long sides showed scenes from the procession (perhaps from the thanksgiving ceremony of 13 BC) of the Senate, the people of Rome, the magistrates, and the family of Augustus. On the two short sides are four panels with mythological themes.

> My song has led me to the Altar of Peace
>   one day from the month's end.
> Peace, be present with the wreath of Actium on your head
>   and stay in kindness through the world.
> Let there be no reason for a triumph—and no enemies:
>   you will bring more glory than war!
> Let the soldier carry arms only to repress arms.
>   Let the trumpet sound only for ceremony.
> Let the ends of the earth stand in awe of the men of Rome:
>   if not fear, let there be love.

Priests, add incense to the flames of Peace,
    strike down the white victim.
May the house which guarantees peace, in peace last for ever—
    be that your prayer to the gods who love piety.

Ovid *Fasti* 1. 709-22
tr. J. Ferguson

E15 The Lupercal

The Lupercal was the site of the sacred cave on the Palatine where the she-wolf had suckled Romulus and Remus (Dionysius of Halicarnassus Roman Antiquities *I. 79. 7-8). Augustus rebuilt the precinct there (RG 19). Among the statues was one dedicated to Drusus, his step-son, brother of Tiberius.*

Also by decree of the equestrian order a statue of Drusus Caesar should be placed in the Lupercal amongst the others, in order that the incredible sorrow of the people be made manifest, that his features be remembered, that the greatest and most numerous honours be paid him, and that his memory be preserved.

CIL 6. 912
tr. K. Chisholm

E16 The Volcanal

Volcanus, or Vulcan, the god of fire, had a precinct and altar at the western end of the Forum Romanum. Augustus dedicated an altar to him in 9 BC; the absence to which he refers was perhaps his stay in Ticinum.

Imperator Caesar Augustus, son of the divine Julius, *pontifex maximus*, acclaimed *imperator* thirteen times, consul eleven times, in the 15th year of his tribunician power, (dedicated this) to Volcanus from the contributions made to him in his absence at the beginning of the year, in which Nero Claudius Drusus and Titus Quinctius Crispinus were consuls.

CIL 6. 457
tr. K. Chisholm

E17 The closing of the temple of Janus

Orosius records the closing and opening of the temple of Janus. His dates must be wrong, and governed by his placing Christ's birth in 2 BC. We know the closure was decreed in 11 BC (Dio Cassius 54. 36. 2) but postponed, presumably to 8 or 7 BC; the reopening must be 1 BC when Gaius Caesar set out for war in the east. Augustus would by then be technically a senex, *having reached sixty.*

(a)
So in the 752nd year after the foundation of Rome Caesar Augustus, having settled all the nations from east to west and south to north within the whole circle of Ocean in a single peace, shut the gates of Janus in person for the third time. Rustiness was actual evidence that they remained closed for about twelve years while peace reigned, and were opened only in Augustus' extreme old age through rebellion at Athens and trouble in Dacia.

(b)
Then, to speak in the words of Cornelius Tacitus 'in Augustus' old age the temple of Janus was opened, while new peoples were being harried at the very ends of the earth, often for profit, and sometimes with loss, and this lasted till the reign of Vespasian.'

Orosius 6. 22. 1; 7. 3. 7
tr. J. Ferguson

(c)   *Written after 27 BC (title of Augustus) and before 23 (further closure)*

When [Numa] had thus become king over a new city founded by virtue of armed force, he prepared to give the city a new foundation based on just laws and practices. As he saw that people could not become accustomed to these foundations while still at war, because warfare turns their natures ferocious, he reckoned that his savage people should be tamed by desisting from war, so he built the temple of Janus at the bottom of the Argilentum as a witness to peace and war, so that when open it indicated a state of war, when closed that all the surrounding people were at peace. It has been closed twice since Numa's reign; the first time when Titus Manlius was consul, after the end of the First Punic war; the second time, granted by heaven for our own age to witness, was when the Emperor Caesar Augustus after the battle of Actium had established peace on land and sea.

Livy 1. 19. 1–3
tr. K. Chisholm and J. Ferguson

E18 The house of Augustus on the Palatine

Augustus lived simply, in a house, not a palace (see also RG 35; Suetonius Augustus 57).

(a)

After his victory Octavian returned to Rome, and announced that he meant to reserve for public use several houses which he had purchased through agents, to allow for more space round his own dwelling. He also promised to build a Temple of Apollo with a colonnade surrounding it, a work which he carried out with princely generosity.

Velleius Paterculus 2. 81. 3
tr. Dudley *Urbs Roma*

(b)

> Phoebus has one part, another is given to Vesta.
>   Augustus himself holds the third, left over by the gods.
> Stand firm laurel of the Palatine, stand firm
>   house wreathed with oak. Three eternal gods live in one house.

Ovid *Fasti* 4. 951-4
tr. K. Chisholm

(c)

Augustus lived first close to the Roman Forum, at the top of the Scalae Anulariae, in a house which had once belonged to the orator Calvus. Later he lived on the Palatine, but even so, in a modest house which had been that of Hortensius. It was not particularly large or elaborate: there were short colonnades, with columns of Alban stone, no marble, nor any elaborate floor mosaics. For more than forty years he used the same bedroom, winter and summer, although he found the winter climate of Rome particularly trying, and although he persistently spent the winter in the city. If he had some particularly secret business on hand, and needed to be free from interruption, there was a private study at the top of the house, which he used to call 'Syracuse' or 'the workshop': there he would go, or also to the suburban villa of one of his freedmen. When he was ill, he would take to bed in the house of Maecenas. His simple taste in fittings and furniture is apparent in the couches and tables that are still preserved, most of which hardly reach the standard of elegance to be expected from a private person.

Suetonius *Augustus* 72. 1-2
tr. Dudley *Urbs Roma*

E19 Livia as builder

(a)

> Where am I going? Augustus can claim that theme.
> > Now for the Great Goddess.
> There is a natural outcrop; hence the name 'the Rock'.
> > It takes up most of the hill.
> Here Remus watched in vain, while the Palatine birds
> > gave his brother the first omens.
> Here the Senators founded a temple, which the eyes of men may not see,
> > on a gentle slope.
> It was dedicated by one who bore the ancient name of the Clausi,
> > a virgin.
> Livia restored it, to imitate her husband
> > and follow him in all things.

(b)

> Livia dedicated a magnificent temple to Concord,
> > and gave it to her husband,
> generations to come must learn that on the site of Livia's columns
> > was once a huge palace,
> comparable to a city, fully as large
> > as many towns.
> It was razed, not for high treason.
> > Its extravagance was dangerous.
> Caesar undertook the overthrow of that vastness
> > and the loss of his inheritance.
> The act of a censor, an example to others,
> > the judge obeying his own laws.

Ovid *Fasti* 5. 147–59; 6. 637–49

tr. J. Ferguson

E20 Dedication and display of paintings

(a) *Nikias and Philochares were Greek painters of the fourth century BC.*

But it was the dictator Caesar who most enhanced the reputation of painting by dedicating pictures of Ajax and Medea in front of the Temple of Venus Genetrix. After him it was Marcus Agrippa, a man whose taste tended toward rustic simplicity rather than refined elegance. There exists, in any case, a magnificent oration by Agrippa, worthy of the greatest of citizens, on the subject of making all statues and painting public property, which would have been a more satisfactory solution than banishing them as exiles to country villas. Nevertheless, the same grim personage bought two pictures, an Ajax and a Venus (Aphrodite) from the people of Kyzikos for 1,200,000 (sesterces). Moreover, he had small painted panels worked into the marble in even the hottest part of his baths; these were removed a short time ago, when they were being restored.

The Divine Augustus surpassed all others when he placed two paintings in the most frequently visited part of his forum; depicted in one of these was the 'Visage of War' and also 'Triumph,' while the other represented the Castors and Victory. He also placed (two) pictures, which we shall discuss in connection with the names of their artists, in the temple of his father Caesar. Furthermore, he had imbedded into the wall in the Curia, which he consecrated in the Comitium, a Nemea seated on a lion and carrying a palm branch, by whom stands an old man with a staff, over whose head hangs a picture of a two-horse chariot—a picture on which Nikias wrote that he did it in the encaustic technique; such was the expression used by Nikias. The admirable point about the other picture is the way in which it shows the resemblance between an aged father and his grown-up son without obscuring the difference in their ages. Philochares has provided evidence to show that this work is by him; and if one were to reckon the effect of this painting alone, it would be proof of the immense power of this art, since thanks to Philochares the Senate of the Roman people has gazed upon Glaukion and his son Aristippos, who would otherwise be unknown, for so many centuries.

Pliny *Natural History* 35. 26-8
tr. Pollitt *The Art of Rome*

(b) *Evidence for the existence of a trade in copies of Greek 'Old Master' paintings*

Finally he [Pausias, a 4th-cent.-BC artist] painted a portrait of the woman herself [Glycera, a maker of chaplets of flowers], seated and wearing a wreath, which is one of the very finest of pictures. . . . A copy (in Greek *apographon*) of this picture was bought by Lucius Lucullus [1st-cent.-BC] at Athens for two talents; <it had been made by> Dionysius at Athens.

Pliny *Natural History* 35. 125
tr. H. Rackham (Loeb 1952)

E21 Wall paintings

(a) *The* praenomen *of Tadius is uncertain. It may be Spurius, Studius, or Ludius.*

Nor must Spurius Tadius also, of the period of his late lamented Majesty Augustus, be cheated of his due, who first introduced the most attractive fashion of painting walls with pictures of country houses and porticoes and landscape gardens, groves, woods, hills, fish-ponds, canals, rivers, coasts, and whatever anybody could desire, together with various sketches of people going for a stroll or sailing in a boat or on land going to country houses riding on asses or in carriages, and also people fishing and fowling or hunting or even gathering the vintage. His works include splendid villas approached by roads across marshes, men tottering and staggering along carrying women on their shoulders for a (*wager*), and a number of humorous drawings of that sort besides, extremely wittily designed. He also introduced using pictures of seaside cities to decorate uncovered terraces, giving a most pleasing effect and at a very small expense.

(b) *Early Italian and Etruscan paintings still visible in the first century AD*

For the art of painting had already been brought to perfection even in Italy. At all events there survive even today in the temples at Ardea paintings that are older than the city of Rome, which to me at all events are incomparably remarkable, surviving for so long a period as though freshly painted, although unprotected by a roof. Similarly at Lanuvium, where there are an Atalanta and a Helena close together, nude figures, painted by the same artist, each of outstanding beauty (the former shown as a virgin), and not damaged even by the collapse of the temple. The Emperor Gaius from lustful motives attempted to remove them, but the consistency of plaster would not allow this to be done. There are pictures surviving at Caere that are even older.

(c) *Wall paintings considered inferior to easel-pictures*

But among artists great fame has been confined to the painters of pictures only [i.e. panel- or easel-pictures], a fact which shows the wisdom of early times to be the more worthy of respect, for they did not decorate walls, merely for owners of property, or houses, which would remain in one place and which could not be rescued in a fire. Protogenes was content with a cottage in his little garden; Apelles had no wall-frescoes in his house; it was not yet the fashion to colour the whole of the walls. With all these artists their art was on the alert for the benefit of cities, and a painter was the common property of the world.

Pliny *Natural History* 35. 116–17; 35. 17–18; 35. 118
tr. H. Rackham (Loeb 1952)

E22 Sculpture

(a) *Pliny has frequent references to Greek statues displayed in Rome (see also K9). Scopas, Praxiteles, and Lysippus were the most famous sculptors of the fourth century BC.*

Equally there is doubt as to whether the Dying Children of Niobe in the temple of the Sosian Apollo was the work of Scopas or of Praxiteles. Similarly, we cannot tell which of the two carved the Father Janus [probably a Hermes] which was dedicated in its rightful temple by Augustus after being brought here from Egypt; and now a covering of gilt has hidden its secret still more.

Pliny *Natural History* 36. 28
tr. D. Eichholz (Loeb 1962)

(b)
... And near the Portico of Octavia there is a statue of Apollo by Philiskos of Rhodes, which stands in his (Apollo's) own shrine, and also a Latona (Leto), a Diana (Artemis), the nine Muses, and another statue of Apollo ... The Pan and Olympos wrestling, which is in the same building and is the second best known symplegma in the world, is by Heliodoros ... The standing Venus is by Polycharmos. It is apparent from the honour given to it that the work of Lysias, which the Divine Augustus dedicated in honour of his father Octavius in an aedicula adorned with columns upon the arch on the Palatine, was held in great esteem. This work consisted of a four-horse chariot group and an Apollo and a Diana (Artemis), all carved from one piece of stone.

Pliny *Natural History* 36. 35-6
tr. Pollitt *The Art of Rome*

(c)
... the sons of Archermus, Bupalus and Athenis... At Rome there are statues by them on the angles of the pediments of the temple of Apollo on the Palatine and on almost all the buildings for which the emperor Augustus... was responsible.

Pliny *Natural History* 36. 13
tr. D. Eichholz (Loeb 1962)

(d)
The sanctuary (at Lugdunum [now Lyon]) which was dedicated to Augustus Caesar by a league of all the Gauls was built before the city at the junction of the two rivers. There is a notable altar with an inscription naming the tribes, which are sixty in number, and also images of these, one for each tribe, as well as another large statue.

Strabo 4. 192
tr. Pollitt *The Art of Rome*

(e)
We have often seen statues of Augustus in solid obsidian, since this stone comes in

sufficiently large pieces for this purpose; Augustus also dedicated as a sort of marvel four obsidian elephants in the temple of Concord.

Pliny *Natural History* 36. 196
tr. Pollitt *The Art of Rome*

E23 Statue of Marsyas

This statue was a notorious place for assignations.

P. Munatius took a chaplet of flowers from the statue of Marsyas, and put it on his head. The triumvirs ordered him to be put in chains for this offence: an appeal to the tribunes brought no intervention . . . the only other example of licence is that of Julia, daughter of the late Emperor Augustus; a letter from him complains that in her night revels she had crowned the statue of Marsyas with a chaplet . . .

Pliny *Natural History*
tr. Dudley *Urbs Roma*

E24 Portraiture

The art of portraiture was highly developed by the Romans. Originally influenced by Italo-Etruscan funerary portraiture and perhaps developed as some form of ancestor-worship, family portraits retained a role of social importance even in Imperial times. Important families displayed portraits of wax or sometimes of more durable material at funeral processions, and these were kept, in some cases permanently on show, in the entrance-halls of their houses. Following this tradition, much Roman portrait-sculpture (especially in the late Republic) was uniquely realistic, and true to the smallest detail of the physical appearance of the individual portrayed. The influence of earlier Greek, and especially Hellenistic, sculpture can also be seen in a more consciously artistic and sometimes more emotional style. With the need for recognizable portraits of the Princeps and his family came a type of sculpted portrait which, though still individualized, was more idealizing in character.

(a)   *Modern habits unfavourably compared with those of earlier times*

The painting of portraits, used to transmit through the ages extremely correct likenesses of persons, has entirely gone out. Bronze shields are now set up as monuments with a design in silver, with a dim outline of men's figures; heads of statues are exchanged for others, about which before now actually sarcastic epigrams have been current: so universally is a display of material preferred to a recognizable likeness of one's own self. And in the midst of all this, people tapestry the walls of their picture-galleries with old pictures, and they prize likenesses of strangers, while as for themselves they imagine that the honour only consists in the price, for their heir to break up the statue and haul it out of the house with a noose. Consequently nobody's likeness lives and they leave behind them portraits that represent their money, not themselves. ..... In the halls of our ancestors it was otherwise; portraits were the objects displayed to be looked at, not statues by foreign artists, nor bronzes nor marbles, but wax models of faces were set out each on a separate sideboard, to furnish likenesses to be carried in procession at a funeral in the clan, and always when some member of it passed away the entire company of his house that had ever existed was present.

(b) *Portrait shields*

But the first person to institute the custom of privately dedicating the shields with portraits in a temple or public place, I find, was Appius Claudius, the consul with Publius Servilius in the 259th year of the city [495 BC]. .... After him Marcus Aemilius, Quintus Lutatius' colleague in the consulship [78 BC], set up portrait shields not only in the Basilica Aemilia but also in his own home. ...

Pliny *Natural History* 35. 4–6; 12–13
tr. H. Rackham (Loeb 1952)

(c) *Portrait statues were set up in many different kinds of places and for many purposes.*

The road [the Via Flaminia] was finished just at this time [27 BC], and for that reason statues to Augustus were made for the arches of the bridge over the Tiber and also at Ariminum [Rimini—where the road ended].

Dio Cassius 53. 22. 2
tr. Pollitt *The Art of Rome*

(d) *Funeral of Drusus, son of Tiberius, in AD 23*

Tacitus (Annals 3.5) also describes the bier of Nero Drusus, brother of Tiberius, surrounded by portrait busts of the Claudii and Julii, at his funeral conducted by Augustus in 9 BC.

The funeral ceremony with the procession of portrait busts was extremely impressive, since Aeneas, the founder of the Julian family, all the Alban kings, Romulus the founder of Rome, and after them the Sabine nobles, Attus Clausus, and portrait busts of all the other Claudii were exhibited in a long procession.

Tacitus *Annals* 4. 9
tr. Pollitt *The Art of Rome*

(e) *Greek and Roman statue-types*

In old days the statues dedicated were simply clad in the toga. Also naked figures holding spears, made from models of Greek young men from the gymnasiums—what are called figures of Achilles—became popular. The Greek practice is to leave the figure entirely nude, whereas Roman and military statuary adds a breastplate: indeed the dictator Caesar gave permission for a statue wearing a cuirass to be erected in his honour in his Forum.

Pliny *Natural History* 34. 18
tr. H. Rackham (Loeb 1952)

E25 Mosaic

Mosaic floors had already begun during the time of Sulla; at least there exists today a floor made of tiny inlaid pieces which he had made for the sanctuary of Fortuna at Praeneste. Afterward these pavements were driven from the floor to vaulted ceilings and began to be made of glass. This too is a rather recent invention. At any rate Agrippa, in the baths which he built at Rome, painted the terracotta work in the hot-rooms in encaustic and decorated the remaining parts with white paint; no doubt he would have made vaulted ceilings inlaid with glass if this technique had already been invented or if it had been adapted from the walls of the stage of Scaurus' theater, which I have mentioned, for use on ceilings.

Pliny *Natural History* 36. 189
tr. Pollitt *The Art of Rome*

E26 Gem-collecting

The first person at Rome to collect a great many gems—the sort of collection which they refer to by the foreign name dactyliotheca—was Sulla's stepson Scaurus. There was for a long time no other until Pompey the Great dedicated among his offerings on the Capitoline those which had belonged to King Mithridates; his collection, as Varro and other authors of that era confirm, was much inferior to that of Scaurus. His example was followed by the dictator Caesar, who consecrated six dactyliothecas in the temple of Venus Genetrix, and by Marcellus (42-23 B.C.), the son of Octavia (and nephew of Augustus), who consecrated one in the temple of Apollo on the Palatine.

Pliny *Natural History* 37. 11
tr. Pollitt *The Art of Rome*

E27 A collector

Gaius Asinius Pollio (76 BC–AD 5), friend of Augustus, was politician, poet, historian, and critic.

Asinius Pollio, being a man of great enthusiasm, naturally wanted his art collection to be seen. In it are Centaurs carrying Nymphs by Arkesilaos, Thespiades (Helikonian Muses) by Kleomenes, Oceanus and Jupiter by Heniochos, Appiades by Stephanos, the Hermerotes by Tauriskos (not the engraver, but rather an artist from Tralles) a Jupiter Hospitalis by Papylos, the pupil of Praxiteles, and a Zethos and Amphion along with Dirke, the bull and the rope—a work by Apollonios and Tauriskos which was brought from Rhodes. . . . In the same place there is a praiseworthy Liber Pater by Eutychides.

Pliny *Natural History* 36. 33
tr. Pollitt *The Art of Rome*

E28 An art gallery

The following passage is from a work of fiction, and therefore cannot be taken too seriously as to detail, but there seems no good reason to doubt its evidence that 'art galleries' open to the public (perhaps like the porticoes of Livia and Octavia at Rome—see F31(b)) existed in other Italian towns. The setting is one of the old Greek colonies on the Bay of Naples; so it looks as if the Campanian wall-painters would have had reasonably easy access to Greek 'Old Masters' if they had wished to study them.

'I went into an art-gallery, which had a wonderful variety of paintings. For instance, I even saw work by Zeuxis still unaffected by the ravages of time. And I examined, not without a certain thrill, some sketches by Protogenes, so life-like they were a challenge to nature herself. I practically worshipped that masterpiece of Apelles that the Greeks call The Goddess on One Knee.'

Petronius, *Satyricon* 83
tr. J. P. Sullivan (Penguin 1965)

E29 Augustus' seal

(a)
After him (Pyrgoteles, the gem carver of Alexander the Great) in renown were

211

Apollonides and Kronios and the man who cut with the utmost exactness that portrait of the divine Augustus which later emperors use as a seal—namely Dioskourides.

(b)

The divine Augustus at the beginning of his career used a seal engraved with a sphinx. He had found among his mother's rings two which were remarkably similar. During the civil war whenever he himself was absent his friends used one of these as a seal on letters and edicts which the conditions of the times made it necessary to issue; and it was a standing wry joke among those who received them to say that the sphinx had come bearing its riddles. And naturally the seal of Maecenas engraved with a frog was an object which caused great terror because it signified that a contribution of money would be demanded.

Pliny *Natural History* 37. 8; 31. 10
tr. Pollitt *The Art of Rome*

(c)

On letters of recommendation, documents, and personal letters he at first used a sphinx as his seal design, later a portrait of Alexander the Great, and finally his own portrait cut by the hand of Dioskourides; the last of these continued to be used by the succeeding emperors.

Suetonius *Augustus* 50
tr. Pollitt *The Art of Rome*

F AUGUSTAN POETRY

The age of Augustus was a period of almost unparalleled brilliance of literary creativity–in both prose and verse. The work of the poets Virgil (F1-6), Horace (F7-27), and Ovid (F28-43) stands out even from such a background. It is great literature in its own right, transcending the poets' own time and environment. While remaining within the literary conventions of the period, which were deeply rooted in Greek and Hellenistic literature, these three poets each possess a strong individual voice, using different forms and varied themes. The Augustan poets were also closely involved in the political events of their time. Virgil would have lost his estates after the civil wars if Augustus had not intervened. Horace, having served under Brutus at Philippi, was reconciled to Octavian and later became a 'poet laureate' of the Princeps. Ovid was exiled by Augustus for a mysterious offence which has never been clarified, but may well have been political in nature. The poems in this section therefore reflect the ideas and ideals of the Augustan Age, and to a certain extent, helped shape them. Literary success depended on the right patronage and Augustus himself was patron to Virgil and Horace. This does not mean that they wrote, to order, the propaganda of a new regime, but that, caught up in the historical events of the civil war and the establishment of the Principate, their poems reflect the hopes of a new 'Golden Age' of peace and prosperity.

F1 The *Life* of Virgil

A number of Lives *of Virgil were written in antiquity, of which the best known, most extensive, and most reliable is that found in the introduction to a commentary on Virgil's* Bucolics *(*Eclogues*) and* Georgics *by the fourth-century-AD grammarian Aelius Donatus. It is very probably taken from a work by Suetonius,* On Famous Men, *which dealt with a number of poets, including Horace (see F7). As the secretary (*ab epistulis*) to the Emperor Hadrian (AD 117–38), Suetonius would have had access to Augustus' private correspondence and other evidence.*

1   Publius Vergilius Maro, a native of Mantua, had parents of humble origin, especially his father, who according to some was a potter, although the general opinion is that he was at first the hired man of a certain Magus, an attendant on the magistrates, later became his son-in-law because of his diligence, and greatly increased his little property by buying up woodlands and raising bees.   2   He was born in the first consulship of Gnaeus Pompeius the Great and Marcus Licinius Crassus, on the Ides of October, in a district called Andes, not far distant from Mantua.   3   While

he was in his mother's womb, she dreamt that she gave birth to a laurel-branch, which on touching the earth took root and grew at once to the size of a full-grown tree, covered with fruits and flowers of various kinds; and on the following day, when she was on the way to a neighbouring part of the country with her husband, she turned aside and gave birth to her child in a ditch beside the road. 4 They say that the infant did not cry at its birth, and had such a gentle expression as even then to give assurance of an unusually happy destiny. 5 There was added another omen; for a poplar branch, which, as was usual in that region on such occasions, was at once planted where the birth occurred, grew so fast in a short time that it equalled in size poplars planted long before. It was called from him 'Vergil's tree' and was besides worshipped with great veneration by pregnant and newly delivered women, who made and paid vows beneath it.

6 Vergil spent his early life at Cremona until he assumed the gown of manhood, upon his fifteenth birthday, in the consulship of the same two men who had been consuls the year he was born; and it chanced that the poet Lucretius died that very same day. 7 Vergil, however, moved from Cremona to Mediolanum, and shortly afterwards from there to Rome. 8 He was tall and of full habit, with a dark complexion and a rustic appearance. His health was variable; for he very often suffered from stomach and throat troubles, as well as with headache; and he also had frequent haemorrhages. 9 He ate and drank but little. He was especially given to passions for boys, and his special favourites were Cebes and Alexander, whom he calls Alexis in the second poem of his 'Bucolics.' This boy was given him by Asinius Pollio, and both his favourites had some education, while Cebes was even a poet. It is common report that he also had an intrigue with Plotia Hieria. 10 But Asconius Pedianus declares that she herself used to say afterwards, when she was getting old that Vergil was invited by Varius to associate with her, but obstinately refused. 11 Certain it is that for the rest of his life he was so modest in speech and thought, that at Naples he was commonly called 'Parthenias,' and that whenever he appeared in public in Rome, where he very rarely went, he would take refuge in the nearest house, to avoid those who followed and pointed him out. 12 Moreover, when Augustus offered him the property of a man who had been exiled, he could not make up his mind to accept it. 13 He possessed nearly ten million sesterces from the generous gifts of friends, and he had a house at Rome on the Esquiline, near the gardens of Maecenas, although he usually lived in retirement in Campania and in Sicily.

14 He was already grown up when he lost his parents of whom his father previously went blind, and two own brothers: Silo, who died in childhood, and Flaccus, who lived to grow up, and whose death he laments under the name of Daphnis.

15 Among other studies he gave attention also to medicine and in particular to mathematics. 16 He pleaded one single case in court too, but no more; for, as Melissus has told us, he spoke very slowly and almost like an uneducated man.

17 He made his first attempt at poetry when he was still a boy . . .

19 Presently he began to write of Roman history, but thinking himself unequal

to the subject, turned to the Bucolics, especially in order to sing the praises of Asinius Pollio, Alfenus Varus, and Cornelius Gallus, because at the time of the assignment of the lands beyond the Po, which were divided among the veterans by order of the triumvirs after the victory at Philippi, these men had saved him from ruin.   20 Then he wrote the Georgics in honour of Maecenas, because he had rendered him aid, when the poet was still but little known, against the violence of one of the veterans, from whom Vergil narrowly escaped death in a quarrel about his farm.   21 Last of all he began the Aeneid, a varied and complicated theme, and as it were a mirror of both the poems of Homer; moreover it treated Greek and Latin personages and affairs in common, and contained at the same time an account of the origin of the city of Rome and of Augustus, which was the poet's special aim.

22   When he was writing the Georgics, it is said to have been his custom to dictate each day a large number of verses which he had composed in the morning, and then to spend the rest of the day in reducing them to a very small number, wittily remarking that he fashioned his poem after the manner of a she-bear, and gradually licked it into shape.   23 In the case of the Aeneid, after writing a first draft in prose and dividing it into twelve books, he proceeded to turn into verse one part after another, taking them up just as he fancied, in no particular order.   24 And that he might not check the flow of his thought, he left some things unfinished, and, so to speak, bolstered others up with very slight words, which, as he jocosely used to say, were put in like props, to support the structure until the solid columns should arrive.

25   The Bucolics he finished in three years, the Georgics in seven, the Aeneid in twelve.   26 The success of the Bucolics on their first appearance was such, that they were even frequently rendered by singers on the stage.   27 When Augustus was returning after his victory at Actium and lingered at Atella to treat his throat, Vergil read the Georgics to him for four days in succession, Maecenas taking his turn at the reading whenever the poet was interrupted by the failure of his voice. 28 His own delivery, however, was sweet and wonderfully effective.   29 In fact, Seneca has said that the poet Julius Montanus used to declare that he would have purloined some of Vergil's work, if he could also have stolen his voice, expression, and dramatic power; for the same verses sounded well when Vergil read them, which on another's lips were flat and toneless.   30 Hardly was the Aeneid begun, when its repute became so great that Sextus Propertius did not hesitate to declare:

> 'Yield, ye Roman writers; yield, ye Greeks;
> A greater than the Iliad is born.'

31   Augustus indeed (for it chanced that he was away on his Cantabrian campaign) demanded in entreating and even jocosely threatening letters that Vergil send him 'something from the "Aeneid"'; to use his own words, 'either the first draft of the poem or any section of it that he pleased.'   32 But it was not until long afterwards, when the material was at last in shape, that Vergil read to him three books in all, the second, fourth, and sixth. The last of these produced a remarkable effect on Octavia, who was present at the reading; for it is said that when he reached the

215

verses about her son, 'Thou shalt be Marcellus,' she fainted and was with difficulty revived. 33 He gave readings also to various others, but never before a large company, selecting for the most part passages about which he was in doubt, in order to get the benefit of criticism. 34 They say that Eros, his amanuensis and freedman, used to report, when he was an old man, that Vergil once completed two half-verses off-hand in the course of a reading. For having before him merely the words 'Misenum Aeoliden,' he added 'quo non praestantior alter,' and again to 'aere ciere viros' he joined 'Martemque accendere cantu,' thrown off with like inspiration, and he immediately ordered Eros to add both half-lines to his manuscript.

35 In the fifty-second year of his age, wishing to give the final touch to the Aeneid, he determined to go away to Greece and Asia, and after devoting three entire years to the sole work of improving his poem, to give up the rest of his life wholly to philosophy. But having begun his journey, and at Athens meeting Augustus, who was on his way back to Rome from the Orient, he resolved not to part from the emperor and even to return with him; but in the course of a visit to the neighbouring town of Megara in a very hot sun, he was taken with a fever, and added to his disorder by continuing his journey; hence on his arrival at Brundisium he was considerably worse, and died there on the eleventh day before the Kalends of October, in the consulship of Gnaeus Sentius and Quintus Lucretius. 36 His ashes were taken to Naples and laid to rest on the via Puteolana less than two miles from the city, in a tomb for which he himself composed this couplet:

> 'Mantua gave me the light, Calabria slew me; now holds me
> Parthenope. I have sung shepherds, the country, and wars.'

37 He named as heirs Valerius Proculus, his half-brother, to one-half of his estate, Augustus to one-fourth, Maecenas to one-twelfth; the rest he left to Lucius Varius and Plotius Tucca, who revised the 'Aeneid' after his death by order of Augustus. 38 With regard to this matter we have the following verses of Sulpicius of Carthage:

> 'Vergil had bidden these songs by swift flame be turned into ashes,
> Songs which sang of thy fates, Phrygia's leader renowned.
> Varius and Tucca forbade, and thou, too, greatest of Caesars,
> Adding your veto to theirs, Latium's story preserved.
> All but twice in the flames unhappy Pergamum perished
> Troy on a second pyre narrowly failed of her doom.'

39 He had arranged with Varius, before leaving Italy, that if anything befell him his friend should burn the 'Aeneid'; but Varius had emphatically declared that he would do no such thing. 40 Therefore in his mortal illness Vergil constantly called for his book-boxes, intending to burn the poem himself; but when no one brought them to him, he made no specific request about the matter, but left his writings jointly to the above mentioned Varius and to Tucca, with the stipulation that they should publish nothing which he himself would not have given to the world. 41 However, Varius published the 'Aeneid' at Augustus' request, making

only a few slight corrections, and even leaving the incomplete lines just as they were. These last many afterwards tried to finish, but failed owing to the difficulty that nearly all the half-lines in Vergil are complete in sense and meaning, the sole exception being 'Quem tibi iam Troia.' . . .

[Suetonius] *Life of Virgil* (abridged)
tr. J. C. Rolfe (Loeb 1914)

F2 The *Messianic Eclogue*

This poem is nicknamed the 'Messianic Eclogue' from the likeness of prophecies of the coming of a child to the foretelling of the birth of Christ in the Old Testament Book of Isaiah. The identity of the child has been, and still is, an endless subject of dispute (see R. Coleman (ed.) Eclogues (Cambridge 1977) pp. 150–4). It may be symbolic. The poem is addressed to Pollio during his consulship of 40 BC, and may draw some of its inspiration from the treaty of Brundisium (see B18) between Antony and Octavian, negotiated by Pollio and Maecenas, which seemed to offer lasting peace. For Eclogue 1 see B50.

    Sicilian Muse, I would try now a somewhat grander theme.
Shrubberies or meek tamarisks are not for all: but if it's
Forests I sing, may the forests be worthy of a consul.
      Ours is the crowning era foretold in prophecy:
Born of Time, a great new cycle of centuries
Begins. Justice returns to earth, the Golden Age
Returns, and its first-born comes down from heaven above.
Look kindly, chaste Lucina, upon this infant's birth,
For with him shall hearts of iron cease, and hearts of gold
Inherit the whole earth—yes, Apollo reigns now.   10
And it's while you are consul—you, Pollio—that this glorious
Age shall dawn, the march of its great months begin.
You at our head, mankind shall be freed from its age-long fear,
All stains of our past wickedness being cleansed away.
This child shall enter into the life of the gods, behold them
Walking with antique heroes, and himself be seen of them,
And rule a world made peaceful by his father's virtuous acts.
      Child, your first birthday presents will come from nature's wild—
Small presents: earth will shower you with romping ivy, foxgloves,
Bouquets of gipsy lilies and sweetly-smiling acanthus.   20
Goats shall walk home, their udders taut with milk, and nobody
Herding them: the ox will have no fear of the lion:

217

Silk-soft blossom will grow from your very cradle to lap you.
But snakes will die, and so will fair-seeming, poisonous plants.
Everywhere the commons will breathe of spice and incense.
    But when you are old enough to read about famous men
And your father's deeds, to comprehend what manhood means,
Then a slow flush of tender gold shall mantle the great plains,
Then shall grapes hang wild and reddening on thorn-trees,
And honey sweat like dew from the hard bark of oaks.   30
Yet there'll be lingering traces of our primal error,
Prompting us to dare the seas in ships, to girdle
Our cities round with walls and break the soil with ploughshares.
A second Argo will carry her crew of chosen heroes,
A second Tiphys steer her. And wars—yes, even wars
There'll be; and great Achilles must sail for Troy again.
    Later, when the years have confirmed you in full manhood,
Traders will retire from the sea, from the pine-built vessels
They used for commerce: every land will be self-supporting.
The soil will need no harrowing, the vine no pruning-knife;   40
And the tough ploughman may at last unyoke his oxen.
We shall stop treating wool with artificial dyes,
For the ram himself in his pasture will change his fleece's colour,
Now to a charming purple, now to a saffron hue,
And grazing lambs will dress themselves in coats of scarlet.
    'Run, looms, and weave this future!'—thus have the Fates spoken.
In unison with the unshakeable intent of Destiny.
    Come soon, dear child of the gods, Jupiter's great viceroy!
Come soon—the time is near—to begin your life illustrious!
Look how the round and ponderous globe bows to salute you,   50
The lands, the stretching leagues of sea, the unplumbed sky!
Look how the whole creation exults in the age to come!
    If but the closing days of a long life were prolonged
For me, and I with breath enough to tell your story,
Oh then I should not be worsted at singing by Thracian Orpheus
Or Linus—even though Linus were backed by Calliope
His mother, and Orpheus by his father, beauteous Apollo.
Should Pan compete with me, and Arcady judge us, even
Pan, great Pan, with Arcadian judges, would lose the contest.
    Begin, dear babe, and smile at your mother to show you know her—   60
This is the tenth month now, and she is sick of waiting.
Begin, dear babe. The boy who does not smile at his mother
Will never deserve to sup with a god or sleep with a goddess.

Virgil Eclogues 4
tr. C. Day Lewis (Oxford 1966)

F3 The *Georgics*

The Georgics *were begun c. 37 BC and recited to Octavian when he came home from the East in 29 BC. Composing what was ostensibly a didactic poem on farming, Virgil takes the opportunity to reveal his feelings about the countryside and its importance in the regeneration of Roman life.*

The first passage is taken from the Invocation (for the convention see H1) in which Octavian is addressed, in fulsome terms, in company with deities and spirits. The second reflects the poet's sickness of war in its destruction of human life and fruitful land, and his anxious trust in the 'young prince' who is, of course, Octavian. The final extract briefly introduces Maecenas ('my friend'), Virgil's patron; Virgil also gives us an interesting clue (lines 46-7) as to his future poetic intentions.

(a)

You too, whatever place in the courts of the Immortals
Is soon to hold you—whether an overseer of cities
And warden of earth you'll be, Caesar, so that the great world
Honour you as promoter of harvest and puissant lord
Of the seasons, garlanding your brow with your mother's myrtle:
Or whether you come as god of the boundless sea, and sailors
Worship your power alone, and the ends of the earth pay tribute,
And Tethys gives all her waves to get you for son-in-law:
Or whether you make a new sign in the Zodiac, where amid the
Slow months a gap is revealed between Virgo and Scorpio
(Already the burning Scorpion retracts his claws to leave you
More than your share of heaven):—

Virgil *Georgics* 1. 24-35
tr. C. Day Lewis (Oxford 1966)

(b)

Thus it ensued that Philippi's field saw Roman armies
Once again engaged in the shock of civil war;
And the High Ones did not think it a shame that we should twice
Enrich with our blood Emathia and the broad plains of Haemus.
   Surely the time will come when a farmer on those frontiers
Forcing through earth his curved plough
Shall find old spears eaten away with flaky rust,
Or hit upon helmets as he wields the weight of his mattock
And marvel at the heroic bones he has disinterred.
O Gods of our fathers, native Gods, Romulus, Vesta
Who mothers our Tuscan Tiber and the Roman Palatine,
At least allow our young prince to rescue this shipwrecked era!

219

Long enough now have we
Paid in our blood for the promise Laomedon broke at Troy.
Long now has the court of heaven grudged you to us, Caesar,
Complaining because you care only for mortal triumphs.
For Right and Wrong are confused here, there's so much war in the world,
Evil has so many faces, the plough so little
Honour, the labourers are taken, the fields untended,
And the curving sickle is beaten into the sword that yields not.
There the East is in arms, here Germany marches:
Neighbour cities, breaking their treaties, attack each other:
The wicked War-god runs amok through all the world.
So, when racing chariots have rushed from the starting-gate,
They gather speed on the course, and the driver tugs at the curb-rein
—His horses runaway, car out of control, quite helpless.

Virgil *Georgics* 1. 489–514
tr. C. Day Lewis (Oxford 1966)

(c)

Meanwhile let us pursue the woodland ways, the virgin
Lawns, my friend, the difficult task you have laid upon me.
Without your help, my spirit lacks high ambition. Come then,
Break up my lassitude! Loud is Cithaeron calling
And the hounds of Taÿgetus and Epidaurus tamer of horses,
And the woods all answer Yes and echo the call again.
Yet soon will I stir myself
To tell of Caesar's furious battles, to give him fame
For as many years as divide his day from the birth of Tithonus.

Virgil *Georgics* 3. 40–8
tr. C. Day Lewis (Oxford 1966)

F4 The *Aeneid*

Virgil composed his last and greatest poem during the last twelve years of his life (see F1 above § 25), and died in 19 BC leaving it lacking the final revision. Overriding what seem to have been the poet's wishes, Augustus had the poem published.

These two passages from Book 1 are both, in different ways, glimpses of the future. Prophecy and revelation constitute a valuable device by which the poet emphasizes the close link between past and present through the idea of the unalterable destiny of the Trojan race. On the first occasion (a), Jupiter comforts Venus, Aeneas' mother, by predicting a successful end to the Trojans' struggle after the destruction of Troy and representing the preordained and glorious unfolding of

Rome's history. Note especially the emphasis on the Romans as predestined rulers of a vast empire, the idea of the Roman conquest of Greece as revenge for Troy, and the prediction that an age of peace will follow. It is a matter of dispute whether here Virgil refers to Julius Caesar or Augustus at lines 286-7. Scholars are evenly divided. The second passage (b) is a revelation of a different kind—a tableau of the future wrought in metal on a shield made for Aeneas by Vulcan, the god of fire and smiths (Virgil uses this method of telling a story elsewhere, cf. esp. the stone doors of the temple of the Sibyl at the beginning of Aeneid 6). The centre-piece is the battle of Actium (see B25) in which Octavian and Agrippa defeated Antony and Cleopatra in a sea-battle off the coast of Greece (31 BC). The poet accentuates the contrast between the solidarity of Roman people and Senate and the barbaric eastern hordes supporting Antony and Cleopatra.

For the Aeneid see also W. A. Camps An Introduction to Virgil's Aeneid (Oxford 1969); M. C. J. Putnam The Poetry of the Aeneid (London 1965); V. Pöschl The Art of Vergil (ET Ann Arbor 1962).

(a)

Fear no more, Cytherea. Take comfort, for your people's
Destiny is unaltered; you shall behold the promised
City walls of Lavinium, and exalt great-hearted Aeneas
Even to the starry skies. I have not changed my mind.
I say it now—for I know these cares constantly gnaw you—
And show you further into the secret book of fate:
Aeneas, mightily warring in Italy, shall crush
Proud tribes, to establish city walls and a way of life,
Till a third summer has seen him reigning in Latium
And winter thrice passed over his camp in the conquered land.
His son Ascanius, whose surname is now Iulus—
Ilus it was, before the realm of Ilium fell—
Ascanius for his reign shall have full thirty years
With all their wheeling months; shall move the kingdom from
Lavinium and make Long Alba his sure stronghold.
Here for three hundred years shall rule the dynasty
Of Hector, until a priestess and queen of Trojan blood,
With child by Mars, shall presently give birth to twin sons.
Romulus, then, gay in the coat of the tawny she-wolf
Which suckled him, shall succeed to power and found the city
Of Mars and with his own name endow the Roman nation.
To these I set no bounds, either in space or time;
Unlimited power I give them. Even the spiteful Juno,
Who in her fear now troubles the earth, the sea and the sky,
Shall think better of this and join me in fostering
The cause of the Romans, the lords of creation, the togaed people.
Thus it is written. An age shall come, as the years glide by,

When the children of Troy shall enslave the children of Agamemnon,
Of Diomed and Achilles, and rule in conquered Argos.
From the fair seed of Troy there shall be born a Caesar—
Julius, his name derived from great Iulus—whose empire
Shall reach to the ocean's limits, whose fame shall end in the stars.
He shall hold the East in fee; one day, cares ended, you shall
Receive him into heaven; him also will mortals pray to.
Then shall the age of violence be mellowing into peace:
Venerable Faith, and the Home, with Romulus and Remus,
Shall make the laws; the grim, steel-welded gates of War
Be locked; and within, on a heap of armaments, a hundred
Knots of bronze tying his hands behind him, shall sit
Growling and bloody-mouthed the godless spirit of Discord.

Virgil *Aeneid* 1. 257–96
tr. C. Day Lewis (Oxford 1966)

(b)

Upon this shield the Fire-god, with knowledge of things to come,
Being versed in the prophets, had wrought events from Italian history
And Roman triumphs; upon it appeared the whole line that would spring from
Ascanius' stock, and the wars they would fight in, one by one.
He had depicted the mother wolf as she lay full length in   630
The green-swarded cave of Mars, with the twin boy babies fondling
And suckling at her udders, fearlessly nuzzling their dam;
She, her graceful neck bent sideways and back, is caressing
Each child in turn with her tongue, licking them into shape.
Nearby he had pictured the Sabine women so unceremoniously
Snatched from among the crowds around the arena at Rome
During the Great Games; then the war that immediately came,
Between Romulus' people and Tatius's hard-living Sabines.
Next, these same two kings, their quarrel laid aside,
Are standing at Jove's altar, armed, with bowls in their hands,   640
Ratifying a treaty by the sacrifice of a sow.
Near this was the scene where chariots, driven apart, had torn
Mettus to pieces (but you should have kept to your word, Alban!)—
Tullus is dragging away the remains of that false-tongued man
Through a wood, and the brambles there are drenched with a bloody dew.
Again, you could see Porsenna telling the Romans to take back
The banished Tarquin, and laying strenuous siege to Rome,
While the sons of Aeneas took up the sword for freedom's sake:
He was pictured there to the life, pouring out threats and wild with
Chagrin, seeing that Cocles dared to break down the bridge   650
And Cloelia had slipped her fetters and was swimming across the river.

At the top of the shield, Manlius, warden of the Tarpeian
Fortress, stood before the temple, guarding the Capitol—
The palace, just built by Romulus, being shown with a rough thatched roof.
Here too a silvery goose went fluttering through a golden
Colonnade, honking out an alarum, that the Gauls are on us:
Under the cover of a dark night, lucky for them, the Gauls
Creep closer through the brushwood, some have already scaled
The citadel's heights: their clothing and hair were done in gold;
The stripes on their cloaks are gleaming; about their fair-skinned throats   660
Are necklaces fastened; each of them brandishes two Alpine
Spears in his hand, and carries a tall, narrow shield for protection.
Vulcan had also embossed the dancing Salii and naked
Luperci, their head-dresses bound with wool, and the shields that fell from
Heaven: a solemn procession of virtuous ladies was moving
In cushioned carriages through the city. Elsewhere the deep gates
Of hell were represented, the domicile of the damned
And the torments they suffer—Catiline hangs from the edge of a terrible
Precipice, shrinking away from the faces of Furies above him:
But the righteous are set apart, with Cato as their law-giver.   670
Among these subjects extended a wide and swelling sea;
It was done in gold, yet it looked like the blue sea foaming with white-caps:
Dolphins, picked out in silver, were cart-wheeling all around,
Lashing the face of the deep with their tails and cleaving the water.
Centrally were displayed two fleets of bronze, engaged in
The battle of Actium; all about Cape Leucas you saw
Brisk movement of naval formations; the sea was a blaze of gold.
On one side Augustus Caesar, high up on the poop, is leading
The Italians into battle, the Senate and People with him,
His home-gods and the great gods: two flames shoot up from his helmet   680
In jubilant light, and his father's star dawns over its crest.
Elsewhere in the scene is Agrippa—the gods and the winds fight for him—
Prominent, leading his column: the naval crown with its miniature
Ships' beaks, a proud decoration of war, shines on his head.
On the other side, with barbaric wealth and motley equipment,
Is Anthony, fresh from his triumphs in the East, by the shores of the Indian
Ocean; Egypt, the powers of the Orient and uttermost Bactra
Sail with him; also—a shameful thing—his Egyptian wife.
The fleets are converging at full speed, the sea is all churned and foaming
As the oarsmen take their long strokes and the trident bows drive on   690
They manœuvre for sea-room: you'd think the Cyclades isles were unmoored
And afloat, or mountains were charging at mountains, to see those massive
Galleys on one side attacking the turreted ships of the other.
Volleys of flaming material and iron missiles fly thick
And fast; a strange new slaughter reddens the plains of Neptune.

In the midst, Cleopatra rallies her fleet with Egyptian timbrel,
For she cannot yet see the two serpents of death behind her.
Barking Anubis, a whole progeny of grotesque
Deities are embattled against Neptune and Minerva
And Venus. Mars is raging in the thick of the fight, his figure   700
Wrought from iron, and ominous Furies look on from above;
Here Discord strides exulting in her torn mantle, and she is
Followed by Bellona wielding a bloodstained scourge.
Viewing this, Apollo of Actium draws his bow
From aloft: it creates a panic; all the Egyptians, all
The Indians, Arabians and Sabaeans now turn tail.
You could see the queen Cleopatra praying a fair wind, making
All sail, in the very act of paying the sheets out and running.
The Fire-god had rendered her, pale with the shadow of her own death,
Amid the carnage, borne on by the waves and the westerly gale;   710
And, over against her, the Nile, sorrowing in all its length,
Throws wide the folds of its watery garment, inviting the conquered
To sail for refuge into that blue, protective bosom.
But Caesar has entered the walls of Rome in triumphal procession,
Three times a victor; he dedicates now a thanks-offering immortal
To Italy's gods—three hundred great shrines all over the city.
The streets resound with cheering, rejoicing and merrymaking:
In all the temples women are chanting, altars are lit up;
At the foot of the altars lie the bodies of sacrificed bullocks.
Caesar, enthroned in the marble-white temple of dazzling Apollo,   720
Inspects the gifts from the nations and hangs them up on the splendid
Portals: subjected tribes pass by in a long procession—
A diversity of tongues, of national dress and equipment.
Here Vulcan had represented the Nomads, the flowing robes of
Africans, here the Leleges, Carians, Gelonian bowmen;
Some carry a picture of Euphrates, its waters pacified;
There go the Morini, furthest of men, the branching Rhine,
The Scythians untamed, the Araxes fretting about its bridge.
       Such were the scenes that Aeneas admired on the shield of Vulcan
His mother gave him. Elated by its portrayal of things   730
Beyond his ken, he shouldered his people's glorious future.

Virgil Aeneid 8.626–731
tr. C. Day Lewis (Oxford 1966)

F5 A letter

This fragment of a letter from Virgil to Augustus is quoted in an academic symposium on the subject of Virgil's poetry by the learned scholar Macrobius. Its importance lies in the evidence it gives us of the poet's attitude to his work. We know from the Life, *(see F1 § 31) that it was probably written in answer to pressure from Augustus to 'deliver'. The 'much more important studies' were philosophy, in which the poet had a lifelong interest.*

Of my Aeneid, if I had anything worth your attention, I would gladly send you something, but the subject on which I have embarked is so vast that I think I must have been almost out of my mind to have started it; all the more, since as you know, there are other and much more important studies which claim my attention.

Macrobius, *Saturnalia* 1. 24
tr. C. J. Emlyn-Jones

F6 *Aeneid* Book 6

For general background, see above, F4 (intro.). The 6th book occupies a central position in the poem. After much wandering, Aeneas and the other survivors from Troy have finally reached the coast of Italy. Aeneas visits the Underworld, draws together his past in meeting dead friends and looks towards the future—immediate fighting in the Sibyl's prophecy and more distant glory in the review of the future heroes of Rome waiting to be reborn. The book falls naturally into three sections, a central section telling of Aeneas' journey through the Underworld flanked by an introduction and a conclusion.

(a) *1st section (1–263)*

The preparations for Aeneas' descent to greet his dead father involve consultation of the priestess of Apollo, the Sibyl, concerning Aeneas' destiny in Italy, and ritual preliminaries. Greek mythological themes (the Cretan doors, parallelism between Aeneas and the events of Homer's Iliad, and precedent for Aeneas' descent or katabasis*) are intertwined with native Roman (the Sibyl, death and burial of Misenus, the Golden Bough). Above all, we learn something of* pius *Aeneas.*

Thus spoke Aeneas, in tears, then gave the ships their head,
And at long last they slid to the shores of Euboean Cumae.
The bows are swung round to face the sea, the vessels made fast with
The biting hook of their anchors, and the sheer sterns are lining
The beach. Now, full of excitement, the heroes tumble out
On the Hesperian shore: some look for the seeds of fire

Hidden in veins of flint, some scour the woods, the tangled
Haunts of wild beasts, for fuel, and point to the springs they have found.
But the god-fearing Aeneas made for the shrine where Apollo
Sits throned on high, and that vasty cave—the deeply-recessed   10
Crypt of the awe-inspiring Sibyl, to whom the god gives
The power to see deep and prophesy what's to come.
Now they passed into Diana's grove and the gold-roofed temple.
    The story is that Daedalus, when he escaped from Minos,
Boldly trusting himself to the air on urgent wings,
An unprecedented mode of travel, went floating northwards
Until he was lightly hovering above the Cumaean hilltop.
Here he came first to earth, hung up his apparatus
Of flight as a thanks-offering to Phoebus, and built a great temple.
On its door was depicted the death of Androgeos; also the legend   20
Of how the Athenians, poor souls, were forced to pay yearly tribute
With seven of their sons—the scene when the lots had just been drawn.
Facing this, there's a bas-relief; with Crete rising out of the waves;
Pasiphae, cruelly fated to lust after a bull,
And privily covered; the hybrid fruit of that monstrous union—
The Minotaur, a memento of her unnatural love:
Here's the insoluble maze constructed by Daedalus;
Yet, sympathizing with Ariadne in her great passion,
He gives her himself the clue to the maze's deceptive windings,
And guides with a thread the blind steps of Theseus. In the artifact   30
Icarus too would have had a prominent place, if his father's
Grief had allowed: but twice, trying to work the boy's fall
In gold, did Daedalus' hands fail him. They'd have pursued
The sculptured tale right through, but that Achates, who had
Been sent ahead, arrived with the priestess of Phoebus and Trivia,
Deiphobe, daughter of Glaucus. She now addressed Aeneas:—
    This is no time for poring over those works of art.
Just now you would do best to sacrifice seven bullocks
That have not been yoked, and as many properly chosen sheep.
    She addressed Aeneas; and he promptly performing the rites she   40
Requested, the priestess summoned them into the lofty temple.
    There's a huge cave hollowed out from the flank of Cumae's hill;
A hundred wide approaches it has, a hundred mouths
From which there issue a hundred voices, the Sibyl's answers.
They had reached its threshold when, time it is to ask your destiny,
The Sibyl cried, for lo! the god is with me. And speaking,
There by the threshold, her features, her colour were all at once
Different, her hair flew wildly about; her breast was heaving,
Her fey heart swelled in ecstasy; larger than life she seemed,
More than mortal her utterance: the god was close and breathing   50

His inspiration through her:—
What? Slow to pay your vows
And say your prayers, Aeneas of Troy? Yet only then
Will the spell work and the doors open,
she cried, and again
Fell silent. An icy shudder ran through their very bones
And Aeneas poured out a prayer from the bottom of his heart:—
   O Phoebus, often you pitied the load Troy had to bear;
You it was who guided the hand and the Trojan arrow
Of Paris against Achilles; you were the guide I followed
Into so many seas, lapping great lands, and through
Remote Massylian peoples, the fields the Syrtes fringe: 60
And now, at long last, we have caught the elusive shores of Italy.
Let Troy's ill luck, that has dogged us so far, follow no further.
Ye too, gods and goddesses all, who could not bear
Ilium and the great fame of the Dardans, it is proper now
For you to spare the Trojans. And, O most holy Sibyl,
Foreseer of future things, grant—I but ask for the kingdom
Owed by my destiny—grant that we Trojans may settle in Latium,
We and our wandering gods, the hard-driven deities of Troy.
Then will I found a temple of solid marble to Phoebus
And Trivia, appointing festival days in Phoebus' honour.   70
You too shall have your holy place in the realm to be,
Where I shall deposit the oracles, the mystic runes you utter
For my own people, ordaining a priesthood to their service,
O gracious one. But do not commit your sayings to leaves,
Lest they become the sport of whisking winds and are scattered:
Speak them aloud, I pray.
Aeneas made an end now.
But the Sibyl, not yet submissive to Phoebus, there in her cavern
Prodigiously struggled, still trying to shake from her brain the powerful
God who rode her: but all the more he exhausted her foaming
Mouth and mastered her wild heart, breaking her in with a firm hand.   80
And now the hundred immense doors of the place flew open
Of their own accord, letting out the Sibyl's inspired responses:—
   O you that at last have done with the dangers of the deep
(Yet graver ones await you on land), the Trojans shall come
To power in Lavinium—be troubled no more about this—
But shall not also be glad that they did. Wars, dreadful wars
I see, and Tiber foaming with torrents of human blood.
You will not escape a Simois, a Xanthus there, a Greek
Encampment; Latium has a new Achilles in store for you,   90
He too a goddess' son: nor yet shall the Trojans anywhere
Be rid of Juno's vendetta. Ah then, in your extremity,

227

What tribes, what townships of Italy shall you not sue for aid!
Once more it's an alien bride, a foreign marriage that's destined
To cause such terrible harm to the Trojans.
But never give way to those evils: face them all the more boldly,
Using what methods your luck allows you. The way of salvation
Begins where you'd least expect it, stems from a Greek city.
    Thus from her sanctum spoke the Cumaean Sibyl, pronouncing
Riddles that awed them; her voice came booming out of the cavern,
Wrapping truth in enigma: she was possessed; Apollo   100
Controlled her, shaking the reins and twisting the goad in her bosom.
As soon as her ecstasy ebbed and her raving mouth was silent,
The hero Aeneas began to speak:—
                          Maiden, there's nothing
New or unexpected to me in such trials you prophesy.
All of them I have forecast, worked out in my mind already.
I have one request: since here is reputed to be the gateway
Of the Underworld and the dusky marsh from Acheron's overflow,
May it befall me to go into my dear father's
Presence—open the hallowed gates and show me the way!
Him through the flames, through a thousand pursuing missiles I rescued   110
Out of the enemy's midst and bore him away on these shoulders:
He voyaged with me, enduring sea after sea, enduring
All menace of sea and storm, weak as he was—great ordeals
Beyond his strength, exceeding the normal lot of old age.
Yes, and he himself most earnestly bade me, more than once,
To come to you here and make this appeal. I pray you, kind one,
Take pity on father and son. You have the power: it was not
For nothing that Hecate put you in charge of the grove of Avernus.
Orpheus, with only the tuneful strings of a Thracian lyre
To aid him, could conjure forth the ghost of his wife; Pollux,   120
Who, turn about, shares life and death with his mortal brother,
Constantly comes and goes this way; I need not mention
Theseus or Hercules; I too am descended from great Jove.
    Thus he was making petition, his hands upon the altar,
When the Sibyl began to speak:—
                         O child of a goddess' womb,
Trojan son of Anchises, the way to Avernus is easy;
Night and day lie open the gates of death's dark kingdom:
But to retrace your steps, to find the way back to daylight—
That is the task, the hard thing. A few, because of Jove's
Just love, or exalted to heaven by their own flame of goodness,   130
Men born from gods, have done it. Between, there lies a forest,
And darkly winds the river Cocytus round the place.
But if so great your love is, so great your passion to cross

The Stygian waters twice and twice behold black Tartarus,
If your heart is set on this fantastic project,
Here's what you must do first. Concealed in a tree's thick shade
There is a golden bough—gold the leaves and the tough stem—
Held sacred to Proserpine: the whole wood hides this bough
And a dell walls it round as it were in a vault of shadow.
Yet none is allowed to enter the land which earth conceals   140
Save and until he has plucked that gold-foil bough from the tree.
Fair Proserpine ordains that it should be brought to her
As tribute. When a bough is torn away, another
Gold one grows in its place with leaves of the same metal.
So keep your eyes roving above you, and when you have found the bough
Just pull it out: that branch will come away quite easily
If destiny means you to go; otherwise no amount of
Brute force will get it, nor hard steel avail to hew it away.
Also—and this you know not—the lifeless corpse of a friend
Is lying unburied, a dead thing polluting your whole expedition,   150
While you are lingering here to inquire about fate's decrees.
Before anything else, you must give it proper burial and make
Sacrifice of black sheep: only when you are thus
Purified, shall you see the Stygian groves and the regions
Untreadable to the living.
                              She spoke, then closed her lips.
Aeneas, eyes downcast, countenance full of sorrow,
Moved off, leaving the cave, pondering much in his heart
On the cryptic issues the Sibyl had raised. Loyal Achates
Walked with him, his gait heavy beneath the same load of trouble.
Many were the conjectures they threw out, one to the other,   160
As to which of their dead friends the Sibyl had meant, and whose body
Must be interred. Now when they drew near the beach, they saw there
The body of Misenus, cut off by cruel death—
Misenus, son of Aeolus, whom none had excelled in firing
The warrior passions of men with thrilling trumpet calls.
He had been a comrade of mighty Hector, at Hector's side
Had fought and won great fame as a trumpeter and a spear-man.
After Achilles had defeated Hector and killed him,
This valiant hero, Misenus, attached himself to Dardan
Aeneas' company, following now no lesser a man.   170
But today, as he sent his horn's notes ringing over the sea,
Most rashly challenging the gods to a musical contest,
Jealous Triton caught him off guard—if we may credit
The story—and plunged him down in the surf among those rocks.
Now they were all standing around him, lamenting loudly,
Not least the good-hearted Aeneas. And now at once they hasten

Weeping to carry out the Sibyl's instructions, piling
Timber up with a will for a towering funeral altar.
Into the age-old forest, where only wild things lurk,
They go: spruces are felled, the holm oak rings with axe blows,   180
Wedges are used to split ash logs and the cleavable wood
Of oaks, immense rowans are rolled down from the heights.
Aeneas himself, in the middle of these activities,
Carrying the same tools as they, encouraged his friends.
But also, sad at heart, gazing up at the huge forest,
He brooded; and then he uttered his thoughts aloud in a prayer:—
    If only I might glimpse that golden bough on its tree
In the great wood this very moment! for all that the Sibyl
Said about you, Misenus, was true, too sadly true.
    The words were hardly out when it befell that two doves   190
Came planing down from above his very eyes
And alighted upon the green turf. The hero recognized
His mother's birds. His heart leapt up and he said a prayer:—
    Show me the way, if way there is! Oh, wing your flight
To that part of the forest where the precious bough overshadows
The fruitful soil. Do not forsake me, heavenly mother,
At this most crucial hour!
                       He spoke; stopped in his tracks
To note what signs they gave and in what direction they'd move.
Now the doves, as they fed, flitted on from spot to spot, but never
So far ahead that one who followed lost sight of them.   200
Then, when they came to the mouth of foul-breathing Avernus,
Swiftly they soared, went gliding through the soft air and settled,
The pair of them, on a tree, the wished-for place, a tree
Amid whose branches there gleamed a bright haze, a different colour—
Gold. Just as in depth of winter the mistletoe blooms
In the woods with its strange leafage, a parasite on the tree,
Hanging its yellow-green berries about the smooth round boles:
So looked the bough of gold leaves upon that ilex dark,
And in a gentle breeze the gold-foil foliage rustled.
Aeneas at once took hold of the bough, and eagerly breaking   210
It off with one pull, he bore it into the shrine of the Sibyl.
Meantime upon the shore the Trojans were still lamenting
Misenus, and praying the last rites to his oblivious dust.
First they laid resinous wood, and upon it sections of oak trees
To build the pyre up high; the sides of the pyre were wattled
With sombre-foliaged boughs; in front they planted funereal
Cypresses, and his shining arms adorned its top.
Some lit fires beneath the cauldrons, and boiled water;

They washed and anointed the corpse of their friend, so cold in death.
All were lamenting. When they had wept him, they laid on the bier   220
His body, covering it with purple drapes and the dead man's
Own clothing. The bearers lifted the bier onto the pyre,
A melancholy office, and in the traditional manner
Averting their eyes, applied the lighted torches. The pile of
Offerings burned—the incense, the meat, the libations of oil.
Now when the ashes had fallen in and the flames died down,
They quenched the remains, the thirsty embers, with wine; and collecting
The bones, Corynaeus put them away in a casket of bronze.
He then moved round his comrades three times, bearing pure water;
Aspersing them with drops he shook from a branch of fruitful   230
Olive, he purified them, and spoke the farewell words.
Aeneas the true now raised over his friend a massive
Tomb, laying on it the man's own arms, his oar and his trumpet,
Beneath that high headland which takes its name from him,
Misenum, and preserves his fame unto all ages.
  This done, Aeneas hastened to follow the Sibyl's directions.
A deep, deep cave there was, its mouth enormously gaping,
Shingly, protected by the dark lake and the forest gloom:
Above it, no winged creatures could ever wing their way
With impunity, so lethal was the miasma which   240
Went fuming up from its black throat to the vault of heaven:
Wherefore the Greeks called it Avernus, the Birdless Place.
Here the Sibyl first lined up four black-skinned bullocks,
Poured a libation of wine upon their foreheads, and then,
Plucking the topmost hairs from between their brows, she placed
These on the altar fires as an initial offering,
Calling aloud upon Hecate, powerful in heaven and hell.
While other laid their knives to these victims' throats, and caught
The fresh warm blood in bowls, Aeneas sacrificed
A black-fleeced lamb to Night, the mother of the Furies,   250
And her great sister, Earth, and a barren heifer to Proserpine.
Then he set up altars by night to the god of the Underworld,
Laying upon the flames whole carcases of bulls
And pouring out rich oil over the burning entrails.
But listen!—at the very first crack of dawn, the ground
Underfoot began to mutter, the woody ridges to quake,
And a baying of hounds was heard through the half-light: the goddess was coming,
Hecate. The Sibyl cried:—
                    Away! Now stand away,
You uninitiated ones, and clear the whole grove!
But you, Aeneas, draw your sword from the scabbard and fare forth!   260

Now you need all your courage, your steadfastness of heart.
    So much she said and, ecstatic, plunged into the opened cave mouth:
Unshrinking went Aeneas step for step with his guide.

(b)   *2nd section (264–678)*

*In descending to the Underworld accompanied by the Sibyl, Aeneas undergoes all
the traditional experiences of the journey, including the crossing of the Styx in
Charon's boat and viewing of the various categories of the dead. But, most important,
he meets again significant people from his past life, the helmsman Palinurus (for
whose loss he was weeping at the beginning of the book) Dido, the Carthaginian
queen whom he had abandoned, and Deiphobus, a Trojan comrade-at-arms who
was treacherously slaughtered during the fall of Troy.*

You gods who rule the kingdom of souls! You soundless shades!
Chaos, and Phlegethon! O mute wide leagues of Night-land!—
Grant me to tell what I have heard! With your assent
May I reveal what lies deep in the gloom of the Underworld!
    Dimly through the shadows and dark solitudes they wended,
Through the void domiciles of Dis, the bodiless regions:
Just as, through fitful moonbeams, under the moon's thin light,   270
A path lies in a forest, when Jove has palled the sky
With gloom, and the night's blackness has bled the world of colour.
See! At the very porch and entrance way to Orcus
Grief and ever-haunting Anxiety make their bed:
Here dwell pallid Diseases, here morose Old Age,
With Fear, ill-prompting Hunger, and squalid Indigence,
Shapes horrible to look at, Death and Agony;
Sleep, too, which is the cousin of Death; and Guilty Joys,
And there, against the threshold, War, the bringer of Death:
Here are the iron cells of the Furies, and lunatic Strife   280
Whose viperine hair is caught up with a headband soaked in blood.
    In the open a huge dark elm tree spreads wide its immemorial
Branches like arms, whereon, according to old wives' tales,
Roost the unsolid Dreams, clinging everywhere under its foliage.
Besides, many varieties of monsters can be found
Stabled here at the doors—Centaurs and freakish Scyllas,
Briareus with his hundred hands, the Lernaean Hydra
That hisses terribly and the flame-throwing Chimaera,
Gorgons and Harpies, and the ghost of three-bodied Geryon.
Now did Aeneas shake with a spasm of fear, and drawing   290
His sword, offered its edge against the creatures' onset:
Had not his learned guide assured him they were but incorporeal
Existences floating there, forms with no substance behind them,
He'd have attacked them, and wildly winnowed with steel mere shadows.
    From here is the road that leads to the dismal waters of Acheron.

Here a whirlpool boils with mud and immense swirlings
Of water, spouting up all the slimy sand of Cocytus.
A dreadful ferryman looks after the river crossing,
Charon: appallingly filthy he is, with a bush of unkempt
White beard upon his chin, with eyes like jets of fire; 300
And a dirty cloak draggles down, knotted about his shoulders.
He poles the boat, he looks after the sails, he is all the crew
Of that rust-coloured wherry which takes the dead across—
An ancient now, but a god's old age is green and sappy.
This way came fast and streaming up to the bank the whole throng:
Matrons and men were there, and there were great-heart heroes
Finished with earthly life, boys and unmarried maidens,
Young men laid on the pyre before their parents' eyes;
Multitudinous as the leaves that fall in a forest
At the first frost of autumn, or the birds that out of the deep sea 310
Fly to land in migrant flocks, when the cold of the year
Has sent them overseas in search of a warmer climate.
So they all stood, each begging to be ferried across first,
Their hands stretched out in longing for the shore beyond the river.
But the surly ferryman embarks now this, now that group,
While others he keeps away at a distance from the shingle.
Aeneas, being astonished and moved by the great stir, said:—
    Tell me, O Sibyl, what means this mustering at the river?
What purpose have these souls? By what distinction are some
Turned back, while other souls sweep over the wan water? 320
    To which the long-lived Sibyl uttered this brief reply:—
    O son of Anchises' loins and true-born offspring of heaven,
What you see is the mere of Cocytus, the Stygian marsh
By whose mystery even the gods, having sworn, are afraid to be forsworn.
All this crowd you see are the helpless ones, the unburied:
That ferryman is Charon: the ones he conveys have had burial.
None may be taken across from bank to awesome bank of
That harsh-voiced river until his bones are laid to rest.
Otherwise, he must haunt this place for a hundred years
Before he's allowed to revisit the longed-for stream at last. 330
    The son of Anchises paused and stood stock still, in deep
Meditation, pierced to the heart by pity for their hard fortune.
He saw there, sorrowing because deprived of death's fulfilment,
Leucaspis and Orontes, the commodore of the Lycian
Squadron, who had gone down, their ship being lost with all hands
In a squall, sailing with him the stormy seas from Troy.
    And look! yonder was roaming the helmsman, Palinurus,
Who, on their recent voyage, while watching the stars, had fallen
From the afterdeck, thrown off the ship there in mid-passage.

A sombre form in the deep shadows, Aeneas barely
Recognized him; then accosted:— 340
                      Which of the gods, Palinurus,
Snatched you away from us and made you drown in the mid-sea?
Oh, tell me! For Apollo, whom never before had I found
Untruthful, did delude my mind with this one answer,
Foretelling that you would make your passage to Italy
Unharmed by sea. Is it thus he fulfils a sacred promise?
    Palinurus replied:—
                    The oracle of Phoebus has not tricked you,
My captain, son of Anchises; nor was I drowned by a god.
It was an accident: I slipped, and the violent shock
Of my fall broke off the tiller to which I was holding firmly 350
As helmsman, and steering the ship. By the wild seas I swear
That not on my own account was I frightened nearly so much as
Lest your ship, thus crippled, its helmsman overboard,
Lose steerage-way and founder amid the mountainous waves.
Three stormy nights did the South wind furiously drive me along
Over the limitless waters: on the fourth day I just
Caught sight of Italy, being lifted high on a wave crest.
Little by little I swam to the shore. I was all but safe,
When, as I clung to the rough-edge cliff top, my fingers crooked
And my soaking garments weighing me down, some barbarous natives 360
Attacked me with swords, in their ignorance thinking that I was a rich prize.
Now the waves have me, the winds keep tossing me up on the shore again.
So now, by the sweet light and breath of heaven above
I implore you, and by your father, by your hopes for growing Ascanius,
Redeem me from this doom, unconquered one! Please sprinkle
Dust on my corpse—you can do it and quickly get back to port Velia:
Or else, if way there is, some way that your heavenly mother
Is showing you (not, for sure, without the assent of deity
Would you be going to cross the swampy Stygian stream), 370
Give poor Palinurus your hand, take me with you across the water
So that at least I may rest in the quiet place, in death.
    Thus did the phantom speak, and the Sibyl began to speak thus:—
    This longing of yours, Palinurus, has carried you quite away.
Shall you, unburied, view the Styx, the austere river
Of the Infernal gods, or come to its bank unbidden?
Give up this hope that the course of fate can be swerved by prayer.
But hear and remember my words, to console you in your hard fortune.
I say that the neighbouring peoples, compelled by portents from heaven
Occurring in every township, shall expiate your death,
Shall give you burial and offer the solemn dues to your grave, 380
And the place shall keep the name of Palinurus for ever.

Her sayings eased for a while the anguish of his sad heart;
He forgot his cares in the joy of giving his name to a region.
    So they resumed their interrupted journey, and drew near
The river. Now when the ferryman, from out on the Styx, espied them
Threading the soundless wood and making fast for the bank,
He hailed them, aggressively shouting at them before they could speak:—
    Whoever you are that approaches my river, carrying a weapon,
Halt there! Keep your distance, and tell me why you are come!
This is the land of ghosts, of sleep and somnolent night: 390
The living are not permitted to use the Stygian ferry.
Not with impunity did I take Hercules,
When he came, upon this water, nor Theseus, nor Pirithous,
Though their stock was divine and their powers were irresistible.
Hercules wished to drag off on a leash the watch-dog of Hades,
Even from our monarch's throne, and dragged it away trembling:
The others essayed to kidnap our queen from her lord's bed-chamber.
    The priestess of Apollo answered him shortly, thus:—
    There is no such duplicity here, so set your mind at rest;
These weapons offer no violence: the huge watch-dog in his kennel   400
May go on barking for ever and scaring the bloodless dead,
Proserpine keep her uncle's house, unthreatened in chastity.
Trojan Aeneas, renowned for war and a duteous heart,
Comes down to meet his father in the shades of the Underworld.
If you are quite unmoved by the spectacle of such great faith,
This you must recognize—
                    And here she disclosed the golden
Bough which was hid in her robe. His angry mood calms down.
No more is said. Charon is struck with awe to see
After so long that magic gift, the bough fate-given;
He turns his sombre boat and poles it towards the bank.   410
Then, displacing the souls who were seated along its benches
And clearing the gangways, to make room for the big frame of Aeneas,
He takes him on board. The ramshackle craft creaked under his weight
And let in through its seams great swashes of muddy water.
At last, getting the Sibyl and the hero safe across,
He landed them amidst wan reeds on a dreary mud flat.
    Huge Cerberus, monstrously couched in a cave confronting them,
Made the whole region echo with his three-throated barking.
The Sibyl, seeing the snakes bristling upon his neck now,
Threw him for bait a cake of honey and wheat infused with   420
Sedative drugs. The creature, crazy with hunger, opened
Its three mouths, gobbled the bait; then its huge body relaxed
And lay, sprawled out on the ground, the whole length of its cave kennel.
Aeneas, passing its entrance, the watch-dog neutralized,

Strode rapidly from the bank of the river of no return.
   At once were voices heard, a sound of mewling and wailing,
Ghosts of infants sobbing there at the threshold, infants
From whom a dark day stole their share of delicious life,
Snatched them away from the breast, gave them sour death to drink.
Next to them were those condemned to death on a false charge.   430
Yet every place is duly allotted and judgement is given.
Minos, as president, summons a jury of the dead: he hears
Every charge, examines the record of each; he shakes the urn.
Next again are located the sorrowful ones who killed
Themselves, throwing their lives away, not driven by guilt
But because they loathed living: how they would like to be
In the world above now, enduring poverty and hard trials!
God's law forbids: that unlovely fen with its glooming water
Corrals them there, the nine rings of Styx corral them in.
Not far from here can be seen, extending in all directions,   440
The vale of mourning—such is the name it bears: a region
Where those consumed by the wasting torments of merciless love
Haunt the sequestered alleys and myrtle groves that give them
Cover; death itself cannot cure them of love's disease.
Here Aeneas descried Phaedra and Procris, sad
Eriphyle showing the wounds her heartless son once dealt her,
Evadne and Pasiphae; with them goes Laodamia;
Here too is Caeneus, once a young man, but next a woman
And now changed back by fate to his original sex.
Amongst them, with her death-wound still bleeding, through the deep wood   450
Was straying Phoenician Dido. Now when the Trojan leader
Found himself near her and knew that the form he glimpsed through the shadows
Was hers—as early in the month one sees, or imagines he sees,
Through a wrack of cloud the new moon rising and glimmering—
He shed some tears, and addressed her in tender, loving tones:—
Poor, unhappy Dido, so the message was true that came to me
Saying you'd put an end to your life with the sword and were dead?
Oh god! was it death I brought you, then? I swear by the stars,
By the powers above, by whatever is sacred in the Underworld,
It was not of my own will, Dido, I left your land.   460
Heaven's commands, which now force me to traverse the shades,
This sour and derelict region, this pit of darkness, drove me
Imperiously from your side. I did not, could not imagine
My going would ever bring such terrible agony on you.
Don't move away! Oh, let me see you a little longer!
To fly from me, when this is the last word fate allows us!
   Thus did Aeneas speak, trying to soften the wild-eyed,
Passionate-hearted ghost, and brought the tears to his own eyes.

She would not turn to him; she kept her gaze on the ground,
And her countenance remained as stubborn to his appeal   470
As if it were carved from recalcitrant flint or a crag of marble.
At last she flung away, hating him still, and vanished
Into the shadowy wood where her first husband, Sychaeus,
Understands her unhappiness and gives her an equal love.
None the less did Aeneas, hard hit by her piteous fate,
Weep after her from afar, as she went, with tears of compassion.
    Then he passed on the appointed way. They came to the last part
Of Limbo, the place set apart for men famous in war.
Here Tydeus met him, here that warrior of high renown
Parthenopaeus, here the pale spectre of Adrastus;   480
Then those for whom lamentation had risen on earth—the fallen
Fighters of Troy; Aeneas groaned aloud when he saw those
Long ranks of death—Glaucus, Medon, Thersilochus,
The three sons of Antenor, Polyphoetes the priest of Ceres,
Idaeus, still with the arms he bore, the chariot he drove once.
To right and left the spirits press thickly around Aeneas.
Not enough just to have seen him once—they want to detain him,
To pace along beside him and find out why he has come there.
But the Greek generals and the regiments of Agamemnon,
When they beheld his armour glinting through the gloom,   490
Were seized with fear and trembling; some turned tail, even as
In the old days they had run for their ships; some uttered a wraith of
A war cry—they tried to shout, but their wide mouths only whimpered.
    Just then Aeneas caught sight of Deiphobus, his whole body
A mass of wounds, most horribly mangled about the face—
The face and both the hands, head mutilated with ears
Torn off, and the nose lopped—a barbarous disfigurement.
The moment he'd recognized that shrinking creature who covered
His ghastly wounds, Aeneas burst out in familiar tones:—
    Deiphobus, great fighter, descended from high-born Teucer,   500
Who was it chose to inflict such atrocious punishment on you?
Who could go to such lengths against you? On Troy's last night
I heard a rumour that, worn out with killing and killing Greeks,
You had sunk down on a huge indiscriminate heap of dead bodies.
Then, myself, I erected by the Rhoetean shore
A cenotaph for you, and thrice invoked your spirit aloud.
Your name and a trophy mark the spot; yourself I could not
Find to inter in your native soil before I departed.
    The son of Priam replied:—
                        Dear friend, you neglected nothing;
All that was needed you've done for Deiphobus and his shade.   510
My destiny and the destructive nature of that Lacaenian

Woman brought me to this: it was she who gave me these souvenirs.
You remember how we spent that last night in rejoicings,
In a fools' paradise; too well, no doubt, you remember it.
When the horse of doom had cleared at a bound the battlements
Of Troy, bearing an armed detachment within its belly,
That woman faked a dance, led the Trojan women around,
Yelling in Bacchanal orgy; under cover of which herself
With a blazing torch in her hand signalled the Greeks from our citadel.
I, worn out by our ordeals and leaden with sleep, was lying   520
In my unlucky bedroom under a coverlet
Of deep, delicious rest, very like the peace of death.
Meantime that nonpareil wife of mine removed all the arms from
Our house, yes, even my trusty sword from beneath my pillow;
Then called Menelaus inside, opened the door to him, hoping—
Vile thing—to make a wonderful present of me to her lover
And thus erase the stigma of her old wicked doings.
No more of this: they burst into the bedroom; Ulysses was with them,
Promoter and compère of crimes. Ye gods, may such deeds recoil
On the Greeks, if my prayer for revenge is made with a clear conscience.   530
But tell me now in turn, what chance has brought you here
Alive. Were you compelled by your wanderings on the ocean,
Or a command from heaven? Or what fate irks you, that you should
Enter this joyless, sunless abode, these vague, vexed regions?

So they conversed, till Aurora, driving her rosy chariot,
Had passed the midway point of the sky in her flying course;
And indeed they might have used up all the allotted time thus,
Had not his guide, the Sibyl, spoken a few words of warning:—
Night comes apace, Aeneas; yet we spend the hours in grieving.
Here is the spot where the way forks, going in two directions;   540
The right-hand leads beneath the battlements of great Dis,
And is our route to Elysium; the left-hand takes the wicked
To Tartarus, their own place, and punishment condign.
Deiphobus said:—
                    Great Sibyl, do not be angry with me.
I will leave you, return to the shades and make their number complete.
Fare on, Aeneas, our pride, and with better luck than mine!
Thus he spoke, and speaking, turned on his heel and went.
Aeneas looked back on a sudden: he saw to his left a cliff
Overhanging a spread of battlements, a threefold wall about them,
Girdled too by a swift-running stream, a flaming torrent—   550
Hell's river of fire, whose current rolls clashing rocks along.
In front, an enormous portal, the door-posts columns of adamant,
So strong that no mortal violence nor even the heaven-dwellers
Could broach it: an iron tower stands sheer and soaring above it,

Whereupon Tisiphone sits, wrapped in a bloodstained robe,
Sleeplessly, day-long, night-long, guarding the forecourt there.
From within can be heard the sounds of groaning and brutal lashing,
Sounds of clanking iron, of chains being dragged along.
Scared by the din, Aeneas halted; he could not move:—
    What kinds of criminals are these? Speak, lady! What punishments   560
Afflict them, that such agonized sounds rise up from there?
    Then the Sibyl began:—
                         O famous lord of the Trojans,
No righteous soul may tread that threshold of the damned:
But, when Hecate appointed me to the Avernian grove,
She instructed me in heaven's punishments, showed me all.
Here Rhadamanthus rules, and most severe his rule is,
Trying and chastising wrongdoers, forcing confessions
From any who, on earth, went gleefully undetected—
But uselessly, since they have only postponed till death their atonement.
At once Tisiphone, the avenger, scourge in hand,   570
Pounces upon the guilty, lashing them, threatening them
With the angry snakes in her left hand, and calls up her bloodthirsty sisters.
Then at last the hinges screech, the infernal gates
Grind open. Do you see the sentry, who she is,
Posted over the forecourt? the shape that guards the threshold?
Within, there dwells a thing more fierce—the fifty-headed
Hydra, with all its black throats agape. Then Tartarus
Goes sheer down under the shades, an abyss double in depth
The height that Olympus stands above a man gazing skyward.
Here Earth's primeval offspring, the breed of Titans, who   580
Were hurled down by Jove's lightning, writhe in the bottomless pit.
Here have I seen the twin sons of Aloeus, the gigantic
Creatures who sought to pull down heaven itself with their own
Bare hands, and to unseat Jove from his throne above.
Salmoneus too have I seen undergoing the rigorous sentence
Imposed when he mimicked the thunder and lightning of Jove almighty:
Drawn by a four-horse team and shaking a lighted torch,
He would go through Greece exulting, even through the middle of Elis
City, claiming the homage due to the gods alone—
Madman, to copy the nonpareil lightning, the thunderstorm   590
With a rumble of bronze wheels and a clatter of hard-hoofed horses!
But the Father almighty, among his serried storm clouds, launched
A weapon—no torches, no smoky light of farthing dips
Was this—and hurled the blasphemer down with the wind of its passage.
Tityos too, the nursling of Earth who mothers all,
Was to be seen, his body pegged out over a full nine
Acres, a huge vulture with hooked beak gnawing for ever

His inexhaustible liver, the guts that are rich in torment,
Pecking away for its food, burrowing deep through the body
It lives in, and giving no rest to the always-replenished vitals.   600
Need I mention the Lapithae, Ixion or Pirithous?
Over them, always about to fall and looking as if it were
Falling, a black crag hangs: banqueting couches gleam with
Golden legs, raised high, and feasts of regal opulence
Are set before damned eyes; but the chief of the Furies, reclining
Nearby, forbids them to stretch out their hands for the food; she leaps up,
Menacing them with her lifted torch, and shouts like thunder.
Here are those who in life hated their own brothers,
Or struck their parents; those who entangled their dependants
In fraudulent dealing; and those who sat tight on the wealth they had won,   610
Setting none aside for their own kin—most numerous of all are these;
Then such as were killed for adultery, took part in militant treason,
Men who made bold to break faith with their masters:—all such await
Punishment, mewed up here. And seek not to know what punishment,
What kind of destined torment awaits each one in the Pit.
Some have to roll huge rocks; some whirl round, spread-eagled
On spokes of wheels: the tragic Theseus sits, condemned to
Spend eternity in that chair: the poor wretch, Phlegyas,
Admonishes all, crying out through the mirk in solemn avowal,
Be warned by me! Learn justice, and not to belittle the gods!   620
One sold his country for gold, putting her under the yoke of
Dictatorship, and corruptly made and unmade her laws;
One entered the bed of his daughter, forced an unholy mating:
All dared some abominable thing, and what they dared they did.
No, not if I had a hundred tongues, a hundred mouths
And a voice of iron, could I describe all the shapes of wickedness,
Catalogue all the retributions inflicted here.
Thus spoke the long-lived priestess of Phoebus, then added this:—
     But come, resume your journey, finish the task in hand!
Let us go quickly on. I can see the bastions, forged in   630
The Cyclops' furnaces, and the arch of the gateway yonder,
Where we are bidden to put down your passport, the golden bough.
     She had spoken. Side by side they went the twilight way,
Rapidly covering the space between, and approached the gateway.
Aeneas stopped at the entrance, sprinkled himself with holy
Water, and placed the bough right at the doorway there.
     Now this was done at last, and Proserpine had her offering,
They went on into the Happy Place, the green and genial
Glades where the fortunate live, the home of the blessed spirits.
What largesse of bright air, clothing the vales in dazzling   640
Light, is here! This land has a sun and stars of its own.

Some exercise upon the grassy playing-fields
Or wrestle on the yellow sands in rivalry of sport;
Some foot the rhythmic dances and chant poems aloud.
Orpheus, the Thracian bard, is there in his long robe,
To accompany their measures upon the seven-stringed lyre
Which he plucks, now with his fingers, now with an ivory plectrum.
Here is the ancient line of Teucer, a breed most handsome,
Great-hearted heroes born in the happier days of old,
Ilus, Assaracus, and Dardanus, founder of Troy.   650
From afar Aeneas marvelled at the arms, the phantom chariots.
Spears stood fixed in the ground, everywhere over the plain
Grazed the unharnessed horses. The pleasure those heroes had felt,
When alive, in their arms and chariots, the care they had taken to pasture
Their sleek horses—all was the same beyond the tomb.
Aeneas noticed others to left and right on the greensward
Feasting and singing a jovial paean in unison
Amidst a fragrant grove of bay trees, whence the river
Eridanus springs, to roll grandly through woods of the world above.
Here were assembled those who had suffered wounds in defence of   660
Their country; those who had lived pure lives as priests; and poets
Who had not disgraced Apollo, poets of true integrity;
Men who civilized life by the skills they discovered, and men whose
Kindness to other people has kept their memory green—
All these upon their temples wore headbands white as snow.
Now the Sibyl addressed the company dotted about there,
And specially Musaeus, for round him a large group
Gazing up at him as he towered head and shoulders above them:—
    Tell me, you blessed spirits, and you, most honoured poet,
Whereabouts can we find Anchises? We have come here,   670
Crossing the great rivers of the Underworld, to see him.
    So did Musaeus make reply with these few words:—
    None of us has a fixed abode: we dwell in shady
Groves, we make our beds on river-banks, reside in
Watersweet meadows. But if your heart's desire is such,
Then climb this rise and I'll set your feet on an easy path.
    He spoke, and leading the way, showed them the luminous plains
Extending below them. Now they went down from the uplands.

3rd section (679-901)

Aeneas' personal encounters culminate in that with his father, Anchises, who then proceeds to reveal to him the secret of the after-life through the transmigration of souls, leading to a review of all the heroic Romans awaiting rebirth. This turns into a pageant of the future glories of Rome, culminating in glorification of Augustus and an assertion of Rome's Imperial destiny.

Deep in a green valley stood father Anchises, surveying
The spirits there confined before they went up to the light of   680
The world above: he was musing seriously, and reviewing
His folk's full tally, it happened, the line of his loved children,
Their destinies and fortunes, their characters and their deeds.
Now, when he saw Aeneas coming in his direction
Over the grass, he stretched out both hands, all eagerness,
And tears poured down his cheeks, and the words were tumbling out:—
     So you have come at last? The love that your father relied on
Has won through the hard journey? And I may gaze, my son,
Upon your face, and exchange the old homely talk with you?
Thus indeed I surmised it would be, believed it must happen,   690
Counting the days till you came: I was not deceived in my hopes, then.
Over what lands, what wide, wide seas you have made your journey!
What dangers have beset you! And now you are here with me.
How I dreaded lest you should come to some harm at Carthage!
     Aeneas replied:—
                              Your image it was, your troubled phantom
That, often rising before me, has brought me to this place.
Our ships are riding at anchor in the Tyrrhene sea. Oh, let me
Take your hand and embrace you, father! Let me! Withdraw not!
     Even as he spoke, his cheeks grew wet with a flood of tears.
Three times he tried to put his arms round his father's neck,   700
Three times the phantom slipped his vain embrace—it was like
Grasping a wisp of wind or wings of a fleeting dream.
     Now did Aeneas descry, deep in a valley retiring,
A wood, a secluded copse whose branches soughed in the wind,
And Lethe river drifting past the tranquil places.
Hereabouts were flitting a multitude without number,
Just as, amid the meadows on a fine summer day,
The bees alight on flowers of every hue, and brim the
Shining lilies, and all the lea is humming with them.
Aeneas, moved by the sudden sight, asked in his ignorance   710
What it might mean, what was that river over there
And all that crowd of people swarming along its banks.
Then his father, Anchises, said:—
                              They are souls who are destined for
Reincarnation; and now at Lethe's stream they are drinking
The waters that quench man's troubles, the deep draught of oblivion.
Long, long have I wanted to tell you of these and reveal them
Before your eyes, to count them over, the seed of my seed,
That you might the more rejoice with me in the finding of Italy.
     But, father, must it be deemed that some souls ascend from here
To our earthly scene? re-enter our dull corporeal existence?   720

242

Why ever should so perverse a craving for earth possess them?
   I will tell you, my son, certainly; I will not keep you in doubt,
Answered Anchises, and then enlarged on each point successively:—
First, you must know that the heavens, the earth, the watery plains
Of the sea, the moon's bright globe, the sun and the stars are all
Sustained by a spirit within; for immanent Mind, flowing
Through all its parts and leavening its mass, makes the universe work.
This union produced mankind, the beasts, the birds of the air,
And the strange creatures that live under the sea's smooth face.
The life-force of those seeds is fire, their source celestial,   730
But they are deadened and dimmed by the sinful bodies they live in—
The flesh that is laden with death, the anatomy of clay:
Whence these souls of ours feel fear, desire, grief, joy,
But encased in their blind, dark prison discern not the heaven-light above.
Yes, not even when the last flicker of life has left us,
Does evil, or the ills that flesh is heir to, quite
Relinquish our souls; it must be that many a taint grows deeply,
Mysteriously grained in their being from long contact with the body.
Therefore the dead are disciplined in purgatory, and pay
The penalty of old evil: some hang, stretched to the blast of   740
Vacuum winds, for others, the stain of sin is washed
Away in a vast whirlpool or cauterized with fire.
Each of us finds in the next world his own level: a few of us
Are later released to wander at will through broad Elysium,
The Happy Fields; until, in the fullness of time, the ages
Have purged that ingrown stain, and nothing is left but pure
Ethereal sentience and the spirit's essential flame.
All these souls, when they have finished their thousand-year cycle,
God sends for, and they come in crowds to the river of Lethe,
So that, you see, with memory washed out, they may revisit   750
The earth above and begin to wish to be born again.
   When Anchises had finished, he drew his son and the Sibyl
Into the thick of the murmuring concourse assembled there
And took his stand on an eminence from which he could scan the long files
Over against him, and mark the features of those who passed.
   Listen, for I will show you your destiny, setting forth
The fame that from now shall attend the seed of Dardanus,
The posterity that awaits you from an Italian marriage—
Illustrious souls, one day to inherit our Trojan name.
That young man there—do you see him?—who leans on an untipped spear,   760
Has been allotted the next passage to life, and first of
All these will ascend to earth, with Italian blood in his veins;
He is Silvius, an Alban name, and destined to be your last child,
The child of your late old age by a wife, Lavinia, who shall

243

Bear him in sylvan surroundings, a king and the father of kings
Through whom our lineage shall rule in Alba Longa.
Next to him stands Procas, a glory to the Trojan line;
Then Capys and Numitor, and one who'll revive your own name—
Silvius Aeneas, outstanding alike for moral rectitude
And prowess in war, if ever he comes to the Alban throne.   770
What fine young men they are! Look at their stalwart bearing,
The oak leaves that shade their brows—decorations for saving life!
These shall found your Nomentum, Gabii and Fidenae,
These shall rear on the hills Collatia's citadel,
Pometii, and the Fort of Inuus, Bola and Cora—
All nameless sites at present, but then they shall have these names.
Further, a child of Mars shall go to join his grandsire—
Romulus, born of the stock of Assaracus by his mother,
Ilia. Look at the twin plumes upon his helmet's crest,
Mars' cognizance, which marks him out for the world of earth!   780
His are the auguries, my son, whereby great Rome
Shall rule to the ends of the earth, shall aspire to the highest achievement,
Shall ring the seven hills with a wall to make one city,
Blessed in her breed of men: as Cybele, wearing her turreted
Crown, is charioted round the Phrygian cities, proud of
Her brood of gods, embracing a hundred of her children's children—
Heaven-dwellers all, all tenants of the realm above.
Now bend your gaze this way, look at that people there!
They are *your* Romans. Caesar is there and all Ascanius'
Posterity, who shall pass beneath the arch of day.   790
And here, here is the man, the promised one you know of—
Caesar Augustus, son of a god, destined to rule
Where Saturn ruled of old in Latium, and there
Bring back the age of gold: his empire shall expand
Past Garamants and Indians to a land beyond the zodiac
And the sun's yearly path, where Atlas the sky-bearer pivots
The wheeling heavens, embossed with fiery stars, on his shoulder.
Even now the Caspian realm, the Crimean country
Tremble at oracles of the gods predicting his advent,
And the seven mouths of the Nile are in a sweat of fear.   800
Not even Hercules roved so far and wide over earth,
Although he shot the bronze-footed deer, brought peace to the woods of
Erymanthus, subdued Lerna with the terror of his bow;
Nor Bacchus, triumphantly driving his team with vines for reins,
His team of tigers down from Mount Nysa, travelled so far.
Do we still hesitate, then, to enlarge our courage by action?
Shrink from occupying the territory of Ausonia?
Who is that in the distance, bearing the hallows, crowned with

A wreath of olive? I recognize—grey hair and hoary chin—
That Roman king who, called to high power from humble Cures,   810
A town in a poor area, shall found our system of law
And thus refound our city. The successor of Numa, destined
To shake our land out of its indolence, stirring men up to fight
Who have grown unadventurous and lost the habit of victory,
Is Tullus. After him shall reign the too boastful Ancus,
Already over-fond of the breath of popular favour.
Would you see the Tarquin kings, and arrogant as they, Brutus
The avenger, with the symbols of civic freedom he won back?
He shall be first to receive consular rank and its power of
Life and death: when his sons awake the dormant conflict,   820
Their father, a tragic figure, shall call them to pay the extreme
Penalty, for fair freedom's sake. However posterity
Look on that deed, patriotism shall prevail and love of
Honour. See over there the Decii, the Drusi, Torquatus
With merciless axe, Camillus with the standards he recovered.
See those twin souls, resplendent in duplicate armour: now
They're of one mind, and shall be as long as the Underworld holds them;
But oh, if ever they reach the world above, what warfare,
What battles and what carnage will they create between them—
Caesar descending from Alpine strongholds, the fort of Monoecus,   830
His son-in-law Pompey lined up with an Eastern army against him.
Lads, do not harden yourselves to face such terrible wars!
Turn not your country's hand against your country's heart!
You, be the first to renounce it, my son of heavenly lineage,
You be the first to bury the hatchet! . . .
That one shall ride in triumph to the lofty Capitol,
The conqueror of Corinth, renowned for the Greeks he has slain.
That one shall wipe out Argos and Agamemnon's Mycenae,
Destroying an heir of Aeacus, the seed of warrior Achilles,
Avenging his Trojan sires and the sacrilege done to Minerva.   840
Who could leave unnoticed the glorious Cato, Cossus,
The family of the Gracchi, the two Scipios—thunderbolts
In war and death to Libya; Fabricius, who had plenty
In poverty; Serranus, sowing his furrowed fields?
Fabii, where do you lead my lagging steps? O Fabius,
The greatest, you the preserver of Rome by delaying tactics!
Let others fashion from bronze more lifelike, breathing images—
For so they shall—and evoke living faces from marble;
Others excel as orators, others track with their instruments
The planets circling in heaven and predict when stars will appear.   850
But, Romans, never forget that government is your medium!
Be this your art:—to practise men in the habit of peace,

Generosity to the conquered, and firmness against aggressors.
   They marvelled at Anchises' words, and he went on:—
   Look how Marcellus comes all glorious with the highest
Of trophies, a victor over-topping all other men!
He shall buttress the Roman cause when a great war shakes it,
Shatter the Carthaginian and rebel Gaul with his cavalry,
Give to Quirinus the third set of arms won in single combat.
   Aeneas interposed, seeing beside Marcellus   860
A youth of fine appearance, in glittering accoutrements,
But his face was far from cheerful and downcast were his eyes:—
   Father, who is he that walks with Marcellus there?
His son? Or one of the noble line of his children's children?
How the retinue murmurs around him! How fine is the young man's presence!
Yet is his head haloed by sombre shade of night.
   Then father Anchises began, tears welling up in his eyes:—
   My son, do not probe into the sorrows of your kin.
Fate shall allow the earth one glimpse of this young man—
One glimpse, no more. Too puissant had been Rome's stock, ye gods,   870
In your sight, had such gifts been granted it to keep.
What lamentations of men shall the Campus Martius echo
To Mars' great city! O Tiber, what obsequies you shall see
One day as you glide past the new-built mausoleum!
No lad of the Trojan line shall with such hopeful promise
Exalt his Latin forebears, nor shall the land of Romulus
Ever again be so proud of one she has given birth to.
Alas for the sense of duty, the old-time honour! Alas for
The hand unvanquished in war! Him would no foe have met
In battle and not rued it, whether he charged on foot   880
Or drove his lathering steed with spurs against the enemy.
Alas, poor youth! If only you could escape your harsh fate!
Marcellus you shall be. Give me armfuls of lilies
That I may scatter their shining blooms and shower these gifts
At least upon the dear soul, all to no purpose though
Such kindness be.
            So far and wide, surveying all,
They wandered through that region, those broad and hazy plains.
After Anchises had shown his son over the whole place
And fired his heart with passion for the great things to come,
He told the hero of wars he would have to fight one day,   890
Told of the Laurentines and the city of Latinus,
And how to evade, or endure, each crisis upon his way.
   There are two gates of Sleep: the one is made of horn,
They say, and affords the outlet for genuine apparitions:
The other's a gate of brightly-shining ivory; this way

The Shades send up to earth false dreams that impose upon us.
Talking, then, of such matters, Anchises escorted his son
And the Sibyl as far as the ivory gate and sent them through it.
Aeneas made his way back to the ships and his friends with all speed,
Then coasted along direct to the harbour of Caieta.   900
Bow-anchors out, the ships are lining the shore with their sterns.

Virgil *Aeneid* 6
tr. C. Day Lewis (Oxford 1966)

F7 *Life* of Horace

This Life, *which comes down to us in some MSS of Horace's poems, derives almost definitely from the same source as Donatus'* Life of Virgil *(F1) namely Suetonius'* On Poets *from* The Lives of Famous Men. *The Horace* Life *is much shorter, and derives a great deal of its information from the works of the poet himself.*

1   Quintus Horatius Flaccus of Venusia had for a father, as he himself writes, a freedman who was a collector of money at auctions; but it is believed that he was a dealer in salted provisions, for a certain man in a quarrel thus taunted Horace: 'How often have I seen your father wiping his nose with his arm!' Horace served as tribune of the soldiers in the war of Philippi, at the instance of Marcus Brutus, one of the leaders in that war. When his party was vanquished, he was pardoned and purchased the position of a quaestor's clerk. Then contriving to win the favour, first of Maecenas and later of Augustus, he held a prominent place among the friends of both. How fond Maecenas was of him is evident enough from the well known epigram: 'If that I do not love you, my own Horace, more than life itself, behold your comrade leaner than Ninnius.' But he expressed himself much more strongly in his last will and testament in this brief remark to Augustus: 'Be as mindful of Horatius Flaccus as of myself.'   2 Augustus offered him the post of secretary, as appears in this letter of his to Maecenas: 'Before this I was able to write my letters to my friends with my own hand; now overwhelmed with work and in poor health, I desire to take our friend Horace from you. He will come then from that parasitic table of yours to my imperial board, and help me write my letters.' Even when Horace declined, Augustus showed no resentment at all, and did not cease his efforts to gain his friendship. We have letters from which I append a few extracts by way of proof: 'Enjoy any privilege at my house, as if you were making your home there; for it will be quite right and proper for you to do so, inasmuch as that was the relation which I wished to have with you, if your health had permitted.' And again, 'How mindful I am of you our friend Septimius can also tell you; for it chanced that I spoke of you in his presence. Even if you were so proud as to scorn my friendship, I do not therefore return your disdain.' Besides

this, among other pleasantries, he often calls him 'a most immaculate libertine' and 'his charming little man,' and he made him well to do by more than one act of generosity.   3 As to his writings, Augustus rated them so high, and was so convinced that they would be immortal, that he not only appointed him to write the Secular Hymn, but also bade him celebrate the victory of his stepsons Tiberius and Drusus over the Vindelici, and so compelled him to add a fourth to his three books of lyrics after a long silence. Furthermore, after reading several of his 'Talks,' the Emperor thus expressed his pique that no mention was made of him: 'You must know that I am not pleased with you, that in your numerous writings of this kind you do not talk with me, rather than with others. Are you afraid that your reputation with posterity will suffer because it appears that you were my friend?' In this way he forced from Horace the selection which begins with these words: 'Seeing that single-handed thou dost bear the burden of tasks so many and so great, protecting Italy's realm with arms, providing it with morals, reforming it by laws, I should sin against the public weal, Caesar, if I wasted thy time with long discourse.'

4   In person he was short and fat, as he is described with his own pen in his satires and by Augustus in the following letter: 'Onysius has brought me your little volume, and I accept it, small as it is, in good part, as an apology. But you seem to me to be afraid that your books may be bigger than you are yourself; but it is only stature that you lack, not girth. So you may write on a pint pot, that the circumference of your volume may be well rounded out, like that of your own belly.'

5   It is said that he was immoderately lustful; for it is reported that in a room lined with mirrors he had harlots so arranged that whichever way he looked, he saw a reflection of venery. He lived for the most part in the country on his Sabine or Tiburtine estate, and his house is pointed out near the little grove of Tiburnus. I possess some elegies attributed to his pen and a letter in prose, supposed to be a recommendation of himself to Maecenas, but I think that both are spurious; for the elegies are commonplace and the letter is besides obscure, which was by no means one of his faults.

6   He was born on the sixth day before the Ides of December in the consulate of Lucius Cotta and Lucius Torquatus, and died on the fifth day before the Kalends of the same month in the consulship of Gaius Marcius Censorinus and Gaius Asinius Gallus, fifty-nine days after the death of Maecenas, in his fifty-seventh year. He named Augustus as his heir by word of mouth, since he could not make and sign a will because of the sudden violence of his ailment. He was buried and laid to rest near the tomb of Maecenas on the farther part of the Esquiline Hill.

[Suetonius] *Life of Horace*
tr. J. C. Rolfe (Loeb 1914)

F8 *Satires* 1. 6

The Roman 'satire' implied poetic composition of relatively free form and content; often, however, the subject tended to be discussion of literary, social and ethical questions with emphasis on 'examples' of virtue and vice (hence the development into what we would now recognize as satire). A prominent feature of Horace's Satires (among his earliest work) is the use of autobiography as a way of introducing reflections on morality and life. The following passage, taken from a poem on social and political ambition, reveals the poet's independence, respect for his father and pride in his lowly origins, while defending himself from a charge of 'social climbing'.

I revert now to myself—only a freedman's son,
run down by everyone as only a freedman's son,
now because I'm a friend of yours, Maecenas, before
because as a military tribune I commanded a Roman legion.
The two factors are different; a person might have reason
to grudge me that rank, but he shouldn't grudge me your friendship too,   50
especially as you are so careful to choose suitable people,
and to hold aloof from twisters on the make. I could never say
I was lucky in the sense that I *just happened* to win your friendship.
It wasn't chance that brought you into my life. In the first place
the admirable Virgil and then Varius told you what I was.
When I met you in person I just gulped out a few words,
for diffidence tied my tongue and stopped me from speaking plainly.
I didn't pretend that I had a distinguished father or possessed
estates outside Tarentum which I rode around on a horse.
I told you what I was. As usual, you answered briefly. I left.   60
Nine months later you asked me back and invited me to join
your group of friends. For me the great thing is that I won
the regard of a discriminating man like you, not by having
a highly distinguished father but by decency of heart and character.

Yet if my faults are not too serious or too many, and if
my nature, apart from such blemishes, in other respects is sound
(just as on a handsome body you might notice a few moles),
if no one can fairly accuse me of greed or meanness or frequenting
brothels, if (to blow my own trumpet) my life is clean
and above reproach, and my friends are fond of me, then the credit   70
is due to my father.
                He was a poor man with a few
scraggy acres, yet he wouldn't send me to Flavius' school
where the important boys, the sons of important sergeant-majors,
used to go, with satchel and slate swinging from the left arm,
clutching their tenpenny fee on the Ides of every month.

Instead he courageously took his boy to Rome, to be taught
the accomplishments which any knight or senator would have his own
progeny taught. Anyone who noticed my clothes and the servants
in attendance (a feature of city life) would have assumed
that the money for these items came from the family coffers.   80
My father himself was the most trustworthy guardian imaginable,
accompanying me to all my classes. In short he preserved my innocence
(which is fundamental in forming a good character), saving me
not only from nasty behaviour but from nasty imputations.
He wasn't worried that someone might fault him later on
if I became an auctioneer or, like himself, a broker,
and didn't make much money; nor would I have complained.
As it is, I owe him all the more respect and gratitude.

> Horace *Satires* 1. 6. 45–88
> tr. N. Rudd (Penguin 1979)

F9 *Epistles* 1. 13

The Epistles, *among Horace's later works, are literary letters which largely continue and enlarge on the themes of the* Satires. *The following is an exception—a witty letter to a messenger but clearly aimed at Augustus. The 'book' is Horace's* Odes *1–3 and the date c. 23 BC.*

As I told you, Vinnius, at length and often, when you were leaving,
be sure to deliver the rolls to Augustus with seal intact,
if he's well and in good form, and *if* he requests them.
Don't blunder out of zeal for me, and by doing your duty
with excessive ardour make my little volumes unwelcome.
If you find the pages heavy and abrasive, throw them away;
but don't, on reaching the right address, go crashing in
with your load like a wild thing, turning the fine old family name
of Ass into a joke, and becoming a subject of gossip.

Use your strength to get over mountain, stream and bog.   10
Then, when you've struggled through and arrived at your destination,
this is how you should hold the parcel—you mustn't carry
the bundle of books under your arm, like a hick with a lamb,
or tipsy Pirria with her stolen ball of wool, or a workman
with cap and slippers at the dinner of a prominent fellow tribesman.
Don't tell all and sundry how much you sweated to carry
poems which I hope Caesar will enjoy reading and hearing.

Those, then, are my many instructions. Press ahead.
Good-bye; and please don't trip and fall down on all you're charged with!

Horace *Epistles* 1. 13
tr. N. Rudd (Penguin 1979)

F10 *Epistles* 2.1

Horace was one of the great literary critics of his day. The following two passages deal with two major preoccupations of Roman poets; first, the theoretical question of Rome's cultural debt to Greece and second, the more practical problem of patronage and how to refuse a commission gracefully. Both extracts are taken from an Epistle *addressed to Augustus, an answer, according to the* Life *(see above F7 § 3) prompted by Augustus' pique at not being mentioned in the* Satires. *The second passage may be seen as a graceful excuse for not giving Augustus a more prominent place in his poetry.*

(a)

When Greece surrendered she took control of her rough invader,   156
and brought the arts to rustic Latium. Then the primitive
metre of Saturn dried up; and the fetid smell gave way
to cleaner air; nevertheless for many years
there remained, and still remain today, signs of the farmyard.
It was late when the Roman applied his brains to Greek writing.
In the peace which followed the Punic wars he began to wonder
if Aeschylus, Thespis and Sophocles had anything useful to offer,
and if he himself could produce an adequate version. He tried,
and liked the result, having grand ideas and natural keenness.
(He did catch some of the tragic spirit and his strokes came off,
but he had the novice's guilty dread of using a rubber.)

(b)

Your own judgement of poets, however, is fully upheld   245
by your favourite writers Virgil and Varius; also the presents
they have received reflect the greatest credit on you.
The truth is that the mind and character of famous men
come through as clearly in a poet's work as the features do
in a bronze statue. For my part, rather than writing talks
that creep on the ground I'd sooner celebrate mighty deeds,
describing the lie of the land, the course of rivers, the setting
of forts on mountain tops, barbarous kingdoms, and then
the ending of strife throughout the world by your command,

Janus guardian of peace locked behind his bars,
and the Parthian overawed by your imperial might—
if only my powers matched my yearning; but a minor poem
is not in keeping with your pre-eminence, and I should be rash
to venture upon a task so far beyond my abilities.

Horace *Epistles* 2. 1. 156–67; 245–59
tr. N. Rudd (Penguin 1979)

F11 *Odes* 1. 1

The first three books of Horace's Odes *were published in 23 BC and were composed over the previous ten years or so. We know nothing about publication (but see F7).*

This poem was written to stand at the head of the collection of Odes *1–3, and was consequently addressed to Horace's patron Maecenas. The poet uses a traditional catalogue of 'lives' in order to assert his own particular calling.*

Maecenas, son of royal stock,
My friend, my honour, my firm rock,
The enthusiastic charioteer
Stirs up the Olympic dust, then, clear-
ing turning-post with red-hot wheels,
Snatches the victor's palm and feels
Lord of the earth, god among men;
The politician glories when
The fickle voters designate
Him three times public magistrate;
A third if in his barns he stores
All Libya's wheat-stacked threshing floors.
The peasant happy with a rake
Scratching his family fields won't take
Even an Attaline reward
To face the terrors of shipboard,
An awkward landsman trying to plough
Salt furrows with a Cyprian prow.
The trader, when the southerly gales
Tussle the waves round Samos, quails
And grumbles for a life of ease,
For his home town and fields and trees,
But, ill-disposed to learn to be
A poor man, soon refits for sea
His tossed ships. One man won't decline

Goblets of vintage Massic wine,
Or stolen time, a solid chunk
Of afternoon, sprawled by the trunk
Of a green arbutus, or spread-
eagled by some quiet fountain-head.
Another likes the life at arms,
The camp's cacophonous alarms—
Bugle and clarion—and the wars
Mothers abominate. Outdoors,
Underneath the freezing skies,
Contentedly the hunter lies,
Oblivious of his sweet young bride
When once his trusty dogs have spied
Deer, or a Marsian wild boar tears
The fine-spun netting of his snares.
But me the crown of ivy, sign
Of poets' brows, denotes divine;
Me the light troop, in the cool glen,
Of nymphs and satyrs screens from men—
While Euterpe still lets me use
Her twin pipes, and her sister Muse
Consents to tune the Lesbian lyre.
And if to the great lyric choir
You add my name, this head, held high,
Will jog the planets in the sky.

The Odes of Horace 1. 1
tr. J. Michie (Penguin 1967, repr. 1978)

F12 *Odes* 1. 4

A characteristic comparison and contrast of seasonal change with the fortunes of human life

Winter relaxes its grip. West winds are a pleasant change. The spring's here.
   The windlasses haul down the dry hulls seaward;
Penned in the stable, the beasts grow fretful; the farmer loves his fire less;
   The fields no longer shine with morning whiteness.
Queening the dance, with a full moon hanging above, the Cytherean
   Leads, and the Nymphs and comely Graces follow,
Stamping the ground to the beat, hands linked. In the Cyclops' sweltering
   workshop

Red-visaged Vulcan sets the forges blazing.
Now heads glossy with oil sport wreaths of the season's vivid myrtle
   Or the few blooms unclenching earth releases.
Time, too, now in the leaf-dark groves for a sacrifice to Faunus—
   A lamb, or else a kid, if he prefers it.
Hold! Pale Death, at the poor man's shack and the pasha's palace kicking
   Impartially, announces his arrival.
Life's brief tenure forbids high hopes to be built in disproportion,
   My lucky Sestius, for Night and Pluto's
Shadowy walls and the ghosts men talk of will soon be crowding round you.
   Once there, you cannot rule the feast by dice-throw
Or give Lycidas long rapt gazes. This year his beauty kindles
   The young men: soon the girls will catch fire also.

The Odes of Horace 1.4
tr. J. Michie (Penguin 1967, repr. 1978)

F13 *Odes* 1. 5

What slim youngster, his hair dripping with fragrant oil,
Makes hot love to you now, Pyrrha, ensconced in a
   Snug cave curtained with roses?
     Who lays claim to that casually

Chic blonde hair in a braid? Soon he'll be scolding the
Gods, whose promise, like yours, failed him, and gaping at
   Black winds making his ocean's
     Fair face unrecognisable.

He's still credulous, though, hugging the prize he thinks
Pure gold, shining and fond, his for eternity.
   Ah, poor fool, but the breeze plays
     Tricks. Doomed, all who would venture to

Sail that glittering sea. Fixed to the temple wall,
My plaque tells of an old sailor who foundered and,
   Half-drowned, hung up his clothes to
     Neptune, lord of the element.

The Odes of Horace 1.5
tr. J. Michie (Penguin 1967, repr. 1978)

F14 *Odes* 1.9

For the subject see F12.

Look how the snow lies deeply on glittering
Soracte. White woods groan and protestingly
    Let fall their branch-loads. Bitter frost has
        Paralysed rivers: the ice is solid.

Unfreeze the cold! Pile plenty of logs in the
Fireplace! And you, dear friend Thaliarchus, come,
    Bring out the Sabine wine-jar four years
        Old and be generous. Let the good gods

Take care of all else. Later, as soon as they've
Calmed down this contestation of winds upon
    Churned seas, the old ash-trees can rest in
        Peace and the cypresses stand unshaken.

Try not to guess what lies in the future, but
As Fortune deals days enter them into your
    Life's book as windfalls, credit items,
        Gratefully. Now that you're young, and peevish

Grey hairs are still far distant, attend to the
Dance-floor, the heart's sweet business; for now is the
    Right time for midnight assignations,
        Whispers and murmurs in Rome's piazzas

And fields, and soft, low laughter that gives away
The girl who plays love's games in a hiding-place—
    Off comes a ring coaxed down an arm or
        Pulled from a faintly resisting finger.

The Odes of Horace 1.9
tr. J. Michie (Penguin 1967, repr. 1978)

F15 *Odes* 1.14

The ode is a political allegory closely modelled on the sixth-century-BC Greek lyric poet, Alcaeus. The date is uncertain—perhaps shortly before Actium (31 BC) but possibly later (there is no sure evidence external to the poem itself).

Beware, good ship! Fresh squalls are taking
You out to sea again. Start making
    For harbour, run in hard.
    Listen—a groaning yard;

And look—both sides stripped, oars gone, mast
Crippled by the sou'wester's blast.
    The hull can scarcely hope,
    Shorn of its girding-rope,

To ride the ungovernable seas;
Your sails are torn; the images
    To which, hard pressed, you turn
    Have vanished from the stern.

Daughter you may be of a fine
Plantation, true-bred Pontic pine,
    But pride of name and wood
    Will do you little good.

No sailor puts his trust in mere
Paintwork in danger. Good ship, steer
    Wisely—or on a rock
    Be the wind's laughing-stock.

O once my worry and despair,
But now my loving charge and care,
    Avoid the Cyclades:
    Bright islands, treacherous seas.

The Odes of Horace 1.14
tr. J. Michie (Penguin 1967, repr. 1978)

F16 *Odes* 1.27

A dramatic sketch of a wine-party

Origins of the theme lie in Greek lyric poetry, more specifically the sixth-century Ionian, Anacreon.

To brawl with cups intended for pleasure is
What men in Thrace do—barbarous habit, to
    Be laid aside. Our modest Bacchus
      Ought to be sheltered from bloody mêlées.

Lamplight and wine make scarcely the setting for
Short Persian dirks drawn drunkenly. Hush, for the
   God's sake less uproar, comrades. Keep your
     Places, your banqueting elbows steady.

I too must down my share of Falernian
Strong wine, you say? All right; but the brother of
   Lyde from Locris has to tell whose
     Arrow has made him a blissful victim.

He's backing down? No, those are my drinking terms.
Come, I'm convinced, whoever's enslaved you, there's
   No need to blush: true love has kindled
     Passionate fires, and we know you always

Prefer a freeborn mistress. Then out with it!
Our ears are safe, no matter who . . . Miserable
   Boy, what a whirlpool's dragged you struggling
     Down! You deserve to be better suited.

What witch, what drug-skilled wizard from Thessaly,
What god indeed knows how to release you from
   That triple hell-hound's fatal clutches?
     Pegasus even could hardly manage.

The Odes of Horace 1. 27
tr. J. Michie (Penguin 1967, repr. 1978)

F17 *Odes* 1. 37

The 'Cleopatra Ode'. Written probably soon after the arrival at Rome in the autumn of 30 BC of the news of Cleopatra's suicide; cf. A. Hardie in Papers of the Liverpool Latin Seminar 1976 (pp. 113-40) who argues for dating this poem to Octavian's triumph of August, 29 BC.

Today is the day to drink and dance on. Dance, then,
Merrily, friends, till the earth shakes. Now let us
   Rival the priests of Mars
With feasts to deck the couches of the gods.

Not long ago it would have been high treason
To fetch the Caecuban from family store-rooms,
   When the wild Queen was still
Plotting destruction to our Capitol

And ruin to the Empire with her squalid
Pack of diseased half-men—mad, wishful grandeur,
    Tipsy with sweet good luck!
But all her fleet burnt, scarcely one ship saved—

That tamed her rage; and Caesar, when his galleys
Chased her from Italy, soon brought her, dreaming
    And drugged with native wine,
Back to the hard realities of fear.

As swiftly as the hawk follows the feeble
Dove, or in snowy Thessaly the hunter
    The hare, so he sailed forth
To bind this fatal prodigy in chains.

Yet she preferred a finer style of dying:
She did not, like a woman, shirk the dagger
    Or seek by speed at sea
To change her Egypt for obscurer shores,

But, gazing on her desolated palace
With a calm smile, unflinchingly laid hands on
    The angry asps until
Her veins had drunk the deadly poison deep,

And, death-determined, fiercer then than ever,
Perished. Was she to grace a haughty triumph,
    Dethroned, paraded by
The rude Liburnians? Not Cleopatra!

The Odes of Horace 1. 37
tr. J. Michie (Penguin 1967, repr. 1978)

F18 *Odes* 2. 1

To Gaius Asinius Pollio (76 BC–AD 5) a man of affairs and historian. As this Ode tells us, Pollio had selected for his historical theme the period from the consulship of Metellus, i.e. 60 BC, the year of the formation of the first triumvirate, up to the supremacy of Augustus.

Your theme is civil warfare since Metellus
Was consul. To describe its causes, phases
    And crimes, Fortune's caprice,
The doomed alliances of triumvirs,

The blood-smeared weapons still unexpiated,
Is to traverse a field sown thick with hazards,
    Pollio: you tread on fire
Still smouldering underneath deceptive ash.

Yet do not leave our theatre long deserted
By your stern tragic Muse. Soon, when the history
    Is ordered on the page,
Renew your high vocation, don again

The Attic buskin—you whom the despairing
Defendant and the pondering Senate lean on,
    You whom the laurel brought
Long-lasting glory in Dalmatia's war.

So now you batter our ear-drums with alarums
Blared from the ominous horn and clarion; arms flash
    And horses panic; fear
Quivers reflected in the rider's face.

I have a vision of the great commanders
Jacketed in grime, their uniform of honour,
    And of a world subdued
Except for Cato's unforgiving soul.

Now Juno and the gods who once befriended
The Africans but had no power to save them
    Reap their revenge and lay
The victors' grandsons at Jugurtha's tomb

As sacrifice. Our fields are rich with Roman
Dead and not one lacks graves to speak against our
    Impious battles. Even
Parthia can hear the ruin of the West.

What lake or river has not had a taste of
Sorrowful war? Our seas are all discoloured
    By slaughter; every beach
Is redder for the spilling of our blood.

Steady, wild Muse! Have you forsworn your light touch?
Simonides wrote better dirges. Come, let's
    Go to the cave of love
And look for music in a jollier key.

The Odes of Horace 2.1
tr. J. Michie (Penguin 1967, repr. 1978)

F19 *Odes* 2.7

To Pompeius, describing their mutual exploits at the battle of Philippi (where Horace served the Republican side) and the joy of reunion

> Pompeius, chief of all my friends, with whom
> I often ventured to the edge of doom
> > When Brutus led our line,
> > With whom, aided by wine
>
> And garlands and Arabian spikenard,
> I killed that afternoon that died so hard—
> > Who has new-made you, then,
> > A Roman citizen
>
> And given you back your native gods and weather?
> We two once beat a swift retreat together
> > Upon Philippi's field,
> > When I dumped my poor shield,
>
> And courage cracked, and the strong men who frowned
> Fiercest were felled, chins to the miry ground.
> > But I, half-dead with fear,
> > Was wafted, airborne, clear
>
> Of the enemy lines, wrapped in a misty blur
> By Mercury, not sucked back, as you were,
> > From safety and the shore
> > By the wild tide of war.
>
> Pay Jove his feast, then. In my laurel's shade
> Stretch out the bones that long campaigns have made
> > Weary. Your wine's been waiting
> > For years: no hesitating!
>
> Fill up the polished goblets to the top
> With memory-drowning Massic! Slave, unstop
> > The deep-mouthed shells that store
> > Sweet-smelling oil and pour!
>
> Who'll run to fit us out with wreaths and find
> Myrtle and parsley, damp and easily twined?
> > Who'll win the right to be
> > Lord of the revelry
>
> By dicing highest? I propose to go
> As mad as a Thracian. It's sheer joy to throw
> > Sanity overboard
> > When a dear friend's restored.

The Odes of Horace 2.7
tr. J. Michie (Penguin 1967, repr. 1978)

F20 *Odes* 2. 15

A characteristic Augustan attitude—nostalgia for bygone 'austerity' and 'public spirit'

>Soon I foresee few acres for harrowing
>Left once the rich men's villas have seized the land;
>   Fishponds that outdo Lake Lucrinus
>   Everywhere; bachelor plane-trees ousting
>
>Vine-loving elms; thick myrtle-woods, violet-beds,
>All kinds of rare blooms tickling the sense of smell,
>   Perfumes to drown those olive orchards
>   Nursed in the past for a farmer's profit;
>
>Quaint garden-screens, too, woven of laurel-boughs
>To parry sunstroke. Romulus never urged
>   This style of life; rough-bearded Cato
>   Would have detested the modern fashions.
>
>Small private wealth, large communal property—
>So ran the rule then. No one had porticoes
>   Laid out with ten-foot builder's measures,
>   Trapping the cool of the northern shadow.
>
>No one in those days sneered at the turf by the
>Roadside; yet laws bade citizens beautify
>   Townships at all men's cost and quarry
>   Glorious marble to roof the temples.

The Odes of Horace 2. 15
tr. J. Michie (Penguin 1967, repr. 1978)

F21 *Odes* 2. 16

>Peace and calm seas the voyager begs the gods for
>When storms blow up in mid-Aegean, and black clouds
>Muffle the moon, and sailors miss the usual
>   Stars in the sky;
>
>And peace is what the battle-maddened Thracians
>And the fierce Parthians with their painted quivers
>Pray for—the peace no gold or gems or purple,
>   Grosphus, can buy.
>
>A pasha's bribes, a consul's rodded lictors
>Can soon disperse a riot of the people,

But not the grey mob of the mind, the worries
    Circling the beams

Of fretted ceilings. He lives well on little
Whose family salt-dish glitters on a plain-laid
Table; no fears or ugly longings steal his
    Innocent dreams.

Why do we aim so high, when time must foil our
Brave archery? Why hanker after countries
Heated by foreign suns? What exile ever
    Fled his own mind?

Care, that contagion, clambers up the bronze-prowed
Galley, keeps level with the galloping squadron,
Outruns the stag and leaves the cloud-compelling
    East wind behind.

Happy with here and now, scorning hereafter,
Heart, with an easy humorousness attemper
The bitterness of things. Nothing is perfect
    Seen from all sides.

Death snatched away Achilles in his glory,
Long-drawn-out age wasted Tithonus inchmeal,
And any day may keep from you some blessing
    Which it provides

Me with. Sicilian cattle moo, a hundred
Herds, in your meadow, mares trained for the race-track
Neigh in your stalls, you dress in Tyrian purple,
    Double-dyed woof;

But I am rich too: Fate, an honest patron,
Has given me a small farm, an ear fine-tuned to
The Grecian Muses, and a mind from vulgar
    Envy aloof.

The Odes of Horace 2. 16
tr. J. Michie (Penguin, 1967, repr. 1978)

F22 *Odes* 3. 5

The 'Regulus Ode'. A poem about honour, culminating with a famous historical exemplum, the conduct of M. Atilius Regulus during the Carthaginian wars. The story of his voluntary return to Carthage had a strong moral appeal for the Romans (cf. Cicero De Officiis *3. 99–115–G13). See further J. Ferguson* Moral Values in the Ancient World *(London 1958) ch. 9.*

Thunder in heaven confirms our faith—Jove rules there;
But here on earth Augustus shall be hailed as
    God also, when he makes
New subjects of the Briton and the dour

Parthian. Did Crassus' troops live in dishonour
With Medish wives and grow grey-headed serving
    (O Roman Senate! O
Custom corrupted!) a barbarian power

And enemy in-laws? Marsians, Apulians,
Forget the Sacred Shields, Rome's name, the toga
    And Vesta's deathless flame,
While Jupiter's temple and the City stood

Unharmed? This was the shame far-seeing Regulus
Guarded against when he refused a base peace
    And spurned the precedent
That would have brought the unborn age no good:

And so the captives forfeited his pity,
The young men died. 'For I have seen our eagles
    Nailed to the Punic shrines,'
Regulus said, 'swords wrested from our men

And no blood spilt; with these eyes I have witnessed
The hands of citizens and free men pinioned
    Behind their backs, the gates
Of Carthage wide, their scarred fields tilled again.

As if a soldier hurried back to battle
Fiercer for being ransomed! Sirs, you are heaping
    Loss upon shame. When wool
Is dipped in purple, farewell to its white

Purity. Courage, likewise, once departed,
Is slow to pay failed hearts a second visit.
    If does, freed from the net,
Make no resistance, will a man show fight

Who gave himself to known perfidious enemies?
Will he take arms again to wear down Carthage
    Who meekly let his wrists
Feel ropes and would not look death in the face?

Blind to his source of safety, he confuses
The qualities of peace and war. Thus honour
 Dies and great Carthage climbs
Higher on Italy's ruin and disgrace!'

They say he drew back from the kiss his true wife
And little children begged, and like a prisoner
 Deprived of civil rights
Bent an austere gaze grimly on the ground,

Until his unexampled admonition
Had fixed the wavering Senate in their purpose
 And he could push through crowds
Of grieving friends, exile- and glory-bound.

And yet he knew what the barbarian torturer
Had ready for him. Kinsmen blocked his passage,
 The people held him back,
But he returned as unconcernedly

As if they were his clients and he'd settled
Some lengthy lawsuit for them and was going
 On to Venafrum's fields
Or to Tarentum, Sparta's colony.

The Odes of Horace 3. 5
tr. J. Michie (Penguin 1967, repr. 1978)

F23 *Odes* 3. 9

'When you loved me, dear Lydia, when
I was preferred and your white neck was
Not for the arms of other men,
I was as happy as the King of Persia then.'

'When you loved me, dear, when I came
First in your heart and Chloe second,
Then Lydia proudly wrote her name
Next to our Roman Ilia's in the roll of fame.'

'Chloe's queen now, my girl from Thrace,
Who sings and plays the lyre divinely.
If Fate would spare that darling face,
I'd suffer death unflinchingly in Chloe's place.'

'Ornytus' son from Thurii
Has fired my heart, and his is burning.
If Fate let him live and doomed me,
I'd die for Calais twice over willingly.'

'What if past love came back and tied
Us teamed to the brass yoke of Venus,
    If blonde Chloe were thrust outside
And jilted Lydia found the door left open wide?'

'Though he's star-bright and you're as mad
As the outrageous Adriatic
    And light as cork, I'd still be glad
To live with you and die with you, come good or bad.'

The Odes of Horace 3.9
tr. J. Michie (Penguin 1967, repr. 1978)

F24 *Odes* 3. 29

To Maecenas: riches contrasted with self-sufficiency in the face of Fortune

Descendant of Etruscan kings, Maecenas,
A jar of mellow wine still to be tilted,
    Choice roses, Syrian oil
Prepared expressly for your hair, all wait

Patiently in my house. Bestir yourself, then!
Why gaze all year towards the brooks of Tibur,
    Aefula's sloping fields
And the high hilltop which the parricide

Telegonus built? Leave your unpleasing plenty,
Leave your cloud-grazing palace, leave admiring
    The glamour of great Rome—
The money and the hubbub and the smoke.

Change for the rich can be a kind of pleasure,
And a plain meal well served in a poor cottage
    (Bare walls, no purple cloth)
Often unties the lines that worry knits.

Now shining Cepheus hoists his constellation
Up from the dark, now Procyon and Leo,
    Fierce, heat-heralding stars,
Glare as the sun brings back the days of drought;

The weary shepherd with his spent flock makes for
Shadow and water and the shaggy wood-god's
    Thickets; the river-bank
Dumbly endures the absence of the breeze.

Yet still you labour to perfect the pattern
Of government, Rome's anxious sentry keeping
    Watch on the farthest East,
Cyrus' old kingdom and the uneasy Don

For plots of war. God, though, has wisely locked up
The outcome in impenetrable darkness,
    And laughs when mortals show
Inquisitive apprehension. I commend

A level mind that grapples with what's here now.
As for the rest, look on it as a river,
    One moment calm and tame,
Gliding to meet the Tuscan sea, the next

Churning a chaos of gouged rocks, torn tree-trunks,
Corpses and rubble of houses, while the mountains
    And forests amplify
The roar and pitiless rain exacerbates

The temper of the water. Call him happy
And lord of his own soul who every evening
    Can say, 'Today I have lived.
Tomorrow Jove may blot the sky with cloud

Or fill it with pure sunshine, yet he cannot
Devalue what has once been held as precious,
    Or tarnish or melt back
The gold the visiting hour has left behind.'

Fortune enjoys her grim work and will never
Give up the cruel game she plays of changing
    Her mind and her rewards:
She loves me, then she loves me not, woos him.

I praise her when she's by, but let her stretch those
Wings, I write off her gifts as losses, pull on
    Philosophy's cloak and court
Poverty, who brings no dowry but is true.

To grovel in prayer because the mast is groaning
Under the gale is not my style; I will not
    Haggle with heaven: 'God save
My bales from Tyre and Cyprus lest they go

To swell the greedy sea's collection!' I just
Bob through the storms of the Aegean, safely
    Tucked in my rowing-boat,
Sped by the weather and the Heavenly Twins.

The Odes of Horace 3.29
tr. J. Michie (Penguin 1967, repr. 1978)

F25 *Odes* 3.30

A formal epilogue

More durable than bronze, higher than Pharaoh's
Pyramids is the monument I have made,
A shape that angry wind or hungry rain
Cannot demolish, nor the innumerable
Ranks of the years that march in centuries.
I shall not wholly die: some part of me
Will cheat the goddess of death, for while High Priest
And Vestal climb our Capitol in a hush,
My reputation shall keep green and growing.
Where Aufidus growls torrentially, where once,
Lord of a dry kingdom, Daunus ruled
His rustic people, I shall be renowned
As one who, poor-born, rose and pioneered
A way to fit Greek rhythms to our tongue.
Be proud, Melpomene, for you deserve
What praise I have, and unreluctantly
Garland my forehead with Apollo's laurel.

The Odes of Horace 3.30
tr. J. Michie (Penguin 1967, repr. 1978)

F26 *Odes* 4.4

The fourth Book of Odes was written c. 13 BC in response to a request from Augustus that Horace should celebrate the military exploits of Drusus and Tiberius in 15 BC. The following poem is directly on this subject, and praises also the guiding paternal hand of Augustus himself.

267

Have you seen the feathered servant of the lightning,
Made by the king of gods king of his wandering
    Kind for his trusty part
In kidnapping the blond boy Ganymede?

Young blood and eagle's energy first launch him
Out of the nest to meet a sky of troubles,
    And the spring winds conspire,
Now storms are past, to teach his timid wings

Airy adventures. Soon his great sweep sends him
Plummeting down to terrify the sheepfold,
    Or, rage- and hunger-driven,
He lugs the wrestling serpent in his grip.

Have you seen a roe-deer browsing in contentment,
And then a lion whelp come upon her, freshly
    Weaned from the tawny teat—
Doomed she looks up, food for his unfleshed tooth?

Eagle or lion was Drusus to the warring
Vindelici among the Rhaetian passes,
    Whose right hands have preferred
The Amazon axe from immemorial time

(Custom whose origin we cannot guess here,
Nor should men sound all knowledge). Long unconquered,
    Victors on many fields,
Their armies scattered by a young man's skill

Have learnt what power accrues when mind and heart are
Fed with religion in a reverent household,
    Learnt what paternal love
Can do, when it is Caesar's, for two boys.

Brave noble men father brave noble children.
In bulls and horses likewise the male's stamp shows
    Clearly; we never find
Fear bred from fierceness, eagles hatching doves.

Yet it is training that promotes the inborn
Talent, and morals that shore up the spirit.
    When laws of conduct fail,
Vice mars what nature once formed excellent.

How deep the debt you owe the clan of Nero,
Rome, the Metaurus witnesses, and routed
    Hasdrubal, and that day
When darkness lifted over Latium

And victory had its first fair Roman dawn since
The terrible African rode through our cities
 Like fire through pine-woods, like
An east wind whipping the Sicilian waves.

From that day Roman manhood plucked momentum
And marched from strength to strength. The shrines that Carthage
 Laid barbarously waste
Refurbished saw their gods stand straight again,

Till the perfidious Hannibal in despair cried,
'We are like deer, predestined prey, who yet would
 Run after ravening wolves.
Triumph for us lies in retreat and stealth.

This race that, risen undaunted from Troy's ashes,
Ferried its gods, old men and children over
 The tossing Tuscan sea
To house them safely in Italian towns,

Is like some tough-grained oak, lopped by the woodman
On Algidus, that dark-boughed, verdurous mountain:
 It bleeds, it feels the shock,
Yet draws in vigour from the very axe,

Flourishing as fiercely as the severed Hydra
Sprouted at chafing Hercules. Old Cadmus'
 Dragon-sown fields at Thebes
Never pushed up a prodigy like this.

Whelm it in water, it will come up brighter.
Throw it, and it will grapple with the winner
 Again and take the applause.
The wars they wage breed tales for wives to tell.

Henceforward I'll no more send home to Carthage
Arrogant messengers to proclaim my triumphs.
 Lost, lost all hope and sunk
Our nation's star now Hasdrubal is dead.'

There's not a feat that cannot be accomplished
By Claudian hands. Jupiter smiles upon their
 Works, and their wise designs
Pilot us through the rapids of our wars.

The Odes of Horace 4.4
tr. J. Michie (Penguin 1967, repr. 1978)

F27 *Odes* 4. 7

On the subject, see F12 above.

Snow's gone away; green grass comes back to the meadows, and green leaves
    Back to the trees, as the earth
Suffers her springtime change. Now last month's torrents, diminished,
    Keep to their channels. The Grace
Dares to unrobe and, the Nymphs and her two sweet sisters attending,
    Ventures a dance in the woods.
Yet be warned: each year gone round, each day-snatching hour says,
    'Limit your hopes: you must die.'
Frost gives way to the warm west winds, soon summer shall trample
    Spring and be trodden in turn
Under the march of exuberant, fruit-spilling autumn, then back comes
    Winter to numb us again,
Moons make speed to repair their heavenly losses, but not so
    We, who, when once we have gone
Downwards to join rich Tullus and Ancus and father Aeneas,
    Crumble to shadow and dust.
Who knows whether the all-high gods intend an addition
    Made to the sum of today?
Give to your own dear self: that gift is the only possession
    Fingers of heirs cannot grasp.
Once you are dead, Torquatus, and Minos delivers his august
    Verdict upon your affairs,
No blue blood, no good deeds done, no eloquent pleading
    Ever shall conjure you back.
Great is the power of Diana and chaste was Hippolytus, yet still
    Prisoned in darkness he lies.
Passionate Theseus was, yet could not shatter the chains Death
    Forged for his Pirithous.

The Odes of Horace 4.7
tr. J. Michie (Penguin 1967, repr. 1978)

F28 Ovid's life: *Tristia* 4. 10

In AD 8, Ovid, a poet of great reputation and assured position in Roman society was exiled for misdemeanour—a 'poem' (the Art of Love*) and a 'mistake' the nature of which (although Ovid alludes to it again and again) remains a mystery. It may be connected with the politics of the Imperial succession or implication in a scandal*

*involving the younger Julia who was banished at about this time. While in exile on
the Black Sea coast at Tomi (modern Constanza), Ovid wrote poems asserting his
innocence and requesting review of his sentence. Among these, collectively called*
Tristia *(poems of sadness), is an autobiography, which is reproduced below.*

Posterity, recognize who it is you're reading,
    the poet of fun, kindness, love.
Born in Sulmo, a land rich in ice-cold water,
    ninety miles from Rome—
there I appeared in the very year when
    both consuls fell in battle.
If it counts for anything, my rank was ancestral, long-standing—
    no knighthood of recent fortune.
I was not the first child, having a brother
10   a year older.
The same star watched both our births,
    two cakes were offered on a single day,
the day among the five of Minerva's festival
    when blood flows in battle.
We began our education young; our father's care
    took us to Rome's men of learning,
My brother inclined to oratory even in his greener years;
    he was born for a war of words.
From my boyhood I loved the rites of the gods,
20   the Muse was secretly claiming me.
Often my father would say 'Why go in for an unprofitable profession?
    Homer died penniless.'
I was stunned by his words, totally abandoned Helicon,
    tried writing prose.
Song came effortlessly in appropriate metres,
    everything I wrote was verse.
Meantime the years passed by with silent step;
    my brother and I donned the toga,
our shoulders wore the broad purple stripe, while
30   our enthusiasms were unchanged.
But my brother doubled a decade and died,
    I lost half of myself.
I received the first office of youth,
    a member of the Board of Three.
There remained the senate; I chose to cut my stripe;
    that was too big for me.
I had no tough physique, no mind for the work,
    I avoided ambition's anxieties.
The Muses kept directing me to retirement.
40   That's what I wanted too.

I followed the poets of the day,
    thought each a god incarnate.
Macer, getting on in years, would read to me of birds,
    poisonous snakes, healing herbs.
Propertius liked declaiming to me of the fires of love,
    a close friend.
Among epic poets Ponticus, among iambic writers Bassus
    were delightful companions.
Horace held my attention by his mastery of metre
50   in Latin lyric.
Vergil I only just saw; the greedy Fates deprived
    Tibullus of my friendship.
Tibullus succeeded you, Gallus; Propertius succeeded Tibullus.
    I came fourth in line.
Younger people showed me the honour I gave my elders;
    my poetry was presently popular.
I first gave public readings of my adolescent verses
    when I'd hardly started to shave.
What moved my talent? Corinna (not her real name)!
60   All Rome was singing of her.
I wrote a great deal, but where I discerned faults
    I gave them to the flames to revise.
In fact, as I went into exile, I burnt stuff which would have given pleasure
    in disgust with my profession.
My heart was impressionable, no match for Cupid's weapons,
    moved by light impulses.
Such I was, inflamed by the tiniest spark—yet
    no scandal touched my name.
When I was but a boy, I was made to marry an unworthy wife—
70   not for long!
Number two was a blameless bedfellow, but only
    briefly with me.
My last wife has stayed with me into old age,
    patient in marriage to an exile.
My daughter, with two children by different husbands,
    made me a grandfather.
My father had fulfilled his destiny, reaching
    the age of ninety.
I mourned him as he would have mourned me.
80   Next my mother died.
Both were happy in dying opportunely
    before my condemnation,
and I am happy that they did not live to see my unhappiness
    or shed tears over me.

Yet if anything besides the name survives death,
  if some shade escapes the pyre,
if news of me reaches my parents' shades,
  if I am arraigned before the court of Hades,
I pray that they may know, in all honesty, that the sentence of banishment
90   was for a mistake not a crime.
So much for the dead. I turn back to those eager to know
  the course of my life.
My best years were past, whiteness strewed
  my younger hairs,
ten times since my birth the olive-crowned charioteer
  had secured the prize at Olympia,
When the Emperor's indignation ordered me to Tomis
  in the Black Sea, on the left side.
Everyone knows—all too clearly—why I fell;
100   no place for words of mine.
What need to tell of the treachery of friends and malice of servants?
  I had plenty to bear as bad as exile!
My spirit refused to give way to disaster, and showed itself
  unconquerable within.
I forgot myself, forgot my life of peace, took up
  the weapons of the moment.
The misfortunes I faced by land and sea outnumbered
  the stars in the sky.
I wandered long, eventually reaching the shores where
110   the Getae adjoin Sarmatia.
Here while the clash of arms rings round me, as I can
  I solace myself with song.
There is no one to listen.
  In pretence I spend the day.
The fact that I am alive, that I put a firm front on hardship,
  that I look sorrow in the face,
I owe to poetry. It offers me comfort,
  rest and remedy,
it is my guide and companion, transporting me from the Danube
120   to Helicon,
it has given me, what few are granted, glory while alive—
  no need to wait for death!
Jealousy, which grudges present glories, has not eaten away
  an atom of my work.
Our age has produced great poets,
  but my reputation stands.
There are many I rank above myself, but others rank me with them,
  and I *am* the best-seller.

If poets have any prophetic gift, were I to die this minute,
130   earth could not claim me.
My reputation may be due to your kindness or my own poetry,
     but, gentle reader, thank you.

Ovid *Tristia* 4. 10
tr. J. Ferguson

F29 *Tristia* 2. 353–370

Ovid seeks to excuse his offence (the writing of the Ars Amatoria*) by emphasizing the distinction between poetry and morality.*

I assure you, my character differs from my verse (my life is moral, my muse is gay), and most of my work, unreal and fictitious, has allowed itself more licence than its author has had. A book is not an evidence of one's soul, but an honourable impulse that presents very many things suited to charm the ear. Else would Accius be cruel, Terence a reveller, or those would be quarrelsome who sing of fierce war.

Moreover, not I alone have written tales of tender love, but for writing of love I alone have been punished. What but the union of love and lavish wine was the teaching of the lyric muse of the aged Tean bard? What did Lesbian Sappho teach the girls if not love? Yet Sappho was secure, the Tean also was secure. It did not injure thee, scion of Battus, that thou didst often in verse confess to the reader thy wanton pleasures. No play of charming Menander is free from love, yet he is wont to be read by boys and girls.

Ovid *Tristia* 2. 353–70
tr. A. L. Wheeler (Loeb 1924)

F30 Ovid's *Metamorphoses* 15. 745–879

Ovid's Metamorphoses, *a poem in fifteen books in which mythological stories involving changes of shape or 'metamorphoses' are related, concludes with a contemporary theme, the transformation of Julius Caesar into a star and the establishment of Augustus, eventually to be deified in his turn.*

On the Metamorphoses *see further L. P. Wilkinson* Ovid Recalled *(Cambridge 1955) ch. 7; B. Otis* Ovid as an Epic Poet *(Cambridge 1970); G. K. Galinsky* Ovid's Metamorphoses *(Oxford 1978).*

The Deification of Caesar

                              The old god
Came to our shrines from foreign lands, but Caesar
Is god in his own city. First in war,
And first in peace, victorious, triumphant,
Planner and governor, quick-risen to glory,
The newest star in Heaven, and more than this,
And above all, immortal through his son.
No work, in all of Caesar's great achievement,
Surpassed this greatness, to have been the father
Of our own Emperor. To have tamed the Britons,
Surrounded by the fortress of their ocean,
To have led a proud victorious armada
Up seven-mouthed Nile, to have added to the empire
Rebel Numidia, Libya, and Pontus
Arrogant with the name of Mithridates,
To have had many triumphs, and deserved
Many more triumphs: this was truly greatness,
Greatness surpassed only by being father
Of one yet greater, one who rules the world
As proof that the immortal gods have given
Rich blessing to the human race, so much so
We cannot think him mortal, our Augustus,
Therefore our Julius must be made a god
To justify his son.
                              And golden Venus
Saw this, and saw, as well, the murder plotted
Against her priest, the assassins in their armor,
And she grew pale with fear. 'Behold,' she cried
To all the gods in turn, 'Behold, what treason
Threatens me with its heavy weight, what ambush
Is set to take Iulus' last descendant!
Must this go on forever? Once again
The spear of Diomedes strikes to wound me,
The walls of Troy fall over me in ruins,
Once more I see my son, long-wandering,
Storm-tossed, go down to the shades, and rise again
To war with Turnus, or to speak more truly,
With Juno. It is very foolish of me
To dwell on those old sufferings, for my fear,
My present fear, has driven them from my mind.
Look: Do you see them whetting their evil daggers?
Avert this crime, before the fires of Vesta
Drown in their high-priest's blood!'

                                        The anxious goddess
Cried these complaints through Heaven, and no one listened.
The gods were moved, and though they could not shatter
The iron mandates of the ancient sisters,
They still gave certain portents of the evil
To come upon the world. In the dark storm-clouds
Arms clashed and trumpets blared, most terrible,
And horns heard in the sky warned men of crime,
And the sun's visage shone with lurid light
On anxious lands. Firebrands were seen to flash
Among the stars, the clouds dripped blood, rust-color
Blighted the azure Morning-Star, and the Moon
Rode in a blood-red car. The Stygian owl
Wailed in a thousand places; ivory statues
Dripped tears in a thousand places, and wailing traveled
The holy groves, and threats were heard. No victim
Paid expiation, and the liver warned
Of desperate strife to come, the lobe found cloven
Among the entrails. In the market place,
Around the homes of men and the gods' temples
Dogs howled by night, and the shadows of the silent
Went roaming, and great earthquakes shook the city.
No warning of the gods could check the plotting
Of men, avert the doom of fate. Drawn swords
Were borne into a temple; nowhere else
In the whole city was suitable for murder
Save where the senate met.
                                        Then Venus beat
Her breast with both her hands, and tried to hide him,
Her Caesar, in a cloud, as she had rescued
Paris from Menelaus, as Aeneas
Fled Diomedes' sword. And Jove spoke to her:
'My daughter, do you think your power alone
Can move the fates no power can ever conquer?
Enter the home of the Three Sisters: there
You will see the records, on bronze and solid iron,
Wrought with tremendous effort, and no crashing
Of sky, no wrath of lightning, no destruction
Shall make them crumble. They are safe, forever.
There you will find engraved on adamant
The destinies of the race, unchangeable.
I have read them, and remembered; I will tell you
So you may know the future. He has finished
The time allotted him, this son you grieve for;

His debt to earth is paid. But he will enter
The Heaven as a god, and have his temples
On earth as well: this you will see fulfilled,
Will bring about, you and his son together.
He shall inherit both the name of Caesar
And the great burden, and we both shall help him
Avenge his father's murder. Under him
Mutina's conquered walls will sue for mercy,
Pharsalia know his power, and Philippi
Run red with blood again, and one more Pompey
Go down to death in the Sicilian waters.
A Roman general's Egyptian woman,
Foolish to trust that liaison, will perish
For all her threats that our own capitol
Would serve Canopus. Need I bring to mind
Barbarian lands that border either ocean?
Whatever lands men live on, the world over,
Shall all be his to rule, and the seas also.
And when peace comes to all the world, his mind
Will turn to law and order, civil justice,
And men will learn from his sublime example,
And he, still looking forward toward the future,
The coming generations, will give order
That his good wife's young son should take his name,
His duty when he lays the burden down,
Though he will live as long as ancient Nestor
Before he comes to Heaven to greet his kinsmen.
Now, in the meantime, from the murdered body
Raise up the spirit, set the soul of Julius
As a new star in Heaven, to watch over
Our market place, our Capitol.'
                                        He ended,
And Venus, all unseen, came to the temple,
Raised from the body of Caesar the fleeting spirit,
Not to be lost in air, but borne aloft
To the bright stars of Heaven. As she bore it,
She felt it burn, released it from her bosom,   *soul of Caesar*
And saw it rise, beyond the moon, a comet
Rising, not falling, leaving the long fire
Behind its wake, and gleaming as a star.
And now he sees his son's good acts, confessing
They are greater than his own, for once rejoicing
In being conquered. But the son refuses
To have his glories set above his father's;

Fame will not heed him, for she heeds no mortal,
Exalts him, much against his will, resists him
In this one instance only. So must Atreus
Defer to Agamemnon; so does Theseus
Surpass Aegeus, and Achilles Peleus,
And—(one more instance where the father's glory
Yields to the son's)—Saturn is less than Jove.
Jove rules the lofty citadels of Heaven,
The kingdoms of the triple world, but Earth
Acknowledges Augustus. Each is father
As each is lord. O gods, Aeneas' comrades,
To whom the fire and sword gave way, I pray you,
And you, O native gods of Italy,
Quirinus, father of Rome, and Mars, the father
Of Rome's unconquered sire, and Vesta, honored
With Caesar's household gods, Apollo, tended
With reverence as Vesta is, and Jove,
Whose temple crowns Tarpeia's rock, O gods,
However many, whom the poet's longing
May properly invoke, far be the day,
Later than our own era, when Augustus
Shall leave the world he rules, ascend to Heaven,
And there, beyond our presence, hear our prayers!

The Epilogue

Now I have done my work. It will endure,
I trust, beyond Jove's anger, fire and sword,
Beyond Time's hunger. The day will come, I know,
So let it come, that day which has no power
Save over my body, to end my span of life
Whatever it may be. Still, part of me,
The better part, immortal, will be borne
Above the stars; my name will be remembered
Wherever Roman power rules conquered lands,
I shall be read, and through all centuries,
If prophecies of bards are ever truthful,
I shall be living, always.

Ovid *Metamorphoses* 15. 745-879
tr. R. Humphries (Indiana 1955)

F31 *Ars Amatoria*

The following extracts are all taken from Ovid's most notorious poem, the Art of Love *(*Ars Amatoria*). The pursuit and capture of a girl is set out as a science in parody of current 'textbook' didactic poetry. The first extract emphasizes the limits of the study and highlights the 'hunt' parallel. The second, long, passage describes the places where girls hang out, dwelling on the theatre and a discreditable element from Rome's 'glorious' past, the rape of the Sabine women. The third and fourth extracts are both parodies, the one, of the 'golden Age' ideal (see Virgil* Aeneid *6. 794), the other of the rape of Helen, where the blame falls squarely on the injured husband.*

(a) *1. 35–52*

> First, my raw recruit, my inexperienced soldier,
>> Take some trouble to find the girl whom you really can love.
> Next, when you see what you like your problem will be how to win her.
>> Finally, strive to make sure mutual love will endure.
> That's as far as I go, the territory I cover,
>> Those are the limits I set: take them or leave them alone.
>
> While you are footloose and free to play the field at your pleasure,
>> Watch for the one you can tell, 'I want no other but you!'
> She is not going to come to you floating down from the heavens:
>> For the right kind of a girl you must keep using your eyes.
> Hunters know where to spread their nets for the stag in his covert,
>> Hunters know where the boar gnashes his teeth in the glade.
> Fowlers know brier and bush, and fishermen study the waters
>> Baiting the hook for the cast just where the fish may be found.
> So you too, in your hunt for material worthy of loving,
>> First will have to find out where the game usually goes.
> I will not tell you to sail searching far over the oceans,
>> I will not tell you to plod any long wearisome road.

(b) *1. 67–162*

> Take your time, walk slow, when the sun approaches the lion.
>> There are porticoes, marbled under the shade,
> Pompey's, Octavia's, or the one in Livia's honor,
>> Or the Danaids' own, tall on the Palatine hill.
> Don't pass by the shrine of Adonis, sorrow to Venus,
>> Where, on the Sabbath day, Syrians worship, and Jews.
> Try the Memphian fane of the Heifer, shrouded in linen;
>> Isis makes many a girl willing as Io for Jove.
> Even the courts of the law, the bustle and noise of the forum,
>> (This may be hard to believe) listen to whispers of love.

Hard by the marble shrine of Venus, the Appian fountain,
    Where the water springs high in its rush to the air,
There, and more than once, your counsellor meets with his betters,
    All his forensic arts proving of little avail;
Others he might defend; himself he cannot; words fail him,
    Making objections in vain; Cupid says, *Overruled!*
Venus, whose temple is near, laughs at the mortified creature,
    Lawyer a moment ago, in need of a counsellor now.
Also, the theater's curve is a very good place for your hunting,
    More opportunity here, maybe, than anywhere else.
Here you may find one to love, or possibly only have fun with,
    Someone to take for a night, someone to have and to hold.
Just as a column of ants keeps going and coming forever,
    Bearing their burdens of grain, just as the flight of the bees
Over the meadows and over the fields of the thyme and the clover,
    So do the women come, thronging the festival games,
Elegant, smart, and so many my sense of judgment is troubled.
    Hither they come, to see; hither they come, to be seen.
This is a place for the chase, not the chaste, and Romulus knew it,
    Started it all, in fact; think of the Sabine girls.
There were no awnings, then, over the benches of marble,
    There were no crimson flowers staining the platform's floor,
Only the natural shade from the Palatine trees, and the stage-set
    Quite unadorned, and the folk sitting on steps of sod,
Shading their foreheads with leaves, studying, watching intently,
    Each for the girl he would have, none of them saying a word.
Then, while the Tuscan flute was sounding its primitive measure,
    While the dancer's foot thrice beat the primitive ground,
While the people roared in uninhibited cheering,
    Romulus gave the sign. They had been waiting. They knew.
Up they leaped, and their noise was proof of their vigorous spirit.
    Never a virgin there was free from the lust of a hand.
Just as the timid doves fly from the swooping of eagles,
    Just as the newest lamb tries to escape from the wolf,
So those girls, fearing men, went rushing in every direction;
    Every complexion, through fright, turning a different hue.
Though their fear was the same, it took on different guises:
    Some of them tore their hair; some of them sat stricken dumb.
One is silent in grief, another calls for her mother,
    One shrieks out, one is still; one runs away, and one stays.
So, they are all carried off, these girls, the booty of husbands,
    While, in many, their fear added endowments of charm.
If one struggled too much, or refused to go with her captor,
    He'd pick her up from the ground, lift her aloft in his arms,

Saying, 'Why do you spoil your beautiful eyes with that crying?
    Wasn't your mother a wife? That's all I want you to be.'
Romulus, you knew the way to give rewards to your soldiers!
    Give me rewards such as these, I would enlist for the wars.
So, to this very day, the theater keeps its tradition:
    Danger is lurking there still waiting for beautiful girls.

Furthermore, don't overlook the meetings when horses are running;
    In the crowds at the track opportunity waits.
There is no need for a code of finger-signals or nodding.
    Sit as close as you like; no one will stop you at all.
In fact, you will have to sit close—that's one of the rules, at a race track.
    Whether she likes it or not, contact is part of the game.
Try to find something in common, to open the conversation;
    Don't care too much what you say, just so that every one hears.
Ask her, 'Whose colors are those?'—that's good for an opening gambit.
    Put your own bet down, fast, on whatever she plays.
Then, when the gods come along in procession, ivory, golden,
    Outcheer every young man, shouting for Venus, the queen.
Often it happens that dust may fall on the blouse of the lady.
    If such dust should fall, carefully brush it away.
Even if there's no dust, brush off whatever there isn't.
    Any excuse will do: why do you think you have hands?
If her cloak hangs low, and the ground is getting it dirty,
    Gather it up with care, lift it a little, so!
Maybe, by way of reward, and not without her indulgence,
    You'll be able to see ankle or possibly knee.
Then look around and glare at the fellow who's sitting behind you,
    Don't let him crowd his knees into her delicate spine.
Girls, as everyone knows, adore these little attentions:
    Getting the cushion just right, that's in itself quite an art;
Yes, and it takes a technique in making a fan of your program
    Or in fixing a stool under the feet of a girl.
Such is the chance of approach the race track can offer a lover.
    There is another good ground, the gladiatorial shows.
On that sorrowful sand Cupid has often contested,
    And the watcher of wounds often has had it himself.
While he is talking, or touching a hand, or studying entries,
    Asking which one is ahead after his bet has been laid,
Wounded himself, he groans to feel the shaft of the arrow;
    He is a victim himself, no more spectator, but show.

(c) *2. 273–86*

> What about sending her poems? A very difficult question.
>> Poems, I am sorry to say, aren't worth so much in this town.
> Oh, they are praised, to be sure; but the girls want something more costly.
>> Even illiterates please, if they have money to burn.
> Ours is a Golden Age, and gold can purchase you honors,
>> All the 'Golden Mean' means is, gold is the end.
> Homer himself, if he came attended by all of the Muses,
>> With no scrip in his purse, would be kicked out of the house.
> There are a few, very few, bright girls with a real education,
>> Some (perhaps) here and there, willing to give it a try.
> So, go ahead, praise both: the worth of the song matters little
>> Just so you make it sound lovely while reading aloud.
> Whether or not she can tell one kind of verse from another,
>> If there's a line in her praise she will assume, 'It's a gift!'

(d) *2. 359–72*

> When Menelaus was gone, and the bed of Helen was lonesome,
>> Paris and warmth were found in the embrace of the night.
> Menelaus, I think, was a fool to go off on a journey,
>> Leaving his wife and his guest housed in identical walls.
> Only a madman would think that the dove was safe with the falcon,
>> Only a madman leave sheep to the mercy of wolves.
> Helen was not to blame, and neither, so help me, was Paris;
>> Given the chance that he had, who would do anything else?
> You were to blame, Menelaus: you gave him the time, the occasion;
>> Why in the world should they not follow the counsel you gave?
> What did you think she would do? Her husband was gone, she was lonely,
>> Paris was far from a boor—why should she sleep all alone?
> I acquit Helen outright, and put the blame on the husband.
>> What did she do but make use of the occasion he gave?

Ovid *Art of Love* (excerpts)
tr. Rolfe Humphries (Indiana 1957)

F32 *Amores* 1. 1

A formal introduction sets the tone of humour and parody. Ovid represents himself as trying to write serious verse, i.e. hexameters, but being undermined by Cupid, who forces him into elegiacs, the metre of love poetry.

282

My epic was under construction—wars and armed violence
in the grand manner, with metre matching theme.

I had written the second hexameter when Cupid grinned
and calmly removed one of its feet.

'You young savage' I protested 'poetry's none of your business.
We poets are committed to the Muses.

Imagine Venus grabbing Minerva's armour
and Minerva brandishing love's torch!

Imagine Ceres queen of the mountain forests
and Diana the huntress running a farm!

Or longhaired Phoebus doing pike drill
and Mars strumming the seven-stringed lyre!

You've a large empire, my boy—too much power already.
Why so eager for extra work?

Or is the whole world yours—the glens of Helicon included?
Can't Phoebus call his lyre his own these days?

Page one line one of my epic rises to noble heights
but line two lowers the tone

and I haven't the right subject for light verse—
a pretty boy or a girl with swept-up hair.'

In reply the god undid his quiver and pulled out
an arrow with my name on it.

'Poet' he said, flexing the bow against his knee,
'I'll give you something to sing about—take that!'

Alas his arrows never miss. My blood's on fire.
Love has moved in as master of my heart.

I choose the couplet—rising six feet, falling five.
Farewell, hexameters and iron wars.

Garland your golden hair with myrtle from the seaside,
hendecametric Muse, my Elegia.

Ovid *Amores* 1. 1
tr. Guy Lee (J. Murray 1968)

F33 *Amores* 1. 2

A parody of the sleepless lover leading to an equally burlesque Triumph of love

What's wrong with me I wonder? This mattress feels so hard.
The blankets won't stay on the bed.

I haven't slept a wink—tossing and turning
all night long. And now I'm aching all over.

Can it be love? Surely I'd know if it were?
Or does love work under cover and strike unobserved?

Yes, those phantom arrows must have pierced my heart
and relentless Cupid is torturing me.

Shall I give in? Or fan the flame by fighting it?
Better give in. Balance makes a burden light.

Shake a torch and it flares up—
leave it alone and it dies.

A bullock restive under the yoke
gets beaten more than his patient partner.

Spirited horses bruise their mouths on the bit;
the docile seldom feel it.

The god of love hits rebels far harder
than his submissive slaves.

Then I submit, Cupid. I'm your latest victim
standing here with my hands up.

The war's over. I'm suing for peace and pardon.
There's no glory in shooting an unarmed man.

Bind your hair with myrtle. Harness your mother's doves.
Vulcan will fit you out with a chariot.

Mount it and steer your doves through the crowd
as they hail you victor.

You too can celebrate a glorious Triumph
with young men and girls as your prisoners of war

and I'll be among them wearing my new chains
nursing this open wound—your abject slave.

Conscience and Common Sense and all Love's enemies
will be dragged along with hands tied behind their backs.

You'll strike fear into all hearts.
The crowd will worship you, chanting *Io Triumphe*.

Your loyal irregulars Flattery Passion and Illusion
will act as bodyguard,

the forces that bring you victory over gods and men,
providing cover for your nakedness.

Your laughing mother will watch the Triumph from Olympus
and clap her hands and shower you with roses

as you ride along, jewels flashing from wings and hair,
a golden boy in a golden chariot,

raising many a fire if I know you,
wounding many a heart as you pass by,

your arrows willy-nilly never resting,
the flame of your torch scorching at close range,

a god mighty as Bacchus along the Ganges,
your doves terrible as tigers.

Then spare me for your Triumph.
Don't waste your strength on me

but imitate your conquering cousin Augustus—
he turns his conquests into protectorates.

Ovid Amores 1.2
tr. Guy Lee (J. Murray 1968)

F34 *Amores* 1.4

A dramatic monologue

Your husband? Going to the same dinner as us?
I hope it chokes him.

So I'm only to gaze at you, darling? Play gooseberry
while another man enjoys your touch?

You'll lie there snuggling up to him? He'll put his arm
round your neck whenever he wants?

No wonder Centaurs fought over Hippodamia
when the wedding wine began to flow.

I don't live in the forest nor am I part horse
but I find it hard to keep my hands off you.

However here's my plan. Listen carefully.
Don't throw my words of wisdom to the winds.

Arrive before him—not that I see what good
arriving first will do but arrive first all the same.

When he takes his place on the couch and you go to join him
looking angelic, secretly touch my foot.

Watch me for nods and looks that talk
and unobserved return my signals

in the language of eyebrows and fingers
with annotations in wine.

Whenever you think of our love-making
stroke that rosy cheek with your thumb.

If you're cross with me, darling,
press the lobe of your ear

but turn your ring round if you're pleased
with anything I say or do.

When you feel like cursing your fool of a husband
touch the table as if you were praying.

If he mixes you a drink, beware—tell him to drink it himself.
then quietly ask the waiter for what you want.

I'll intercept the glass as you hand it back
and drink from the side you drank from.

Refuse all food he has tasted first—
it has touched his lips.

Don't lean your gentle head against his shoulder
and don't let him embrace you

or slide a hand inside your dress
or touch your breasts. Above all don't kiss him.

If you do I'll cause a public scandal,
grab you and claim possession.

I'm bound to see all this. It's what I shan't see
that worries me—the goings on under your cloak.

Don't press your thigh or your leg against his
or touch his coarse feet with your toes.

I know all the tricks. That's why I'm worried.
I hate to think of him doing what I've done.

We've often made love under your cloak, sweetheart,
in a glorious race against time.

You won't do that, I know. Still,
to avoid all doubt don't wear one.

286

Encourage him to drink but mind—no kisses.
Keep filling his glass when he's not looking.

If the wine's too much for him and he drops off
we can take our cue from what's going on around us.

When you get up to leave and we all follow
move to the middle of the crowd.

You'll find me there—or I'll find you
so touch me anywhere you can.

But what's the good? I'm only temporizing.
Tonight decrees our separation.

Tonight he'll lock you in and leave me
desolated at your door.

Then he'll kiss you, then go further,
forcing his right to our secret joy.

But you *can* show him you're acting under duress.
Be mean with your love—give grudgingly—in silence.

He won't enjoy it if my prayers are answered.
And if they're not, at least assure me you won't.

But whatever happens tonight tell me tomorrow
you didn't sleep with him—and stick to that story.

Ovid *Amores* 1.4
tr. Guy Lee (J. Murray 1968)

F35 *Amores* 1.5

Siesta time in sultry summer.
I lay relaxed on the divan.

One shutter closed, the other ajar,
made sylvan semi-darkness,

a glimmering dusk, as after sunset,
or between night's end and day's beginning—

the half light shy girls need
to hide their hesitation.

At last—Corinna. On the loose in a short dress,
long hair parted and tumbling past the pale neck—

lovely as Lais of the many lovers,
Queen Semiramis gliding in.

I grabbed the dress; it didn't hide much,
but she fought to keep it,

only half-heartedly though.
Victory was easy, a self-betrayal.

There she stood, faultless beauty
in front of me, naked.

Shoulders and arms challenging eyes and fingers.
Nipples firmly demanding attention.

Breasts in high relief above the smooth belly.
Long and slender waist. Thighs of a girl.

Why list perfection?
I hugged her tight.

The rest can be imagined—we fell asleep.
Such afternoons are rare.

Ovid *Amores* 1.5
tr. Guy Lee (J. Murray 1968)

F36 *Amores* 1.11 and 12

Napë, the coiffeuse,
no ordinary maid,

backstage-manager of my love-life,
my silent prompter,

keeper of Corinna's conscience,
averting crisis—

please, Napë, take her this note,
immediately.

You're flesh and blood,
no fool.

You must have suffered in Cupid's wars
so help a comrade in arms.

If she asks about me, say I live for our next meeting.
This note will explain.

But I'm wasting time. Hand it to her when she's free,
make sure she reads it then and there,

and watch her face meanwhile—
there's prophecy in faces.

See she replies at once—a long letter.
Blank wax is a bore.

Get her to space the lines close and fill the margins
so it takes me longer to read.

Wait. Why tire her fingers pushing a stylus?
YES will do, in huge block capitals.

I'll garland those writing-tablets with Victory's laurel
and hang them up in the temple of Venus

above this dedication:
'From Naso—in wooden gratitude.'

Weep for my failure—writing-tablets returned
with a sorry answer: *Can't manage today.*

The superstitious are right. Napë stubbed her toe
on the step as she left.

You must have been drinking, my girl.
Next time be more careful, and pick your feet up.

Damn those obstructive lumps of wood,
this wax frustration

obviously extracted
from Corsican hemlock honey.

coloured with cinnabar, I'm told,
but in fact—bloody.

The gutter's the place for this lumber
to be crunched under passing wheels.

I'm sure the man who made them
had felon's hands.

The tree they came from hanged a suicide—
supplied the executioner with crosses.

Horned owls hooted in its branches,
vultures and screech-owls brooded there.

I was mad to entrust these
with tender messages.

They were meant for deadly legal instruments
in the hands of some commissioner for oaths,

or to be wedged among a usurer's ledgers,
recording his bad debts.

Double-tablets? Double crossers!
They say two's an unlucky number.

God rot their wood with worm
and their wax with white mildew!

Ovid *Amores* 1. 11 and 12
tr. Guy Lee (J. Murray 1968)

F37 *Amores* 1. 13

Here she comes, over the sea from her poor old husband,
frosty axle turning, bringing the yellow day.

Why hurry, Aurora? Hold your horses, for Memnon's sake
and the annual sacrifice of his birds.

Now's the time when I love to lie in my love's soft arms,
the time of times to feel her body close to mine,

the time when sleep is heavy, the air cold,
and birdsong sweetest.

Why hurry? Lovers hate your company.
Tighten the reins in your rosy fingers.

Before your coming sailors can better watch their stars
and keep their course in open waters.

Travellers however tired rise when you appear
and soldiers reach for their weapons.

Your eye first lights on peasants shouldering their mattocks
and drags oxen under the yoke.

You rob children of sleep, condemn them
to classrooms and the cruel cane.

You send the unwary down to the Forum
to give their one-word promise and lose thousands.

Learned counsel deprecate your summons
to rise and shine again in court.

Back to the distaff and the daily stint
you call the housewife when her hands could idle.

I could stand all this, but pretty girls rising at dawn—
no lover can endure it.

If only night would defy you,
and the stars stare you out!

If only the wind would break your axle,
or frozen cloud give your team a fall!

Why hurry, spoil-sport?—Does Memnon's black skin
reflect the colour of his mother's heart?

I wish Tithonus could gossip about you—
he'd kill your heavenly reputation.

You run away from him because he's old—
he hates you getting up so early.

But if you slept with Cephalus, you'd shout
'Oh gallop slow, you midnight horses!'

I know your husband's senile, but why should my love suffer?
Did I arrange your marriage?

The Moon let her Endymion sleep for years—
and she's quite as beautiful as you are.

Even Jupiter couldn't stand the sight of you
that time he joined two nights of love together—

My final thrust. She must have heard me—she turned pink.
But the sun came up on time—as usual.

Ovid *Amores* 1.13
tr. Guy Lee (J. Murray 1968)

F38 *Amores* 2.5

Cupid, pack up your quiver. Is any love worth while
if it makes me long with all my heart for death?

And I long to die, my hell on earth, my darling,
when I think how you deceived me.

No secret notes, no presents smuggled in
laid bare your infidelity.

I only wish I couldn't prove it.
Why oh why is my case so good?

A man's in luck if his girl can say *Not Guilty*
and he can defend her with confidence.

It's callous and vindictive
to fight for a costly verdict against a sweetheart.

But I saw you both, with my own eyes. I was cold sober,
not, as you thought, asleep—though the wine was flowing.

I watched a conspiracy of eyebrows,
a confabulation of nods.

I could hear your eyes and decipher your fingers
and read the proposals you tabled in wine.

None of your innocent remarks escaped me—
the code was obvious.

When all the other guests had gone,
except a few young men, dead to the world,

I saw you kissing one another—
tongues deeply involved.

No sisterly kisses those,
but long and passionate—

the sort Venus gives Mars,
not Diana Phoebus.

'Stop' I shouted. 'That pleasure's mine.
I shall claim my rights.

You and I enjoy them in common.
Third parties are out.'

As I went on angrily speaking my mind
her face turned a guilty red—

red as the sky when Aurora paints it
or a girl first meeting her betrothed

red as a rose among pale lilies
or the harvest moon bewitched

or tinted Lydian ivory
that time never yellows.

Her blush was one of these, or maybe all.
She'd never looked more lovely—unintentionally.

She stared remorsefully at the ground—
remorseful staring suited her.

I felt like pulling her hair (it was perfectly set)
and scratching her eyes out

but when I saw her face my arms fell,
foiled by the feminine.

Anger vanished. I found myself begging
for kisses as good as those I'd watched.

She burst out laughing and treated me to her best—
they'd make an angry Jupiter drop his bolt.

Did the other man have my luck? The thought torments me.
I wish they'd been less good.

They were far better than the ones I taught her—
she must have had extra tuition.

It's a pity they gave me such pleasure,
a pity our tongues ever met.

because now I have two worries: kisses, yes,
but not only kisses.

That sort must have been learnt in bed;
so at least one teacher has been well paid.

Ovid *Amores* 2.5
tr. Guy Lee (J. Murray 1968)

F39 *Amores* 2.7 and 8

Ovid defends himself against an accusation of infidelity only to reveal that the accusation is really true

So that's my role—the professional defendant?
I'm sick of standing trial—though I always win.

At the theatre I've only to glance at the back rows
and your jealous eye pin-points a rival.

A pretty girl need only look at me
and you're sure the look is a signal.

I compliment another woman—you grab my hair.
I criticize her—and you think I've something to hide.

If I'm looking well I don't love you.
If pale, I'm pining for someone else.

I wish to God I had been unfaithful—
the guilty can take their punishment.

As it is you accuse me blindly, believing anything.
It's your own fault your anger cuts no ice.

Remember the donkey, putting his long ears back—
the more he's beaten the slower he goes.

So that's the latest count against me—
I'm carrying on with your maid Cypassis?

Good God, if I wanted variety
is it likely I'd pick on a drudge like her?

What man of breeding would sleep with a slave
or embrace a body scarred by the lash?

Besides, she's your coiffeuse—her skill
makes her a favourite of yours.

I'd be mad to ask a maid so devoted to you.
She'd only turn me down and tell.

By Venus and Cupid's bow,
I'm innocent—I swear it!

Cypassis, incomparable coiffeuse
who should start a *salon* on Olympus,

no country lass, as I know from our encounters,
but Corinna's treasure and my treasure-hunt—

who was it told her about *us*?
How does she know we slept together?

I didn't blush though, did I? Said nothing by mistake
to betray our secret?

I may have argued no one in his right mind
would have an affair with a maid.

but Achilles adored his maid Briseis
and Agememnon fell for his slave Cassandra.

I can't claim to be greater than those two.
What goes for royalty is good enough for me.

Corinna looked daggers at *you* though.
And how you blushed! I saw you.

But I saved the day, you must admit,
by swearing my Venus oath.

—Dear goddess, bid the warm south winds
blow that white lie over the ocean!—

So in return, my black beauty,
reward me today with your sweet self.

Why shake your head? The danger's over.
Don't be ungrateful. Remember your duty to *me*.

If you're stupid enough to refuse I'll have to confess
and betray myself for betraying her.

I'll tell your mistress where and when we met, Cypassis,
and what we did and how many times and how we did it.

Ovid *Amores* 2. 7 and 8
tr. Guy Lee (J. Murray 1968)

F40 *Amores* 2.10

Graecinus, I blame *you*. Yours that memorable remark
'No one can love two girls at once'.

I trusted you and dropped my guard. The result
is too embarrassing—a double love-life.

They're both beautiful, both sophisticated.
It's hard to say which has more to offer.

Certainly one is more attractive—but which one?
I love each more than the either.

torn by a schizophrenic passion,
a catamaran in contrary winds.

Great Aphrodite, one girl's hell enough on earth—
why double-damn me?

Why add leaves to trees, stars to the Milky Way,
water to the deep blue sea?

Still, two loves are better than none at all.
God send my enemies a moral life,

single sleep and limbs relaxed
in mid-mattress.

But give *me* ruthless love—to interrupt my slumbers
with company in bed.

Let woman be my undoing—one if one's enough—
otherwise two.

I can take it. I may be thin and under weight
but I've muscle and stamina.

Pleasure's a food that builds me up.
I've never disappointed a girl.

Many's the night I've spent in love
and been fighting fit the morning after.

To die in love's duel—what final bliss!
It's the death I should choose.

Let soldiers impale their hearts on a pike
and pay down blood for glory.

Let seafaring merchants make their millions
till they and their lies are shipwrecked at last.

But when *I* die let me faint in the to and fro of love
and fade out at its climax.

> I can just imagine the mourners' comment:
> 'Death was the consummation of his life.'

Ovid *Amores* 2. 10
tr. Guy Lee (J. Murray 1968)

F41 *Amores* 3. 2

> It's not the horses that bring me here
> though I hope your favourite wins.
>
> To sit with you and talk with you is why I've come—
> I've come to tell you I'm in love.
>
> If I watch you and you watch the races
> we'll both enjoy watching a winner.
>
> How I envy your charioteer!
> He's a lucky man to be picked by you.
>
> I wish it was me. I'd get my team
> off to a flying start,
>
> crack the whip, give them their heads
> and shave the post with my nearside wheel.
>
> But if I caught sight of *you* in the race
> I'd drop the reins and lose ground.
>
> Poor Pelops was nearly killed at Pisa
> gazing in Hippodamia's eyes,
>
> but being her favourite of course he won
> as I hope your driver and I will.—
>
> It's no good edging away. The line brings us together—
> that's the advantage of the seating here.
>
> You on the right, sir—please be careful.
> Your elbow's hurting the lady.
>
> And you in the row behind—sit up, sir!
> Your knees are digging into her back.
>
> My dear, your dress is trailing on the ground.
> Lift it up—or there you are, I've done it for you.
>
> What mean material to hide those legs!
> Yes, the more one looks the meaner it seems.
>
> Legs like Atalanta,
> Milanion's dream of bliss.

A painter's model for Diana
running wilder than the beasts.

My blood was on fire before. What happens now?
You're fuelling a furnace, flooding the Red Sea.

I'm sure that lightweight dress is hiding
still more delightful revelations.

But what about a breath of air while we wait?
This programme will do as a fan.

Is it really as hot as I feel? Or merely my imagination
fired by your sultry presence?

Just then a speck of dust fell on your white dress.
Forgive me—out, damned spot!

But here's the procession. Everybody hush.
Give them a hand. The golden procession's here.

First comes Victory, wings outstretched.
Goddess, grant me victory in love!

Neptune next. Salute him, sailors.
Not for me the ocean—I'm a landlover.

Soldiers, salute Mars. I'm a disarmer,
all for peace and amorous plenty.

There's Phoebus for the soothsayers, Phoebe for the hunters,
Minerva for the master craftsmen.

Farmers can greet Bacchus and Ceres,
boxers pray to Pollux and knights to Castor.

But I salute the queen of love and the boy with the bow.
Venus, smile on my latest venture.

Make my new mistress willing—or weak-willed.
A lucky sign—the goddess nodded

giving her promise. And now I'm asking for yours.
With Venus' permission I'll worship *you*.

By all these witnesses, divine and human,
I swear I want you to be mine for ever.

But the seat's a bit too high for you.
Why not rest your feet on the railing in front?

Now, they've cleared the course. The Praetor's starting the first race.
Four-horse chariots. Look—they're off.

There's your driver. Anyone *you* back is bound to win.
Even the horses seem to know what you want.

My God, he's taking the corner too wide.
What are you doing? The man behind is drawing level.

What are you doing, wretch? Breaking a poor girl's heart.
For pity's sake pull on your left rein!

We've backed a loser. Come on everyone, all together,
flap your togas and signal a fresh start.

Look, they're calling them back. Lean your head against me
so the waving togas don't disarrange your hair.

Now, they're off again—plunging out of the stalls,
rushing down the course in a clash of colours.

Now's your chance to take the lead. Go all out for that gap.
Give my girl and me what we want.

Hurrah, he's done it! You've got what you wanted, sweetheart.
That only leaves me—do I win too?

She's smiling. There's a promise in those bright eyes.
Let's leave now. You can pay my bet in private.

Ovid *Amores* 3.2
tr. Guy Lee (J. Murray 1968)

F42 *Amores* 3.11

To hell with love! I've been a martyr long enough.
You're quite impossible.

I've slipped my shackles. Yes, I'm now a free man—
I can blush to remember how I forgot myself.

Victory at last. I've planted my foot on Cupid's neck.
I didn't know I had it in me.

'Stick to it' I tell myself, 'don't weaken.
It's painful, but think of the pain as medicine.'

Did I really lie down like a tramp on the pavement
all those nights you locked me out?

Did I really stand guard at your door like a slave
while you were hugging another man?

I well remember seeing your lover leave the house
and stagger home—invalided out.

The worst of it was that he saw me—
I could wish my enemies nothing worse.

Was there a single day when I didn't report for duty
as your personal escort, your friend, your lover?

My company made everybody love you.
My passion for you started a male fashion.

I can't forget the lies you fed me,
the promises you fooled me with,

the nods to lover-boys at parties,
the sly remarks in obvious code.

Once, I heard you were ill, rushed to your house in a panic
and found you in bed—yes, in the arms of my rival.

These and other unspeakable insults have made me hard.
Find someone else to play the martyr.

My ship's in harbour, garlands hanging from the stern,
deaf to the roar of the rising storm.

Don't waste sweet words and bygone witchery on me.
I've learnt some common sense at last.

Love and hate, here in my heart, at tug of war—
and love I suppose will find a way to win.

I'd sooner hate. If I can't I'll be the reluctant lover—
the dumb ox bearing the yoke he loathes.

Your behaviour drives me away, your beauty draws me back.
I adore your face and abhor your failings.

With or without you life's impossible
and I can't decide what I want.

Why can't you be less lovely or more true?
Why must your faults and your figure clash?

I love what you are and hate what you do—
but your self, alas, outweighs your selfishness.

By the bed we shared, by all the gods
who let you take their names in vain,

by your face my holy icon, by your eyes that ravished mine,
take pity on me.

Be what you will you'll still be mine—but you must choose—
do you want me to want to love you or be forced to?

Make life plain sailing for me please
by helping me love what I can't help loving.

Ovid Amores 3.11
tr. Guy Lee (J. Murray 1968)

F43 *Amores* 3. 14

Your loveliness, I don't deny, needs lovers,
but spare me facts and figures—please.

My moral code does not require you to be chaste,
but it does demand concealment.

Any woman who pleads Not Guilty is innocent;
only confession gives her a bad name.

What madness to parade your nightlife in the daylight
and publicize your private affairs!

Even prostitutes insist on privacy
and lock the door before obliging a client.

Will *you* expose your naked guilt to scandalmongers
and give full details of your own misconduct?

Have *some* decency, please—or at least pretend to have,
so I can think you're faithful even if you aren't.

Carry on as before, but don't admit it,
and don't be ashamed of decorum in public.

There's a proper place for impropriety—
enjoy it there, shedding your inhibitions.

But don't forget them when you leave.
Confine your faults to bed.

It's no disgrace to undress there,
press thigh to thigh,

kiss as you please, and figure out
love's total variety,

moaning and whispering sweet words,
shaking the bedstead in abandon.

But when you dress put on your moral make-up too
and wear the negative look of virtue.

Take whoever you please—provided you take me in.
Don't enlighten me. Let me keep my illusions.

Need I see those notes coming and going?
That double hollow in the bed?

Your hair in sleepless disarray?
Those love-bites on your neck?

You'll soon be committing adultery before my very eyes.
Destroy your good name if you must, but spare my feelings.

These endless confessions bring me out in a cold sweat—
honestly, they're killing me.

My love becomes frustrated hate for what I can't help loving.
I'd gladly die—if only you'd die with me.

I'll ask no questions, I promise, and ferret out no secrets
if you'll do me the simple favour of deceit.

But if ever I catch you in the act,
if ever I'm forced to see the worst,

then flatly deny I saw what I did,
and your words shall stand in for my eyes.

It's so easy for you to beat a willing loser.
Only remember to say Not Guilty.

Two words can clear you—speak them and win.
Your case may be weak but your judge is weaker.

Ovid *Amores* 3.14
tr. Guy Lee (J. Murray 1968)

Part 2

G   CICERO *DE OFFICIIS* BOOK 3

De Officiis tackles the age-old ethical problem of the relationship between means and end from the point of view of a member of the Roman Establishment. Not only is it an important source for the assimilation and adaptation of Greek ideas within the conceptual framework of Roman society, but in its affirmation of good faith and justice in both public and private life, it stands along with the *Philippics* in Cicero's defiance of the destroyers of the Republic. The word *officium* (pl. *officia*) is commonly translated as 'duty'. Strictly it meant 'appropriate action'.

Cicero's overall aim in Book 3 was to complete the ethical enquiry foreshadowed by Panaetius. Books 1 and 2 followed Panaetius' outline (cf. G4a, 6 (intro.), 7, 13) by considering questions of judgement about right and wrong in the moral sense (Book 1) and questions of judgement about expediency and inexpediency (Book 2). In Book 3 Cicero considers how decisions can be reached when the imperatives of morality (*honestas*) and expediency (*utilitas*) appear to conflict. The structure of Book 3 attempts to follow that of the two previous books in taking the four virtues (wisdom, justice, courage, and moderation) and examining each in turn for its bearing on possible conflict between *honestas* and *utilitas*, but in practice Cicero's approach is more diffuse and is dictated by his assumption that this problem of conflict exists for men of imperfect understanding who may best be guided by general rules. Cicero's discussion of the base for these rules of conduct examines the role of law, tradition, and conscience and makes notable use of *exempla* drawn from Roman history and from the myths and history of Greece, all of which were part of the cultural background of educated Romans. In Book 3 not only does Cicero make his distinctive contribution to the discussion of conflict between *honestas* and *utilitas*, outlined initially by Panaetius, but he also does so through the medium of discussion of Roman upper-class values. The book is therefore an important source for social values as well as for the Roman adaptation of Greek philosophical sources.

For text with introduction, commentary, and notes see H.A. Holden (7th edn. Cambridge 1891). For a translation in modern idiom (with glossary) see J. Higginbotham *Cicero on Moral Obligation* (Faber & Faber 1967). On Cicero see H.A.K. Hunt *The Humanism of Cicero* (Melbourne 1954); M.L. Clarke *The Roman Mind* (London 1956); A.E. Douglas in T.A. Dorey (ed.) *Cicero* (London 1965); J. Ferguson in *Studies in Cicero* (Rome 1962).

G1   Two verdicts on Cicero

Cicero's political achievement may not have been as great as he himself imagined, but his prominence and skill as an orator gained him influence and many supporters as well as creating powerful enemies; for his opposition to Antony, see B7, 15; for his relationship with Octavian, B6–8. For his political career, see D. Stockton Cicero, A Political Biography (Oxford 1971).

(a)

This passage refers to Clodius' attack on Cicero and gives important insight into the strengths and weaknesses of Cicero's political position, which rested on rhetorical skill rather than on other attributes, such as birth. Clodius Pulcher, a member of the noble Claudian family and tribune in 58 BC, passed a measure exiling Cicero; a corrupt opportunist, he used violence to further his aims.

But since he decided that it was not easy to overthrow a man who had very great influence in the state by reason of his skill in speaking, he proceeded to conciliate not only the populace, but also the knights and the senate, by whom Cicero was held in the highest regard. His hope was that if he could make these men his own, he might easily cause the downfall of the orator, whose strength lay rather in the fear than in the good-will which he inspired. For Cicero annoyed great numbers by his speeches, and those whom he aided were not so thoroughly won to his side as those whom he injured were alienated; for most men are more ready to feel irritation at what displeases them than to feel grateful to any one for kindnesses, and they think that they have paid their advocates in full with their fee, while their chief concern is to get even with their opponents in some way or other. Cicero, moreover, made for himself very bitter enemies by always striving to get the better of even the most powerful men and by always employing an unbridled and excessive frankness of speech toward all alike; for he was in pursuit of a reputation for sagacity and eloquence such as no one else possessed, even in preference to being thought a good citizen. As a result of this and because he was the greatest boaster alive and regarded no one as equal to himself, but in his words and life alike looked down upon everybody and would not live as any one else did, he was wearisome and burdensome, and was consequently both disliked and hated even by those very persons whom he otherwise pleased.

Dio Cassius 38. 12,
tr. E. Cary (Loeb 1914)

(b)

Cicero became consul in 63 BC and was hailed as the saviour of Rome for defeating the conspiracy of Catiline, an ambitious aristocrat who had organized disaffected elements throughout Italy in an attempt to gain power; Cicero, finding proof of this, denounced the conspirators and had some of them put to death without a trial. This was used against him by Clodius.

Although Cicero was not expressly named in the wording of the bill, it was aimed at him alone. And so this man, who had earned by his great services the gratitude of his country, gained exile as his reward for saving the state. Caesar and Pompey were not free from the suspicion of having had a share in the fall of Cicero. Cicero seemed to have brought upon himself their resentment by refusing to be a member of the commission of twenty charged with the distribution of lands in Campania. Within two years Cicero was restored to his country and to his former status, thanks to the interest of Gnaeus Pompeius—somewhat belated, it is true, but effective when once exerted—and thanks to the prayers of Italy, the decrees of the senate, and the zealous activity of Annius Milo, tribune of the people. Since the exile and return of Numidicus no one had been banished amid greater popular disapproval or welcomed back with greater enthusiasm. As for Cicero's house, the maliciousness of its destruction by Clodius was now compensated for by the magnificence of its restoration by the senate.

Velleius Paterculus 2. 45. 1-3
tr. F.W. Shipley (Loeb 1924)

G2 Conflict and values in the late Republic

(a)

The speech was prepared in defence of Publius Sestius, a tribune of the plebs, who was prosecuted at the instigation of Clodius in 56 BC. The context is therefore that of the struggle between the factions of the Optimates and Populares during the declining years of the Republic. The extract is important for its identification of the qualities ascribed to the Optimates with the gloria *of Rome's Imperial expansion. For a detailed discussion of the relationship between social values and Imperial attitudes see P.A. Brunt 'Laus Imperii' in (eds.) P.A. Garnsey and C.R. Whittaker* Imperialism in the Ancient World (*Cambridge 1978*).

Those, then, who seek to win the praise of men of standing, which alone deserves the name of honour, must ever strive to win for others the peace and pleasures which they must deny themselves. They must toil and sweat for the common good; they must face hostility and often endure danger for the sake of the *res publica*; they must wrestle with many unscrupulous rascals and scoundrels; and sometimes they must even challenge the men of power. Such was the policy, such the achievement of our most distinguished statesmen; it is a tale made familiar to all of us by legend, tradition, and history. And, I ask you, do we ever find held up as paragons for emulation men who have at any time incited the people to revolution, or clouded their innocent judgement by wholesale distributions of largesse, or heaped calumny on any man of courage or distinction who served the *res publica* well? The general verdict of our citizens has always been that such men were irresponsible, reckless, criminal, subversive, while those who thwarted their attacks and assaults, those whose authority, integrity, determination, and high resolve stood firm against the counsels of Rome's enemies, those are the men whom they have always called our men of principle, our most influential members, our leaders, and the sources of our great imperial achievement.

Cicero *Pro Sestio* 139 tr. W.K. Lacey and B.W.J.G. Wilson
Res Publica: Roman Society and Politics according to Cicero (Bristol/Oxford 1978)

(b)
On the desire for peace after the civil wars see also B27

But just at the present time there is no reason for the People to disagree with their picked and chief men. They demand nothing, they do not desire revolution, they delight in their own peace, in the honour of the 'Best Men,' and in the glory of the whole State. And so those who are for revolution and riot, unable any longer to arouse the Roman People by state-bounty, because the common folk, after passing through so many serious insurrections and disorders, welcome peace—they now hold meetings packed with hirelings, nor is it their aim to say or propose what those present wish to hear, but they use corruption and bribery to make it appear that everything they say is listened to with pleasure.

Cicero *Pro Sestio* 104
tr. R. Gardner (Loeb 1958)

G3 Standing for public office

The Short Guide to Electioneering (Commentariolum Petitionis) *a pamphlet on how to seek election to the consulship, is attributed to Quintus, Marcus Cicero's brother. It may indeed have been written by Quintus, or by a contemporary, or even by a later author imitating the style and language of the late Republic (see M.I. Henderson 'De Commentariolo Petitionis' JRS 40 (1950) 8–21). There are many similarities to Marcus Cicero's speech* In Toga Candida, *delivered a few days before the elections of 64 BC. A* novus homo *(pl.* novi homines*) was literally a new man; someone who sought public office from outside the ruling Senatorial class. Although influential in their own area, Cicero's family were Equestrian (equites), and, although Equestrians could enter the Senate by being elected to a lower magistracy, it was almost unheard for a new man to seek the consulship (cf. Velleius Paterculus, 2, 76, 4). The* publicani *were very rich Equestrian businessmen who bid for public contracts tendered by the censors;* collegia *here refers to the politically active societies of the late Republic;* amici *were friends with political influence or political allies. The* municipia *were towns in Italy with independent municipal administrations.*

2   Consider what city this is, what you are seeking, who you are. Almost every day as you go down to the forum, you must bear this in mind—'I am a *novus homo*. I am seeking the consulship. This is Rome.'

The fact that you are a *novus homo* will be made considerably less harsh by the reputation of your oratory; for oratory has always conferred great distinction. A man who is thought worthy to be the advocate of men of consular rank cannot be considered unworthy of the consulship. Since you have this reputation to start with, and your position, whatever it is, is the result of this, come prepared to speak as though in each individual case a verdict were to be made on your whole character and ability.

3   See that the aids to this ability which I know are your special gifts are ready and available: remind yourself time and again of what Demetrius wrote about the study and practice of Demosthenes. Secondly see that people know how many friends you have and what sort of men they are. For what *novi homines* have possessed the advantages which you have? You have all the *publicani*, virtually all the *equites*, many *municipia* loyal to you alone, many men of every class whom you have defended, several *collegia*, and in addition very many young men who have been won over to you by the study of oratory, and a large and constant circle of *amici* in daily attendance.

> [Q. Cicero] *A Short Guide to Electioneering* 2-3
> tr. D.W. Taylor and J. Murrell *LACTOR* 3 (1968)

G4 Cicero on writing philosophy

Titus Pomponius, nicknamed Atticus, a wealthy equestrian, was a loyal and devoted friend to Cicero. Their edited correspondence is full of information about their characters, families, friends, and occupations, as well as being a rich source for the political and social life of their times. For text, translation and commentary, see D. R. Shackleton Bailey Cicero's Letters to Atticus; Cicero's Letters to his Friends *(Cambridge 1965-8; 1977).*

(a)
The De Officiis *was published in November 44 BC; Quintus Cicero was married to Atticus' sister, not very happily.*

4   Now to your more recent letter. I have completed the subject of Duty, so far as Panaetius goes, in two books. He has three. He begins by dividing the enquiries on Duty into three categories: (*a*) when the question is whether an action is right or wrong; (*b*) whether it is expedient or inexpedient; and (*c*) how to judge in cases of apparent conflict between the two, e.g. that of Regulus—right to go back, expedient to remain. He gives an excellent exposition of *a* and *b*; *c* he promises to

discuss in due course but never actually did so. That topic was followed up by Posidonius. I have sent for his book and have also written to Athenodorus the Bald asking him to send me an abstract, for which I am now waiting. Would you please give him a push, ask him to send it as soon as possible? It includes a section on 'Duty depending on given circumstances'. As for your query about the title, I make no doubt that [*kathēkon*] is 'duty', unless you have some other suggestion. But the fuller title is 'On Duties'. I address it to my son Marcus. That seemed not inappropriate. . . .

6 I have not buried myself down at Pompeii as I wrote that I should, partly because the weather is abominable, partly because I get letters every day from Octavian urging me to put my shoulder to the wheel, come to Capua, save the Republic a second time, and at all events return to Rome at once. 'Durst not refuse for shame, for fear accept.' He has certainly shown, and continues to show, plenty of energy, and he will go to Rome with a large following; but he is very much a boy. Thinks the Senate will meet at once. Who will come? And who, supposing he comes, will run up against Antony in so uncertain a situation? On the Kalends of January he may be some protection; or perhaps the issue will be fought out before then. The boy is remarkably popular in the towns. On his way to Samnium he passed through Cales and stayed the night at Teanum. Amazing receptions and demonstrations of encouragement. Would you have thought it? For this reason I shall return to Rome sooner than I had intended. I shall write as soon as I decide definitely. . . .

> Cicero *To Atticus* 16. 11. 4; 6 (5 Nov. 44 from Puteoli)
> tr. D. R. Shackleton Bailey (Cambridge 1965–8)

(b)

Cicero was aware of the difficulties inherent in translating Greek philosophical concepts into Latin; (cf. also Cicero Academica *1. 6. 24).*

1 I have really nothing to write about. It was a different story at Puteoli, when every day brought something afresh about Octavian and much (some of it untrue) about Antony. In answer to what you write (I got three letters from you on the 11th), I strongly agree with you that if Octavian were to have much power the tyrant's measures would be far more solidly approved than in the temple of Tellus, and that this will be bad for Brutus. On the other hand, if he is beaten, you can see that Antony will be intolerable, so one can't tell which to prefer. . . .

3 But, one thing leading to another, I don't feel any doubt that what the Greeks call [*kathēkon*] is our 'duty'. Why do you doubt that it would apply perfectly well to public, as well as private, life? We talk of the Consuls' duty, don't we, or the Senate's duty, or a general's duty? It fits perfectly—or give me something better.

> Cicero *To Atticus* 16. 14. 1; 3 (12(?) Nov. 44 from Arpinum)
> tr. D. R. Shackleton Bailey (Cambridge 1965–8)

G5 Cicero justifies turning to philosophy

The De Officiis *(conventionally translated as 'On Duties') is written in the form of advice given to Cicero's son Marcus (whom he addresses as Cicero, often 'my Cicero'). It was among his last works composed between 45 and 44 BC. The following passages provide an indication of Cicero's attitude to philosophical pursuits (cf. also Cicero* Academica *2. 5-6, on the appropriateness of Greek learning and philosophy for public men).*

(a)

2   Although my books have aroused in not a few men the desire not only to read but to write, yet I sometimes fear that what we term philosophy is distasteful to certain worthy gentlemen, and that they wonder that I devote so much time and attention to it.

Now, as long as the state was administered by the men to whose care she had voluntarily entrusted herself, I devoted all my effort and thought to her. But when everything passed under the absolute control of a despot and there was no longer any room for statesmanship or authority of mine; and finally when I had lost the friends who had been associated with me in the task of serving the interests of the state, and who were men of the highest standing, I did not resign myself to grief, by which I should have been overwhelmed, had I not struggled against it; neither, on the other hand, did I surrender myself to a life of sensual pleasure unbecoming to a philosopher.

3   I would that the government had stood fast in the position it had begun to assume and had not fallen into the hands of men who desired not so much to reform as to abolish the constitution. For then, in the first place, I should now be devoting my energies more to public speaking than to writing, as I used to do when the republic stood; and in the second place, I should be committing to written form not these present essays but my public speeches, as I often formerly did. But when the republic, to which all my care and thought and effort used to be devoted, was no more, then, of course, my voice was silenced in the forum and in the senate.

(b)

5   Therefore, amid all the present most awful calamities I yet flatter myself that I have won this good out of evil—that I may commit to written form matters not at all familiar to our countrymen but still very much worth their knowing. For what, in the name of heaven, is more to be desired than wisdom? What is more to be prized? What is better for a man, what more worthy of his nature? Those who seek after it are called philosophers; and philosophy is nothing else, if one will translate the word into our idiom, than 'the love of wisdom.' Wisdom, moreover, as the word has been defined by the philosophers of old, is 'the knowledge of things human and divine and of the causes by which those things are controlled.' And if the man lives who would belittle the study of philosophy, I quite fail to see what in the world he would see fit to praise.

Cicero *De Officiis* 2. 2-3; 5
tr. W. Miller (Loeb 1913)

G6 The subject of *De Officiis*

Cicero begins the work by drawing a distinction between the kind of officium *which entails a moral obligation and the kind of* officium *in which decisions are made on practical grounds. He explores the relationship between the two kinds of* officium, *the criteria on which decisions about each kind are made, and the conflicts which may arise between them.*

The Stoics were members of a Hellenistic school of philosophy based on the teachings of Zeno of Citium (335-263 BC). Stoicism was brought to the Romans by Panaetius (185-109 BC) and his pupil Posidonius. The early Stoics held that to do what is right is the only good; Panaetius was interested in problems of practical morality, and rejected the rigidity of the Stoic paradox that only the perfectly good could lead the good life. He adapted Stoicism by developing the distinction between perfectum *and* medium officium *and by extending the meaning of* officium. *Aristo and Erillus were Stoics holding extreme views, Pyrrho of Elis was the founder of the Sceptics, who held that truth and knowledge are unattainable. See further A.A. Long* Hellenistic Philosophy *(Duckworth 1974); and see H.A.K. Hunt* The Humanism of Cicero *(Melbourne 1954) for a discussion of the place of* De Officiis *among Cicero's philosophical works.*

4   But since I have decided to write you a little now (and a great deal by and by), I wish, if possible, to begin with a matter most suited at once to your years and to my position. Although philosophy offers many problems, both important and useful, that have been fully and carefully discussed by philosophers, those teachings which have been handed down on the subject of moral duties seem to have the widest practical application. For no phase of life, whether public or private, whether in business or in the home, whether one is working on what concerns oneself alone or dealing with another, can be without its moral duty; on the discharge of such duties depends all that is morally right, and on their neglect all that is morally wrong in life.

5   Moreover, the subject of this inquiry is the common property of all philosophers; for who would presume to call himself a philosopher, if he did not inculcate any lessons of duty? But there are some schools that distort all notions of duty by the theories they propose touching the supreme good and the supreme evil. For he who posits the supreme good as having no connection with virtue and measures it not by a moral standard but by his own interests—if he should be consistent and not rather at times over-ruled by his better nature, he could value neither friendship nor justice nor generosity; and brave he surely cannot possibly be that counts pain the supreme evil, nor temperate he that holds pleasure to be the supreme good.

6   Although these truths are so self-evident that the subject does not call for discussion, still I have discussed it in another connection. If, therefore, these schools should claim to be consistent, they could not say anything about duty; and no fixed, invariable, natural rules of duty can be posited except by those who say that moral

goodness is worth seeking solely or chiefly for its own sake. Accordingly, the teaching of ethics is the peculiar right of the Stoics, the Academicians, and the Peripatetics; for the theories of Aristo, Pyrrho, and Erillus have been long since rejected; and yet they would have the right to discuss duty if they had left us any power of choosing between things, so that there might be a way of finding out what duty is. I shall, therefore, at this time and in this investigation follow chiefly the Stoics, not as a translator, but, as is my custom, I shall at my own option and discretion draw from those sources in such measure and in such manner as shall suit my purpose.

7 Since, therefore, the whole discussion is to be on the subject of duty, I should like at the outset to define what duty is, as, to my surprise, Panaetius has failed to do. For every systematic development of any subject ought to begin with a definition, so that everyone may understand what the discussion is about.

Every treatise on duty has two parts: one, dealing with the doctrine of the supreme good; the other, with the practical rules by which daily life in all its bearings may be regulated. The following questions are illustrative of the first part: whether all duties are absolute; whether one duty is more important than another; and so on. But as regards special duties for which positive rules are laid down, though they are affected by the doctrine of the supreme good, still the fact is not so obvious, because they seem rather to look to the regulation of everyday life; and it is these special duties that I propose to treat at length in the following books.

Cicero *De Officiis* 1. 4b, 5-7
tr. W. Miller (Loeb 1913)

G7 The distinction between *medium officium* and *perfectum officium*

8 And yet there is still another classification of duties: we distinguish between 'mean' duty, so-called, and 'absolute' duty. Absolute duty we may, I presume, call 'right,' for the Greeks call it [*katorthōma*], while the ordinary duty they call [*kathēkon*]. And the meaning of those terms they fix thus: whatever is right they define as 'absolute' duty, but 'mean' duty, they say, is duty for the performance of which an adequate reason may be rendered.

9 The consideration necessary to determine conduct is, therefore, as Panaetius thinks, a threefold one: first, people question whether the contemplated act is morally right or morally wrong; and in such deliberation their minds are often led to widely divergent conclusions. And then they examine and consider the question whether the action contemplated is or is not conducive to comfort and happiness in life, to the command of means and wealth, to influence, and to power, by which they may be able to help themselves and their friends; this whole matter turns upon a question of expediency. The third type of question arises when that which seems

313

to be expedient seems to conflict with that which is morally right; for when expediency seems to be pulling one way, while moral right seems to be calling back in
the opposite direction, the result is that the mind is distracted in its inquiry and
brings to it the irresolution that is born of deliberation.

10   Although omission is a most serious defect in classification, two points have
been overlooked in the foregoing: for we usually consider not only whether an
action is morally right or morally wrong, but also, when a choice of two morally
right courses is offered, which one is morally better; and likewise, when a choice of
two expedients is offered, which one is more expedient. Thus the question which
Panaetius thought threefold ought, we find, to be divided into five parts. First,
therefore, we must discuss the moral—and that, under two sub-heads; secondly, in
the same manner, the expedient; and finally, the cases where they must be weighed
against each other.

Cicero *De Officiis* 1. 8–10
tr. W. Miller (Loeb 1913)

G8 A defence of Scepticism

*The Academics were members of the philosophical school founded by Plato in the
fourth century BC. The attitude of the Academy towards Scepticism changed in
the third and second centuries BC; Carneades, the most important Academic of the
late second – early first centuries, rejected dogmatism, doubted the validity of the
Stoic theory of knowledge, and pointed to an ethical theory based on probability
and common sense. In Cicero's time the New Academy was under Philo of Larissa
and Antiochus of Ascalon (130–68 BC); Antiochus moved away from scepticism
towards a combination of the Stoic theory of knowledge and Peripatetic Ethics.*

*Cratippus was a member of the Peripatetic school, founded by Aristotle's pupil
Theophrastus. The later Peripatetics did not have the wide range of interests of
Aristotle and Theophrastus; in the first century BC under the leadership of Andro-
nicus of Rhodes they were not sharply distinguished from the Stoics.*

7   But people raise other objections against me—and that, too, philosophers and
scholars—asking whether I think I am quite consistent in my conduct: for although
our school maintains that nothing can be known for certain, yet, they urge, I make
a habit of presenting my opinions on all sorts of subjects and at this very moment
am trying to formulate rules of duty. But I wish that they had a proper understanding of our position. For we Academicians are not men whose minds wander
in uncertainty and never know what principles to adopt. For what sort of mental
habit, or rather what sort of life would that be which should dispense with all rules
for reasoning or even for living? Not so with us; but, as other schools maintain that
some things are certain, others uncertain, we, differing with them, say that some
things are probable, others improbable.

8   What, then, is to hinder me from accepting what seems to me to be probable, while rejecting what seems to be improbable, and from shunning the presumption of dogmatism, while keeping clear of that recklessness of assertion which is as far as possible removed from true wisdom? And as to the fact that our school argues against everything, that is only because we could not get a clear view of what is 'probable,' unless a comparative estimate were made of all the arguments on both sides.

But this subject has been, I think, quite fully set forth in my 'Academics.' And although, my dear Cicero, you are a student of that most ancient and celebrated school of philosophy, with Cratippus as your master—and he deserves to be classed with the founders of that illustrious sect—still I wish our school, which is closely related to yours, not to be unknown to you.

Cicero *De Officiis* 2. 7–8
tr. W. Miller (Loeb 1913)

G9   The derivation of moral obligation

This passage illustrates the way in which Cicero's philosophical concern with the derivation of moral obligation from wisdom slides into an assertion that moral obligation is in fact derived from justice, indeed from Cicero's own concept of justice.

153   My view, therefore, is that those duties are closer to Nature which depend upon the social instinct than those which depend upon knowledge; and this view can be confirmed by the following argument: (1) suppose that a wise man should be vouchsafed such a life that, with an abundance of everything pouring in upon him, he might in perfect peace study and ponder over everything that is worth knowing, still, if the solitude were so complete that he could never see a human being, he would die. And then, the foremost of all virtues is wisdom—what the Greeks call [*sophia*]; for by prudence, which they call [*phronēsis*], we understand something else, namely, the practical knowledge of things to be sought for and of things to be avoided. (2) Again, that wisdom which I have given the foremost place is the knowledge of things human and divine, which is concerned also with the bonds of union between gods and men and the relations of man to man. If wisdom is the most important of the virtues, as it certainly is, it necessarily follows that that duty which is connected with the social obligation is the most important duty. And (3) service is better than mere theoretical knowledge, for the study and knowledge of the universe would somehow be lame and defective, were no practical results to follow. Such results, moreover, are best seen in the safeguarding of human interests. It is essential, then, to human society; and it should, therefore, be ranked above speculative knowledge.

154   Upon this all the best men agree, as they prove by their conduct. For who is so absorbed in the investigation and study of creation, but that, even though he were working and pondering over tasks never so much worth mastering and even though he thought he could number the stars and measure the length and breadth of the universe, he would drop all those problems and cast them aside, if word were suddenly brought to him of some critical peril to his country, which he could relieve or repel? And he would do the same to further the interests of parent or friend or to save him from danger.

155   From all this we conclude that the duties prescribed by justice must be given precedence over the pursuit of knowledge and the duties imposed by it; for the former concern the welfare of our fellow-men; and nothing ought to be more sacred in men's eyes than that.

> Cicero *De Officiis* 1. 153–5
> tr. W. Miller (Loeb 1913)

G10 Examples from Book 2

In Book 2 Cicero considers the officia *concerned in the achievement of the aims of those in public life. Cicero discusses these* officia *in terms of* utilitas *(expediency). The following passages are important as sources for Roman social values and for Cicero's own political attitudes. Cicero uses specific examples from Greek and Roman history, as well as from his own time, to illustrate his points.*

(a) *On friendship and fame*

Laelius was a Stoic, pupil of Panaetius, whose friendship with Africanus was extolled by Cicero.

30   But we do not all feel this need to the same extent; for it must be determined in conformity with each individual's vocation in life whether it is essential for him to have the affection of many or whether the love of a few will suffice. Let this then be settled as the first and absolute essential—that we have the devotion of friends, affectionate and loving, who value our worth. For in just this one point there is but little difference between the greatest and the ordinary man; and friendship is to be cultivated almost equally by both.

31   All men do not, perhaps, stand equally in need of political honour, fame, and the good-will of their fellow-citizens; nevertheless, if these honours come to a man, they help in many ways, and especially in the acquisition of friends.

But friendship has been discussed in another book of mine, entitled 'Laelius.' Let us now take up the discussion of Glory, although I have published two books on that subject also. Still, let us touch briefly on it here, since it is of very great help in the conduct of more important business.

The highest, truest glory depends upon the following three things: the affection, the confidence, and the mingled admiration and esteem of the people. Such sentiments, if I may speak plainly and concisely, are awakened in the masses in the same way as in individuals. But there is also another avenue of approach to the masses, by which we can, as it were, steal into the hearts of all at once.

Cicero *De Officiis* 2. 30-1
tr. W. Miller (Loeb 1913)

(b) *On public games*

Theophrastus succeeded Aristotle as the head of the Peripatos, and followed him in his range of interests; he was perhaps more interested in the sciences than in metaphysics. P. Crassus was father to the triumvir M. Licinius Crassus; Lucius Crassus was a famous orator, consul in 95; Publius Lentulus, consul in 57, helped Cicero return from exile; M. Aemilius Scaurus was defended by Cicero for maladministration in Sardinia; Pompey was Cn. Pompeius Magnus the triumvir.

(b)
55 There are, in general, two classes of those who give largely: the one class is the lavish, the other the generous. The lavish are those who squander their money on public banquets, doles of meat among the people, gladiatorial shows, magnificent games, and wild-beast fights—vanities of which but a brief recollection will remain, or none at all.

56 The generous, on the other hand, are those who employ their own means to ransom captives from brigands, or who assume their friends' debts or help in providing dowries for their daughters, or assist them in acquiring property or increasing what they have. And so I wonder what Theophrastus could have been thinking about when he wrote his book on 'Wealth.' It contains much that is fine; but his position is absurd, when he praises at great length the magnificent appointments of the popular games, and it is in the means for indulging in such expenditures that he finds the highest privilege of wealth. But to me the privilege it gives for the exercise of generosity, of which I have given a few illustrations, seems far higher and far more certain.

How much more true and pertinent are Aristotle's words, as he rebukes us for not being amazed at this extravagant waste of money, all to win the favour of the populace. 'If people in time of siege,' he says, 'are required to pay a mina for a pint of water, this seems to us at first beyond belief, and all are amazed; but, when they think about it, they make allowances for it on the plea of necessity. But in the matter of this enormous waste and unlimited expenditure we are not very greatly astonished, and that, too, though by it no extreme need is relieved, no dignity is enhanced, and the very gratification of the populace is but for a brief, passing moment; such pleasure as it is, too, is confined to the most frivolous, and even in these the very memory of their enjoyment dies as soon as the moment of gratification is past.'

57 His conclusion, too, is excellent: 'This sort of amusement pleases children,

silly women, slaves, and the servile free; but a serious-minded man who weighs such matters with sound judgement cannot possibly approve of them.'

And yet I realize that in our country, even in the good old times, it had become a settled custom to expect magnificent entertainments, from the very best men in their year of aedileship. So both Publius Crassus, who was not merely surnamed 'The Rich' but was rich in fact, gave splendid games in his aedileship; and a little later Lucius Crassus (with Quintus Mucius, the most unpretentious man in the world, as his colleague) gave most magnificent entertainments in his aedileship. Then came Gaius Claudius, the son of Appius, and after him, many others—the Luculli, Hortensius, and Silanus. Publius Lentulus, however, in the year of my consulship, eclipsed all that had gone before him, and Scaurus emulated him. And my friend Pompey's exhibitions in his second consulship were the most magnificent of all. And so you see what I think about all this sort of thing.

Cicero *De Officiis* 2. 55–7
tr. W. Miller (Loeb 1913)

(c) *Expenditure on public works*

Lucius Philippus, a distinguished orator, was tribune in 104 BC; Gaius Cotta, consul in 75, is one of the characters in Cicero's work De Natura Deorum; *Curio was consul in 76; Demetrius of Phalerum, a pupil of Theophrastus, was both orator and philosopher; Pericles was the most eminent Athenian statesman of the fifth century BC.*

The justification for gifts of money, therefore, is either necessity or expediency. 59 And, in making them even in such cases, the rule of the golden mean is best. To be sure, Lucius Philippus, the son of Quintus, a man of great ability and unusual renown, used to make it his boast that without giving any entertainments he had risen to all the positions looked upon as the highest within the gift of the state. Cotta could say the same, and Curio. I, too, may make this boast my own—to a certain extent; for in comparison with the eminence of the offices to which I was unanimously elected at the earliest legal age—and this was not the good fortune of any one of those just mentioned—the outlay in my aedileship was very inconsiderable.

60 Again, the expenditure of money is better justified when it is made for walls, docks, harbours, aqueducts, and all those works which are of service to the community. There is, to be sure, more of present satisfaction in what is handed out, like cash down; nevertheless public improvements win us greater gratitude with posterity. Out of respect for Pompey's memory I am rather diffident about expressing any criticism of theatres, colonnades, and new temples; and yet the greatest philosophers do not approve of them—our Panaetius himself, for example, whom I am following, not slavishly translating, in these books; so, too, Demetrius of Phalerum, who denounces Pericles, the foremost man of Greece, for throwing away so much money on the magnificent, far-famed Propylaea. But this whole theme is discussed at length in my books on 'The Republic.'

To conclude, the whole system of public bounties in such extravagant amount is intrinsically wrong; but it may under certain circumstances be necessary to make them; even then they must be proportioned to our ability and regulated by the golden mean.

Cicero *De Officiis* 2. 59-60
tr. W. Miller (Loeb 1913)

(d) *Private property*

Cicero asserts that it is a statesman's prime duty to safeguard the rights of private property. His outburst may have been prompted by Mark Antony's second agrarian law of 44 BC, by which commissioners were given power to expropriate land which would then be used for settlement by Caesar's discharged veterans and also by the urban poor, for whose favour Antony was vying with Octavian (cf. B19 and I39). For a detailed discussion see J. M. Carter 'Cicero: Politics and Philosophy, in Cicero and Vergil', Studies in Honour of Harold Hunt *ed. J. R. C. Martyn (Hakkert 1972).*

73 The man in an administrative office, however, must make it his first care that everyone shall have what belongs to him and that private citizens suffer no invasion of their property rights by act of the state. It was a ruinous policy that Philippus proposed when in his tribuneship he introduced his agrarian bill. However, when his law was rejected, he took his defeat with good grace and displayed extraordinary moderation. But in his public speeches on the measure he often played the demagogue, and that time viciously, when he said that 'there were not in the state two thousand people who owned any property.' That speech deserves unqualified condemnation, for it favoured an equal distribution of property; and what more ruinous policy than that could be conceived? For the chief purpose in the establishment of constitutional state and municipal governments was that individual property rights might be secured. For, although it was by Nature's guidance that men were drawn together into communities, it was in the hope of safeguarding their possessions that they sought the protection of cities.

74 The administration should also put forth every effort to prevent the levying of a property tax, and to this end precautions should be taken long in advance. Such a tax was often levied in the times of our forefathers on account of the depleted state of their treasury and their incessant wars. But, if any state (I say 'any,' for I would rather speak in general terms than forebode evils to our own; however, I am not discussing our own state but states in general)—if any state ever has to face a crisis requiring the imposition of such a burden, every effort must be made to let all the people realize that they must bow to the inevitable, if they wish to be saved. And it will also be the duty of those who direct the affairs of the state to take measures that there shall be an abundance of the necessities of life. It is needless to discuss the ordinary ways and means; for the duty is self-evident; it is necessary only to mention the matter. . . .

319

78   But they who pose as friends of the people, and who for that reason either attempt to have agrarian laws passed, in order that the occupants may be driven out of their homes, or propose that money loaned should be remitted to the borrowers, are undermining the foundations of the commonwealth: first of all, they are destroying harmony, which cannot exist when money is taken away from one party and bestowed upon another; and second, they do away with equity, which is utterly subverted, if the rights of property are not respected. For, as I said above, it is the peculiar function of the state and the city to guarantee to every man the free and undisturbed control of his own particular property.

79   And yet, when it comes to measures so ruinous to public welfare, they do not gain even that popularity which they anticipate. For he who has been robbed of his property is their enemy; he to whom it has been turned over actually pretends that he had no wish to take it ; and most of all, when his debts are cancelled, the debtor conceals his joy, for fear that he may be thought to have been insolvent; whereas the victim of the wrong both remembers it and shows his resentment openly. Thus even though they to whom property has been wrongfully awarded be more in number than they from whom it has been unjustly taken, they do not for that reason have more influence; for in such matters influence is measured not by numbers but by weight. And how is it fair that a man who never had any property should take possession of lands that had been occupied for many years or even generations, and that he who had them before should lose possession of them?

Cicero *De Officiis* 2. 73–4; 78
tr. W. Miller (Loeb 1913)

G11 Rejection of the 'Social Contract'

In this passage Cicero rejects the theory that men come together in communities by mutual agreement in order to satisfy common needs such as food, defence, shelter, in favour of the view that men possess social instincts by nature. He maintains that it is this natural sociability, and not expediency, which gives the dominant tone to social values and political action.

157   And again, as swarms of bees do not gather for the sake of making honeycomb but make the honeycomb because they are gregarious by nature, so human beings—and to a much higher degree—exercise their skill together in action and thought because they are naturally gregarious. And so, if that virtue [Justice] which centres in the safeguarding of human interests, that is, in the maintenance of human society, were not to accompany the pursuit of knowledge, that knowledge would seem isolated and barren of results. In the same way, courage [Fortitude], if unrestrained by the uniting bonds of society, would be but a sort of brutality and savagery. Hence it follows that the claims of human society and the

bonds that unite men together take precedence of the pursuit of speculative knowledge.

158   And it is not true, as certain people maintain, that the bonds of union in human society were instituted in order to provide the the needs of daily life; for, they say, without the aid of others we could not secure for ourselves or supply to others the things that Nature requires; but if all that is essential to our wants and comfort were supplied by some magic wand, as in the stories, then every man of first-rate ability could drop all other responsibility and devote himself exclusively to learning and study. Not at all. For he would seek to escape from his loneliness and to find someone to share his studies; he would wish to teach, as well as to learn; to hear, as well as to speak. Every duty, therefore, that tends effectively to maintain and safeguard human society should be given the preference over that duty which arises from speculation and science alone.

159   The following question should, perhaps, be asked: whether this social instinct, which is the deepest feeling in our nature, is always to have precedence over temperance and moderation also. I think not. For there are some acts either so repulsive or so wicked, that a wise man would not commit them, even to save his country. Posidonius has made a large collection of them; but some of them are so shocking, so indecent, that it seems immoral even to mention them. The wise man, therefore, will not think of doing any such thing for the sake of his country; no more will his country consent to have it done for her. But the problem is the more easily disposed of because the occasion cannot arise when it could be to the state's interest to have the wise man do any of those things.

160   This, then, may be regarded as settled: in choosing between conflicting duties, that class takes precedence which is demanded by the interests of human society. [And this is the natural sequence; for discreet action will presuppose learning and practical wisdom; it follows, therefore, that discreet action is of more value than wise (but inactive) speculation.]

So much must suffice for this topic. For, in its essence, it has been made so clear, that in determining a question of duty it is not difficult to see which duty is to be preferred to any other. Moreover, even in the social relations themselves there are gradations of duty so well defined that it can easily be seen which duty takes precedence of any other: our first duty is to the immortal gods; our second, to country; our third, to parents; and so on, in a descending scale, to the rest.

Cicero *De Officiis* 1. 157–60
tr. W. Miller (Loeb 1913)

G12 The distinction between human and civic obligations

51   This, then, is the most comprehensive bond that unites together men as men and all to all; and under it the common right to all things that Nature has produced

for the common use of man is to be maintained, with the understanding that, while everything assigned as private property by the statutes and by civil law shall be so held as prescribed by those same laws, everything else shall be regarded in the light indicated by the Greek proverb: 'Amongst friends all things in common.' Furthermore, we find the common property of all men in things of the sort defined by Ennius; and, though restricted by him to one instance, the principle may be applied very generally:

> 'Who kindly sets a wand'rer on his way
> Does e'en as if he lit another's lamp by his:
> No less shines his, when he his friend's hath lit.'

In this example he effectively teaches us all to bestow even upon a stranger what it costs us nothing to give.

52   On this principle we have the following maxims:

'Deny no one the water that flows by;' 'Let anyone who will take fire from our fire;' 'Honest counsel give to one who is in doubt;'

for such acts are useful to the recipient and cause the giver no loss. We should, therefore, adopt these principles and always be contributing something to the common weal. But since the resources of individuals are limited and the number of the needy is infinite, this spirit of universal liberality must be regulated according to that test of Ennius—'No less shines his'—in order that we may continue to have the means for being generous to our friends.

Cicero *De Officiis* 1. 51–2
tr. W. Miller (Loeb 1913)

G13 Cicero *De Officiis* Book 3

1   Cato, who was of about the same years, Marcus, my son, as that Publius Scipio who first bore the surname of Africanus, has given us the statement that Scipio used to say that he was never less idle than when he had nothing to do and never less lonely than when he was alone. An admirable sentiment, in truth, and becoming to a great and wise man. It shows that even in his leisure hours his thoughts were occupied with public business and that he used to commune with himself when alone; and so not only was he never unoccupied, but he sometimes had no need for company. The two conditions, then, that prompt others to idleness— leisure and solitude—only spurred him on. I wish I could say the same of myself and say it truly. But if by imitation I cannot attain to such excellence of character, in aspiration, at all events, I approach it as nearly as I can; for as I am kept by force of armed treason away from practical politics and from my practice at the bar, I am now leading a life of leisure. For that reason I have left the city and, wandering in the country from place to place, I am often alone.

2   But I should not compare this leisure of mine with that of Africanus, nor this solitude with his. For he, to find leisure from his splendid services to his

country, used to take a vacation now and then and to retreat from the assemblies and the throngs of men into solitude, as into a haven of rest. But my leisure is forced upon me by want of public business, not prompted by any desire for repose. For now that the senate has been abolished and the courts have been closed, what is there, in keeping with my self-respect, that I can do either in the senate-chamber or in the forum?

3 So, although I once lived amid throngs of people and in the greatest publicity, I am now shunning the sight of the miscreants with whom the world abounds and withdrawing from the public eye as far as I may, and I am often alone. But I have learned from philosophers that among evils one ought not only to choose the least, but also to extract even from these any element of good that they may contain. For that reason, I am turning my leisure to account—thought it is not such repose as the man should be entitled to who once brought the state repose from civil strife—and I am not letting this solitude, which necessity and not my will imposes on me, find me idle . . .

5 But, my dear Cicero, while the whole field of philosophy is fertile and productive and no portion of it barren and waste, still no part is richer or more fruitful than that which deals with moral duties; for from these are derived the rules for leading a consistent and moral life. And therefore, although you are, as I trust, diligently studying and profiting by these precepts under the direction of our friend Cratippus, the foremost philosopher of the present age, I still think it well that your ears should be dinned with such precepts from every side and that, if it could be, they should hear nothing else.

6 These precepts must be laid to heart by all who look forward to a career of honour, and I am inclined to think that no one needs them more than you. For you will have to fulfil the eager anticipation that you will imitate my industry, the confident expectation that you will emulate my course of political honours, and the hope that you will, perhaps, rival my name and fame. You have, besides, incurred a heavy responsibility on account of Athens and Cratippus: for, since you have gone to them for the purchase, as it were, of a store of liberal culture, it would be a great discredit to you to return empty-handed, thereby disgracing the high reputation of the city and of your master. Therefore, put forth the best mental effort of which you are capable; work as hard as you can (if learning is work rather than pleasure); do your very best to succeed; and do not, when I have put all the necessary means at your disposal, allow it to be said that you have failed to do your part.

But enough of this. For I have written again and again for your encouragement. Let us now return to the remaining section of our subject as outlined.

7 Panaetius, then, has given us what is unquestionably the most thorough discussion of moral duties that we have, and I have followed him in the main—but with slight modifications. He classifies under three general heads the ethical problems which people are accustomed to consider and weigh: first, the question whether the matter in hand is morally right or morally wrong; second, whether it is expedient or inexpedient; third, how a decision ought to be reached, in case that

which has the appearance of being morally right clashes with that which seems to be expedient. He has treated the first two heads at length in three books; but, while he has stated that he meant to discuss the third head in its proper turn, he has never fulfilled his promise.

[*Paragraphs 8-10 summarize the evidence in favour of the view that Panaetius intended to complete the third part of the discussion.*]

11   In regard to Panaetius's real intentions, therefore, no doubt can be entertained. But whether he was or was not justified in adding this third division to the inquiry about duty may, perhaps, be a matter for debate. For whether moral goodness is the only good, as the Stoics believe, or whether, as your Peripatetics think, moral goodness is in so far the highest good that everything else gathered together into the opposing scale would have scarcely the slightest weight, it is beyond question that expediency can never conflict with moral rectitude. And so, we have heard, Socrates used to pronounce a curse upon those who first drew a conceptual distinction between things naturally inseparable. With this doctrine the Stoics are in agreement in so far as they maintain that if anything is morally right, it is expedient, and if anything is not morally right, it is not expedient.

12   But if Panaetius were the sort of man to say that virtue is worth cultivating only because it is productive of advantage, as do certain philosophers who measure the desirableness of things by the standard of pleasure or of absence of pain, he might argue that expediency sometimes clashes with moral rectitude. But since he is a man who judges that the morally right is the only good, and that those things which come in conflict with it have only the appearance of expediency and cannot make life any better by their presence nor any worse by their absence, it follows that he ought not to have raised a question involving the weighing of what seems expedient against what is morally right.

13   Furthermore, when the Stoics speak of the supreme good as 'living conformably to Nature,' they mean, as I take it, something like this: that we are always to be in accord with virtue, and from all other things that may be in harmony with Nature to choose only such as are not incompatible with virtue. This being so, some people are of the opinion that it was not right to introduce this counterbalancing of right and expediency and that no practical instruction should have been given on this question at all.

And yet moral goodness, in the true and proper sense of the term, is the exclusive possession of the wise and can never be separated from virtue; but those who have not perfect wisdom cannot possibly have perfect moral goodness, but only a semblance of it.

14   And indeed these duties under discussion in these books the Stoics call 'mean duties'; they are a common possession and have wide application; and many people attain to the knowledge of them through natural goodness of heart and through advancement in learning. But that duty which those same Stoics call 'right' is perfect and absolute and 'satisfies all the numbers,' as that same school says, and is attainable by none except the wise man.

15   On the other hand, when some act is performed in which we see 'mean' duties manifested, that is generally regarded as fully perfect, for the reason that the common crowd does not, as a rule, comprehend how far it falls short of real perfection; but, as far as their comprehension does go, they think there is no deficiency. This same thing ordinarily occurs in the estimation of poems, paintings, and a great many other works of art: ordinary people enjoy and praise things that do not deserve praise. The reason for this, I suppose, is that those productions have some point of excellence which catches the fancy of the uneducated, because these have not the ability to discover the points of weakness in any particular piece of work before them. And so, when they are instructed by experts, they readily abandon their former opinion.

The performance of the duties, then, which I am discussing in these books, is called by the Stoics a sort of second-grade moral goodness, not the peculiar property of their wise men, but shared by them with all mankind.

16   Accordingly, such duties appeal to all men who have a natural disposition to virtue. And when the two Decii or the two Scipios are mentioned as 'brave men' or Fabricius [or Aristides] is called 'the just,' it is not at all that the former are quoted as perfect models of courage or the latter as a perfect model of justice, as if we had in one of them the ideal 'wise man.' For no one of them was wise in the sense in which we wish to have 'wise' understood; neither were Marcus Cato and Gaius Laelius wise, though they were so considered and were surnamed 'the wise.' Not even the famous Seven were 'wise.' But because of their constant observance of 'mean' duties they bore a certain semblance and likeness to wise men.

17   For these reasons it is unlawful either to weigh true morality against conflicting expediency, or common morality, which is cultivated by those who wish to be considered good men, against what is profitable; but we every-day people must observe and live up to that moral right which comes within the range of our comprehension as jealously as the truly wise men have to observe and live up to that which is morally right in the technical and true sense of the word. For otherwise we cannot maintain such progress as we have made in the direction of virtue.

So much for those who have won a reputation for being good men by their careful observance of duty.

18   Those, on the other hand, who measure everything by a standard of profits and personal advantage and refuse to have these outweighed by considerations of moral rectitude are accustomed, in considering any question, to weigh the morally right against what they think the expedient; good men are not. And so I believe that when Panaetius stated that people were accustomed to hesitate to do such weighing, he meant precisely what he said—merely that 'such was their custom,' not that such was their duty. And he gave it no approval; for it is most immoral to think more highly of the apparently expedient than of the morally right, or even to set these over against each other and to hesitate to choose between them.

What, then, is it that may sometimes give room for a doubt and seem to call for consideration? It is, I believe, when a question arises as to the character of an action under consideration.

19 For it often happens, owing to exceptional circumstances, that what is accustomed under ordinary circumstances to be considered morally wrong is found not to be morally wrong. For the sake of illustration, let us assume some particular case that admits of wider application: what more atrocious crime can there be than to kill a fellow-man, and especially an intimate friend? But if anyone kills a tyrant—be he never so intimate a friend—he has not laden his soul with guilt, has he? The Roman People, at all events, are not of that opinion; for of all glorious deeds they hold such a one to be the most noble. Has expediency, then, prevailed over moral rectitude? Not at all; moral rectitude has gone hand in hand with expediency.

Some general rule, therefore, should be laid down to enable us to decide without error, whenever what we call the expedient seems to clash with what we feel to be morally right; and, if we follow that rule in comparing courses of conduct, we shall never swerve from the path of duty.

20 That rule, moreover, shall be in perfect harmony with the Stoics' system and doctrines. It is their teachings that I am following in these books and for this reason: the older Academicians and your Peripatetics (who were once the same as the Academicians) give what is morally right the preference over what seems expedient; and yet the discussion of these problems, if conducted by those who consider whatever is morally right also expedient and nothing expedient that is not at the same time morally right, will be more illuminating than if conducted by those who think that something not expedient may be morally right and that something not morally right may be expedient. But our New Academy allows us wide liberty, so that it is within my right to defend any theory that presents itself to me as most probable. But to return to my rule.

21 Well then, for a man to take something from his neighbour and to profit by his neighbour's loss is more contrary to Nature than is death or poverty or pain or anything else that can affect either our person or our property. For, in the first place, injustice is fatal to social life and fellowship between man and man. For, if we are so disposed that each, to gain some personal profit, will defraud or injure his neighbour, then those bonds of human society, which are most in accord with Nature's laws, must of necessity be broken.

22 Suppose, by way of comparison, that each one of our bodily members should conceive this idea and imagine that it could be strong and well if it should draw off to itself the health and strength of its neighbouring member, the whole body would necessarily be enfeebled and die; so, if each one of us should seize upon the property of his neighbours and take from each whatever he could appropriate to his own use, the bonds of human society must inevitably be annihilated. For, without any conflict with Nature's laws, it is granted that everybody may prefer to secure for himself rather than for his neighbour what is essential for the conduct of life; but Nature's laws do forbid us to increase our means, wealth, and resources by despoiling others.

23   But this principle is established not by Nature's laws alone (that is, by the common rules of equity), but also by the statutes of particular communities, in accordance with which in individual states the public interests are maintained. In all these it is with one accord ordained that no man shall be allowed for the sake of his own advantage to injure his neighbour. For it is to this that the laws have regard; this is their intent, that the bonds of union between citizens should not be impaired; and any attempt to destroy these bonds is repressed by the penalty of death, exile, imprisonment, or fine.

Again, this principle follows much more effectually directly from the Reason which is in Nature, which is the law of gods and men. If anyone will hearken to that voice (and all will hearken to it who wish to live in accord with Nature's laws), he will never be guilty of coveting anything that is his neighbour's or of appropriating to himself what he has taken from his neighbour.

24   Then, too, loftiness and greatness of spirit, and courtesy, justice, and generosity are much more in harmony with Nature than are selfish pleasure, riches, and life itself; but it requires a great and lofty spirit to despise these latter and count them as naught, when one weighs them over against the common weal. [But for anyone to rob his neighbour for his own profit is more contrary to Nature than death, pain, and the like.]

25   In like manner it is more in accord with Nature to emulate the great Hercules and undergo the greatest toil and trouble for the sake of aiding or saving the world, if possible, than to live in seclusion, not only free from all care, but revelling in pleasures and abounding in wealth, while excelling others also in beauty and strength. Thus Hercules denied himself and underwent toil and tribulation for the world, and, out of gratitude for his services, popular belief has given him a place in the council of the gods.

The better and more noble, therefore, the character with which a man is endowed, the more does he prefer the life of service to the life of pleasure. Whence it follows that man, if he is obedient to Nature, cannot do harm to his fellow-man.

26   Finally, if a man wrongs his neighbour to gain some advantage for himself, he must either imagine that he is not acting in defiance of Nature or he must believe that death, poverty, pain, or even the loss of children, kinsmen, or friends, is more to be shunned than an act of injustice against another. If he thinks he is not violating the laws of Nature, when he wrongs his fellow-men, how is one to argue with the individual who takes away from man all that makes him man? But if he believes that, while such a course should be avoided, the other alternatives are much worse—namely, death, poverty, pain—he is mistaken in thinking that any ills affecting either his person or his property are more serious than those affecting his soul.

This, then, ought to be the chief end of all men, to make the interest of each individual and of the whole body politic identical. For, if the individual appropriates to selfish ends what should be devoted to the common good, all human fellowship will be destroyed.

27   And further, if Nature ordains that one man shall desire to promote the

interests of a fellow-man, whoever he may be, just because he is a fellow-man, then it follows, in accordance with that same Nature, that there are interests that all men have in common. And, if this is true, we are all subject to one and the same law of Nature; and, if this also is true, we are certainly forbidden by Nature's law to wrong our neighbour. Now the first assumption is true; therefore the conclusion is likewise true.

28   For that is an absurd position which is taken by some people, who say that they will not rob a parent or a brother for their own gain, but that their relation to the rest of their fellow-citizens is quite another thing. Such people contend in essence that they are bound to their fellow-citizens by no mutual obligations, social ties, or common interests. This attitude demolishes the whole structure of civil society.

Others again who say that regard should be had for the rights of fellow-citizens, but not of foreigners, would destroy the universal brotherhood of mankind; and, when this is annihilated, kindness, generosity, goodness, and justice must utterly perish; and those who work all this destruction must be considered as wickedly rebelling against the immortal gods. For they uproot the fellowship which the gods have established between human beings, and the closest bond of this fellowship is the conviction that it is more repugnant to Nature for man to rob a fellow-man for his own gain than to endure all possible loss, whether to his property or to his person . . . or even to his very soul—so far as these losses are not concerned with justice; for this virtue is the sovereign mistress and queen of all the virtues.

29   But, perhaps, someone may say: 'Well, then, suppose a wise man were starving to death, might he not take the bread of some perfectly useless member of society?' [Not at all; for my life is not more precious to me than that temper of soul which would keep me from doing wrong to anybody for my own advantage.] 'Or again; supposing a righteous man were in a position to rob the cruel and inhuman tyrant Phalaris of clothing, might he not do it to keep himself from freezing to death?'

30   These cases are very easy to decide. For, if merely for one's own benefit one were to take something away from a man, though he were a perfectly worthless fellow, it would be an act of meanness and contrary to Nature's law. But suppose one would be able, by remaining alive, to render signal service to the state and to human society—if from that motive one should take something from another, it would not be a matter for censure. But, if such is not the case, each one must bear his own burden of distress rather than rob a neighbour of his rights. We are not to say, therefore, that sickness or want or any evil of that sort is more repugnant to Nature than to covet and to appropriate what is one's neighbour's; but we do maintain that disregard of the common interests is repugnant to Nature; for it is unjust.

31   And therefore Nature's law itself, which protects and conserves human interests, will surely determine that a man who is wise, good, and brave, should in emergency have the necessaries of life transferred to him from a person who is idle and worthless; for the good man's death would be a heavy loss to the common weal; only let him beware that self-esteem and self-love do not find in such a transfer of possessions a pretext for wrong-doing. But, thus guided in his decision,

the good man will always perform his duty, promoting the general interests of human society on which I am so fond of dwelling.

32   As for the case of Phalaris, a decision is quite simple: we have no ties of fellowship with a tyrant, but rather the bitterest feud; and it is not opposed to Nature to rob, if one can, a man whom it is morally right to kill;—nay, all that pestilent and abominable race should be exterminated from human society. And this may be done by proper measures; for, as certain members are amputated, if they show signs themselves of being bloodless and virtually lifeless and thus jeopardize the health of the other parts of the body, so those fierce and savage monsters in human form should be cut off from what may be called the common body of humanity.

Of this sort are all those problems in which we have to determine what moral duty is, as it varies with varying circumstances.

[*In paragraphs 33 and 34 Cicero claims his discussion is in accordance with Paneatius' intentions.*]

35   Now when we meet with expediency in some specious form or other, we cannot help being influenced by it. But if upon closer inspection one sees that there is some immorality connected with what presents the appearance of expediency, then one is not necessarily to sacrifice expediency but to recognize that there can be no expediency where there is immorality. But if there is nothing so repugnant to Nature as immorality (for Nature demands right and harmony and consistency and abhors their opposites), and if nothing is so thoroughly in accord with Nature as expediency, then surely expediency and immorality cannot coexist in one and the same object.

Again: if we are born for moral rectitude and if that is either the only thing worth seeking, as Zeno thought, or at least to be esteemed as infinitely outweighing everything else, as Aristotle holds, then it necessarily follows that the morally right is either the sole good or the supreme good. Now, that which is good is certainly expedient; consequently, that which is morally right is also expedient.

36   Thus it is the error of men who are not strictly upright to seize upon something that seems to be expedient and straightway to dissociate that from the question of moral right. To this error the assassin's dagger, the poisoned cup, the forged wills owe their origin; this gives rise to theft, embezzlement of public funds, exploitation and plundering of provincials and citizens; this engenders also the lust for excessive wealth, for despotic power, and finally for making oneself king even in the midst of a free people; and anything more atrocious or repulsive than such a passion cannot be conceived. For with a false perspective they see the material rewards but not the punishment—I do not mean the penalty of the law, which they often escape, but the heaviest penalty of all, their own demoralization.

37   Away, then, with questioners of this sort (for their whole tribe is wicked and ungodly), who stop to consider whether to pursue the course which they see is morally right or to stain their hands with what they know is crime. For there is guilt in their very deliberation, even though they never reach the performance of

the deed itself. Those actions, therefore, should not be considered at all, the mere consideration of which is itself morally wrong.

Furthermore, in any such consideration we must banish any vain hope and thought that our action may be covered up and kept secret. For if we have only made some real progress in the study of philosophy, we ought to be quite convinced that, even though we may escape the eyes of gods and men, we must still do nothing that savours of greed or of injustice, of lust or of intemperance.

[*Paragraphs 38 and 39a examine the story of Gyges as related by Plato.*]

39b   For when we ask what they would do, if they could escape detection, we are not asking whether they can escape detection; but we put them as it were upon the rack: should they answer that, if impunity were assured, they would do what was most to their selfish interest, that would be a confession that they are criminally minded; should they say that they would not do so, they would be granting that all things in and of themselves immoral should be avoided. . . .

But let us now return to our theme.

40   Many cases oftentimes arise to perplex our minds with a specious appearance of expediency: the question raised in these cases is not whether moral rectitude is to be sacrificed to some considerable advantage (for that would of course be wrong), but whether the apparent advantage can be secured without moral wrong. When Brutus deposed his colleague Collatinus from the consular office, his treatment of him might have been thought unjust; for Collatinus had been his associate, and had helped him with word and deed in driving out the royal family. But when the leading men of the state had determined that all the kindred of Superbus and the very name of the Tarquins and every reminder of the monarchy should be obliterated, then the course that was expedient—namely, to serve the country's interests—was so pre-eminently right, that it was even Collatinus's own duty to acquiesce in its justice. And so expediency gained the day because of its moral rightness; for without moral rectitude there could have been no possible expediency.

41   Not so in the case of the king who founded the city: it was the specious appearance of expediency that actuated him; and when he decided that it was more expedient for him to reign alone than to share the throne with another, he slew his brother. He threw to the winds his brotherly affection and his human feelings, to secure what seemed to him—but was not—expedient; and yet in defence of his deed he offered the excuse about his wall—a specious show of moral rectitude, neither reasonable nor adequate at all. He committed a crime, therefore, with due respect to him let me say so, be he Quirinus or Romulus.

42   And yet we are not required to sacrifice our own interests and surrender to others what we need for ourselves, but each one should consider his own interests, as far as he may without injury to his neighbour's. 'When a man enters the foot-race,' says Chrysippus with his usual aptness, 'it is his duty to put forth all his strength and strive with all his might to win; but he ought never with his foot to trip, or with his hand to foul a competitor. Thus in the stadium of life, it is not

unfair for anyone to seek to obtain what is needful for his own advantage, but he has no right to wrest it from his neighbour.'

43   It is in the case of friendships, however, that men's conceptions of duty are most confused; for it is a breach of duty either to fail to do for a friend what one rightly can do, or to do for him what is not right. But for our guidance in all such cases we have a rule that is short and easy to master: apparent advantages—political preferment, riches, sensual pleasures, and the like—should never be preferred to the obligations of friendship. But an upright man will never for a friend's sake do anything in violation of his country's interests or his oath or his sacred honour, not even if he sits as judge in a friend's case; for he lays aside the role of friend when he assumes that of judge. Only so far will he make concessions to friendship, that he will prefer his friend's side to be the juster one and that he will set the time for presenting his case, as far as the laws will allow, to suit his friend's convenience. 44   But when he comes to pronounce the verdict under oath, he should remember that he has God as his witness—that is, as I understand it, his own conscience, than which God himself has bestowed upon man nothing more divine. From this point of view it is a fine custom that we have inherited from our forefathers (if we were only true to it now), to appeal to the juror with this formula—'to do what he can consistently with his sacred honour.' This form of appeal is in keeping with what I said a moment ago would be morally right for a judge to concede to a friend. For supposing that we were bound to do everything that our friends desired, such relations would have to be accounted not friendships but conspiracies.

45   But I am speaking here of ordinary friendships; for among men who are ideally wise and perfect such situations cannot arise.

They say that Damon and Phintias, of the Pythagorean school, enjoyed such ideally perfect friendship, that when the tyrant Dionysius had appointed a day for the execution of one of them, and the one who had been condemned to death requested a few days' respite for the purpose of putting his loved ones in the care of friends, the other became surety for his appearance, with the understanding that if his friend did not return, he himself should be put to death. And when the friend returned on the day appointed, the tyrant in admiration for their faithfulness begged that they would enrol him as a third partner in their friendship.

46   Well then, when we are weighing what seems to be expedient in friendship against what is morally right, let apparent expediency be disregarded and moral rectitude prevail; and when in friendship requests are submitted that are not morally right, let conscience and scrupulous regard for the right take precedence of the obligations of friendship. In this way we shall arrive at a proper choice between conflicting duties—the subject of this part of our investigation.

Through a specious appearance of expediency wrong is very often committed in transactions between state and state, as by our own country in the destruction of Corinth. A more cruel wrong was perpetrated by the Athenians in decreeing that the Aeginetans, whose strength lay in their navy, should have their thumbs cut off. This seemed to be expedient; for Aegina was too grave a menace, as it was close to the Piraeus. But no cruelty can be expedient; for cruelty is most abhorrent to human nature, whose lead we ought to follow.

47   They, too, do wrong who would debar foreigners from enjoying the advantages of their city and would exclude them from its borders, as was done by Pennus in the time of our fathers, and in recent times by Papius. It may not be right, of course, for one who is not a citizen to exercise the rights and privileges of citizenship; and the law on this point was secured by two of our wisest consuls. Crassus and Scaevola. Still, to debar foreigners from enjoying the advantages of the city is altogether contrary to the laws of humanity.
was secured by two of our wisest consuls, Crassus and Scaevola. Still, to debar foreigners from enjoying the advantages of the city is altogether contrary to the laws of humanity.

There are splendid examples in history where the apparent expediency of the state has been set at naught out of regard for moral rectitude. Our own country has many instances to offer throughout her history, and especially in the Second Punic War, when news came of the disaster at Cannae, Rome displayed a loftier courage than ever she did in success; never a trace of faint-heartedness, never a mention of making terms. The influence of moral right is so potent, that it eclipses the specious appearance of expediency.

[*Paragraphs 48 and 49 draw on examples from Greek history.*]

49   . . . Let it be set down as an established principle, then, that what is morally wrong can never be expedient—not even when one secures by means of it that which one thinks expedient; for the mere act of thinking a course expedient, when it is morally wrong, is demoralizing.

50   But, as I said above, cases often arise in which expediency may seem to clash with moral rectitude; and so we should examine carefully and see whether their conflict is inevitable or whether they may be reconciled. The following are problems of this sort: suppose, for example, a time of dearth and famine at Rhodes, with provisions at fabulous prices; and suppose that an honest man has imported a large cargo of grain from Alexandria and that to his certain knowledge also several other importers have set sail from Alexandria, and that on the voyage he has sighted their vessels laden with grain and bound for Rhodes; is he to report the fact to the Rhodians or is he to keep his own counsel and sell his own stock at the highest market price? I am assuming the case of a virtuous, upright man, and I am raising the question how a man would think and reason who would not conceal the facts from the Rhodians if he thought that it was immoral to do so, but who might be in doubt whether such silence would really be immoral.

51   In deciding cases of this kind Diogenes of Babylonia, a great and highly esteemed Stoic, consistently holds one view; his pupil Antipater, a most profound scholar, holds another. According to Antipater all the facts should be disclosed, that the buyer may not be uninformed of any detail that the seller knows; according to Diogenes the seller should declare any defects in his wares, in so far as such a course is prescribed by the common law of the land; but for the rest, since he has

goods to sell, he may try to sell them to the best possible advantage, provided he is guilty of no misrepresentation.

'I have imported my stock,' Diogenes's merchant will say; 'I have offered it for sale; I sell at a price no higher than my competitors—perhaps even lower, when the market is overstocked. Who is wronged?'

52 'What say you?' comes Antipater's argument on the other side: 'it is your duty to consider the interests of your fellow-men and to serve society; you were brought into the world under these conditions and have these inborn principles which you are in duty bound to obey and follow, that your interest shall be the interest of the community and conversely that the interest of the community shall be your interest as well; will you, in view of all these facts, conceal from your fellow-men what relief in plenteous supplies is close at hand for them?'

'It is one thing to conceal,' Diogenes will perhaps reply; 'not to reveal is quite a different thing. At this present moment I am not concealing from you, even if I am not revealing to you, the nature of the gods or the highest good; and to know these secrets would be of more advantage to you than to know that the price of wheat was down. But I am under no obligation to tell you everything that it may be to your interest to be told.'

53 'Yea,' Antipater will say, 'but you are, as you must admit, if you will only bethink you of the bonds of fellowship forged by Nature and existing between man and man.'

'I do not forget them,' the other will reply; 'but do you mean to say that those bonds of fellowship are such that there is no such thing as private property? If that is the case, we should not sell anything at all, but freely give everything away.'

In this whole discussion, you see, no one says, 'However wrong morally this or that may be, still, since it is expedient, I will do it'; but the one side asserts that a given act is expedient, without being morally wrong, while the other insists that the act should not be done, because it is morally wrong.

54 Suppose again that an honest man is offering a house for sale on account of certain undesirable features of which he himself is aware but which nobody else knows; suppose it is unsanitary, but has the reputation of being healthful; suppose it is not generally known that vermin are to be found in all the bedrooms; suppose, finally, that it is built of unsound timber and likely to collapse, but that no one knows about it except the owner; if the vendor does not tell the purchaser these facts but sells him the house for far more than he could reasonably have expected to get for it, I ask whether his transaction is unjust or dishonourable.

55 'Yes,' says Antipater, 'it is; for to allow a purchaser to be hasty in closing a deal and through mistaken judgment to incur a very serious loss, if this is not re-fusing "to set a man right when he has lost his way" (a crime which at Athens is prohibited on pain of public execration), what is? It is even worse than refusing to set a man on his way: it is deliberately leading a man astray.'

'Can you say,' answers Diogenes, 'that he compelled you to purchase, when he did not even advise it? He advertised for sale what he did not like; you bought what you did like. If people are not considered guilty of swindling when they place upon their placards FOR SALE: A FINE VILLA, WELL BUILT, even when it is neither good nor properly built, still less guilty are they who say nothing in praise of their house. For where the purchaser may exercise his own judgment, what fraud can there be on the part of the vendor? But if, again, not all that is expressly stated has to be made good, do you think a man is bound to make good what has not been said? What, pray, would be more stupid than for a vendor to recount all the faults in the article he is offering for sale? And what would be so absurd as for an auctioneer to cry, at the owner's bidding, "Here is an unsanitary house for sale"?'

56   In this way, then, in certain doubtful cases moral rectitude is defended on the one side, while on the other side the case of expediency is so presented as to make it appear not only morally right to do what seems expedient, but even morally wrong not to do it. This is the contradiction that seems often to arise between the expedient and the morally right. But I must give my decision in these two cases; for I did not propound them merely to raise the questions, but to offer a solution.

57   I think, then, that it was the duty of that grain-dealer not to keep back the facts from the Rhodians, and of this vendor of the house to deal in the same way with his purchaser. The fact is that merely holding one's peace about a thing does not constitute concealment, but concealment consists in trying for your own profit to keep others from finding out something that you know, when it is for their interest to know it. And who fails to discern what manner of concealment that is and what sort of person would be guilty of it? At all events he would be no candid or sincere or straightforward or upright or honest man, but rather one who is shifty, sly, artful, shrewd, underhand, cunning, one grown old in fraud and subtlety. Is it not inexpedient to subject oneself to all these terms of reproach and many more besides?

[Paragraphs 58–62 examine further Roman examples.]

63   Now I observe that Hecaton of Rhodes, a pupil of Panaetius, says in his books on 'Moral Duty' dedicated to Quintus Tubero that 'it is a wise man's duty to take care of his private interests, at the same time doing nothing contrary to the civil customs, laws, and institutions. But that depends on our purpose in seeking prosperity; for we do not aim to be rich for ourselves alone but for our children, relatives, friends, and, above all, for our country. For the private fortunes of individuals are the wealth of the state.' Hecaton could not for a moment approve of Scaevola's act, which I cited a moment ago; for he openly avows that he will abstain from doing for his own profit only what the law expressly forbids. Such a man deserves no great praise nor gratitude.

64   Be that as it may, if both pretence and concealment constitute 'criminal fraud,' there are very few transactions into which 'criminal fraud' does not enter; or, if he only is a good man who helps all he can, and harms no one, it will certainly be no easy matter for us to find the good man as thus defined.

To conclude, then, it is never expedient to do wrong, because wrong is always immoral; and it is always expedient to be good, because goodness is always moral.

65   In the laws pertaining to the sale of real property it is stipulated in our civil

code that when a transfer of any real estate is made, all its defects shall be declared as far as they are known to the vendor. According to the laws of the Twelve Tables it used to be sufficient that such faults as had been expressly declared should be made good and that for any flaws which the vendor expressly denied, when questioned, he should be assessed double damages. A like penalty for failure to make such declaration also has now been secured by our jurisconsults: they have decided that any defect in a piece of real estate, if known to the vendor but not expressly stated, must be made good by him.   66   For example, the augurs were proposing to take observations from the citadel and they ordered Tiberius Claudius Centumalus, who owned a house upon the Caelian Hill, to pull down such parts of the building as obstructed the augurs' view by reason of their height. Claudius at once advertised his block for sale, and Publius Calpurnius Lanarius bought it. The same notice was served also upon him. And so, when Calpurnius had pulled down those parts of the building and discovered that Claudius had advertised it for sale only after the augurs had ordered them to be pulled down, he summoned the former owner before a court of equity to decide 'what indemnity the owner was under obligation "in good faith" to pay and deliver to him.' The verdict was pronounced by Marcus Cato, the father of our Cato (for as other men receive a distinguishing name from their fathers, so he who bestowed upon the world so bright a luminary must have his distinguishing name from his son); he, as I was saying, was presiding judge and pronounced the verdict that 'since the augurs' mandate was known to the vendor at the time of making the transfer and since he had not made it known, he was bound to make good the purchaser's loss.'

67   With this verdict he established the principle that it was essential to good faith that any defect known to the vendor must be made known to the purchaser. If his decision was right, our grain-dealer and the vendor of the unsanitary house did not do right to suppress the facts in those cases. But the civil code cannot be made to include all cases where facts are thus suppressed; but those cases which it does include are summarily dealt with. [*Another illustration from contemporary events is here omitted.*]

What is the purpose of these illustrations? To let you see that our forefathers did not countenance sharp practice.

68   Now the law disposes of sharp practices in one way, philosophers in another: the law deals with them as far as it can lay its strong arm upon them; philosophers, as far as they can be apprehended by reason and conscience. Now reason demands that nothing be done with unfairness, with false pretence, or with misrepresentation. Is it not deception, then, to set snares, even if one does not mean to start the game or to drive it into them? Why, wild creatures often fall into snares undriven and unpursued. Could one in the same way advertise a house for sale, post up a notice 'To be sold,' like a snare, and have somebody run into it unsuspecting?

69   Owing to the low ebb of public sentiment, such a method of procedure, I find, is neither by custom accounted morally wrong nor forbidden either by statute or by civil law; nevertheless it is forbidden by the moral law. For there is a bond of

fellowship—although I have often made this statement, I must still repeat it again and again—which has the very widest application, uniting all men together and each to each. This bond of union is closer between those who belong to the same nation, and more intimate still between those who are citizens of the same city-state. It is for this reason that our forefathers chose to understand one thing by the universal law and another by the civil law. The civil law is not necessarily also the universal law; but the universal law ought to be also the civil law. But we possess no substantial, life-like image of true Law and genuine Justice; a mere outline sketch is all that we enjoy. I only wish that we were true even to this; for, even as it is, it is drawn from the excellent models which Nature and Truth afford.

70　For how weighty are the words: 'That I be not deceived and defrauded through you and my confidence in you'! How precious are these: 'As between honest people there ought to be honest dealing, and no deception'! But who are 'honest people,' and what is 'honest dealing'—these are serious questions.

It was Quintus Scaevola, the pontifex maximus, who used to attach the greatest importance to all questions of arbitration to which the formula was appended 'as good faith requires'; and he held that the expression "good faith" had a very extensive application, for it was employed in trusteeships and partnerships, in trusts and commissions, in buying and selling, in hiring and letting—in a word, in all the transactions on which the social relations of daily life depend; in these, he said, it required a judge of great ability to decide the extent of each individual's obligation to the other, especially when counter-claims were admissible in most cases.

71　Away, then, with sharp practice and trickery, which desires, of course, to pass for wisdom, but is far from it and totally unlike it. For the function of wisdom is to discriminate between good and evil; whereas, inasmuch as all things morally wrong are evil, trickery prefers the evil to the good.

It is not only in the case of real estate transfers that the civil law, based upon a natural feeling for the right, punishes trickery and deception, but also in the sale of slaves every form of deception on the vendor's part is disallowed. For by the aediles' ruling the vendor is answerable for any deficiency in the slave he sells, for he is supposed to know if his slave is sound, or if he is a runaway, or a thief. The case of those who have just come into the possession of slaves by inheritance is different.

72　From this we come to realize that since Nature is the source of right, it is not in accord with Nature that anyone should take advantage of his neighbour's ignorance. And no greater curse in life can be found than knavery that wears the mask of wisdom. Thence come those countless cases in which the expedient seems to conflict with the right. For how few will be found who can refrain from wrong-doing, if assured of the power to keep it an absolute secret and to run no risk of punishment!

73　Let us put our principle to the test, if you please, and see if it holds good in those instances in which, perhaps, the world in general finds no wrong; for in this connection we do not need to discuss cut-throats, poisoners, forgers of wills, thieves, and embezzlers of public moneys, who should be repressed not by lectures and discussions of philosophers, but by chains and prison walls; but let us study here the conduct of those who have the reputation of being honest men.

Certain individuals brought from Greece to Rome a forged will, purporting to be that of the wealthy Lucius Minucius Basilus. The more easily to procure validity for it, they made joint-heirs with themselves two of the most influential men of the day, Marcus Crassus and Quintus Hortensius. Although these men suspected that the will was a forgery, still, as they were conscious of no personal guilt in the matter, they did not spurn the miserable boon procured through the crime of others. What shall we say, then? Is this excuse competent to acquit them of guilt? I cannot think so, although I loved the one while he lived, and do not hate the other now that he is dead.

74 Be that as it may, Basilus had in fact desired that his nephew Marcus Satrius should bear his name and inherit his property. (I refer to the Satrius who is the present patron of Picenum and the Sabine country—and oh, what a shameful stigma it is upon the times!) And therefore it was not right that two of the leading citizens of Rome should take the estate and Satrius succeed to nothing except his uncle's name. For if he does wrong who does not ward off and repel injury when he can—as I explained in the course of the First Book—what is to be thought of the man who not only does not try to prevent wrong, but actually aids and abets it? For my part, I do not believe that even genuine legacies are moral, if they are sought after by designing flatteries and by attentions hypocritical rather than sincere.

And yet in such cases there are times when one course is likely to appear expedient and another morally right.

75 The appearance is deceptive; for our standard is the same for expediency and for moral rectitude. And the man who does not accept the truth of this will be capable of any sort of dishonesty, any sort of crime. For if he reasons, 'That is, to be sure, the right course, but this course brings advantage,' he will not hesitate in his mistaken judgment to divorce two conceptions that Nature has made one; and that spirit opens the door to all sorts of dishonesty, wrong-doing, and crime.

Suppose, then, that a good man had such power that at a snap of his fingers his name could steal into rich men's wills, he would not avail himself of that power —no, not even though he could be perfectly sure that no one would ever suspect it. Suppose, on the other hand, that one were to offer a Marcus Crassus the power, by the mere snapping of his fingers, to get himself named as heir, when he was not really an heir, he would, I warrant you, dance in the forum. But the righteous man, the one whom we feel to be a good man, would never rob anyone of anything to enrich himself. If anybody is astonished at this doctrine, let him confess that he does not know what a good man is.

76 If, on the other hand, anyone should desire to unfold the idea of a good man which lies wrapped up in his own mind, he would then at once make it clear to himself that a good man is one who helps all whom he can and harms nobody, unless provoked by wrong. What shall we say, then? Would he not be doing harm who by a kind of magic spell should succeed in displacing the real heirs to an estate

and pushing himself into their place? 'Well,' someone may say, 'is he not to do what is expedient, what is advantageous to himself?' Nay, verily; he should rather be brought to realize that nothing that is unjust is either advantageous or expedient; if he does not learn this lesson, it will never be possible for him to be a 'good man.'

77   When I was a boy, I used to hear my father tell that Gaius Fimbria, an ex-consul, was judge in a case of Marcus Lutatius Pinthia, a Roman knight of irreproachable character. On that occasion Pinthia had laid a wager to be forfeited 'if he did not prove in court that he was a good man.' Fimbria declared that he would never render a decision in such a case, for fear that he might either rob a reputable man of his good name, if he decided against him, or be thought to have pronounced someone a good man, when such a character is, as he said, established by the performance of countless duties and the possession of praiseworthy qualities without number.

To this type of good man, then, known not only to a Socrates but even to a Fimbria, nothing can possibly seem expedient that is not morally right. Such a man, therefore, will never venture to think—to say nothing of doing—anything that he would not dare openly to proclaim. Is it not a shame that philosophers should be in doubt about moral questions on which even peasants have no doubts at all? For it is with peasants that the proverb, already trite with age, originated: when they praise a man's honour and honesty, they say, 'He is a man with whom you can safely play at odd and even in the dark.' What is the point of the proverb but this—that what is not proper brings no advantage, even if you can gain your end without anyone's being able to convict you of wrong?

78   Do you not see that in the light of this proverb no excuse is available either for the Gyges of the story or for the man who I assumed a moment ago could with a snap of his fingers sweep together everybody's inheritance at once? For as the morally wrong cannot by any possibility be made morally right, however successfully it may be covered up, so what is not morally right cannot be made expedient, for Nature refuses and resists.

79   'But stay,' someone will object, 'when the prize is very great, there is excuse for doing wrong.'

Gaius Marius had been left in obscurity for more than six whole years after his praetorship and had scarcely the remotest hope of gaining the consulship. It looked as if he would never even be a candidate for that office. He was now a lieutenant under Quintus Metellus, who sent him on a furlough to Rome. There before the Roman People he accused his own general, an eminent man and one of our first citizens, of purposely protracting the war and declared that if they would make him consul, he would within a short time deliver Jugurtha alive or dead into the hands of the Roman People. And so he was elected consul, it is true, but he was a traitor to his own good faith and to justice; for by a false charge he subjected to popular disfavour an exemplary and highly respected citizen, and that too, although he was his lieutenant and under leave of absence from him.

80   Even our kinsman Gratidianus failed on one occasion to perform what would be a good man's duty: in his praetorship the tribunes of the people

summoned the college of praetors to council, in order to adopt by joint resolution a standard of value for our currency; for at that time the value of money was so fluctuating that no one could tell how much he was worth. In joint session they drafted an ordinance, defining the penalty and the methods of procedure in cases of violation of the ordinance, and agreed that they should all appear together upon the rostra in the afternoon to publish it. And while all the rest withdrew, some in one direction, some in another, Marius (Gratidianus) went straight from the council-chamber to the rostra and published individually what had been drawn up by all together. And that coup, if you care to know, brought him vast honour; in every street statues of him were erected; before these incense and candles burned. In a word, no one ever enjoyed greater popularity with the masses.

81   It is such cases as these that sometimes perplex us in our consideration, when the point in which justice is violated does not seem so very significant, but the consequences of such slight transgression seem exceedingly important. For example, it was not so very wrong morally, in the eyes of Marius, to overreach his colleagues and the tribunes in turning to himself alone all the credit with the people; but to secure by that means his election to the consulship, which was then the goal of his ambition, seemed very greatly to his interest. But for all cases we have one rule, with which I desire you to be perfectly familiar: that which seems expedient must not be morally wrong; or, if it is morally wrong, it must not seem expedient. What follows? Can we account either the great Marius or our Marius Gratidianus a good man? Work out your own ideas and sift your thoughts so as to see what conception and idea of a good man they contain. Pray, tell me, does it coincide with the character of your good man to lie for his own profit, to slander, to overreach, to deceive? Nay, verily; anything but that!

82   Is there, then, any object of such value or any advantage so worth the winning that, to gain it, one should sacrifice the name of a 'good man' and the lustre of his reputation? What is there that your so-called expediency can bring to you that will compensate for what it can take away, if it steals from you the name of a 'good man' and causes you to lose your sense of honour and justice? For what difference does it make whether a man is actually transformed into a beast or whether, keeping the outward appearance of a man, he has the savage nature of a beast within?

Again, when people disregard everything that is morally right and true, if only they may secure power thereby, are they not pursuing the same course as he who wished to have as a father-in-law the man by whose effrontery he might gain power for himself? He thought it advantageous to secure supreme power while the odium of it fell upon another; and he failed to see how unjust to his country this was, and how wrong morally. But the father-in-law himself used to have continually upon his lips the Greek verses from the Phoenissae, which I will reproduce as well as I can—awkwardly, it may be, but still so that the meaning can be understood:

> 'If wrong may e'er be right, for a throne's sake
> Were wrong most right:—be God in all else feared!'

Our tyrant deserved his death for having made an exception of the one thing that was the blackest crime of all.

83   Why do we gather instances of petty crime—legacies criminally obtained and fraudulent buying and selling? Behold, here you have a man who was ambitious to be king of the Roman People and master of the whole world; and he achieved it! The man who maintains that such an ambition is morally right is a madman; for he justifies the destruction of law and liberty and thinks their hideous and detestable suppression glorious. But if anyone agrees that it is not morally right to be kind in a state that once was free and that ought to be free now, and yet imagines that it is advantageous for him who can reach that position, with what remonstrance or rather with what appeal should I try to tear him away from so strange a delusion? For, oh ye immortal gods! can the most horrible and hideous of all murders—that of fatherland—bring advantage to anybody, even though he who has committed such a crime receives from his enslaved fellow-citizens the title of 'Father of his Country'? Expediency, therefore, must be measured by the standard of moral rectitude, and in such a way, too, that these two words shall seem in sound only to be different but in real meaning to be one and the same.

84   What greater advantage one could have, according to the standard of popular opinion, than to be a king, I do not know; when, however, I begin to bring the question back to the standard of truth, then I find nothing more disadvantageous for one who has risen to that height by injustice. For can occasions for worry, anxiety, fear by day and by night, and a life all beset with plots and perils be of advantage to anybody?

'Thrones have many foes and friends untrue, but few devoted friends,' says Accius. But of what sort of throne was he speaking? Why, one that was held by right, handed down from Tantalus and Pelops. Aye, but how many more foes, think you, had that king who with the Roman People's army brought the Roman People themselves into subjection and compelled a state that not only had been free but had been mistress of the world to be his slave.

85   What stains do you think he had upon his conscience, what scars upon his heart? But whose life can be advantageous to himself, if that life is his on the condition that the man who takes it shall be held in undying gratitude and glory? But if these things which seem so very advantageous are not advantageous because they are full of shame and moral wrong, we ought to be quite convinced that nothing can be expedient that is not morally right. [*Further examples in 86 and 87, omitted here, contain actions said to be expedient for the state; the increased revenues refer to taxes from states which were forced to pay tribute although they had paid money to be granted exemption.*] 'But,' someone will say, 'the revenues were increased, and therefore it was expedient.' How long will people venture to say that a thing that is not morally right can be expedient?

88   Furthermore, can hatred and shame be expedient for any government? For government ought to be founded upon fair fame and the loyalty of allies.

On this point I often disagreed even with my friend Cato; it seemed to me that he was too rigorous in his watchful care over the claims of the treasury and the revenues; he refused everything that the farmers of the revenue asked for and much that the allies desired; whereas, as I insisted, it was our duty to be generous to the allies and to treat the publicans as we were accustomed individually to treat our tenants—and all the more, because harmony between the orders was essential to the welfare of the republic. Curio, too, was wrong, when he pleaded that the demands of the people beyond the Po were just, but never failed to add, 'Let expediency prevail.' He ought rather to have proved that the claims were not just, because they were not expedient for the republic, than to have admitted that they were just, when, as he maintained, they were not expedient.

89   The sixth book of Hecaton's 'Moral Duties' is full of questions like the following: 'Is it consistent with a good man's duty to let his slaves go hungry when provisions are at famine prices?'

Hecaton gives the argument on both sides of the question; but still in the end it is by the standard of expediency, as he conceives it, rather than by one of human feeling, that he decides the question of duty.

Then he raises this question: supposing a man had to throw part of his cargo overboard in a storm, should he prefer to sacrifice a high-priced horse or a cheap and worthless slave? In this case regard for his property interest inclines him one way, human feeling the other.

'Suppose that a foolish man has seized hold of a plank from a sinking ship, shall a wise man wrest it away from him if he can?'

'No,' says Hecaton; 'for that would be unjust.'

'But how about the owner of the ship? Shall he take the plank away because it belongs to him?'

'Not at all; no more than he would be willing when far out at sea to throw a passenger overboard on the ground that the ship was his. For until they reach the place for which the ship is chartered, she belongs to the passengers, not to the owner.'

90   'Again; suppose there were two to be saved from the sinking ship—both of them wise men—and only one small plank, should both seize it to save themselves? Or should one give place to the other?'

'Why of course, one should give place to the other, but that other must be the one whose life is more valuable either for his own sake or for that of his country.'

'But what if these considerations are of equal weight in both?'

'Then there will be no contest, but one will give place to the other, as if the point were decided by lot or at a game of odd and even.' [*90b, 91 and 92 contain further examples.*]

92   The question arises also whether agreements and promises must always be kept, 'when,' in the language of the praetors' edicts, 'they have not been secured through force or criminal fraud.'

If one man gives another a remedy for the dropsy, with the stipulation that, if he is cured by it, he shall never make use of it again; suppose the patient's health is restored by the use of it, but some years later he contracts the same disease once more; and suppose he cannot secure from the man with whom he made the agreement permission to use the remedy again, what should he do? That is the question. Since the man is unfeeling in refusing the request, and since no harm could be done to him by his friend's using the remedy, the sick man is justified in doing what he can for his own life and health.

93   Again: suppose that a millionaire is making some wise man his heir and leaving him in his will a hundred million sesterces; and suppose that he has asked the wise man, before he enters upon his inheritance, to dance publicly in broad daylight in the forum; and suppose that the wise man has given his promise to do so, because the rich man would not leave him his fortune on any other condition; should he keep his promise or not? I wish he had made no such promise; that, I think, would have been in keeping with his dignity. But, seeing that he has made it, it will be morally better for him, if he believes it morally wrong to dance in the forum, to break his promise and refuse to accept his inheritance rather than to keep his promise and accept it—unless, perhaps, he contributes the money to the state to meet some grave crisis. In that case, to promote thereby the interests of one's country, it would not be morally wrong even to dance, if you please, in the forum. [*94–95a introduce examples from Greek mythology.*]

95   Promises are, therefore, sometimes not to be kept; and trust are not always to be restored. Suppose that a person leaves his sword with you when he is in his right mind, and demands it back in a fit of insanity; it would be criminal to restore it to him; it would be your duty not to do so. Again, suppose that a man who has entrusted money to you proposes to make war upon your common country, should you restore the trust? I believe you should not; for you would be acting against the state, which ought to be the dearest thing in the world to you. Thus there are many things which in and of themselves seem morally right, but which under certain circumstances prove to be not morally right: to keep a promise, to abide by an agreement, to restore a trust may, with a change of expediency, cease to be morally right.

With this I think I have said enough about those actions which masquerade as expedient under the guise of prudence, while they are really contrary to justice.

96   Since, however, in Book One we derived moral duties from the four sources of moral rectitude, let us continue the same fourfold division here in pointing out how hostile to virtue are those courses of conduct which seem to be, but really are not, expedient. We have discussed wisdom, which cunning seeks to counterfeit, and likewise justice, which is always expedient. There remain for our discussion two divisions of moral rectitude, the one of which is discernible in the greatness and pre-eminence of a superior soul, the other, in the shaping and regulation of it by temperance and self-control.

[*97–99a contain further examples from Greek mythology.*]

99   But let us leave illustrations both from story and from foreign lands and turn

to real events in our own history. Marcus Atilius Regulus in his second consulship was taken prisoner in Africa by the stratagem of Xanthippus, a Spartan general serving under the command of Hannibal's father Hamilcar. He was sent to the senate on parole, sworn to return to Carthage himself, if certain noble prisoners of war were not restored to the Carthaginians. When he came to Rome, he could not fail to see the specious appearance of expediency, but he decided that it was unreal, as the outcome proves. His apparent interest was to remain in his own country, to stay at home with his wife and children, and to retain his rank and dignity as an ex-consul, regarding the defeat which he had suffered as a misfortune that might come to anyone in the game of war. Who says that this was not expedient? Who, think you? Greatness of soul and courage say that it was not.

100   Can you ask for more competent authorities? The denial comes from those virtues, for it is characteristic of them to await nothing with fear, to rise superior to all the vicissitudes of earthly life, and to count nothing intolerable that can befall a human being. What, then, did he do? He came into the senate and stated his mission; but he refused to give his own vote on the question; for, he held, he was not a member of the senate so long as he was bound by the oath sworn to his enemies. And more than that, he said—'What a foolish fellow,' someone will say, 'to oppose his own best interests'—he said that it was not expedient that the prisoners should be returned; for they were young men and gallant officers, while he was already bowed with age. And when his counsel prevailed, the prisoners were retained and he himself returned to Carthage, affection for his country and his family failed to hold him back. And even then he was not ignorant of the fact that he was going to a most cruel enemy and to exquisite torture; still, he thought his oath must be sacredly kept. And so even then, when he was being slowly put to death by enforced wakefulness, he enjoyed a happier lot than if he had remained at home an aged prisoner of war, a man of consular rank forsworn.

101   'But,' you will say, 'it was foolish of him not only not to advocate the exchange of prisoners but even to plead against such action.'

How was it foolish? Was it so, even if his policy was for the good of the state? Nay; can what is inexpedient for the state be expedient for any individual citizen?

People overturn the fundamental principles established by Nature, when they divorce expediency from moral rectitude. For we all seek to obtain what is to us expedient; we are irresistibly drawn toward it, and we cannot possibly be otherwise. For who is there that would turn his back upon what is to him expedient? Or rather, who is there that does not exert himself to the utmost to secure it? But because we cannot discover it anywhere except in good report, propriety, and moral rectitude, we look upon these three for that reason as the first and the highest objects of endeavour, while what we term expediency we account not so much an ornament to our dignity as a necessary incident to living.

102   'What significance, then,' someone will say, 'do we attach to an oath? It is not that we fear the wrath of Jove, is it? Not at all; it is the universally accepted view of all philosophers that God is never angry, never hurtful. This is the doctrine not only of those who teach that God is Himself free from troubling cares and that

He imposes no trouble upon others, but also of those who believe that God is ever working and ever directing His world. Furthermore, suppose Jupiter had been wroth, what greater injury could He have inflicted upon Regulus than Regulus brought upon himself? Religious scruple, therefore, had no such preponderance as to outweigh so great expediency.'

'Or was he afraid that his act would be morally wrong? As to that, first of all, the proverb says, "Of evils choose the least." Did that moral wrong, then, really involve as great an evil as did that awful torture? And secondly, there are the lines of Accius:

> *Thyestes.* "Hast thou broke thy faith?"
> *Atreus.* "None have I giv'n; none give I ever to the faithless."

Although this sentiment is put into the mouth of a wicked king, still it is illuminating in its correctness.'

103 Their third argument is this: just as we maintain that some things seem expedient but are not, so they maintain, some things seem morally right but are not. 'For example,' they contend, 'in this very case it seems morally right for Regulus to have returned to torture for the sake of being true to his oath. But it proves not to be morally right, because what an enemy extorted by force ought not to have been binding.'

As their concluding argument, they add: whatever is highly expedient may prove to be morally right, even if it did not seem so in advance.

These are in substance the arguments raised against the conduct of Regulus. Let us consider them each in turn.

104 'He need not have been afraid that Jupiter in anger would inflict injury upon him; he is not wont to be angry or hurtful.'

This argument, at all events, has no more weight against Regulus's conduct than it has against the keeping of any other oath. But in taking an oath it is our duty to consider not what one may have to fear in case of violation but wherein its obligation lies: an oath is an assurance backed by religious sanctity; and a solemn promise given, as before God as one's witness, is to be sacredly kept. For the question no longer concerns the wrath of the gods (for there is no such thing) but the obligations of justice and good faith. For, as Ennius says so admirably:

> 'Gracious Good Faith, on wings upborne;
> thou oath in Jupiter's great name!'

Whoever, therefore, violates his oath violates Good Faith; and, as we find it stated in Cato's speech, our forefathers chose that she should dwell upon the Capitol 'neighbour to Jupiter Supreme and Best.'

105 'But,' objection was further made, 'even if Jupiter had been angry, he could not have inflicted greater injury upon Regulus than Regulus brought upon himself.'

Quite true, if there is no evil except pain. But philosophers of the highest authority assure us that pain is not only not the supreme evil but no evil at all. And pray do not disparage Regulus, as no unimportant witness—nay, I am rather inclined to think he was the very best witness—to the truth of their doctrine. For what more competent witness do we ask for than one of the foremost citizens of Rome, who voluntarily faced torture for the sake of being true to his moral duty?

Again, they say, 'Of evils choose the least'—that is, shall one 'choose moral wrong rather than misfortune,' or is there any evil greater than moral wrong? For if physical deformity excites a certain amount of aversion, how offensive ought the deformity and hideousness of a demoralized soul to seem!

106   Therefore, those who discuss these problems with more rigour make bold to say that moral wrong is the only evil, while those who treat them with more laxity do not hesitate to call it the supreme evil.

Once more, they quote the sentiment:

'None have I given, none give I ever to the faithless.'

It was proper for the poet to say that, because, when he was working out his Atreus, he had to make the words fit the character. But if they mean to adopt it as a principle, that a pledge given to the faithless is no pledge, let them look to it that it be not a mere loophole for perjury that they seek.

107   Furthermore, we have laws regulating warfare, and fidelity to an oath must often be observed in dealings with an enemy: for an oath sworn with the clear understanding in one's own mind that it should be performed must be kept; but if there is no such understanding, it does not count as perjury if one does not perform the vow. For example, suppose that one does not deliver the amount agreed upon with pirates as the price of one's life, that would be accounted no deception—not even if one should fail to deliver the ransom after having sworn to do so; for a pirate is not included in the number of lawful enemies, but is the common foe of all the world; and with him there ought not to be any pledged word nor any oath mutually binding.

108   For swearing to what is false is not necessarily perjury, but to take an oath 'upon your conscience,' as it is expressed in our legal formulas, and then fail to perform it, that is perjury. For Euripides aptly says:

'My tongue has sworn; the mind I have has sworn no oath.'

But Regulus had no right to confound by perjury the terms and covenants of war made with an enemy. For the war was being carried on with a legitimate, declared enemy; and to regulate our dealings with such an enemy, we have our whole fetial code as well as many other laws that are binding in common between nations. Were this not the case, the senate would never have delivered up illustrious men of ours in chains to the enemy.

109   And yet that very thing happened. Titus Veturius and Spurius Postumius in their second consulship lost the battle at the Caudine Forks, and our legions were sent under the yoke. And because they made peace with the Samnites, those

generals were delivered up to them, for they had made the peace without the approval of the people and senate. And Tiberius Numicius and Quintus Maelius, tribunes of the people, were delivered up at the same time, because it was with their sanction that the peace had been concluded. This was done in order that the peace with the Samnites might be annulled. And Postumius, the very man whose delivery was in question, was the proposer and advocate of the said delivery. [*A similar instance is here omitted.*]

110 'But,' they argued against Regulus, 'an oath extorted by force ought not to have been binding.' As if force could be brought to bear upon a brave man!

'Why, then, did he make the journey to the senate, especially when he intended to plead against the surrender of the prisoners of war?'

Therein you are criticizing what is the noblest feature of his conduct. For he was not content to stand upon his own judgment but took up the case, in order that the judgment might be that of the senate; and had it not been for the weight of his pleading, the prisoners would certainly have been restored to the Carthaginians; and in that case, Regulus would have remained safe at home in his country. But because he thought this not expedient for his country, he believed that it was therefore morally right for him to declare his conviction and to suffer for it.

When they argued also that what is highly expedient may prove to be morally right, they ought rather to say not that it 'may prove to be' but that it actually is morally right. For nothing can be expedient which is not at the same time morally right; neither can a thing be morally right just because it is expedient, but it is expedient because it is morally right.

From the many splendid examples in history, therefore, we could not easily point to one either more praiseworthy or more heroic than the conduct of Regulus.

111 But of all that is thus praiseworthy in the conduct of Regulus, this one feature above all others calls for our admiration: it was he who offered the motion that the prisoners of war be retained. For the fact of his returning may seem admirable to us nowadays, but in those times he could not have done otherwise. That merit, therefore, belongs to the age, not to the man. For our ancestors were of the opinion that no bond was more effective in guaranteeing good faith than an oath. That is clearly proved by the laws of the Twelve Tables, by the 'sacred' laws, by the treaties in which good faith is pledged even to the enemy, by the investigations made by the censors and the penalties imposed by them; for there were no cases in which they used to render more rigorous decisions than in cases of violation of an oath.

[*112 contains another Roman example, omitted here.*]

113 Now, as Regulus deserves praise for being true to his oath, so those ten whom Hannibal sent to the senate on parole after the battle of Cannae deserve censure, if it is true that they did not return; for they were sworn to return to the camp which had fallen into the hands of the Carthaginians, if they did not succeed in negotiating an exchange of prisoners. Historians are not in agreement in regard to the facts. Polybius, one of the very best authorities, states that of the ten eminent nobles

who were sent at that time, nine returned when their mission failed at the hands of the senate. But one of the ten, who, a little while after leaving the camp, had gone back on the pretext that he had forgotten something or other, remained behind at Rome; he explained that by his return to the camp he was released from the obligation of his oath. He was wrong; for deceit does not remove the guilt of perjury—it merely aggravates it. His cunning that impudently tried to masquerade as prudence was, therefore, only folly. And so the senate ordered that the cunning scoundrel should be taken back to Hannibal in chains.

114 But the most significant part of the story is this: the eight thousand prisoners in Hannibal's hands were not men that he had taken in the battle or that had escaped in the peril of their lives, but men that the consuls Paulus and Varro had left behind in camp. Though these might have been ransomed by a small sum of money, the senate voted not to redeem them, in order that our soldiers might have the lesson planted in their hearts that they must either conquer or die. When Hannibal heard this news, according to that same writer, he lost heart completely, because the senate and the people of Rome displayed courage so lofty in a time of disaster. Thus apparent expediency is outweighed when placed in the balance against moral rectitude.

115 Gaius Acilius, on the other hand, the author of a history of Rome in Greek, says that there were several who played the same trick of returning to the camp to release themselves thus from the obligation of their oath, and that they were branded by the censors with every mark of disgrace.

Let this be the conclusion of this topic. For it must be perfectly apparent that acts that are done with a cowardly, craven, abject, broken spirit, as the act of Regulus would have been if he had supported in regard to the prisoners a measure that seemed to be advantageous for him personally, but disadvantageous for the state, or if he had consented to remain at home—that such acts are not expedient, because they are shameful, dishonourable, and immoral.

116 We have still left our fourth division, comprising propriety, moderation, temperance, self-restraint, self-control.

Can anything be expedient, then, which is contrary to such a chorus of virtues? And yet the Cyrenaics, adherents of the school of Aristippus, and the philosophers who bear the name of Anniceris find all good to consist in pleasure and consider virtue praiseworthy only because it is productive of pleasure. Now that these schools are out of date, Epicurus has come into vogue—an advocate and supporter of practically the same doctrine. Against such a philosophy we must fight it out 'with horse and foot,' as the saying is, if our purpose is to defend and maintain our standard of moral rectitude.

117 For if, as we find it in the writings of Metrodorus, not only expediency but happiness in life depends wholly upon a sound physical constitution and the reasonable expectation that it will always remain sound, then that expediency—and, what is more, the highest expediency, as they estimate it—will assuredly clash with moral rectitude. For, first of all, what position will wisdom occupy in that

system? The position of collector of pleasures from every possible source? What a sorry state of servitude for a virtue—to be pandering to sensual pleasure! And what will be the function of wisdom? To make skilful choice between sensual pleasures? Granted that there may be nothing more pleasant, what can be conceived more degrading for wisdom than such a role?

Then again, if anyone hold that pain is the supreme evil, what place in his philosophy has fortitude, which is but indifference to toil and pain? For, however many passages there are in which Epicurus speaks right manfully of pain, we must nevertheless consider not what he says, but what it is consistent for a man to say who has defined the good in terms of pleasure and evil in terms of pain.

And further, if I should listen to him, I should find that in many passages he has a great deal to say about temperance and self-control; but 'the water will not run,' as they say. For how can he commend self-control and yet posit pleasure as the supreme good? For self-control is the foe of the passions, and the passions are the handmaids of pleasure.

118   And yet when it comes to these three cardinal virtues, those philosophers shift and turn as best they can, and not without cleverness. They admit wisdom into their system as the knowledge that provides pleasures and banishes pain; they clear the way for fortitude also in some way to fit in with their doctrines, when they teach that it is a rational means for looking with indifference upon death and for enduring pain. They bring even temperance in—not very easily, to be sure, but still as best they can; for they hold that the height of pleasure is found in the absence of pain. Justice totters or rather, I should say, lies already prostrate; so also with all those virtues which are discernible in social life and the fellowship of human society. For neither goodness nor generosity nor courtesy can exist, any more than friendship can, if they are not sought of and for themselves, but are cultivated only for the sake of sensual pleasure or personal advantage.

Let us now recapitulate briefly.

119   As I have shown that such expediency as is opposed to moral rectitude is no expediency, so I maintain that any and all sensual pleasure is opposed to moral rectitude. And therefore Calliphon and Dinomachus, in my judgment, deserve the greater condemnation; they imagined that they should settle the controversy by coupling pleasure with moral rectitude; as well yoke a man with a beast! But moral rectitude does not accept such a union; she abhors it, spurns it. Why, the supreme good, which ought to be simple, cannot be a compound and mixture of absolutely contradictory qualities. But this theory I have discussed more fully in another connection; for the subject is a large one. Now for the matter before us.

120   We have, then, fully discussed the problem how a question is to be decided, if ever that which seems to be expediency clashes with moral rectitude. But if, on the other hand, the assertion is made that pleasure admits of a show of expediency also, there can still be no possible union between it and moral rectitude. For, to make the most generous admission we can in favour of pleasure, we

will grant that it may contribute something that possibly gives some spice to life, but certainly nothing that is really expedient.

121 Herewith, my son Marcus, you have a present from your father—a generous one, in my humble opinion; but its value will depend upon the spirit in which you receive it. And yet you must welcome these three books as fellow-guests, so to speak, along with your notes on Cratippus's lectures. But as you would sometimes give ear to me also, if I had come to Athens (and I should be there now, if my country had not called me back with accents unmistakable, when I was half-way there), so you will please devote as much time as you can to these volumes, for in them my voice will travel to you; and you can devote to them as much time as you will. And when I see that you take delight in this branch of philosophy, I shall then talk further with you—at an early date, I hope, face to face—but as long as you are abroad, I shall converse with you thus at a distance.

Farewell, my dear Cicero, and be assured that, while you are the object of my deepest affection, you will be dearer to me still, if you find pleasure in such counsel and instruction.

Cicero *De Officiis* 3 (abridged)
tr. W. Miller (Loeb 1913)

H LUCRETIUS *ON THE NATURE OF THE UNIVERSE*

On the Nature of the Universe (*De Rerum Natura*) is a philosophical poem in six books, the only work of Titus Lucretius Carus (*c*.94–55 BC) a learned Epicurean, probably of aristocratic birth. Although, following convention, the poem is addressed to a patron, the statesman C. Memmius, Lucretius clearly aims to convert his fellow-Romans in general to the philosophy of peace of mind which the Greek, Epicurus (341–270 BC), had expounded. Lucretius was not a major influence in his time; but his poem was read and probably edited after his death by Cicero (H13, 14), and its substance and style were an influence on the early development of Virgil and Horace some twenty or thirty years later. The standard edition of the poem is that of C. Bailey, 3 vols. (Oxford 1947), and useful introductions to many aspects of Lucretius in D.R. Dudley (ed.) 'Lucretius' in *Studies in Latin Literature and its Influence* (London 1965). For a short lucid account of Epicureanism, see A. A. Long, *Hellenistic Philosophy* (London 1974) ch. 2. The translation (R. Latham, Penguin) is in prose, but reproduces accurately and effectively the style of the original. We have divided the poem into sections and paragraphs for convenience of reference.

H1 Invocation to Venus

In a formal introduction, Lucretius invokes Venus, a deity closely associated with Epicureanism as goddess of Peace and Love, addresses his patron, and introduces the main theme of his poem, the removal of superstition (fear of the gods and of death) through reasoned exposition of the true nature of the universe.

1 Mother of Aeneas and his race, delight of men and gods, life-giving Venus, it is your doing that under the wheeling constellations of the sky all nature teems with life, both the sea that buoys up our ships and the earth that yields our food. Through you all living creatures are conceived and come forth to look upon the sunlight. Before you the winds flee, and at your coming the clouds forsake the sky. For you the inventive earth flings up sweet flowers. For you the ocean levels laugh, the sky is calmed and glows with diffused radiance. When first the day puts on the aspect of spring, when in all its force the fertilizing breath of Zephyr is unleashed, then, great goddess, the birds of air give the first intimation of your entry; for yours is the power that has pierced them to the heart. Next the cattle run wild, frisk through the lush pastures and swim the swift-flowing streams. Spell-bound by your charm, they follow your lead with fierce desire. So throughout seas and

uplands, rushing torrents, verdurous meadows and the leafy shelters of the birds, into the breasts of one and all you instil alluring love, so that with passionate longing they reproduce their several breeds.

2   Since you alone are the guiding power of the universe and without you nothing emerges into the shining sunlit world to grow in joy and loveliness, yours is the partnership I seek in striving to compose these lines *On the Nature of the Universe* for my noble Memmius. For him, great goddess, you have willed outstanding excellence in every field and everlasting fame. For his sake, therefore, endow my verse with everlasting charm.

3   Meanwhile, grant that this brutal business of war by sea and land may everywhere be lulled to rest. For you alone have power to bestow on mortals the blessing of quiet peace. In your bosom Mars himself, supreme commander in this brutal business, flings himself down at times, laid low by the irremediable wound of love. Gazing upward, his neck a prostrate column, he fixes hungry eyes on you, great goddess, and gluts them with love. As he lies outstretched, his breath hangs upon your lips. Stoop, then, goddess most glorious, and enfold him at rest in your hallowed bosom and whisper with those lips sweet words of prayer, beseeching for the people of Rome untroubled peace. In this evil hour of my country's history, I cannot pursue my task with a mind at ease, as an illustrious scion of the house of Memmius cannot at such a crisis withhold his service from the common weal.

4   For what is to follow, my Memmius, lay aside your cares and lend undistracted ears and an attentive mind to true reason. Do not scornfully reject, before you have understood them, the gifts I have marshalled for you with zealous devotion. I will set out to discourse to you on the ultimate realities of heaven and the gods. I will reveal those *atoms* from which nature creates all things and increases and feeds them and into which, when they perish, nature again resolves them. . . .

5   When human life lay grovelling in all men's sight, crushed to the earth under the dead weight of superstition whose grim features loured menacingly upon mortals from the four quarters of the sky, a man of Greece was first to raise mortal eyes in defiance, first to stand erect and brave the challenge. Fables of the gods did not crush him, nor the lightning flash and the growling menace of the sky. Rather, they quickened his manhood, so that he, first of all men, longed to smash the constraining locks of nature's doors. The vital vigour of his mind prevailed. He ventured far out beyond the flaming ramparts of the world and voyaged in mind throughout infinity. Returning victorious, he proclaimed to us what can be and what cannot: how a limit is fixed to the power of everything and an immovable frontier post. Therefore superstition in its turn lies crushed beneath his feet, and we by his triumph are lifted level with the skies.

6   One thing that worries me is the fear that you may fancy yourself embarking on an impious course, setting your feet on the path of sin. Far from it. More often it is this very superstition that is the mother of sinful and impious deeds. Remember how at Aulis the altar of the Virgin Goddess was foully stained with the blood of Iphigeneia by the leaders of the Greeks, the patterns of chivalry.

351

The headband was bound about her virgin tresses and hung down evenly over both her cheeks. Suddenly she caught sight of her father standing sadly in front of the altar, the attendants beside him hiding the knife and her people bursting into tears when they saw her. Struck dumb with terror, she sank on her knees to the ground. Poor girl, at such a moment it did not help her that she had been first to give the name of father to a king. Raised by the hands of men, she was led trembling to the altar. Not for her the sacrament of marriage and the loud chant of Hymen. It was her fate in the very hour of marriage to fall a sinless victim to a sinful rite, slaughtered to her greater grief by a father's hand, so that a fleet might sail under happy auspices. Such are the heights of wickedness to which men are driven by superstition.

7 You yourself, if you surrender your judgement at any time to the blood-curdling declamations of the prophets, will want to desert our ranks. Only think what phantoms they can conjure up to overturn the tenor of your life and wreck your happiness with fear. And not without cause. For, if men saw that a term was set to their troubles, they would find strength in some way to withstand the hocus-pocus and intimidations of the prophets. As it is, they have no power of resistance, because they are haunted by the fear of eternal punishment after death. They know nothing of the nature of the spirit. Is it born, or is it implanted in us at birth? Does it perish with us, dissolved by death, or does it visit the murky depths and dreary sloughs of Hades? . . .

8 I must therefore give an account of celestial phenomena, explaining the movements of sun and moon and also the forces that determine events on earth. Next, and no less important, we must look with keen insight into the makeup of spirit and mind: we must consider those alarming phantasms that strike upon our minds when they are awake but disordered by sickness, or when they are buried in slumber, so that we seem to see and hear before us men whose dead bones lie in the embraces of earth.

I am well aware that it is not easy to elucidate in Latin verse the obscure discoveries of the Greeks. The poverty of our language and the novelty of the theme compel me often to coin new words for the purpose. But your merit and the joy I hope to derive from our delightful friendship encourage me to face any task however hard. This it is that leads me to stay awake through the quiet of the night, studying how by choice of words and the poet's art I can display before your mind a clear light by which you can gaze into the heart of hidden things.

Lucretius 1. 1–57; 62–115; 127–45
tr. R. E. Latham (Penguin 1951)

H2 The nature of matter

Lucretius begins with the nature of matter. Taking the dictum that matter cannot be created or destroyed he shows that the only constituent elements of the universe are atoms (tiny impenetrable particles) and void (emptiness).

1   This dread and darkness of the mind cannot be dispelled by the sunbeams, the shining shafts of day, but only by an understanding of the outward form and inner workings of nature. In tackling this theme, our starting-point will be this principle: *Nothing can ever be created by divine power out of nothing.* The reason why all mortals are so gripped by fear is that they see all sorts of things happening on the earth and in the sky with no discernible cause, and these they attribute to the will of a god. Accordingly, when we have seen that nothing can be created out of nothing, we shall then have a clearer picture of the path ahead, the problem of how things are created and occasioned without the aid of the gods.

2   First then, if things were made out of nothing, any species could spring from any source and nothing would require seed. Men could arise from the sea and scaly fish from the earth, and birds could be hatched out of the sky. Cattle and other domestic animals and every kind of wild beast, multiplying indiscriminately, would occupy cultivated and waste lands alike. The same fruits would not grow constantly on the same trees, but they would keep changing; any tree might bear any fruit. . . .

3   The second great principle is this: *nature resolves everything into its component atoms and never reduces anything to nothing.* If anything were perishable in all its parts, anything might perish all of a sudden and vanish from sight. There would be no need of any force to separate its parts and loosen its links. In actual fact, since everything is composed of indestructible seeds, nature obviously does not allow anything to perish till it has encountered a force that shatters it with a blow or creeps into chinks and unknits it.

4   If the things that are banished from the scene by age are annihilated through the exhaustion of their material, from what source does Venus bring back the several races of animals into the light of life? And, when they are brought back, where does the inventive earth find for each the special food required for its sustenance and growth? From what fount is the sea replenished by its native springs and the streams that flow into it from afar? . . .

5   . . . showers perish when father ether has flung them down into the lap of mother earth. But the crops spring up fresh and gay; the branches on the trees burst into leaf; the trees themselves grow and are weighed down with fruit. Hence in turn man and brute draw nourishment. Hence we see flourishing cities blest with children and every leafy thicket loud with new broods of songsters. Hence in lush pastures cattle wearied by their bulk fling down their bodies, and the white milky juice oozes from their swollen udders. Hence a new generation frolic friskily on wobbly legs through the fresh grass, their young minds tipsy with undiluted milk. Visible objects therefore do not perish utterly, since nature repairs one thing from another and allows nothing to be born without the aid of another's death.

6   Well, Memmius, I have taught you that things cannot be created out of nothing nor, once born, be summoned back to nothing. Perhaps, however, you are becoming mistrustful of my words, because these atoms of mine are not visible to the eye. Consider, therefore, this further evidence of *bodies whose existence you must acknowledge though they cannot be seen.* First, wind, when its force is roused, whips up waves, founders tall ships and scatters cloud-rack. Sometimes scouring

plains with hurricane force it strews them with huge trees and batters mountain peaks with blasts that hew down forests. Such is wind in its fury, when it whoops aloud with a mad menace in its shouting. Without question, therefore, there must be invisible particles of wind which sweep sea and land and the clouds in the sky, swooping upon them and whirling them along in a headlong hurricane. In the way they flow and the havoc they spread they are no different from a torrential flood of water when it rushes down in a sudden spate from the mountain heights, swollen by heavy rains, and heaps together wreckage from the forest and entire trees. Soft though it is by nature, the sudden shock of oncoming water is more than even stout bridges can withstand, so furious is the force with which the turbid storm-flushed torrent surges against their piers. With a mighty roar it lays them low, rolling huge rocks under its waves and brushing aside every obstacle from its course. Such, therefore, must be the movement of blasts of wind also. When they have come surging along some course like a rushing river, they push obstacles before them and buffet them with repeated blows; and sometimes, eddying round and round, they snatch them up and carry them along in a swiftly circling vortex. Here then is proof upon proof that winds have invisible bodies, since in their actions and behaviour they are found to rival great rivers, whose bodies are plain to see. . . .

7   Again, in the course of many annual revolutions of the sun a ring is worn thin next to the finger with continual rubbing. Dripping water hollows a stone. A curved ploughshare, iron though it is, dwindles imperceptibly in the furrow. We see the cobble-stones of the highway worn by the feet of many wayfarers. The bronze statues by the city gates show their right hands worn thin by the touch of travellers who have greeted them in passing. We see that all these are being diminished, since they are worn away. But to perceive what particles drop off at any particular time is a power grudged to us by our ungenerous sense of sight.

8   To sum up, whatever is added to things gradually by nature and the passage of days, causing a cumulative increase, eludes the most attentive scrutiny of our eyes. Conversely, you cannot see what objects lose by the wastage of age—sheer sea-cliffs, for instance, exposed to prolonged erosion by the mordant brine—or at what time the loss occurs. It follows that nature works through the agency of invisible bodies.

9   On the other hand, things are not hemmed in by the pressure of solid bodies in a tight mass. This is because *there is vacuity in things*. A grasp of this fact will be helpful to you in many respects and will save you from much bewildered doubting and questioning about the universe and from mistrust of my teaching. Well then, by vacuity I mean intangible and empty space. If it did not exist, things could not move at all. For the distinctive action of matter, which is counteraction and obstruction, would be in force always and everywhere. Nothing could proceed, because nothing would give it a starting-point by receding. As it is, we see with our own eyes at sea and on land and high up in the sky that all sorts of things in all sorts of ways are on the move. If there were no empty space, these things would be denied the power of restless movement—or rather, they could not possibly have come into existence, embedded as they would have been in motionless matter.

10   Besides, there are clear indications that things that pass for solid are in fact porous. Even in rocks a trickle of water seeps through into caves, and copious drops ooze from every surface. Food percolates to every part of an animal's body. Trees grow and bring forth their fruit in season, because their food is distributed throughout their length from the tips of the roots through the trunk and along every branch. Noises pass through walls and fly into closed buildings. Freezing cold penetrates to the bones. If there were no vacancies through which the various bodies could make their way, none of these phenomena would be possible.

11   Again, why do we find some things outweigh others of equal volume? If there is as much matter in a ball of wool as in one of lead, it is natural that it should weigh as heavily, since it is the function of matter to press everything downwards, while it is the function of space on the other hand to remain weightless. Accordingly, when one thing is not less bulky than another but obviously lighter, it plainly declares that there is more matter in it and much less empty space. We have therefore reached the goal of our diligent inquiry: there is in things an admixture of what we call vacuity. . . .

12   *Material objects are of two kinds, atoms and compounds of atoms. The atoms themselves cannot be swamped by any force, for they are preserved indefinitely by their absolute solidity.* Admittedly, it is hard to believe that anything can exist that is absolutely solid. The lightning stroke from the sky penetrates closed buildings, as do shouts and other noises. Iron glows molten in the fire, and hot rocks are cracked by untempered scorching. Hard gold is softened and melted by heat; and bronze, ice-like, is liquefied by flame. Both heat and piercing cold seep through silver, since we feel both alike when a cooling shower of water is poured into a goblet that we hold ceremonially in our hands. All these facts point to the conclusion that nothing is really solid. But sound reasoning and nature itself drive us to the opposite conclusion. Pay attention, therefore, while I demonstrate in a few lines that there exist certain bodies that are absolutely solid and indestructible, namely those atoms which according to our teaching are the seeds or prime units of things from which the whole universe is built up.

13   In the first place, we have found that nature is twofold, consisting of two totally different things, matter and the space in which things happen. Hence each of these must exist by itself without admixture of the other. For, where there is empty space (what we call vacuity), there matter is not; where matter exists, there cannot be a vacuum. Therefore the prime units of matter are solid and free from vacuity.

Lucretius 1. 146-66; 215-31; 250-97; 311-69, 483-510
tr. R. E. Latham (Penguin 1951)

H3 Introduction to Book 2

In this introductory passage, interspersed with the reasoned exposition, and osten-sibly digressionary, are Lucretius' observations on the moral and social consequences of ignoring his message.

1 What joy it is, when out at sea the stormwinds are lashing the waters, to gaze from the shore at the heavy stress some other man is enduring! Not that anyone's afflictions are in themselves a source of delight; but to realize from what troubles you yourself are free is joy indeed. What joy, again, to watch opposing hosts marshalled on the field of battle when you have yourself no part in their peril! But this is the greatest joy of all: to stand aloof in a quiet citadel, stoutly fortified by the teaching of the wise, and to gaze down from that elevation on others wandering aimlessly in a vain search for the way of life, pitting their wits one against another, disputing for precedence, struggling night and day with unstinted effort to scale the pinnacles of wealth and power. O joyless hearts of men! O minds without vision! How dark and dangerous the life in which this tiny span is lived away! Do you not see that nature is clamouring for two things only, a body free from pain, a mind released from worry and fear for the enjoyment of pleasurable sensations?

2 So we find that the requirements of our bodily nature are few indeed, no more than is necessary to banish pain. To heap pleasure upon pleasure may heighten men's enjoyment at times. But what matter if there are no golden images of youths about the house, holding flaming torches in their right hands to illumine banquets prolonged into the night? What matter if the hall does not sparkle with silver and gleam with gold, and no carved and gilded rafters ring to the music of the lute? Nature does not miss these luxuries when men recline in company on the soft grass by a running stream under the branches of a tall tree and refresh their bodies pleasurably at small expense. Better still if the weather smiles upon them and the season of the year stipples the green herbage with flowers. Burning fevers flee no swifter from your body if you toss under figured counterpanes and coverlets of crimson than if you must lie in rude home-spun.

3 If our bodies are not profited by treasures or titles or the majesty of king-ship, we must go on to admit that neither are our minds. Or tell me, Memmius, when you see your legions thronging the Campus Martius in the ardour of mimic warfare, supported by ample auxiliaries, magnificently armed and fired by a common purpose, does that sight scare the terrors of superstition from your mind? Does the fear of death retire from your breast and leave it carefree at the moment when you sight your warships ranging far and wide? Or do we not find such resources absurdly ineffective? The fears and anxieties that dog the human breast do not shrink from the clash of arms or the fierce rain of missiles. They stalk unabashed among princes and potentates. They are not awe-struck by the gleam of gold or the bright sheen of purple robes. . . .

Lucretius 2. 1–52
tr. R. E. Latham (Penguin 1951)

H4 The Swerve

In the following passage Lucretius attempts to explain (a) combination of atoms to form compounds (b) individual free will. His solution to the apparent problem of the continuous downward movement and non-collision of the atoms is to introduce a slight swerve which ensures their collision and combination to form the world as we know it. The theory of the swerve is not found in the extant writings of Epicurus; how precisely Lucretius relates the atomic swerve to voluntary human action is not clear (see also Cicero's criticism (H15) and D. J. Furley Two Studies in the Greek Atomists *(Princeton 1967) pp. 161–237).*

1   In this connexion there is another fact that I want you to grasp. *When the atoms are travelling straight down through empty space by their own weight, at quite indeterminate times and places they swerve ever so little from their course,* just so much that you can call it a change of direction. If it were not for this swerve, everything would fall downwards like rain-drops through the abyss of space. No collision would take place and no impact of atom on atom would be created. Thus nature would never have created anything.

2   If anyone supposes that heavier atoms on a straight course through empty space could outstrip lighter ones and fall on them from above, thus causing impacts that might give rise to generative motions, he is going far astray from the path of truth. The reason why objects falling through water or thin air vary in speed according to their weight is simply that the matter composing water or air cannot obstruct all objects equally, but is forced to give way more speedily to heavier ones. But empty space can offer no resistance to any object in any quarter at any time, so as not to yield free passage as its own nature demands. Therefore, through undisturbed vacuum all bodies must travel at equal speed though impelled by unequal weights. The heavier will never be able to fall on the lighter from above or generate of themselves impacts leading to that variety of motions out of which nature can produce things. We are thus forced back to the conclusion that the atoms swerve a little—but only a very little, or we shall be caught imagining slantwise movements, and the facts will prove us wrong. For we see plainly and palpably that weights, when they come tumbling down, have no power of their own to move aslant, so far as meets the eye. But who can possibly perceive that they do not diverge in the very least from a vertical course?

3   Again, if all movement is always interconnected, the new arising from the old in a determinate order—if the atoms never swerve so as to originate some new movement that will snap the bonds of fate, the everlasting sequence of cause and effect—what is the source of the free will possessed by living things throughout the earth? What, I repeat, is the source of that will-power snatched from the fates, whereby we follow the path along which we are severally led by pleasure, swerving from our course at no set time or place but at the bidding of our own hearts? There is no doubt that on these occasions the will of the individual originates the movements that trickle through his limbs. Observe, when the starting barriers are flung

back, how the race-horses in the eagerness of their strength cannot break away as suddenly as their hearts desire. For the whole supply of matter must first be mobilized throughout every member of the body: only then, when it is mustered in a continuous array, can it respond to the prompting of the heart. So you may see that the beginning of movements is generated by the heart; starting from the voluntary action of the mind, it is then transmitted throughout the body and the limbs. Quite different is our experience when we are shoved along by a blow inflicted with compulsive force by someone else.

4   In that case it is obvious that all the matter of our body is set going and pushed along involuntarily, till a check is imposed through the limbs by the will. Do you see the difference? Although many men are driven by an external force and often constrained involuntarily to advance .or to rush headlong, yet there is within the human breast something that can fight against this force and resist it. At its command the supply of matter is forced to take a new course through our limbs and joints or is checked in its course and brought once more to a halt. So also in the atoms you must recognize the same possibility: besides weight and impact there must be a third cause of movement, the source of this inborn power of ours, since we see that nothing can come out of nothing. For the weight of an atom prevents its movements from being completely determined by the impact of other atoms. But the fact that the mind itself has no internal necessity to determine its every act and compel it to suffer in helpless passivity—this is due to the slight swerve of the atoms at no determinate time or place.

Lucretius 2. 216–93
tr. R. E. Latham (Penguin 1951)

H5   Philosophy in verse

Here, in the introduction to Book 4, Lucretius reveals his reasons for using the verse medium for a philosophical subject.

I am blazing a trail through pathless tracts of the Muses' Pierian realm, where no foot has ever trod before. What joy it is to light upon virgin springs and drink their waters. What joy to pluck new flowers and gather for my brow a glorious garland from fields whose blossoms were never yet wreathed by the Muses round any head. This is my reward for teaching on these lofty topics, for struggling to loose men's minds from the tight knots of superstition and shedding on dark corners the bright beam of my song that irradiates everything with the sparkle of the Muses. My art is not without a purpose. Physicians, when they wish to treat children with a nasty dose of wormwood, first smear the rim of the cup with a coat of yellow honey. The children, too young as yet for foresight, are lured by the sweetness at their lips into swallowing the bitter draught. So they are tricked but not trapped; for the treatment

1. Bronze bust of Augustus with inlaid eyes of marble and glass, from Meroë, Sudan. Early first century AD.

2a. Detail from the inscription of the *Res Gestae* on the *Monumentum Ancyranum*, Ankara, showing the first lines of the Latin text.

2b. Inscription from the Mausoleum of Augustus in Rome, built in 28 BC as a family tomb. The epitaphs are of Marcellus (d. 23 BC), Augustus' son-in-law, and of Octavia (d. 11 BC), Augustus' sister and mother of Marcellus.

3a. Bust of Marcus Tullius Cicero, probably a copy dating from the early Empire, showing the orator in middle age. Much restored.

3b. The Augustan *rostra* (orators' platforms) in the Forum in Rome. The dowel-holes for attaching the ships' beaks are visible. The Temple of Saturn is on the left.

4. Statue of Augustus in armour from the villa of Livia at Prima Porta, probably a contemporary marble copy of a bronze original. The breast-plate records the recovery of the Roman standards from Parthia.

5a. Coin showing the Arch of Augustus, voted by the Senate in 19 BC to commemorate the return of the Roman standards captured by the Parthians.

5b. Copy of the *Clupeus Virtutis* of Augustus found in Arles. The original, a golden shield commemorating Augustus' valour, clemency, justice and piety, was set up in the Senate house after the settlement of 27 BC.

SENATVS
POPVLVSQVE ROMANVS
IMP CAESARI DIVI F AVGVSTO
COS VIII DEDIT CLVPEVM
VIRTVTIS CLEMENTIAE
IVSTITIAE PIETATIS ERGA
DEOS PATRIAMQVE

6. The Forum of Augustus, Rome, dedicated in 2 BC, showing the Temple of Mars Ultor and part of the massive boundary wall separating it from Subura.

7a. Arch, dating from 27 BC, commemorating the restoration of the major roads of Italy by Augustus, placed where the Via Flaminia enters Rimini (Ariminum).

7b. Fortified gate in Turin (Augusta Taurinorum), an Augustan colony founded c. 25 BC.

8a. Commemorative arch erected in honour of Augustus in 9–8 BC in Susa (Segusio) by the tribes of the Cottian Alps.

8b. Monument of La Turbie (Alpes Maritimes), the *Tropaea Augusti* built in 7–6 BC to commemorate Augustus' subjugation of the Alpine tribes.

9*a*. The Maison Carrée at Nîmes (Nemausus) begun in *c*. 19 BC, a beautifully preserved temple in the classical style. The acanthus frieze echoes that of the Ara Pacis in Rome.

9*b*. The aqueduct of Nîmes, known as the Pont du Gard, late first century BC. The upper tier contains the actual water conduit.

10. The theatre at Orange (Arausio), begun in the reign of Tiberius. Part of the auditorium and the stage building with a three-storeyed scenery wall (*scaenae frons*) are visible.

11. The Augustan market at Lepcis Magna, built in 8 BC. The two pavilions, circular chambers with octagonal porticoes, were originally limestone structures.

12. Detail from the Ara Pacis, dedicated in 9 BC. Panel from the west side depicting the sacrifice by Aeneas of the white sow. Aeneas is shown as a tall bearded figure with veiled head.

13. Group from the south frieze of the Ara Pacis. The central veiled figure is most probably Agrippa. The female figure following him has been identified as Livia.

14*a*. Bust of Tiberius, made to look like a youthful Augustus, probably dating from after AD 4.

14*b*. Green basanite portrait bust of a Julio-Claudian prince, probably Germanicus, made about AD 19-37, from Egypt. The cross on the forehead is a Christian addition made in late antiquity.

15a. Onyx cameo of Claudius and his family. On the left are Claudius and his wife Agrippina, facing them probably Tiberius and Livia.

15b. A sardonyx cameo known as the 'Gemma Augustea'. Occupying the centre of the scene are the seated figures of Augustus and Roma. The figure descending from the chariot is probably Tiberius, and the young man standing next to Roma may be Gaius Caesar.

Gaius Julius Caesar

Scribonia — m² — Augustus — m³ — Livia — m — Tiberius Claudius Nero

Julia — m² — Agrippa   Tiberius   Drusus

Gaius and Lucius   Agrippina — m — Germanicus   Claudius

Gaius

16. The Julio-Claudians

Gaius Julius Caesar (101–44 BC) adopted his nephew Gaius Octavius, the future **Augustus** (63 BC–AD 14). Augustus had only one child, his daughter Julia (39 BC–AD 14), by his second wife Scribonia. He had two stepsons, **Tiberius** (42 BC–AD 37) and Nero Claudius Drusus, children of his third wife **Livia** (57 BC–AD 29), from her marriage to Tiberius Claudius Nero. Augustus adopted **Gaius** (20 BC–AD 4) and **Lucius** (17 BC–AD 2), sons of his daughter Julia by her second marriage to **M. Agrippa** (63–12 BC), and brought them up as his heirs, but their early deaths meant that he was succeeded by Tiberius whom he adopted. Tiberius' own son Drusus died young, and Tiberius was succeeded by **Gaius** (AD 12–41), son of **Germanicus** (15 BC–AD 9) and **Agrippina** (d. AD 33) and grandson of Tiberius' brother Drusus. Gaius was succeeded by his uncle **Claudius** (10 BC–AD 54), brother of Germanicus.

restores them to health. In the same way our doctrine often seems unpalatable to those who have not sampled it, and the multitude shrink from it. That is why I have tried to administer it to you in the dulcet strains of poesy, coated with the sweet honey of the Muses. My object has been to engage your mind with verses while you gain insight into the nature of the universe and learn to appreciate the profit you are reaping.

Lucretius 4. 1–25
tr. R. E. Latham (Penguin 1951)

H6   Sensation

In Book 4 Lucretius turns from the external world to the human mind and body. The working of the human senses is related to atomic 'skins' which peel off the object and hit the eye, ear, etc., thereby producing a sense-impression. Lucretius goes on to develop, at some length, the Epicurean belief that all knowledge whatever is based upon sensation, an assumption which lies at the heart of Epicurus' materialism (see also H7).

1   Now I will embark on an explanation of a highly relevant fact, *the existence of what we call 'images' of things*, a sort of outer skin perpetually peeled off the surface of objects and flying about this way and that through the air. It is these whose impact scares our minds, whether waking or sleeping, on those occasions when we catch a glimpse of strange shapes and phantoms of the dead. Often, when we are sunk in slumber, they startle us with the notion that spirits may get loose from Hades and ghosts hover about among the living, and that some part of us may survive after death when body and mind alike have been disintegrated and dissolved into their component atoms.

2   I maintain therefore that replicas or insubstantial shapes of things are thrown off from the surface of objects. These we must denote as an outer skin or film, because each particular floating image wears the aspect and form of the object from whose body it has emanated. This you may infer, however dull your wit, from the following facts.

3   In the first place, within the range of vision, many objects give off particles. Some of these are rarefied and diffused, such as the smoke emitted by logs or the heat by fire. Others are denser and more closely knit: cicadas, for instance, in summer periodically shed their tubular jackets; calves at birth cast off cauls from the surface of their bodies; the slippery snake sloughs off on thorns the garment we often see fluttering on a briar. Since these things happen, objects must also give off a much flimsier film from the surface of their bodies. For, since those more solid emanations fall off, no reason can be given why such flimsy ones should not. Besides, we know that on the surface of objects there are lots of tiny particles, which

359

could be thrown off without altering the order of their arrangement or the outline of their shape, and all the faster because, being relatively few and lying right on the outside, they are less liable to obstruction.

4 We certainly see that many objects throw off matter in abundance, not only from their inmost depths, as we have said before, but from their surfaces in the form of colour. This is done conspicuously by the awnings, yellow, scarlet and maroon, stretched flapping and billowing on poles and rafters over spacious theatres. The crowded pit below and the stage with all its scenery are made to glow and flow with the colours of the canopy. The more completely the theatre is hemmed in by surrounding walls, the more its interior, sheltered from the daylight, is irradiated by this flood of colour. Since canvasses thus give off colour from their surface, all objects must give off filmy images as a result of spraying particles from their surfaces this way and that. Here then, already definitely established, we have indications of images, flying about everywhere, extremely fine in texture and individually invisible.

5 Again, the reason why smell, smoke, heat and the like come streaming out of objects in shapeless clouds is that they originate in the inmost depths; so they are split up in their circuitous journey, and there are no straight vents to their channels through which they may issue directly in close formation. When the thin film of surface colour, on the other hand, is thrown off, there is nothing to disrupt it, since it lies exposed right on the outside.

Lucretius 4. 29–97
tr. R. E. Latham (Penguin 1951)

H7   Optical illusions and knowledge

1 *When we see the square towers of a city in the distance, they often appear round.* This is because every angle seen at a distance is blunted or even is not seen as an angle at all. Its impact is nullified and does not penetrate as far as our eyes, because films that travel through a great deal of air lose their sharp outlines through frequent collisions with it. When every angle has thus eluded our sense, the result is as though the square ashlars were rounded off on the lathe—not that they resemble really round stones seen close up, but in a sketchy sort of way they counterfeit them.

2 Again, *our shadow in the sunlight seems to us to move* and keep step with us and imitate our gestures, incredible though it is that unillumined air should walk about in conformity with a man's movements and gestures. For what we commonly call a shadow can be nothing but air deprived of light. Actually the earth is robbed of sunlight in a definite succession of places wherever it is obstructed by us in our progression, and the part we have left is correspondingly replenished with it. That is why the successive shadows of our body seem to be the same shadow following us along steadily step by step. New particles of radiance are always

streaming down and their predecessors are consumed, as the saying goes, like wool being spun into the fire. So the earth is easily robbed of light and is correspondingly replenished and washed off the black stains of shadow.

3   Here, as always, *we do not admit that the eyes are in any way deluded*. It is their function to see where light is, and where shadow. But whether the shadow . that was here is moving over there, or whether on the other hand what really happens is what I have just described—that is something to be discerned by the reasoning power of the mind. The nature of phenomena cannot be understood by the eyes. You must not hold them responsible for this fault of the mind. . . .

4   When we gaze from one end down the whole length of a colonnade, though its structure is perfectly symmetrical and it is propped throughout on pillars of equal height, yet it contracts by slow degrees in a narrowing cone that draws roof to floor and left to right till it unites them in the imperceptible apex of the cone. . . .

5   To landsmen ignorant of the sea, ships in harbour seem to be riding crippled on the waves, with their poops broken. So much of the oars as projects above the waterline is straight, and so is the upper part of the rudder. But all the submerged parts appear refracted and wrenched round in an upward direction and almost as though bent right back so as to float on the surface. . . .

6   We have many other paradoxical experiences of the same kind, all of which seem bent on shaking our faith in the senses. But all to no purpose. Most of this illusion is due to the mental assumptions which we ourselves superimpose, so that things not perceived by the senses pass for perceptions. There is nothing harder than to separate the facts as revealed from the questionable interpretations promptly imposed on them by the mind. . . .

7   You will find, in fact, that the concept of truth was originated by the senses and that the senses cannot be rebutted. The testimony that we must accept as more trustworthy is that which can spontaneously overcome falsehood with truth. What then are we to pronounce more trustworthy than the senses? Can reason derived from the deceitful senses be invoked to contradict them, when it is itself wholly derived from the senses? If they are not true, then reason in its entirety is equally false. Or can hearing give the lie to sight, or touch to hearing? Can touch in turn be discredited by taste or refuted by the nostrils or rebutted by the eyes? This, in my view, is out of the question. Each sense has its own distinctive faculty, its specific function. There must be separate discernment of softness and cold and heat and of the various colours of things and whatever goes with the colours; separate functioning of the palate's power of taste; separate generation of scents and sounds. This rules out the possibility of one sense confuting another. It will be equally out of the question for one sense to belie itself, since it will always be entitled to the same degree of credence. Whatever the senses may perceive at any time is all alike true. Suppose that reason cannot elucidate the cause why things that were square when close at hand are seen as round in the distance. Even so, it is better, in default of reason, to assign fictitious causes to the two shapes than to let things clearly apprehended slip from our grasp. This is to attack belief at its very roots—to tear up the entire foundation on which the maintenance of life is built. It is not only

reason that would collapse completely. If you did not dare trust your senses so as to keep clear of precipices and other such things to be avoided and make for their opposites, there would be a speedy end to life itself.

Lucretius 4. 353–86; 426–31; 436–42; 462–8; 478–510
tr. R. E. Latham (Penguin 1951)

H8 Death is nothing to us

These passages are taken from Book 3. In a 'digressionary' introduction, the fate of the 'superstitious' is vividly described. The bulk of the book, however, is taken up with stating one of Lucretius' central beliefs, the mortality of the soul, a hypothesis for which Lucretius feels the need to furnish twenty-nine different proofs (below are three representative samples, H9). The final section, a climax, contrasts vividly the conventional and the Epicurean attitude to death (H10).

1   You, who out of black darkness were first to lift up a shining light, revealing the hidden blessings of life—you are my guide, O glory of the Grecian race. In your well-marked footprints now I plant my resolute steps. It is from love alone that I long to imitate you, not from emulous ambition. Shall the swallow contend in song with the swan, or the kid match its rickety legs in a race with the strong-limbed steed? You are my father, illustrious discoverer of truth, and give me a father's guidance. From your pages, as bees in flowery glades sip every blossom, so do I crop all your Golden Sayings—golden indeed, and for ever worthy of everlasting life.

2   As soon as your reasoning, sprung from that god-like mind, lifts up its voice to proclaim the nature of the universe, then the terrors of the mind take flight, the ramparts of the world roll apart, and I see the march of events throughout the whole of space. The majesty of the gods is revealed and those quiet habitations, never shaken by storms nor drenched by rain-clouds nor defaced by white drifts of snow which a harsh frost congeals. A cloudless ether roofs them, and laughs with radiance lavishly diffused. All their wants are supplied by nature, and nothing at any time cankers their peace of mind. But nowhere do I see the halls of Hell, though the earth is no barrier to my beholding all that passes underfoot in the space beneath. At this I am seized with a divine delight, and a shuddering awe, that by your power nature stands thus unveiled and made manifest in every part.

3   I have already shown what the component bodies of everything are like; how they vary in shape; how they fly spontaneously through space, impelled by a perpetual motion; and how from these all objects can be created. The next step now is evidently to elucidate in my verses the nature of mind and of life. In so doing I shall drive out neck and crop that fear of Hell which blasts the life of man from its very foundations, sullying everything with the blackness of death and leaving no pleasure pure and unalloyed. I know that men often speak of sickness or

of shameful life as more to be dreaded than the terrors of Hell; they profess to know that the mind consists of blood, or maybe wind, if that is how the whim takes them, and to stand in no need whatever of our reasoning. But all this talk is based more on a desire to show off than on actual proof, as you may infer from their conduct. These same men, though they may be exiled from home, banished far from the sight of their fellows, soiled with some filthy crime, a prey to every torment, still cling to life. Wherever they come in their tribulation, they make propitiatory sacrifices, slaughter black cattle and dispatch offerings to the Departed Spirits. The heavier their afflictions, the more devoutly they turn their minds to superstition. Look at a man in the midst of doubt and danger, and you will learn in his hour of adversity what he really is. It is then that true utterances are wrung from the recesses of his breast. The mask is torn off; the reality remains.

4   Consider too the greed and blind lust of power that drive unhappy men to overstep the bounds of right and may even turn them into accomplices or instruments of crime, struggling night and day with unstinted effort to scale the pinnacles of wealth. These running sores of life are fed in no small measure by the fear of death. For abject ignominy and irksome poverty seem far indeed from the joy and assurance of life, and in effect loitering already at the gateway of death. From such a fate men revolt in groundless terror and long to escape far, far away. So in their greed of gain they amass a fortune out of civil bloodshed: piling wealth on wealth, they heap carnage on carnage. With heartless glee they welcome a brother's tragic death. They hate and fear the hospitable board of their own kin. Often, in the same spirit and influenced by the same fear, they are consumed with envy at the sight of another's success: he walks in a blaze of glory, looked up to by all, while they curse the squalor in which their own lives are bogged. Some sacrifice life itself for the sake of statues and a title. Often from fear of death mortals are gripped by such a hate of living and looking on the light that with anguished hearts they do themselves to death. They forget that this very fear is the fountainhead of their troubles; this it is that harasses conscience, snaps the bonds of friendship and hurls down virtue from the heights. Many a time before now men have betrayed their country and their beloved parents in an effort to escape the halls of Hell.

Lucretius 3. 1–86
tr. R. E. Latham (Penguin 1951)

H9 The mortality of the soul

1   First of all, then, I have shown that spirit is flimsy stuff composed of tiny particles. Its atoms are obviously far smaller than those of swift-flowing water or mist or smoke, since it far outstrips them in mobility and is moved by a far slighter impetus. Indeed, it is actually moved by images of smoke and mist. So, for instance, when we are sunk in sleep, we may see altars sending up clouds of steam and giving

off smoke; and we cannot doubt that we are here dealing with images. Now, we see that water flows out in all directions from a broken vessel and the moisture is dissipated, and mist and smoke vanish into thin air. Be assured, therefore, that spirit is similarly dispelled and vanishes far more speedily and is sooner dissolved into its component atoms once it has been let loose from the human frame. When the body, which served as a vessel for it, is by some means broken and attenuated by loss of blood from the veins, so as to be no longer able to contain it, how can you suppose that it can be contained by any kind of air, which must be far more tenuous than our bodily frame? . . .

2   Furthermore, as the body suffers the horrors of disease and the pangs of pain, so we see the mind stabbed with anguish, grief and fear. What more natural than that it should likewise have a share in death? Often enough in the body's illness the mind wanders. It raves and babbles distractedly. At times it drifts on a tide of drowsiness, with drooping eyelids and nodding head, into a deep and endless sleep, from which it cannot hear the voices or recognize the faces of those who stand around with streaming eyes and tear-stained cheeks, striving to recall it to life. Since the mind is thus invaded by the contagion of disease, you must acknowledge that it is destructible. For pain and sickness are the artificers of death, as we have been taught by the fate of many men before us. . . .

3   Again, mind and body as a living force derive their vigour and vitality from their conjunction. Without body, the mind alone cannot perform the vital motions. Bereft of vital spirit, the body cannot persist and exercise its senses. As the eye up-rooted and separated from the body cannot see, so we perceive that spirit and mind by themselves are powerless. It is only because their atoms are held in by the whole body, intermingled through veins and flesh, sinews and bones, and are not free to bounce far apart, that they are kept together so as to perform the motions that generate sentience. After death, when they are expelled out of the body into the gusty air, they cannot perform the sensory motions because they are no longer held together in the same way. The air indeed will itself be a body, and an animate one at that, if it allows the vital spirit to hang together and keep up these motions which it used to go through before in the sinews and the body itself. Here then is proof upon proof. You must perforce admit that, when the whole bodily envelope crumbles after the expulsion of the vital breath, the senses of the mind and the spirit likewise disintegrate, since body and mind are effects of the same cause.

Lucretius 3. 425–44; 459–75; 558–94
tr. R. E. Latham (Penguin 1951)

H10   The Epicurean attitude to death

1   From all this it follows that *death is nothing to us* and no concern of ours, since our tenure of the mind is mortal. In days of old, we felt no disquiet when the

hosts of Carthage poured in to battle on every side—when the whole earth, dizzied by the convulsive shock of war, reeled sickeningly under the high ethereal vault, and between realm and realm the empire of mankind by land and sea trembled in the balance. So, when we shall be no more—when the union of body and spirit that engenders us has been disrupted—to us, who shall then be nothing, nothing by any hazard will happen any more at all. Nothing will have power to stir our senses, not though earth be fused with sea and sea with sky. . . .

2   If the future holds travail and anguish in store, the self must be in existence, when that time comes, in order to experience it. But from this fate we are re-deemed by death, which denies existence to the self that might have suffered these tribulations. Rest assured, therefore, that we have nothing to fear in death. One who no longer is cannot suffer, or differ in any way from one who has never been born, when once this mortal life has been usurped by death the immortal.

3   When you find a man treating it as a grievance that after death he will either moulder in the grave or fall a prey to flames or to the jaws of predatory beasts, be sure that his utterance does not ring true. Subconsciously his heart is stabbed by a secret dread, however loudly the man himself may disavow the belief that after death he will still experience sensation. I am convinced that he does not grant the admission he professes, nor the grounds of it; he does not oust and pluck himself root and branch out of life, but all unwittingly makes something of himself linger on. When a living man confronts the thought that after death his body will be mauled by birds and beasts of prey, he is filled with self-pity. He does not banish himself from the scene nor distinguish sharply enough between himself and that abandoned carcass. He visualizes that object as himself and infects it with his own feelings as an onlooker. That is why he is aggrieved at having been created mortal. He does not see that in real death there will be no other self alive to mourn his own decease—no other self standing by to flinch at the agony he suffers lying there being mangled, or indeed being cremated. For if it is really a bad thing after death to be mauled and crunched by ravening jaws, I cannot see why it should not be dis-agreeable to roast in the scorching flames of a funeral pyre, or to lie embalmed in honey, stifled and stiff with cold, on the surface of a chilly slab, or to be squashed under a crushing weight of earth.

4   'Now it is all over. Now the happy home and the best of wives will welcome you no more, nor winsome children rush to snatch the first kiss at your coming and touch your heart with speechless joy. No chance now to further your fortune or safeguard your family. Unhappy man,' they cry, 'unhappily cheated by one treach-erous day out of all the uncounted blessings of life!' But they do not go on to say: 'And now no repining for these lost joys will oppress you any more.' If they per-ceived this clearly with their minds and acted according to the words, they would free their breasts from a great load of grief and dread.

5   'Ah yes! *You* are at peace now in the sleep of death, and so you will stay to the end of time. Pain and sorrow will never touch you again. But to us, who stood weeping inconsolably while you were consumed to ashes on the dreadful pyre—to us no day will come that will lift the undying sorrow from our hearts.' Ask the

speaker, then, what is so heart-rending about this. If something returns to sleep and peace, what reason is that for pining in inconsolable grief? . . .

6   Here is something that you might well say to yourself from time to time: 'Even good king Ancus looked his last on the daylight—a better man than you, my presumptuous friend, by a long reckoning. Death has come to many another monarch and potentate, who lorded it over mighty nations. . . . And the Master himself, when his daylit race was run, Epicurus himself died, whose genius out-shone the race of men and dimmed them all, as the stars are dimmed by the rising of the fiery sun. And will *you* kick and protest against your sentence? You, whose life is next-door to death while you are still alive and looking on the light. You, who waste the major part of your time in sleep and, when you are awake, are snoring still and dreaming. You, who bear a mind hag-ridden by baseless fear and cannot find the commonest cause of your distress, hounded as you are, poor creature, by a pack of troubles and drifting in a drunken stupor upon a wavering tide of fantasy.'

7   Men feel plainly enough within their minds, a heavy burden, whose weight depresses them. If only they perceived with equal clearness the causes of this depression, the origin of this lump of evil within their breasts, they would not lead such a life as we now see all too commonly—no one knowing what he really wants and everyone for ever trying to get away from where he is, as though mere loco-motion could throw off the load. Often the owner of some stately mansion, bored stiff by staying at home, takes his departure, only to return as speedily when he feels himself no better off out of doors. Off he goes to his country seat, driving his carriage and pair hot-foot, as though in haste to save a house on fire. No sooner has he crossed its doorstep than he starts yawning or retires moodily to sleep and courts oblivion, or else rushes back to revisit the city. In so doing the individual is really running away from himself. Since he remains reluctantly wedded to the self whom he cannot of course escape, he grows to hate him, because he is a sick man ignorant of the cause of his malady. If he did but see this, he would cast other thoughts aside and devote himself first to studying the nature of the universe. It is not the fortune of an hour that is in question, but of all time—the lot in store for mortals through-out the eternity that awaits them after death.

8   What is this deplorable lust of life that holds us trembling in bondage to such uncertainties and dangers? A fixed term is set to the life of mortals, and there is no way of dodging death. In any case the setting of our lives remains the same through-out, and by going on living we do not mint any new coin of pleasure. So long as the object of our craving is unattained, it seems more precious than anything besides. Once it is ours, we crave for something else. So an unquenchable thirst for life keeps us always on the gasp. There is no telling what fortune the future may bring—what chance may throw in our way, or what upshot lies in waiting. By prolonging life, we cannot subtract or whittle away one jot from the duration of our death. The time after our taking off remains constant. However many generations you may add to your store by living, there waits for you none the less the same eternal death. The time of not-being will be no less for him who made an end of life

with yesterday's daylight than for him who perished many a moon and many a year before.

Lucretius 3. 830–42; 862–911; 1024–8; 1042–end
tr. R. E. Latham (Penguin 1951)

H11 The gods

Lucretius attempts to show that belief in the power of the gods is absurd and that it came about through erroneous conclusions drawn from visions seen in sleep and startling natural phenomena such as thunder and lightning. The gods do exist, but they enjoy an untroubled existence far away from our world, in which they have neither the power nor the inclination to intervene. (The Epicurean explanation of the nature of the gods is not one of the strongest points of the system. For passages both supporting and opposing the Epicurean explanation of how we perceive the gods, a subject into which Lucretius does not delve deeply, see H16, 17.)

1   Furthermore, you must not suppose that the holy dwelling-places of the gods are anywhere within the limits of the world. For the flimsy nature of the gods, far removed from our senses, is scarcely visible even to the perception of the mind. Since it eludes the touch and pressure of our hands, it can have no contact with anything that is tangible to us. For what cannot be touched cannot touch. Therefore their dwelling-places also must be unlike ours, of the same flimsy texture as their bodies, as I will prove to you at length later on.

2   Next, the theory that they deliberately created the world in all its natural splendour for the sake of man, so that we ought to praise this eminently praiseworthy piece of divine workmanship and believe it eternal and immortal and think it a sin to unsettle by violence the everlasting abode established for mankind by the ancient purpose of the gods and to worry it with words and turn it topsy-turvy— this theory, Memmius, with all its attendant fictions is sheer nonsense. For what benefit could immortal and blessed beings reap from our gratitude, that they should undertake any task on our behalf? Or what could tempt those who had been at peace so long to change their old life for a new? The revolutionary is one who is dissatisfied with the old order. But one who has known no trouble in the past, but spent his days joyfully—what could prick such a being with the itch for novelty? Or again, what harm would it have done us to have remained uncreated? Are we to suppose that our life was sunk in gloom and grief till the light of creation blazed forth? True that, once a man is born, he must will to remain alive so long as beguiling pleasure holds him. But one who has never tasted the love of life, or been enrolled among the living, what odds is it to him if he is never created? . . .

3   Even if I knew nothing of the atoms, I would venture to assert on the evidence of the celestial phenomena themselves, supported by many other arguments,

367

that the universe was certainly not created for us by divine power: it is so full of imperfections. In the first place, of all that is covered by the wide sweep of the sky, part has been greedily seized by mountains and the woodland haunts of wild beasts. Part is usurped by crags and desolate bogs and the sea that holds far asunder the shores of the lands. Almost two-thirds are withheld from mankind by torrid heat and perennial deposits of frosts. The little that is left of cultivable soil, if the force of nature had its way, would be choked with briars, did not the force of man oppose it. It is man's way, for the sake of life, to groan over the stout mattock and cleave the earth with down-pressed plough. Unless we turn the fruitful clods with the coulter and break up the soil to stimulate the growth of the crops, they cannot emerge of their own accord into the open air. Even so, when by dint of hard work all the fields at last burst forth into leaf and flower, then either the fiery sun withers them with intemperate heat, or sudden showers and icy frosts destroy them and gales of wind batter them with hurricane force. Again, why does nature feed and breed the fearsome brood of wild beasts, a menace to the human race by land and sea? Why does untimely death roam abroad? The human infant, like a shipwrecked sailor cast ashore by the cruel waves, lies naked on the ground, speechless, lacking all aids to life, when nature has first tossed him with pangs of travail from his mother's womb upon the shores of the sunlit world. He fills the air with his piteous wailing, and quite rightly, considering what evils life holds in store for him. But beasts of every kind, both tame and wild, have no need of rattles or a nurse to lull them with inarticulate babble. They do not want to change their clothes at every change in the weather. They need no armaments or fortifications to guard their possessions, since all the needs of all are lavishly supplied by mother earth herself and nature, the great artificer. . . .

4   Let us now consider why *reverence for the gods* is widespread among the nations. What has crowded their cities with altars and inaugurated those solemn rites that are in vogue today in powerful states and busy resorts? What has implanted in mortal hearts that chill of dread which even now rears new temples of the gods the wide world over and packs them on holy days with pious multitudes? The explanation is not far to seek. Already in those early days men had visions when their minds were awake, and more clearly in sleep, of divine figures, dignified in mien and impressive in stature. To these figures they attributed sentience, because they were seen to move their limbs and give voice to lordly utterances appropriate to their stately features and stalwart frames. They further credited them with eternal life, because the substance of their shapes was perpetually renewed and their appearance unchanging and in general because they thought that beings of such strength could not lightly be subdued by any force. They pictured their lot as far superior to that of mortals, because none of them was tormented by the fear of death, and also because in dreams they saw them perform all sorts of miracles without the slightest effort.

5   Again, men noticed the orderly succession of celestial phenomena and the round of the seasons and were at a loss to account for them. So they took refuge in handing over everything to the gods and making everything dependent on their

whim. They chose the sky to be the home and head-quarters of the gods because it is through the sky that the moon is seen to tread its cyclic course with day and night and night's ominous constellations and the night-flying torches and soaring flames of the firmament, clouds and sun and rain, snow and wind, lightning and hail, the sudden thunder-crash and the long-drawn intimidating rumble.

6   Poor humanity, to saddle the gods with such responsibilities and throw in a vindictive temper! What griefs they hatched then for themselves, what festering sores for us, what tears for our posterity! This is not piety, this oft-repeated show of bowing a veiled head before a graven image; this bustling to every altar; this kow-towing and prostration on the ground with palms outspread before the shrines of the gods; this deluging of altars with the blood of beasts; this heaping of vow on vow. True piety lies rather in the power to contemplate the universe with a quiet mind.

7   When we gaze up at the supernal regions of this mighty world, at the ether poised above, studded with flashing stars, and there comes into our minds the thought of the sun and moon and their migrations, then in hearts already racked by other woes a new anxiety begins to waken and rear up its head. We fall to wondering whether we may not be subject to some unfathomable divine power, which speeds the shining stars along their various tracks. It comes as a shock to our faltering minds to realize how little they know about the world. Had it a birth and a beginning? Is there some limit in time, beyond which its bastions will be unable to endure the strain of jarring motion? Or are they divinely gifted with everlasting surety, so that in their journey through the termless tract of time they can mock the stubborn strength of illimitable age? . . .

8   . . . picture a storm at sea, the wind scouring the water with hurricane force and some high admiral of the fleet swept before the blast with all his lavish com-plement of troops and battle elephants. How he importunes the peace of the gods with vows! How fervently he prays in his terror that the winds, too, may be at peace and favouring breezes blow! But, for all his prayers, the tornado does not relax its grip, and all too often he is dashed upon the reefs of death. So irresistibly is human power ground to dust by some unseen force, which seems to mock at the majestic rods and ruthless axes of authority and trample on them for its sport.

9   Lastly, when the whole earth quakes beneath their feet, when shaken cities fall in ruins or hang hesitantly tottering, what wonder if mortal men despise them-selves and find a place in nature for super-human forces and miraculous divine powers with supreme control over the universe?

Lucretius 5. 146–80; 195–234; 1161–1217; 1226–40
tr. R. E. Latham (Penguin 1951)

H12   The origins of civilization

In this long extract from Book 5 Lucretius deals with the origins of civilization. As

§1ff. reveals, the origin of man is seen as a natural sequel to the appearance of vegetation. Vegetable and animal originated in the same way, i.e., out of the earth. The progress of man is seen as a gradual evolution from primitive existence to economic and social co-operation and ultimately to developed political institutions.

1   First of all, the earth girdled its hills with a green glow of herbage, and over every plain the meadows gleamed with verdure and with bloom. Then trees of every sort were given free rein to join in an eager race for growth into the gusty air. As feathers, fur and bristles are generated at the outset from the bodies of winged and four-footed creatures, so then *the new-born earth first flung up herbs and shrubs. Next in order it engendered the various breeds of mortal creatures*, manifold in mode of origin as in form. The animals cannot have fallen from the sky, and those that live on land cannot have emerged from the briny gulfs. We are left with the conclusion that the name of mother has rightly been bestowed on the earth, since out of the earth everything is born.

2   Even now multitudes of animals are formed out of the earth with the aid of showers and the sun's genial warmth. So it is not surprising if more and bigger ones took shape and developed in those days, when earth and ether were young. First, the various breeds of winged birds were hatched out of eggs in the spring season, just as now the cicadas in summer crawl out spontaneously from their tubular integuments in quest of sustenance and life. Then it was that the earth brought forth the first mammals. There was a great superfluity of heat and moisture in the soil. So, wherever a suitable spot occurred, there grew up wombs, clinging to the earth by roots. These, when the time was ripe, were burst open by the maturation of the embryos, rejecting moisture now and struggling for air. Then nature directed towards that spot the pores of the earth making it open its veins and exude a juice resembling milk, just as nowadays every female when she has given birth is filled with sweet milk because all the flow of nourishment within her is directed into the breasts. The young were fed by the earth, clothed by the warmth and bedded by the herbage, which was then covered with abundance of soft down. The childhood of the world provoked no hard frosts or excessive heats or winds of boisterous violence. For all things keep pace in their growth and the attainment of their full strength. Here then, is further proof that the name of mother has rightly been bestowed on the earth, since it brought forth the human race and gave birth at the appointed season to every beast that runs wild among the high hills and at the same time to the birds of the air in all their rich variety.

3   Then, because there must be an end to such parturition, the earth ceased to bear, like a woman worn out with age. For the nature of the world as a whole is altered by age. Everything must pass through successive phases. Nothing remains for ever what it was. Everything is on the move. Everything is transformed by nature and forced into new paths. One thing, withered by time, decays and dwindles. Another emerges from ignominy, and waxes strong. So the nature of the world as a whole is altered by age. The earth passes through successive phases, so that it can no longer bear what it could, and it can now what it could not before...

4 In those days, again, many species must have died out altogether and failed to reproduce their kind. Every species that you now see drawing the breath of life has been protected and preserved from the beginning of the world either by cunning or by prowess or by speed. In addition, there are many that survive under human protection because their usefulness has commended them to our care. The surly breed of lions, for instance, in their native ferocity have been preserved by prowess, the fox by cunning and the stag by flight. The dog, whose loyal heart is alert even in sleep, all beasts of burden of whatever breed, fleecy sheep and horned cattle, over all these, my Memmius, man has established his protectorate. They have gladly escaped from predatory beasts and sought peace and the lavish meals, procured by no effort of theirs, with which we recompense their service. But those that were gifted with none of these natural assets, unable either to live on their own resources or to make any contribution to human welfare, in return for which we might let their race feed in safety under our guardianship—all these, trapped in the toils of their own destiny, were fair game and an easy prey for others, till nature brought their race to extinction. . . .

5 The human beings that peopled these fields were far tougher than the men of today, as became the offspring of tough earth. They were built on a framework of bigger and solider bones, fastened through their flesh to stout sinews. They were relatively insensitive to heat and cold, to unaccustomed diet and bodily ailments in general. Through many decades of the sun's cyclic course they lived out their lives in the fashion of wild beasts roaming at large. No one spent his strength in guiding the curved plough. No one knew how to cleave the earth with iron, or to plant young saplings in the soil or lop the old branches from tall trees with pruning hooks. Their hearts were well content to accept as a free gift what the sun and showers had given and the earth had produced unsolicited. Often they stayed their hunger among the acorn-laden oaks. Arbutus berries, whose scarlet tint now betrays their winter ripening, were then produced by the earth in plenty and of a larger size. In addition the lusty childhood of the earth yielded a great variety of tough foods, ample for afflicted mortals. Rivers and springs called to them to slake their thirst, as nowadays a clamorous cataract of water, tumbling out of the high hills, summons from far away the thirsty creatures of the wild. They resorted to those woodland sanctuaries of the nymphs, familiar to them in their wandering, from which they knew that trickling streams of water issued to bathe the dripping rocks in a bountiful shower, sprinkled over green moss, and gushed out here and there over the open plain.

6 They did not know as yet how to enlist the aid of fire, or to make use of skins, or to clothe their bodies with trophies of the chase. They lived in thickets and hillside caves and forests and stowed their rugged limbs among bushes when driven to seek shelter from the lash of wind and rain.

They could have no thought of the common good, no notion of the mutual restraint of morals and laws. The individual, taught only to live and fend for himself, carried off on his own account such prey as fortune brought him. Venus coupled the bodies of lovers in the greenwood. Mutual desire brought them together, or the male's mastering might and overriding lust, or a payment of acorns or arbutus berries or choice pears. Thanks to their surpassing strength of hand and foot, they hunted the woodland beasts by hurling stones and wielding ponderous clubs. They were more than a match for many of them; from a few they took refuge in hiding-places.

7   When night overtook them, they flung their jungle-bred limbs naked on the earth like bristly boars, and wrapped themselves round with a coverlet of leaves and branches. It is not true that they wandered panic-stricken over the country-side through the darkness of night, searching with loud lamentations for the day-light and the sun. In fact they waited, sunk in quiet sleep, till the sun with his rose-red torch should bring back radiance to the sky. Accustomed as they were from infancy to seeing the alternate birth of darkness and light, they could never have been struck with amazement or misgiving whether the withdrawal of the sun-light might not plunge the earth in everlasting night. They were more worried by the peril to which unlucky sleepers were often exposed from predatory beasts. Turned out of house and home by the intrusion of a slavering boar or a burly lion, they would abandon their rocky roofs at dead of night and yield up their leaf-strewn beds in terror to the savage visitor.

8   The proportion of mortal men that relinquished the dear light of life before it was all spent was not appreciably higher then than now. Then it more often happened that an individual victim would furnish living food to a beast of prey: engulfed in its jaws, he would fill thicket and mountainside and forest with his shrieks, at the sight of his living flesh entombed in a living sepulchre. Those who saved their mangled bodies by flight would press trembling palms over ghastly sores, calling upon death in heart-rending voices, till life was wrenched from them by racking spasms. In their ignorance of the treatment that wounds demand, they could not help themselves. But it never happened then that many thousands of men following the standards were led to death on a single day. Never did the ocean levels, lashed into tumult, hurl ships and men together upon the reefs. Here, time after time, the sea would rise and vainly vent its fruitless ineffectual fury, then lightly lay aside its idle threats. The crafty blandishment of the unruffled deep could not tempt any man to his undoing with its rippling laughter. Then, when the mariner's presumptuous art lay still unguessed, it was lack of food that brought failing limbs at last to death. Now it is superfluity that proves too much for them. The men of old, in their ignorance, often served poison to themselves. Now, with greater skill, they administer it to others.

9   As time went by, men began to build huts and to use skins and fire. Male and female learnt to live together in a stable union and to watch over their joint pro-geny. Then it was that humanity first began to mellow. Thanks to fire, their chilly bodies could no longer so easily endure the cold under the canopy of heaven. Venus subdued brute strength. Children by their wheedling easily broke down their parents' stubborn temper. Then neighbours began to form mutual alliances, wishing neither to do nor to suffer violence among themselves. They appealed on behalf of their children and womanfolk, pointing out with gestures and inarticulate cries that

it is right for everyone to pity the weak. It was not possible to achieve perfect unity of purpose. Yet a substantial majority kept faith honestly. Otherwise the entire human race would have been wiped out there and then instead of being propagated, generation after generation, down to the present day. . . .

10   Here is the answer to another question that you may be putting to yourself. *The agent by which fire was first brought down to earth* and made available to mortal man was lightning. To this source every hearth owes its flames. Think how many things we see ablaze with heaven-sent flame, when a stroke from heaven has endowed them with heat. There is also, however, another possible source. When a branching tree, tossed by the wind, is swaying and surging to and fro and stooping to touch the branches of another tree, the violent friction squeezes out seeds of fire, till sometimes from the rubbing of bough against bough, trunk against trunk, there flashes out a blazing burst of flame. Either of these occurrences may have given fire to mortals. Later it was the sun that taught them to cook food and soften it by heating on the flames, since they noticed in roaming through the fields how many things were subdued and mellowed by the impact of its ardent rays.

11   As time went by, men learnt to change their old ways of life by means of fire and other new inventions, instructed by those of outstanding ability and mental energy. *Kings began to found cities* and establish citadels for their own safeguard and refuge. They parcelled out cattle and lands, giving to each according to his looks, his strength and his ability; for good looks were highly prized and strength counted for much. Later came the invention of property and the discovery of gold, which speedily robbed the strong and the handsome of their pre-eminence. The man of greater riches finds no lack of stalwart frames and comely faces to follow in his train. And yet, if a man would guide his life by true philosophy, he will find ample riches in a modest livelihood enjoyed with a tranquil mind. Of that little he need never be beggared. Men craved for fame and power so that their fortune might rest on a firm foundation and they might live out a peaceful life in the enjoyment of plenty. An idle dream. In struggling to gain the pinnacle of power they beset their own road with perils. And then from the very peak, as though by a thunder-bolt, they are cast down by envy into a foul abyss of ignominy. For envy, like the thunderbolt, most often strikes the highest and all that stands out above the common level. Far better to lead a quiet life in subjection than to long for sovereign authority and lordship over kingdoms. So leave them to the blood and sweat of their wearisome unprofitable struggle along the narrow pathway of ambition. Since they savour life through another's mouth and choose their target rather by hearsay than by the evidence of their own senses, it avails them now, and will avail them, no more than it has ever done.

12   So the kings were killed. Down in the dust lay the ancient majesty of thrones, the haughty sceptres. The illustrious emblem of the sovereign head, dabbled in gore and trampled under the feet of the rabble, mourned its high estate. What once was feared too much is now as passionately down-trodden. So the conduct of affairs sank back into the turbid depths of mob-rule, with each man struggling to win dominance and supremacy for himself. Then some men showed how to form a

constitution, based on fixed rights and recognized laws. Mankind, worn out by a life of violence and enfeebled by feuds, was the more ready to submit of its own free will to the bondage of laws and institutions. This distaste for a life of violence came naturally to a society in which every individual was ready to gratify his anger by a harsher vengeance than is now tolerated by equitable laws. Ever since then the enjoyment of life's prizes has been tempered by the fear of punishment. A man is enmeshed by his own violence and wrong-doing, which commonly recoil upon their author. It is not easy for one who breaks by his acts the mutual compact of social peace to lead a peaceful and untroubled life. Even if he hides his guilt from gods and men, he must feel a secret misgiving that it will not rest hidden for ever. He cannot forget those oft-told tales of men betraying themselves by words in dreams or delirium that drag out long-buried crimes into the daylight.

> Lucretius 5. 783–836; 855–77; 925–1027; 1091–1160
> tr. R. E. Latham (Penguin 1951)

H13 Cicero on Lucretius

In 54 BC Lucretius' poem had probably just been published, possibly prepared for publication by Cicero himself (H14). This, the only extant contemporary comment on the poem, is frustrating in its brevity (it is one of two brief postscripts to Cicero's main letter).

The poems of Lucretius are just as you write—with frequent flashes of genius and yet exceedingly artistic.

> Cicero *Letter to his brother Quintus* 2. 10. 3
> tr. W. Glyn Williams (Loeb 1972)

H14 St. Jerome on Lucretius

The following is an addition by St. Jerome to the historical chronicle of the Christian writer Eusebius under the year 94 BC. The famous story of Lucretius' suicide is passed over in silence by Cicero. Its origin may have been Christian animosity, strengthened by some observations on love in Book 4 of the poem itself. The extent of Cicero's hand in the appearance of the poem is doubtful. 'Corrected' is probably nearer the truth than 'emended' or 'edited'. Cicero, normally so informative about his activities, makes no mention of this task (see H13).

[In the year 94 BC] Titus Lucretius the poet was born who, after being driven mad by a love potion, composed in his lucid intervals some writings (which afterwards Cicero corrected). He died, by his own hand, aged forty-four.

St. Jerome Chronicle
tr. C. J. Emlyn Jones

H15 Cicero on Epicureanism

Cicero, philosophically eclectic, did not really approve, either morally or intellectually, of Epicureanism, but gave it a fair hearing. The 'clever fellow' is Epicurus (although we do not find the theory of the swerve in Epicurus' extant writings). In De Finibus, *Cicero presents fairly and at some length arguments for and against Epicureanism, and in this particular passage exposes what he feels to be one of its weaknesses.*

He believes that these same indivisible solid bodies are borne by their own weight perpendicularly downward, which he holds is the natural motion of all bodies; but thereupon this clever fellow, being met with the difficulty that if they all travelled downwards in a straight line, and, as I said, perpendicularly, no one atom would ever be able to overtake any other atom, accordingly introduced an idea of his own invention: he said that the atom makes a very tiny swerve—the smallest divergence possible; and so are produced entanglements and combinations and cohesions of atoms with atoms, which result in the creation of the world and all its parts, and of all that in them is. Now not only is the whole of this affair a piece of childish fancy, but it does not even achieve the result that its author desires. The swerving is itself an arbitrary fiction; for Epicurus says the atoms swerve without a cause,—yet this is the capital offence in a natural philosopher, to speak of something taking place uncaused. Then also he gratuitously deprives the atoms of what he himself declared to be the natural motion of all heavy bodies, namely, movement in a straight line downwards, and yet he does not attain the object for the sake of which this fiction was devised. For, if all the atoms swerve, none will ever come to cohere together; or if some swerve while others travel in a straight line, by their own natural tendency, in the first place this will be tantamount to assigning to the atoms their different spheres of action, some to travel straight and some sideways; while secondly (and this is a weak point with Democritus also) this riotous hurly-burly of atoms could not possibly result in the ordered beauty of the world we know.

Cicero De Finibus 1. 18–20
tr. H. Rackham (Loeb 1914)

H16 Differing views on the gods

In this literary dialogue, Cicero represents the views of the different philosophical schools on the nature of the gods. In this particular passage, the Epicurean Velleius contrasts the wild superstition of conventional belief with the rationalism of Epicurus.

Anyone pondering on the baseless and irrational character of these doctrines ought to regard Epicurus with reverence, and to rank him as one of the very gods about whom we are inquiring. For he alone perceived, first, that the gods exist, because nature herself has imprinted a conception of them on the minds of all mankind. For what nation or what tribe of men is there but possesses untaught some 'preconception' of the Gods? Such notions Epicurus designates by the word *prolepsis*, that is, a sort of preconceived mental picture of a thing, without which nothing can be understood or investigated or discussed. The force and value of this argument we learn in that work of genius, Epicurus's *Rule or Standard of Judgement*. You see therefore that the foundation (for such it is) of our inquiry has been well and truly laid. For the belief in the gods has not been established by authority, custom or law, but rests on the unanimous and abiding consensus of mankind; their existence is therefore a necessary inference, since we possess an instinctive or rather an innate concept of them; but a belief which all men by nature share must necessarily be true; therefore it must be admitted that the gods exist. And since this truth is almost universally accepted not only among philosophers but also among the unlearned, we must admit it as also being an accepted truth that we possess a 'preconception', as I called it above, or 'prior notion', of the gods. (For we are bound to employ novel terms to denote novel ideas, just as Epicurus himself employed the word *prolepsis* in a sense in which no one had ever used it before.) We have then a preconception of such a nature that we believe the gods to be blessed and immortal. For nature, which bestowed upon us an idea of the gods themselves, also engraved on our minds the belief that they are eternal and blessed. If this is so, the famous maxim of Epicurus truthfully enunciates that 'that which is blessed and eternal can neither know trouble itself nor cause trouble to another, and accordingly cannot feel either anger or favour, since all such things belong only to the weak.'

Cicero *De Natura Deorum* 1. 43–4
tr. H. Rackham (Loeb 1933)

H17 Cicero's criticism of the Epicurean view of the gods

In this passage, from the same work as H16, Cicero advances a position critical to the Epicurean hypothesis concerning the human conception of the gods.

Your assertion was that the form of god is perceived by thought and not in the senses, that it has no solidity nor numerical persistence, and that our perception of it is such that it is seen owing to similarity and succession, a never-ceasing stream of similar forms arriving continually from the infinite number of atoms, and that thus it results that our mind, when its attention is fixed on these forms, conceives the divine nature to be happy and eternal.

Now in the name of the very gods about whom we are talking, what can possibly be the meaning of this? If the gods only appeal to the faculty of thought, and have no solidity or definite outline, what difference does it make whether we think of a god or of a hippocentaur? Such mental pictures are called by all other philosophers mere empty imaginations, but you say they are the arrival and entrance into our minds of certain images. Well, then, when I seem to see Tiberius Gracchus in the middle of his speech in the Capitol producing the ballot-box for the vote on Marcus Octavius, I explain this as an empty imagination of the mind, but your explanation is that the images of Gracchus and Octavius have actually remained on the spot, so that when I come to the Capitol these images are borne to my mind; the same thing happens, you say, in the case of god, whose appearance repeatedly impinges on men's minds, and so gives rise to the belief in happy and eternal deities. Suppose that there are such images constantly impinging on our minds: but that is only the presentation of a certain form—surely not also of a reason for supposing that this form is happy and eternal?

Cicero *De Natura Deorum* 1. 105–7
tr. H. Rackham (Loeb 1933)

H18 Diodorus Siculus on the creation of man

Diodorus, a younger contemporary of Lucretius, wrote a World History, *of which the following passage represents the origin and earliest years of mankind. Its close resemblance to Lucretius' account (see esp. H12) suggests a common source or sources, possibly Epicurus himself.*

But the first men to be born, they say, led an undisciplined and bestial life, setting out one by one to secure their sustenance and taking for their food both the tenderest herbs and the fruits of wild trees. Then, since they were attacked by the wild beasts, they came to each other's aid, being instructed by expediency, and when gathered together in this way by reason of their fear, they gradually came to recognize their mutual characteristics. And though the sounds which they made were at first unintelligible and indistinct, yet gradually they came to give articulation to their speech, and by agreeing with one another upon symbols for each thing which presented itself to them, made known among themselves the significance which was to be attached to each term. But since groups of this kind arose over every part of the inhabited world, not all men had the same language, inasmuch as every group organized the elements of its speech by mere chance. This is the explanation of the present existence of every conceivable kind of language, and furthermore, out of these first groups to be formed came all the original nations of the world.

Now the first men, since none of the things useful for life had yet been discovered, led a wretched existence, having no clothing to cover them, knowing not the use of dwelling and fire, and also being totally ignorant of cultivated food. For since they were ignorant of the harvesting of the wild food, they laid by no store of its fruits against their needs; consequently large numbers of them perished in the winters because of the cold and the lack of food. Little by little, however, experience taught them both to take to the caves in winter and to store such fruits as could be preserved. And when they had become acquainted with fire and other useful things, the arts also and whatever else is capable of furthering man's social life were gradually discovered. Indeed, speaking generally, in all things it was necessity itself that became man's teacher, supplying in appropriate fashion instruction in every matter to a creature which was well endowed by nature and had, as its assistants for every purpose, hands and speech and sagacity of mind.

Diodorus Siculus 1. 8. 1–9
tr. C. H. Oldfather (Loeb 1933)

I THE ROMAN OUTLOOK

Social history covers such a wide variety of topics that it is not possible, nor indeed academically desirable, to compartmentalize 'social historical' sources neatly into one section. All material in this sourcebook provides evidence for one aspect or another of Roman society, and the starting-point of the social historian will be governed by the problem he wishes to investigate. This section concentrates on providing: (i) sources which illuminate topics and themes raised in other sections (e.g. slavery and freedmen, D19-21, K24; political settlement and the land problem, B10, 19); (ii) primary evidence for looking at certain themes from the point of view of a social historian (e.g. cultural assimilation, I14-27; the relationship between urban and rural life, I34-44, patterns of land use, I35-7); (iii) sources which illuminate the conceptual framework of the Romans (e.g. cult and belief, I5-11; the values of the ruling class, I1, 49-56). Cross-references provide a link with related source material. The section should therefore be regarded as a pointer towards other sections of the book rather than as a definitive collection of sources or themes.

I1 Propertius' Rome

Propertius (born between 54 and 47 BC and died before 2 BC) came from a prominent family from Assisi. His family lost much of its property in Octavian's confiscations of 41-40 and in that year a relative was killed at Perusia. Book 1 of the Elegies *was probably published before late 28 BC after which he gained the patronage of Maecenas. Book 4 may have been published posthumously, though the latest events mentioned belong to 16 BC. See also D26, E10.*

(a) *1.22*

> Tullus, you ask in our long friendship's name
> What rank, what birth, what household gods I claim.
> You know Perusia, where sepultured lie
> The Italian dead—our country's cemetery
> In those ungentle times when feud at home
> Hounded to war the citizens of Rome—
> Earth of Etruria! How this thought must be
> Bitter, beyond the common grief, to me:
> You left my kinsman's outcast corpse to lie
> Craving the shroud of soil which you deny.
> Where fertile Umbria spreads her opulent earth
> Nearest the plain below, she gave me birth.

(b) *1.21*

Soldier, hot-foot your comrades' fate to shun,
As wounded from the Etrurian lines you run,
Why do you, when my groanings reach your ear,
Glare so on me, a friend-in-arms most near?
Go safe, to glad your parents' eyes; and shed
No tears, to tell your sister how I bled;
How Gallus came from Caesar's swords unscarred,
And by base hands was taken off his guard.
Let him that finds the scattered bones that lie
On Tuscan hills, pass mine in ignorance by.

(c) *2.15.41-9*

If all men, covetous of a life like mine,
Drank deep, and lay with limbs weighed down with
    wine,
No wounding steel, no warships would there be,
Nor would our bones be tossed in Actium's sea,
Nor would war-wearied Rome, with hair unbound,
Be by her conquests, as by foes, hemmed round.
For this posterity may praise us long:
The cups we drank have done the gods no wrong.
Cling to life's joys, while daylight lasts for you

(d) *4.10.27-37*

Nomentum then was Rome's remotest spoil,
And the few roods of Cora's captured soil.
Not yet across the Tiber then had gone
The sound of war—but now there follows on
Cossus, by whom Tolumnius, Veii's king,
Was slain, when Veii took some conquering.
Veii of old had monarchs of her own,
And in her forum stood a golden throne:
Now in her walls the plodding shepherd's horn
Sings, and amid her bones men reap the corn.

(e) *3.4*

Arms for the East! Rich India's hour is near,
When Caesar's godlike purpose shall appear:
His fleet shall cleave the gem-filled sea, to gain
The last grand prize, earth's ultimate domain,
Which now prepares for Tiber's triumph-day,
When running low, Euphrates owns his sway.
Beneath Italian fasces, men of Rome,

A tributary land shall Parthia come,
Surely though late, and trophies won from her
Shall learn to know the Latian Jupiter.   10
Set sail, you veteran ships; you armoured steeds,
Do for the cause your customary deeds.
Go with my blessing: serve Rome's history well:
Make expiation where the Crassi fell.
O father Mars, O Vestal fires that sway
The fates, prolong my life to see the day
When Caesar's chariot, crammed with spoils, goes by,
The horses checking at the people's cry;
With captured towns, whose names I'll see displayed,
While on my lady's breast my head is laid;   20
The Parthian shaft, the trousered warrior's bow,
And captured leaders with their arms on show.
Venus, preserve your own, immortal be
The scion of Aeneas whom you see.
Theirs be this spoil who won it: I shall play
My part by cheering in the Sacred Way.

(f) *3.9.48–end*

I'll be content to give delight, and thus
Ranked with Philetas and Callimachus,   50
Like one divine win worship and acclaim
From boys and girls, whom songs like theirs inflame.
   Yet if you give a lead, my verse shall go
To sing of Jove in arms against the foe;
Of Phlegra's hills, whereon Eurymedon
And Coeus breathed their threats against his throne;
Of brother kings whom those wild teats had fed;
Of walls made firm, when Remus' blood was shed;
Of Roman steers, that grazed on Palatine—
My wit shall soar to sing what you assign: 60
The victory cars that roll from shore to shore
Sped by my song; the Parthian bow no more
Bent in feigned flight: Pelusium's forts that feel
The devastating force of Roman steel;
And Antony's death-dealing hands, whose weight
His own life felt—all these will I relate.
Give me your gracious help in manhood's race:
Nay, take the reins and speed my chariot's pace.
Maecenas, all the fame I have—to be
Called your adherent—is your gift to me.   70

tr. A. E. Watts (Penguin 1966)

12 Contrasting attitudes to the empire

(a) *Virgil emphasizes the contribution of men from different parts of Italy to Rome's Imperial expansion.*

> Veins of silver and copper Italy too has revealed
> And rivers running with gold.
> Active her breed of men—the Marsians and Sabellians,
> Ligurians used to hardship, Volscian javelin-throwers;
> Mother she is of the Decii, Marii, great Camilli,
> The Scipios relentless in war; and of you, most royal Caesar,
> Who now triumphant along the furthest Asian frontiers
> Keep the war-worthless Indians away from the towers of Rome

> Virgil *Georgics* 2. 165–76
> tr. C. Day Lewis (Oxford 1966)

(b) *Horace expresses a detachment both from the problems and advantages of empire.*

> 'Is warlike Spain hatching a plot?'
> You ask me anxiously. 'And what
> Of Scythia?' My dear Quinctius,
> There's a whole ocean guarding us.
> Stop fretting: life has simple needs.
> Behind us smooth-cheeked youth recedes,
> Good looks go too, and in our beds
> Dry wizened skins and grizzled heads
> Wait to put easy sleep to rout
> And drive love's sensuous pleasures out.
> Buds lose their springtime gloss, and soon
> The full becomes the thin-faced moon.
> Futurity is infinite:
> Why tax the brain with plans for it?
> Better by this tall plane or pine
> To sprawl and, while we may, drink wine
> And grace with Syrian balsam drops
> And roses these fast-greying tops.
> Bacchus shoos off the wolves of worry.
> Ho, slaves! Which one of you will hurry
> Down to the nearby brook to tame
> The heat of this Falernian's flame?
> Who'll coax from home to join our feast
> Lyde, of easy girls the least

Easy to get? Bid her bestir
Herself and bring along with her
The ivory lyre, wearing her curls
Neat-braided like a Spartan girl's.

Horace *Odes* 2. 11
tr. J. Michie (Penguin 1967 rev. 1978)

13 The Religious Traditions

This passage from Livy is put into the mouth of Camillus and refers to the pro-
posal to emigrate to Veii after the sack of Rome by the Gauls in 390 BC. The
historical allusions date to the fourth century but the account is written under the
impact of Augustus' reassertion of religious values. Note the importance of the
Capitol (a religious centre as well as a citadel), of the pomerium, *or religious bound-*
ary of the city, of auspices and auguries, of the religious aspect of political as-
semblies, of the Vestals and the priest of Jupiter. Aius Locutius, the Power of the
Speaking Voice, is a typical example of the numina *or* Sondergötter, *gods of a*
limited function. In general see J. H. W. G. Liebeschütz Continuity and Change in
Roman Religion *(Oxford 1979).*

'If we had no religious traditions established with the city's foundation and passed
down from hand to hand, it would still be clear in the present crisis that divine
power has defended Rome and I should think it impossible for men to neglect
religious observances. Consider the successes and failures of recent years: you will
find that obedience to the gods has led to success, indifference to failure.

Think what a difference there is between us and our predecessors! They passed
on to us some ceremonies to be performed on the Alban Hill and in Lavinium.
There was a tabu on transferring these ceremonies from enemy cities to Rome; can
we without breaking a tabu transfer ceremonies from here to the enemy city of
Veii? Remember how often ceremonies have to be repeated because through fault
or accident, some detail has been omitted from the traditional ritual. After the
portent of the Alban Lake, at a time when our country was engaged in war with
Veii, it was simply the repetition of the ceremonies and auspices which brought us
new life. More, it is in full mindfulness of the religion of our fathers that we have
introduced foreign gods to Rome and established fresh gods. Juno the Queen was
recently brought from Veii on to the Aventine. What a marvellous day that was!
The crowds! The enthusiasm of the ladies! We have given instructions for a temple
to be built to Aius Locutius in honour of the voice from heaven heard on the Via
Nova. We have added the Capitoline Games to the other annual festivals, and established on the authority of the Senate a new college of priests to control it. What

383

need was there for these new enterprises if we proposed to join the Gauls in with-drawing from the city of Rome? Did we remain in the Capitol through all those months of siege not of our own free will, but out of fear of the enemy? We are talking about ceremonies and temples. How about priests? Does the degree of your impiety ever cross your mind? There is only one place for the Vestals to live and nothing but the sack of the city has ever caused them to stir from it. There is a tabu preventing Jupiter's priest from spending even a single night outside the city. Are you going to make them into priests of Veii instead of Rome? Vesta, are your own Vestals going to abandon you? Is the Priest going to live abroad and night after night pile up the guilt for himself and his country? Almost all public business has to be transacted within the city's boundaries after taking auspices. Is this to be for-gotten and ignored? The *comitia curiata*, which takes decisions about war, and the *comitia centuriata*, which elects consuls and military tribunes, can only meet in the traditional places after auspices have been taken. Are we going to transfer these to Veii? Or are the people to congregate at great inconvenience in this city, when it has been abandoned by gods and men, simply for the formal assemblies? . . .

Here stands the Capitol where men discovered a human head, to receive divine assurance that in that place lay the head and crown of empire. Here, when the Capitol was liberated and the auguries were being taken, to the great joy of your elders, the gods of Youth and the Boundary refused to be shifted. Here are the fires of Vesta; here are the shields which came down from heaven, here are all the gods and their favour—if you stand firm.'

Livy 5. 51. 4-10; 52; 54. 7.
tr. J. Ferguson

I4 The Laws of War

The passage emphasizes the status of the oath and of the exact observance of religious ritual in ensuring that warfare was both legal and propitious. Strictly the Fetial Code regulated treaty obligations. It did not apply to civil war.

As for war, humane laws touching it are drawn up in the fetial code of the Roman People under all the guarantees of religion; and from this it may be gathered that no war is just, unless it is entered upon after an official demand for satisfaction has been submitted or warning has been given and a formal declaration made. Popilius was general in command of a province. In his army Cato's son was serving on his first campaign. When Popilius decided to disband one of his legions, he discharged also young Cato, who was serving in that same legion. But when the young man out of love for the service stayed on in the field, his father wrote to Popilius to say that if he let him stay in the army, he should swear him into service with a new oath of allegiance, for in view of the voidance of his former oath he could not legally fight the foe. So extremely scrupulous was the observance of the laws in regard to the conduct of war. There is extant, too, a letter of the elder Marcus Cato to his son Marcus, in which he writes that he has heard that the youth has been discharged by the consul, when he was serving in Macedonia in the war with Perseus. He warns him, therefore, to be careful not to go into battle; for, he says, the man who is not legally a soldier has no right to be fighting the foe.

Cicero *De Officiis* 1. 36
tr. W. Miller (Loeb 1913)

I5 Cicero on Religious Law

Only three books from Cicero's De Legibus (On Laws) *survive. The work is prescriptive and expounds the Stoic notion of divinely sanctioned law based on reason, with special reference to Roman practice in magistracies and in religion.*

No one shall have gods to himself, either new gods or alien gods, unless recognized by the state. Privately they shall worship those gods whose worship they have duly received from their ancestors. In cities they shall have shrines; they shall have groves in the country and homes for the Lares. They shall preserve the rites of their families and their ancestors. They shall worship as gods both those who have always been regarded as dwellers in heaven, and also those whose merits have admitted them to heaven: Hercules, Liber, Aesculapius, Castor, Pollux, Quirinus: also those qualities through which an ascent to heaven is granted to mankind; Intellect, Piety, Virtue, Good Faith. To their praise there shall be shrines, but not to vices.

They shall perform the established rites . . . On holidays the priests shall offer on behalf of the state the prescribed grains and fruits; this shall be done according to prescribed rites on prescribed days . . . . Those who are ignorant of the methods and rites suitable to these public and private sacrifices shall seek instructions from the public priests . . . . Of the ancestral rites, the best shall be preserved . . . Vows shall be scrupulously performed; there shall be a penalty for the violation of the law. . . . The sacred rites of families shall remain for ever.

Cicero *Laws* 2. 8. 19 ff. (abridged)
tr. Ancient History Bureau (Occasional Paper RP1)

I6 The Roman Gods

St. Augustine, writing in the early fifth century AD, preserves evidence from Varro about Roman religion. Not included in this extract is a lengthy description of individual gods and spirits associated with individual activities, feelings, and aspects of nature and agriculture, on the basis of which St. Augustine points out the difference between local rural religion and the state cults.

Next let us inquire, if you like, which god or which gods, out of the mighty throng worshippéd by the Romans, they believe did most to extend and preserve their empire. . . . I do not record them all, for I am bored by all this, though they are not ashamed of it.

But I wanted to show by this very small sample that they by no means venture to assert that it was these deities who founded, extended and preserved the Roman Empire. These were so occupied, each with his special duties, that no one thing as a whole was entrusted to any one of them. So how could Segetia care for the empire, when she was not allowed to take care of the grain crop and of trees at the same time? How could Cunina think of weapons, when they did not permit her charge to reach beyond the cradled babies? How could Nodutus help in war, when he was not concerned with the follicle of wheat, but only with the node on the joint? Everyone has a single doorkeeper for his house, and since he is a man, that is quite sufficient. But they put three gods there: Forculus for the doors (*fores*), Cardea for the hinges (*cardo*) and Limentinus for the threshold (*limen*). Thus Forculus was not competent to guard both the hinge and the threshold along with the door.

We must therefore leave this throng of little gods, or put them aside for a while, and examine the role of the greater gods, by which Rome became so great as to rule so long over so many nations. Well, undoubtedly this is the work of Jupiter. For he is the one whom they represent as king of all the gods and goddesses; this is the meaning of his sceptre, and of the Capitol on its high hill. Of this god they declare that it was most aptly said, though by a poet: 'All things are full of Jupiter.' Varro believes that he is worshipped even by those who worship one God only, without an image, though he is called by another name. If this is true, why was he so badly treated in Rome, and also by other peoples, that an image was made for him? This fact displeased even Varro so much that, although he was bound by the perverse custom of his great city, he still never scrupled to say and write that those who had set up images for their peoples had both subtracted reverence and added error.

St. Augustine *City of God* 4. 32 (abridged)
tr. W. M. Green (Loeb 1963)

I7 Polybius on Roman Religion

Polybius, the Greek historian of Rome's rise to world power, was a member of the Scipionic circle (although a captive in Rome) and became an admirer of Roman Imperial expansion. See in general F. W. Walbank Commentary on Polybius *(Oxford 1957-79).*

But the quality in which the Roman commonwealth is most distinctly superior is in my opinion the nature of their religious convictions. I believe that it is the very thing which among other peoples is an object of reproach, I mean superstition, which maintains the cohesion of the Roman State. These matters are clothed in such pomp and introduced to such an extent into their public and private life that nothing could exceed it, a fact which will surprise many. My own opinion at least is that they have adopted this course for the sake of the common people. It is a course which perhaps would not have been necessary had it been possible to form a state composed of wise men, but as every multitude is fickle, full of lawless desires, unreasoned passion, and violent anger, the multitude must be held in by invisible terrors and suchlike pageantry. For this reason I think, not that the ancients acted rashly and at haphazard in introducing among the people notions concerning the gods and beliefs in the terrors of hell, but that the moderns are most rash and foolish in banishing such beliefs. The consequence is that among the Greeks, apart from other things, members of the government, if they are entrusted with no more than a talent, though they have ten copyists and as many seals and twice as many witnesses, cannot keep their faith; whereas among the Romans those who as magistrates and legates are dealing with large sums of money maintain correct conduct just because they have pledged their faith by oath. Whereas elsewhere it is a rare thing to find a man who keeps his hands off public money, and whose record is clean in this respect, among the Romans one rarely comes across a man who has been detected in such conduct. . . .

Polybius 6. 56
tr. W. R. Paton (Loeb 1923)

18 Augury

The college of augurs was one of the four leading priestly collegia *at Rome. Appointment was a political honour. Cicero emphasizes that the role of the augurs in his day was not to foretell the future but to observe and interpret signs by which the gods' approval of a proposed public action could be judged. The political utility of the office was therefore considerable.*

Enough has been said of portents; auspices remain and so do lots—I mean 'lots' that are drawn, and not those uttered by prophets, and more correctly styled 'oracles.' I shall speak of oracles when I get to natural divination. In addition I must discuss the Chaldeans. But first let us consider auspices. 'To argue against auspices is a hard thing,' you say, 'for an augur to do.' Yes, for a Marsian, perhaps; but very easy for a Roman. For we Roman augurs are not the sort who foretell the future by observing the flights of birds and other signs. And yet, I admit that Romulus, who founded the city by the direction of auspices, believed that augury was an art

387

useful in seeing things to come—for the ancients had erroneous views on many subjects. But we see that the art has undergone a change, due to experience, education, or the long lapse of time. However, out of respect for the opinion of the masses and because of the great service to the State we maintain the augural practices, discipline, religious rites and laws, as well as the authority of the augural college.

Cicero *de Divinatione* 2. 33. 70
tr. W. A. Falconer (Loeb 1923)

19 Roman traditional piety

Both Livy and Horace, in contrasting traditional with present-day practice, follow the convention of associating Rome's past success with the pious observation of the state cults.

(a) *Livy contrasts the mid-fifth century BC with his own time.*

But there had not yet come about that contempt for the gods which possesses the present generation; nor did everybody seek to construe oaths and laws to suit himself, but rather shaped his own practices by them.

Livy 3. 20. 5
tr. B. O. Foster (Loeb 1927)

(b)

Roman, though guiltless, thou must expiate
    Thy father's sins until thou build'st again
The temples, and the statues, desecrate
    With sooty smoke, and every fallen fane.

Thou reign'st because the gods are over thee.
    From them all policies and all success.
The gods neglected gave to Italy,
    Sorrowful country, many a distress.

Pacorus and Monaeses twice have smote
    Our expeditions, that with auspices
Unfavourable marched, and now they gloat
    To add our loot to their mean necklaces.

The Dacian and the Aethiop near won
    The City, when immersed in strife were we:
With navies formidable was the one,
    The other with a better archery.

This age so rife with wrong contaminates
   First marriage, then the race, and then the home.
And from this spring disaster percolates
   And overwhelms the populace and Rome.

With grown-up girls it now is all the rage
   To learn Ionic dances and to train
Their limbs for them, and from an early age
   To dream of loves from which they should abstain.

And younger lovers one will look for soon,
   And even where her husband drinks his wine;
Nor does she care to whom she gives the boon
   Of lawless love, where only dim lights shine,

But goes where bidden, in the sight of all,
   Even her husband knowing where she goes,
Whether it is some pedlar gives the call
   Or Spanish captain, who great pay bestows.

Not of these parents came that youthful band
   Who dyed the sea with Carthaginian gore,
And killed Antiochus and Pyrrhus and
   The dreadful Hannibal in days of yore:

But they were soldiers of a manly stock,
   Well skilled to turn the clods with Samnite spade,
Who brought cut logs, when shadows of the rock
   Grew long, to their stern mothers, as they bade.

Then would the setting sun from labouring
   And weary oxen take the yoke away,
And comes the friendly hour of evening
   And into night the Chariot rolls from day.

What is it withering time does not abate?
   Our fathers' age, worse than our grandsires' days,
Bore us still worse, soon a more profligate
   Posterity will take our wretched place.

Horace *Odes* 3.6
tr. Lord Dunsany and M. Oakley (J.M. Dent 1961)

110 Augustus' religious policy

The religious policy of Augustus emphasized the revival of traditional cults; cf. D2, 3.

As for religious matters, he did not allow the Egyptian rites to be celebrated inside the pomerium, but made provision for the temples; those which had been built by private individuals he ordered their sons and descendants, if any survived, to repair, and the rest he restored himself.

Dio Cassius 53. 2. 4
tr. E. Cary (Loeb 1977)

(b) *An indication of the fine distinctions behind Augustus' relgious policy. As well as stressing Augustus' respect for tradition, Suetonius might have pointed out that in the cults mentioned this is also reflected in a distinction between Hellenic and non-Hellenic practices.*

Augustus showed great respect towards all ancient and long-established foreign rites, but despised the rest. Once, for example, after becoming an adept in the Eleusinian Mysteries at Athens, he judged a case in which the privileges of Demeter's priests were questioned. Since certain religious secrets had to be quoted in the evidence, he cleared the court, dismissed his legal advisers and settled the dispute *in camera*. On the other hand, during his journey through Egypt he would not go out of his way, however slightly, to honour the divine Apis bull; and praised his grandson Gaius for not offering prayers to Jehovah when he visited Jerusalem.

Suetonius *Augustus* 93
tr. R. Graves (Penguin 1957)

I11 Benefactor cult

(a) *The* Natural History *of Pliny the Elder was published in AD 77 and dedicated to the Emperor Titus, to whom, as to Vespasian, Pliny was an* amicus. *The passage is cited here for its evidence on historical precedent relating to benefactor cult.*

For mortal to aid mortal—this is god; and this is the road to eternal glory; by this road went our Roman chieftains, by this road now proceeds with heavenward step, escorted by his children, the greatest ruler of all time, His Majesty Vespasian, coming to the succour of an exhausted world. To enrol such men among the deities is the most ancient method of paying them gratitude for their benefactions. In fact the names of the other gods, and also of the stars that I have mentioned above, originated from the services of men: at all events who would not admit that it is the interpretation of men's characters that prompts them to call each other Jupiter or Mercury or other names, and that originates the nomenclature of heaven?

Pliny *Natural History* 2. 18. 19
tr. H. Rackham (Loeb 1938)

(b) *Cicero takes up a favourite theme, his moral rectitude in provincial adminis-tration (cf. C17, 31). Note especially here his rejection of the material aspects of benefactor cult. Such rejection would not have been expected by either provincials or Romans.*

I myself left Tarsus for Asia on the Nones of January amid really indescribable enthusiasm among the Cilician communities, especially the people of Tarsus. After crossing the Taurus I found a marvellous eagerness for my arrival in the districts of Asia under me, which in the six months of my administration had not received a single letter of mine or seen a compulsory guest. Before my time that part of the year had regularly been occupied with profiteering of this sort. The richer commu-nities used to give large sums to avoid having troops quartered on them. The Cypriots gave 200 Attic talents. While I am governor the island will not be asked for a penny—that is not hyperbole, it is the naked truth. In return for these benefits, which dumbfound the provincials, I allow none but verbal honours to be decreed to me. I forbid statues, temples, chariots. Nor do I impose myself upon the com-munities in any other way—but perhaps I do upon you when I blow my own trumpet like this. Put up with it if you love me; after all it was you who wanted me to act so.

Cicero *Letters to Atticus* 5.21.7
tr. D. R. Shackleton Bailey (Cambridge 1968)

I12 The Sibylline Oracle

During the fifth century BC the Romans started to consult the oracle of the Sibyl of Cumae, the most northern Greek city in Campania, and later the Sacred Books (written in Greek) were put in the care of a priestly college, resulting in the pro-gressive Hellenization of the Roman state religion, including the introduction of new gods and rites. The last religious innovation was the introduction of the wor-ship of Magna Mater from Asia Minor in 205 BC. During the last century of the Republic the college became embroiled in political machination (see Cicero De Divinatione *2.54). Augustus took care to regularize the content of the books (see E10). See further W. Warde Fowler* The Religious Experience of the Roman People (*London 1911*).

Since the expulsion of the kings, the commonwealth, taking upon itself the guarding of these oracles, entrusts the care of them to persons of great distinction, who hold this office for life, being exempt from military service and from all civil em-ployment, and it assigns public slaves to assist them, in whose absence the others are not permitted to inspect the oracles. In short, there is no possession of the Romans, sacred or profane, which they guard so carefully as they do the Sibylline oracles. They consult them, by order of the senate, when the state is in the grip of party strife or some great misfortune has happened to them in war, or some important prodigies or apparitions have been seen which are difficult of interpretation, as has often happened. . . . In all this I am following the account given by Varro in his work on religion.

Dionysius of Halicarnassus *Roman Antiquities* 4. 62
tr. Lewis and Reinhold vol. 1

I13 Letter of the consuls concerning Bacchic associations

In the early second century BC the secret orgiastic rites of the Greek cult of Bacchus spread north from southern Italy, reaching Rome in 186 BC. Converts included members of the lower classes and slaves and it was probably fear of political conspiracy (as well as religious conservatism) which prompted the action of the Senate. Note especially that this senatorial decree applies to the whole of Italy, thus constituting direct control over the affairs of the Allies, and that the worship of Bacchus continued to be tolerated on an individual basis. For an account of the rumoured ritual see Livy 39. 8 ff. On Roman distrust of lower-class participation in organizations see also I57, 58.

[Letter of the consuls transmitting the decree of the senate concerning
Bacchic associations]
The consuls Quintus Marcius son of Lucius, and Spurius Postumius son of Lucius consulted the senate on the 7th day of October in the temple of Bellona. Present at the writing [of the decree] were Marcus Claudius son of Marcus, Lucius Valerius son of Publius, and Quintus Minucius son of Gaius.

In the matter of Bacchic orgies they passed a decree that the following proclamation should be issued to those who are allied with the Romans by treaty:

'Let none of them be minded to maintain a place of Bacchic worship. Should there be some who say they must needs maintain a place of Bacchic worship, they must come to the urban praetor at Rome, and our senate, when it has heard what they have to say, shall make decision on these matters, provided that at least one hundred senators be present when the matter is deliberated. Let no man, whether Roman citizen or of the Latin name or one of the allies, be minded to attend a meeting of Bacchant women without approaching the urban praetor and obtaining his authorization with the approval of the senate, provided that not fewer than one hundred senators be present when the matter is deliberated. Adopted.

'Let no man be a priest. Let not any man or woman be a master; nor let any of them be minded to keep a common fund; nor let any person be minded to make either man or woman a master or vice-master, or be minded henceforth to exchange oaths, vows, pledges, or promises with others, or be minded to plight faith with others. Let no one be minded to perform ceremonies in secret; nor let anyone be minded to perform ceremonies, whether in public or in private or outside the city, without approaching the urban praetor and obtaining his authorization with the approval of the senate, provided that not fewer than one hundred senators be present when the matter is deliberated. Adopted....

'Let no one be minded to hold services in a group larger than five men and women together, and let not more than two men and three women be minded to attend there among, except on authorization of the urban praetor and the senate as recorded above.'

You shall proclaim these orders at a public meeting for a period covering not less than three market days, and that you may be cognizant of the decree of the senate, the decree was as follows: They decreed that should there be any persons who act contrary to the provisions recorded above, proceedings for capital offense must be taken against them; and the senate deemed it right and proper that you engrave this on a bronze tablet and that you order it to be fastened up where it can most easily be read; and that within ten days after the delivery of this letter to you, you see to it that those places of Bacchic worship which may exist are dismantled, as recorded above, except if there be anything holy therein. Ager Teuranus.

> *CIL* 1² 581
> tr. Lewis and Reinhold vol. 1

I14 The cult of Aesculapius

The passage refers to the importation of the Greek god of medicine into the Roman Pantheon in 293 BC. This is important because it is the first extant example of cult being brought direct from Greece. Previous influence had been via the cults of the Latin and Greek cities of Italy.

The Romans on account of a pestilence, at the instructions of the Sibylline books, sent ten envoys under the leadership of Quintus Ogulnius to bring Aesculapius from Epidaurus. When they had arrived there and were marveling at the huge statue of the god, a serpent glided from the temple, an object of veneration rather than of horror, and to the astonishment of all made its way through the midst of the city to the Roman ship, and curled itself up in the tent of Ogulnius. The envoys sailed to Antium, carrying the god, where through the calm sea the serpent made its way to a nearby temple of Aesculapius, and after a few days returned to the ship. And when the ship was sailing up the Tiber, the serpent leaped on the nearby island, where a temple was established to him. The pestilence subsided with astonishing speed.

> Anonymous *On Famous Men* 22.1.1–3
> tr. Lewis and Reinhold vol. 1

I15 The cult of Isis and Serapis

The Hellenized Egyptian cult of Isis and Serapis came to the Greek cities in the south of Italy in the third century BC. It encountered the usual Roman suspicion for alien and secretive cults but was eventually recognized by Gaius. This extract is taken from an imaginative work of the second century AD and describes one of the cult festivals, symbolizing the spring opening of the navigation season. See also R. Witt Isis in the Graeco-Roman World *(Thames & Hudson 1971)*; Isis among the Greeks and Romans *(Harvard 1979)*.

Now the special procession of the savior goddess was moving by. Women resplendent in white garments, rejoicing in varied ornaments and wearing wreaths of spring flowers, strewed with blossoms from their bosoms the path along which the sacred procession was passing. Others turned shining mirrors, held behind their backs, toward the goddess as she came, to demonstrate their reverence on the way. Others, carrying ivory combs, with the gestures of their arms and the movements of their fingers went through the motions of combing and adorning the queenly hair. Others also sprinkled the streets with various ointments, including delightful balsam scattered drop by drop. In addition, there came a great number, of both sexes, with lamps, torches, wax tapers and other lights, propitiating with light the offspring of the celestial stars. Then pleasant harmonies sounded, pipes and flutes in the sweetest tones. These were followed by a delightful chorus of very select young men, resplendent in white garments and festal array, repeating a charming song. . . . There came, too, the trumpeters devoted to great Serapis, who with slanting reeds stretched to the right ear repeated the familiar melody of the temple and god. And there were many who called for free room for the sacred rites. Then poured in masses of initiates in the divine rites, men and women of every rank and every age, who glistened in their pure white linen garb. The women had their hair anointed and decked with a bright covering, but the men, their hair completely shaven, had glistening pates . . . and with timbrels of bronze, silver, aye and gold, they made a loud shrill jingling. But the principal priests, overseers of the sacred rites, who were appareled in surplices tightly girt round with white linen cloth and hanging down to the ground, carried the splendid trappings of the most powerful gods. . . .

Presently the gods came forth, deigning to walk on human feet. Here was Anubis, the awful messenger of the gods above and below, his face partly black and partly golden, lofty, raising up on high his dog's head, and bearing in his left hand his wand, and in his right hand shaking the green palm. Directly after followed, raised to an upright position, the image of the goddess, that is, the fruitful mother of all. . . . Another carried a spacious box of secrets concealing within the mysteries of the glorious religion. Another bore in his happy bosom the venerable image of the highest godhead, not like any beast, bird, wild animal or even human being, but made by a clever discovery, and therefore to be revered, an emblem ineffable of a somehow higher religion, one to be guarded with great silence. . . .

Meanwhile, amid the hubbub of the festive prayers, proceeding little by little we reached the sea. . . . There, after the images were duly arranged, we saw a boat skillfully wrought and variegated round about with the marvelous paintings of the Egyptians. This boat, most scrupulously purified, the high priest named after and dedicated to the goddess, intoning the most solemn prayers from his holy lips and purifying it with a glowing torch, an egg, and sulphur. The gleaming sail of this blessed bark bore the words of a vow woven into it; these words renewed the vow concerning the prosperous navigation of the new sailing season. The mast rose up high, made of pine, round and splendid, conspicuous for its remarkable masthead; the poop, fashioned in the shape of a goose's neck, gleamed with its covering of gold plate; and the whole ship, finished with bright citron wood, was magnificent. Then all the people, both priestly and lay, vied in heaping winnowing fans loaded with spices and such like offerings, and poured over the waves libations of these offerings mixed with milk, until the ship was filled with abundant devotions and propitious prayers; then it was loosened from its cables and given to the sea with a special serene breeze. And when we had lost sight of it because of the distance it had gone, each of them that bore the holy objects took up again and carried what he had brought, and eagerly took his way back to the shrine, maintaining the same order of procession.

When we came to the temple itself, the high priest, those who carried the divine images, and especially those who had long been initiated in the venerable secrets went into the chamber of the goddess and arranged in due fashion the lifelike images. Then one of these, whom all call the secretary, taking his place before the doors, summoned to a kind of meeting the company of the *pastophori*, which is the name of the holy college. From a raised platform he read forth from a book, offering propitious vows for the great emperor, the senate, the *equites*, the entire Roman people, and for the sailors and ships under the control and sovereignty of our world. Then he pronounced in the Greek tongue and manner, "*Ploiaphesia.*" The ensuing shout of the people indicated that this word brings good luck to all. And then, gleaming with joy, the populace, carrying leafy boughs, twigs, and garlands, kissed the places on the steps where the silver statue of the goddess had rested, and departed to their homes.

> Apuleius *The Golden Ass* (*Metamorphoses*) 11. 9–11; 16–17
> tr. Lewis and Reinhold vol. 2

116 Juvenal on Foreign rites

Juvenal is a late source. His first extant satires were not published until sometime between AD 100 and AD 110 when he was middle-aged and thus do not provide direct evidence for social attitudes under the Julio-Claudians. They are, however, useful as comparative material indicating the extent to which a biting satirist could vilify the importation into Rome of alien culture and practice which was already

attracting attention in earlier sources (cf. I10). See in general G. Highet Juvenal
the Satirist (Oxford 1954); J. Ferguson (ed.) *Juvenal (London 1979).*

> . . . And now in comes a procession,
> Devotees of the frenzied Bellona, and Cybele, Mother of Gods
> Led by a giant eunuch, the idol of his lesser
> Companions in obscenity. Long ago, with a sherd,
> He sliced off his genitals: now neither the howling rabble
> Nor the kettledrums can outshriek him. His plebeian cheeks
> Are framed in a Phrygian mitre. With awesome utterance
> He bids her beware of September and its siroccos—
> Unless, that is, she lays out a hundred eggs
> For purificatory rites, and makes him a present
> Of some old clothes, russet-coloured, so that any calamity,
> However sudden or frightful, may pass into the garments—
> A package-deal expiation, valid for twelve whole months.
> In winter she'll break the ice, descend into the river,
> And thrice, before noon, let the eddies of Tiber close
> Over her timorous head; then crawl out, naked, trembling,
> And shuffle on bleeding knees, by way of penance,
> Across the Field of Mars. Indeed, if white Io so orders,
> She'll make a pilgrimage to the ends of Egypt,
> Fetch water from tropic Meroë for the aspersion
> Of Isis's temple, that stands beside those ancient sheep-pens
> The public polling-booths. She believes that she's summoned
> By the voice of the Lady herself—just the sort of rare
> Mind and spirit, no doubt, that a god *would* choose to talk to
> In the small hours! That's why high praise and special honours
> Go to her dogheaded colleague, Anubis, who runs through the streets
> With a shaven-pated crew dressed in linen robes, and mocks
> The people's grief for Osiris. He it is who intercedes
> For wives who fail to abstain from sex on the prescribed
> And ritual days, exacting huge penalties
> When the marriage-bed is polluted, or when the silver
> Serpent appears to nod. His tears and professional
> Mutterings—after Osiris has been bribed with a fat goose
> And some sacrificial cake—will guarantee absolution.
> No sooner has *he* pushed off than a palsied Jewess,
> Parking her haybox outside, comes round soliciting alms
> In a breathy whisper. She knows, and can interpret,
> The Laws of Jerusalem: a high-priestess-under-the-trees,
> A faithful mediator of Heaven on earth. She too
> Fills her palm, but more sparingly: Jews will sell you
> Whatever dreams you like for a few small coppers.

Then there are fortune-tellers, Armenians, Syrians,
Who'll pry out the steaming lungs of a pigeon, predict
A young lover for the lady, or a good fat inheritance
From some childless millionaire. They'll probe a chicken's
Bosom, unravel the guts of a puppy: sometimes
They even slaughter a child. The seer can always
Turn informer on his client.
                         Chaldaean astrologers
Will inspire more confidence: their every pronouncement
Is a straight tip, clients believe, from the oracular fountain
Of Ammon. (Now that Delphi has fallen silent
The human race is condemned to murky unknowing
Of what the future may bring.) The most successful
Have been exiled on several occasions—like you-know-who
With his venal friendship and rigged predictions, who settled
The hash of that great citizen dreaded by Otho . . .

Juvenal *Satires* 6. 512–58
tr. P. Green (Penguin 1967)

(b) *Juvenal's emphasis is on the influx of aliens from the Hellenized east (cf. I19).*

'Now let me turn to that race which goes down so well
With our millionaires, but remains *my* special pet aversion,
And not mince my words. I cannot, citizens, stomach
A Greek-struck Rome. Yet what fraction of these sweepings
Derives, in fact, from Greece? For years now Syrian
Orontes has poured its sewerage into our native Tiber—
Its lingo and manners, its flutes, its outlandish harps
With their transverse strings, its native tambourines,
And the whores who hang out round the race-course.
        (That's where to go
If you fancy a foreign piece in one of those saucy toques.)
Our beloved Founder should see how his homespun rustics
Behave today, with their dinner-pumps—*trechedipna*
They call them—not to mention their *niceteria*
(Decorations to you) hung round their *ceromatic* (that's
Well-greased) wrestlers' necks.

Juvenal *Satires* 3. 59–67
tr. P. Green (Penguin 1967)

I17 Augustus' treatment of the Jews in Rome

By the 'sacred money' Philo means the annual tax paid by all adult male Jews throughout the world for the upkeep of the Temple.

Augustus knew that the large district of Rome beyond the Tiber was owned and inhabited by Jews. The majority of them were Roman freedmen. They had been brought to Italy as prisoners of war and manumitted by their owners, and had not been made to alter any of their national customs. Augustus therefore knew that they had synagogues and met in them, especially on the Sabbath, when they received public instruction in their national philosophy. He also knew that they collected sacred money from their 'first-fruits' and sent it up to Jerusalem by the hand of envoys who would offer the sacrifices. But despite this he did not expel them from Rome or deprive them of their Roman citizenship because they remembered their Jewish nationality also. He introduced no changes into their synagogues, he did not prevent them from meeting for the exposition of the Law, and he raised no objection to their offering of the 'first-fruits'. On the contrary, he showed such reverence for our traditions that he and almost all his family enriched our Temple with expensive dedications. He gave orders for regular sacrifices of holocausts to be made daily in perpetuity at his own expense, as an offering to the Most High God. These sacrifices continue to this day, and will continue always, as a proof of his truly imperial character. Moreover, at the monthly distributions in Rome, when all the people in turn receive money or food, he never deprived Jews of this bounty, but if the distribution happened to be made on the Sabbath, when it is forbidden to receive or give anything or to do any of the ordinary things of life in general, especially commercial life, he instructed the distributors to reserve the Jews' share of the universal largesse until the next day.

Philo *Legatio* 155–8
tr. E. M. Smallwood (E. J. Brill 1970)

I18 A decree of Augustus about the rights of the Jews (AD 2/3)

The reference at the end to Censorinus, proconsul of Asia AD 2/3, dates the document.

'Caesar Augustus, Pontifex Maximus with tribunician power, decrees as follows. Since the Jewish nation has been found well-disposed to the Roman people not only at the present time but also in time past, and especially in the time of my father the emperor Caesar, as has their high priest Hyrcanus, it has been decided by me and my council under oath, with the consent of the Roman people, that the Jews may follow their own customs in accordance with the law of their fathers, just as they followed them in the time of Hyrcanus, high priest of the Most High God, and that their sacred monies shall be inviolable and may be sent up to Jerusalem and delivered to the treasurers in Jerusalem, and that they need not give bond to appear in court on the Sabbath or on the day of preparation for it after the ninth hour. And if anyone is caught stealing their sacred books or their sacred monies from a synagogue or an ark of the Law, he shall be regarded as sacrilegious, and his property shall be confiscated to the public treasury of the Romans. As for the resolution which was offered by them in my honour concerning the piety which I show to all men, and on behalf of C. Marcius Censorinus, I order that it and the present edict be set up in the most conspicuous part of the temple assigned to me by the federation of Asia in Ancyra. If anyone transgresses any of the above ordinances, he shall suffer severe punishment.' This was inscribed on a pillar in the temple of Caesar.

Josephus *AJ* 16. 162–5
tr. R. Marcus and A. Wikgren (Loeb 1963)

119 The case against Greek influence

(a) *Cato illustrates an extreme case of the opposition among traditionalists to the increasing influence of Greek culture and philosophy in Rome in the second century BC. The visit described took place in 155 BC. Note that opposition was based on moral scruples. In the same work (12) Plutarch attributes to Cato 'the words of the Romans come from their hearts while those of the Greeks come from their lips'; cf. also Athenaeus,* Savants at Dinner *12. 547a: 'The Romans, therefore, the most virtuous men in all things, did a good job when they banished the Epicureans [173 BC] . . . because of the pleasures which they introduced.'*

When Cato was already an old man, Carneades the Academic and Diogenes the Stoic came as envoys from Athens to Rome. . . . The most studious of the youth at once went to wait upon these men, and frequently heard them speak with admiration. But the charm of Carneades, which had boundless power and a reputation equal to it, won large and sympathetic audiences, and filled the city with its sound, like a wind. The report spread far and wide that a Greek of amazing talent, who charmed and disarmed everybody, had infused a powerful passion into the young men, so that forsaking their other pleasures and pursuits, they were in ecstasies about philosophy. This pleased the other Romans, and they were glad to see the youth participating in Greek culture and consorting with such remarkable men. But Cato, when this passion for discussion came flowing into the city, from the beginning was distressed, fearing lest the youth, by diverting their ambitions in this direction, should prefer a reputation for speaking well before that of deeds and military campaigns. And when the fame of the philosophers increased in the city,

399

and a distinguished man, Gaius Acilius, at his own request became their interpreter to the senate at their first audience, Cato determined, under a specious pretext, to have all philosophers cleared out of the city. And coming into the senate he blamed the magistrates for letting those envoys stay so long a time without settling the matter, though they were such persuasive persons that they could easily secure anything they wished; that therefore a decision should be made and a vote taken on the embassy as soon as possible, so that they might go home again to their own schools and lecture to the sons of the Greeks, while the Roman youth listened, as hitherto, to their own laws and magistrates.

He did this not out of hostility, as some think, to Carneades, but because he wholly despised philosophy, and out of a patriotic zeal mocked all Greek culture and learning. . . . And to prejudice his son against anything that was Greek, in a rasher voice than became one of his age, he declared, as it were with the voice of a prophet or seer, that the Romans would lose their empire when they began to be infected with Greek literature. But indeed time has shown the vanity of this prophecy of doom, for while the city was at the zenith of her empire she made all Greek learning and culture her own.

Plutarch *Life of Cato the Elder* 22-23b (abridged)
tr. Lewis and Reinhold vol. 1

120 Cicero acknowledges Greek influence

Though I wrote and read and declaimed daily with unflagging interest, yet I was not satisfied to confine myself only to rhetorical exercises. . . . For the study of civil law I attached myself to Quintus Scaevola, the son of Quintus; he took no pupils, but the legal opinions given to his clients taught those who wished to hear him. The year following this was the consulship of Sulla and Pompey. Publius Sulpicius was tribune at that time and addressed the people daily, so that I came to know his style thoroughly. At this time Philo, then head of the Academy, along with a group of loyal Athenians, had fled from Athens because of the Mithridatic War and had come to Rome. Filled with great enthusiasm for the study of philosophy, I gave myself up wholly to his instruction. In so doing I tarried with him the more faithfully, for though the variety and sublimity of his subject delighted and held me, yet it appeared as if the whole institution of courts of justice had vanished for ever. . . . At this time too I devoted myself to study at Rome with Molo of Rhodes, famous as a pleader and teacher. . . .

For a space of about three years the city was free from the threat of arms. . . . During all this time I spent my days and nights in study of every kind. I worked with Diodotus the Stoic, who made his residence in my house, and after a life of long intimacy died there only a short time ago. From him, apart from other subjects, I received thorough training in dialectic, which may be looked upon as a contracted or compressed eloquence. Without it you too, Brutus, have held that eloquence properly so called (which your philosophers tell us is an expanded dialectic) is impossible. But though I devoted myself to his teaching and to the wide range of subjects at his command, yet I allowed no day to pass without some rhetorical exercises. I prepared and delivered declamations (the term now in vogue), most often with Marcus Piso and Quintus Pompeius, or indeed with anyone, daily. This exercise I practiced much in Latin, but more often in Greek, partly because Greek, offering more opportunity for stylistic embellishment, accustomed me to a similar habit in using Latin, but partly too because the foremost teachers, knowing only Greek, could not, unless I used Greek, correct my faults nor convey their instruction.

Meantime, in the process of restoring orderly government, violence broke out again. . . . Measures were enacted for the reconstitution of the courts and stable government was at length restored. . . . It was not until this time that I first began to undertake cases both civil and criminal, for it was my ambition, not (as most do) to learn my trade in the Forum, but so far as possible to enter the Forum already trained. At this time too I devoted myself to study with Molo; for it chanced that he came to Rome in the dictatorship of Sulla as a member of a commission to the senate with regard to the reimbursement of Rhodes. Thus my first criminal case, spoken in behalf of Sextus Roscius, won such favorable comment that I was esteemed not incompetent to handle any litigation whatsoever. There followed then in quick succession many other cases which I brought into court, carefully worked out, and, as the saying is, smelling somewhat of the midnight oil. . . .

However, having come to the conclusion that with relaxation and better control of my voice, as well as with modification of my general style of speaking, I should at once avoid risk to my health and acquire a more tempered style—to effect this change in habit of speaking was the reason for my departure for Asia Minor. Thus I had been active in practice for two years and my name was already well known in the Forum at the time when I left Rome.

Arriving at Athens I spent six months with Antiochus, the wise and famous philosopher of the Old Academy, and with him as my guide and teacher I took up again the study of philosophy, which from my early youth I had pursued, and had made some progress in, and had never wholly let drop. But at the same time at Athens I continued zealously with rhetorical exercises under the direction of Demetrius the Syrian, an experienced teacher of eloquence not without some reputation. Afterwards I traveled through all of Asia Minor and was with the most distinguished orators of the region, who were generous in giving me opportunity to practice declamatory exercises with them. The chief of these was Menippus of Stratonicea, in my judgment the most eloquent man of all Asia in that time; and certainly, if to speak without affectation and without offense to good taste is Attic, he was an orator who could justly be placed in that category. But the one most constantly with me was Dionysius of Magnesia. There were also Aeschylus of Cnidus and Xenocles of Adramyttium. These men were at that time accounted the principal teachers of oratory in Asia. However, not content with them, I went to Rhodes and attached myself to Molo, whom I had already heard at Rome. . . . Thus I came back after two years' absence not only better trained, but almost transformed.

Cicero *Brutus* 89–91
tr. G. L. Hendrickson and G. M. Hubbell (Loeb) abridged Lewis and Reinhold vol. 1

I21 Cicero emphasizes the moral role of literature

For if anyone thinks that the glory won by the writing of Greek verse is naturally less than that accorded to the poet who writes in Latin, he is entirely in the wrong. Greek literature is read in nearly every nation under heaven, while the vogue of Latin is confined to its own boundaries, and they are, we must grant, narrow. Seeing, therefore, that the activities of our race know no barrier save the limits of the round earth, we ought to be ambitious that whithersoever our arms have penetrated there also our fame and glory should extend; for the reason that literature exalts the nation whose high deeds it sings, and at the same time there can be no doubt that those who stake their lives to fight in honour's cause find therein a lofty incentive to peril and endeavour.

Cicero *pro Archia Poeta* 10. 23
tr. M. H. Watts (Loeb 1923)

I22 A need for Roman historiography

Cicero, his brother Quintus, and friend Atticus discuss the need for a Roman historiography to rival that of the Greeks.

Q. As I understand it, then, my dear brother, you believe that different principles are to be followed in history and in poetry.

M. Certainly, Quintus; for in history the standard by which everything is judged is the truth, while in poetry it is generally the pleasure one gives; however, in the works of Herodotus, the Father of History, and in those of Theopompus, one finds innumerable fabulous tales.

A. I now have an opportunity which I have been wanting, and I shall not let it pass.

M. What do you mean, Titus?

A. There has long been a desire, or rather a demand, that you should write a history. For people think that, if you entered that field, we might rival Greece in this branch of literature also. And to give you my own opinion, it seems to me that you owe this duty not merely to the desires of those who take pleasure in literature, but also to your country, in order that the land which you have saved you may also glorify. For our national literature is deficient in history, as I realize myself and as I frequently hear you say. But you can certainly fill this gap satisfactorily, since, as you at least have always believed, this branch of literature is closer than any other to oratory. Therefore take up the task, we beg of you, and find the time for a duty which has hitherto been either overlooked or neglected by our countrymen. For after the annals of the chief pontiffs, which are records of the driest possible character, when we come to Fabius, or to Cato (whose name is always on your lips), or to Piso, Fannius, or Vennonius, although one of these may display more vigour than another, yet what could be more lifeless than the whole group? Fannius' contemporary, Antipater, to be sure, blew a somewhat more forceful strain, and showed some power, though of a rough and rustic character, lacking in polish and the skill that comes from training; nevertheless he might have served as a warning to his successors that they should take greater pains with their writing. But lo and behold, his successors were those fine specimens, Clodius and Asellio! These two are not to be compared with Coelius, but rather with the feebleness and clumsiness of our earlier historians. And why should I even mention Macer? His long-winded style shows indeed some little acumen (though borrowed not from the Greeks' wealth of knowledge, but from the Roman copyists), but his speeches contain many absurdities, and his elevated passages are exaggerated beyond all bounds. His friend Sisenna has easily surpassed all our other historians up to the present time, with the exception of those whose works may not yet have been published, and therefore cannot be estimated. Yet he has never been considered an orator of your rank, and in his historical writing he has an almost childish purpose in view, for it seems that Clitarchus is absolutely the only Greek author whom he has read, and that his sole desire is to imitate him. And even if he had succeeded in this, he would still be considerably below the highest standards. Therefore this task is yours; its accomplishment is expected of you—that is, if Quintus agrees with me.

Cicero *Laws* 1. 5-7
tr. C. W. Keyes (Loeb 1928)

123 Hellenic Values

1   Famous sportsmen who win victories at Olympia, Corinth and Nemea, have been assigned such great distinctions by the ancestors of the Greeks that they not only receive praise publicly at the games, as they stand with palm and crown, but also when they go back victorious to their own people they ride triumphant with their four-horse chariots into their native cities, and enjoy a pension for life from the State. When I observe this, I am surprised that similar or even greater distinctions are not assigned to those authors who confer infinite benefits on mankind throughout

the ages. For this is the more worthy of enactment, in that while sportsmen make their own bodies stronger, authors not only cultivate their own perceptions, but by the information in their books prepare the minds of all to acquire knowledge and thus to stimulate their talents.

2   For in what respect could Milo of Croton advantage mankind because he was unconquered, or others who won victories in the same kind, except that in their lifetime they enjoyed distinction among their fellow-citizens? But the daily teachings of Pythagoras, Democritus, Plato, Aristotle, and other thinkers, elaborated as they were by unbroken application, furnish ever-fresh and flowering harvests, not only to their fellow-citizens but also to all mankind. Those who from tender years are satisfied thence with abundance of knowledge, acquire the best habits of thought, institute civilised manners, equal rights, laws without which no state can be secure. 3. Since, therefore, such boons have been conferred on individuals and communities by wise writers, not only do I think that palms and crowns should be awarded to them, but that triumphs also should be decreed and that they should be canonised in the mansions of the gods.

I will propose, as examples taken from a great number, several conceptions of a few thinkers which have helped the furnishing of human life, in order that the consideration of these may lead mankind to confess that honours should be conferred upon their inventors.

Vitruvius 9. 1–3
tr. F. Granger (Loeb 1934)

I24   Changes in the function and characteristics of oratory

(a) *A selection of captions to rhetorical exercises from the handbooks of Seneca the Elder (c. 55 BC — c. 37–41 AD). Notice that some of the captions reflect his attachment to the traditional subject areas of politics and morality.*

Three hundred Spartans sent against Xerxes, when the contingents of three hundred sent from all [the rest of] Greece had fled, deliberate whether they too should flee.
    Cicero deliberates whether he should beg Antony for mercy.
    Cicero deliberates whether he should burn his writings since Antony promises he will be unharmed if he does.

A priestess must be supremely chaste and pure. A maiden was captured by pirates and sold. She was bought by a procurer and made a prostitute. But she prevailed upon those who came to her to pay her her fee [without intercourse]. When she could not prevail upon a soldier who had come to her, and he struggled with her and attacked her, she killed him. She was indicted, acquitted, and returned to her people. She seeks to become a priestess. The petition is opposed.

A man was captured by pirates and wrote to his father for ransom; he was not ransomed. The daughter of the pirate chief made him swear that he would marry her if he were released, and he swore it. She left her father and eloped with the young man. He returned to his father and married her. A rich widow crosses their path. The father orders him to divorce the daughter of the pirate chief and marry the widow. He refuses and is disinherited.

A blind man is entitled to receive 1,000 *denarii* from the public treasury. Ten young men, when they had dissipated their fortunes, drew lots under an agreement that the one whose name was drawn would be blinded and thus get 1,000 *denarii*. The lot of one was drawn, and he was blinded. He applies for the 1,000 *denarii*. The application is denied.

Injury of known origin is actionable. A man whose life was wrecked, his three children and wife lost when his house burned, hanged himself. A passer-by cut down the noose. He is prosecuted by the released man for injury.

Seneca the Elder *Suasoriae* and *Controversiae* (extracts)
tr. Lewis and Reinhold vol. 2

(b) *The authorship of the dialogue, probably composed in the last years of the first century AD, has been disputed by some scholars. What is important here is the historical perspective underlying the strictures about the divorce of oratory from its political basis.*

Only he is an orator who can speak on any topic with beauty and elegance and in a manner that carries conviction, in keeping with the importance of the subject, appropriately to the circumstances, with pleasure to the audience. The men of earlier days were convinced of this. They understood that to accomplish this required, not declaiming in rhetoricians' schools, not exercising merely the tongue and the voice in fictitious debates without any sort of approach to reality, but imbuing the mind with those disciplines that deal with good and evil, honor and dishonor, right and wrong; for this is the orator's subject matter. . . . The accomplished speakers of modern times are so completely unconcerned about this that you can detect in their pleadings the unseemly and shameful defects of modern colloquial speech. And also, they know nothing of legislation, have no grasp of the decrees of the senate, actually scoff at the civil law, and have a positive horror of the study of philosophy and the teachings of the sages. They have banished oratory, as it were, from her rightful realm and reduce her to a handful of commonplace and narrow platitudes, so that she who was once mistress of all the arts and imbued our minds with her noble retinue is now clipped and docked, without state, without esteem, I almost said without her free birthright, and is learned like one of the meanest handicrafts. This, then, is in my opinion the prime and principal reason why we have degenerated to such an extent from the eloquence of the orators of old.

Tacitus *Dialogue on Oratory* 30–2 (selections)
tr. Lewis and Reinhold vol. 2

125 Art collecting or luxury?

(a) *Cicero here, for forensic purposes, presents art collecting from the conquered as a form of corruption. The two speeches against Verres are important sources for the study of provincial administration and its abuse in the late Republic. Ironically, Verres was later proscribed by Antony, who coveted his art treasures.*

Among all the treasures that so richly adorn this beautiful city of ours, is there one statue, one picture, that has not been captured and brought hither from the enemies we have defeated in war? And the country houses of our wealthy men are furnished to overflowing with the countless beautiful things stripped from our most loyal allies. . . . Believe me, gentlemen—though I am quite sure that you have yourselves heard what I am about to tell you—in spite of all the disasters that in recent years have befallen both our allies and foreign peoples, and all the wrongs they have suffered, nothing is causing or has caused more distress to the Greek populations than such plunderings of temples and towns.

Cicero *Against Verres* 2. 5. 48. 127; 4. 59. 132
tr. Lewis and Reinhold vol. 1

(b) *The Epicurean Lucullus was the brother-in-law of Clodius and had a distinguished career as soldier and administrator, attaining the consulate in 74 BC. In 59 his unhappy relationship with Caesar prompted him to retire to pursue his love of literature, the arts, and luxury. He died insane. On luxury and the sumptuary laws of Augustus cf. D16–17.*

And, indeed, Lucullus' life, like the Old Comedy, presents us at the beginning with political acts and military commands, and at the end with drinking bouts and banquets, and what were practically orgies, and torch races, and all manner of frivolity. For I count as frivolity his sumptuous buildings, porticoes, and baths, still more his paintings and statues, and all his enthusiasm for these arts, which he collected at vast expense, lavishly pouring out on them the vast and splendid wealth which he acquired in his campaigns. Even now, with all the advance of luxury, the Lucullan gardens are counted the most costly of the imperial gardens. When Tubero the Stoic saw Lucullus' works on the seashore and near Naples, where he suspended hills over vast tunnels, encircling his residences with moats of sea water and with streams for breeding fish, and built villas into the sea, he called him Xerxes in a toga. . . .

Lucullus' daily dinners were ostentatiously extravagant—not only their purple coverlets, beakers adorned with precious stones, choruses, and dramatic recitations, but also their display of all sorts of meats and daintily prepared dishes—making him an object of envy to the vulgar. . . . Once when he dined alone, he became angry because only one modest course had been prepared, and called the slave in charge. When the latter said that he did not think that there would be need of anything expensive since there were no guests, Lucullus said, 'What, do you not know that today Lucullus dines with Lucullus?'

Plutarch *Life of Lucullus* 39.1–41.2
abridged and tr. Lewis and Reinhold vol. 1

126 The cost of luxury

The Natural History *is the only surviving work among the Elder Pliny's vast output (AD 23/4–79). Completed towards the end of his life his encyclopaedic work draws on material obtained from studies and travel during a busy military, legal, and administrative career in the Equestrian* cursus. *It is also an important source for the study of Roman agriculture (cf. 134 ff.).*

At the lowest reckoning India, China, and the Arabian peninsula drain our Empire of 100,000,000 sesterces every year—that is what our luxuries and womenfolk cost us.

Pliny *Natural History* 12.41.84
tr. Lewis and Reinhold vol. 2

127 The increase of luxury

(a) *The context is that of the increase in luxury (see I25–6) and the apparently un-successful sumptuary legislation of Augustus (D16–17). The consuls had drawn Tiberius' attention to the effect of gluttony on the price of necessities. Dio Cassius also refers to legislation by Tiberius in AD 16 forbidding the wearing of silk clothing by men and the use of golden tableware except for religious purposes (57.15.1).*

. . . What am I to start with prohibiting and cutting down to the standard of old? The vast size of the country manors? The number of slaves of every nationality? The weight of silver and gold? The marvels in bronze and painting? The indiscriminate dress of men and women, or that luxury peculiar to the women alone which, for the sake of jewels, diverts our riches to foreign and even hostile peoples?

I am not unaware that at dinner parties and social gatherings these excesses are condemned and a limit is demanded. But let anyone enact a law imposing penalties, and those very same persons will clamor that the state is being subverted, that this means ruin for every member of high society, that no one is guiltless.

Tacitus *Annals* 3. 53–4 (abridged)
tr. Lewis and Reinhold vol. 2

(b) *Gaul as a source of wealth*

Rome's relations with the provinces and client kingdoms were interrelated at many levels, economic, military, cultural (cf. I30–3 and C10 ff.).

Domitius and Fabius, son of Paulus, who was surnamed Allobrogicus, first entered the Gauls with an army; later these provinces cost us much blood in our attempts at conquest alternating with our loss of them. In all these operations the work of Caesar is the most brilliant and most conspicuous. Reduced under his auspices and generalship, they pay almost as much tribute into the treasury as the rest of the world.

Velleius Paterculus 2. 39
tr. F. W. Shipley (Loeb 1924)

I28 Trade

Strabo (64/3 BC – AD 21 or later) was a Greek of partly Asiatic origin. His Histori-cal Sketches are lost. His Geography in seventeen books survives. For a geographer he was surprisingly little travelled and his work emphasizes the use of geography in public affairs, rather than its scientific aspects. Turdetania was a region in the south-western part of the Iberian peninsula. Elsewhere (Geog. 3. 2. 5) Strabo says 'all their foreign trade is carried on with Italy and Rome'. Synnada is in Asia.

(a)
There are exported from Turdetania large quantities of grain and wine, and also olive oil, not only in large quantities but also of best quality. And further, wax, honey, and pitch are exported from there, and large quantities of kermes, and ruddle which is not inferior to the Sinopean earth. And they build their ships there out of native timber; and they have salt quarries in their country, and not a few streams of salt water. Not unimportant, either, is the fish-salting industry that is carried on, not only from this region but also from the rest of the seaboard outside the Pillars [Strait of Gibraltar], and the product is not inferior to that of the Pontus [Black Sea]. Formerly much cloth came from Turdetania, but now wool,

especially of the raven-black sort, which is surpassingly beautiful; at all events, the rams are bought for breeding purposes at a talent apiece. Surpassing, too, are the delicate fabrics which are woven by the people of Salacia. Turdetania also has a great abundance of cattle of all kinds, and of game. . . . The abundance of the exports of Turdetania is indicated by the size and the number of the ships, for merchantmen of the greatest size sail from this region to Puteoli and to Ostia, the seaport of Rome. . . .

(b)

Synnada is not a large city; but there lies in front of it a plain planted with olives, about sixty stadia in circuit [?]. And beyond it is Docimaea, a village, and also the quarry of 'Synnadic' marble (so the Romans call it, though the natives call it 'Docimite' or 'Docimaean'). At first this quarry yielded only stones of small size, but on account of the present extravagance of the Romans great monolithic pillars are taken from it, which in their variety of colors are so nearly like the alabastrite marble; so that, although the transportation of such heavy burdens to the sea is difficult, still, both pillars and slabs, remarkable for their size and beauty, are conveyed to Rome. . . .

Strabo *Geography* 3. 2. 6; 12. 8. 14, 16 (abridged)
tr. H. L. Jones (Loeb 1923, 1928) Lewis and Reinhold vol. 2

129 Travel and trade by sea

(a)

Two prefects of Egypt, Galerius and Balbillus, made the passage from the Straits of Sicily to Alexandria in under seven and six days, respectively. Fifteen years later Valerius Marianus, a senator of praetorian rank, made Alexandria from Puteoli in less than nine days, in summertime, on a very light breeze. To think that [commerce] brings Cádiz, by the Strait of Gibraltar, within seven days of Ostia, Hither Spain within four days, the province of Narbonese Gaul within three, and Africa, even on a very gentle breeze, within two (as happened to Gaius Flavius, legate of the proconsul Vibius Crispus)!

Pliny *Natural History* 19. 1. 3-4
tr. Lewis and Reinhold vol. 2

(b)

The work of the jurist Gaius (2nd century AD) is characterized by an interest in historical explanation (sometimes mistaken). The reference here is to Junian Latins and the validity of the passage is supported by Suetonius Claudius 19. *Note that Rome relied on private ship-owners* (navicularii) *to transport supplies to Rome and to the army. It was not until the third century AD that they were absorbed into the Imperial service.*

Likewise, by an edict of Claudius, Latins acquire Roman citizenship if they build a seagoing vessel of a capacity of not less than 10,000 *modii* of grain, and if that ship, or another in its place, carries grain to Rome for six years.

Gaius *Institutes* 1. 32 c
tr. Lewis and Reinhold vol. 2

I30 Wheat from the provinces

Nothing is more prolific than wheat. Nature has given it this attribute since she nourishes man chiefly on it. A single *modius* of wheat, if the soil is suitable, like that of the Byzacium plain in Africa, yields 150 *modii*. From that region the deified Augustus received from his procurator—incredible as it seems—a shipment of almost 400 shoots grown from a single grain (the correspondence on this matter is still extant). Nero, similarly, received 360 stalks grown from one grain. The plains of Leontini and elsewhere in Sicily, the whole of Baetic Spain, and especially Egypt, yield wheat a good hundredfold.

Pliny *Natural History* 18. 21
tr. Lewis and Reinhold vol. 2

I31 Claudius' dispositions in the provinces

(a) *For the strategic importance of client states see further C10, 13.*

Next Claudius restored Commagene to Antiochus, since Gaius, though he had him-self given him the district, had taken it away again; and Mithridates the Iberian, whom Gaius had summoned and imprisoned, was sent home again to resume his throne. To another Mithridates, a descendant of Mithridates the Great, he granted the kingdom of Bosporus, giving to Polemo some land in Cilicia in place of it. He enlarged the domain of Agrippa of Palestine, who, happening to be in Rome, had helped him to become emperor, and he bestowed on him the rank of consul; and to his brother Herod he gave the rank of praetor and a principality. And he permitted them to enter the senate and to express thanks to him in Greek.

Dio Cassius *Roman History* 60. 8. 1–3
tr. E. Cary (Loeb 1924) Lewis and Reinhold vol. 2

(b) *The passage refers to AD 49 and highlights another episode in Claudius' relations with the provincial aristocracy. Special permission was normally necessary for Senators to visit their estates outside Italy.*

Also condemned at this time was Gaius Cadius Rufus, a governor of Bithynia, who was charged by its people for extortion. Another province, Narbonese Gaul, received a privilege for its deferential attitude to the senate: senators originating from it were allowed to visit their homes without the emperor's permission, as was already permitted to members from Sicily. Ituraea and Judaea, on the deaths of their monarchs, Sohaemus and Agrippa respectively, were incorporated in the province of Syria.

Tacitus *Annals* 12. 22–3
tr. M. Grant (Penguin 1971)

132 Armenia

Armenia had been in dispute between Rome and Parthia for many years. Thus prestige to Nero achieved by Tiridates' acceptance of Roman overlordship was enormous (Tiridates was the brother of the ruler of the Parthian Empire. For the emotive significance of earlier relations with Parthia cf. E6).

Tiridates set out for Rome, bringing with him not only his own sons but also those of Vologeses, Pacorus, and Monobazus. Their progress all the way from the Euphrates was like a triumphal procession. . . . The prince covered the whole distance as far as Italy on horseback, and beside him rode his wife, wearing a golden helmet in place of a veil, so as not to go counter to her native customs by letting her face be seen. In Italy he was conveyed in a chariot sent by Nero and met the emperor at Naples. . . . He refused, however, to obey the order to lay aside his sword when he approached the emperor, but fastened it to the scabbard with nails. Yet he knelt upon the ground, and with arms crossed called him master, and did obeisance. . . .

After this Nero conducted him to Rome and set the diadem upon his head. The entire city had been decorated with torches and garlands, and great crowds of people were to be seen everywhere, the Forum being especially full. . . . Everything had been prepared during the night; and at daybreak Nero, wearing the triumphal garb and accompanied by the senate and the Praetorian Guards, entered the Forum. He ascended the *Rostra* and seated himself upon a chair of state. Next Tiridates and his retinue passed between lines of armed troops drawn up on either side, took their stand before the *Rostra*, and did obeisance to the emperor as they had done before. At this a great roar went up, which so alarmed Tiridates that for some moments he stood speechless, in terror of his life. Then, silence having been proclaimed, he recovered courage and quelling his pride made himself subservient to the necessities of the occasion, caring little how humbly he spoke, in view of the prize he hoped to obtain. These were his words: 'Master, I am the descendant of Arsaces, brother of the kings Vologeses and Pacorus, and thy slave. And I have come to thee, my god, to worship thee as I do Mithras. Whatever destiny thou spinnest for me shall be mine; for thou art my fate and my fortune.' Nero replied to him as follows: 'Well hast thou done to come hither in person, that meeting me face to face thou mayest enjoy my grace. For what neither thy father left thee nor thy brothers gave and preserved for thee, this do I grant thee. King of Armenia I now declare thee, that both thou and they may understand that I have the power to take away kingdoms and to bestow them.' At the close of these words he bade him ascend by the approach which had been built in front of the *Rostra* expressly for this occasion, and when Tiridates had been made to sit beneath his feet, he placed the diadem upon his head.

> Dio Cassius *Roman History* 63. 1. 2–5. 4 (abridged)
> tr. E. Cary (Loeb 1924) adapted Lewis and Reinhold vol. 2

I33 Prosecution of a provincial governor

The trial occurred in AD 100/1; for Pliny see I41, introduction.

To Cornelius Minicianus

At last I can give you a full account of all the trouble I have had over the public action brought by the province of Baetica, a most complicated case which after several hearings ended in a variety of sentences: the reason for which you shall hear.

Caecilius Classicus had been governor of Baetica in the same year that Marius Priscus was in Africa. His rapacity during this time was matched by his brutality, for he was a scoundrel who made no secret of his evil ways. It so happened that Priscus came from Baetica and Classicus from Africa; hence the joke current among the Baetici (for exasperation often breaks out into wit)—'I got as bad as I gave'. However, Priscus was brought to trial by a single city along with several private individuals, whereas Classicus was attacked by the entire province. He forestalled the trial by his death, which might have been accidental or self-inflicted; there was much general suspicion but no definite proof, for, though it seemed likely that he intended to die since he could not defend himself, it is surprising that he should have died to escape the shame of condemnation for deeds which he was not ashamed to do. Nevertheless, the Baetici continued with their action after his death. (This was legally permissible, but the practice had lapsed, and was revived on this occasion after a long interval.) In addition to Classicus, they extended their charges to his friends and accomplices, demanding an individual investigation in each case.

I appeared for the Baetici, supported by Lucceius Albinus, a fluent and elegant orator whom I have long admired; since our association on this occasion I have come to feel a warm affection for him. The will to succeed implies some reluctance to share success, and especially where forensic oratory is concerned; but in our case there was no rivalry nor competition. We both put the needs of the case before personal considerations in a combined effort, for we felt that the importance of the issue and its outcome demanded that we did not assume such responsibility in a single speech from each of us. . . .

Pliny *Epistles* 3. 9
tr. Betty Radice (Penguin 1963)

134 The importance of farming

(a) *Note that Cicero emphasizes he is conveying the 'conventional wisdom' on the subject. The professions have greater prestige than trades but by implication they are not suitable occupations for Senators. Agriculture is praised both as a source of wealth and on moral grounds (cf. G9).*

Now in regard to trades and other means of livelihood, which ones are to be considered becoming to a gentleman and which ones are vulgar, we have been taught, in general, as follows. First, those means of livelihood are rejected as undesirable which incur people's ill-will, as those of tax-gatherers and usurers. Unbecoming to a gentleman, too, and vulgar are the means of livelihood of all hired workmen whom we pay for mere manual labour, not for artistic skill; for in their case the very wage they receive is a pledge of their slavery. Vulgar we must consider those also who buy from wholesale merchants to retail immediately; for they would get no profits without a great deal of downright lying; and verily, there is no action that is meaner than misrepresentation. And all mechanics are engaged in vulgar trades; for no workshop can have anything liberal about it. Least respectable of all are those trades which cater for sensual pleasures:

'Fishmongers, butchers, cooks, and poulterers,
And fishermen,'

as Terence says. Add to these if you please, the perfumers, dancers, and the whole *corps de ballet*!

But the professions in which either a higher degree of intelligence is required or from which no small benefit to society is derived—medicine and architecture, for example, and teaching—these are proper for those whose social position they become. Trade, if it is on a small scale, is to be considered vulgar; but if wholesale and on a large scale, importing large quantities from all parts of the world and distributing to many without misrepresentation, it is not to be greatly disparaged. Nay, it even seems to deserve the highest respect, if those who are engaged in it, satiated, or rather, I should say, satisfied with the fortunes they have made, make

413

their way from the port to a country estate, as they have often made it from the sea into port. But of all the occupations by which gain is secured, none is better than agriculture, none more profitable, none more delightful, none more becoming to a freeman.

Cicero *De Officiis* 1.150–1
tr. W. Miller (Loeb 1913)

(b)

It is true that to obtain money by trade is sometimes more profitable, were it not so hazardous; and likewise money-lending, if it were as honourable. Our ancestors held this view and embodied it in their laws, which required that the thief be mulcted double and the usurer fourfold; how much less desirable a citizen they considered the usurer than the thief, one may judge from this. And when they would praise a worthy man their praise took this form: 'good husbandman,' 'good farmer'; one so praised was thought to have received the greatest commendation.

Cato *On Agriculture* 1.1
tr. W. D. Hooper, rev. H. B. Ash (Loeb 1934)

I35 The Elder Cato on agriculture

The Elder Cato's work on agriculture is the first work on the subject in Latin. Although early (it was written in the middle of the second century BC) a short extract is included here for comparison with Varro and Columella. Like the later writers, Cato is concerned with investment farming not subsistence agriculture. Most of the work is devoted to practical advice. For a detailed analysis of the contents see K. D. White (1970) Roman Farming *(Thames & Hudson) Appendix A.*

Moreover, it is from among the farmers that the sturdiest men and keenest soldiers come, and the gain they make is the most blameless of all, the most secure, and the least provocative of envy, and the men engaged in this pursuit are least given to disaffection. . . .

If you ask me what sort of farm is best, I will say this: one hundred *iugera* of land consisting of every kind of cultivated field, and in the best situation; the vineyard is of first importance if the wine is good and the yield is great; the irrigated garden is in the second place, the willow plantation in the third, the olive orchard in the fourth, the meadow in the fifth, the grain land in the sixth, forest trees to furnish foliage in the seventh, the vineyard trained on trees in the eighth, the acorn wood in the ninth. . . .

When the head of the household comes to the farmhouse, on the same day, if possible, as soon as he has paid respect to the god of the household, he should make the round of the farm; if not on the same day, at least on the next. When he has learned in what way the farm work has been done and what tasks are finished and what not yet finished, he should next day summon the foreman and inquire how much of the work is done, how much remains, whether the different operations have been completed in good season and whether he can complete what remains, and what is the situation as to wine and grain and all other produce. . . . let him sell the old work oxen, the blemished cattle, the blemished sheep, the wool, the skins, the old wagon, the worn-out tools, the aged slave, the slave that is diseased, and everything else that he does not need. An owner should be a man who is a seller rather than a buyer. . . .

Cato On Agriculture
tr. E. Brehaut Cato the Censor on Farming (New York 1933)
abridged Lewis and Reinhold vol. 1

136 Varro on agriculture

De Re Rustica was published in 37 BC when Varro was over eighty and is one of his few surviving works. In contrast to Cato's work it stands out for its great learning and references to earlier authorities, combined with a willingness to experiment. It pays special attention to the extension of the cultivation of vines and fruit trees and to animal husbandry. In an important passage Varro laments the passing of the traditional agricultural basis to society and morals (praised by Cato) in response to political and social change and the pressures of urbanization. For analysis of the agricultural contents see K. D. White Roman Farming *and J. M. Frayn* Subsistence Farming in Roman Italy *(Centaur 1979).*

Equipped with this knowledge, the farmer should aim at two goals, profit and pleasure; the object of the first is material return, and of the second enjoyment. The profitable plays a more important role than the pleasurable; and yet for the most part the methods of cultivation which improve the aspect of the land, such as planting of fruit and the olive trees in rows, make it not only more profitable but also more salable, and add to the value of the estate. . . . Farms which have suitable means near by of transporting their products to market and convenient means of transporting thence those things needed on the farm are for that reason profitable. For many have among their holdings some into which grain or wine or the like which they lack must be brought, and on the other hand not a few have those from which a surplus must be sent away. And so it is profitable near a city to have gardens on a large scale; for instance, of violets and roses and many other products for which there is a demand in a city; while it would not be profitable to raise the same products on a distant farm where there is no market to which products can be carried. Again, if there are towns or villages in the neighborhood, or even well-furnished lands and farmsteads of rich owners, from which you can purchase at a reasonable price what you need for the farm, and to which you can sell your surplus, such as props, or poles, or reeds, the farm will be more profitable than if they must be fetched from a distance; sometimes, in fact, more so than if you can supply them yourself by raising them on your own place. For this reason farmers in such circumstances prefer to have in their neighborhood men whose services they can call upon under a yearly contract—physicians, fullers, and other artisans—rather than to have such men of their own on the farm; for sometimes the death of one artisan wipes out the profit of a farm. This department of a great estate rich owners are wont to entrust to their own people; for if towns or villages are too far away from the estate, they supply themselves with smiths and other necessary artisans to keep on the place, so that their farm hands may not leave their work and lounge around holiday-making on working days, rather than make the farm more profitable by attending to their duties.

Slaves should be neither cowed nor high-spirited. They ought to have men over them who know how to read and write and have some little education, who are dependable and older than the hands whom I have mentioned; for they will be more respectful to these than to men who are younger. Furthermore, it is especially important that the foremen be men who are experienced in farm operations; for the foreman must not only give orders but also take part in the work, so that his subordinates may follow his example but also understand that there is good reason for his being over them—the fact that he is superior to them in knowledge. They are not to be allowed to control their men with whips rather than with words, if only you can achieve the same result. Avoid having too many slaves of the same nation, for this is a fertile source of domestic quarrels. The foremen are to be made more zealous by rewards, and care must be taken that they have a bit of property of their own, and mates from among their fellow slaves to bear them children; for by this means they are made more steady and more attached to the place. . . .

It was not without reason that those great men, our ancestors, put the Romans who lived in the country ahead of those who lived in the city. For as in the country those who live in the villa are lazier than those who are engaged in carrying out work on the land, so they thought that those who settled in town were more indolent than those who dwelt in the country. Hence they so divided the year that they attended to their town affairs only on the ninth days and dwelt in the country on the remaining seven. So long as they kept up this practice they attained both objects—keeping their lands most productive by cultivation, and themselves enjoying better health and not requiring the citified gymnasia of the Greeks. . . . As therefore in these days practically all the heads of families have sneaked within the walls, abandoning the sickle and the plow, and would rather busy their hands in the theater and in the circus than in the grain fields and the vineyards, we hire a man to bring us from Africa and Sardinia the grain with which to fill our stomachs, and the vintage we store comes in ships from the islands of Cos and Chios. And so, in a land where the shepherds who founded the city taught their offspring the cultivation of the earth, there, on the contrary, their descendants, from greed and in the face of the laws, have made pastures out of grain lands—not knowing that agriculture and grazing are not the same thing. . . .

Varro *On Landed Estates*
tr. W. D. Hooper, rev. H. B. Ash Loeb, abridged Lewis and Reinhold vol. 1

137 Columella on running a farm

Columella's work is a systematic treatise in 12 books written between AD 60 and AD 65. He came from a Spanish family of landowners and held estates in central Italy, combining a practical approach with frequent reference to Greek and Latin authors including Virgil. Columella's aim is to advise the owners of fairly large estates worked for profit and he therefore devotes special attention to handling of the workforce and to the problems of the absentee landlord. The emphasis of the work also suggests that cereal production had continued to decline and pasturage increased. For a detailed discussion see K. D. White (op. cit.).

The size of the villa and the number of its parts should be proportioned to the whole enclosure, and it should be divided into three groups: the *villa urbana* (manor house), the *villa rustica* (farmhouse), and the *villa fructuaria* (storehouse) . . . the master must give special attention, among other things, to laborers; and these are either tenant farmers or slaves (unfettered or in chains). He should be civil in dealing with his tenant farmers, should show himself affable, and should be more exacting in the matter of work than of payments, as this gives less offense yet is, generally speaking, more profitable. For when land is carefully tilled, it usually brings a profit, and never a loss except when it is assailed by unusually severe weather or robbers; and therefore the tenant does not venture to ask for reduction of his rent. But the master should not be insistent on his rights in every particular to which he has bound his tenant, such as the exact day for payment of money, or the matter of demanding firewood and other trifling contributions; attention to such matters causes country folk more trouble than expense. . . . I myself remember having heard Publius Volusius, an old man who had been consul and was very wealthy, declare that estate to be most fortunate which had natives of the place as tenant farmers and which held them by reason of long association, even from the cradle, as if born on their own father's property. So I am decidedly of the opinion that repeated re-letting of a farm is a bad thing, but that a worse thing is the tenant farmer who lives in town and prefers to till the land through his slaves rather than by his own hand. . . .

The next point is with regard to slaves—over what duty it is proper to place each, and to what sort of tasks to assign them. So my advice at the start is not to appoint an overseer from the sort of slaves who are physically attractive, and certainly not from that class which has been engaged in the voluptuous occupations of the city.

417

This lazy and sleepy-headed class of slaves, accustomed to idling, to the Field of Mars, the circus and the theaters, to gambling, to taverns, to bawdy houses, never ceases to dream of these follies; and when they carry them over into their farming, the master suffers not so much loss in the slave himself as in his whole estate. A man should be chosen who has been hardened by farm work from his infancy, one who has been tested by experience. . . .

But be the overseer what he may, he should be given a woman companion to keep him within bounds and moreover in certain matters to be a help to him. . . . He must be urged to take care of the equipment and the iron tools, and to keep in repair and stored away twice as many as the number of slaves requires, so that there will be no need of borrowing from a neighbor; for the loss in slave labor exceeds the cost of articles of this sort. In the care and clothing of the slave household he should have an eye to usefulness rather than appearance, taking care to keep them fortified against wind, cold, and rain, all of which are warded off with long-sleeved leather tunics, garments of patchwork, or hooded cloaks. If this be done, no weather is so unbearable but that some work may be done in the open. . . .

Also, to women who are unusually prolific, and who ought to be rewarded for the bearing of a certain number of offspring, I have granted exemption from work and sometimes even freedom after they have reared many children: a mother of three children received exemption from work, a mother of more, her freedom as well. Such justice and consideration on the part of the master contributes greatly to the increase of his estate. . . .

Those devoted to the study of agriculture must be informed of one thing first of all—that the return from vineyards is a very rich one . . . We can hardly recall a time when grain crops, throughout at least the greater part of Italy, returned a yield of four to one.

Columella *On Agriculture* 1. 6–9; 3. 3
tr. H. B. Ash (Loeb) abridged and adapted Lewis and Reinhold vol. 2

I38 An agricultural Calendar

Month of January. 31 days. The Nones fall on the fifth day. The day has 9¾ hours. The night has 14¼ hours. The sun is in the sign of Capricorn. The month is under the protection of Juno. Stakes are sharpened. Willow and reeds are cut. Sacrifices to the household gods.

Month of February. 28 days. The Nones fall on the fifth day. The day has 10¾ hours. The night has 13¼ hours. The sun is in the sign of Aquarius. The month is under the protection of Neptune. The grain fields are weeded. The part of the vines above ground is tended. Reeds are burned. Parentalia, Lupercalia, Dear Relatives' Day, Terminalia.

Month of March. 31 days. The Nones fall on the seventh day. The day has 12 hours. The night has 12 hours. The equinox falls on the twenty-fifth day. The sun is in the sign of Pisces. The month is under the protection of Minerva. The vines are propped up in trenched ground and pruned. Three-month wheat is sown. The bark of Isis. Sacrifices to Mamurius. Liberalia, Quinquatria, Bathing.

Month of April. 30 days. The Nones fall on the fifth day. The day has 13½ hours. The night has 10½ hours. The sun is in the sign of Aries. The month is under the protection of Venus. The lustration of the sheep is made. Sacrifices to the Isis of Pharus. Also festival of Sarapis.

Month of May. 31 days. The Nones fall on the seventh day. The day has 14½ hours. The night has 9½ hours. The sun is in the sign of Taurus. The month is under the protection of Apollo. The grain fields are cleared of weeds. The sheep are shorn. The wool is washed. Young steers are put under the yoke. The vetch for fodder is cut. The lustration of the grain fields is made. Sacrifices to Mercury and Flora.

Month of June. 30 days. The Nones fall on the fifth day. The day has 15 hours. The night has 9 hours. The solstice falls on the twenty-fourth day. The sun is in the sign of Gemini. The month is under the protection of Mercury. The hay is mown. The vines are cultivated. Sacrifice to Hercules and Fors Fortuna.

Month of July. 31 days. The Nones fall on the seventh day. The day has 14¼ hours. The night has 9¾ hours. The sun is in the sign of Cancer. The month is under the protection of Jupiter. Barley and beans are harvested. Apollinaria, Neptunalia.

Month of August. 31 days. The Nones fall on the fifth day. The day has 13 hours. The night has 11 hours. The sun is in the sign of Leo. The month is under the protection of Ceres. The stakes are prepared. Cereals are harvested, likewise the wheat. The stubble is burned. Sacrifices to Hope, Safety, and Diana. Volcanalia.

Month of September. 30 days. The Nones fall on the fifth day. The day has 12 hours. The night has 12 hours. The equinox falls on the twenty-fourth day. The sun is in the sign of Virgo. The month is under the protection of Vulcan. The casks are smeared with pitch. Fruits are gathered. The earth around the trees is dug up. Feast of Minerva.

Month of October. 31 days. The Nones fall on the seventh day. The day has 10¾ hours. The night has 13¼ hours. The sun is in the sign of Libra. The month is under the protection of Mars. Grape gathering. Sacrifices to Bacchus.

Month of November. 30 days. The Nones fall on the fifth day. The day has 9½ hours. The night has 14½ hours. The sun is in the sign of Scorpion. The month is under the protection of Diana. Sowing of wheat and barley. Digging of trenches for trees. Feast of Jupiter. Discovery.

Month of December. 31 days. The Nones fall on the fifth day. The day has 9 hours. The night has 15 hours. The sun is in the sign of Sagittarius. The month is under the protection of Vesta. Beginning of winter, or winter solstice. The vines are matured. Beans are sown. Wood is cut. Olives are gathered and also sold. Saturnalia.

CIL 6. 2305
tr. Lewis and Reinhold vol. 2

I39 Civil War and the land problem

(a)

Appian of Alexandria gained Roman citizenship and became an advocate at Rome. Writing in Greek in the mid-second century AD *he was an admirer of Roman Imperialism and drawing on earlier sources Book 1 of the* Civil Wars *contributes useful evidence about the impact of empire and war on Italy at the fall of the Republic. See also B5 ff., G1–3.*

The Romans, as they subdued the Italian peoples successively in war, used to seize a part of their lands and build towns there, or enroll colonists of their own to occupy those already existing, with the idea of using these as outposts; but of the land acquired by war they assigned the cultivated part forthwith to the colonists, or sold or leased it. Since they had no leisure as yet to allot the part which then lay desolated by war (this was generally the greater part), they made proclamation that in the meantime those who were willing to work it might do so for a toll of the yearly crops, namely a tenth of the grain and a fifth of the fruit. From those who kept flocks was required a toll of the animals, both oxen and small cattle. They did these things in order to multiply the Italian people, whom they considered very hardy, so that they might have plenty of allies at home. But the very opposite thing happened; for the rich, taking possession of the greater part of the undistributed lands and being emboldened by the lapse of time to believe that they would never be dispossessed, absorbing any adjacent strips and their poor neighbors' allotments partly by purchase under persuasion and partly by force, came to cultivate vast tracts instead of single estates, using purchased slaves as agricultural laborers and herdsmen, since free laborers could be drawn from agriculture into the army. At the same time the ownership of slaves brought them great gain from the multitude of their progeny, who increased free from danger because they were exempt from military service. Thus certain powerful men became extremely rich and the class of slaves multiplied throughout the country, while the Italian people dwindled in numbers and strength, oppressed by penury, taxes, and military service. If they had any respite from these evils, they passed their time in idleness, because the land was held by the rich, who employed slaves instead of freemen as cultivators.

Appian *Civil Wars* 1.1.7
tr. H. White (Loeb 1913)

(b)

To encourage the army with expectation of booty they promised them, besides other gifts, eighteen cities of Italy as colonies—cities which excelled in wealth, in the splendor of their estates and houses, and which were to be divided among them (land, buildings, and all) just as though they had been captured from an enemy in war. The most renowned among these were Capua, Regium, Venusia, Beneventum, Nuceria, Ariminum, and Vibo. Thus were the most beautiful parts of

Italy marked out for the soldiers. But they decided to destroy their personal enemies beforehand, so that the latter should not interfere with their arrangements while they were carrying on war abroad. Having come to these decisions, they reduced them to writing, and Octavian as consul communicated them to the soldiers— all except the list of proscriptions. When the soldiers heard them they applauded and embraced each other in token of mutual reconciliation.

Appian *Civil Wars* 4. 1. 3
tr. H. White (Loeb 1913)

140 A poetic contrast

Horace contrasts the simple life of a small farmer with the luxury supported by large estates.

(a)

> Soon I foresee few acres for harrowing
> Left once the rich men's villas have seized the land;
>   Fishponds that outdo Lake Lucrinus
>   Everywhere; bachelor plane-trees ousting
>
> Vine-loving elms; thick myrtle-woods, violet-beds,
> All kinds of rare blooms tickling the sense of smell,
>   Perfumes to drown those olive orchards
>   Nursed in the past for a farmer's profit;
>
> Quaint garden-screens, too, woven of laurel-boughs
> To parry sunstroke. Romulus never urged
>   This style of life; rough-bearded Cato
>   Would have detested the modern fashions.
>
> Small private wealth, large communal property—
> So ran the rule then. No one had porticoes
>   Laid out with ten-foot builder's measures,
>   Trapping the cool of the northern shadow.
>
> No one in those days sneered at the turf by the
> Roadside; yet laws bade citizens beautify
>   Townships at all men's cost and quarry
>   Glorious marble to roof the temples.

Horace *Odes* 2. 15
tr. J. Michie (Penguin 1967 repr. 1978)

(b)

No gold or ivory gleams
On panelled ceilings in my house; no marble beams
    Hewn on Hymettus press
Great columns quarried from the Libyan wilderness;
    No eastern millionaire
Ever made me his palace's unwitting heir;
    No well-born ladies dressed
In Spartan purple wait on me. Yet I am blessed
    With honesty and a streak
Of golden talent, and, though poor, rich people seek
    Me out. I do not task
The charity of the gods, nor from my patron ask
    Greater reward than this:
My one dear Sabine farm is wealth enough and bliss.
    Day dispossesses day,
Moons hurry to be born and race to their decay;
    Yet you, blind to the fact
Of imminent death, with one foot in the grave contract
    For marble to build more
Villas and, not content to own the mainland shore,
    Push out your property
From Baiae's beaches to displace the growling sea.
    Nor is that all. You rip
Marking-posts out of neighbours' fields and greedily skip
    Into your tenants' lands.
Next day they leave, their household gods clutched in their hands,
    Their ragged children held
Tight in their arms, a homeless man and wife, expelled.
    Be warned, though. No hall waits
More surely for its lord than the predestined gates
    Of greedy Death. Why toil
To add to your possessions? The impartial soil
    Opens herself to take
The pauper and the prince alike. No bribe could make
    Hell's ferryman alter course
To row clever Prometheus back. Death holds by force
    Proud Tantalus and the clan
Of Tantalus. He, when work is done and the poor man
    Begs him to ease his lot,
Comes to the call; indeed he comes, called for or not.

Horace *Odes* 2. 18
tr. J. Michie (Penguin 1967 repr. 1978)

I41 The younger Pliny's villa

Pliny the Younger (c. AD 61 – c. AD 112) was the nephew and adopted son of Pliny the Elder (see I26). His uncle was an eques *but he himself entered the Senate, his career culminating as* legatus Augusti *in Bithynia–Pontus under Trajan; Pliny published nine books of literary letters between 100 and 109 and a tenth book containing official correspondence with Trajan about the administration of Bithynia. Pliny's letters are an invaluable source for the study of society and administration in the late first century AD. The passage quoted here is relevant to studies of the earlier part of the century in that it confirms trends in agricultural practice and in the attitude of prosperous city-dwellers–themes identified by Varro and Columella. The remainder of the letter contains a detailed description of Pliny's villa.*

You may wonder why my Laurentine place (or my Laurentian, if you like that better) is such a joy to me, but once you realize the attractions of the house itself, the amenities of its situation, and its extensive sea-front, you will have your answer. It is seventeen miles from Rome, so that it is possible to spend the night there after necessary business is done, without having cut short or hurried the day's work, and it can be approached by more than one route; the roads to Laurentum and Ostia both lead in that direction, but you must leave the one at the fourteenth milestone and the other at the eleventh. Whichever way you go, the side road you take is sandy for some distance and rather heavy and slow-going if you drive, but soft and easily covered on horseback. The view on either side is full of variety, for sometimes the road narrows as it passes through the woods, and then it broadens and opens out through wide meadows where there are many flocks of sheep and herds of horses and cattle driven down from the mountains in winter to grow sleek on the pastures in the springlike climate.

Pliny *Letters* 2. 17 (extract)
tr. Betty Radice (Penguin 1963)

I42 The Younger Pliny's wife

A late source which confirms the persistence of traditional upper-class attitudes to the accomplishments and conduct required of women as well as indicating an appreciation of a well-educated companion. Compare the politically emancipated women of the leading families (B58, 61; K6, 25) and for a full discussion of the position of women from all sections of society see J. P. V. D. Balsdon Roman Women (*Bodley Head 1962*).

She is highly intelligent and a careful housewife, and her devotion to me is a sure indication of her virtue. In addition, this love has given her an interest in literature:

she keeps copies of my works to read again and again and even learn by heart. She is so anxious when she knows that I am going to plead in court, and so happy when all is over! (She arranges to be kept informed of the sort of reception and applause I receive, and what verdict I win in the case.) If I am giving a reading she sits behind a curtain near by and greedily drinks in every word of appreciation. She has even set my verses to music and sings them, to the accompaniment of her lyre, with no musician to teach her but the best of masters, love.

All this gives me the highest reason to hope that our mutual happiness will last for ever and go on increasing day by day, for she does not love me for my present age nor my person, which will gradually grow old and decay, but for my aspirations to fame; nor would any other feelings be suitable for one brought up by your hands and trained in your precepts, who has seen only what was pure and moral in your company and learned to love me on your recommendation. For you respected my mother like a daughter, and have given me guidance and encouragement since my boyhood; you always foretold that I should become the man I am now in the eyes of my wife. Please accept our united thanks for having given her to me and me to her as if chosen for each other.

Pliny *Letters* 4. 19 (extract)
tr. Betty Radice (Penguin 1963)

I43 Metal for tools and agricultural implements

Diodorus' world history was composed between c. 60-30 BC. Here, he describes the iron mines at Elba (Aethalia in Greek). Puteoli was the main centre for the iron industry in Italy.

Off the city of Etruria known as Populonia there is an island which men call Aethalia. It is about 100 stades distant from the coast and received the name it bears from the smoke (*aethalus*) which lies so thick about it. For the island possesses a great amount of iron ore, which they quarry in order to melt and cast and thus secure the iron, and they possess a great abundance of this ore. Now those who are engaged in the working of the ore crush the rock and burn the lumps which they have thus broken in certain igneous furnaces; and in these they smelt the lumps by means of a great fire and form them into pieces of moderate size which are in their appearance like large sponges. These are bought up by traders in exchange [for money or goods] and are then transported to Puteoli or the other trading stations, where there are men who purchase such cargoes and who, with the aid of a multitude of artisans in metal whom they have collected, work it further and manufacture iron objects of every description. Some of these are worked into the shape of armor, and others are ingeniously fabricated into shapes well suited for two-pronged forks and sickles and other such tools; and these are then transported by traders to every region, and thus many parts of the inhabited world have a share in the usefulness which accrues from these products.

Diodorus Siculus *Historical Library* 5. 13. 1-2
tr. C. H. Oldfather (Loeb) adapted Lewis and Reinhold vol. 2

144 The grain supply

(a)

The problem of the grain supply worsened with the decline of cereal production in Italy from the second century BC and Rome came to rely on supplies from overseas provinces. Augustus made the cura annonae *the responsibility of the Princeps, the prefecture being an Equestrian post. The handling of grain imports prompted Claudius' attempts to improve harbour facilities at Ostia (AD 42).*

The excessive price of grain led practically to insurrection, and for several days the theater was the scene of many demands shouted with greater boldness than was customary toward the emperor. Aroused by this, Tiberius upbraided the magistrates and the senators for failing to restrain the populace by the authority of the state, and reminded them of the provinces from which he imported the supply of grain and of how much greater a supply it was than Augustus had provided.

Tacitus *Annals* 6. 13. 1-2
tr. J. Jackson (Loeb) in Lewis and Reinhold vol. 2

(b)

Claudius always gave scrupulous attention to the care of the city and the supply of grain. . . . When there was a scarcity of grain because of long-continued droughts, he was once stopped in the middle of the Forum by a mob and so pelted with abuse and at the same time with pieces of bread that he was barely able to make his escape to the palace by a back door. After this experience he resorted to every possible means to bring supplies to Rome, even in the winter season. To the importers he held out the certainty of profit by assuming the expense of any loss that they might suffer from storms. To those who built merchant ships he accorded great benefits adapted to the conditions of each, namely, to a citizen, exemption from the Papian-Poppaean Law; to one of Latin rights, full citizenship; to women, the privileges of mothers of four children. And all these provisions are in force today.

Suetonius *Claudius* 18-19
tr. J. C. Rolphe (Loeb) adapted Lewis and Reinhold vol. 2

I45 Games

The material in this section mainly falls outside Augustus' reign and is included for illustrative or comparative purposes.

The letter (a) refers to the games given by Pompey to celebrate the dedication of his theatre and the temple of Venus Victrix (55 BC during Pompey's second consulship). The other passages (b–d) emphasize the prestige to be gained through the provision of public donations and entertainments.

(a)

If you ask me, the games were of course most magnificent; but they would not have been to your taste; that I infer from my own feelings. . . . For any feeling of cheerfulness was extinguished by the spectacle of such magnificence—a magnificence which, I am sure, it will not disturb you in the least to have missed seeing. For what pleasure can there be in the sight of 600 mules in the *Clytaemnestra*, or of 3,000 bowls in the *Trojan Horse*, or of the varied accoutrements of foot and horse in some big battle? . . .

There remain the wild-beast hunts, two a day for five days—magnificent; there is no denying it. But what pleasure can it possibly be to a man of culture, when either a puny human being is mangled by a most powerful beast, or a splendid beast is transfixed with a hunting spear? And even if all this is something to be seen, you have seen it more than once; and I, who was a spectator, saw nothing new in it. The last day was that of the elephants, and on that day the mob and crowd was greatly impressed, but manifested no pleasure. Indeed the result was a certain compassion and a kind of feeling that that huge beast has a fellowship with the human race.

Cicero *Letters to Friends* 7. 1
tr. W. Glyn Williams (Loeb) abridged Lewis and Reinhold vol. 2

(b)

The next year Agrippa agreed to be made aedile and without taking anything from the public treasury repaired all the public buildings and all the streets, cleaned out the sewers, and sailed through them underground into the Tiber. . . . Furthermore, he distributed olive oil and salt to all, and furnished baths free of charge throughout the year for the use of both men and women; and in connection with the many festivals of all kinds which he gave . . . he hired barbers, so that no one should be at any expense for their services. Finally he rained upon the heads of the people in the theater tickets that were good for money in one case, for clothes in another, and again for something else, and he also set out immense quantities of various wares for all comers and allowed the people to scramble for these things.

Dio Cassius 49. 43 1–4
tr. E. Cary (Loeb) adapted Lewis and Reinhold vol. 2

(c)

The principal events between Tiberius's coming of age and his accession to the throne may be summarized as follows. He staged a gladiatorial contest in memory of his father Nero, and another in memory of his grandfather Drusus. The first took place in the Forum, the second in the amphitheatre; and he persuaded some retired gladiators to appear with the rest, by paying them 1,000 gold pieces each. There were theatrical performances, too, but Tiberius did not attend them. Livia and Augustus financed these lavish entertainments.

Suetonius *Tiberius* 7
tr. R. Graves (Penguin 1957)

(d)

Claudius often distributed largesse to the people, and gave numerous magnificent public shows; not only the traditional ones in the customary places, but others, including novelties and ancient revivals, where nobody had ever seen them staged before.

Pompey's Theatre was damaged by fire, and when Claudius held Games at its rededication he first sacrificed in the Temple of Victorious Venus and in the shrines of Honour, Virtue and Felicity—all of which were built above the auditorium—and then walked down the aisle between packed and silent tiers, to inaugurate the Games from a raised seat in the orchestra.

He also celebrated Saecular Games, on the excuse that Augustus had staged them before they were really due; though his own *History* mentions how much trouble Augustus took to reckon the intervals separating their occurrences in the past, and to recommence the series, after the tradition had long been broken, when the correct year came round once more.

Suetonius *Claudius* 21
tr. R. Graves (Penguin 1957)

146 Election notices

These are a small selection from the hundreds of 'graffiti' painted or scratched on buildings in Pompeii; (b)–(d) refer to municipal elections for aedile.

(a)

The fruit dealers together with Helvius Vestalis unanimously urge the election of Marcus Holconius Priscus as duovir with judicial power.

(b)

I ask you to elect Gaius Julius Polybius aedile. He gets good bread.

(c)

The worshippers of Isis unanimously urge the election of Gnaeus Helvius Sabinus as aedile.

(d)

I ask you to elect Marcus Cerrinius Vatia to the aedileship. All the late drinkers support him. Florus and Fructus wrote this.

(e)

I wonder, O wall, that you have not fallen in ruins from supporting the stupidities of so many scribblers.

> CIL 4. 202; 429; 787; 581; 1904
> tr. Lewis and Reinhold vol. 2

147 A show of violence

The letter dates from after Seneca's retirement from political prominence (AD 62).

I chanced to stop in at a midday show, expecting fun, wit, and some relaxation, when men's eyes take respite from the slaughter of their fellow men. It was just the reverse. The preceding combats were merciful by comparison; now all trifling is put aside and it is pure murder. The men have no protective covering. Their entire bodies are exposed to the blows, and no blow is ever struck in vain. . . . In the morning men are thrown to the lions and the bears, at noon they are thrown to their spectators. The spectators call for the slayer to be thrown to those who in turn will slay him, and they detain the victor for another butchering. The outcome for the combatants is death; the fight is waged with sword and fire. This goes on while the arena is free. 'But one of them was a highway robber, he killed a man!' Because he killed he deserved to suffer this punishment, granted. . . . 'Kill him! Lash him! Burn him! Why does he meet the sword so timidly? Why doesn't he kill boldly? Why doesn't he die game? Whip him to meet his wounds! Let them trade blow for blow, chests bare and within reach!' And when the show stops for intermission, 'Let's have men killed meanwhile! Let's not have nothing going on!'

> Seneca *Moral Epistles* 7. 3–5
> tr. Lewis and Reinhold vol. 2

148 A triumph

The triumph was celebrated jointly by Vespasian and Titus in AD 71 after Rome's eventual victory in the Jewish war (see §0). The example is cited here both for its intrinsic interest and as an example of an Imperial triumph, reserved for the Princeps or his family. Under the Republic the celebration of a triumph by a victorious general was a highly coveted honour, but this came to an end under Augustus. M. Agrippa refused all triumphs voted him and the last military triumph was recorded in 19 BC in the Calendar of Triumphs *which forms part of the* Fasti.

Previous notice having been given of the day on which the triumphal procession would take place, not a soul among the countless multitude in the city remained at home; all issued forth and occupied every position where it was at all possible to stand, leaving only room for the necessary passage of those upon whom they were to gaze.

The troops, while it was still night, had all marched out in centuries and cohorts under their commanders. . . . About the time dawn was breaking Vespasian and Titus issued forth, crowned with laurel and clad in the traditional purple robes, and proceeded to the porticoes of Octavia; for here the senate and the chief magistrates and those of equestrian rank were awaiting their coming. A platform had been erected in front of the porticoes, with chairs of ivory placed for them upon it; to these they mounted and took their seats. Instantly, acclamations rose from the troops, all bearing ample testimony to their valor. The princes were unarmed, in silk robes, and crowned with laurel. Vespasian, having acknowledged their acclamations, which they wished to prolong, gave the signal for silence. Then, amidst profound and universal stillness, he rose and, covering most of his head with his mantle, recited the customary prayers, Titus also praying in like manner. . . The princes . . . having donned their triumphal robes and sacrificed to the gods . . . sent the procession on its way, driving off through the theaters, in order to give the crowds a better view.

It is impossible adequately to describe the multitude of those spectacles and their magnificence . . . for the collective exhibition on that day of almost everything that men who have ever been blessed by fortune have one by one acquired . . . displayed the majesty of the Roman Empire. . . .

The war was shown in numerous representations, in separate sections, affording a very vivid picture of its episodes. Here was to be seen a prosperous country being devastated, there whole battalions of the enemy slaughtered; here a party in flight, there others being led into captivity; walls of surpassing size demolished by engines, mighty fortresses overpowered; cities with well-manned defenses completely mastered and an army pouring within the ramparts, an area all deluged with blood, the hands of those incapable of resistance raised in supplication; temples being set on fire, houses pulled down over their owners' heads; and, after general desolation and woe, rivers flowing, not over a cultivated land, nor supplying drink to man and beast, but across a country still on every side in flames. . . .

The spoils in general were borne in promiscuous heaps; but conspicuous above all stood out those captured in the temple at Jerusalem. These consisted of a golden table, many talents in weight, and a candelabrum, likewise made of gold. . . . After these, and last of all the spoils, was carried a copy of the Law of the Jews.

429

Then followed a large party carrying images of victory, all made of ivory and gold. Behind them drove first Vespasian, followed by Titus; while Domitian rode alongside them, in magnificent apparel and mounted on a horse that was a remarkable sight.

The triumphal procession ended at the temple of Jupiter Capitolinus, on reaching which they halted, for it was a time-honored custom to wait there until the execution of the enemy's general was announced. This was Simon bar Giora, who had just figured in the procession among the prisoners, and then, with a noose around him and scourged meanwhile by his escorts, had been dragged to the spot abutting on the Forum, where Roman law requires that malefactors condemned to death should be executed. After the announcement that Simon was no more and the shouts of universal applause which greeted it, the princes began the sacrifices and, having duly offered these with the customary prayers, withdrew to the palace.

Josephus *BJ* 7. 5. 122–56 (abridged)
tr. Lewis and Reinhold vol. 2

149 Duty under bad rule

The extract is from Tacitus' account of the career of his father-in-law Agricola, a successful legatus in Britain under Domitian from AD 78 (see also § N). The immediate context is a passage in which Tacitus uses an account of Domitian's supposedly churlish treatment of Agricola to introduce a meditation on the duty of public men to serve Rome honourably, even under tyrannical principes.

Let those whose way it is to admire only what is forbidden learn from him that great men can live even under bad rulers; and that submission and moderation, if animation and energy go with them, reach the same pinnacle of fame, whither more often men have climbed by perilous courses but, with no profit to the state, have earned their glory by an ostentatious death.

Tacitus *Agricola* 42
tr. M. Hutton, rev. R. M. Ogilvie (Loeb 1970)

150 The trial of Marcus Scribonius Libo Drusus (AD 16)

Libo was a descendant of Pompey and also of Augustus' first wife Scribonia and combined veneration for his ancestors with an interest in astrologers' predictions about his future prospects. In the preceding passage Tacitus points out that Tiberius was so anxious to obtain damning evidence that he ordered Libo's slaves to be sold to the Treasury Agent so that they could be interrogated under torture about Libo's political plans. (An ancient decree of the Senate forbade the use of such evidence when the slaves' master was on a capital charge.) Libo then killed himself. (see K8).

In the senate, however, the prosecution continued with undiminished earnestness. Tiberius pronounced on oath that, whatever Libo's guilt, he himself would have interceded for his life if he had not so hastily killed himself. Libo's property was divided among the accusers, and those of them who were senators received supernumerary praetorships. Then Marcus Aurelius Cotta Maximus Messallinus proposed that Libo's statue should be excluded from his descendants' funeral-parades, and Cnaeus Cornelius Lentulus that no Scribonius should ever again bear the name of Drusus. On the motion of Lucius Pomponius Flaccus, days were appointed for public thanksgiving. Lucius Munatius Plancus, Gaius Asinius Gallus, Marcus Papius Mutilus, and Lucius Apronius voted thank-offerings to Jupiter, Mars, and Concord, and a resolution that 13 September—the day of Libo's suicide—should become a public holiday. I have listed these distinguished proposers and their servilities to show how long ago this national disgrace started. The senate also ordered the expulsion of astrologers and magicians from Italy. One, Lucius Pituanius, was thrown from the Tarpeian Rock, another, Publius Marcius, executed by the consuls in traditional fashion to the sound of the bugle, outside the Esquiline Gate.

Tacitus *Annals* 2. 32
tr. M. Grant (Penguin 1971)

I51 The Condemnation of Silius

The passage refers to AD 24. The charges of extortion and connivance in the rebellion of Sacrovir were initiated by Sejanus against Silius because of Silius' friendship for Germanicus, his honorary triumph in Germany, and the consequent boast that Tiberius owed his throne to the loyalty of Silius' legions. In addition, Silius' wife was a friend of Agrippina.

Silius anticipated imminent condemnation by suicide. But his property was dealt with unmercifully. It is true that the provincial taxpayers received nothing back (and none of them requested a refund). But gifts by Augustus were deducted, and the claims of the emperor's personal estate enforced item by item. Never before had Tiberius gone to such pains regarding other men's property. Gaius Asinius Gallus proposed Sosia's banishment, moving that half of her property should be confiscated and the other half left to her children. Marcus Aemilius Lepidus, however, counter-proposed that a quarter should go to the accusers—as the law required —but that her children should have the rest.

431

I find that this Marcus Lepidus played a wise and noble part in events. He often palliated the brutalities caused by other people's sycophancy. And he had a sense of proportion—for he enjoyed unbroken influence and favour with Tiberius. This compels me to doubt whether, like other things, the friendships and enmities of rulers depend on destiny and the luck of a man's birth. Instead, may not our personalities play some part, enabling us to steer a way, safe from intrigues and hazards, between perilous insubordination and degrading servility?

However, Lepidus was contradicted by Marcus Aurelius Cotta Maximus Messallinus, who was of equally noble birth but very different character. At his proposal the senate decreed that officials, however free of guilt or knowledge of guilt themselves, should be punished for their wives' wrongdoing in the provinces as though it were their own.

Tacitus *Annals* 4. 20
tr. M. Grant (Penguin 1971)

I52 The prosecution of Cremutius Cordus

The passage refers to AD 25. The immediate context is Tacitus' study of the autocracy of the principate and the difficulties this presents for the historian. Metellus Pius was the father-in-law of Pompey, Lucius Afranius one of his generals. Pollio was a consular and historian of republican sympathies (for Horace's warning to him see F18) Corvinus was an orator and man of letters who became a supporter of Augustus.

But I must return to my subject. In the following year the consuls were Cossus Cornelius Lentulus and Marcus Asinius Agrippa. The year began with the prosecution of Aulus Cremutius Cordus on a new and previously unheard-of charge: praise of Brutus in his *History*, and the description of Cassius as 'the last of the Romans'. The prosecutors were Satrius Secundus and Pinarius Natta, dependants of Sejanus; that was fatal to the accused man. So was the grimness of Tiberius' face as he listened to the defence. This is how Cremutius, resigned to death, conducted it:

'Senators, my words are blamed. My actions are not blameworthy. Nor were these words of mine aimed against the emperor or his parent, whom the law of treason protects. I am charged with praising Brutus and Cassius. Yet many have written of their deeds—always with respect. Livy, outstanding for objectivity as well as eloquence, praised Pompey so warmly that Augustus called him "the Pompeian". But their friendship did not suffer. And Livy never called Quintus Caecilius Metellus Pius Scipio, Lucius Afranius, and this same pair, bandits and parricides— their fashionable designations today. He described them in language appropriate to distinguished men.

'Gaius Asinius Pollio gave a highly complimentary account of them. Marcus

Valerius Messalla Corvinus called Cassius "my commander". Both lived out wealthy and honoured lives. When Cicero praised Cato to the skies, the dictator Julius Caesar reacted by writing a speech against him—as in a lawsuit. Antony's letters, Brutus' speeches, contain scathing slanders against Augustus. The poems of Marcus Furius Bibaculus and Catullus—still read—are crammed with insults against the Caesars. Yet the divine Julius, the divine Augustus endured them and let them be. This could well be interpreted as wise policy, and not merely forbearance. For things unnoticed are forgotten; resentment confers status upon them.'

Tacitus *Annals* 4. 34
tr. M. Grant (Penguin 1971)

153 Tiberius' fear of political conspiracy

Much evidence is extant, not only of the hatred that Tiberius earned but of the state of terror in which he himself lived, and the insults heaped upon him. He forbade anyone to consult soothsayers, except openly and with witnesses present; and even attempted to suppress all oracles in the neighbourhood of Rome—but desisted for fear of the miraculous power shown by the sacred Lots, which he brought to Rome in a sealed chest from the Temple of Fortune at Palestrina. They vanished and did not become visible again until returned to the same temple.

Suetonius *Tiberius* 63
tr. R. Graves (Penguin 1957)

154 Claudius' history

Claudius' historical interests were subject to political control.

While still a boy Claudius had started work on a Roman history, encouraged by the famous historian Livy, and assisted by Sulpicius Flavus. But when he gave his first public reading to a packed audience he found it difficult to hold their attention because at the very beginning of his performance a very fat man came in, sat down, and broke a bench—which sent several of his neighbours sprawling—and excited considerable merriment. Even when silence had been restored Claudius could not help recalling the sight and going off into peals of laughter.

As Emperor he continued work on this history, from which a professional gave frequent readings. It opened with the murder of Julius Caesar, then skipped a few years and started again at the close of the Civil Wars; because he realized, from his mother's and grandmother's lectures, that he would not be allowed to publish a free and unvarnished report on the intervening period. Of the first part two volumes survive; of the second, forty-one.

Suetonius Claudius 41
tr. R. Graves (Penguin 1957)

155 Accusation against Publius Suillius Rufus

The extract refers to AD 58 and is part of a series of accusations and counter-accusations of extortion and embezzlement of provincial funds. Eventually Suillius was exiled and half his estate confiscated (cf. 133).

Now came the condemnation of Publius Suillius Rufus. He had earned much hatred in his stormy career. Nevertheless his fall brought discredit upon Seneca. Under Claudius the venal Suillius had been formidable. Changed times had not brought him as low as his enemies wished. Indeed, he envisaged himself as agressor rather than suppliant. It was to suppress him—so it was said—that the senate had revived an old decree under the Cincian law, penalizing advocates who accepted fees. Suillius protested abusively, reviling Seneca with characteristic ferocity and senile outspokenness.

'Seneca hates Claudius' friends,' said Suillius. 'For under Claudius he was most deservedly exiled! He only understands academic activities and immature youths. So he envies men who speak out vigorously and unaffectedly for their fellow-citizens. I was on Germanicus' staff while Seneca was committing adultery in his house! Is the acceptance of rewards a dependant offers voluntarily, for an honourable job, a worse offence than seducing imperial princesses? What branch of learning, what philosophical school, won Seneca three hundred million sesterces during four years of imperial friendship? In Rome, he entices into his snares the childless and their legacies. His huge rates of interest suck Italy and the provinces dry. I, on the other hand, have worked for my humble means. I will endure prosecution, trial, and everything else rather than have my lifelong efforts wiped out by this successful upstart!'

Tacitus Annals 13.42
tr. M. Grant (Penguin 1971)

156 The death of Thrasea Paetus

The passage refers to AD 66. Note the role of informers and paid accusers and the variety of the charges. For the killing of the nobilis *Rubellius Plautus see Tacitus*

Annals 14. 56 ff. Unlike Rubellius Plautus (who had Julio-Claudian blood) Thrasea Paetus did not represent a threat as an alternative Princeps. The main characteristic of the Stoic martyrs was that they rejected the manner and tone in which the Princeps exercised authority. For a detailed comparison of a number of examples, see J. M. C. Toynbee 'Dictators and Philosophers in the first century AD. (Greece & Rome 13 (1944) 43-58); D. R. Dudley A History of Cynicism (London 1937) *ch. 7.*

After the massacre of so many distinguished men, Nero finally coveted the destruction of Virtue herself by killing Thrasea and Marcius Barea Soranus. He had long hated them both. Against Thrasea there were additional motives. He had, as I mentioned, walked out of the senate during the debate about Agrippina. He had also been inconspicuous at the Youth Games. This gave all the more offence because during Games (the festival instituted by Antenor the Trojan) at his birthplace, Patavium, he had participated by singing in tragic costume. Besides, on the day when the praetor Antistius Sosianus was virtually condemned to death for writing offensive verses about Nero, he had proposed and carried a more lenient sentence. Again, after Poppaea's death, he had deliberately stayed away when divine honours were voted to her, and was not present at her funeral.

Cossutianus Capito kept these memories fresh. For that criminal bore Thrasea a grudge for helping a Cilician deputation to convict him for extortion. So now Capito added further charges: 'At the New Year, Thrasea evaded the regular oath. Though a member of the Board of Fifteen for Religious Ceremonies, he absented himself from the national vows. He has never sacrificed for the emperor's welfare or his divine voice. Once an indefatigable and invariable participant in the senate's discussions—taking sides on even the most trivial proposal—now, for three years, he has not entered the senate. Only yesterday, when there was universal competition to strike down Lucius Junius Silanus Torquatus and Lucius Antistius Vetus, he preferred to take time off helping his dependants.

'This is party-warfare against the government. It is secession. If many more have the same impudence, it is war. As this faction-loving country once talked of Caesar versus Cato, so now, Nero, it talks of you versus Thrasea. And he has his followers—or his courtiers rather. They do not yet imitate his treasonable voting. But they copy his grim and gloomy manner and expression: they rebuke your amusements. He is the one man to whom your safety is immaterial, your talents unadmired. He dislikes the emperor to be happy. But even your unhappiness, your bereavements, do not appease him. Disbelief in Poppaea's divinity shows the same spirit as refusing allegiance to the acts of the divine Augustus and divine Julius. Thrasea rejects religion, abrogates law.

'In every province and army the official Gazette is read with special care—to see what Thrasea has refused to do. If his principles are better, let us adopt them. Otherwise, let us deprive these revolutionaries of their chief and champion. This is the school which produced men like Quintus Aelius Tubero and Marcus Favonius—unpopular names even in the old Republic. They acclaim Liberty to destroy the imperial régime. Having destroyed it, they will strike at Liberty too. Your removal of a Cassius was pointless if you propose to allow emulators of the Brutuses to multiply and prosper. Finally—write no instructions about Thrasea yourself. Leave the senate to decide between us.' Nero whipped up Cossutianus' hot temper still further, and associated with him the bitingly eloquent Titus Clodius Eprius Marcellus.

The prosecution of Marcius Barea Soranus had been claimed by Ostorius Sabinus, a knight, on the grounds of alleged incidents during the defendant's governorship of Asia. The energy and fairness of Barea Soranus in that post had increased the emperor's malevolence. He had industriously cleared the harbour of Ephesus, and had refrained from punishing Pergamum for forcibly preventing an ex-slave of Nero called Acratus from removing its statues and pictures. However the charges against him were friendship with Rubellius Plautus and courting the provincials with revolutionary intentions. His conviction was timed just before Tiridates' arrival to receive the Armenian crown. This was to divert attention from domestic outrages to foreign affairs—or, perhaps, to display imperial grandeur to the visitor by a truly royal massacre of distinguished men.

All Rome turned out to welcome the emperor and inspect the king. Thrasea's presence, however, was forbidden. Undismayed, he wrote to Nero inquiring what the charges against him were and insisting that he would clear himself if he were told them and given an opportunity to dispose of them. Nero took the letter eagerly, hoping Thrasea had been frightened into some humiliating statement that would enhance the imperial prestige. But this was not so. Indeed, it was Nero who took fright, at the innocent Thrasea's spirited independence; so he convened the senate.

Thrasea consulted his friends whether he should attempt or disdain to defend himself. The advice he received was contradictory. Some said he should attend the senate. 'We know you will stand firm,' they said. 'Everything you say will enhance your renown! A secret end is for the feeble-spirited and timid. Let the people see a man who can face death. Let the senate hear inspired, superhuman utterances. Even Nero might be miraculously moved. But if his brutality persists, at least posterity will distinguish a noble end from the silent, spiritless deaths we have been seeing.'

Other friends, while equally complimentary to himself, urged him to wait at home, forecasting jeers and insults if he attended the senate. 'Avert your ears from taunts and slanders,' they advised. 'Cossutianus and Eprius are not the only criminals. Others are savage enough not to stop at physical violence—and fear makes even decent men follow their lead. You have been the senate's glory. Spare them this degrading crime: leave their verdict on Thrasea uncertain. To make Nero ashamed of his misdeeds is a vain hope. Much more real is the danger of his cruelty to your wife and daughter and other dear ones. No—die untarnished, unpolluted, as gloriously as those in whose footsteps and precepts you have lived!'

One of those present, the fervent young Lucius Junius Arulenus Rusticus, sought glory by proposing, as tribune, to veto the senate's decree. Thrasea rejected his enthusiastic plan as futile—fatal to its author, and not even any help to the accused. 'My time is finished,' he said. 'I must not abandon my longstanding, unremitting way of life. But you are starting your official career. Your future is uncompromised, so you must consider carefully beforehand what political cause you intend to adopt in such times.' The advisability of his own presence or absence he reserved for personal decision.

Next morning, two battalions of the Guard, under arms, occupied the temple of Venus Genetrix. The approach to the senate-house was guarded by a gang of civilians openly displaying their swords. Troops too were arrayed round the principal forums and the law-courts. Under their menacing glares, the senators entered the building. The emperor's address was read by his quaestor. Without mentioning any name he rebuked members for neglecting their official duties and setting the knights a slovenly example. What wonder, he said, if senators from distant provinces stayed away, when many ex-consuls and priests showed greater devotion to the embellishment of their gardens?

The accusers seized the weapon which this gave them. Cossutianus began the attack. Eprius Marcellus, following with even greater violence, claimed that the issue was one of prime national importance. The emperor's indulgence, he said, was hampered by the insubordination of those beneath him, and the senate had hitherto been overlenient. 'For you have allowed yourselves', he said, 'to be ridiculed with impunity—by the rebellious Thrasea, his equally infatuated son-in-law Helvidius Priscus, Gaius Paconius Agrippinus (heir to his father's hatred of emperors), and that scribbler of detestable verses Curtius Montanus. I insist that a former consul should attend the senate; a priest take the national vows; a citizen swear the oath of allegiance. Or has Thrasea renounced our ancestral customs and rites in favour of open treachery and hostility?

'In a word: let this model senator, this protector of the emperor's critics, appear and specify the reforms and changes that he wants. His detailed carpings would be more endurable than the universal censure of his silence. Does world-peace give him no satisfaction, or victories won without a Roman casualty? Do not gratify the perverted ambitions of a man who deplores national success, thinks of courts, theatres, and temples as deserts—and threatens to exile himself. Here is a man to whom senatorial decrees, public office, Rome itself, mean not a thing. Let him sever all connection with the place he has long since ceased to love, and has now ceased even to honour with his attendance!'

While Eprius Marcellus spoke in this vein, grim and blustering as ever, fanatical of eye, voice, and features, the senators did not feel any genuine sadness: repeated perils had made the whole business all too familiar. And yet as they saw the Guardsmen's hands on their weapons, they felt a new, sharper terror. They thought of Thrasea's venerable figure. Some also pitied Helvidius, to suffer for his guiltless marriage relationship. And what was there against Agrippinus except his father's downfall?—for he too, though as innocent as his son, had succumbed to imperial cruelty under Tiberius. The worthy young Montanus, too, was no libellous poet. The cause of his banishment was his manifest talent.

Next Ostorius Sabinus, the accuser of Barea Soranus, entered and began to speak. He denounced the defendant's friendship with Rubellius Plautus, and claimed

437

that Barea's governorship of Asia had been planned not to serve the public interest but to win popularity for himself—by encouraging the cities to rebellion. That was stale. But there was also a new charge involving Barea's daughter, Servilia, in his ordeal. She was said to have given large sums to magicians. This was true; but the cause was filial affection. Young and imprudent, she had consulted the magicians out of love for her father—but only about the prospects of her family's survival, and of Nero's compassion, and of a happy outcome to the senate's investigation. So she too was summoned before the senate. There, at opposite ends of the consul's dais, stood the elderly father and his teenage daughter, unconsolable for the loss of her exiled husband Annius Pollio—and unable even to look at her father, whose perils she had clearly intensified.

The accuser demanded whether she had sold her *trousseau* and taken the necklace from her neck in order to raise money for magical rites. At first she collapsed on the ground, weeping incessantly and not answering. But then she grasped the altar and its steps, and cried: 'Never have I called upon forbidden gods or spells! My unhappy prayers have had a single aim: that you, Caesar, and you, senators, should spare my dear father. I gave my jewels and clothes—the things that a woman in my position owns—as I would have given my blood and my life if the magicians had wanted them! I did not know the men before. They must answer for their own reputations and methods; that is not for me to do. I never mentioned the emperor except as a god. And everything was done without my poor father's knowledge. If it was a crime, I alone am to blame!'

Soranus broke in with the plea that she had not gone with him to the province, was too young to have known Rubellius Plautus, and was unimplicated in the charges against her husband. 'Her only crime is too much family affection,' he urged. 'Take her case separately—for me any fate will be acceptable.' Then he moved towards his daughter to embrace her, and she towards him. But attendants intervened and kept them apart.

Evidence was then heard. The brutality of the prosecution aroused compassion—which was only equalled by the indignation felt against one of the witnesses, Publius Egnatius Celer. He was a dependant of Soranus bribed to ruin his friend. Though professing the Stoic creed, he was crafty and deceitful at heart, using a practised demeanour of rectitude as a cover for viciousness and greed. But money was capable of stripping off the mask. Egnatius became a standard warning that men of notorious depravity or obvious deceit yield nothing in nastiness to hypocritical pseudo-philosophers and treacherous friends. However, the same day provided a model of integrity—Cassius Asclepiodotus, the richest man in Bithynia. Having honoured Soranus when he prospered, he would not desert him in his fall. So he was deprived of his whole fortune and ordered into exile—thus affording a demonstration of heaven's impartiality between good and evil.

Thrasea, Soranus, and Servilia were allowed to choose their own deaths. Helvidius and Paconius were banned from Italy. Montanus was spared for his father's sake, with the stipulation that his official career should be discontinued. The accusers Eprius and Cossutianus received five million sesterces each, Ostorius twelve hundred thousand and an honorary quaestorship.

The consul's quaestor, sent to Thrasea, found him in the evening in his garden. In his company were numerous distinguished men and women. His attention, however, was concentrated on a Cynic professor, Demetrius. To judge from Thrasea's earnest expression, and audible snatches of their conversation, they were discussing the nature of the soul and the dichotomy of spirit and body. A close friend, Domitius Caecilianus, came and informed him of the senate's decision. Thrasea urged the weeping and protesting company to leave rapidly and avoid the perils of association with a doomed man. His wife Arria, like Arria her mother, sought to share his fate. But he told her to stay alive and not deprive their daughter of her only protection.

Thrasea walked to the colonnade. There the quaestor found him, happy rather than sorrowful, because he had heard that his son-in-law Helvidius Priscus was merely banned from Italy. Then, taking the copy of the senate's decree, he led Helvidius and Demetrius into his bedroom, and offered the veins of both his arms. When the blood began to flow, he sprinkled it on the ground, and called the quaestor nearer. 'This is a libation', he said, 'to Jupiter the Liberator. Look, young man! For you have been born (may heaven avert the omen!) into an age when examples of fortitude may be a useful support.'

Tacitus *Annals* 16. 19 – end
tr. M. Grant (Penguin 1971)

157 Fear of associations

The Younger Pliny's correspondence with Trajan is a late source (AD 100-9). It is useful here as a detailed example of the persistence of official fear that associations might involve political conspiracy or rioting.

[Pliny to the Emperor Trajan]

While I was making a tour of another part of the province, an enormous fire at Nicomedia destroyed many private dwellings and two public structures—the old men's shelter and the temple of Isis—though they stood on opposite sides of the street. It spread so far firstly owing to the force of the wind, and secondly to the inactivity of the people, who, it is clear, stood idle and motionless spectators of such a terrible calamity; and in any case the city possessed not a single pump or fire bucket or any equipment at all for fighting fires. These will, however, be procured, as I have already ordered. Do you, my lord, consider whether you think it well to organize an association of firemen, not to exceed 150 members. I will see to it that none but firemen are admitted into it, and that the privileges granted shall not be abused for any other purpose; and since they would be so few, it would not be difficult to keep them under surveillance.

[Trajan to Pliny]

You are of course thinking of the examples of a number of other places in suggesting that an association of firemen might be organized in Nicomedia. But we must remember that the peace of your province, and particularly of those cities, has been repeatedly disturbed by organizations of this kind. Whatever name we give them, and for whatever purpose, men who have gathered together will all the same become a political association before long. It is therefore better to provide equipment which can be helpful for controlling fires, advise property owners to use these themselves, and, if the situation warrants it, call on the populace for assistance.

[Pliny to the Emperor Trajan]

The free allied city of Amisus enjoys, by benefit of your indulgence, the use of its own laws. A petition having been presented to me there concerning mutual-benefit societies, I append it to this letter, that you may consider, my lord, whether and to what extent these are either to be permitted or prohibited.

[Trajan to Pliny]

As to Amisus, whose petition you appended to your letter, if they are permitted by their laws, which they enjoy by virtue of their treaty, to maintain a mutual-benefit society, we cannot prevent them from having one, especially if the contributions are employed not for the purposes of rioting and illicit gatherings but for the support of the indigent. In other cities, however, which are subject to our laws, organizations of this nature are to be prohibited.

Pliny *Letters* 10. 33–4; 92–3
tr. Lewis and Reinhold vol. 2

I58 A burial society

The inscription dates from AD 136 and gives details of the financial arrangements and practices of a burial society (which might include slave members). The extract emphasizes that the meetings of such societies were strictly controlled. The society feels obliged to emphasise its allegiance to the Emperor (Hadrian).

Clause from the Decree of the Senate of the Roman People

These are permitted to assemble, convene, and maintain a society: those who desire to make monthly contributions for funerals may assemble in such a society, but they may not assemble in the name of such society except once a month for the sake of making contributions to provide burial for the dead.

May this be propitious, happy and salutary to the Emperor Caesar Trajanus Hadrian Augustus and to the entire imperial house, to us, to ours, and to our society, and may we have made proper and careful arrangements for providing decent obsequies at the departure of the dead! Therefore we must all agree to contribute faithfully, so that our society may be able to continue in existence a long time. You, who desire to enter this society as a new member, first read the by-laws carefully before entering, so as not to find cause for complaint later or bequeath a lawsuit to your heir.

CIL 14. 2112 (abridged)
tr. Lewis and Reinhold vol. 2

159 Honours from the city of Veii to a freedman of Augustus

The inscription is important for an estimation of the status of Imperial freedmen. Compare K24, D20 ff. and for a detailed treatment of the social mobility of the familia Caesaris *see P. R. C.* Weaver Familia Caesaris *(Cambridge 1972) and 'Imperial Freedmen and slaves' in (ed.) M. I.* Finley Studies in Ancient Society *(Routledge & Kegan Paul 1974).*

When the town council of Augustan Veii met in Rome at the temple of Venus Genetrix, they decided unanimously that, until the decree should be put in writing, in the meantime, Gaius Julius Gelos, freedman of Augustus, who not only helped the town of Veii at all times with his advice and influence, but also wanted to make it famous with his resources and through his son, be allowed to be decreed the most fitting honour: that he be ranked among the priests of Augustus just as if he enjoyed that honour, and be allowed to sit on the special seat of honour among the priests of the cult of Augustus at all the games in our town and to take part in all public feasts among the town councillors. They decided likewise that no tax imposed by the town of Augustan Veii should be exacted from him or his children.

There were present: Gaius Scaevius Curiatius, Lucius Perperna Priscus, duovirs; Marcus Flavius Rufus, quaestor; Titus Vettius Rufus, quaestor, Marcus Tarquitius Saturninus, Lucius Maecilius Scrupus, Lucius Favonius Lucanus, Gnaeus Octavius Sabinus, Titus Sempronius Gracchus, Publius Acuvius, son of Publius of the tribe *Tromentina*, Gaius Veianius Maximus, Titus Tarquitius Rufus, Gaius Julius Merula. Transacted in the consulship of Gaetulicus and Calvisius Sabinus.

ILS 6579
tr. LACT *Inscriptions of the Roman Empire AD 14–117*
eds. B. H. Warmington and S. H. Miller (LACTOR 8, 19--)

I60 Dedicatory Inscriptions

(a) *Dedicatory inscription by the* ministri Fortunae Augustae

The cult of Fortuna Augusta was established at Pompeii with the dedication of a temple in AD 3. This inscription probably dates from the reign of Gaius, c. AD 39/40. The dedicators named are all freedmen of wealthy Pompeiian families, but slaves could also be ministri *(see (b)).*

Lucius Numisius Primus, Lucius Numisius Optatus and Lucius Melissaeus Plocamus, ministers of the cult of Fortuna Augusta, (made this dedication) in accordance with the decree of the decurions, on the instruction of Lucius Julius Ponticus and Publius Gavius Pastor, chief magistrates, and of Quintus Poppaeus and Caius Vibius, aediles, during the consulship of Quintus Futius and Publius Calvisius.

CIL 10. 817
tr. J. Ward-Perkins and A. Claridge

(b) *Dedicatory inscription by the* ministri Augusti

Membership of this collegium *was open to slaves as well as freedmen. Officials served for one year and records date from 2 BC. This inscription probably dates from the early first century AD and is of particular interest because Narcissus' master Popidius Moschus, a freedman of an influential family, was named as one of the* ministri *in 2 BC (CIL 10. 890), an example of the operation of patronage in the service of the Imperial cult.*

Narcissus, slave of Popidius Moschus, and Nymphodotus, slave of Caprasius Jucundus, ministers of the cult of Augustus, (made this dedication) by decree of the decurions, on the instructions of Publius Vettius Celer and Decimus Alfidius.

CIL 10. 908
tr. J. Ward-Perkins and A. Claridge

(c) *Inscribed slab recording the rebuilding of the temple of Isis*

The father of the donor was a wealthy freedmen of the Popidius family and was debarred from election to the council of decurions because he had been a slave. The wealth and status of this freedman is further attested by the dedication of a statue of Dionysus (indentified here with Osiris) and a pavement in an adjoining room.

'Numerius Popidius Celsinus, son of Numerius, at his own expense rebuilt from its foundations the Temple of Isis, which had been totally destroyed by earthquake. In recognition of his generosity the city council elected him to their number without any further fee, although he was only six years old'.

CIL 10. 846
tr. J. Ward-Perkins and A. Claridge

I61 Claudius rules on the protection of sick slaves

On slavery see K. Hopkins Conquerors and Slaves *Sociological Studies in Roman History vol. 1 (Cambridge 1978); P. A. Brunt* Italian Manpower 225 BC–AD 14 *(Oxford 1971); M. I. Finley (ed.)* Slavery in Classical Antiquity *(Heffer 1960, Barnes & Noble 1968).*

Finding that a number of sick or worn-out slaves had been marooned by their owners on the Island of Aesculapius in the Tiber, to avoid the trouble of giving them proper medical attention, Claudius freed them all and ruled that none who got well again should return to the control of his former owner; furthermore, that any owner who made away with a sick slave, for the same mean reason, should be charged with murder.

> Suetonius *Claudius* 25. 2
> tr. R. Graves (Penguin 1957)

I62 The murder of the City Prefect

The passage refers to the murder of the City Prefect in AD 61 and is significant for its evidence about the persistence of upper-class fear of slave treachery and for the indication of the size of the household concerned. The opposition of arguments from utilitas *and* humanitas *is taken up in I64.*

One of his own slaves murdered the prefect of the city [Rome], Pedanius Secundus, either because he had been refused his freedom after the price had been agreed upon, or because in the passion of an infatuation for a catamite he was unable to brook his master's rivalry. In any case, according to ancient custom the whole slave household which had dwelt under the same roof was to be led to execution, but a sudden massing of the populace, which was bent on protecting so many innocent lives, brought matters to the point of insurrection, and the senate was besieged. In the senate itself there was a strong feeling on the part of some who were averse to excessive severity, but most held that no change should be made. One of these, Gaius Cassius, in stating his view, argued to the following effect:
'. . . An ex-consul has been murdered in his own home by a slave's treachery which no one reported. . . . Certainly, decree impunity! But whom will rank shield, when it did not avail the prefect of the city? Whom will a large number of slaves keep safe, when four hundred did not protect Pedanius Secundus? . . . Many clues precede a crime; if our slaves report these, we may live singly amid numbers, safe amid an insecure throng, and, if perish we must, not unavenged, at least, upon the guilty. To our ancestors the temper of their slaves was always suspect, even when they were born on the same farm or under the same roof, and acquired an affection

for their masters forthwith. But now that we have in our households foreigners with customs different from our own, with alien religions or none at all, you will not restrain such a motley rabble except by fear. But, it will be said, innocent lives will be lost. Well, when every tenth man of a routed army is felled by the club, the lot falls on the brave also. In every wholesale punishment there is some injustice to individuals, which is compensated by the advantage to the state.'

While no one member dared to oppose Cassius' view, a din of voices rose in reply from those who pitied the number, age, or sex of the victims, and the undoubted innocence of the great majority. Nevertheless, the side which was for decreeing their execution prevailed. But the decision could not be complied with, because a dense crowd had gathered, threatening to use stones and firebrands. Then the emperor reprimanded the people by edict, and when the condemned were being led to punishment he had the whole route lined with detachments of soldiers.

> Tacitus *Annals* 14. 42-5 (abridged)
> tr. Lewis and Reinhold vol. 2

163 A potential danger

On one occasion a proposal was made by the Senate to distinguish slaves from freedmen by their dress; it then became apparent how great would be the impending danger if our slaves began to count our numbers.

> Seneca *On Clemency* 1. 24. 1
> tr. Lewis and Reinhold vol. 2

164 Seneca on slaves

Seneca was writing after his retirement from public life. The extract gives an insight into his repugnance for luxuria *and the degeneration of the patron–client relationship as well as into the implications for slavery of the Stoic doctrine of the brotherhood of man.*

I am glad to learn, through those who come from you, that you live on friendly terms with your slaves. This befits a sensible and well educated man like yourself. 'They are slaves,' people declare. Nay, rather they are men. 'Slaves!' No, companions. 'Slaves!' No, they are unpretentious friends. . . .

As a result of [their] high-handed treatment the proverb is current: 'As many enemies as you have slaves.' They are not enemies when we acquire them; we make them enemies. I shall pass over the other cruel and inhuman conduct toward them;

for we maltreat them, not as if they were men, but as if they were beasts of burden. When we recline at a banquet, one slave mops up the disgorged food, another crouches beneath the table and gathers up the leftovers of the tipsy guests. Another carves the priceless game birds; with unerring strokes and skilled hand he cuts choice morsels along the breast and rump. . . . Another, who serves the wine, must dress like a woman and wrestle with his advancing years; he cannot get away from his boyhood, but is dragged back to it; and though he has already acquired a soldier's figure, he is kept beardless by having his hair smoothed away or plucked out by the roots, and he must remain awake throughout the night, dividing his time between his master's drunkenness and his lust—in the bedchamber he must be a man, at the feast a boy. Another, whose duty it is to put a valuation on the guests, must stick to his task, poor fellow, and watch to see whose flattery and whose immodesty, whether of appetite or of language, is to get them an invitation for tomorrow. . . .

Seneca *Moral Epistles* 47
tr. R. M. Gunmore (Loeb) abridged and adapted Lewis and Reinhold vol. 2

J ON ARCHITECTURE

This section includes literary and epigraphic sources relating to the architecture of Rome (J2–5), but is principally devoted to the writings of Vitruvius Pollio, who is known to us only through his treatise on architecture. From it we discover that he had been a military engineer under Julius Caesar and later Octavian (Book 1 Preface 2). He was clearly aware of the Princeps' plans for reconstruction and his book may well have been written around 27 BC. in an attempt to promote himself as one of the architects to be employed. The work is a mixture of down-to-earth instructions for builders and the reproduction of Hellenistic theories of proportion and design from older sources which Vitruvius quotes. He clearly intended to show that architecture was a demanding and intellectual pursuit though his work is no literary masterpiece, the Latin being distinctly vernacular in places; and his descriptions of some of the Hellenistic theories are obscure and confusing. Nevertheless his book is the only surviving treatise by an ancient artist and its effect on the subsequent course of European architecture has been enormous.

J1 Dedicatory inscriptions

Most major buildings were provided with dedicatory inscriptions which often record who paid for the building and in whose honour it was erected. Details such as cost or names of the architects are very seldom recorded but the inscriptions are an invaluable means of identifying actual structures referred to in the literature and often help us to fix precise dates for known buildings. This selection of inscriptions from Rome shows the sort of information they relay. The texts (a)–(d) are in Ehrenberg and Jones[2].

(a)
This inscription was found in the bed of the Tiber. The words in italics are later additions to the text. It was a dedication of an altar of Augustus to the gods, set up nine years after the beginning of the organization of vicomagistri. *The date is AD 1.*

To Mercury, to the eternal God Jupiter, Queen Juno, Minerva, Sol, Luna, Apollo, Diana, Fortuna . . . Ops, Isis, Pi(ety?) . . . to the divine fates that this enterprise turn out beneficial, fortunate, and favourable to Imperator Caesar Augustus, to his rule, and that of the Senate and people of Rome, and to the inhabitants of the world; in the 9th year which is beginning propitiously with the consulship of Gaius

446

Caesar and Lucius Paullus, Lucius Lucretius Zethus, freedman of Lucius, by command of Jupiter, erected the altar of Augustus. *Salus (Health) Semonia, and the Victory of the People.*

ILS 3090

(b) *The arch of Augustus*

This inscription was discovered in the mid-sixteenth century in Rome; O. Richter (Jahrbuch des arch. Instituts 1889 p. 153) concludes that it stood before the triumphal arch of Augustus next to the temple of divine Julius. It refers to the year 29 BC in which Octavian celebrated a triple triumph (see also B26).

The Senate and the people of Rome in honour of Imperator Caesar son of the divine Julius, consul for the fifth time, consul designate for the sixth, for having saved the Republic.

ILS 81

(c) *An inscription from 4 BC found on a statue-base under the Palatine in Rome*

Sacred to the public Lares. Caesar Augustus *pontifex maximus* (dedicates this), in the 19th year of his tribunician power, from offerings brought for him in his absence by the people on 1 January, when Gaius Calvisius Sabinus and Lucius Passienus Rufus were consuls.

ILS 99

(d) *An inscription from the base of a golden statue of Augustus found in the Forum Augusti*

To Imperator Caesar Augustus father of his country (dedicated by) the province of further Spain (Baetica) because the province was given peace by his aid and constant care. One hundred pounds of gold.

ILS 103

(e) *This inscription was found on an altar in the ruins of a small shrine on the Esquiline. Suetonius Augustus 57 describes the habit of bringing New Year's presents for Augustus even in his absence. Iullus Antonius and Fabius Maximus were consuls in 10 BC when, according to Dio Cassius (54. 36) Augustus was away in Gaul.*

Imperator Caesar Augustus, son of the divine (Julius), *pontifex maximus*, consul eleven times, in the 14th year of his tribunician power, (dedicated this) shrine from contributions presented to him in his absence by the people of Rome on 1 January, when Iullus Antonius and Africanus Fabius were consuls; sacred to Mercury.

ILS 92
tr. K. Chisholm

(f)

This open space, as enclosed within the limits of this ring of *cippi*, and the altar which is below, were dedicated by the emperor Caesar Domitianus Augustus Germanicus, in discharge of a vow undertaken, but long neglected and not honoured, for the purpose of preventing fires, when the City burned for nine days in the reign of Nero. It is dedicated on condition that no-one may within these limits be permitted to build a house, remain, carry on a trade, plant a tree or any other crop; also that the praetor to whom charge of this district of the city shall fall by lot, or some other magistrate, shall at the Festival of Volcanus on the 23rd of August in every year offer a red calf and a boar. . . .

CIL 6. 826
tr. Dudley *Urbs Roma*

J2 Aqueducts

See also C35, 36.

(a) Tiberius Claudius Augustus etc. etc. (A.D. 46), having dug channels from the Tiber in the course of harbour works, and led them to the sea, freed the city from the danger of floods.

CIL 14. 85

(b) But let us go on to describe marvels whose real value makes them incontestable. Q. Marcius Rex, being ordered by the Senate to repair the conduits of the Aqua Appia, the Anio, and the Tepula, tunnelled through the mountains to bring to Rome a new water-supply that bore his name and was finished during his praetorship. Again, Agrippa as aedile added to these the Aqua Virgo, repaired and restored the others, and constructed 700 basins, besides 500 fountains and 130 distribution points, many of which were finely decorated. To these works he added 300 statues of bronze or marble and 400 columns of marble; all this was done in a year. In the account he wrote of his aedileship he added that games lasting 59 days were celebrated in honour of this achievement, and that the 170 baths were thrown open to the public *gratis*—a number now of course very greatly increased. But all previous aqueducts have been completely outclassed by the very lavish schemes begun by the Emperor Gaius and completed by Claudius, by which the water from the Curtian and Caerulean Springs, as well as the Anio Novus, were conducted into Rome from the 40th milestone at such a high altitude as to supply all the seven hills of Rome. 350 million sesterces were expended on this project. If we take careful account of all the abundant supply of water for public buildings, baths, settling-tanks, pools, private mansions, gardens, and country estates close to the city, and of the distance the water travels before entering the city, the height of the arches, the tunnelling of mountains, the levelling of routes across deep valleys, one must rate all this as the most remarkable achievement anywhere in the world.

Pliny *Natural History* 36. 121-2
tr. Dudley *Urbs Roma*

J3 The Great Fire

Actual descriptions of Rome or other towns are rare but the historians provide a number of glimpses particularly when some extreme disaster occurred or an unusually great building was erected. The great fire of Rome in AD 64 and Nero's subsequent rebuilding plans provided ample material.

Disaster followed, in the form of the most terrible and destructive fire Rome has ever known. Whether this was accidental, or elaborately contrived by the Emperor, is uncertain; historians give both versions. It began in the part of the Circus Maximus which is close to the Palatine and Caelian Hills, and among shops whose wares included inflammable goods. The fire took hold at once, and the wind very quickly spread it the length of the Circus, where there were no palaces with outer walls nor temples within precincts nor indeed anything else to check it. First it swept through all the level ground, then climbed the hills, then returned again to destroy the lower districts. The speed with which it spread, and the all-too-inflammable nature of the old city, with its narrow winding streets and irregular buildings, nullified all attempts to contain it. All movement was blocked by the terrified, shrieking women, by helpless old people or children, by those who sought their own safety or tried to help others—some carrying invalids, others waiting for them to catch up, some rushing headlong, others rooted to the spot. When people looked back, outbreaks of fire threatened them from the front or the flanks. When they reached a neighbouring quarter, that too was alight: even what they had supposed to be remote districts were found to be affected. Finally, utterly at a loss as to what to avoid or where to go, they filled the streets, or collapsed in the fields. Some died because they had lost everything they had—even their food for the day. Others had lost their loved ones in the flames, and preferred death, though they could have escaped. No one dared to fight the flames. Menacing gangs threatened anyone who dared to put out the fire; indeed, some men openly cast on torches, and said they had their instructions. They may have been acting under orders, they may simply have wanted a freer hand to loot.

Nero was then at Antium. He did not return to Rome until the flames were threatening the house he had built to link the Palatine with the Gardens of Maecenas. But the fire could not be checked before it had destroyed the Palatine itself, the palace, and everything in the vicinity. As a refuge for the terrified, homeless people he threw open the Campus Martius and the buildings of Agrippa. He also

449

opened his own gardens, and constructed emergency huts to house the thousands of helpless refugees. Supplies were brought in from Ostia and the neighbouring towns, and the price of corn was reduced to 3 sesterces a peck. These were meant to be popular measures, but they earned no gratitude, for a widespread report had it that as the city was burning Nero entered his private theatre and sang 'The Fall of Troy', comparing the modern with the ancient calamity.

The fire was brought to a halt on the sixth day at the foot of the Esquiline, where enormous demolition of houses faced its unbroken violence with open space and bare ground. But before terror was allayed, or hope could revive in the people, there was a fresh outbreak in the more open parts of the city. Here actual loss of life was less, but the destruction of temples and amenities such as colonnades was even more widespread. This second fire was the more suspicious because it started on the estates of Tigellinus in the Aemilian district. Nero, it seemed, longed for the glory of founding a new city, and giving it his own name. For indeed, of the fourteen regions into which Rome was divided, only four remained intact, three were destroyed to ground level; in the other seven a few houses survived, but half-burned and severely damaged.

It would be a long task to enumerate all the palaces, blocks of apartments, and temples that were destroyed. Among famous and ancient shrines, there perished Servius Tullius' Temple of the Moon-Goddess, the Great Altar and Shrine which Evander dedicated to Hercules, the Temple of Jupiter Stator, the Regia, the work of Romulus and of Numa, and above all, the Shrine of Vesta and the Penates of the Roman People. There perished too the spoils of so many victories, the masterpieces of Greek art, and the ancient and authentic manuscripts of so many of the great writers of Roman literature. For all the beauty of the re-built city, there are many of an older generation who remember those losses as unique and irreplaceable. It was noted in some quarters that the fire began on July 19th, the very day on which the Senonian Gauls burned the city. Others inquired so as to discover that between the two fires there elapsed the same number of years, plus months, plus days.

Tacitus *Annals* 15. 38–41
tr. Dudley *Urbs Roma*

J4 The Golden House

*Nero's Golden House (*Domus Aurea*) provides the fullest account we have of a large palace from the early Empire.*

(a)
The entrance hall was designed for a colossal statue, 120 feet high, bearing Nero's head. So vast were the grounds, that triple colonnades ran for a mile. There was, too, an enormous lake, surrounded by buildings made to look like cities. The

parklands contained fields, vineyards, pastures and woodlands; there were a great variety of animals, domestic and wild. Some parts of the palace were overlaid with gold, and studded with jewels and mother-of-pearl. The dining rooms had ceilings of ivory, with sliding panels to allow flowers and perfumes to be showered down upon the guests. The main dining room was a rotunda, which revolved slowly, day and night, like the vault of heaven itself. There were baths with a lavish supply of both sea-water and sulphur water. When the palace was completed on this sumptuous scale, Nero's approval as he dedicated it was confined to the remark 'At last I can begin to live like a human being!'

Suetonius *Nero* 31

(b)

Nero made good use of this disaster to his country. For he built himself a palace, remarkable not so much for its gold and jewels—these are the usual trappings of luxury and have become commonplace—as for its meadows, its lakes, its artificial wilderness, now of woods and now of open spaces, and its vistas. Severus and Celer were the architects and engineers.

Tacitus *Annals* 15. 42

(c)

Here, where the glistening colossus views the stars at short range, where the scaffolding rises in the middle of the Sacred Way—here stretched wide the haughty entrance halls of the cruel tyrant, and a single great estate stood in the whole of Rome. Here, where the noble mass of the great amphitheatre is being built, was the lake of Nero. Here, where we admire the Thermae of Titus—that gift so quickly given—Nero's proud park had swallowed the cottages of the poor. Where the colonnade of Claudius' (temple) spreads its spacious shades, were the furthest bounds of that unfinished palace. Rome is restored to herself, and under your rule, Caesar, the people's pleasure is what once belonged to their lord and master.

Martial *Spectacula* 1. 2
tr. Dudley *Urbs Roma*

(d) *A painter who worked on Nero's Golden House and was perhaps one of the inventors of the 'Fourth Style'*

More recently there was the serious and severe, but at the same time overly florid painter Famulus [or Fabullus] . By his hand there was a Minerva which continued to face the viewer no matter from what angle he looked at it. He used to paint for only a few hours a day, but this was done with great gravity, since he always wore a toga, even when he was in the midst of his painter's equipment. The *Domus Aurea* was the prison for his artistry, and for that reason there are not many other examples of his work extant.

Pliny *Natural History* 35. 120
tr. Pollitt *The Art of Rome*

J5 The Capitol

The Capitol was the citadel of Rome, site of the temple of Jupiter Best and Greatest, one of the major cult centres of the city. The destruction of the temple by fire occurred in AD 69, a result of the clash between partisans of Vitellius and Vespasian. Tacitus' description of the restoration makes plain the pervasiveness of ritual in Roman life and its close connection with public architecture.

The task of restoring the Capitol was entrusted to Lucius Vestinus, an equestrian, but commanding a power and reputation second to none. The *haruspices* he consulted advised that the remains of the old building should be carted off to the marshes, but the temple re-erected on the former site: the gods were averse to any change in its design. On the 21st of June, in fine weather, the whole area to be consecrated for the temple was surrounded with wreaths and garlands. Soldiers entered, men of lucky names, carrying branches from propitious trees. Then Vestal Virgins, with boys and girls whose parents were both alive, purified the whole space with water drawn from sacred springs and rivers. Then Helvidius Priscus, the praetor, having hallowed the whole area by the sacrifice of a bull, a stallion, and a boar, and placed the entrails on the altar, solemnly repeated after the Chief Pontiff, Plautius Aelianus, a prayer to Jupiter, Juno, and Minerva, and the gods who protect the Empire, to enlist their support for the project, and to bring divine aid to prosper the plans for their temple which had been begun by the efforts of man. He then touched the wreaths with which the foundation stone and the ropes around it were bound. At the same time the other magistrates, the priests, the senate, the knights, and a large part of the common people, vied with each other in their zeal to drag along the huge stone. In every part of the foundations were placed ores of gold and silver, never melted down, but in their original state. The augurs had forbidden that any metal or stone intended for some other purpose should be allowed to profane their work. The height of the building was increased: this was the sole innovation that religion would allow, and the only respect in which the ancient temple seemed less than magnificent.

Tacitus *Histories* 4. 53
tr. Dudley *Urbs Roma*

J6 Vitruvius On Architecture

This work is wide ranging and its structure is often surprising. The ten books are arranged as follows:
Book 1 Preface; education of the architect; fundamental principles of architecture; departments of architecture; site of a city; city walls; layout of streets and remarks on the winds; sites for public buildings.

Book 2 Introduction; origins of the house; the nature of primordial substance; brick; sand; lime; pozzolana; stone; methods of building walls; timber; highland and lowland fir.

Book 3 Introduction; symmetry in temples and the human body; classification of temples; proportions and spacing of columns; foundations; proportions of the Ionic order.

Book 4 Introduction; origins of the three orders and proportions of the Corinthian capital; ornaments of the orders; proportions of Doric temples; the cella and pronaos; orientation of temples; doorways of temples; Tuscan temples; circular temples and other varieties; altars.

Book 5 Introduction; forum and basilica; treasury, prison, and senate house; theatre-site, foundations, and acoustics; harmonics; sounding vases in the theatre; theatre plan; Greek theatres; acoustics of the theatre site; colonnades and walks; baths; the palaestra; harbours, breakwaters, and shipyards.

Book 6 Introduction; climate and the style of house; symmetry and modifications to suit the site; proportions of the principal rooms; proper aspects of rooms; housing for different ranks of society; farm buildings; the Greek house; foundations and substructures.

Book 7 Introduction; floors; preparation of stucco; vaults and stucco; stucco in damp places; wall painting; use of marble in stucco; natural colours; vermilion and quicksilver; vermilion; black; blue; yellow ochre; white, green and red leads; purple; artificial colours.

Book 8 Introduction; the Zodiac and the planets; phases of the moon; the sun's course through the signs; northern constellations; southern constellations; astrology; the principles of dialling; sundials and water clocks.

Book 10 Introduction; machines and instruments; hoisting machines; elements of motion; machines for raising water; water wheels and water mills; the water screw; Ctesibius' pump; the water organ; measuring a journey; catapults; ballistae; stringing and tuning of catapults; siege machines; the tortoise; Hegetor's tortoise; defensive machinery.

The following passages are from the Loeb translation by F. Granger (1934).

Book 1 Preface: Vitruvius' dedication to Augustus

1   When your Highness's divine mind and power, O Caesar, gained the empire of the world, Rome gloried in your triumph and victory. For all her enemies were crushed by your invincible courage and all mankind obeyed your bidding; the Roman people and senate were not only freed from fear but followed your guidance, inspired as it was by a generous imagination. Amid such affairs I shrank from publishing my writings on architecture in which I displayed designs made to a large scale, for I feared lest by interrupting at an inconvenient time, I should be found a hindrance to your thoughts.

2   But I observed that you cared not only about the common life of all men, and the constitution of the state, but also about the provision of suitable public buildings; so that the state was not only made greater through you by its new

provinces, but the majesty of the empire also was expressed through the eminent dignity of its public buildings. Hence I conceived that the opportunity should be taken at once of bringing before you my proposals about these things: the more so, because I had been first known to your father herein, whose virtues I revered. When, however, the Council of Heaven gave him an abode in the mansion of the immortals and placed in your power your father's empire, that same zeal of mine which had remained faithful to his memory found favour also with you.

Therefore, along with M. Aurelius and P. Minidius and Cn. Cornelius, I was put in charge of the construction and repair of *balistae* and *scorpiones* and other engines of war, and, along with my colleagues, received advancement. After first granting me this surveyorship, you continued it by the recommendation of your sister.

3   Since, then, I was indebted to you for such benefits that to the end of life I had no fear of poverty, I set about the composition of this work for you. For I perceived that you have built, and are now building, on a large scale. Furthermore, with respect to the future, you have such regard to public and private buildings, that they will correspond to the grandeur of our history, and will be a memorial to future ages. I have furnished a detailed treatise so that, by reference to it, you might inform yourself about the works already complete or about to be entered upon. In the following books I have expounded a complete system of architecture.

J7 1. 1. 1–11: On the training of architects

1   The science of the architect depends upon many disciplines and various apprenticeships which are carried out in other arts. His personal service consists in craftsmanship and technology. Craftsmanship is continued and familiar practice, which is carried out by the hands in such material as is necessary for the purpose of a design. Technology sets forth and explains things wrought in accordance with technical skill and method.

2   So architects who without culture aim at manual skill cannot gain a prestige corresponding to their labours, while those who trust to theory and literature obviously follow a shadow and not reality. But those who have mastered both, like men equipped in full armour, soon acquire influence and attain their purpose.

3   Both in general and especially in architecture are these two things found; that which signifies and that which is signified. That which is signified is the thing proposed about which we speak; that which signifies is the demonstration unfolded in systems of precepts. Wherefore a man who is to follow the architectural profession manifestly needs to have experience of both kinds. He must have both a natural gift and also readiness to learn. (For neither talent without instruction nor instruction without talent can produce the perfect craftsman.) He should be a man of letters, a skilful draughtsman, a mathematician, familiar with historical studies, a diligent student of philosophy, acquainted with music; not ignorant of

medicine, learned in the responses of jurisconsults, familiar with astronomy and astronomical calculations.

4   The reasons why this should be so are these. An architect must be a man of letters that he may keep a record of useful precedents. By his skill in draughtsmanship he will find it easy by coloured drawings to represent the effect desired. Mathematics again furnishes many resources to architecture. It teaches the use of rule and compass and thus facilitates the laying out of buildings on their sites by the use of set-squares, levels and alignments. By optics, in buildings, lighting is duly drawn from certain aspects of the sky. By arithmetic, the cost of building is summed up; the methods of mensuration are indicated; while the difficult problems of symmetry are solved by geometrical rules and methods. 5   Architects ought to be familiar with history because in their works they often design many ornaments about which they ought to render an account to inquirers. For example, if anyone in his work sets up, instead of columns, marble statues of long-robed women which are called caryatids, and places mutules and cornices above them, he will thus render an account to inquirers. Caria, a Peloponnesian state, conspired with the Persian enemy against Greece. Afterwards the Greeks, gloriously freed from war by their victory, with common purpose went on to declare war on the inhabitants of Caria. The town was captured; the men were killed; the state was humiliated. Their matrons were led away into slavery and were not allowed to lay aside their draperies and ornaments. In this way, and not at one time alone, were they led in triumph. Their slavery was an eternal warning. Insult crushed them. They seemed to pay a penalty for their fellow-citizens. And so the architects of that time designed for public buildings figures of matrons placed to carry burdens; in order that the punishment of the sin of the Cariatid women might be known to posterity and historically recorded.   6   Not less the Spartans under the command of Pausanias, son of Agesilas, having conquered with a small force an infinitely large army of Persians, gloriously celebrated a triumph with spoils and plunder, and, from the booty, built the Persian Colonnade to signify the merit and courage of the citizens and to be a trophy of victory to their descendants. There they placed statues of their captives in barbaric dress—punishing their pride with deserved insults—to support the roof, that their enemies might quake, fearing the workings of such bravery, and their fellow-citizens looking upon a pattern of manhood might by such glory be roused and prepared for the defence of freedom. Therefrom many have set up Persian statues to support architraves and their ornaments. This motive has supplied for their works some striking variations. There are also other narratives of the same kind with which architects should possess acquaintance.   7   Philosophy, however, makes the architect high-minded, so that he should not be arrogant but rather urbane, fair-minded, loyal, and what is most important, without avarice; for no work can be truly done without good faith and clean hands. Let him not be greedy nor have his mind busied with acquiring gifts; but let him with seriousness guard his dignity by keeping a good name. And such are the injunctions of philosophy. Philosophy, moreover, explains the 'nature of things' (and this in Greek is *physiologia*), a subject which it is necessary to have studied carefully because it

presents many different natural problems, as, for example, in the case of water-supply. For in the case of water-courses, where there are channels or bends or where water is forced along on a levelled plane, natural air-pockets are produced in different ways, and the difficulties which they cause cannot be remedied by anyone unless he has learnt from philosophy the principles of nature. So also the man who reads the works of Ctesibius or Archimedes and of others who have written manuals of the same kind will not be able to perceive their meaning, unless he has been instructed herein by philosophers.   8   A man must know music that he may have acquired the *acoustic* and mathematical relations and be able to carry out rightly the adjustments of *balistae, catapultae* and *scorpiones*. For in the cross-beams on right and left are holes 'of half-tones' (*hemitonia*) through which ropes twisted out of thongs are stretched by windlasses and levers. And these ropes are not shut off nor tied up, unless they make clear and equal sounds in the ear of the craftsman. For the arms which are shut up under those strains, when they are stretched out, ought to furnish an impetus evenly, and alike on either side. But if they do not give an equal note, they will hinder the straight direction of the missiles. 9   In theatres, also, are copper vessels and these are placed in chambers under the rows of seats in accordance with mathematical reckoning. The Greeks call them *echeia*. The differences of the sounds which arise are combined into musical symphonies or concords: the circle of seats being divided into fourths and fifths and the octave. Hence, if the delivery of the actor from the stage is adapted to these contrivances, when it reaches them, it becomes fuller, and reaches the audience with a richer and sweeter note. Or again, no one who lacks a knowledge of music can make water-engines or similar machines.   10   Again, he must know the art of medicine in its relation to the regions of the earth (which the Greeks call *climata*); and to the characters of the atmosphere, of localities (wholesome or pestilential), of water-supply. For apart from these considerations, no dwelling can be regarded as healthy. He must be familiar with the rights or easements which necessarily belong to buildings with party walls, as regards the range of eaves-droppings, drains and lighting. The water-supply, also, and other related matters, ought to be familiar to architects: so that, before building is begun, precautions may be taken, lest on completion of the works the proprietors should be involved in disputes. Again, in writing the specifications, careful regard is to be paid both to the employer and to the contractor. For if the specification is carefully written, either party may be released from his obligations to the other, without the raising of captious objections. By astronomy we learn the east, the west, the south and the north; also the order of the heavens, the equinox, the solstice, the course of the planets. For if anyone is unfamiliar with these, he will fail to understand the construction of clocks.

11   Since, therefore, so great a profession as this is adorned by, and abounds in, varied and numerous accomplishments, I think that only these persons can forthwith justly claim to be architects who from boyhood have mounted by the steps of these studies and, being trained generally in the knowledge of arts and the sciences, have reached the temple of architecture at the top.

J8 1. 2. 1–9: Of what things architecture consists

Vitruvius outlines five areas of architecture offering a technical vocabulary to describe methods of drawing.

Most of the technical terms here derive from Greek. The whole system of designing and measuring rests on the relationship of parts to each other. Usually the base diameter of the column was taken as a module and all other dimensions calculated as multiples or fractions of that which give the whole design a unity of proportion. This method underlies all classical architecture, and is reinforced by the stress on symmetry—not simply making one half a mirror image of the other (which is axial symmetry) but with each item balanced by a corresponding member. Such a system tended not to value novelty but rather led to a stress on convention and precedent.

1   Now architecture consists of Order, which in Greek is called *taxis*, and of Arrangement, which the Greeks name *diathesis*, and of Proportion and Symmetry and Decor and Distribution which in Greek is called *oeconomia*.

2   Order is the balanced adjustment of the details of the work separately, and, as to the whole, the arrangement of the proportion with a view to a symmetrical result. This is made up of Dimension, which in Greek is called *posotes*. Now Dimension is the taking of modules from the parts of the work; and the suitable effect of the whole work arising from the several subdivisions of the parts.

Arrangement, however, is the fit assemblage of details, and, arising from this assemblage, the elegant effect of the work and its dimensions, along with a certain quality or character. The kinds of the arrangement (which in Greek are called *ideae*) are these: ichnography (plan); orthography (elevation); scenography (perspective). Ichnography (plan) demands the competent use of compass and rule; by these plans are laid out upon the sites provided. Orthography (elevation), however, is the vertical image of the front, and a figure slightly tinted to show the lines of the future work. Scenography (perspective) also is the shading of the front and the retreating sides, and the correspondence of all lines to the vanishing point, which is the centre of a circle. These three (plan, elevation and perspective) arise from imagination and invention. Imagination rests upon the attention directed with minute and observant fervour to the charming effect proposed. Invention, however, is the solution of obscure problems; the treatment of a new undertaking disclosed by an active intelligence. Such are the outlines of Arrangement.

3   Proportion implies a graceful semblance; the suitable display of details in their context. This is attained when the details of the work are of a height suitable to their breadth, of a breadth suitable to their length; in a word, when everything has a symmetrical correspondence.

4   Symmetry also is the appropriate harmony arising out of the details of the work itself; the correspondence of each given detail among the separate details to the form of the design as a whole. As in the human body, from cubit, foot, palm, inch and other small parts comes the symmetric quality of eurhythmy; so is it in

457

the completed building. First, in sacred buildings, either from the thickness of columns, or a triglyph, or the module; of a balista by the perforation which the Greeks call *peritreton*; by the space between the rowlocks in a ship which is called *dipechyaia*: so also the calculation of symmetries, in the case of other works, is found from the details.

5 Decor demands the faultless ensemble of a work composed, in accordance with precedent, of approved details. It obeys convention, which in Greek is called *thematismos*, or custom or nature. . . .

6 With reference to fashion, decor is thus expressed; when to magnificent interiors vestibules also are made harmonious and elegant. For if the interior apartments present an elegant appearance, while the approaches are low and uncomely, they will not be accompanied by fitness. Again, if, in Doric entablatures, dentils are carved on the cornices, or if with voluted capitals and Ionic entablatures, triglyphs are applied, characteristics are transferred from one style to another: the work as a whole will jar upon us, since it includes details foreign to the order. . . .

OF DOORS AND WINDOWS IN BATHS AND ELSEWHERE

Also there will be natural seemliness if light is taken from the east for bedrooms and libraries; for baths and winter apartments, from the wintry sunset; for picture galleries and the apartments which need a steady light, from the north, because that quarter of the heavens is neither illumined nor darkened by the sun's course but is fixed unchangeable throughout the day.

ON THE QUALITIES OF SITES AND SUPPLIES FOR THE WORKS

8 Distribution or Economy, however, is the suitable disposal of supplies and the site, and the thrifty and wise control of expense in the works. This will be guarded if, in the first place, the architect does not require what can only be supplied and prepared at great cost. For it is not everywhere that there is a supply of quarry sand or hewn stone, or fir or deal or marble. Different things are found in different places, the transport of them may be difficult and costly. Now where there is no quarry sand we must use washed river or sea sand; the need for fir or deal will be met by using cypress, poplar, elm, pine; other difficulties will be solved in a like fashion. 9 The second stage in Economy comes, when buildings are variously disposed for the use of owners or with a view to the display of wealth or lofty enough to suit the most dignified eloquence. For manifestly houses should be arranged in one way in towns; in another way for persons whose income arises from country estates; not the same for financiers; in another way for the wealthy men of taste; for the powerful, however, by whose ideas the state is governed, there must be special adjustment to their habits. And generally the distribution of buildings is to be adapted to the vocations of their owners.

J9 1. 3. 1-2: On the parts of architecture

Vitruvius sets out the arrangement of his work. The section on building is obvious enough but it is interesting to find a whole book on dialling (astrology and calculations for sundials and the like) and on mechanics (water power and military equipment). It is also significant that the sections on building begin with military structures; and the basis of all building in the much quoted recipe of strength, utility, and grace is tantalizingly indefinable.

1   The parts of architecture itself are three: Building (Books 1-VIII), Dialling (Book IX), and Mechanics (Book X). Building in turn is divided into two parts; of which one is the placing of city walls, and of public buildings on public sites (Books I-V); the other is the setting out of private buildings (Books VI-VIII). Now the assignment of public buildings is threefold: one, to defence; the second, to religion; the third, to convenience. The method of defence by walls, towers and gates has been devised with a view to the continuous warding off of hostile attacks; to religion belongs the placing of the shrines and sacred temples of the immortal gods; to convenience, the disposal of public sites for the general use, such as harbours, open spaces, colonnades, baths, theatres, promenades, and other things which are planned, with like purposes, in public situations.

2   Now these should be so carried out that account is taken of strength, utility, grace. Account will be taken of *strength* when the foundations are carried down to the solid ground, and when from each material there is a choice of supplies without parsimony; of *utility*, when the sites are arranged without mistake and impediment to their use, and a fit and convenient disposition for the aspect of each kind; of *grace*, when the appearance of the work shall be pleasing and elegant, and the scale of the constituent parts is justly calculated for symmetry.

J10 1. 5. 1-5: On the foundations of walls and the establishment of towns

1   When, therefore, by these methods there shall be ensured healthiness in the laying out of the walls; and districts shall be chosen abounding in fruit to feed the citizens; and roads duly laid out, or convenient rivers, or supplies by sea through the harbours, shall have ready transport to the ramparts: then the foundations of the towers and walls are to be laid. If such foundations can be found, they are to be dug down to the solid and in the solid, as may seem proportionate to the amplitude of the work, of a breadth greater than that of the walls which shall be above the ground; and these foundations are to be filled with as solid structure as possible.

2   Towers, moreover, are to be projected on the outer side, in order that when the enemy wishes to approach the wall in an attack, he may be wounded on his exposed flanks by weapons on the right and left from the towers. And it seems that

care must especially be taken that the approach be not easy for an enemy block-ading the wall. The approach must be made to wind along the steep places, and so devised that the ways to the gates are not straight, but on the left of the wall. For when it is so done, then as the troops approach, their right side will be next the wall and will not be protected by the shield. Moreover, towns are not to be planned square nor with projecting angles, but on the round, so that the enemy be seen from several sides. For when angles run out, defence is difficult, because the angle defends the enemy rather than the townsmen.   3   But I think the width of the wall should be so made that armed men meeting one another above can pass without hindrance. Then, in the width, through-timbers of charred olive wood should be put very frequently, in order that both fronts of the wall, being tied together by these timbers, as though by pins, may have everlasting strength. For such timber cannot be injured by decay or weather or age; even when it is covered with soil or placed in water, it remains unimpaired and useful for ever. And so not only the city wall, but the substructures, and those dividing walls which are made to be of the thickness of fortifications, when united in this manner, will not quickly be de-cayed.   4   The distances between the towers are so to be made that one is not further from another than a bowshot; so that if a tower is besieged anywhere, then, by 'scorpions' and other missile engines from the towers right and left, the enemy may be thrown back. And also opposite the lower part of the towers, the wall is to be divided by intervals as wide as a tower; and these intervals opposite the interior parts of the towers shall be joined with planks. These, however, are not to be fixed with iron nails. For if the enemy occupies any part of the wall, the defenders shall cut them down, and if they manage it quickly, they will not suffer the enemy to penetrate the rest of the towers and wall, unless he is willing to throw himself head-long.   5   The towers therefore are to be made round or polygonal. For engines more quickly demolish square towers, because the battering-rams beat and break the angles; whereas in the case of rounded surfaces, even when they drive the battering-rams wedge-fashion towards the centre, they cannot hurt them. Further, the fortifications of the wall and towers especially when joined by embankments are safer, because neither battering-rams nor undermining nor other contrivances avail to injure them.

J11 1. 6. 1; 3; 6–8: Respecting the division of works inside the walls

Vitruvius lays much stress on the importance of designing to fit with prevailing winds. He gives precise instructions for determining the direction of the main street (cardo maximus) *by means of a diagram and thus establishing the grid for a new town. Vitruvius recommends a plan that will exclude winds on medical grounds. It is interesting that 300 years later Oribasius recommends the exact opposite—that winds should be allowed to blow through and air a town.*

RESPECTING THE DIVISION OF THE WORKS WHICH ARE INSIDE THE WALLS
AND THEIR ARRANGEMENT SO THAT THE NOXIOUS BREATH OF THE
WINDS MAY BE AVOIDED

1　When the walls are set round the city, there follow the divisions of the sites
within the walls, and the layings out of the broad streets and the alleys with a view
to aspect. These will be rightly laid out if the winds are carefully shut out from the
alleys. For if the winds are cold they are unpleasant; if hot, they infect; if moist,
they are injurious. Wherefore this fault must be avoided and guarded against, lest
there happen what in many cities is not infrequent. For example in the island of
Lesbos, the town of Mytilene is magnificently and elegantly built, but not situated
with prudence. For in this city when the South wind blows men fall ill; when the
North-west, they cough; when the North, they are restored to health; but they cannot stand in the alleys and streets because of the vehemence of the cold. . . .　3
Suppose they are excluded. Not only will this render a place healthy for sound
persons; but also if any diseases shall happen to arise from other infections, those
who in other healthy places find cure from counteracting medicine, in these, on
account of the moderate climate and by the exclusion of the winds, will be still
more quickly cured. For the diseases which are cured with difficulty in the regions
which are described above are these: cold in the windpipe, cough, pleurisy, phthisis,
spitting of blood, and others which are cured by strengthening remedies rather
than by purgings. These ailments are treated with difficulty, first because they are
caught from chills, secondly because when the strength is worn out by disease the
air is agitated; it is thinned by the agitation of the winds; at the same time it draws
the sap from diseased persons and renders them thinner. On the other hand, a
smooth and thick air which is free from the passage of draughts and does not move
backwards and forwards, builds up their limbs by its steadiness, and so nourishes
and refreshes those who are caught by these diseases. . . .　6　Let there be placed
to a level a marble dial, somewhere in the middle of the city; or let a space be so
polished to rule and level that the marble dial is not wanted. Above the middle
point of that place, let there be put a bronze indicator to track the shadow (which
in Greek is called *sciotheres*). Before midday, at about the fifth hour, the end of the
shadow of the indicator is to be taken and marked with a point. Then a radius being
taken from the indicator to the point which marks the length of the shadow, with
that, from the indicator as centre, a circumference is to be drawn. After midday the
growing shadow of the indicator, when it touches the line of the circle and marks a
post-meridian shadow equal to the ante-meridian, is to be marked with a point.
7　From these two points, two intersecting circles are to be described. Through
the intersection and the centre of the circle first described, a line is to be carried
through to the end so that the southern and northern quarters may be indicated.
Next we take as radius the sixteenth part of the circumference of the circle. From
centres given by the meridian line at the two points where it touches the circle, and
with that radius, points are to be marked right and left in the circle, both on the
southern and on the northern part. Then from these four points, intersecting lines

are to be drawn through the middle centre from one side of the circumference to the other. Thus both for the south wind and for the north wind we shall have marked out the eighth part of the circumference. The remaining parts in the whole round, three on the right and three on the left, are to be distributed equally, so that equal divisions of the eight winds are marked out in the figure. Then the angles between two quarters of the winds will determine the laying out both of the streets and of the alleys. 8 For by these methods and this division, troublesome winds will be excluded from the dwellings and the streets. For when the quarters of the city are planned to meet the winds full, the rush of air and the frequent breezes from the open space of the sky will move with mightier power, confined as they are in the jaws of the alleys. Wherefore the directions of the streets are to avoid the quarters of the winds, so that when the winds come up against the corners of the blocks of buildings they may be broken, driven back and dissipated.

J12 1.7.1: On the sites of public buildings

After apportioning the alleys and settling the main streets, the choice of sites for the convenience and common use of citizens has to be explained; for sacred buildings, the forum, and the other public places. And if the ramparts are by *the sea*, a site where the forum is to be put is to be chosen next the harbour; but if *inland*, in the middle of the town. But for sacred buildings of the gods under whose protection the city most seems to be, both for Jupiter and Juno and Minerva, the sites are to be distributed on the highest ground from which the most of the ramparts is to be seen. To Mercury, however, in the forum, or also, as to Isis and Serapis, in the business quarter; to Apollo and Father Bacchus against the theatre; to Hercules, in cities which have no gymnasia nor amphitheatres, at the circus; to Mars outside the walls but in the parade ground; and also to Venus near the harbour.

J13 2.1–5: The origin of building

The speculative account of the history of building may be related, in its evolutionary approach, to writers such as Lucretius. It is important in that it sets out to show that the forms of Roman architecture are rooted in natural law.

1 Men, in the old way, were born like animals in forests and caves and woods, and passed their life feeding on the food of the fields. Meanwhile, once upon a time, in a certain place, trees, thickly crowded, tossed by storms and winds and rubbing their branches together, kindled a fire. Terrified by the raging flame, those who were about that place were put to flight. Afterwards when the thing was quieted down, approaching nearer they perceived that the advantage was great for

their bodies from the heat of the fire. They added fuel, and thus keeping it up, they brought others; and pointing it out by signs they showed what advantages they had from it. In this concourse of mankind, when sounds were variously uttered by the breath, by daily custom they fixed words as they had chanced to come. Then, indicating things more frequently and by habit, they came by chance to speak according to the event, and so they generated conversation with one another.   2   Therefore, because of the discovery of fire, there arose at the beginning, concourse among men, deliberation and a life in common. Many came together into one place, having from nature this boon beyond other animals, that they should walk, not with head down, but upright, and should look upon the magnificence of the world and of the stars. They also easily handled with their hands and fingers whatever they wished. Hence after thus meeting together, they began, some to make shelters of leaves, some to dig caves under the hills, some to make of mud and wattles places for shelter, imitating the nests of swallows and their methods of building. Then observing the houses of others and adding to their ideas new things from day to day, they produced better kinds of huts.   3   Since men were of an imitative and teachable nature, they boasted of their inventions as they daily showed their various achievements in building, and thus, exercising their talents in rivalry, were rendered of better judgment daily. And first, with upright forked props and twigs put between, they wove their walls. Others made walls, drying moistened clods which they bound with wood, and covered with reeds and leafage, so as to escape the rain and heat. When in winter-time the roofs could not withstand the rains, they made ridges, and smearing clay down the sloping roofs, they drew off the rain-water.

   4   That these things were so practised from the beginnings above described we can observe, seeing that to this day buildings are constructed for foreign nations of these materials, as in Gaul, Spain, Portugal, Aquitaine, with oak shingles or thatch. . . . Not less also at Marseilles we can observe roofs without tiles, made of earth and kneaded with straw. At Athens there is an ancient type of building, on the Areopagus, to this day covered with mud. Also in the Capitolium the Hut of Romulus, and in the Citadel, shrines covered with straw, can remind us, and signify the customs and the antiquities of Rome.

J14 2. 3. 1–4: On bricks

*This and the following chapters read more like a builder's manual though they are still interspersed with conventional antiquarian asides on Greek terms and practices. Vitruvius uses the word for sun-dried bricks (*lateres*) which had been more common in Republican times although kiln-baked bricks (*testae*) were replacing them in the reign of Augustus.*

1   Therefore, first I will speak about bricks, and from what kind of clay they ought to be brought. For they ought not to be made from sandy nor chalky soil nor

gravelly soil: because when they are got from these formations, first they become heavy, then, when they are moistened by rain showers in the walls, they come apart and are dissolved. And the straw does not stick in them because of their roughness. But bricks are to be made of white clayey earth or of red earth, or even of rough gravel. For these kinds, because of their smoothness, are durable. They are not heavy in working, and are easily built up together.   2   Now bricks are to be made either in the spring or autumn, that they may dry at one and the same time. For those which are prepared at the summer solstice become faulty for this reason: when the sun is keen and overbakes the top skin, it makes it seem dry, while the interior of the brick is not dried. And when afterwards it is contracted by drying, it breaks up what was previously dried. Thus bricks crack and are rendered weak. But, most especially, they will be more fit for use if they are made two years before. For they cannot dry throughout before. Therefore when they are built in fresh and not dry, and the plaster is put on and becomes rigid, they remain solid only on the surface. Hence they settle and cannot keep the same height as the plaster. For by contraction and the consequent movement they cease to stick to the plaster, and are separated from their union with it. Therefore the wall-surfaces are separated from the wall itself, and because of their thinness cannot stand of themselves and are broken, and the walls settling haphazard, become faulty. That is why the citizens of Utica use no bricks for building walls, unless the magistrate has approved them as being dry and made five years before.   3   Now there are three kinds of bricks: one which in Greek is called *Lydion*, that is the one which we use, a foot and a half long, a foot wide. Greek buildings are constructed with the other two. Of these, one is called *pentadoron*, the other *tetradoron*. Now the Greeks call the palm *doron*, because the giving of gifts is called *doron*, and this is always done by means of the palm of the hand. Thus the brick that is of five palms every way is called pentadoron; of four palms, tetradoron. Public buildings are erected with the former; private buildings with the latter.   4   Along with these bricks, half-bricks also are made. When these are built to the line of the face, on one side courses are laid with bricks, on the other side half-bricks are laid. The walls are bound together by the alternate facings; and the middle of the bricks, being placed above the joints, produces firmness, and a not unpleasing appearance on either side.

J15 2. 4. 1–3: On sand

Vitruvius' word for rubble structures (caementicia structura) *shows that he is talking of walls built of Roman concrete, that is to say an aggregate of cement and lumps of rubble (cf. 2. 8–J18). The quality of sand and lime was crucial to their strength since it was in effect the cement mortar that held the wall up while the rubble aggregate merely provided the mass.*

1   Now in rubble structures we must first inquire about the sand, that it be suitable for mixing material into mortar, and without the admixture of earth. Now the

kinds of quarried sand are these: black, white, red, and from lignite. Of these, that which makes a noise when rubbed in the hand will be best; but that which is earthy will not have a like roughness. Also, if it is covered up in a white cloth, and afterwards shaken up or beaten, and does not foul it, and the earth does not settle therein, it will be suitable.   2   But if there are no sand-pits whence it may be dug, then it must be sifted out from the river bed or from gravel, not less also from the sea-shore. But such sand has these faults in buildings: it dries with difficulty, nor does the wall allow itself to be loaded continuously without interruptions for rest, nor does it allow of vaulting. But in the case of sea sand, when plastered surfaces are laid upon walls, the walls discharge the salt of the sands and are broken up. 3   But quarry sand quickly dries in buildings, and the surface lasts; and it admits of vaulting, but only that which is fresh from the pit. For if after being taken out it lies too long, it is weathered by the sun and the moon and the hoar frost, and is dissolved and becomes earthy. Thus when it is thrown into the rubble, it cannot bind together the rough stones, but these collapse and the loads give way which the walls cannot maintain. But while fresh pit sand has such virtues in buildings, it is not useful in plaster work; because owing to its richness, the lime when mingled with straw cannot, because of its strength, dry without cracks. But river sand because of its fineness (like that from Signia), when it is worked over with polishing tools, acquires solidity in the plaster.

J16 2. 6. 1–6: On Pozzolana

Pozzolana *was a form of volcanic ash giving great strength when mixed in cement. The first deposits were found near Puteoli (hence its name) but there are in fact widespread deposits of similar ash over southern Italy and in and around Rome. Although it was in common use under Augustus, Vitruvius' concentration on the geology and geography suggests that he was not able to draw on any craft tradition of recipes for its use.*

1   There is also a kind of powder which, by nature, produces wonderful results. It is found in the neighbourhood of Baiae and in the lands of the municipalities round Mount Vesuvius. This being mixed with lime and rubble, not only furnishes strength to other buildings, but also, when piers are built in the sea, they set under water. Now this seems to happen for this reason: that under these mountainous regions there are both hot earth and many springs. And these would not be unless deep down they had huge blazing fires of sulphur, alum or pitch. Therefore the fire and vapour of flame within, flowing through the cracks, makes that earth light. And the tufa which is found to come up there is free from moisture. Therefore, when three substances formed in like manner by the violence of fire come into one mixture, they suddenly take up water and cohere together. They are quickly hardened by the moisture and made solid, and can be dissolved neither by the

465

waves nor the power of water. 2 But that there are fervent heats in these districts may be proved by this circumstance. In the hills of Baiae which belong to Cumae sites are excavated for sweating-rooms. In these hot vapour rising deep down perforates the soil by the violence of its heat, and passing through it rises in these places, and so produces striking advantages in sweating-rooms. Not less also let it be recorded, that heats in antiquity grew and abounded under Mount Vesuvius, and thence belched forth flame round the country. And therefore now that which is called 'sponge-stone' or Pompeian pumice seems to be brought to this general quality from another kind of stone when it is subjected to heat. 3 But that kind of sponge stone which is taken thence is not found in all places, only round Etna and on the hills of Mysia (which is called *Catacecaumene* by the Greeks), and if there are in any other places properties of that kind. If, therefore, in these places there are found hot springs, and in all excavations, warm vapours, and if the very places are related by the ancients to have had fires ranging over the fields, it seems to be certain that by the violence of fire, moisture has been removed from the tufa and earth just as from lime in kilns. 4 Therefore, when unlike and unequal substances are caught together and brought into one nature, the hot desiccation, suddenly saturated with water, seethes together with the latent heat in the bodies affected, and causes them to combine vehemently and to gain rapidly one strong solidity.

Since in Etruria also there are frequent springs of hot water, there will remain the inquiry why there also the powder is not found, from which in the same manner walling may set under water. Therefore it seemed good, before inquiry was made on these matters, to set forth how they seemed to come about. 5 Neither the same kinds of soil nor the same rocks are found in all places and regions, but some are earthy, others of gravel, others pebbly, in other places sandy material; and generally there are found in the earth qualities of unlike and unequal kind with the various regions. But we may regard the matter especially in this way: almost everywhere, where the Apennine range encloses the regions of Italy and Etruria, sand-pits are found; whereas across the Apennines, where the land adjoins the Adriatic, none are found. Generally also it is not indeed even named across the sea in Achaia and Asia. Therefore not in all places in which frequent hot springs boil up can the same conveniences arise; but all things are generated as the Nature of Things has determined, not for the pleasure of man, but disparate as though by chance. 6 Therefore wherever mountains are not of earth but of a woody kind, the force of fire escaping through the veins burns it up. It burns out what is soft and tender, but leaves what is rough. Therefore just as in Campania, burnt-out earth becomes ashes, so in Etruria, charred stone becomes carbuncular. Both are excellent in walling. But some materials have advantages in buildings on land, and others in piers built into the sea. The nature of wood is softer than tufa, more solid than the earth; and when this is burnt deep down by the violence of vapour, there is generated in some places that kind of sand which is called lignite (carbunculus).

J17 2. 7. 1–5: On stone

Vitruvius begins by distinguishing two types of stonework—ashlar (a smooth sur-
face built with squared stones) and rubble (irregular courses and a rough face)—
before discussing the different qualities of stone from different quarries. The harder
stone was better but more expensive because it was more difficult to work. Two
main kinds of building stone were common in Rome and Italy. The softest was
tufa, a porous volcanic rock which was easily worked and much used under the
Republic. There were also harder limestones, notably Travertine from Tivoli and
the harder fire-resistant Peperino from Mons Albanus. These were increasingly used
in the late Republic and common in the early Empire. There were tufa quarries in
and around Rome and many limestone quarries in the hills up to 20 miles inland.
Architects would normally specify the quarry from which they wanted stone
brought; Vitruvius names a number of them. Marble from Luna (Carrara) began to
be used under Augustus but mostly for decoration or in thin sheets for facing (but
see 7. 6. 1–J30).

1   I have spoken of lime and sand, both of what varieties they are and what virtues
they possess. Next in order comes the description of the quarries from which both
squared stone and supplies of rubble are taken and furnished for buildings. Now
these are found to be of unequal and unlike virtues. For some are soft, as they are
in the neighbourhood of the city at Grotta Rossa, Palla, Fidenae and Alba; others
are medium, as at Tivoli, Amiternum, Soracte, and those which are of these kinds;
some hard, like lava. There are also many other kinds, as red and black tufa in
Campania; in Umbria and Picenum and in Venetia, white stone which indeed is cut,
like wood, with a toothed saw.   2   But all these quarries which are of soft stone
have this advantage: when stones are taken from these quarries they are easily
handled in working, and if they are in covered places, they sustain their burden, but
if they are in open and exposed places, they combine with ice and hoar frost, are
turned to powder and are dissolved: along the sea-coast, also, being weathered by
the brine, they crumble and do not endure the heat. Travertine, however, and all
stones which are of the same kind, withstand injury from heavy loads and from
storms; but from fire they cannot be safe; as soon as they are touched by it they
crack and break up. And the reason is that by the nature of their composition they
have little moisture and also not much earth, but much air and fire. Therefore,
since there is less moisture and earth in these, then also the fire, when the air has
been expelled by the contact and violence of the heat, following far within and
seizing upon the empty spaces of the fissures, seethes and produces, from its own
substance, similar burning bodies.   3   But there are also several quarries in the
neighbourhood of Tarquinii, known as the Anician, in colour like those of Alba,
of which the workings are mostly round the lake of Bolsena, and also in the prefecture of Statonia. These also have infinite virtues; for they can neither be injured by weathering under frost nor by the approach of fire. But the stone is firm
and wears well over a long time, because it has little air and fire in its natural

467

mixture, a medium amount of moisture, and much of the earthy. Thus solidified by its close composition, it is injured neither by weathering nor by the violence of fire.   4   Now this we may especially judge from the monuments, which are about the municipality of Ferentum, made from these quarries. For they have large statues strikingly made, and lesser figures and flowers and acanthus finely carved. These, old as they are, appear as fresh as if they were just made. None the less also, coppersmiths in their bronze castings get moulds from these quarries, and find great advantages from them for casting bronze. And if these were near the city, it would be worth while to execute all works from these stoneyards.   5   Since then, because of their nearness, necessity compels the use of supplies from the quarries of Grotta Rossa and Palla, and others which are nearest to the city, we must take precautions if we wish to complete our work without faults. When we have to build, let the stone be got out two years before, not in winter but in summer, and let it lie and stay in exposed places. Those stones, however, which in the two years suffer damage by weathering, are to be thrown into the foundations. Those which are not faulty are tested by Nature, and can endure when used in building above ground. And these precautions are to be taken not only in the case of squared stones, but also for rough stone or rubble walling.

J18 2. 8. 1–2; 7–9; 16–18; 20: On walling

By the time of Augustus, walls were most commonly built as a concrete core held in place until it set by some sort of facing. Once the concrete was set it and not the facing provided the strength. The wall may be named after the surface pattern achieved by setting bricks or stones into the aggregate of the core. Net-pattern work (opus reticulatum) was the regular form by the late Republic and the pattern was formed by small square-faced blocks set diamond wise. However it is clear that a variety of walling methods, stone, brick, and rubble were all in use in the insulae (which Augustus limited to 70 feet) where solid sun-dried brick walls would be too massive.

(a)
1   There are two kinds of walling; one like net-work, *opus reticulatum*, which all use now, and the old manner which is called *opus incertum*. Of these the reticulatum is more graceful, but it is likely to cause cracks because it has the beds and joints in every direction. The 'uncertain' rough work, *opus incertum*, lying course above course and breaking joints, furnishes walling which is not pleasing but is stronger than the reticulatum.   2   Both kinds of walling are to be built with very minute stones; so that the walls, thoroughly saturated with mortar of lime and sand, may hold longer together. For since the stones are of a soft and open nature, they dry up the moisture by sucking it out of the mortar. But when the supply of lime and sand is abundant, the wall having more moisture will not quickly become

perishable, but holds together. When once, also, the moist power has been sucked out of the mortar, through the loose structure of the rubble, and the lime separates from the sand and is dissolved, the rubble also cannot cohere with them, but renders the walls ruinous with lapse of time.

7   But people nowadays, being eager for speedy building, attend only to the facing, setting the stones on end, and fill it up in the middle with broken rubble and mortar. Thus three slices are raised in this walling, two of the facings, and a middle one of the filling in. Not so the Greeks who lay the stones level and put the headers and stretchers alternately. Thus they have not to fill in the middle, but with their through facing stones they render solid the unbroken and single thickness of the walls. In addition to the rest, they insert special stones facing on either front of un-broken thickness. These they call *diatonos* (through-stones), and they, by bonding, especially strengthen the solidity of the wall.

8   Therefore if anyone will from these commentaries observe and select a style of walling, he will be able to take account of durability. For those which are of soft rubble with a thin and pleasing facing cannot fail to give way with lapse of time. Therefore when arbitrators are taken for party-walls, they do not value them at the price at which they were made, but when from the accounts they find the tenders for them, they deduct as price of the passing of each year the 80th part, and so—in that from the remaining sum repayment is made for these walls—they pronounce the opinion that the walls cannot last more than 80 years.   9   There is no deduction made from the value of brick walls provided that they remain plumb; but they are always valued at as much as they were built for.

(b)

16   Since, therefore, kings of very great power have not disdained walls built of brick (in cases where wealth gained by taxation and plunder allowed the use not only of rubble or squared stone, but even of marble), I do not think that buildings which are made of brick walls are to be disregarded so long as they are duly roofed. But why this fashion ought not to be followed out by the Roman people in the city I will set forth, and will not omit the causes and reasons of this.   17   Public statutes do not allow a thickness of more than a foot and a half to be used for party walls. But other walls also are put up of the same thickness lest the space be too much narrowed. Now brick walls of a foot and a half—not being two or three bricks thick—cannot sustain more than one story. Yet with this greatness of the city and the unlimited crowding of citizens, it is necessary to provide very numerous dwellings. Therefore since a level site could not receive such a multitude to dwell in the city, circumstances themselves have compelled the resort to raising the height of buildings. And so by means of stone pillars, walls of burnt brick, party walls of rubble, towers have been raised, and these being joined together by frequent board floors produce upper stories with fine views over the city to the utmost advantage. Therefore walls are raised to a great height through various stories, and the Roman people has excellent dwellings without hindrance.

18   Now, therefore, the reason is explained why, because of the limited space

in the city, they do not allow walls to be of sun-dried bricks. When it shall be necessary to use them, outside the city, such walls will be sound and durable after the following manner. At the top of the walls let walling of burnt brick be put beneath the tiles, and let it have a projecting cornice. So the faults which usually happen here can be avoided. For when tiles in the roof are broken or thrown down by the wind (where rain-water could pass through from showers), the burnt brick shield will not allow the brickwork to be damaged; but the projection of the cornices will throw the drippings outside the facing line, and in that way will keep intact the structure of brick walls. . . .

20   I could wish that walls of wattlework had not been invented. For however advantageous they are in speed of erection and for increase of space, to that extent are they a public misfortune, because they are like torches ready for kindling. Therefore it seems better to be at greater expense by the cost of burnt brick than to be in danger by the convenience of wattlework walls: for these also make cracks in the plaster covering owing to the arrangement of the uprights and cross-pieces. For when the plaster is applied, they take up the moisture and swell, then when they dry they contract, and so they are rendered thin, and break the solidity of the plaster. But since haste, or lack of means, or partitions made over an open space, sometimes require this construction, we must proceed as follows. Let the foundation be laid high up, so that it is untouched by the rough stones of the pavement; for when they are fixed in these, they become rotten in time; then they settle, and falling forward they break through the surface of the plaster.

J19 5. 1. 1–10: On the forum and basilica

The forum was the commercial and administrative centre of a Roman town. There might be several fora *but the main one would be in the form of an open square, usually at the crossing of the two main streets. At one end would be temples dedicated to the tutelary deity and often to Rome and Augustus, and the administrative offices would be housed in the basilica, a large public hall often with balconies and* exedrae *and frequently with separate offices attached.*

1   The Greeks plan the forum on the square with most ample double colonnades and close-set columns; they ornament them with stone or marble architraves, and above they make promenades on the boarded floors. But in the cities of Italy we must not proceed on the same plan, because the custom of giving gladiatorial shows in the forum has been handed down from our ancestors.   2   For that reason more roomy intercolumniations are to be used round the spectacle; in the colonnades, silver-smiths' shops; and balconies, rightly placed for convenience and for public revenue, are to be placed on the upper floors.

The dimensions of the forum ought to be adjusted to the audience lest the space be cramped for use, or else, owing to a scanty attendance, the forum should seem too large. Now let the breadth be so determined that when the length is divided into three parts, two are assigned to the breadth. For so the plan will be oblong, and the arrangement will be adapted to the purpose of the spectacles. 3   The upper columns are to be a quarter less than the lower ones; because the lower columns ought to be stronger for bearing weight than the upper ones. Not less one ought also to imitate the natural growth of trees, as in tapering trees, the fir, the cypress, the pine, of which everyone is thicker at the roots. Then diminishing it rises on high, by a natural contraction growing evenly to the summit. Therefore since the nature of growing plants so demands, things are rightly arranged both in height and thickness, if the higher are more contracted than the lower.

4   The sites of basilicas ought to be fixed adjoining the fora in as warm a quarter as possible, so that in the winter, business men may meet there without being troubled by the weather. And their breadth should be fixed at not less than a third, nor more than half their length, unless the nature of the site is awkward and forces the proportions to be changed. When the site is longer than necessary, the committee rooms are to be placed at the end of the basilica, as they are in the Basilica Julia at Aquileia.   5   The columns of basilicas are to be of a height equal to the width of the aisle. The aisle is to have a width one third of the nave. The columns of the upper story are to be less than those below as herein above specified. The parapet between the upper and lower columns ought to be one fourth less than the upper columns, so that people walking on the first floor may not be seen by persons engaged in business. The architraves, friezes and cornices are to be designed in accordance with the columns, as we have prescribed in the third book.

6   At the Julian Colony of Fano, I let out for contract and superintended the building of a basilica not inferior to these in dignity and grace. Its proportions and harmonies are as follows: There is a vaulted nave between the columns 120 feet long and 60 broad. The aisle between the columns of the nave and the outside wall, is 20 feet wide. The columns are of an unbroken height, including the capitals, of 50 feet with a diameter of 5 feet. Behind them adjoining the aisle are pilasters 20 feet high, 2½ feet wide and 1½ feet thick. These carry the beams under the flooring. Above, there are pilasters 18 feet high, 2 feet wide and 1 foot thick, which take the beams which carry the principals of the main roof, and the roofs of the aisles which are lower than the vaulting of the nave.   7   The space which remains in the intercolumniations, above the pilasters and below the tops of the columns, admits the necessary lighting. In the width of the nave counting the angle columns right and left, there are four columns at each end. On the side adjoining the forum, there are eight, including the angle columns. On the other side there are six, including the angle columns. The two columns in the middle are omitted, so as not to obstruct the view of the pronaos of the Temple of Augustus which is situated in the middle of the side wall of the basilica and faces the middle of the forum and the Temple of Jupiter.   8   The tribunal which is in the former temple, is in the shape of the segment of a circle. The width of the segment in front is 46 feet; its depth is 15 feet; so that those who come before the magistrates may not interfere with persons on business in the basilica. Above the columns are beams made of three

2 foot joists bolted together. These return from the third column on either side of the opening to the antae of the pronaos, and adjoin the curve of the tribunal right and left. 9 Above the beams vertically over the capitals, piers are placed on supports, 3 feet high and 4 feet square. Above them, beams formed of two 2 foot joists, carefully wrought, are carried round the basilica. Thereon over against the shafts of the columns, and the antae and walls of the pronaos, cross-beams and struts support the whole ridge of the basilica, and a second ridge running out from the middle of the main ridge, over the pronaos of the temple. 10 Thus there arises from the roof a double arrangement of gables. This gives a pleasing effect both to the exterior of the roof and to the high vaulting within. Further, we dispense with the ornaments of the entablatures and the provision of the upper columns and parapets. We are relieved from laborious details and escape a large expenditure, while the carrying up of the columns without a break to the beams of the vault seems to give a sumptuous magnificence and impressiveness to the work.

J20 5.3.3–5: On the site of the theatre

Vitruvius spends a great deal of time on theatres which were enormous structures holding several thousand spectators. Unlike Greek theatres, Roman theatres were often free-standing buildings on flat sites and their semicircular auditoria were enclosed by a high wall backing the stage. Permanent theatres of this sort first appeared in towns like Pompeii around 80 BC. and the first permanent theatre in Rome was the theatre of Pompey (55 BC.) which was one of the major monuments of Rome in Vitruvius' time.

3 If the theatre is on a hillside, the construction of the foundations will be easier. But if they have to be laid on level or marshy ground, piles and substructures must be used as we have written in the third book concerning the foundations of temples. Above the foundations, the stepped seats ought to be built up from the substructure in stone or marble. 4 The curved level gangways, it seems, should be made proportionately to the height of the theatre; and each of them not higher at the back, than is the breadth of the passage of the gangway. For if they are taller, they will check and throw out the voice into the upper part of the theatre. Neither will they allow the endings of words to come with a clear significance to the ears of the people in their seats above the gangways. In brief the section of the theatre is to be so managed that if a line is drawn touching the lowest and the top rows, it shall also touch the front angles of all the rows. Thus the voice will not be checked. 5 Many and spacious stepped passages must be arranged between the seats; but the upper ones ought to be discontinuous with the lower. Everywhere, each passage (upper or lower) must be continuous and straight without bends; so that when the audience is dismissed from the spectacle, it may not be cramped, but may find everywhere separate and uninterrupted exits.

Great care is also to be taken that the place chosen does not deaden the sound, but that the voice can range in it with the utmost clearness. And this can be brought about if a site is chosen where the passage of sound is not hindered.

J21 5. 9. 1–3; 5; 7–9: On colonnades and passages behind the scenes

It is interesting to note how Vitruvius considers the provision of large colonnades at the rear of a theatre as an integral part of the design. Such colonnades formed a part of Pompey's theatre (the Senate was meeting there when Caesar was assassinated) and can still be seen in the Forum of the Corporations behind the theatre at Ostia.

1 Behind the stage, colonnades are to be planned so that when the play is interrupted by sudden showers, the audience may have a place of refuge; the colonnades may also furnish room to set up the stage machinery. At Rome there are the Colonnades of Pompey; at Athens there are the Colonnades of Eumenes, the Temple of Bacchus, and as you leave the theatre, on the left-hand side there is the Odeum. . . . In other cities also which have had skilful architects there are colonnades and walks adjoining the theatres. 2 These, it appears, should be so planned that they are double, having Doric columns on the outside finished with architraves and ornaments in due proportion. The width of the colonnades should be arranged as follows. Taking the height of the outer columns, this will give the width from the lower part of the outer columns to the middle columns and from the middle columns to the walls which surround the walks of the colonnades. The middle columns are to be designed one fifth higher than the outer ones, and either in the Ionic or Corinthian style. 3 The proportions and symmetries of the columns will not be calculated in the same way as I have described for sacred edifices. In the temples of the gods dignity should be aimed at; in colonnades and other similar works, elegance. And so if the columns are in the Doric style, their height including the capitals is to be divided into 15 parts of which one is to be the module. The planning of the whole work is to be calculated to this module. The thickness of the column at the foot is to be of two modules. The intercolumniation is to be $5\frac{1}{2}$ modules. The height of the column excluding the capital is to be 14 modules. The height of the capital is to be one module; the width $2\frac{1}{6}$ modules. The proportions of the rest of the work are to be completed as laid down in the fourth book for sacred edifices. . . .

5 The open spaces which are between the colonnades under the open sky, are to be arranged with green plots; because walks in the open are very healthy, first for the eyes, because from the green plantations, the air being subtle and rarefied, flows into the body as it moves, clears the vision, and so by removing the thick humour from the eyes, leaves the glance defined and the image clearly marked. Moreover, since in walking the body is heated by motion, the air extracts the

humours from the limbs, and diminishes repletion, by dissipating what the body has, more than it can carry. . . .

7 In order that these walks may be always dry and free from mud, the following measures should be taken. They are to be dug and emptied out as deeply as possible. Drains are to be constructed right and left. In the walls of these, which are on the side of the parade, pipes are to be fixed inclined to the drains. When this is complete, the place is to be filled with charcoal; then above this the walks are to be covered with sand and levelled. Thus by the natural porosity of the charcoal, and by the insertion of the pipes, the overflow of the water will be taken off. Thus the parades will be dry and without moisture.

8 Moreover in these buildings, custom included depots for stores required by the cities. In times of siege, the provision of everything else is more easy than that of wood. Salt is easily brought in beforehand. Corn is quickly gathered by the community and by individuals. If it fails, provision can be made with green vegetables, meat or beans. Water is obtained by the digging of wells; in sudden storms it is received from the sky by the roof tiles. But the provision of fire-wood, which is most necessary for cooking food, is difficult and troublesome. For it takes time to collect and is used in large quantities. 9 In times of siege the walks are thrown open, and wood is distributed to each citizen according to his tribe. Thus walks in the open air serve two outstanding purposes: health in time of peace, and security in war. In this way the laying out of walks, not only behind the stage of the theatre but also for the temples of all the gods, can furnish cities with great advantages.

Since these topics seem to us to be enough explained, there will now follow a description of the planning of baths.

J22 5. 10. 1–5: On baths

Vitruvius pays little attention to the planning of bathing establishments because in his day they were not grandiose buildings in their own gardens (like Caracalla's baths) but often merely suites of rooms within larger blocks. There was little chance for display except in decoration and Vitruvius concentrates on the structure and services. His description of the under-floor heating (hypocaust) is particularly clear.

1 Firstly a site must be chosen as warm as possible, that is, turned away from the north and east. Now the hot and tepid baths are to be lighted from the winter west; but if the nature of the site prevents, at any rate from the south. For the time of bathing is fixed between midday and evening. We must also take care that the hot baths for men and for women are adjacent and planned with the same aspects. For in this way it will follow that the same furnace and heating system will serve for both baths and for their fittings. Three bronze tanks are to be placed above the furnace: one for the hot bath, a second for the tepid bath, a third for the cold bath.

They are to be so arranged that the hot water which flows from the tepid bath into the hot bath, may be replaced by a like amount of water flowing down from the cold into the tepid bath. The vaulted chambers which contain the basins, are to be heated from the common furnace. 2 The hanging floors of the hot baths are to be made as follows: first the ground is to be paved with eighteen inch tiles sloping towards the furnace, so that when a ball is thrown in it does not rest within, but comes back to the furnace room of itself. Thus the flame will more easily spread under the floor. On this pavement, piers of eight inch bricks are to be built at such intervals that two foot tiles can be placed above. The piers are to be two feet high. They are to be laid in clay worked up with hair, and upon them two foot tiles are to be placed to take the pavement.   3   The vaulted ceilings will be more convenient if they are made of concrete. But if they are of timber, they should be tiled underneath, in the following fashion. Iron bars or arches are to be made and hung on the timber close together with iron hooks. And these rods or arches are to be placed so far apart that the tiles without raised edges may rest upon, and be carried by them; thus the whole vaulting is finished resting upon iron. Of these vaulted ceilings the upper joints are to be stopped with clay and hair kneaded together. The under side, which looks to the pavement below, is to be first plastered with potsherds and lime pounded together, and then finished with stucco or fine plaster. Such vaulting over hot baths will be more convenient if it is made double. For the moisture from the heat cannot attack the wood of the timbering but will be dispersed between the two vaults.   4   Now the size of the baths is to be proportioned to the number of persons, and is to be thus arranged. Apart from the apse containing the bathing tub and the basin in which it stands, the breadth is to be two thirds of the length. The bathing tub should be placed under the light so that the bystanders do not obscure the light with their shadows. The apses for the bathing tubs should be spacious so that when the first comers have taken their places, the others watching their turn may stand conveniently. Now the width of the basin between the wall and the parapet, should be not less than six feet, from which the lower step and the 'cushion,' are to take two feet.   5   The domed sweating chamber should adjoin the tepid bath. The height to the springing of the dome should be equal to the width. In the middle of the dome a light is to be left. From this a bronze tray is hung with chains; by the raising and lowering of the tray from the opening, the sweating is adjusted. The tray should be circular, so that the force of the flame and the heat may be diffused equally from the centre over the rounded curve.

J23 5. 12. 1-4; 5-7: On harbours and shipyards

Harbours were important to Rome relying, as she did, on the import of corn from Sicily. The River Tiber was fast flowing and barely navigable, though there was a small harbour at Ostia at the river mouth and a moderately safe roadstead for trans-

shipment. Julius Caesar had plans to reorganize the port and the river outlet but in the event nothing was done until the reign of Claudius. It is tempting to read into Vitruvius' detailed treatment some knowledge of the proposed development and hope of employment.

1   It remains to deal with the suitable arrangement of harbours, and to explain by what means, in these, ships are protected from stormy weather. There are great advantages if they are well placed by nature and have headlands (acroteria) jutting out, behind which bays or creeks are formed owing to the nature of the place. For round these colonnades either docks are to be made, or approaches from the colonnades to the warehouses. On either side towers are to be built from which chains (across the harbour) can be drawn by machinery.

2   But if we have no natural harbour suitable for protecting ships from a stormy sea, we must proceed as follows. If there is an anchorage on one side without any river mouth to interfere, piers are to be constructed on the other side by masonry or embankments in order to form an enclosed harbour. The masonry which is to be in the sea must be constructed in this way. Earth is to be brought from the district which runs from Cumae to the promontory of Minerva, and mixed, in the mortar, two parts to one of lime.   3   Then in the place marked out, cofferdams, formed of oak piles and tied together with chains, are to be let down into the water and firmly fixed. Next, the lower part between them under the water is to be levelled and cleared with a platform of small beams laid across and the work is to be carried up with stones and mortar as above described, until the space for the structure between the dams is filled. Such is the natural advantage of the places described above. . . .

5   Where, however, the earth in question is not found, we must proceed as follows. Double coffer-dams bound together with planks and chains are to be put in the place marked out. Between the supports, clay in hampers made of rushes is to be pressed down. When it is well pressed down and as closely as possible, the place marked out by the enclosure is to be emptied with waterscrews and waterwheels with drums, and so dried. Here the foundations are to be dug. If the foundations are on the sea bottom, they are to be emptied and drained to a greater width than the wall to be built upon them, and then the work is to be filled in with concrete of stone lime and sand.   6   But if the bottom is soft the foundations are to be charred piles of alder and olive filled in with charcoal, as prescribed for the foundations of theatres and the city walls. The wall is then raised of squared stone with joints as long as possible, so that the middle stones may be well tied together by the jointing. The inside of the wall is then to be filled in with rubble or masonry. Thus it may be possible for a tower to be built upon it.

7   Subsequently the shipyards are to be built and with a northern aspect, as a rule. For southern aspects because of their warmth generate dry rot, wood worms and ship worms with other noxious creatures, and feed and maintain them. Further, such buildings should have very little wood in them because of fire. As to their dimensions no rule should be laid down. They are to be made to take the

largest vessels; so that even if such vessels are drawn ashore, they may have a roomy berth.

In this book I have described how the works required for public purpose in cities are to be planned and carried out. The next book will consider the requirements of private buildings and their due proportions.

J24 6. 3. 1–9; 11: On the plan of a house

Both the layout and the dimensions make it clear that Vitruvius is talking of the houses of the aristocracy or of the very wealthy such as are familiar from Pompeii. The buildings retain elements of Etruscan and Greek building traditions as well as other influences. There was a good deal of variety though certain elements were central. The roofed courtyard (atrium) derives from Etruscan farmhouse building and is always built with the tablinum, a descendant of the Etruscan farmhouse, at one end facing the entry and wings each side of what was originally the farm yard. Vitruvius describes the ways in which the roof might be supported. The longest tradition, Tuscan, was for a projecting roof without columns. Tetrastyle has four columns at the corners while the most elaborate, Corinthian, has intermediate columns as well. In displuviate atria the water drains outward, away from the central opening. Vaulted atria were rarer because the majority of houses of this type were largely single storey. The atrium was the focus of life and the tablinum provided an office for the patronus or master of the house (alcove is a misleading translation except that the room was usually open to both atrium and peristyle); the alae flanked the atrium and were also open to it. Entrance, atrium and tablinum would normally lie on an axis which ran through to the peristyle or garden court, a Greek derivative that would be laid out at right angles to the principal axis of the house.

Because there was so much open planning in Roman houses room shapes might be elaborated for variety. The plain rectangle was commonest but grandeur could be added by the provision of apsed recesses, exedrae. Vitruvius is very specific about the proportions of rooms and one should notice the considerable height made necessary by the Italian climate.

The oeci, described by Vitruvius as though they were a normal part of the house, give rise to some problems of interpretation; the word appears to derive from the Greek for house but Vitruvius describes palatial audience chambers which he rightly likens to basilicas. Again it is tempting to see his description aimed at patronage on an Imperial scale.

1   The courtyards of houses are of five different styles, and the names of them are as follows: Tuscan, Corinthian, Tetrastyle, Displuviate, Vaulted. The Tuscan are those in which the beams which are carried across the atrium have trimmers to them and valleys running down from the angles of the walls to the angles of the

beams; thus there is a delivery of the rainfall from the eaves into the middle of the court. In the Corinthian manner, the beams and open space are arranged in the same way, but the beams, starting from the walls, are fixed upon columns surrounding the open space. The tetrastyle courtyards have angle columns under the beams, which gain thereby in usefulness and strength, because they are not compelled to bear great pressure and are not loaded by the trimmers.

2 Displuviate courtyards are those in which the rafters which support the frame of the opening carry the gutters down. They are very advantageous for winter apartments because the central openings are raised and do not impede the lights of the triclinia. But there is this disadvantage in the upkeep: when the rainwater flows down, the pipes round the walls receive it, but do not quickly take the water flowing from the channels; as they receive it, they are clogged with the surplus water. Consequently the joiner's work and the walls are damaged. Vaulted courtyards are employed when the span is not great, and they furnish roomy apartments in the story above.

3 The length and breadth of the *atrium* is planned in three ways. The first arrangement is to divide the length into five parts, and to give three of these to the width; the second divides the length into three parts and assigns two to the width; in the third arrangement a square is described upon the width, and the diagonal of the square is drawn: whatever is the size of the diagonal supplies the length of the atrium. 4 The height of the atrium to the underside of the beams is to be three-quarters of the length. The remaining quarter is to be assigned as the dimension of the ceiling and of the roof, above the beams.

The width of the *alae* or wings, on the right and the left, is to be one-third of the length of the atrium when it is from 30 to 40 feet; from 40 to 50 feet the length is to be divided into three parts and a half, and one is to be given to the alae. When the length is from 50 to 60 feet, a fourth part is to be assigned to the alae. From 60 to 80 feet let the length be divided into four parts and a half: of these one is to be the width of the alae. From 80 to 100 feet the length divided into five parts will determine the breadth of the alae. The lintel beams are to be placed so high, that, in height, the alae are equal to their breadth.

5 The *tablinum* or alcove, if the breadth of the atrium is 20 feet, must be two-thirds in width. If the breadth of the atrium is 30 to 40 feet, half is to be given to the alcove. When the breadth is from 40 to 60, two-fifths are to be assigned to the alcove. For the smaller atria cannot have the same kind of symmetry as the larger. For if we use the symmetry of the larger atria in the smaller, it cannot be useful for the alcove or the wing. But if we use the symmetry of the smaller in the larger, the details will be huge and monstrous. Therefore I thought that according to their kinds the exact dimensions should be registered with a view both to use and to effect. 6 The height of the alcove to the cornice is to be one-eighth more than its breadth. The panelled ceiling is to be raised higher than the cornices by one-third of the breadth.

The main entrance for smaller atria is to be two-thirds of the width of the alcove; for larger atria, one-half. The portraits with their ornaments are to be fixed above at a height equal to the breadth of the alae.

The relation of the breadth to the height of the doors is to be in the Doric manner for Doric buildings, in the Ionic, for Ionic buildings, as in the case of Greek doorways of which the symmetrical relations have been set out in the fourth book.

The width of the opening of the compluvium is to be not less than a fourth, nor more than a third, of the width of the atrium; the length, in proportion to the atrium.

7   The peristyles lie crosswise, and should be one-third wider than they are deep. The height of the columns is to be the same as the breadth of the colonnade of the peristyle. The inter-columniations are to extend not less than three or more than four diameters of the columns. But if the columns in the peristyle are to be in the Doric style, the modules are to be taken as I described in the fourth book about Doric detail, and the columns and triglyphs arranged accordingly.

8   The length of *triclinia*, or dining-rooms, must be twice their width. The height of all apartments which are oblong must be so arranged that the length and breadth are added together; of this sum half is taken, and this gives the height. But if they shall be exedrae or square *oeci*, the height is to be one and a half times the width. Picture galleries (like exedrae) are to be made of ample dimensions. Corinthian and tetrastyle halls and those which are called Egyptian, are to have the same proportion of length and breadth as in the description of the triclinia, but owing to the use of columns they are to be more spacious.

9   There is this difference between a Corinthian and an Egyptian oecus. The Corinthian has one row of columns placed either upon a stylobate or upon the ground. Above, it is to have architraves and cornices either of fine joinery or plaster, and above the cornices, curved ceilings rounded to a circular section. In the Egyptian saloons, however, architraves are placed above the columns, and floor joists are to be carried from the architraves to the walls opposite. On the floor boards a pavement is to be laid that there may be a balcony in the open. Then above the architrave, and perpendicularly above the lower columns, columns one-fourth shorter are to be placed. Above their architraves and ornaments they have panelled ceilings, and windows are placed between the upper columns. Thus the Egyptian halls resemble basilicas rather than Corinthian apartments. . . .

11   In buildings of this kind, all the rules of symmetry must be followed, which are allowed by the site, and the windows will be easily arranged unless they are darkened by high walls opposite. But if they are obstructed by the narrowness of the street or by other inconveniences, skill and resource must alter the proportions by decreasing or adding, so that an elegance may be attained in harmony with the proper proportions.

J25 6. 5. 1–3: On building suitably for different ranks of society

The careful assignment of building for rank fits well with the conventions of Roman society and Vitruvius makes clear the physical requirements for the working of the patron–client system. It is also worth noting the close relationship between agri-culture and commerce and that shops and stores and even workshops were regularly accommodated in houses.

1   When we have arranged our plan with a view to aspect, we must go on to con-sider how, in private buildings, the rooms belonging to the family, and how those which are shared with visitors, should be planned. For into the private rooms no one can come uninvited, such as the bedrooms, dining-rooms, baths and other apartments which have similar purposes. The common rooms are those into which, though uninvited, persons of the people can come by right, such as vestibules, courtyards, peristyles and other apartments of similar uses. Therefore magnificent vestibules and alcoves and halls are not necessary to persons of a common fortune, because they pay their respects by visiting among others, and are not visited by others.   2   But those who depend upon country produce must have stalls for cattle and shops in the forecourt, and, within the main building, cellars, barns, stores and other apartments which are for the storage of produce rather than for an elegant effect. Again, the houses of bankers and farmers of the revenue should be more spacious and imposing and safe from burglars. Advocates and professors of rhetoric should be housed with distinction, and in sufficient space to accommodate their audiences. For persons of high rank who hold office and magistracies, and whose duty it is to serve the state, we must provide princely vestibules, lofty halls and very spacious peristyles, plantations and broad avenues finished in a majestic manner; further, libraries and basilicas arranged in a similar fashion with the mag-nificence of public structures, because, in such palaces, public deliberations and private trials and judgments are often transacted.

3   Therefore if buildings are planned with a view to the status of the client, as was set forth in the first book under the head of decor, we shall escape censure. For our rules will be convenient and exact in every respect. Moreover, we shall take account of these matters, not only when we build in town, but in the coun-try; except that, in town, the halls adjoin the entrance, in the country the peri-styles of mansions built town-fashion come first, then the atria surrounded by paved colonnades overlooking the palaestra and the promenades.

I have set forth as I am able the general methods of building in town. I will now state the methods of building in the country, with a view to convenience in use, and especially to the disposition of the site.

J26 6. 8. 1–5; 8–10: On the stability of buildings

(See also J10, 18.) The extent of settlement in large load-bearing structures is often considerable and Vitruvius points out obvious good practice to minimize the problem. The emphasis on vertical thrust through the centres of walls is important but would often be difficult to test in complex buildings especially if there were

shared walls or divided ownership. The 'open spaces' refer to the possibility of over-
hanging upper stories. The practice of opening up the ground floors to shops often
meant that the weight of the structure was effectively carried on short sections of
the wall or piers. The use of wedge-shaped 'voussoirs' and the building of relieving
arches over openings remain standard in brick buildings to this day.

1   Buildings which start from the level of the ground, if the foundations are so
laid, as we have explained in previous books with reference to city walls and theatres, will assuredly be solid and durable. But if there are spaces underground and
vaulted cellars, the foundations must be wider than the structures in the upper
parts of the building. The party walls, the piers, the columns, are to be placed with
their centres perpendicularly above the lower parts, so as to correspond to the
solid. For if the weight of the dividing walls or of the columns is over open spaces,
it cannot be permanently sustained.

2   Further, if supports are put for the piers and pilasters between the windows,
these faults will be avoided. For when lintels and bressumers are loaded with
walling, they sag in the middle and cause fractures by settlement; but when piers
are placed underneath and wedged up, they do not allow the beams to settle and
injure the structure above.

3   We must also contrive to relieve the weight of the walling by arches with
their voussoirs, and their joints directed to a centre. For when arches, with their
voussoirs, are carried outside the beams and lintels, in the first place the wood relieved of its burden will not sag; in the second place, if it decays in course of time,
it will easily be replaced without the labour of shoring up.

4   Moreover, when buildings rest upon piers, and arches are constructed with
voussoirs and with joints directed to a centre, the end piers in the buildings are to
be set out of greater width, so that they may be stronger and resist when the
voussoirs, being pressed down by the weight of the walling owing to the jointing,
thrust towards the centre and push out the imposts. Therefore if the angle piers
are of wide dimensions, they will restrain the thrust and give stability to the buildings.

5   When proper attention has been given herein that such care be taken, we
must not less be on our guard that every part of a building maintains its perpen-
dicular and that no part leans over. But the greatest care must be taken in the substructures, because, in these, immense damage is caused by the earth piled against
them. For it cannot remain of the same weight as it usually has in the summer: it
swells in the winter by absorbing water from the rains. Consequently by its weight
and expansion it bursts and thrusts out the retaining walls. . . .

8   How buildings can be carried out so as to avoid failure, and how precautions
must be taken in the first stages, has been explained. For the same care is not needful in repairing roof tiling, or principals or rafters, which if faulty are easily repaired, as in the foundations. I have also described how those parts of a building
which are not considered to belong to the solid can be made stable, and how they
are to be constructed.

9   An architect cannot control the kinds of material which it is necessary to

use, for the reason that not all kinds of material occur in all places, as was explained in the last book. Besides, the client decides whether he is to build in brick or rubble or ashlar. Therefore the test of all building is held to be threefold: fine workmanship, magnificence, architectural composition. When a building has a magnificent appearance, the expenditure of those who control it, is praised. When the craftsmanship is good, the supervision of the works is approved. But when it has a graceful effect due to the symmetry of its proportions, the site is the glory of the architect. 10 His work is duly accomplished when he submits to receive advice from his workmen and from laymen. For all men, and not only architects, can approve what is good. But there is this difference between the architect and the layman, that the layman cannot understand what is in hand unless he sees it already done; the architect, when once he has formed his plan, has a definite idea how it will turn out in respect to grace, convenience, and propriety.

I have described, as explicitly as I can, the details which are useful in private buildings and how they are to be carried out. In the next book I will treat of the methods of finishing the work, so that they may be ornamental, free from defects and permanent.

J27 7. 3. 1–8: On stucco

Even today stucco is one of the commonest surface finishes in Italy. It is remarkably durable and being applied wet allows of moulding far more cheaply than by carving stone. Once again Vitruvius' recipe reads like a detailed craftsman's instruction manual.

1 When, therefore, curved ceilings are in question, we must proceed as follows. Parallel laths are to be put not more than two feet apart. They are to be of cypress wood; deal is soon affected by decay and by age. The laths being fixed to the shape of an arch, are to be secured by wooden ties to the floor or roof above, and fastened with an abundance of iron nails. The ties are to be of timber unaffected by decay or age or damp, such as boxwood, juniper, olive, winter oak, cypress and the like, except the common oak, which warps and causes cracks where it is used. 2 When the ribs are in their place, Greek reeds are to be bruised and bound to the ribs with cords of Spanish broom as the shape of the curve requires. Further, on the upper surface of the arch, mortar, mixed with lime and sand, is to be spread, so that if any drippings fall from the floor or roof above, they may be held up. If there be no supply of Greek reed, thin reeds are to be collected from the marshes, and are to be made up in bundles with cords of rough thread to the right length and of equal thickness, provided that not more than two feet separates the knots of the bundles. These then are to be fixed with cord to the ribs as already described, and wooden pins are to be driven through them. Everything else is to be done as already described. 3 When the arched surfaces are fixed and interwoven with the reeds, the under surface is to be rough cast; then sand is to be applied and afterwards finished with hair mortar or marble.

When the coved surfaces are finished, the cornices must be carried along the springing below them, and these must be made as light and slender as possible. For when they are large, they settle under their own weight and cannot keep their place. Gypsum should not be employed, but selected marble of uniform texture, lest the gypsum by setting too soon prevent the work from drying uniformly. Further, we must avoid in these arched ceilings the old arrangements, because, in them, the projecting surfaces of the cornices overhang dangerously with their heavy weight.   4   Now there are other and more elaborate forms of cornice. In apartments, however, where there is a fire and lamps, the cornices should be plain so that they may be the more easily dusted. They can be carved in summer rooms and exedrae where there is very little smoke and soot cannot do any damage. For plaster work, with its glittering whiteness, takes up the smoke that comes from other buildings as well as from the owner's.

5   When the cornices are finished, the walls are to be rough-cast as coarsely as possible, and when the rough-cast is nearly dry, the surface of sand must be shaped in such a way that the lengths are set out by the rule and square, the heights by the plummet, the corners by the set-square. For in this way the designs of the fresco-paintings will not be interfered with. A second and third coat is to be applied, as the one underneath dries. Thus when the solidity of the plaster is the more established from the application of the coats of sand, it is the more stable and enduring.

6   When in addition to the rough-cast, not less than three coats of sand have been laid, then coats of powdered marble are to be worked up, and the mortar is to be so mixed, that when it is worked up it does not adhere to the trowel, but the iron comes clean from the mortar. When a thick layer has been spread and is drying, a second thin coat is to be spread. And when this has been worked up and rubbed over, a still finer coat is to be applied. When the walls have been made solid with three coats of sand and also of marble, they will not be subject to cracks or any other fault.

7   After they are rendered solid by the use of the plasterer's tools and polished to the whiteness of marble, they will show a glittering splendour when the colours are laid on with the last coat. When the colours are carefully laid upon the wet plaster, they do not fail but are permanently durable, because the lime has its moisture removed in the kilns, and becoming attenuated and porous, is compelled by its dryness to seize upon whatever happens to present itself. It gathers seeds or elements by with whatever parts it is formed, it dries together so that it seems to have the qualities proper to its kind.

8   Stucco, therefore, when it is well made, does not become rough in lapse of time, nor lose its colours when they are dusted, unless they have been laid on carelessly and on a dry surface. When, therefore, stucco has been executed on walls in accordance with these instructions, it will retain its firmness and brilliance and fine quality. But when only one coat of sand and one of sifted marble is applied, the thin stucco cannot resist damage and is easily broken, and it does not keep a finish of proper brilliance because of its inadequate thickness.

J28 7. 4. 4–5: On stucco in damp places

It is interesting that, besides offering detailed recipes for mixing stucco and for applying it in damp places, Vitruvius sees the craft as necessarily dominating the design and is quite clear about the functional appropriateness of particular designs.

4   The craftsmen, again, in the stucco-work, must keep the designs in accordance with 'decor,' that they may have a character fitted to their place and adjusted to the differences of style. In winter dining-rooms, painting of detail is not useful in the composition, nor fine mouldings in the cornice under the vault, because they are damaged by the smoke from the fire and the frequent soot from the lamps. In these rooms, immediately above the dado, panels of black are to be worked up and finished with strips of yellow ochre or vermilion intervening. The arched ceilings have a plain finish. As to the pavements, it will not be unsatisfactory if we observe the arrangement of Greek winter apartments. A useful construction is not at all expensive.   5   For inside the levelled surface of the triclinium a depth of about two feet is dug. The ground is well rammed and a pavement of rubble or pounded brick is laid with a fall towards the gutter and its outlets. Then charcoal is collected and crushed by treading, and a mixture six inches thick of ashes, sand and lime is laid. The top surface is then rubbed with stone to rule and level, and has the appearance of a black pavement. At banquets, therefore, the wine which is thrown from the cups or spit out after tasting dries as it falls. And although the servants who are employed there are barefooted, their feet are not stained by the wine-lees on this kind of pavement.

J29 7. 5. 1–4: On wall painting

Vitruvius is firmly conservative in his assessment of styles of wall painting. Four 'styles' were identified by Mau in his excavations at Pompeii in the 1880s which though not a chronological sequence nor entirely separate, form the basis of much later criticism. Vitruvius describes the 'first style', imitating marble inlay, very briefly–it was quite superseded by his day. The 'second style' was more illusionistic, dissolving the wall surface into a variety of vistas seen through cleverly painted fictive architecture. It was still in regular use in the early Augustan period but was rapidly giving way to the more elegant decorative and florid 'third style' of which Vitruvius thoroughly disapproved. (For painting see also E20, 21.)

1   In other apartments for use in spring, autumn or summer, and also in atria and cloisters, the ancients used definite methods of painting definite objects. For by painting an image is made of what is, or of what may be; for example, men, buildings, ships, and other objects; of these definite and circumscribed bodies, imitations are taken and fashioned in their likeness. Hence the ancients who first used

polished stucco, began by imitating the variety and arrangement of marble inlay; then the varied distribution of festoons, ferns, coloured strips.

2   Then they proceeded to imitate the contours of buildings, the outstanding projections of columns and gables; in open spaces, like exedrae, they designed scenery on a large scale in tragic, comic, or satyric style; in covered promenades, because of the length of the walls, they used for ornament the varieties of land-scape gardening, finding subjects in the characteristics of particular places; for they paint harbours, headlands, shores, rivers, springs, straits, temples, groves, hills, cattle, shepherds. In places, some have also the anatomy of statues, the images of the gods, or the representations of legends; further, the battles of Troy and the wanderings of Ulysses over the countryside with other subjects taken in like manner from Nature.

3   But these which were imitations based upon reality are now disdained by the improper taste of the present. On the stucco are monsters rather than definite representations taken from definite things. Instead of columns there rise up stalks; instead of gables, striped panels with curled leaves and volutes. Candelabra uphold pictured shrines and above the summits of these, clusters of thin stalks rise from their roots in tendrils with little figures seated upon them at random. Again, slender stalks with heads of men and of animals attached to half the body.

4   Such things neither are, nor can be, nor have been. On these lines the new fashions compel bad judges to condemn good craftsmanship for dullness. For how can a reed actually sustain a roof, or a candelabrum the ornaments of a gable? or a soft and slender stalk, a seated statue? or how can flowers and half-statues rise alternately from roots and stalks? Yet when people view these falsehoods, they approve rather than condemn, failing to consider whether any of them can really occur or not. Minds darkened by imperfect standards of taste cannot discern the combination of impressiveness with a reasoned scheme of decoration. For pictures cannot be approved which do not resemble reality. Even if they have a fine and craftsmanlike finish, they are only to receive commendation if they exhibit their proper subject without transgressing the rules of art.

J30 7. 6. 1: On the use of marble

Crushed marble was used in the stucco to give a hard mix capable of retaining a smooth surface and crisp detail in the mouldings. It slowed down the setting process so that there was less danger of cracking.

Marble is not found of the same kind in all regions. In some places, blocks occur with shining flakes, as of salt. And these being crushed and ground are of use. But where there are no such supplies, marble-rubble, or splinters as they are called, which the marble workers throw down from their benches, are crushed and ground. This material when sifted the plasterers use in their work. Elsewhere, for example between the boundaries of Magnesia and Ephesus, there are places where it is dug up ready for use, and need not be ground nor sifted. It is as fine as if it had been crushed by hand and sifted.

There are other coloured materials which occur in a natural state in certain places, and are dug up from mines. Yet others are composed of different substances and are treated and blended so as to serve the same purposes in buildings.

J31 7. 9. 1–4: On the preparation of vermilion

In the days when colour could not be bought ready made, architects and painters needed a detailed knowledge of the chemistry and commercial processes involved. The palette was limited and Vitruvius gives detailed recipes for all the main colours. The method of polishing the walls to retain the brightness of the colours is also interesting and was important since in the bright sunshine of Italy, it is likely that untreated paintings would fade almost beyond recognition in five to ten years.

1   I will now return to the preparation of vermilion. When the ore is dry, it is bruised with iron rammers, and by frequent washing and heating, the waste is removed and the colour is produced. When, therefore, the quicksilver has thus been removed, minium loses its natural virtues, and becomes soft and friable.   2   And so when it is used in the finishing of enclosed apartments, it remains of its own colour without defects; but in open places like peristyles and exedrae and so forth, where the sun and moon can send their brightness and their rays, the part so affected is damaged and becomes black, when the colour loses its strength. Among the many instances of this is the case of the public official Faberius. He wished to have his palace on the Aventine elegantly finished, and had all the walls of the peristyle covered with vermilion. In a month the walls turned to an unpleasant and uneven colour; and so he was the first to let a contract for laying on other colours.

3   But if anyone proceeds in a less crude fashion, and wishes a vermilion surface to keep its colour after the finishing of the wall is dry, let him apply with a strong brush Punic wax melted in the fire and mixed with a little oil. Then putting charcoal in an iron vessel, and heating the wall with it, let the wax first be brought to melt, and let it be smoothed over, then let it be worked over with waxed cord and clean linen cloths, in the same way as naked marble statues; this process is called *ganōsis* in Greek.   4   Thus a protective coat of Punic wax does not allow the brilliance of the moon or the rays of the sun to remove the colour from these finished surfaces by playing on them.

J32 8. 6. 1–10: On aqueducts, leaden and earthen pipes

The water supply to Rome was another important area of public expenditure, in which Augustus was deeply involved, and had a considerable effect on the development of urban life in the Roman world generally. The problems of supply to the individual houses of the wealthy continued to make difficulties (aqueducts themselves were illegally tapped). The surveying skill and the cost of building aqueducts for a gravity flow must have been considerable but Vitruvius is noticably cautious about the use of pressure pipes.

1   The supply of water is made by three methods: by conduits along artificial channels, or by lead pipes, or by earthenware tubes. And they are arranged as follows. In the case of channels, the structure must be on a very solid foundation; the bed of the current must be levelled with a fall of not less than 6 inches in 100 feet. The channels are to be arched over to protect the water from the sun. When they come to the city walls, a reservoir is to be made. To this a triple receptacle is to be joined, to receive the water; and three pipes of equal size are to be put in the reservoir, leading to the adjoining receptacles, so that when there is an overflow from the two outer receptacles, it may deliver into the middle receptacle.

2   From the middle receptacle pipes will be taken to all pools and fountains; from the second receptacle to the baths, in order to furnish a public revenue; to avoid a deficiency in the public supply, private houses are to be supplied from the third: for private persons will not be able to draw off the water, since they have their own limited supply from their receptacle. The reason why I have made this division, is in order that those who take private supplies into their houses may contribute by the water rate to the maintenance of the aqueducts.   3   If there are hills between the city and the fountain head, we must proceed as follows. Tunnels are to be dug underground and levelled to the fall already described. If the formation of the earth is of tufa or stone, the channel may be cut in its own bed; but if it is of soil or sand the bed and the walls with the vaulting are to be constructed in the tunnel through which the water is to be brought. Air shafts are to be at the distance of one actus (120 feet) apart.

4   But if the supply is to be by lead pipes, first of all a reservoir is to be built at the fountain head. Then the section of the pipe is to be determined for the supply of water, and the pipes are to be laid from the reservoir to a reservoir in the city. The pipes are to be cast in lengths of not less than 10 feet. If the lead is 100 inches wide, they are to weigh 1200 lbs. each; if 80 inches, 960 lbs.; if 50 inches, 600 lbs.; if 40 inches, 480 lbs.; if 30 inches, 360 lbs.; if 20 inches, 240 lbs.; if 15 inches, 180 lbs.; if 10 inches, 120 lbs.; if 8 inches, 100 lbs.; if 5 inches, 60 lbs. The pipes receive the names of the sizes from the width of the sheets of lead in inches, before they are bent round into pipes. For when a pipe is made of a sheet of lead 50 inches wide, it is called a fifty-inch pipe, and similarly the rest.

5   When, however, an aqueduct is made with lead pipes it is to have the following arrangement. If from the fountain head there is a fall to the city, and the

intervening hills are not so high as to interrupt the supply, and if there are valleys, we must build up the pipes to a level as in the case of open channels. If the way round the hills is not long, a circuit is to be used; if the valleys are wide-spreading, the course will be down the hill, and when it reaches the bottom, it is carried on a low substructure so that it may be levelled as far as possible. This will form a U-shaped bend which the Greeks call *koilia*. When the bend comes uphill after a gentle swelling spread over the long space of the bend, the water is to be forced to the height of the top of the hill.

6   But if the bend is not made use of in the valleys, or if the pipe is not brought up to a level, and there is an elbow, the water will burst through and break the joints of the pipes. Further, stand-pipes are to be made in the bend, by which the force of the air may be relaxed. In this way the supply of water by lead pipes may be carried out in the best manner, because the descent, the circuit, the bend, the compression of the air, can be thus managed when there is a regular fall from the fountain head to the city.

7   Again, it is not without advantage to put reservoirs at intervals of 200 actus (24,000 feet), so that if a fault arises anywhere, neither the whole load of water nor the whole structure may be disturbed, but it may be more easily found where the fault is. But these reservoirs are to be neither in the descent nor on the level portion of the bend, nor on the rise, nor generally in valleys, but on unbroken level ground.

8   But if we wish to employ a less expensive method, we must proceed as follows. Earthenware pipes are to be made not less than two inches thick, and so tongued that they may enter into and fit one another. The joints are to be coated with quicklime worked up with oil. At the descents to the bend, a block of red stone is to be placed at the actual elbow, and pierced so that the last pipe on the incline, and the first from the level of the bend, may be jointed in the stone. In the same way uphill: the last from the level of the bend, and the first of the ascent, are to be jointed in the same way in the hollow of the red stone.

9   Thus, by adjusting the level of the tubes, the work will not be forced out of its place at the downward inclines and the ascents. For a strong current of air usually arises in the passage of water, so that it even breaks through rocks, unless, to begin with, the water is evenly and sparingly admitted from the fountain head, and controlled at the elbows and turns by bonding joints or a weight of ballast. Everything else is to be fixed as for lead pipes. Further, when the water is first sent from the fountain head, ashes are to be put in first, so that if any joints are not sufficiently coated, they may be grouted with the ashes.

10   Water-supply by earthenware pipes has these advantages. First, if any fault occurs in the work, anybody can repair it. Again, water is much more wholesome from earthenware pipes than from lead pipes. For it seems to be made injurious by lead, because white lead is produced by it; and this is said to be harmful to the human body. Thus if what is produced by anything is injurious, it is not doubtful but that the thing is not wholesome in itself.

tr. F. Granger (Loeb 1934)

K THE SUCCESSION

Augustus had so firmly established the Principate as a form of government that when he died, Tiberius, his adopted son and heir (K1-14) took over the reins of government smoothly. In theory the Senate could have taken control and re-established a government with two heads of state and all the checks against the accumulation of power by one individual. In practice Tiberius, a mature and experienced military commander, had served Augustus loyally for years, and already shared his *tribunicia potestas* and his *imperium*.

The development of the Principate under the Julio-Claudians is clouded in our sources by the personalities of the *principes*. Tiberius, dour and embittered, came from a noble family distinguished in Republican times and could expect high office because of his military achievements alone. Gaius (K15-18) was a young un-tried boy and Claudius (K19-26) an infirm elderly man when they succeeded to supreme power at Rome. Our main sources for the period, Tacitus and Suetonius, have stamped their own interpretation of events and characters on the political and constitutional developments and we must learn to allow for their assumptions and possible bias. The account in Tacitus' *Annals* of Tiberius' reign reads like the death knell of a whole class—the Roman ruling aristocratic families. Suetonius sees perversion and madness as dominating the behaviour of Gaius. Both look back at a period when rule by one man was a dynamically developing institution from a time when Empire was the established form of government.

K1 Tacitus on the writing of history

(a)
On Tacitus generally see R. Syme Tacitus *(Oxford 1958) and on the* Annals, *B. Walker* The Annals of Tacitus *(Manchester 1952).*

32 I am aware that much of what I have described, and shall describe, may seem unimportant and trivial. But my chronicle is quite a different matter from histories of early Rome. Their subjects were great wars, cities stormed, kings routed and captured. Or, if home affairs were their choice, they could turn freely to conflicts of consuls with tribunes, to land- and corn-laws, feuds of conservatives and com-mons. Mine, on the other hand, is a circumscribed, inglorious field. Peace was scarcely broken—if at all. Rome was plunged in gloom, the ruler uninterested in expanding the empire.

Yet even apparently insignificant events such as these are worth examination.

For they often cause major historical developments. 33 This is so whether a country (or city) is a democracy, an oligarchy, or an autocracy. For it is always one or the other—a mixture of the three is easier to applaud than to achieve, and besides, even when achieved, it cannot last long. When there was democracy, it was necessary to understand the character of the masses and how to control them. When the senate was in power, those who best knew its mind—the mind of the oligarchs—were considered the wisest experts on contemporary events. Similarly, now that Rome has virtually been transformed into an autocracy, the investigation and record of these details concerning the autocrat may prove useful. Indeed, it is from such studies—from the experience of others—that most men learn to distinguish right and wrong, advantage and disadvantage. Few can tell them apart instinctively.

So these accounts have their uses. But they are distasteful. What interests and stimulates readers is a geographical description, the changing fortune of a battle, the glorious death of a commander. My themes on the other hand concern cruel orders, unremitting accusations, treacherous friendships, innocent men ruined—a conspicuously monotonous glut of downfalls and their monotonous causes. Besides, whereas the ancient historian has few critics—nobody minds if he over-praises the Carthaginian (or Roman) army—the men punished or disgraced under Tiberius have numerous descendants living today. And even when the families are extinct, some will think, if their own habits are similar, that the mention of another's crimes is directed against them. Even glory and merit make enemies—by showing their opposites in too sharp and critical relief.

(b)

65 The only proposals in the senate that I have seen fit to mention are particularly praiseworthy or particularly scandalous ones. It seems to me a historian's foremost duty to ensure that merit is recorded, and to confront evil deeds and words with the fear of posterity's denunciations. But this was a tainted, meanly obsequious age. The greatest figures had to protect their positions by subserviency; and, in addition to them, all ex-consuls, most ex-praetors, even many junior senators competed with each other's offensively sycophantic proposals. There is a tradition that whenever Tiberius left the senate-house he exclaimed in Greek, 'Men fit to be slaves!' Even he, freedom's enemy, became impatient of such abject servility.

> Tacitus *Annals* 4. 32-3; 3. 65
> tr. Michael Grant (Penguin 1977)

K2 Tiberius' early career

Tiberius became praetor at twenty-six years of age (16 BC) and accompanied Augustus to Gaul. On Agrippa's death he took over the command in Pannonia

(12 BC). For his retirement to Rhodes in 6 BC see further Dio Cassius 55. 9. 2 ff. Detailed accounts of Tiberius' life and career can be found in F. B. Marsh The Reign of Tiberius *(London 1931); B. Levick* Tiberius the Politician *(Thames & Hudson 1976); R. Seager* Tiberius *(Eyre Methuen 1972).*

Tiberius married Vipsania Agrippina, daughter of Augustus's admiral Marcus Agrippa and grand-daughter of Caecilius Atticus, the Roman knight to whom Cicero addressed many of his letters. It proved a happy marriage; but when Vipsania had already borne him a son, Drusus, whose paternity he acknowledged, and found herself pregnant again, he was required to divorce her and hurriedly marry Augustus's daughter Julia. Tiberius took this very ill. He loved Vipsania and strongly disapproved of Julia, realizing, like everyone else, that she had felt an adulterous passion for him while still married to his father-in-law Agrippa. Tiberius continued to regret the divorce so heartily that when, one day, he accidentally caught sight of Vipsania and followed her with tears in his eyes and intense unhappiness written on his face, precautions were taken against his ever seeing her again.

At first he lived on good terms with Julia and dutifully reciprocated her love; but gradually conceived such a loathing for her that, after their child had died in infancy at Aquileia, he broke off marital relations. On the death in Germany of his brother Drusus, Tiberius brought the body back to Rome, walking in front of the coffin all the way. . . .

9 His first campaign was fought against the Cantabrians, as an infantry colonel; next, he took an army to Armenia, where he restored King Tigranes, personally crowning him on his throne of judgement; then he proceeded to collect at the Parthian Court the standards, captured from Marcus Crassus at Carrhae and from Mark Antony's lieutenants in a later war, which Augustus had required him to surrender. For a year or so after this Tiberius governed the 'Long-Haired' province of Transalpine Gaul, where barbarian raids and feuds between the Gallic chieftains had caused considerable unrest. After that he fought consecutively in the Alps, Pannonia, and Germany. The first of these campaigns brought about the subjugation of the Raetians and Vindelicans; the second that of the Breucians and Dalmatians; and in the third he took some 40,000 German prisoners, whom he brought across the Rhine and settled in new homes on the Gallic bank. Tiberius's exploits were rewarded with an ovation, followed by a regular triumph; and it seems that what was then a novel honour had previously been conferred on him, namely triumphal regalia. He became in turn quaestor, praetor, and Consul, and always before he was old enough to qualify officially as a candidate. A few years later he held another consulship, and was given the tribunicial power for a five-year period.

10 Yet, though in the prime of life, in excellent health, and at the height of his career, Tiberius suddenly decided to retire as completely as possible from state affairs. His motive may have been an inveterate dislike of Julia, whom he dared not charge with adultery or divorce on any other grounds; or it may have been a decision not to bore his fellow-countrymen by remaining too long in the public

491

eye—perhaps he even hoped to increase his reputation by a prolonged absence from Rome, so that if the need of his services were ever felt he would be recalled. Another view is that since Augustus's grandchildren Gaius and Lucius, now also his adopted sons, had recently come of age, Tiberius voluntarily resigned his established position as second man in the Empire and left the political field open for them. This was, in fact, the reason which he afterwards gave, and their father Agrippa had done much the same when Augustus's nephew Marcellus began his official career— retiring to the island of Mytilene so as not to overshadow Marcellus by his great reputation, or be mistaken for a rival. At the time, however, Tiberius applied for leave of absence merely on the ground that he was weary of office and needed a rest; nor would he consider either Livia's express pleas for him to stay, or Augustus's open complaints in the Senate that this was an act of desertion. On the contrary, he defeated their vigorous efforts to blunt his resolution, by a four days' hunger-strike. In the end he sailed off: and leaving Julia and Drusus, his son by Vipsania, behind at Rome, hurried down to Ostia without saying a word to any of the friends who came to say goodbye, and kissing only very few of them before he went aboard his ship.

11   As Tiberius coasted past Campania, news reached him that Augustus was ill; so he cast anchor for awhile. But when tongues began to wag, accusing him of standing by in the hope of seizing the throne, he at once made the best of his way to Rhodes, though the wind was almost dead against him. He had cherished pleasant memories of that beautiful and healthy island since touching there, during his return voyage from Armenia, many years before; and contented himself with a modest town house and a near-by country villa which was not on a grand scale either. Here he behaved most unassumingly: after dismissing his lictors and runners he would often stroll about the gymnasium where he greeted and chatted with simple Greeks almost as if they were his social equals. . . .

Soon afterwards, Tiberius learned that Julia had been banished for immoral and adulterous behaviour, and that his name had been used by Augustus on the bill of divorce sent her. The news delighted him, but he felt obliged to send a stream of letters urging a reconciliation between Augustus and her; and though well aware that Julia deserved all she got, allowed her to keep whatever presents she had at any time received from him. When the term of his tribunicial power expired he asked Augustus's leave to return and visit his family, whom he greatly missed; and confessed at last that he had settled in Rhodes only because he wished to avoid the suspicion of rivalry with Gaius and Lucius. Now that both were fully grown and the acknowledged heirs to the throne, he explained his reasons for keeping away from Rome were no longer valid. Augustus, however, turned down the plea, telling him to abandon all hope of visiting his family, whom he had been so eager to desert.

12   Thus Tiberius remained, most unwillingly, in Rhodes; and could hardly persuade Livia to wheedle him the title of ambassador from Augustus, as an official cloak for his disfavour.

His days were now clouded with anxiety. Although he lived a quiet private life in the country, avoiding contact with all important men who landed, unwelcome attentions continued to be paid him; because no general or magistrate sailing along the southern coast of Asia Minor ever failed to break his journey at Rhodes. The anxiety was well founded. When Tiberius had visited Samos to greet his step-son Gaius Caesar, Governor of the East, the slanders spread by Marcus Lollius, Gaius's guardian, ensured him a chilly welcome. Again, some centurions of Tiberius's creation, who had returned to camp from leave, were said to have circulated mysterious messages, apparently incitements to treason, emanating from him. When Augustus informed Tiberius of this suspicion, he answered with reiterated demands that some responsible person, of whatever rank, should be detailed to visit Rhodes and there keep unceasing watch on what he did and said.

13 Tiberius discontinued his usual exercise on horseback and on foot in the parade ground; wore a Greek cloak and slippers instead of the Roman dress suitable to a man of his standing; and for two years, or longer, grew daily more despised and shunned—until the people of Nimes, whom he had once governed, were encouraged to overturn his statues and busts. One day, at a private dinner party attended by Gaius Caesar, Tiberius's name cropped up, and a guest rose to say that if Gaius gave the order he would sail straight to Rhodes and 'fetch back the Exile's head'—for he had come to be known simply as 'the Exile'. This incident brought home to Tiberius the extreme danger of his situation, and he pleaded most urgently for a recall to Rome; Livia supported him with equal warmth, and Augustus at last gave way. But this was partly due to a fortunate chance: Augustus had left the final decision on Tiberius's case to Gaius, who happened at the time to be on rather bad terms with Lollius, and therefore did as Augustus wished, though stipulating that Tiberius should take no part, and renounce all interest, in politics.

Suetonius *Tiberius* 7–13 (abridged)
tr. R. Graves (Penguin 1957)

K3 Augustus' opinion of Tiberius

Soon afterwards the Consuls introduced a measure which gave Tiberius joint control of the provinces with Augustus, and the task of assisting him to carry out the next five-year census. When the usual purificatory sacrifices had completed the census Tiberius set off for Illyricum; but was immediately recalled by Augustus, whom he found in the throes of his last illness. They spent a whole day together in confidential talk. I am well aware of the story that, when Tiberius finally took his departure, Augustus gasped to his attendants: 'Poor Rome, doomed to be masticated by those slow-moving jaws!' I am also aware that, according to some writers, he so frankly disliked Tiberius's dour manner as to interrupt his own careless chatter whenever he entered; and that, when begged by Livia to adopt her son, he is suspected of having agreed the more readily because he foresaw that, with a successor like Tiberius, his death would be increasingly regretted as the years went by. Yet how could so prudent and farsighted an Emperor have acted as blindly as this in a matter of such importance? My belief is that Augustus weighed Tiberius's good qualities against the bad, and decided that the good tipped the scale; he had, after all, publicly sworn that his adoption of Tiberius was in the national interest, and had often referred to him as an outstanding general and the only one capable of defending Rome against her enemies. In support of my contention let me quote the following passages from Augustus's correspondence:

. . . Goodbye, my very dear Tiberius, and the best of luck go with you in your battles on my behalf—and the Muses! Goodbye, dearest and bravest of men and the most conscientious general alive! If anything goes wrong with you, I shall never smile again!

. . . Your summer campaigns, dear Tiberius, deserve my heartiest praise; I am sure that no other man alive could have conducted them more capably than yourself in the face of so many difficulties and the war-weariness of the troops. All those who served with you agree with me that Ennius's well-known line about Quintus Fabius Cunctator should be amended in your favour, from: *Alone he saved us by his cautious ways,* to: *Alone he saved us by his watchful eye.*

. . . If any business comes up that demands unusually careful thought, or that annoys me, I swear by the God of Truth that I miss my dear Tiberius more than I can say. And the Homeric tag runs in my head:

If he came with me, such his wisdom is,
We should escape the fury of the fire.

. . . When people tell me, or I read, that constant campaigning is wearing you out, damnation take me if I don't get gooseflesh in sympathy! I beg you to take things easy, because if you were to fall ill the news would kill your mother and me, and the whole country would be endangered by doubts about the succession.

. . . My state of health is of little importance compared with yours. I pray that the Gods will always keep you safe and sound for us, if they have not taken an utter aversion to Rome.

Suetonius *Tiberius* 21
tr. R. Graves (Penguin 1957)

K4 Tiberius' appearance

Tiberius was strongly and heavily built, and above average height. His shoulders and chest were broad, and his body perfectly proportioned from top to toe. His left hand was more agile than the right, and so strong that he could poke a finger through a sound, newly-plucked apple or into the skull of a boy or young man. He had a handsome, fresh-complexioned face, though subject to occasional rashes of pimples. The letting his back hair grow down over the nape seems to have been a family habit of the Claudians. Tiberius's eyes were remarkably large and possessed the un-usual power of seeing in the dark, when he first opened them after sleep; but this phenomenon disappeared after a minute or two. His gait was a stiff stride, with the neck poked forward, and if ever he broke his usual stern silence to address those walking with him, he spoke with great deliberation and eloquent move-ments of the fingers. Augustus disliked these mannerisms and put them down to pride, but frequently assured both the Senate and the commons that they were physical, not moral, defects. Tiberius enjoyed excellent health almost to the end of his reign, although after the age of thirty he never called in a doctor or asked one to send him medicine.

Suetonius *Tiberius* 68
tr. R. Graves (Penguin 1957)

K5 The Accession of Tiberius

(a)

Tiberius may well have taken time to consider how far to follow the forms and titles used by Augustus but he already possessed the tribunicia potestas *and a proconsular* imperium. *On the chronology of the mutiny in Pannonia and Tiberius' accession see B. Levick* Tiberius the Politician *pp. 72 ff.; P. A. Brunt* JRS *1961 p. 238; for the mutiny on the Rhine see also K6 and M9.*

124   There was, however, in one respect what might be called a struggle in the state, as, namely, the senate and the Roman people wrestled with Caesar to induce him to succeed to the position of his father, while he on his side strove for per-mission to play the part of a citizen on a parity with the rest rather than that of an emperor over all. At last he was prevailed upon rather by reason than by the honour, since he saw that whatever he did not undertake to protect was likely to perish. He is the only man to whose lot it has fallen to refuse the principate for a longer time, almost, than others had fought to secure it. . . .

125   The state soon reaped the fruit of its wise course in desiring Tiberius, nor was it long before it was apparent what we should have had to endure had our request been refused, and what we had gained in having it granted. For the army serving in Germany, commanded by Germanicus in person, and the legions in Illyricum, seized at the same moment by a form of madness and a deep desire to throw everything into confusion, wanted a new leader, a new order of things, and a new republic. Nay, they even dared to threaten to dictate terms to the senate and to the emperor. They tried to fix for themselves the amount of their pay and their period of service. They even resorted to arms; the sword was drawn; their con-viction that they would not be punished came near to breaking out into the worst excesses of arms. All they needed was someone to lead them against the state; there

was no lack of followers. But all this disturbance was soon quelled and suppressed by the ripe experience of the veteran commander, who used coercion in many cases, made promises where he could do so with dignity, and by the combination of severe punishment of the most guilty with milder chastisement of the others.

In this crisis, while in many respects the conduct of Germanicus was not lacking in rigour, Drusus employed the severity of the Romans of old. Sent by his father into the very midst of the conflagration, when the flames of mutiny were already bursting forth, he preferred to hold to a course which involved danger to himself than one which might prove a ruinous precedent, and used the very swords of those by whom he had been besieged to coerce his besiegers.

Velleius Paterculus 2. 124. 2–125 (abridged)
tr. F. W. Shipley (Loeb 1924)

(b)
Tacitus is a major source for Tiberius' principate. On the theory that Augustus may have been considering other successors see Syme, RR p. 433 and n. 4.

After an appropriate funeral, Augustus was declared a god and decreed a temple. 11 But the target of every prayer was Tiberius. Addressing the senate, he offered a variety of comments on the greatness of the empire and his own unpretentiousness. Only the divine Augustus, he suggested, had possessed a personality equal to such responsibilities—he himself, when invited by Augustus to share his labours, had found by experience what hard hazardous work it was to rule the empire. Besides, he said, a State which could rely on so many distinguished personages ought not to concentrate the supreme power in the hands of one man—the task of government would be more easily carried out by the combined efforts of a greater number.

But grand sentiments of this kind sounded unconvincing. Besides, what Tiberius said, even when he did not aim at concealment, was—by habit or nature—always hesitant, always cryptic. And now that he was determined to show no sign of his real feelings, his words became more and more equivocal and obscure. But the chief fear of the senators was that they should be seen to understand him only too well. So they poured forth a flood of tearful lamentations and prayers, gesticulating to heaven and to the statue of Augustus, and making reverent gestures before Tiberius himself.

At this juncture he gave instructions for a document to be produced and read. It was a list of the national resources. It gave the numbers of regular and auxiliary troops serving in the army; the strength of the navy; statistics concerning the provinces and dependent kingdoms; direct and indirect taxation; recurrent expenditure and gifts. Augustus had written all this out in his own hand. Furthermore, he had added a clause advising that the empire should not be extended beyond its present frontiers. Either he feared dangers ahead, or he was jealous.

12 The senate now wallowed in the most abject appeals. Tiberius remarked

incidentally that, although he did not feel himself capable of the whole burden of government, he was nevertheless prepared to take on any branch of it that might be entrusted to him. 'Then I must ask, Caesar,' called out Gaius Asinius Gallus, 'which branch you desire to have handed over to you.' This unexpected question threw Tiberius off his stride. For some moments he said nothing. Then, recovering his balance, he replied that, since he would prefer to be excused from the responsibility altogether, he felt much too diffident to choose or reject this or that part of it. Gallus, however, who had guessed from Tiberius' looks that he had taken offence, protested that the purpose of his question had not been to parcel out functions which were inseparable; it had been to obtain from the lips of Tiberius himself the admission that the State was a single organic whole needing the control of a single mind. Gallus went on to praise Augustus and remind Tiberius of his own victories, and his long and splendid achievements as a civilian. All the same he failed to appease the indignation he had caused. Tiberius had hated him for years, feeling that Gallus' marriage to his own former wife, Marcus Agrippa's daughter Vipsania, was a sign that Gallus had the arrogance of his father Gaius Asinius Pollio—and was over-ambitious.

13   Next Lucius Arruntius spoke in rather the same vein as Gallus. He too gave offence. Tiberius, in his case, had no longstanding hostility. But he was suspicious of Arruntius, whose wealth, activity, and talents were celebrated. Augustus, in one of his last conversations, had gone over the names of men who would be fit and willing to become emperor, or unfit and unwilling, or fit but unwilling. He had described Marcus Aemilius Lepidus as suitable but disdainful, Gaius Asinius Gallus as eager but unsuitable, and Lucius Arruntius as both fit and capable of making the venture, if the chance arose. (There is agreement about the first two names; but in some versions Arruntius is replaced by Cnaeus Calpurnius Piso.) All those mentioned, apart from Lepidus, were soon struck down on one charge or another, at the instigation of Tiberius. Others who chafed his suspicious temperament were Quintus Haterius and Mamercus Aemilius Scaurus. What Haterius did was to ask: 'How long, Caesar, will you allow the State to have no head?' The fault of Scaurus was to say that, since Tiberius had not vetoed the consuls' motion by his tribune's power, there was hope that the senate's prayers would not be unrewarded. Tiberius lost no time in abusing Haterius. But the intervention of Scaurus, against whom his anger was more implacable, he passed over in silence.

Finally, exhausted by the general outcry and individual entreaties, he gradually gave way—not to the extent of admitting that he had accepted the throne, but at least to the point of ceasing to be urged and refuse.

Tacitus *Annals* 1. 11–13
tr. Michael Grant (Penguin 1977)

(c)

Dio's account is close to that of Tacitus. Agrippa was Agrippa Postumus, son of Julia and Marcus Agrippa, exiled because of his vicious nature according to Velleius Paterculus 2. 112. 7; for a different view see E. Hohl Hermes *(1935) 360 n. 1.*

Tiberius was a patrician of good education, but he had a most peculiar nature. He never let what he desired appear in his conversation, and what he said he wanted he usually did not desire at all. On the contrary, his words indicated the exact opposite of his real purpose; he denied all interest in what he longed for, and urged the claims of what he hated. He would exhibit anger over matters that were very far from arousing his wrath, and make a show of affability where he was most vexed. He would pretend to pity those whom he severely punished, and would retain a grudge against those whom he pardoned. Sometimes he would regard his bitterest foe as if he were his most intimate companion, and again he would treat his dearest friend like the veriest stranger. In short, he thought it bad policy for the sovereign to reveal his thoughts; this was often the cause, he said, of great failures, whereas by the opposite course far more and greater successes were attained. Now if he had merely followed this method quite consistently, it would have been easy for those who had once come to know him to be on their guard against him; for they would have taken everything by exact contraries, regarding his seeming indifference to anything as equivalent to his ardently desiring it, and his eagerness for anything as equivalent to his not caring for it. But, as it was, he became angry if anyone gave evidence of understanding him, and he put many to death for no other offence than that of having comprehended him. While it was a dangerous matter, then, to fail to understand him,—for people often came to grief by approving what he said instead of what he wished,—it was still more dangerous to understand him, since people were then suspected of discovering his practice and consequently of being displeased with it. Practically the only sort of man, therefore, that could maintain himself,—and such persons were very rare,—was one who neither misunderstood his nature nor exposed it to others; for under these conditions men were neither deceived by believing him nor hated for showing that they understood his motives. He certainly gave people a vast amount of trouble whether they opposed what he said or agreed with him; for inasmuch as he really wished one thing to be done but wanted to appear to desire something different, he was bound to find men opposing him from either point of view, and therefore was hostile to the one class because of his real feelings, and to the other for the sake of appearances.

It was due to this characteristic, that, as emperor, he immediately sent a dispatch from Nola to all the legions and provinces, though he did not claim to be emperor; for he would not accept this name, which was voted to him along with the others, and though taking the inheritance left him by Augustus, he would not adopt the title 'Augustus.' At a time when he was already surrounded by the bodyguards, he actually asked the senate to lend him assistance so that he might not meet with any violence at the burial of the emperor; for he pretended to be afraid that people might catch up the body and burn it in the Forum, as they had done with that of Caesar. When somebody thereupon facetiously proposed that he be given a guard, as if he had none, he saw through the man's irony and answered: 'The soldiers do not belong to me, but to the State.' Such was his action in this matter; and similarly he was administering in reality all the business of the empire while declaring that he did not want it at all. At first he kept saying he would give up the rule entirely on account of his age (he was fifty-six) and of his near-sighted-ness (for although he saw extremely well in the dark, his sight was very poor in the daytime); but later he asked for some associates and colleagues, though not with the intention that they should jointly rule the whole empire, as in an oligarchy, but rather dividing it into three parts, one of which he would retain himself, while giving up the remaining two to others. One of these portions consisted of Rome and the rest of Italy, the second of the legions, and the third of the subject peoples outside. When now he became very urgent, most of the senators still opposed his expressed purpose, and begged him to govern the whole realm; but Asinius Gallus, who always employed the blunt speech of his father more than was good for him, replied: 'Choose whichever portion you wish.' Tiberius rejoined: 'How can the same man both make the division and choose?' Gallus, then, perceiving into what a plight he had fallen, tried to find words to please him and answered: 'It was not with the idea that you should have only a third, but rather to show the impossibility of the empire's being divided, that I made this suggestion to you.'. . .

Tiberius acted in this way at that time, chiefly because it was his nature to do so and because he had determined upon that policy, but partly also because he was suspicious of both the Pannonian and Germanic legions and feared Germanicus, then governor of the province of Germany and beloved by them. For he had pre-viously made sure of the soldiers in Italy by means of the oaths of allegiance estab-lished by Augustus; but as he was suspicious of the others, he was ready for either alternative, intending to save himself by retiring to private life in case the legions should revolt and prevail. For this reason he often feigned illness and remained at home, so as not to be compelled to say or do anything definite. I have even heard that when it began to be said that Livia had secured the rule for him contrary to the will of Augustus, he took steps to let it appear that he had not received it from her, whom he cordially hated, but under compulsion from the senators by reason of his surpassing them in excellence. Another story I have heard is to the effect that when he saw that people were cool toward him, he waited and delayed until he had be-come complete master of the empire, lest in the hope of his voluntarily resigning it they should rebel before he was ready for them. Still, I do not mean to record these stories as giving the true causes of his behaviour, which was due rather to his regular disposition and to the unrest among the soldiers. Indeed, he immediately sent from Nola and caused Agrippa to be put to death. He declared, to be sure, that this had not been done by his orders and made threats against the perpetrator of the deed; yet he did not punish him at all, but allowed men to invent their own versions of the affair, some to the effect that Augustus had put Agrippa out of the way just before his death, others that the centurion who was guarding him had slain him on his own responsibility for some revolutionary dealings, and still others that Livia instead of Tiberius had ordered his death.

This rival, then, he got rid of at once, but of Germanicus he stood in great fear.

Dio Cassius 57. 1–4. 1 (abridged)
tr. E. Cary (Loeb 1924)

K6 Germanicus and the mutiny on the Rhine

Nero Claudius Germanicus, son of Tiberius' brother Nero Claudius Drusus (Drusus) and Antonia minor, was adopted by Tiberius in AD 4 on Augustus' instructions. His popularity seems to have been largely due to his father's reputation and his own pleasant personality. For the events following the mutiny see also M9.

33   At this time Germanicus, as I have said, was engaged upon assessments in Gaul. There he learnt that Augustus was dead. Germanicus was married to his grand-daughter Agrippina and had several children by her; and since he was the son of Tiberius' brother Nero Drusus, one of his grandparents was the Augusta. Yet Germanicus suffered from the fact that his grandmother and uncle hated him, for reasons which were unfair but all the more potent. For Nero Drusus still lived on in Roman memories. It was believed that if he had obtained control of the empire he would have brought back the free Republic. The hopes and goodwill thus en-gendered passed to his son, Germanicus. For this young man's unassuming per-sonality and popular manner were very different from the haughty, ambiguous looks and words of Tiberius. Ill-feeling among the women made things worse. The Augusta had a stepmother's aversion to Agrippina. Agrippina herself was deter-mined, and rather excitable. But she turned this to good account by her devoted faithfulness to her husband.

34   At all events Germanicus' proximity to the summit of ambition only made him work more enthusiastically on behalf of Tiberius. After taking the oath of loyalty himself, he administered it to his immediate subordinates and to the Belgic communities. Then came the news that the army was rioting. He set out for it hurriedly.

The men met him outside the camp. They kept their eyes fixed on the ground, ostensibly remorseful. As soon as he entered their lines, however, they assailed him with all manner of complaints. Some grasped his hand as though to kiss it, but instead thrust his fingers into their mouths to make him touch their toothless gums. Others showed how old age had deformed them. They crowded round him to listen—in no sort of order. Germanicus told them to divide into their units. But they shouted back that they would hear better where they were. He said that they must at least bring their standards to the front so that it could be seen which battalion was which. Slowly they obeyed. Then Germanicus, after paying a reverent tribute to Augustus' memory, praised the victories and triumphs of Tiberius and, by way of climax, his glorious achievements in German lands with those very brigades. He spoke appreciatively of Italy's unanimous support for the government, and of the loyalty of the Gauls—of the perfect harmony and order prevailing everywhere.

This was received in silence or with indistinct muttering.   35   But then Ger-manicus passed on to the mutiny. What on earth had happened, he asked, to their famous, traditional military discipline, and where had they driven their colonels and company-commanders? The soldiers' reply was to tear off their clothes one after another, and point abusively to the scars left by their wounds and floggings.

There was a confused roar about their wretched pay, the high cost of exemptions from duty, and the hardness of the work. Specific references were made to earth-works, excavations, foraging, collecting timber and firewood, and every other camp task that is either necessary or invented to occupy spare time. The most violent outcry came from the old soldiers, who pointed to their thirty years' service and more, and appealed for relief from their exhaustion before death overtook them in the same old drudgery. 'End this crushing service!' they begged. 'Give us rest— before we are utterly destitute!'

Some asked Germanicus for the legacies which the divine Augustus had left them—adding expressions of personal support for Germanicus. If he wanted the throne, they showed they were for him. At this point he leapt off the dais as if their criminal intentions were polluting him, and moved away. But they blocked his path and menaced him until he went back. Then, however, shouting that death was better than disloyalty, he pulled the sword from his belt and lifted it as though to plunge it into his chest. The men round him clutched his arm and stopped him by force. But the close-packed masses at the back of the crowd, and even, remark-ably enough, certain individuals who had pushed themselves into prominent positions, encouraged him to strike. A soldier called Calusidius even drew his own sword and offered it, remarking that it was sharper. But even in their demented frame of mind the men found this a brutal and repellent gesture. There was a pause; and Germanicus' friends had time to hurry him into his tent.

36   There they considered what was to be done. The soldiers were reported to be organizing a deputation to bring over the army of Upper Germany. They were also, it was said, planning to destroy the capital of the Ubii, and after that taste of looting to burst into the Gallic provinces and plunder them too. The situation was all the more alarming because the Germans knew of the mutiny in the Roman army: the abandonment of the Rhine bank would mean invasion. Yet to arm auxiliaries and loyal tribesmen against the rebellious regulars would be civil war. Severity appeared dangerous. But large concessions would be criminal. It would be just as desperately risky for Rome to give way about everything or about nothing. When all the arguments had been weighed and compared, it was decided to make a statement in the emperor's name. In this, demobilization was promised after twenty years' service. Men who had served sixteen years were to be released but kept with the colours with no duties except to help beat off enemy attacks. Moreover, the legacies which they had requested were to be paid—twice over.

37   The soldiers saw that these concessions were hastily improvised and de-manded their immediate implementation. The discharges were speedily arranged by the senior officers. The cash payments, however, were held up until the troops reached winter camps. Two brigades, the fifth and the twenty-first, refused to move from their summer quarters until, there and then, the whole sum was paid. It had to be scraped together from the travelling funds of Germanicus himself and his staff. The general Caecina took the remaining two brigades, the first and the twentieth, back to the Ubian capital. It was a scandalous march—Eagle, standards, and the cash stolen from the commander, all were carried along together.

Then Germanicus moved on to the army of Upper Germany. He had no difficulty in inducing the second, thirteenth and sixteenth brigades to take the oath; the fourteenth only took it after hesitation. Though there were no demands for discharges and money payments, both were conceded.   38   In the territory of the Chauci, however, a fresh outbreak occurred, among a garrison consisting of detachments from the insubordinate brigades. The trouble was soon stamped out by two prompt executions. This illegal but salutary measure was carried out on the orders of the corps chief-of-staff Manius Ennius. Then, as the mutiny began to swell, he got away. But he was discovered. Relying on a bold course for the safety which his hiding-place had failed to provide, he cried out that their offence was not just against an officer, it was against Germanicus their commander—against Tiberius their emperor! At the same time, intimidating all opposition, he seized the standard and pointed it towards the Rhine. Then, shouting that everyone who fell out would be treated as a deserter, he conducted his men back to their winter camp—still rebellious, but frustrated.

39   Meanwhile the senate's mission to Germanicus found him back at the Ubian altar and capital. The first and the twentieth brigades were in winter quarters there, and also the soldiers who had recently been released but not yet demobilized. Mad with anxiety and bad conscience, these men were also terrified that the concessions which they had won by mutinous methods would be cancelled by the senatorial delegation. Crowds habitually find scapegoats, however unjustifiably, and now they attacked the chief envoy, the former consul Lucius Munatius Plancus, charging him with instigating sanctions against them in the senate. Early in the night they began to clamour for their standard, which was kept in Germanicus' residence. They rushed the door and forced him to get up and—under threat of death—to hand it over. Then, roaming the streets, they encountered the members of the delegation, who had heard the uproar and were on their way to Germanicus. The soldiers heaped abuse on them. Indeed they had it in mind to kill them, and especially Plancus. His high rank made it impossible for him to run away; and in his extreme danger the only available refuge was the camp of the first brigade. There he found sanctuary, grasping the Eagle and standards. But if a colour-sergeant named Calpurnius had not protected him from his fate, then, without precedent even between enemies, the altars of the gods would have been stained with the blood of an emissary of the Roman people, in a Roman camp.

At last morning arrived; and commanders and private soldiers, and the night's doings, were seen for what they were. Germanicus came into the camp and ordered Plancus to be brought to him. Escorting him on to the dais, he assailed this disastrous, maniacal revival of violence. 'It shows how angry the gods are', he said, 'rather than the soldiers!' Then he explained why the delegation had come, and spoke with gloomy eloquence about the rights of envoys, and the deplorable and unfair treatment of Plancus himself—a disgrace to the brigade. The gathering was hardly pacified, but it was cowed; and Germanicus sent the delegates away under the protection of auxiliary cavalry.

40   In this alarming situation Germanicus was generally criticized for not

proceeding to the upper army, which obeyed orders and would help against the rebels. Enough and more than enough mistakes had been made, it was felt, by releases and payments and mild measures. And even if he did not value his own life, people asked why, among these madmen who had broken every law, he kept with him his baby son and his pregnant wife. Surely he owed it to the nation and their imperial grandfather to send them back! Germanicus was long hesitant. His wife scorned the proposal, reminding him that she was of the blood of the divine Augustus and would live up to it, whatever the danger. Then he burst into tears—and clasping to him the expectant mother and their child, persuaded her to go. It was a pitiable feminine company that set out. The supreme commander's own wife, a refugee, clutched his infant son to her breast. Her escorts, his friends' wives—forced to leave with her—were in tears. Those who remained were equally mournful. 41 The scene suggested a captured city rather than a highly successful Caesar in his own camp.

The women's sobbing and lamentation attracted the attention of the soldiers, who came out of their tents and asked why they were crying and what was wrong. Here were these distinguished ladies with no staff-officers or soldiers to look after them, none of the usual escort or other honours due to the supreme commander's wife. And they were off to the Treviri, to be looked after by foreigners! The men felt sorry for them, and ashamed, when they thought of her ancestry—her father was Agrippa, her grandfather Augustus, her father-in-law Nero Drusus—and of her impressive record as wife and mother. Besides, there was her baby son, Gaius, born in the camp and brought up with the regular troops as his comrades. In their army fashion they had nicknamed him 'little Boots' (Caligula), because as a popular gesture he was often dressed in miniature army boots. But their jealousy of the Treviri was what affected them most.

[*Tacitus' account of the reconciliation between Germanicus and the mutineers, here omitted, is highly dramatic and includes an emotional speech by Germanicus.*]

44 At this they petitioned for mercy. Admitting the justice of his rebuke, they begged him to punish the guilty, and forgive those who had slipped. He must lead them against the enemy, they urged. And first his wife must be summoned back— the boy they bred must also return, and not be given to Gauls as a hostage. Germanicus agreed that his son should return, but excused his wife since her confinement was at hand, and so was winter. The rest, he said, was up to them. Changed men, they hastened round arresting the leading rebels and dragging them before the commander of the first brigade, Gaius Caetronius. Each ringleader in turn was tried and punished by him in the following fashion. The men, with drawn swords, stood in a mass. One after another the prisoners were paraded on the platform by a colonel. If they shouted 'Guilty', he was thrown down and butchered. The soldiers revelled in the massacre as though it purged them of their offences. And Germanicus, though the orders had not been his, did not intervene. For the disgust caused by this savagery would be directed against its perpetrators, and not against him.

The discharged men acted similarly. Soon afterwards, they were sent to Raetia. The pretext was defence against a threat from the Suebi; but the real intention was to remove them from a camp with hateful memories of crimes and of their equally appalling retribution. Then Germanicus revised the roll of company-commanders. Each in turn came before him and reported his name, company, birth-place, length of service, and any battle distinctions and decorations. If the colonels and men spoke favourably of his work and character, then the company-commander kept his job. If, however, he was unanimously described as grasping and brutal, he was dismissed from the service.

45　This relieved the immediate crisis. But there was still equally serious trouble from the truculent attitude of the fifth and twenty-first brigades wintering sixty miles away at Vetera. It was they who had started the mutiny and committed the worst atrocities. Now they were as angry as ever, undeterred by the punishment and contrition of their fellow-soldiers. So Germanicus, ready to use force if his authority were set aside, prepared to transport auxiliary troops and arms down the Rhine.

46　When Rome heard of the rebellion in Germany—before the final developments in Illyricum were known—the whole population rounded panic-stricken on Tiberius. Here was he with his insincere hesitation, making fools of the helpless, unarmed senate and Assembly; while the soldiers mutinied! Two half-grown boys, they felt, could not control these rebellions. Tiberius ought to have gone himself, and confronted them with his imperial dignity: they would have given way when they saw their experienced emperor, with sovereign powers of retribution and reward. It was recalled that Augustus had made several visits to the Germanies in later life—yet here was Tiberius, in his prime, sitting in the senate quibbling at members' speeches! The enslavement of Rome, men said, was well in hand. Now something must be done to calm the troops and make peace.

47　Such talk made no impression on Tiberius. He was determined not to jeopardize the nation and himself by leaving the capital. His worries were various. Germany had the stronger army, Pannonia the nearer. The former had Gaul's resources behind it, the latter threatened Italy. So which should he visit first? And what if the one placed second should take serious offence? Whereas, through his sons, he could deal with both simultaneously and keep intact his imperial dignity— which was, indeed, more awe-inspiring at a distance. Besides, it was excusable for the young Germanicus and Drusus to refer some points to their father, and resistance offered to them could be conciliated or broken by himself. If, on the other hand, the emperor were treated contemptuously, no expedient was left.

All the same, as though he were going to start at any moment, he chose his staff, collected equipment, and prepared ships. Then, however, he offered various excuses about the weather, and pressure of business. The deception worked—on intelligent people for a while, on most people for some time, and on those in the provinces for longest of all.

48　Germanicus had brought his troops together and was ready for countermeasures against the mutineers. But he decided to give them more time in case they might profit by the example of the other brigades. So he sent word to Caecina saying that he was coming with a strong force and that, unless they first punished the agitators, he would execute them indiscriminately. Caecina read the letter privately to the colour-sergeants and sergeant-majors and other reliable elements in the camp, and appealed to them to save the army's honour, and their own lives. 'In peace-time', he said, 'backgrounds and justifications are considered; but when war comes, the innocent fall with the guilty.' Sounding the men whom they thought reliable, they found that the greater part of the two brigades was loyal. So in consultation with the general, they fixed a time at which the grossest offenders were to be struck down. At a given signal, they burst into the tents, and surprised and killed their victims. Only those in the secret knew how the massacre had begun—or where it would end.

49   This was unlike any other civil war. It was not a battle between opposing forces. Men in the same quarters, who had eaten together by day and rested together by night, took sides and fought each other. The shrieks, wounds, and blood were unmistakable. But motives were mysterious, fates unpredictable. There were casualties among the loyalists, too; for the culprits also had seized weapons when they realized who were being attacked. Generals, colonels, offered no restraining hand. Mass vengeance was indulged and glutted.

Soon afterwards Germanicus arrived in the camp. Bursting into tears, he cried: 'This is no cure; it is a catastrophe!' Then he ordered the bodies to be cremated.

Tacitus *Annals* 1. 33–49 (abridged)
tr. Michael Grant (Penguin 1977)

K7   Favourable assessments of the early years of Tiberius' principate

(a)
Dio attributes these events to AD 14.

Now when no further news of any rebellious moves came and the whole Roman world had acquiesced securely in his leadership, Tiberius accepted the rule without further dissimulation, and exercised it, so long as Germanicus lived, in the way I am about to describe. He did little or nothing on his own responsibility, but brought all matters, even the slightest, before the senate and communicated them to that body. In the Forum a tribunal had been erected on which he sat in public to dispense justice, and he always associated with himself advisers, after the manner of Augustus; nor did he take any step of consequence without making it known to the rest. After setting forth his own opinion he not only granted everyone full liberty to speak against it, but even when, as sometimes happened, others voted in opposition to him, he submitted; for he often would cast a vote himself. Drusus used to act just like the rest, now speaking first, and again after some of the others. As for Tiberius, he would sometimes remain silent and sometimes give his opinion first, or after a few others, or even last; in some cases he would speak his mind directly, but generally, in order to avoid appearing to take away their freedom of speech, he would say: 'If I had been giving my views, I should have proposed this or that.' This method was just as effective as the other and yet the rest were not thereby prevented from stating their views. On the contrary, he would frequently express one opinion and those who followed would prefer something different, and sometimes they actually prevailed; yet for all that he harboured anger against no one. He held court himself, as I have stated, but he also attended the courts presided over by the magistrates, not alone when invited by them, but also when not invited. He would allow them to sit in their regular places, while he himself took his seat on the bench facing them and as an assessor made any remarks that seemed good to him.

In all other matters, too, he behaved in this same way. Thus, he would not allow himself to be called master by the freemen, nor *imperator* except by the soldiers; the title of Father of his Country he rejected absolutely; that of Augustus he did not assume,—in fact he never permitted it to be even voted to him,—but he did not object to hearing it spoken or to reading it when written, and whenever he sent messages to kings, he would regularly include this title in his letters. In general he was called Caesar, sometimes Germanicus (from the exploits of Germanicus), and Chief of the Senate,—the last in accordance with ancient usage and even by himself. He would often declare: 'I am master of the slaves, *imperator* of the soldiers, and chief of the rest.' He would pray, as often as occasion for praying arose, that he might live and rule so long only as should be to the advantage of the State. And he was so democratic in all circumstances alike, that he would not permit any special observance to be made of his birthday and would not allow people to swear by his Fortune, and if anybody after swearing by it incurred the charge of perjury, he would not prosecute him. . . .

Not only in the ways just related were his actions democratic, but no sacred precinct was set apart for him either by his own choice or in any other way,—at that time, I mean,—nor was anybody allowed to set up an image of him; for he promptly and expressly forbade any city or private citizen to do so. To this prohibition, it is true; he attached the proviso, 'unless I grant permission,' but he added, 'I will not grant it.' For he would not by any means have it appear that he had been insulted or impiously treated by anybody (they were already calling such conduct *maiestas* and were bringing many suits on that ground), and he would not hear of any such indictment being brought on his own account, though he paid tribute to the majesty of Augustus in this matter also. At first, to be sure, he did not punish any of those, even, that had incurred charges for their actions in regard to his predecessor, and he actually released some against whom complaint was made that they had perjured themselves after swearing by the Fortune of Augustus; but as time went on, he put great numbers to death. . . .

Such was Tiberius' behaviour in all matters as long as Germanicus lived; but after his death he changed his course in many respects. Perhaps he had been at heart from the first what he later showed himself to be, and had been merely shamming while Germanicus was alive, because he saw his rival lying in wait for the sovereignty;

or perhaps he was excellent by nature, but drifted into vice when deprived of his rival.

Dio Cassius 57. 7–8. 4; 9; 13. 6
tr. E. Cary (Loeb 1924)

(b)

Tacitus attributes these events to AD 15; on the trial of Cassius Severus, a brilliant but provoking orator, see also Seneca Controv. *3 praef.;* Tacitus Dial. *19 and 26. Romanius Hispo appears to have been a rhetorician who became a professional informer. Suetonius* Tiberius *58 gives a different ending to the trial of Marcellus. Gnaeus Calpurnius Piso became governor of Syria in AD 17.*

72   In spite of repeated popular pressure, Tiberius refused the title 'Father of his Country'. He also declined the senate's proposal that obedience should be sworn to his enactments. All human affairs were uncertain, he protested, and the higher his position the more slippery it was.

Nevertheless, he did not convince people of his Republicanism. For he revived the treason law. The ancients had employed the same name, but had applied it to other offences—to official misconduct damaging the Roman State, such as betrayal of an army or incitement to sedition. Action had been taken against deeds, words went unpunished. The first who employed this law to investigate written libel was Augustus, provoked by Cassius Severus, an immoderate slanderer of eminent men and women. Then Tiberius, asked by a praetor, Quintus Pompeius Macer, whether cases under the treason law were to receive attention, replied: *the laws must take their course.* Like Augustus he had been annoyed by anonymous verses. These had criticized his cruelty, arrogance, and bad relations with his mother.

73   The tentative charges against Falanius and Rubrius, members of the order of knights, are worth recording. For they illustrate the beginnings of this disastrous institution—which Tiberius so cunningly insinuated, first under control, then bursting into an all-engulfing blaze. Falanius was charged, first, with admitting among the worshippers of Augustus, in the cult maintained by households on the analogy of priestly orders, an actor in musical comedies named Cassius who was a male prostitute, and, secondly, with disposing of a statue of Augustus when selling some garden property. Rubrius was charged with perjury by the divinity of Augustus.

When Tiberius heard of these accusations, he wrote to the consuls saying that Augustus had not been voted divine honours in order to ruin Roman citizens. The actor, he observed, together with others, had regularly taken part in the Games which his mother the Augusta had instituted in Augustus' honour—and to include the latter's statues (like those of other gods) in sales of houses or gardens was not sacrilegious. As regards the perjury, it was parallel to a false oath in Jupiter's name: the gods must see to their own wrongs.

74   Shortly afterwards Marcus Granius Marcellus, governor of Bithynia, was accused of treason by his own assistant, Aulus Caepio Crispinus. But it was the latter's partner Romanius Hispo who created a career which was to be made

notorious by the villainous products of subsequent gloomy years. Needy, obscure, and restless, he wormed his way by secret reports into the grim emperor's confidence. Then everyone of any eminence was in danger from him. Over one man he enjoyed an ascendancy; all others loathed him. His was the precedent which enabled imitators to exchange beggary for wealth, to inspire dread instead of contempt, to destroy their fellow-citizens—and finally themselves.

He alleged that Marcus Granius Marcellus had told scandalous stories about Tiberius. The charge was damning. The descriptions the accuser imputed to him recounted the most repulsive features in the emperor's character. Since these were not fictitious it seemed plausible that Marcellus should have described them. Hispo added that Marcellus had placed his own effigy above those of the Caesars, and that on one statue he had cut off the head of Augustus and replaced it by Tiberius.

The emperor lost his temper and, voluble for once, exclaimed that he personally would vote, openly and on oath. This would have compelled other senators to do the same. But, since there still remained some traces of declining freedom, Cnaeus Calpurnius Piso asked a question; 'Caesar, will you vote first or last? If first, I shall have your lead to follow; if last, I am afraid of inadvertently voting against you.' This struck home, and Tiberius, regretting his impetuous outburst, meekly voted for acquittal on the treason counts. Charges of embezzlement were referred to the proper court.

75   However, investigations in the senate were not enough for Tiberius. He also began to sit in the law courts—at the side of the platform, so as not to oust the praetor from his official chair. His presence successfully induced many verdicts disregarding influential pressure and intrigue. Nevertheless, it also infringed on the independance of judges.

At about this time also, a junior senator named Aurelius Pius protested that his house had been undermined by the government's construction of a road and aqueduct. He appealed to the senate. The praetors in charge of the Treasury resisted the claim, but Tiberius came to his help and paid him the value of his house. For the emperor was prepared to spend in a good cause, and kept this good quality long after his others were gone. When an ex-praetor, Propertius Celer, asked to resign from the senate on grounds of poverty, Tiberius, finding that his lack of means was inherited, presented him with one million sesterces. Others then applied. But he requested them to prove their case to the senate. Even when he acted fairly his austerity made a harsh impression; and the applicants preferred silent impoverishment to subsidization accompanied by publicity.

76   In the same year the Tiber, swollen by persistent rain, flooded lowlying parts of the city. When it receded, much loss of life and buildings was apparent. Gaius Asinius Gallus proposed consultation of the Sibylline Books. Tiberius, with his preference for secrecy—in heavenly as in earthly matters—demurred. Instead, Gaius Ateius Capito and Lucius Arruntius were instructed to control the water-level.

A gladiator-show was given in the names of Germanicus and Drusus. The latter was abnormally fond of bloodshed. Admittedly it was worthless blood, but the public were shocked and his father was reported to have reprimanded him. Tiberius himself kept away. Various reasons were given—his dislike of crowds, or his natural glumness, or unwillingness to be compared with Augustus, who had cheerfully attended. It was also suggested, though I would scarcely believe it, that he deliberately gave his son a chance to show his forbidding character—and win unpopularity.

Tacitus *Annals* 1. 72–6
tr. Michael Grant (Penguin 1977)

K8 Trials under Tiberius

(a)
The trial of M. Scribonius Libo Drusus took place in AD 16; Suetonius (Tiberius 25) gives it as one of the reasons for Tiberius' hesitation to succeed to Augustus' position, but from Tacitus' account it appears that Libo, praetor in 15, was already under suspicion in 14. There is some controversy over the importance of the conspiracy; Seneca (Epistles 70. 10) agrees with Tacitus' estimation of Libo as a lightweight; Velleius Paterculus (2. 129. 2) sees Libo as an important threat (cf. also Dio Cassius 57. 15. 4); see also B. Levick Tiberius the Politician *(Thames & Hudson 1976) p. 150 and F. Marsh* The Reign of Tiberius *(Oxford 1931) p. 59; for a detailed and comprehensive study of trials under Tiberius see R. S. Rogers* Criminal Trials and Criminal Legislation under Tiberius *(Connecticut 1935). (Cf. I50 for the end of the trial.)*

27   It was about now that Marcus Scribonius Libo Drusus was accused of subversive plotting. Since this case initiated an evil which for many years corroded public life, I will give details of its beginnings, progress, and conclusion. Libo was a fatuous young man with a taste for absurdities. One of his closest friends, a junior senator named Firmius Catus, interested him in astrologers' predictions, magicians' rites, and readers of dreams. Catus reminded Libo that the Caesars were his cousins —besides being a great-grandson of Pompey, he was grand-nephew of Scribonia, at one time the wife of Augustus—and that his own house, too, was full of ancestral statues.
By encouraging Libo's extravagances and debts and sharing his dissipations and embarrassments, Catus accumulated damning evidence.   28   When he had collected enough witnesses—including slaves to corroborate the account—he requested an interview with the emperor. Tiberius already knew who was accused, and why, through a knight, Vescularius Flaccus, who was more intimate with the emperor than Catus was. Tiberius did not refuse the information of Catus but declined personal contact, indicating that they could continue to communicate through the knight as intermediary. Meanwhile he made Libo praetor and invited him to dinner. No unfriendliness was apparent in Tiberius' expression or talk. His malevolence was completely concealed. He could have stopped all Libo's actions and words. Instead, he preferred to note them.

Finally, however, a certain Junius whom Libo had approached to practise necromancy reported him to Lucius Fulcinius Trio, a man known for his talents as a prosecutor—and eager for notoriety. Trio immediately pounced on Libo, applied to the consuls, and demanded an inquiry by the senate: which was summoned, to discuss (it was added) a grave and terrible matter.   29   Meanwhile Libo put on mourning and, with an escort of aristocratic ladies, went from house to house appealing to his wife's relatives and seeking for an advocate in his perilous position. Everyone refused. Their excuses were different, but they were all afraid. On the day of the meeting he was prostrate with fear and ill-health (possibly, as some said, assumed), and had to be carried in a litter to the senate-house door. Leaning on his brother's arm he stretched out his hand to Tiberius and cried for mercy. The emperor, without altering his expression, read out the accusation and its signatures in a toneless voice calculated neither to aggravate nor to extenuate the charges.

30   Trio and Catus had now been joined by further accusers, Fonteius Agrippa and Gaius Vibius Serenus. They all competed for the principal speech. Finally, as none of them would give way and Libo was undefended, Vibius announced that he would take the charges one by one; and he produced the documents. They were preposterous. In one, Libo asked a fortune-teller if he would become rich enough to pave the Via Appia with money as far as Brundisium. Other stupidities were equally pointless—indeed, if indulgently regarded, pitiable. But in one paper, mysterious or sinister marks against the names of imperial personages and senators were alleged by the prosecutor to be in Libo's handwriting. Libo denied this. But slaves identified his hand; and it was decided to interrogate them under torture. Since, however, there was an ancient senatorial decree forbidding such investigations of slaves in capital charges against their masters, Tiberius—by an astute legal innovation—ordered the slaves to be sold individually to the Treasury Agent. And all this in order to use slaves' evidence against a man of Libo's position, without infringing a senatorial decree!

The defendant thereupon requested an adjournment until the following day, and left for his home. He entrusted his relative Publius Sulpicius Quirinius with a final appeal to Tiberius.   31   The emperor's answer was that Libo should apply to the senate. Meanwhile his house was surrounded by Guardsmen. The sound and sight of them, clanking about in front of the door, plagued the dinner-party which Libo had arranged as his last pleasure on earth. Gripping his slaves' hands and thrusting his sword into their grasp, he cried out for someone to kill him. The slaves shrank away in terror, and knocked over the table-lamp. For Libo it was the darkness of death. He stabbed himself twice in the stomach, and fell moaning. Ex-slaves ran up. The soldiers saw he was dead, and left.

Tacitus *Annals* 2. 27–31
tr. Michael Grant (1977)

(b)

The trial of Appuleia Varilla, grand-daughter of the elder Octavia, took place in AD 17.

Meanwhile, the treason law was maturing. Appuleia Varilla was charged under it for speaking insultingly about the divine Augustus (whose sister was her aunt), as well as about Tiberius and his mother, and for committing adultery. The latter offence was ruled to be a matter for the Julian adultery law. As regards the treason, Tiberius insisted on a distinction between disrespectful remarks about Augustus—for which she should be condemned—and about himself, on which he desired no inquiry to be held. Asked by the consul what his ruling was about Appuleia's alleged slanders against his mother, he did not reply. But at the next meeting of the senate he requested in his mother's name also that no words uttered against her should in any circumstances be made the subject of a charge. He released Appuleia from liability under the treason law. For her adultery he deprecated the severer penalty, but recommended that according to traditional practice her relatives should remove her two hundred miles from Rome. Her lover, Manlius by name, was banned from Italy and Africa.

Tacitus *Annals* 2. 50
tr. Michael Grant (Penguin 1977)

(c)

It is not certain whether the Equestrian Clutorius Priscus was accused of maiestas *for, in effect, predicting the death of Drusus. (Cf. Dio Cassius 57. 20. 3 f.; also Koestermann* Historia *4 (1955) 101.)*

49   At the end of the year [AD 21] an informer attacked the knight Clutorius Priscus, who had been subsidized by Tiberius for writing a well-known poem about Germanicus' death. Clutorius was now accused of composing another poem while Drusus was ill, for even more lucrative publication if the prince died. Clutorius had bragged of this in the house of Publius Petronius, before his host's mother-in-law Vitellia and many leading women. When the accuser came forward, the other women were intimidated into admitting this. Vitellia alone said she had heard nothing. However, the damning evidence was more widely believed, and the consul-elect Decimus Haterius Agrippa moved for the death penalty.

50   Marcus Aemilius Lepidus opposed this motion. 'If, senators,' he argued, 'we only consider the outrageous utterance with which Clutorius Priscus had degraded himself and his hearers, prison and the noose—or even the tortures reserved for slaves—are not enough for him. Yet, however deplorable and outrageous the offence, the emperor's moderation and your own ancient and modern precedents indicate the mitigation of penalties. Besides, folly is distinguished from crime—and words from deeds. For these reasons, it is legitimate to propose a punishment which will cause us to regret neither over-leniency nor harshness. I have often heard our emperor

511

deploring suicides, since they prevent the exercise of his clemency. Clutorius is still alive. His survival will not endanger the State; and his death will convey no lesson. His compositions are senseless, but they are insignificant and ephemeral. A man who betrays his own outrages to impress not men but mere females is no very great danger. I propose, therefore, that we expel him from the city, outlaw him, and confiscate his property, as if he were guilty under the treason law.'

51   A single ex-consul, Gaius Rubellius Blandus, agreed. But the rest supported Haterius. So Clutorius Priscus was imprisoned and immediately executed.

This drew from Tiberius a characteristically cryptic reproof of the senate. While praising their loyalty in so vigorously avenging even minor offences against the emperor, he deprecated so hasty a punishment of a mere verbal lapse. He commended Lepidus—but refrained from criticizing Haterius. The result was a decision that no senatorial decree should be registered at the Treasury for nine days, executions to be delayed for that period. But the senate lacked the freedom to reconsider. And the intervals never softened Tiberius.

Tacitus *Annals* 3. 49–51
tr. Michael Grant (Penguin 1977)

K9 Popular Agitation

(a) *The corn subsidy of AD 19*

Popular agitation was often expressed at the theatre (cf. Tacitus Annals *6. 13. 1). The supply of corn may have been affected by the rebellion in Africa (B. Levick* Tiberius the Politician *p. 121). On Tiberius' dislike of being called* dominus *see further Suetonius* Tiberius *27.*

There was popular agitation against the terrible expense of corn. Tiberius fixed the sale price and promised a subsidy of two sesterces a bushel for dealers. But he still rejected the title 'Father of his Country', which was not offered him again because of this. He also severely reproved people who spoke of his occupations as 'divine' and himself as 'master'. So the paths of speech were narrow and slippery. For though the emperor dreaded freedom, he detested flattery.

Tacitus *Annals* 2. 87
tr. Michael Grant (Penguin 1977)

(b) *An anecdote which, if based on fact, indicates a widespread interest in art!*

Lysippus [a famous Greek sculptor of the 4th cent. BC] as we have said was a most prolific artist and made more statues than any other sculptor, among them the Man using a Body-scraper [*Apoxyomenos*] which Marcus Agrippa gave to be set up in front of his warm baths and of which the emperor Tiberius was remarkably fond.

Tiberius, although at the beginning of his principate he kept some control of himself, in this case could not resist the temptation, and had the statue removed to his bedchamber, putting another one in its place at the baths; but the public were so obstinately opposed to this that they raised an outcry at the theatre, shouting 'Give us back the *Apoxyomenos*', and the Emperor, although he had fallen quite in love with the statue, had to restore it.

Pliny *Natural History* 34. 62
tr. H. Rackham (Loeb 1952)

K10 Tiberius rejects honours from Spain

*Tacitus dates this to AD 25; the temple in Asia was also dedicated to the Senate
(Annals 4. 15) and Tiberius' refusal of Spain's request could be taken as indicative
of his attitude to personal worship. His name was however often linked with that
of Augustus in cults and dedications both in Italy and the provinces (R. Seager,
Tiberius p. 244).*

37   This was the time when Farther Spain sent a delegation to the senate, applying to follow Asia's example and build a shrine to Tiberius and his mother. Disdainful of compliment, Tiberius saw an opportunity to refute rumours of his increasing self-importance. 'I am aware, senators,' he said, 'that my present opposition has been widely regarded as inconsistent with my acquiescence in a similar proposal by the cities of Asia. So I will justify both my silence on that occasion and my intentions from now onwards.

'The divine Augustus did not refuse a temple at Pergamum to himself and the City of Rome. So I, who regard his every action and word as law, followed the precedent thus established—the more readily since the senate was to be worshipped together with myself. One such acceptance may be pardonable. But to have my statue worshipped among the gods in every province would be presumptuous and arrogant. Besides, the honour to Augustus will be meaningless if it is debased by indiscriminate flattery.   38   As for myself, senators, I emphasize to you that I am human, performing human tasks, and content to occupy the first place among men. 'That is what I want later generations to remember. They will do more than justice to my memory if they judge me worthy of my ancestors, careful of your interests, steadfast in danger and fearless of animosities incurred in the public service. Those are my temples in your hearts, those my finest and most lasting images. Marble monuments, if the verdict of posterity is unfriendly, are mere neglected sepulchres. So my requests to provincials and Roman citizens, and heaven, are these. To heaven—grant me, until I die, a peaceful mind and an understanding of what is due to gods and men. To mortals—when I am dead, remember my actions and my name kindly and favourably.'

Later, too, even in private conversation, he persisted in rejecting such veneration. Some attributed this to modesty, but most people thought it was uneasiness. It was also ascribed to degeneracy, on the grounds that the best men aimed highest—that was how Romulus, like Hercules and Liber (Bacchus) among the Greeks, had been admitted to the gods. 'Augustus had done better than Tiberius', it was said, 'by hoping. Rulers receive instantly everything else they want. One thing only needs to be untiringly worked for—a fair name for the future. Contempt for fame means contempt for goodness.'

Tacitus *Annals* 4. 37–8
tr. Michael Grant (Penguin 1977)

K11 Sejanus

Tacitus sees the year AD 23 as a turning-point in Tiberius' rule, which is why he introduces Sejanus at this point. It is difficult to ascertain how far Sejanus was responsible for this deterioration (cf. Suetonius Tiberius *55; 66. 1; and the discussion in B. Levick* Tiberius the Politician *p. 158 ff.).*

(a)

1 In the consulships of Gaius Asinius Pollio and Gaius Antistius Vetus, Tiberius now began his ninth year of national stability and domestic prosperity (the latter, he felt, augmented by Germanicus' death). But then suddenly Fortune turned disruptive. The emperor himself became tyrannical—or gave tyrannical men power. The cause and beginning of the change lay with Lucius Aelius Sejanus, commander of the Guard. I have said something of his influence, and will now describe his origins and personality—and his criminal attempt on the throne.

Sejanus was born at Vulsinii. His father, Lucius Seius Strabo, was a Roman knight. After increasing his income—it was alleged—by a liaison with a rich debauchee named Marcus Gavius Apicius, the boy joined, while still young, the suite of Augustus' grandson Gaius Caesar. Next by various devices he obtained a complete ascendancy over Tiberius. To Sejanus alone the otherwise cryptic emperor spoke freely and unguardedly. This was hardly due to Sejanus' cunning; in that he was outclassed by Tiberius. The cause was rather heaven's anger against Rome—to which the triumph of Sejanus, and his downfall too, were catastrophic. Of audacious character and untiring physique, secretive about himself and ever ready to incriminate others, a blend of arrogance and servility, he concealed behind a carefully modest exterior an unbounded lust for power. Sometimes this impelled him to lavish excesses, but more often to incessant work. And that is as damaging as excess when the throne is its aim.

2 The command of the Guard had hitherto been of slight importance. Sejanus enhanced it by concentrating the Guard battalions, scattered about Rome, in one

camp. Orders could reach them simultaneously, and their visible numbers and strength would increase their self-confidence and intimidate the population. His pretexts were, that scattered quarters caused unruliness; that united action would be needed in an emergency; and that a camp away from the temptations of the city would improve discipline. When the camp was ready, he gradually insinuated himself into the men's favour. He would talk with them addressing them by name. And he chose their company- and battalion-commanders himself. Senators' ambitions, too, he tempted with offices and governorships for his dependants.

Tiberius was readily amenable, praising him in conversation—and even in the senate and Assembly—as 'the partner of my labours', and allowing honours to his statues in theatres, public places, and brigade headquarters. 3 Yet Sejanus' ambitions were impeded by the well-stocked imperial house, including a son and heir—in his prime—and grown-up grandchildren. Subtlety required that the crimes should be spaced out: it would be unsafe to strike at all of them simultaneously. So subtle methods prevailed. Sejanus decided to begin with Drusus, against whom he had a recent grudge. For Drusus, violent-tempered and resentful of a rival, had raised a hand against him during a fortuitous quarrel and, when Sejanus resisted, had struck him in the face.

After considering every possibility, Sejanus felt most inclined to rely on Drusus' wife Livilla, the sister of Germanicus. Unattractive in earlier years, she had become a great beauty. Sejanus professed devotion, and seduced her. Then, this first guilty move achieved—since a woman who has parted with her virtue will refuse nothing—he incited her to hope for marriage, partnership in the empire, and the death of her husband. So the grand-niece of Augustus, daughter-in-law of Tiberius, mother of Drusus' children, degraded herself and her ancestors and descendants with a small-town adulterer; she sacrificed her honourable, assured position for infamy and hazard. The plot was communicated to Eudemus, Livilla's friend and doctor, who had professional pretexts for frequent interviews. Sejanus encouraged his mistress by sending away his wife Apicata, the mother of his three children. Nevertheless the magnitude of the projected crime caused misgivings, delays, and (on occasion) conflicting plans.

4   Meanwhile, at the beginning of the year Drusus Caesar, one of Germanicus' children, assumed adult clothing, and the senate's decrees in honour of his brother Nero Caesar were repeated. Tiberius spoke as well, warmly praising his own son Drusus for his fatherly affection to the sons of his 'brother' Germanicus. For, though lofty positions are not easily compatible with friendliness, Drusus was believed to like the young men or at least not to dislike them. . . .

6   This, the year in which Tiberius' rule began to deteriorate, seems an appropriate moment to review the other branches of the government also, and the methods by which they had been administered since his accession. In the first place, public business—and the most important private business—was transacted in the senate. Among its chief men, there was freedom of discussion: their lapses into servility were arrested by the emperor himself. His conferments of office took into consideration birth, military distinction, and civilian eminence, and the

choice manifestly fell on the worthiest men. The consuls and praetors maintained their prestige. The lesser offices, too, each exercised their proper authority. Moreover, the treason court excepted, the laws were duly enforced.

Levies of grain, indirect taxation, and the other revenues belonging to the State were managed by associations of Roman knights. But the imperial property was entrusted by the emperor to carefully selected agents—some known to him by reputation only. Once appointed, these were kept on indefinitely, often becoming old in the same jobs. The public suffered, it is true, from oppressive food prices. But that was not the emperor's fault. Indeed, he spared neither money nor labour in combating bad harvests and stormy seas. He ensured also that the provinces were not harassed by new impositions and that old impositions were not aggravated through official acquisitiveness or brutality; beatings and confiscations did not exist. His estates in Italy were few, his slaves unobtrusive, his household limited to a few ex-slaves. Any disputes that he had with private citizens were settled in the law courts.

7   Tiberius, in his ungracious fashion—grim and often terrifying as he was—maintained this policy until the death of Drusus reversed it. While Drusus lived, the same methods were employed, because Sejanus in the early stages of his power wanted to gain a reputation for enlightened policy. Moreover, there was an alarming potential avenger in Drusus, who openly showed his hatred and repeatedly complained that the emperor, though he had a son, went elsewhere for his collaborator. Soon, Drusus reflected, the collaborator would be called a colleague—the first steps of an ambitious career are difficult, but once they are achieved helpers and partisans emerge. 'Already Sejanus has secured this new camp—where the Guard are at the disposal of their commander. His statue is to be seen in Pompey's Theatre. The grandsons of us Drususes will be his grandsons too. What can we do now except trust his moderation and pray he will be forbearing?' Drusus often talked like this and many heard him. But even his confidences were betrayed by his wife—to her lover.

8   So Sejanus decided to act. He chose a poison with gradual effects resembling ordinary ill-health. It was administered to Drusus (as was learnt eight years later) by the eunuch Lygdus. All through his son's illness, Tiberius attended the senate. Either he was unalarmed or he wanted to display his will-power. Even when Drusus had died and his body was awaiting burial, Tiberius continued to attend. The consuls sat on ordinary benches as a sign of mourning. But he reminded them of their dignity and rank. The senators wept. But he silenced them with a consoling oration. . .

'Senators: on my behalf as well as your own, adopt and guide these youths, whose birth is so glorious—these great-grandchildren of Augustus. Nero and Drusus Caesars: these senators will take the place of your parents. For, in the station to which you are born, the good and bad in you is of national concern.'   9   This speech was greeted by loud weeping among the senators, followed by heartfelt prayers for the future. Indeed, if Tiberius had stopped there, he would have left his audience sorry for him and proud of their responsibility. But by reverting to empty discredited talk about restoring the Republic and handing the government to the consuls or others, he undermined belief even in what he had said sincerely and truthfully. However, Drusus was voted the same posthumous honours as Germanicus—with the additions expected of flattery's second attempt. The funeral was noteworthy for its long procession of ancestral effigies—Aeneas, originator of the Julian line; all the kings of Alba Longa; Romulus, founder of Rome; then the Sabine nobility with Attus Clausus; finally the rest of the Claudian house.

10   In describing Drusus' death I have followed the most numerous and repu- table authorities. . . .

11   Besides, the real story of the murder was later divulged by Sejanus' wife Apicata, and corroborated under torture by Eudemus and Lygdus; and no historian, however unfriendly to Tiberius, however tendentious an investigator of his doings, has accused him of this crime. My own motive in mentioning and refuting the rumour has been to illustrate by one conspicuous instance the falsity of hearsay gossip, and to urge those who read this book not to prefer incredible tales—how- ever widely current and readily accepted—to the truth unblemished by marvels.

12   When Tiberius pronounced his son's funeral eulogy from the platform, the attitudes and tones of mourning exhibited by the senate and public were insincere and unconvincing. Secretly they were glad that the house of Germanicus was reviving. However, this awakening popularity, and Agrippina's ill-concealed maternal ambitions, only hastened the family's ruin. For when Sejanus saw that Drusus' death brought no retribution upon the murderers and no national grief, his criminal audacity grew. The succession of the children of Germanicus was now certain. So he considered how they could be removed.

To poison all three was impracticable, since their attendants were loyal—and the virtue of their mother Agrippina unassailable. Her insubordination, however, gave Sejanus a handle against Agrippina. He played on the Augusta's longstanding animosity against her, and on Livilla's new complicity. These ladies were to notify Tiberius that Agrippina, proud of her large family and relying on her popularity, had designs on the throne. To this end Sejanus employed skilful slanderers. Notable among them was Julius Postumus, whose adulterous liaison with Mutilia Prisca made him a close friend of the Augusta and particularly apt for Sejanus' purposes; for Prisca had great influence over the old lady, whose jealousy she could use against Agrippina, her granddaughter not by blood like Livilla, but by marriage. Meanwhile Agrippina's closest friends were induced to accentuate her restlessness by malevolent talk.

13   Tiberius derived comfort from his work. He remained fully occupied with public business—legal cases concerning citizens, and petitions from the provinces. On his initiative, the senate decreed three years' remission of tribute to two cities ruined by earthquakes, Cibyra and Aegium. A governor of Farther Spain, Gaius Vibius Serenus, was convicted of violence and deported as a bad character to the island of Amorgos. . . .

15   The senate still handled all manner of business. Even the emperor's agent in Asia, Lucilius Capito, had to defend himself before it when the people of the province prosecuted him. Tiberius insisted that he had only given the agent power

over his personal slaves and revenues, and if Capito had assumed the governor's authority and employed military force he was exceeding his instructions: the provincials must be heard. The case was tried, and Capito condemned.

For this act of justice, and the punishment of Gaius Junius Silanus in the previous year, the cities of Asia decreed a temple to Tiberius, his mother, and the senate. Permission was granted. Germanicus' son Nero Caesar expressed the thanks of the cities to the senate and his grandfather—a welcome experience to his listeners, whose still fresh memories of Germanicus created the illusion that it was he whom they were seeing and hearing. And the young man's princely looks and modest bearing were all the more attractive because Sejanus was known to hate him.

Tacitus *Annals* 4. 1–15 (abridged)
tr. Michael Grant (Penguin 1977)

(b)

Velleius Paterculus may well have been connected with Sejanus, and affected by his fall.

It is but rarely that men of eminence have failed to employ great men to aid them in directing their fortune . . . With these examples before him, Tiberius Caesar has had and still has as his incomparable associate in all the burdens of the principate Sejanus Aelius, son of a father who was among the foremost in the equestrian order, but connected, on his mother's side, with old and illustrious families and families distinguished by public honours, while he had brothers, cousins, and an uncle who had reached the consulship. He himself combined with loyalty to his master great capacity for labour, and possessed a well-knit body to match the energy of his mind; stern but yet gay, cheerful but yet strict; busy, yet always seeming to be at leisure. He is one who claims no honours for himself and so acquires all honours, whose estimate of himself is always below the estimate of others, calm in expression and in his life, though his mind is sleeplessly alert.

In the value set upon the character of this man, the judgement of the whole state has long vied with that of the emperor. . . . It was but the natural following of precedent that impelled Caesar to put Sejanus to the test, and that Sejanus was induced to assist the emperor with his burdens, and that brought the senate and the Roman people to the point where they were ready to summon for the preservation of its security the man whom they regarded as the most useful instrument.

Velleius Paterculus 2. 127. 3–128. 4 (abridged)
tr. F. W. Shipley (Loeb 1924)

(c) *Dio's estimate of Sejanus' power*

Sejanus was so great a person by reason both of his excessive haughtiness and of his vast power, that, to put it briefly, he himself seemed to be emperor and Tiberius a kind of island potentate, inasmuch as the latter spent his time on the island of

Capreae. There was rivalry and jostling about the great man's doors, the people fearing not merely that they might not be seen by their patron, but also that they might be among the last to appear before him; for every word and every look, especially in the case of the most prominent men, was carefully observed.

Dio Cassius 58. 5. 1-2
tr. E. Cary (Loeb 1924)

K12 Tiberius leaves Rome

(a) 57   Now, after long consideration and frequent postponements, Tiberius at last left for Campania. His ostensible purpose was the dedication of temples to Jupiter and Augustus at Capua and Nola respectively. But he had decided to live away from Rome. Like most historians, I attribute his withdrawal to Sejanus' intrigues. Yet, since he maintained this seclusion for six years after Sejanus' execution, I often wonder whether it was not really caused by a desire to hide the cruelty and immorality which his actions made all too conspicuous. It was also said that in old age he became sensitive about his appearance. Tall and abnormally thin, bent and bald, he had a face covered with sores and often plaster. His retirement at Rhodes had accustomed him to unsociability and secretive pleasures.

According to another theory he was driven away by his mother's bullying: to share control with her seemed intolerable, to dislodge her impracticable—since that control had been given him by her. For Augustus had considered awarding the empire to his universally loved grand-nephew Germanicus. But his wife had induced him to adopt Tiberius instead (though Tiberius was made to adopt Germanicus). The Augusta harped accusingly on this obligation—and exacted repayment.

58   Tiberius left with only a few companions: one senator and ex-consul, Marcus Cocceius Nerva the jurist, one distinguished knight, Curtius Atticus—and Sejanus. The rest were literary men, mostly Greeks whose conversation diverted him. The astrologers asserted that the conjunction of heavenly bodies under which he had left Rome precluded his return. This proved fatal to many who deduced, and proclaimed, that his end was near. For they did not foresee the unbelievable fact that his voluntary self-exile would last eleven years. Time was to show how narrow is the dividing-line between authentic prediction and imposture: truth is surrounded by mystery. For the first assertion proved authentic—though he came to adjacent points of the countryside or coast, and often approached the city's very walls. But the prophets' foreknowledge was limited, for he lived to a great age.

59   A dangerous accident to Tiberius at this time stimulated idle gossip, and gave him reason for increased confidence in Sejanus' friendship and loyalty. While they were dining at a villa called The Cave, in a natural cavern between the sea at Amyclae and the hills of Fundi, there was a fall of rock at the cave-mouth. Several servants were crushed, and amid the general panic the diners fled. But Sejanus,

braced on hands and knees, face to face, warded the falling boulders off Tiberius. That is how the soldiers who rescued them found him. The incident increased Sejanus' power. Tiberius believed him disinterested and listened trustingly to his advice, however disastrous.

(b) *Whatever the reasons were for Tiberius' withdrawal to Capri, his absence left Sejanus a free hand at Rome.*

67   Tiberius was dedicating the temples in Campania. He issued an edict forbidding the disturbance of his privacy, and troops were posted in the towns to prevent crowds. He detested these towns, and indeed the whole mainland. So he took refuge on the island of Capreae, separated from the tip of the Surrentum promontory by three miles of sea. Presumably what attracted him was the isolation of Capreae. Harbourless, it has few roadsteads even for small vessels; sentries can control all landings. In winter the climate is mild, since hills on the mainland keep off gales. In summer the island is delightful, since it faces west and has open sea all round. The bay it overlooks was exceptionally lovely, until Vesuvius' eruption transformed the landscape. This was an area of Greek colonization, and tradition records that Capreae had been occupied by the Teleboi.

On this island then, in twelve spacious, separately named villas, Tiberius took up residence. His former absorption in State affairs ended. Instead he spent the time in secret orgies, or idle malevolent thoughts. But his abnormally credulous suspicions were unabated. Sejanus, who had encouraged them even at Rome, whipped them up, and now openly disclosed his designs against Agrippina and Nero Caesar. Soldiers attached to them reported with a historian's precision their correspondence, visitors, and doings private and public. Agents incited them to flee to the German armies, or—in the Forum at its peak hour—to grasp the divine Augustus' statue, and appeal to senate and public. They dismissed such projects: but were accused of them.

Tacitus *Annals* 4. 57–9; 67
tr. Michael Grant (Penguin 1977)

K13   The fall of Sejanus

(a)

Livia died in AD 29 and the next year saw Sejanus at the height of his power. Agrippina and Nero were exiled in AD 29 and Drusus was imprisoned at Rome in AD 30 (Dio Cassius 58. 3. 8; cf. Tacitus Annals *6. 23). The consulship of 31 with Tiberius as his partner was the culmination of Sejanus' career. It is not certain when Tiberius' suspicions were first aroused. It was perhaps a letter from Germanicus' mother Antonia that turned Tiberius against him (Josephus AJ 18. 181 ff.). The official reason given for Sejanus' fall was a plot against Tiberius and Gaius (cf. ILS 157, 158, 159; but see also Dio Cassius 58. 4. 1 ff). On a possible conspiracy against Tiberius see further F. B. Marsh* The Reign of Tiberius *pp. 504 ff.; Syme* Tacitus *pp. 405 f., 752 f.; Koestermann* Hermes *83 (1955) 350 ff.; cf. also the discussions in R. Seager* Tiberius *pp. 214 ff., and B. Levick* Tiberius the Politician *p. 173 and n. 130 on pp. 278-9.*

Tiberius, however, who was no longer ignorant of anything that concerned his minister, was planning how he might put him to death; but, not finding any way of doing this openly and safely, he handled both Sejanus himself and the Romans in general in a remarkable fashion, so as to learn exactly what was in their minds. He kept sending despatches of all kinds regarding himself both to Sejanus and to the senate, now saying that he was in a bad state of health and almost at the point of death, and now that he was exceedingly well and would arrive in Rome directly. At one moment he would heartily praise Sejanus, and again would as heartily denounce him; and, while honouring some of Sejanus' friends out of regard for him, he would be disgracing others. Thus Sejanus, filled in turn with extreme elation and extreme fear, was in constant suspense; for it never occurred to him, on the one hand, to be afraid and so attempt a revolution, inasmuch as he was still held in honour, nor, on the other hand, to be bold and attempt some desperate venture, inasmuch as he was frequently abased. So also with the people at large: they kept hearing alternately the most contradictory reports which came at brief intervals, and so were unable either to regard Sejanus any longer with admiration or, on the other hand, to hold him in contempt, while as for Tiberius, they were kept guessing whether he was going to die or return to Rome; consequently they were in a continual state of doubt. . . . Privately they kept a sharp eye to their own safety, but publicly they paid court to him, the more so as Tiberius had made both Sejanus and his son priests along with Gaius. So they gave him the proconsular power, and also voted that the consuls of each year should be instructed to emulate him in their conduct of the office. As for Tiberius, though he honoured him with the priesthoods, yet he did not send for him; instead, when Sejanus requested permission to go to Campania, pleading as an excuse that his betrothed was ill, the emperor directed him to remain where he was, because he himself was going to arrive in Rome almost immediately.

This was one reason, then, why Sejanus was again becoming alienated; there was also the fact that Tiberius, after appointing Gaius priest, praised him and gave some indications that he intended to make him his successor to the throne. Sejanus would therefore have set on foot a rebellion, especially as the soldiers were ready to obey him in everything, had he not perceived that the populace was immensely pleased at the compliments paid to Gaius, out of reverence for the memory of Germanicus, his father. For he had previously supposed that they, too, were on his side, and now, finding them earnest supporters of Gaius, he became dejected, and regretted that he had not begun a rebellion during his consulship. The rest [were becoming alienated from him], not only for these reasons, but also because Tiberius quashed an indictment against an enemy of Sejanus, a man who had been chosen ten years before to govern Spain, and was now, thanks to the influence of Sejanus, being brought to trial on certain charges; whereupon, because of this case, he granted a general immunity from such suits, during the interval before taking office, to all who were designated to govern provinces or to perform any other public business. And in a letter to the senate about the death of Nero he referred to Sejanus by that name simply, without the addition of the customary titles. Moreover, because sacrifices were being offered to Sejanus, he forbade such offerings to be made to any human being; and because many honours were being voted to Sejanus, he forbade the consideration of any measure which proposed honours for himself. He had, to be sure, forbidden this practice still earlier, but now, because of Sejanus, he renewed his injunction; for one who allowed nothing of the sort to be done in his own case would naturally not permit it in the case of another.

In view of all this, people began to hold Sejanus more and more in contempt; in fact they even avoided meeting him or being left alone with him, and that in a manner too marked not to be noticed. When, therefore, Tiberius learned of this, he took courage, believing that he should have the populace and the senate on his side, and attacked him. And first, in order to take him off his guard as completely as possible, he spread the report that he was going to give him the tribunician power. Then he sent a communication against him to the senate by the hands of Naevius Sertorius Macro, whom he had already secretly appointed to command the bodyguards and had instructed in regard to all that required to be done. Macro entered Rome by night, as if on some different errand, and communicated his instructions to Memmius Regulus, then consul (his colleague sided with Sejanus), and to Graecinius Laco, commander of the night-watch. At dawn Macro ascended the Palatine (for the senate was to sit in the temple of Apollo), and encountering Sejanus, who had not yet gone in, and perceiving that he was troubled because Tiberius had sent him no message, he encouraged him, telling him aside and in confidence that he was bringing him the tribunician power. Overjoyed at this announcement, Sejanus rushed into the senate-chamber. Macro now sent back to their camp the Pretorians that were guarding Sejanus and the senate, after revealing to them his authority and declaring that he bore a letter from Tiberius which bestowed rewards upon them. Then, after stationing the night-watch about the temple in their place, he went in, delivered the letter to the consuls, and came out again before a word was read. He then instructed Laco to keep guard there and himself hurried away to the camp to prevent any uprising.

In the meantime the letter was read. It was a long one, and contained no wholesale denunciation of Sejanus, but first some other matter, then a slight censure of his conduct, then something else, and after that some further objection to him; and at the close it said that two senators who were among his intimate associates must be punished and that he himself must be kept under guard. For Tiberius refrained from giving orders outright to put him to death, not because he did not wish to give such orders, but because he feared that some disturbance might result from such a course. At any rate, he pretended that he could not with safety even make the journey to Rome, and therefore summoned one of the consuls to him. Now the letter disclosed no more than this; but one could observe both by sight and hearing many and various effects produced by it. At first, before it was read, they had been lauding Sejanus, thinking that he was about to receive the tribunician power, and had kept cheering him, anticipating the honours for which they hoped and making it clear to him that they would concur in bestowing them. When, however, nothing of the sort appeared, but they heard again and again just the reverse of what they had expected, they were at first perplexed, and then thrown into deep dejection. Some of those seated near him actually rose up and left him; for they now no longer cared to share the same seat with the man whom previously they had prized having as their friend. Then praetors and tribunes surrounded him, to prevent his causing any disturbance by rushing out, as he certainly would have done, if he had been startled at the outset by hearing any general denunciation. As it was, he paid no great heed to the successive charges as they were read, thinking each one a slight matter which stood alone, and hoping that, at best, no further charge, or, in any event, none that could not be disposed of, was contained in the letter; so he let the time slip by and remained in his seat.

Meanwhile Regulus summoned him to go forward, but he paid no heed, not out of contempt—for he had already been humbled—but because he was unaccustomed to having orders addressed to him. But when the consul, raising his voice and also pointing at him, called the second and the third time, 'Sejanus, come here,' he merely asked him, 'Me? you are calling me?' At last, however, he stood up, and Laco, who had now returned, took his stand beside him. When finally the reading of the letter was finished, all with one voice denounced and threatened him, some because they had been wronged, others through fear, some to conceal their friendship for him, and still others out of joy at his downfall. Regulus did not put the vote to all the senators nor propose to any the death penalty, fearing opposition from some quarter and a disturbance in consequence; for Sejanus had numerous relatives and friends. He merely asked a single senator if he should not be imprisoned, and when he got an affirmative answer, he led Sejanus out of the senate, and together with the other magistrates and Laco took him down to the prison.

Thereupon one might have witnessed such a surpassing proof of human frailty as to prevent one's ever again being puffed up with conceit. For the man whom at dawn they had escorted to the senate-hall as a superior being, they were now dragging to prison as if no better than the worst; on him whom they had previously thought worthy of many crowns, they now laid bonds; him whom they were wont to protect as a master, they now guarded like a runaway slave, uncovering his head when he would fain cover it; him whom they had adorned with the purple-bordered toga, they struck in the face; and him whom they were wont to adore and worship with sacrifices as a god, they were now leading to execution. The populace also assailed him, shouting many reproaches at him for the lives he had taken and many jeers for the hopes he had cherished. They hurled down, beat down, and dragged down all his images, as though they were thereby treating the man himself with contumely, and he thus became a spectator of what he was destined to suffer. For the moment, it is true, he was merely cast into prison; but a little later, in fact that very day, the senate assembled in the temple of Concord not far from the jail, when they saw the attitude of the populace and that none of the Pretorians was about, and condemned him to death. By their order he was executed and his body cast down the Stairway, where the rabble abused it for three whole days and afterwards threw it into the river. His children also were put to death by decree, the girl (whom he had betrothed to the son of Claudius) having been first outraged by the public executioner on the principle that it was unlawful for a virgin to be put to death in the prison. His wife Apicata was not condemned, to be sure, but on learning that her children were dead, and after seeing their bodies on the Stairway, she withdrew and composed a statement about the death of Drusus, directed against Livilla, his wife, who had been the cause of a quarrel between herself and her husband, resulting in their separation; then, after sending this document to Tiberius, she committed suicide. It was in this way that Tiberius came to read her statement; and when he had obtained proof of the information given, he put to death Livilla and all the others therein mentioned. I have, indeed, heard that he spared Livilla out of regard for her mother Antonia, and that Antonia herself of her own accord killed her daughter by starving her. These events, however, were later.

At the time of our narrative a great uproar took place in the city; for the populace slew anyone it saw of those who had possessed great influence with Sejanus and had committed acts of insolence to please him. The soldiers, too, angered because they had been suspected of friendliness for Sejanus and because the nightwatch had been preferred to them for loyalty to the emperor, proceeded to burn and plunder, despite the fact that all the officials were guarding the whole city in accordance with Tiberius' command. Moreover, not even the senate remained quiet; but those of its members who had paid court to Sejanus were greatly disturbed by their fear of vengeance; and those who had accused or borne witness against others were filled with terror, because of the prevailing suspicion that their victims had been destroyed in the interest of Sejanus rather than of Tiberius. Very small, indeed, was the courageous element that remained free from these terrors and expected that Tiberius would become milder. For, as usually happens, they laid the responsibility for their previous misfortunes upon the man who had perished, and charged the emperor with few or none of them; as for most of these things, they said he had either been ignorant of them or had been forced to do them against his will. Privately this was the attitude of the various groups; but publicly they voted, as if they had been freed from a tyranny, not to hold any mourning over the deceased and to have a statue of Liberty erected in the Forum.

Dio Cassius 58. 6. 2–5; 7. 4–12. 4
tr. E. Cary (Loeb 1924)

(b)
Juvenal writing c. 70 years later, makes Sejanus an example of destructive ambition.

> Some men are overthrown by the envy their great power
> Arouses; it's that long and illustrious list of honours
> That sinks them. The ropes are heaved, down come the statues,

Axes demolish their chariot-wheels, the unoffending
Legs of their horses are broken. And now the fire
Roars up in the furnace, now flames hiss under the bellows:
The head of the people's darling glows red-hot, great Sejanus
Crackles and melts. That face only yesterday ranked
Second in all the world. Now it's so much scrap-metal,
To be turned into jugs and basins, frying-pans, chamber-pots.
Hang wreaths on your doors, lead a big white sacrificial
Bull to the Capitol! They're dragging Sejanus along
By a hook, in public. Everyone cheers. 'Just look at that
Ugly stuck-up face,' they say. 'Believe me, I never
Cared for the fellow.' 'But what was his crime? Who brought
The charges, who gave evidence? How did they prove him guilty?'
'Nothing like that: a long and wordy letter arrived
From Capri.' 'Fair enough: you need say no more.'
                                                    And what
Of the commons? They follow fortune as always, and detest
The victims, the failures. If a little Etruscan luck
Had rubbed off on Sejanus, if the doddering Emperor
Had been struck down out of the blue, this identical rabble
Would now be proclaiming that carcase an equal successor
To Augustus. But nowadays, with no vote to sell, their motto
Is 'Couldn't care less'. Time was when their plebiscite elected
Generals, Heads of State, commanders of legions: but now
They've pulled in their horns, there's only two things that concern them:
Bread and the Games.

Juvenal *Satires* 10. 56–81
tr. P. Green (Penguin 1967)

K14 The end of Tiberius' rule

(a)
Tiberius died on 16 March AD 37, aged seventy-seven.

45   In the same year there was a serious fire at Rome. The Aventine and adjacent parts of the Circus Maximus were devastated. Tiberius acquired prestige from the calamity by defraying the value of the houses and apartment-blocks destroyed. This generosity cost him one hundred million sesterces. It was all the more popular be-cause his own building activities were slight. . . . The emperor was voted every compliment that senators' ingenuity could devise. But his reactions, favourable or negative, were never known. For his end was near. . . .

525

Macro had become excessively powerful. Never neglectful of Gaius' favour, now Macro cultivated him more strenuously every day. After the death of Junia Claudilla —whose wedding with Gaius I recorded elsewhere—Macro induced his own wife Ennia to pretend she loved the prince and entice him into a promise of marriage. Gaius had no objection if it helped him towards the throne. Temperamental though he was, intimacy with his grandfather had taught him dissimulation.

46   The emperor knew this—and hesitated about the succession. First, there were his grandsons. Drusus' son Tiberius Gemellus was nearer to him in blood, and dearer. But he was still a boy. Gaius was in the prime of early manhood. He was also popular, being Germanicus' son. So his grandfather hated him. Claudius too was considered. He was middle-aged and well-meaning, but his weakmindedness was an objection. Tiberius feared that to nominate a successor outside the imperial house might bring contempt and humiliation upon Augustus' memory and the name of the Caesars. He cared more for posthumous appreciation than for immediate popularity.

Soon, irresolute and physically exhausted, Tiberius left the decision to fate. It was beyond him. Yet, by certain comments, he showed understanding of the future. When he reproached Macro for abandoning the setting for the rising sun, his meaning was clear. And when Gaius, in casual discussion, slighted the memory of Sulla, Tiberius foretold that Gaius would have all Sulla's faults and none of his virtues. Then, weeping bitterly and clasping his grandson Tiberius Gemellus, he said to the frowning Gaius: 'You will kill him! And someone else will kill you!' However, despite failing health, Tiberius did not ration his sensualities. He was making a show of vigour to conceal his illness; and he kept up his habitual jokes against the medical profession, declaring that no man over thirty ought to need advice about what was good or bad for him. . . .

50   Tiberius' health and strength were now failing. But his stern will and vigorous speech and expression remained. So did his powers of dissimulation. To conceal his obvious decline, he assumed an affable manner. . . .

However, Charicles assured Macro that Tiberius was sinking and would not last more than two days. There were conferences, and dispatches to imperial governors and generals, hurriedly making all arrangements. On March 16th the emperor ceased to breathe, and was believed to be dead. Gaius, surrounded by a congratulatory crowd, issued forth to begin his reign. But then it was suddenly reported that Tiberius had recovered his speech and sight, and was asking for food to strengthen him after his fainting-fit. There was a general panic-stricken dispersal. Every face was composed to show grief—or unawareness. Only Gaius stood in stupefied silence, his soaring hopes dashed, expecting the worst. Macro, unperturbed, ordered the old man to be smothered with a heap of bed-clothes and left alone.

So Tiberius died, in his seventy-eighth year.   51   The son of Tiberius Claudius Nero, he was a Claudian on both sides (his mother was successively adopted into the Livian and the Julian families). From birth he experienced contrasts of fortune. After following his proscribed father into exile, he entered Augustus' family as his stepson—only to suffer from many competitors, while they lived: first Marcellus and Agrippa, then Gaius Caesar and Lucius Caesar. His own brother Nero Drusus was more of a popular favourite. But Tiberius' position became most delicate of all after his marriage to Augustus' daughter Julia. For he had to choose between enduring her unfaithfulness or escaping it. He went to Rhodes. When he returned, he was undisputed heir in the emperor's home for twelve years. Then he ruled the Roman world for nearly twenty-three.

His character, too, had its different stages. While he was a private citizen or holding commands under Augustus, his life was blameless; and so was his reputation. While Germanicus and Drusus still lived, he concealed his real self, cunningly affecting virtuous qualities. However, until his mother died there was good in Tiberius as well as evil. Again, as long as he favoured (or feared) Sejanus, the cruelty of Tiberius was detested, but his perversions unrevealed. Then fear vanished, and with it shame. Thereafter he expressed only his own personality—by unrestrained crime and infamy.

> Tacitus *Annals* 6. 45–51 (abridged)
> tr. Michael Grant (Penguin 1977)

(b)

73 Some believe that he had been given a slow, wasting poison by Gaius Caligula; others that, when convalescent after fever, he demanded food but was refused it. According to one account, he fainted and on regaining consciousness asked for the seal-ring which had meanwhile been removed from his left hand. Seneca writes that Tiberius, realizing how near his end was, removed the ring himself, as if as a present for someone; but then clung to it awhile before replacing it on his finger; that he afterwards lay quiet for some little time with the fist clenched, until summoning his servants; and that, when no one answered, he got out of bed, collapsed, and died.

75 The first news of his death caused such joy at Rome that people ran about yelling: 'To the Tiber with Tiberius!' and others offered prayers to Mother Earth and the Infernal Gods to give him no home below except among the damned.... However, the soldiers carried the corpse on to Rome, where it was cremated with due ceremony.

76 Two years before his death Tiberius had drawn a will in his own handwriting; an identical copy was also found in the handwriting of a freedman. Both these documents had been signed and sealed by witnesses of the very lowest class. In them, Gaius son of Germanicus and Tiberius son of Drusus were named as Tiberius's co-heirs; and if either should die, the survivor was to be the sole heir. Tiberius left legacies to several other persons, including the Vestals; with a bounty for every serving soldier in the army and every member of the Roman commons. Separate bequests to the City wardmasters were added.

> Suetonius *Tiberius* 73; 75–6 (abridged)
> tr. R. Graves (Penguin 1957)

K15 'The beginning of Gaius' principate

Tacitus' account of the reign of Gaius and the first six years of Claudius has been lost. This passage from Suetonius gives some idea of the relief and joy felt on Gaius' accession. For a detailed account of the principate see J. P. V. D. Balsdon The Emperor Gaius *(Oxford 1934).*

13   Gaius' accession seemed to the Roman people—one might almost say, to the whole world—like a dream come true. The memory of Germanicus and compassion for a family that had been practically wiped out by successive murders, made most provincials and soldiers, many of whom had known him as a child, and the entire population of Rome as well, show extravagant joy that he was now Emperor. . . .

14   On his arrival in the City the Senate (and a mob of commoners who had forced their way into the House) immediately and unanimously conferred absolute power upon him. They set aside Tiberius's will—which made his other grandson, then still a child, joint-heir with Gaius—and so splendid were the celebrations that 160,000 victims were publicly sacrificed during the next three months, or perhaps even a shorter period. . . .

15   Gaius strengthened his popularity by every possible means. He delivered a funeral speech in honour of Tiberius to a vast crowd, weeping profusely all the while; and gave him a magnificent burial. But as soon as this was over he sailed for Pandataria and the Pontian Islands to fetch back the remains of his mother and his brother Nero; and during rough weather, too, in proof of devotion. He approached the ashes with the utmost reverence and transferred them to the urns with his own hands. Equally dramatic was his gesture of raising a standard on the poop of the bireme which brought the urns to Ostia, and thence up the Tiber to Rome. He had arranged that the most distinguished knights available should carry them to the Mausoleum, about noon, when the streets were at their busiest; also appointing an annual day of remembrance, marked by Circus games, at which Agrippina's image would be paraded in a covered carriage. He honoured his father's memory by re-naming the month of September 'Germanicus'; and sponsored a senatorial decree which awarded his grandmother Antonia, at a blow, all the honours won by Livia Augusta in her entire lifetime. As fellow-Consul he chose his uncle Claudius, who had hitherto been a mere knight; and adopted young Tiberius when he came of age, giving him the official title of 'Youth Leader'. . . .

A similar bid for popularity was to recall all exiles, and dismiss all criminal charges whatsoever that had been pending since the time of Tiberius. The batches of written evidence in his mother's and brothers' cases were brought to the Forum at his orders, and burned, to set at rest the minds of such witnesses and informers as had testified against them; but first he swore before Heaven that he had neither read nor abstracted a single document. He also refused to examine a report supposedly concerning his own safety, on the ground that nobody could have any reason to hate him, and that he therefore had no time to peruse idle memoranda of this sort.

16   Gaius drove the spintrian perverts from the City, and could with difficulty be restrained from drowning the lot. He gave permission for the works of Titus Labienus, Cremutius Cordus, and Cassius Severus, which had been banned by order of the Senate, to be routed out and republished—making his desire known that posterity should be in full possession of all historical facts; also, he revived Augustus's practice, discontinued by Tiberius, of publishing an Imperial budget; invested the magistrates with full authority, not requiring them to apply for his confirmation of sentences; and scrupulously scanned the list of knights but, though publicy dismounting any who had behaved in a wicked or scandalous manner, was not unduly severe with those guilty of lesser misbehaviour—he merely omitted their names from the list which he read out. Gaius' creation of a fifth judicial division aided jurors to keep abreast of their work; his reviving of the electoral system was designed to restore popular control over the magistracy. He honoured every one of the bequests in Tiberius's will, though this had been set aside by the Senate, and in that of his maternal grandmother Julia, which Tiberius had suppressed; abolished the Italian half-per-cent auction tax; and paid compensation to a great many people whose houses had been damaged by fire. Any king whom he restored to the throne was awarded the taxes that had accumulated since his deposition—Antiochus of Commagene, for example, got a refund of a million gold pieces from the Public Treasury. . . .

17   Gaius held four consulships: the earliest for two months, from 1 July; the next for the whole month of January; the third for the first thirteen days of January; and the fourth for the first seven. Only the last two were in sequence. He assumed his third consulship without a colleague. Some historians describe this as a high-handed breach of precedent; but unfairly, because he was then quartered at Lyons, where the news that his fellow Consul-elect had died in Rome, just before the New Year, had not reached him in time. He twice presented every member of the commons with three gold pieces; and twice invited all the senators and knights, with their wives and children, to an extravagant banquet. At the first of these banquets he gave every man a gown and every woman a red or purple scarf. He also added to the gaiety of Rome by extending the customary four days of the Saturnalia, which begin on 17 December, with a fifth, known as 'Youth Day'.

19   One of his spectacles was on such a fantastic scale that nothing like it had ever been seen before. He collected all available merchant ships and anchored them in two lines, close together, the whole way from Baiae to the mole at Puteoli, a distance of little more than three Roman miles. Then he had the ships boarded over, with earth heaped on the planks, and made a kind of Appian Way along which he trotted back and forth for two consecutive days.

22   So much for Gaius the Emperor; the rest of this history must needs deal with Gaius the Monster.

Suetonius <i>Gaius</i> 13–17; 19; 22 (abridged)
tr. R. Graves (Penguin 1957)

K16 An oath of allegiance

In all provinces and armies an oath of allegiance was taken personally to Gaius. This oath, from Assus in the province of Asia, did not have an individual proposer, and refers to Gaius as a god.

In the consulship of Gnaeus Acerronius Proculus and Gaius Pontius Petronius Nigrinus.

Decree of the Assians on motion of the people

Whereas the rule of Gaius Caesar Germanicus Augustus, hoped and prayed for by all men, has been proclaimed and the world has found unbounded joy and every city and every people has been eager for the sight of the god since the happiest age for mankind has now begun, it was decreed by the council and the Roman business-men among us and the people of Assus to appoint an embassy chosen from the foremost and most distinguished Romans and Greeks to seek an audience and congratulate him, and beg him to remember the city with solicitude, as he personally promised when together with his father Germanicus he first set foot in our city's province.

Oath of the Assians

We swear by Zeus the Savior and by the deified Caesar Augustus and by the ancestral Holy Maiden to be loyal to Gaius Caesar Augustus and all his house and to regard as friends whomever he chooses and as enemies whomever he censures. If we remain faithful to our oath may it go well with us; if we swear falsely, the opposite.

SIG no. 797
tr. Lewis and Reinhold vol. 2

K17 Gaius receives the embassy of Alexandrian Jews

Philo was head of the embassy to Gaius in AD 40 (see O28 ff.).

It is right that I should record also both what we saw and what we heard when we were summoned to take a part in the contention of our citizenship. The moment we entered we knew from his look and movements that we had come into the presence not of a judge but of an accuser more hostile than those arrayed against us. . . . The actual proceedings showed a ruthless tyrant with a menacing frown on his despotic brow. Instead of doing anything that I have just mentioned he sent for the stewards of the two gardens belonging to Maecenas and Lamia near to each other and the city, in which gardens he had been spending three or four days. For this was the stage where the tragedy which was aimed against our whole nation was to be performed with us who were present as the immediate victims. He ordered them to leave all the villas completely open as he wished to make a careful survey of each of them. When we were brought into his presence the moment we saw him we bowed our heads to the ground with all respect and timidity and saluted him addressing him as Emperor Augustus. The mildness and kindness with which he replied to our greeting was such that we gave up not only our case but our lives for lost! In a sneering, snarling way he said, 'Are you the god-haters who do not believe me to be a god, a god acknowledged among all the other nations but not to be named by you?' And stretching out his hands towards heaven he gave utterance to an invocatory address which it was a sin even to listen to, much more to reproduce in the actual words. How vast was the delight which at once filled the envoys on the other side! They thought that Gaius's first utterance had secured the success of their mission. They gesticulated, they danced about and invoked blessings on him under the names of all the gods. . . . While he was saying this he was going on with his survey of the houses, the different chambers, men's or women's, the ground floors, the upper floors, all of them, and some he censured as defective in structure, and for others he made his own plans and gave orders that they should be more magnificent. Then driven along we followed him up and down mocked and reviled by our adversaries, as they do in the mimes at the theatres. . . .

Under such befooling and reviling we were helpless. Then tardily going on a different tack he said, 'We want to hear what claims you make about your citizenship.' We started to speak and give him the information, but when he had had a taste of our pleading and recognized that it was by no means contemptible, he cut short our earlier points before we could bring in the stronger ones, and dashed at high speed into the large room of the house, and walked round it and ordered the windows all round to be restored with transparent stones, [which in the same way as white glass do not obstruct the light but keep off the wind and the scorching sun.] Then he advanced in a leisurely way and said in a more moderate tone, 'What is it that you say?' and when we began on the points which came next in the thread of our argument he ran again into another room and ordered original pictures to be put up there. So with the statement of our case thus mangled and disjointed, one may almost say cut short and crushed to pieces, we gave up. . . And God taking compassion on us turned his spirit to mercy; he relaxed into a softer mood and said just this, 'They seem to me to be people unfortunate rather than wicked and to be foolish in refusing to believe that I have got the nature of a god,' and saying this he went off bidding us be gone also.

Philo *Legatio* 349–67 (abridged)
tr. F. H. Colson (Loeb 1962)

K18 The death of Gaius

Gaius was killed on the last day of the Palatine Games, 24 January AD 41. Cassius Chaerea, a tribune who had shown great bravery in the Rhine mutiny of AD 14, was one of the leading conspirators; Cornelius Sabinus, also a tribune in the praetorian guard, was another (cf. Dio Cassius 59. 29. 1). According to Dio (loc. cit.) there were many conspirators including the prefect of the praetorians and the freedman Callistus.

56 Such frantic and reckless behaviour roused murderous thoughts in certain minds. One or two plots for his assassination were discovered; others were still maturing, when two Guards colonels put their heads together and succeeded in killing him, thanks to the co-operation of his most powerful freedmen and some other Guards officers . . . the principal part in this drama of blood being claimed by Cassius Chaerea. Gaius had persistently teased Cassius, who was no longer young, for his supposed effeminacy.

58 On 24 January then, just past midday, Gaius, seated in the Theatre, could not make up his mind whether to rise for luncheon; he still felt a little queasy after too heavy a banquet on the previous night. However, his friends persuaded him to come out with them, along a covered walk; and there he found some boys of noble family whom he had summoned from Asia, rehearsing the Trojan war-dance. He stopped to watch and encourage them, and would have taken them back to the Theatre and held the performance at once, had their principal not complained of a cold. Two different versions of what followed are current. Some say that Chaerea came up behind Gaius as he stood talking to the boys and, with a cry of 'Take this!' gave him a deep sword-wound in the neck, whereupon Gaius Sabinus, the other colonel, stabbed him in the breast. The other version makes Sabinus tell certain centurions implicated in the plot to clear away the crowd and then asked Gaius for the day's watch-word. He is said to have replied: 'Juppiter', whereupon Chaerea, from his rear, yelled: 'So be it!'—for Juppiter deals sudden death—and split his jaw-bone as he turned his head. Gaius lay twitching on the ground. 'I am still alive!' he shouted; but word went round: 'Strike again!' and he succumbed to further wounds, including sword-thrusts through the genitals. Caesonia was murdered by a centurion at the same time, and little Julia Drusilla's brains were dashed out against a wall. Gaius' bearers rushed to help him, using their litter-poles as spears; and soon his German bodyguard appeared, too late to be of any service, though they killed several of the assassins and a few innocent senators into the bargain.

59 He died at the age of twenty-nine after ruling for three years, ten months and eight days. His body was moved secretly to the Lamian Gardens, half-cremated on a hastily-built pyre, and then buried beneath a shallow covering of sods. Later, when his sisters returned from exile they exhumed, cremated, and entombed it. But all the City knew that the Gardens had been haunted until then by his ghost, and that something horrible appeared every night at the scene of the murder until at last the building burned down.

60   The terror inspired by Gaius' reign could be judged by the sequel: everyone was extremely reluctant to believe that he had really been assassinated, and suspected that the story was invented by himself to discover what people thought of him. The conspirators had no particular candidate for Emperor in mind, and most senators were so bent on restoring the Republic that the Consuls summoned the first assembly not to the House, because it was named the Julian Building, but to the Capitol. Some wanted all memory of the Caesars obliterated, and their temples destroyed. People commented on the fact that every Caesar named 'Gaius' had died by the sword, beginning with Gaius Julius Caesar Strabo, murdered in Cinna's day.

> Suetonius *Gaius* 56; 58–60
> tr. R. Graves (Penguin 1957)

K19 Claudius

The exact nature of Claudius' physical and mental disabilities is a subject of great controversy; T. de C. Ruth in The Problem of Claudius *(Baltimore 1924) provides a useful survey of the various theories. It is certain that his disabilities, greatly exaggerated by tradition, were a real handicap to his political career. The evidence for his scholarship and learning collected by A. Momigliano in* Claudius *(Oxford 1934, new edn. Heffer 1961) suggests that Claudius was physically rather than mentally disabled. Suetonius' rather confused picture of Claudius reflects perhaps a conflict in his sources.*

2   Claudius—Tiberius Claudius Drusus—was born at Lyons, in the consulship of Iullus Antonius and Fabius Africanus, on 1 August, 10 BC, the very day when the first altar was dedicated there to Augustus the God; Drusus died in the following year. Claudius took the surname Germanicus after his brother had been engrafted in the Julian House as Tiberius's adopted son. Nearly the whole of his childhood and youth was so troubled by various diseases that he grew dull-witted and had little physical strength; and on reaching the age at which he should have won a magistracy or chosen a private career, was considered by his family incapable of doing either.

Even the wearing of a man's gown did not free him from the supervision of a tutor, about whom he later wrote: 'The man was a barbarian, an ex-transport officer who had been assigned the task of punishing me savagely whatever I might do.' Claudius's weak health also accounted for his being muffled in a cloak—an unprecedented sight—while presiding at the gladiatorial games given by Germanicus and himself to honour their father's memory; and, at his coming of age, he was taken up to the Capitol in a litter, about midnight, without the customary solemn procession.

3   Though he applied himself seriously to literature while still a child, and

published several samples of his proficiency in its various departments, this did not
advance him to public office or inspire the family with brighter hopes for his future.

Claudius's mother often called him 'a monster: a man whom Mother Nature had
begun to work upon but then flung aside'; and if she ever accused anyone of
stupidity, would exclaim: 'He is a bigger fool even than my son Claudius!' Livia
Augusta, his grandmother, never failed to treat him with the deepest scorn, and
seldom addressed him personally; her reproofs came in the form of brief, bitter
letters or oral messages. When his sister Livilla heard someone predict that he would
one day succeed to the throne, she prayed aloud that the Roman people might be
spared so cruel and undeserved a misfortune. Finally, to show what his great-uncle
Augustus, thought of him, I quote the following extracts from the Imperial
correspondence:

4   My dear Livia,
As you suggested, I have now discussed with Tiberius what we should do about
your grandson Claudius at the coming Festival of Mars the Avenger. We both agreed
that an immediate decision ought to be taken. The question is whether he has—shall
I say?—full command of his five senses. If so, I can see nothing against sending him
through the same degrees of office as his brother; but should he prove physically
and mentally deficient, the public (which is always amused by trifles) must not be
given a chance of laughing at him and us. I fear that we shall find ourselves in constant trouble if the question of his fitness to officiate in this or that capacity keeps
cropping up. We should therefore decide in advance whether he can or cannot be
trusted with offices of state generally.

As regards the immediate question in your last letter, I have no objection to his
taking charge of the priests' banquet at the Festival, if he lets his cousin, young
Silvanus, stand by to see that he does not make a fool of himself. But I am against
his watching the Games in the Circus from the Imperial box, where the eyes of the
whole audience would be on him. I am also against his being made Germanicus's
assistant during the Latin Festival on the Alban Mount, merely to avoid the embarrassment of appointing him City Prefect at Rome while the Senate is absent;
because if capable of the former appointment, he is also capable of the latter.

In short, my dear Livia, I am anxious that a decision should be reached on this
matter once and for all, to save us from further alternations of hope and despair.
You are at liberty to show this to Antonia. . .

Augustus wrote to Livia on another occasion:

. . . While you are away, I shall certainly invite young Tiberius Claudius to dine
every afternoon; rather than leave him to the exclusive company of his tutors
Athenodorus and Sulpicius. If only he would show greater concentration and behave with less capriciousness!—What he needs is someone to imitate: someone who
holds himself up properly, walks well, and has graceful gestures. I am sorry for the
poor fellow, because in serious matters, when not wool-gathering, he shows considerable nobility of principle.

And again:

My dear Livia,
I'll be damned if your grandson Tiberius Claudius hasn't given me a very pleasant
surprise! How on earth anyone who talks so confusedly can nevertheless speak so

well in public—with such clearness, saying all that needs to be said—I simply do not understand.

However, it is clear what decision Augustus eventually took; because he gave Claudius no honours except a seat in the College of Augurs...

Suetonius *Claudius* 2-4
tr. R. Graves (Penguin 1957)

K20 Early Career

Claudius did not follow the Senatorial cursus *but seems to have been liked and respected by the Equestrian order, to which he belonged (cf. Dio Cassius 59. 6. 6) until his consulship in AD 37 with Gaius.*

6   The Knights twice chose Claudius as head of a deputation to the Consuls: the first time was when they requested the privilege of carrying Augustus's body back to Rome on their shoulders; the second, when Sejanus's conspiracy had been suppressed and they were offering felicitations. . . .

7   As soon as Claudius's nephew Gaius became Emperor and tried every means of gaining popularity, Claudius entered on his belated public career as Gaius' colleague in a two-months' consulship; and when he first entered the Forum with the consular rods, an eagle swooped down and perched on his shoulder. He also drew lots for a second consulship, and won one that would fall due four years later. Claudius often presided as Gaius' substitute at the Games, where the audience greeted him with: 'Long live the Emperor's Uncle!' and 'Long live Germanicus's Brother!'

Suetonius *Claudius* 6-7 (abridged)
tr. R. Graves (Penguin 1957)

K21 The Accession of Claudius

On the death of Gaius, Claudius was made Emperor by the Praetorian Guard. He held no magistracies or powers; his only qualification seems to have been his relationship to Germanicus.

(a)
Having spent the better part of his life in circumstances like these, Claudius became Emperor, at the age of fifty, by an extraordinary accident. When the assassins ordered Gaius' courtiers to disperse, pretending that he wished to be alone, Claudius went off with the rest and retired to a room called the Hermaeum; but pre-

535

sently heard about the murder and slipped away in alarm to a near-by balcony, where he hid trembling behind the door curtains. A Guardsman, wandering vaguely through the Palace, noticed a pair of feet beneath the curtain, pulled their owner out for identification and recognized him. Claudius dropped on the floor and clasped the soldier's knees, but found himself acclaimed Emperor. He was then taken to the Palace guard-house where the men were angry, confused, and at a loss what to do; however, they placed him in a litter and, because his own bearers had decamped, took turns at carrying him to General Headquarters. Claudius looked the picture of terror and despair; in his passage through the streets everyone cast him pitying glances as if he were an innocent man being hurried to execution. Once safely in the Guards' Camp, Claudius spent the night among the sentries, confident now that no immediate danger threatened, but feeling little hope for the future since the Consuls, with the approval of the Senate and the aid of City militiamen, had seized the Forum and Capitol, and were determined on restoring the Republic.

When the tribunes of the people summoned him to visit the House and there clarify the situation, Claudius replied that he was being forcibly detained and could not come. The Senate, however, were far from unanimous on questions of practical policy; tiresome recriminations prolonged the debate and prevented the passing of any decree. Meanwhile, crowds surrounded the building and demanded a monarchy, expressly calling for Claudius; so he allowed the Guards to acclaim him Emperor and to swear allegiance. He also promised every man 150 gold pieces, which made him the first of the Caesars to purchase the loyalty of his troops.

Suetonius *Claudius* 10
tr. R. Graves (Penguin 1957)

(b)

This account of Claudius' accession in Josephus' AJ *is much fuller than that of his* BJ *(2. 204–33) and presents a very different picture of Claudius. For a discussion of possible reasons for the discrepancies between the two accounts see V. M. Scramuzza* The Emperor Claudius *(Harvard 1940) p. 12.*

Now Claudius, as I said above, had broken away from the route taken by Gaius, and since the palace was thrown into an uproar by the death of Caesar, he had no means to secure his own safety. He was in a narrow passage when cut off and concealed himself there, though he could see no cause, other than his noble rank, for alarm. For in private life he bore himself modestly and was satisfied with what he had. He pursued his studies, especially in Greek, and abstained completely from the kind of action that could lead to any disturbance. But now the crowd was panic-stricken, and the soldiers raged throughout the palace in their fury, while the emperor's body-guards reverted to a timidity and lack of discipline worthy of civilians. These troops, called the praetorian guard, being the cream of the army, were in session debating their next move. Such as were present were little concerned to avenge Gaius, reasoning that he had justly met his fate. They were rather investigating what course would redound to their advantage. Even the German troops were engaged in vengeance on the assassins more to gratify their own ferocity than to promote the general good of all. Claudius was disturbed by all this and alarmed for his own safety, especially as he had seen the spectacle when the heads of Asprenas and the others were carried past. There he stood in an alcove to which a few steps led, making himself as small as he could in the gloom. Gratus, one of the palace guard, caught sight of him, but was unable to make out his features well enough to recognize him in the dim light. Still he was not so far afield as not to determine that the lurking creature was human. He approached nearer, and when Claudius asked him to withdraw, he pounced upon him and caught him. On recognizing him, he cried to his followers: 'Here is a Germanicus: let us set him up as emperor and move fast.' Claudius saw that they were prepared to carry him off; and fearing that he might be put to death for the slaying of Gaius, he asked them to spare him, reminding them that he had never given them offence, and that he had had no part in planning the course of events. Gratus broke into a smile, tugged at his right arm, and said: 'Stop this niggling about saving your life, when you should be making big plans to gain the empire. The gods have taken it from Gaius and granted it to you for your virtue because they wished to promote the welfare of mankind. Do come and accept the throne of your ancestors that is your due.' So off he carried him, for Claudius was utterly unable to walk, from both fear and joy at what Gratus had said. . . . But when they had come to the open area of the Palatine—legend has it that this was the first site of the city of Rome to receive a settlement—and were just reaching the Treasury, there was a far larger concourse of soldiers, who were overjoyed at the sight of Claudius and who were determined to proclaim him emperor because of the popularity of his brother Germanicus, who had left behind him an immense reputation among all who had known him. They reflected on the rapacity of the powerful members of the senate, and what errors the senate had committed when it was in power before. Moreover, they took into account the impracticability of having the senate handle affairs, and also considered that if the government again passed into the hands of a single ruler they would take a risk upon themselves since one individual would have gained the throne for himself, whereas it was possible for Claudius to receive it by their motion and support. And Claudius would then show his appreciation by an honorarium adequate to such a service.

They expounded their views to one another, pondered them in their own minds, and reported them to each group as it came in. They, on hearing the report, welcomed the summons to action. They closed their ranks about Claudius, wheeled around and proceeded towards the camp, taking his litter on their shoulders in order that there might be no drag on their speed. The will of the people and that of the senators were at variance. The latter were eager to regain their former prestige and earnestly aspired, since after long years they now had the chance, to escape a slavery brought upon them by the insolence of the tyrants. The people, on the other hand, were jealous of the senate, recognizing in the emperors a curb upon the senate's encroachments and a refuge for themselves. They rejoiced in the seizure of

Claudius, and supposed that his securing the throne would avert from them any civil strife such as had occurred in Pompey's day. The senate, having learned that Claudius had been brought into the camp by the soldiers, sent some of their men of superior character to impress on him that he must not take forcible action to put himself on the throne. On the contrary, they said, he should yield to the senate, submitting, as a single individual, to so large a number of men, and allowing the law to provide for the organization of the commonwealth. . . .

This message was delivered by the envoys Veranius and Brocchus, both tribunes of the people, who fell on their knees and besought him on no account to involve the city in wars and calamities; for they saw that Claudius was under protection of a large army and that the consuls were as nothing in comparison with him. They went on to say that if he sought the throne, he should receive it as a gift from the senate, for he would exercise it more auspiciously and more fortunately if he obtained it not by violence but by favour of the donors.

Claudius knew with what contumacy they had been sent, but was for the present moved by their views to greater moderation. Nevertheless, he had recovered from his fear of them both because of the bold action of the soldiers and because of the advice of King Agrippa not to let slip through his hands such an office which had come unsought. . . .

Claudius accordingly replied that he did not wonder that the senate was not pleased at the prospect of submitting to authority because they had been oppressed by the brutality of those who had previously held the imperial office. But he promised to behave with such propriety that they would taste for themselves the savour of an era of fair dealing; that only nominally would the government be his, that in reality it would be thrown open to all in common. Seeing that he had passed through many vicissitudes of fortune before their eyes, they would do well not to distrust him. The envoys, conciliated by the words that they heard, were ushered out. Claudius assembled and addressed the army, binding them by oath that they would remain loyal to him. He presented the praetorian guard with five thousand drachmas apiece and their officers with a proportionate sum and promised similar amounts to the armies wherever they were.

The consuls then called together the senate in the Temple of Jupiter Victor while it was still night. Some of the senators who were in hiding in the city hesitated when they heard the summons; others had departed to their private estates, foreseeing how it would all come out. These latter despaired of liberty and deemed it far better to live out their lives free from the perils of servitude and with leisure from toil than to maintain the dignity of their fathers and have no assurance of surviving. Nevertheless, one hundred—no more—assembled; and, as they were deliberating about the matter in hand, suddenly a shout arose from the soldiers who had stood by them, bidding the senate choose an emperor and not to ruin the empire by entrusting it to a multitude of rulers. The senate replied that they agreed that the government must be in the hands not of everyone but of a single man, but they must see to it that they put it in charge of someone who was worthy of such pre-eminence. Thus the position of the senators was much more distressing because they had not retained the liberty about which they were so eloquent and because they were afraid of Claudius. Nevertheless, there were some who aspired to the throne by reason both of their distinguished birth and of their marriage connexions. For instance, Marcus Vinicius had a good claim both because of his own noble birth and by his marriage to Gaius' sister Julia. He was eager to compete for the highest office but was restrained by the consuls, who brought up one pretext after another. Valerius Asiaticus was restrained by Vinicianus, who was one of Gaius' assassins, from similar designs. There would have been a massacre second to none had those who coveted the empire been allowed to range themselves against Claudius. Above all, there were gladiators—and their number was considerable—and the soldiers of the night watch in the city and all the rowers of the fleet who were streaming into the camp. And so, of those who were candidates for the office, some withdrew in order to spare the city, others out of fear for themselves. . . .

Such was the situation in the senate. Meanwhile, from all quarters men came hurrying towards the camp to pay their respects. One of the two consuls, Quintus Pomponius, was especially guilty in the eyes of the troops for summoning the senate in the cause of liberty. Drawing swords they rushed at him and would have murdered him had not Claudius intervened. Having rescued the consul from peril, Claudius took his seat beside him, but he did not receive the rest of the senators who accompanied Quintus with like honour. Some of them even received blows from the soldiers, who repulsed their attempts to get an audience with him. Aponius retired wounded, and they were all in danger. King Agrippa then approached Claudius, and besought him to take a kinder attitude to the senators; for if any harm came to the senate, he would have no other subjects over whom to rule. Claudius agreed and summoned the senate to the Palatine, whither he was borne through the city, escorted by the soldiers, who dealt very harshly with the crowd.

Josephus *AJ* 19. 212–67 (abridged)
tr. L. H. Feldman (Loeb 1965)

K22 The letter to the Alexandrians

The discovery of this letter in 1920/1 caused a reappraisal of Claudius' abilities as a statesman. The letter, published in November of AD *41, contains Claudius' answers to matters put before him earlier that year by three embassies from Alexandria, one Greek and two Jewish. Claudius deprecates the recent violence in that city and apportions the responsibility equally to both sides; he reaffirms the Jews' right to religious liberty, which he himself had provisionally restored, but does not allow them to improve their civic status.*

Lucius Aemilius Rectus [prefect of Egypt] declares: Since the whole of the city, owing to its numbers, was unable to be present at the reading of the most sacred and most beneficent letter to the city, I have deemed it necessary to display the letter publicly in order that reading it individually you may admire the majesty of our god Caesar and feel gratitude for his good will toward the city. Year 2 of the Emperor Tiberius Claudius Caesar Augustus Germanicus, 14th of New Augustus.

The Emperor Tiberius Claudius Caesar Augustus Germanicus, *pontifex maximus*, holder of the tribunician power, consul designate, to the city of Alexandria, greeting. Tiberius Claudius Barbillus, Apollonius son of Artemidorus, Chaeremo son of Leonidas, Marcus Julius Asclepiades, Gaius Julius Dionysius, Tiberius Claudius Phanias, Pasio son of Potamo, Dionysius son of Sabbio, Tiberius Claudius Archibius, Apollonius son of Aristo, Gaius Julius Apollonius, Hermaiscus son of Apollonius, your envoys, delivered your decree to me and discoursed at length concerning the city, directing my attention to your good will toward us, which from long ago, you may be sure, had been stored up to your advantage in my memory; for you are by nature reverent toward the emperors, as I have come to know well from many things, and in particular you have taken a warm interest— warmly reciprocated—in my house, of which fact (to mention the latest instance, passing over the others) the supreme witness is my brother Germanicus Caesar when he addressed you in franker tones [by word of mouth].

Wherefore I gladly accepted the honors given to me by you, though I am not partial to such things. And first I permit you to keep my birthday as an Augustan day in the manner you have yourselves proposed, and I agree to the erection by you in their several places of the statues of myself and my family; for I see that you were zealous to establish on every side memorials of your reverence for my house. Of the two golden statues, the one made to represent the Claudian Augustan Peace, as my most honored Barbillus suggested and persisted in when I wished to refuse for fear of being thought too offensive, shall be erected at Rome, and the other according to your request shall be carried in procession on my name days in your city; and it shall be accompanied in the procession by a throne, adorned with whatever trappings you wish. It would perhaps be foolish, while accepting such great honors, to refuse the institution of a Claudian tribe and the establishment of sacred groves after the manner of Egypt; wherefore I grant you these requests as well, and if you wish you may also erect the equestrian statues given by Vitrasius Pollio my procurator. As for the erection of the statues in four-horse chariots which you wish to set up to me at the entrances to the country, I consent to let one be placed at the town called Taposiris, in Libya, another at Pharus in Alexandria, and a third at Pelusium in Egypt. But I deprecate the appointment of a high priest for me and the building of temples, for I do not wish to be offensive to my contemporaries, and my opinion is that temples and the like have by all ages been granted as special honors to the gods alone.

Concerning the requests which you have been eager to obtain from me, I decide as follows. All those who have become ephebes up to the time of my principate I confirm and maintain in possession of the Alexandrian citizenship with all the privileges and indulgences enjoyed by the city, excepting those who by fraud have contrived to become ephebes though born of slaves. And it is equally my will that

540

all the other privileges shall be confirmed which were granted to you by the emperors before me, and by the kings and by the prefects, as the deified Augustus also confirmed them. It is my will that the overseers of the temples of the deified Augustus in Alexandria shall be chosen by lot in the same way as those of the same deified Augustus in Canopus are chosen by lot. With regard to the municipal magistracies being made triennial, your proposal seems to me to be very good; for through fear of being called to account for any misrule your magistrates will behave with greater circumspection during their term of office. Concerning the city council, what your custom may have been under the ancient kings I have no means of saying, but that you had no council under the former emperors you are well aware. As this is the first broaching of a novel project, whose utility to the city and to my interests is not evident, I have written to Aemilius Rectus to hold an inquiry and inform me whether in the first place it is right that the body should be constituted, and, if it should be right to create one, in what manner this is to be done.

As for which party was responsible for the riot and feud (or rather, if the truth must be told, the war) with the Jews, although your envoys, particularly Dionysius son of Theo, confronting [your opponents] put your case with great zeal, nevertheless I was unwilling to make a strict inquiry, though guarding within me a store of immutable indignation against any who renewed the conflict; and I tell you once for all that unless you put a stop to this ruinous and obstinate enmity against each other, I shall be driven to show what a benevolent emperor can be when turned to righteous indignation. Wherefore once again I conjure you that, on the one hand, the Alexandrians show themselves forbearing and kindly toward the Jews, who for many years have dwelt in the same city, and dishonor none of the rights observed by them in the worship of their god but allow them to observe their customs as in the time of the deified Augustus, which customs I also, after hearing both sides, have confirmed. And, on the other hand, I explicitly order the Jews not to agitate for more privileges than they formerly possessed, and in the future not to send out a separate embassy as if they lived in a separate city—a thing unprecedented—and not to force their way into gymnasiarchic or cosmetic games, while enjoying their own privileges and sharing a great abundance of advantages in a city not their own, and not to bring in or admit Jews from Syria or those who sail down from Egypt, a proceeding which will compel me to conceive serious suspicions; otherwise I will by all means proceed against them as fomentors of what is a general plague of the whole world. If, desisting from these courses, you both consent to live with mutual forbearance and kindliness, I on my side will exercise a solicitude of very long standing for the city, as one bound to us by ancestral friendship. I bear witness to my friend Barbillus of the solicitude which he has always shown for you in my presence and of the extreme zeal with which he has now advocated your cause, and likewise to my friend Tiberius Claudius Archibius. Farewell.

British Museum Papyrus no. 1912
tr. adapted from Hunt and Edgar (eds) *Select Papyri* (Loeb) Lewis and Reinhold vol. 2

K23 Senators from Gaul

Claudius, censor in AD 48, proposed to fill some of the vacancies in the Senate with prominent Gaulish citizens from Gallia Comata. Tacitus records the speech defending his proposal ((b) below) and we are fortunate in being able to compare Tacitus' account with a record of the same speech ((a) below) inscribed on a bronze tablet, found at Lyon in 1598. A detailed comparison is made by K. Wellesley 'Can you trust Tacitus?' Greece & Rome 1² 2nd ed. (1934) 13-33.

(a)

The speech begins with a typically Claudian historical approach to the issues (omitted here), in an attempt to establish precedents in Roman tradition for the inclusion of foreigners to the Senate. Introducing eminent provincials to the Senate was an important step in the development of a stable Roman Empire.

. . . Surely both my great-uncle, the deified Augustus, and my uncle, Tiberius Caesar, were following a new practice when they desired that all the flower of the colonies and the municipalities everywhere—that is, the better class and the wealthy men—should sit in this senate house. You ask me: Is not an Italian senator preferable to a provincial? I shall reveal to you in detail my views on this matter when I come to obtain approval for this part of my censorship. But I think that not even provincials ought to be excluded, provided that they can add distinction to this senate house.

Look at that most distinguished and most flourishing colony of Vienna [Vienne], how long a time already it is that it has furnished senators to this house! From that colony comes that ornament of the equestrian order—and there are few to equal him—Lucius Vestinus, whom I cherish most intimately and whom at this very time I employ in my affairs. And it is my desire that his children may enjoy the first step in the priesthoods, so as to advance afterwards, as they grow older, to further honors in their rank. . . . I can say the same of his brother, who because of this wretched and most shameful circumstance cannot be a useful senator for you.

The time has now come, Tiberius Caesar Germanicus, now that you have reached the farthest boundaries of Narbonese Gaul, for you to unveil to the members of the senate the import of your address. All these distinguished youths whom I gaze upon will no more give us cause for regret if they become senators than does my friend Persicus, a man of most noble ancestry, have cause for regret when he reads among the portraits of his ancestors the name Allobrogicus. But if you agree that these things are so, what more do you want, when I point out to you this single fact, that the territory beyond the boundaries of Narbonese Gaul already sends you senators, since we have men of our order from Lyons and have no cause for regret. It is indeed with hesitation, members of the senate, that I have gone outside the borders of the provinces with which you are accustomed and familiar, but I must now plead openly the cause of Gallia Comata. And if anyone, in this connection, has in mind that these people engaged the deified Julius in war for ten years, let him set against that the unshakable loyalty and obedience of a hundred years, tested to the full in many of our crises. When my father Drusus was subduing Germany, it was they who by their tranquillity afforded him a safe and securely peaceful rear, even at a time when he had been summoned away to the war from the task of organizing the census which was still new and unaccustomed to the Gauls. How difficult such an operation is for us at this precise moment we are learning all too well from experience, even though the survey is aimed at nothing more than an official record of our resources. [The rest is lost.]

CIL 13. 1668 col. 2
tr. Lewis and Reinhold vol. 2

(b)
23   In the following year the consuls were Aulus Vitellius and Lucius Vipstanus Poplicola. During debates that were now held about enlarging the senate, the chief men of 'long-haired' (northern and central) Gaul—belonging to the tribes with long-standing treaties with Rome, of which they themselves were citizens—claimed the right to hold office in the capital. The question aroused much discussion, and the opposing arguments were put to the emperor.

'Italy is not so decayed', said some, 'that she cannot provide her own capital with a senate. In former times even peoples akin to us were content with a Roman senate of native Romans only; and the government of those days is a glorious memory. To this day, people cite the ancient Roman character for the models of courage and renown.

'Is it not enough that Venetian and Insubrian Gauls have forced their way into the senate? Do we have to import foreigners in hordes, like gangs of prisoners, and leave no careers for our own surviving aristocracy, or for impoverished senators from Latium? Every post will be absorbed by the rich men whose grandfathers and great-grandfathers commanded hostile tribes, assailed our armies in battle, besieged the divine Julius Caesar at Alesia. Those are recent memories. But are we to forget our men who, beside Rome's Capitoline citadel, were killed by the ancestors of these very Gauls? Let them, by all means, have the title of Roman citizens. But the senate's insignia, the glory of office, they must not cheapen.'

24   These and similar arguments did not impress Claudius. He contradicted them on the spot, and then summoned the senate and made this speech:

'The experience of my own ancestors, notably of my family's Sabine founder Clausus who was simultaneously made a Roman citizen and a patrician, encourage me to adopt the same national policy, by bringing excellence to Rome from whatever source. For I do not forget that the Julii came from Alba Longa, the Coruncanii from Camerium, the Porcii from Tusculum; and, leaving antiquity aside, that men from Etruria, Lucania, and all Italy have been admitted into the senate; and that finally Italy herself has been extended to the Alps, uniting not merely individuals but whole territories and peoples under the name of Rome.

'Moreover, after the enfranchisement of Italy across the Po, our next step was to make citizens of the finest provincials too: we added them to our ex-soldiers in settlements throughout the world, and by their means reinvigorated the exhausted empire. This helped to stabilize peace within the frontiers and successful relations with foreign powers. Is it regretted that the Cornelii Balbi immigrated from Spain, and other equally distinguished men from southern Gaul? Their descendants are with us; and they love Rome as much as we do. What proved fatal to Sparta and Athens, for all their military strength, was their segregation of conquered subjects as aliens. Our founder Romulus, on the other hand, had the wisdom—more than once—to transform whole enemy peoples into Roman citizens within the course of a single day. Even some of our kings were foreign. Similarly, the admission to former office of the sons of slaves is not the novelty it is alleged to be. In early times it happened frequently.

‘ "The Senonian Gauls fought against us," it is objected. But did not Italians, Vulsci and Aequi, as well? "The Gauls captured Rome" you say. But we also lost battles to our neighbours—we gave hostages to the Etruscans, we went beneath the Samnites' yoke. Actually, a review of all these wars shows that the Gallic war took the shortest time of all—since then, peace and loyalty have reigned unbroken. Now that they have assimilated our customs and culture and married into our families, let them bring in their gold and wealth rather than keep it to themselves. Senators, however ancient any institution seems, once upon a time it was new! First, plebeians joined patricians in office. Next, the Latins were added. Then came men from other Italian peoples. The innovation now proposed will, in its turn, one day be old: what we seek to justify by precedents today will itself become a precedent.’

25   The senate approved the emperor's speech. The first Gauls who thereby obtained the right to become Roman senators were the Aedui. They owed this privilege to their ancient treaty with Rome and their position as the only Gallic community entitled 'Brothers of the Roman People'. At this period Claudius also elevated senators of particularly long standing and illustrious birth to patrician rank, which few surviving families possessed. They comprised what Romulus had called 'the Greater' and Lucius Junius Brutus 'the Lesser' Houses. Even the families which the dictator Caesar and Augustus promoted in their place, under the Cassian and Saenian laws respectively, had died out. The action of Claudius was welcomed as beneficial, and the imperial censor enjoyed performing it.

But Claudius was worried about how to expel notorious bad characters from the senate. Rejecting old-fashioned severity in favour of a lenient modern method, he advised individuals concerned to consider their own cases and apply for permission to renounce senatorial rank—which would readily be granted. He would then publish expulsions by the censors *and* resignations in a single list—so that the humiliation of those expelled should be mitigated by association with those who had modestly volunteered to withdraw. For this one of the consuls, Lucius Vipstanus Poplicola, proposed that Claudius should be called Father of the Senate—since others too were called Father of the Country, whereas new services to the country deserved new titles. But the emperor vetoed the proposal as too flattering. Then he concluded the ritual of the census, which showed a citizen body of 5,984,072 persons.

Tacitus *Annals* 11.23–5
tr. Michael Grant (Penguin 1977)

K24 The Freedmen

The employment of freedmen in the service of the state had its origins in the need of Romans while in office to carry on using their own private staff as secretaries, accountants and the like. There was no corps of civil servants though some magistracies did have permanent administrative assistants (see A. H. M. Jones, 'The Roman Civil Service' in Studies in Roman Government and Law *(Oxford 1968)). Augustus and Tiberius used their personal staff, including freedmen, to deal with the administrative business of state. This custom became an organized system under Claudius, with freedmen in charge of major 'departments' dealing with the Emperor's secretariat, the treasury, and lawsuits. For an interesting analysis of Claudius' image in the sources as a tool in the hands of women and freedmen see S. K. Dickinson 'Claudius Saturnalicius Princeps' in* Latomus 36 (1977) 634 ff.

28   Among Claudius's favourite freedmen were Posides the eunuch, to whom he actually awarded, at his British triumph, the honour of a headless spear, along with soldiers who had fought in the field. For Felix he had an equally high regard, giving him command of infantry battalions and cavalry squadrons, and the Governorship of Judaea; this Felix married three queens. Then there was Harpocras, who earned the privileges of riding through Rome in a litter and staging public entertainments as though he were a knight. Claudius had an even higher regard for Polybius, his literary mentor, who often walked between the two Consuls. But his firmest devotion was reserved for Narcissus, his secretary, and Pallas, his treasurer, whom he encouraged the Senate to honour with large gifts of money and the insignia of quaestors and praetors as well. They were able to acquire such riches, by legitimate and illegitimate means, that when one day Claudius complained how little cash was left in the Privy Purse, someone answered neatly that he would have heaps of pocket money if only his two freedmen took him into partnership.

29   As I mention above, Claudius fell so deeply under the influence of these freedmen and wives that he seemed to be their servant rather than their emperor; and distributed titles, army commands, indulgences or punishments according to their wishes, however capricious, seldom even aware of what he was about. I need not dwell on matters of lesser importance: how he revoked grants, cancelled edicts, brazenly amended the texts of letters-patent he had issued, or at least substituted new versions for the old. Suffice it to record that he executed his father-in-law Appius Silanus; Julia, daughter of Tiberius's son Drusus; and Julia, daughter of his own brother Germanicus—all on unsupported charges and without the right to

plead in self-defence. Gnaeus Pompey, who had married his daughter Antonia, was stabbed to death while in bed with a favourite catamite; and Lucius Silanus, whom Claudius had betrothed to his daughter Octavia, lost his praetorship and, four days later, had orders to commit suicide; this was the very New Year's Day on which Claudius married Agrippina. He executed thirty-five senators and 300 Roman knights, with so little apparent concern that once, when a centurion reported that So-and-so the ex-Consul was now duly despatched, and Claudius denied having given any such command, his freedmen satisfied him that the soldiers had done right not to wait for instructions before taking vengeance on a public enemy. It is very difficult, however, to believe that they tricked Claudius into signing the marriage contract between Messalina and her lover Silius by an assurance that the marriage was a mere fiction: a transference of portended dangers threatening 'Messalina's husband', from himself to someone else.

Suetonius *Claudius* 28–9
tr. R. Graves (Penguin 1957)

K25 Messalina

Claudius married Messalina, his third wife, in AD 39 when she was fifteen years old. A plot to overthrow Claudius was probably behind the false marriage to C. Silius, whose father committed suicide when accused of conspiracy against Tiberius (Tacitus Annals 4. 18–19), but Messalina's involvement has been questioned (Scramuzza The Emperor Claudius p. 95). Callistus, Pallas and Narcissus were freedmen who held important posts; Lucius Vitellius was a close friend of Claudius, consul three times (AD 34, 43, and 47), and legate of Syria under Tiberius.

25   And now ended Claudius' ignorance of his own domestic affairs. Now he had, ineluctably, to discover and punish his wife's excesses (as a preliminary to coveting an incestuous substitute).   26   Messalina's adultery was going so smoothly that she was drifting, through boredom, into unfamiliar vices. But now fate seemed to have unhinged Gaius Silius; or perhaps he felt that impending perils could only be met by perilous action. He urged that concealment should be dropped. 'We do not have to wait until the emperor dies of old age!' he told her. 'Besides, only innocent people can afford long-term plans. Flagrant guilt requires audacity. And we have accomplices who share our danger. I am without wife or child. I am ready to marry, and to adopt Britannicus. Your power will remain undiminished. Peace of mind will only be yours if we can forestall Claudius. He is slow to discover deception—but quick to anger.'

Messalina was unenthusiastic. It was not that she loved her husband. But she feared that Silius, once supreme, might despise his mistress, and see the crime prompted by an emergency in its true colours. However, the idea of being called his wife appealed to her owing to its sheer outrageousness—a sensualist's ultimate satisfaction. So, waiting only until Claudius had left to sacrifice at Ostia, she celebrated a formal marriage with Silius.

27   It will seem fantastic, I know, that in a city where nothing escapes notice or comment, any human beings could have felt themselves so secure. Much more so that, on an appointed day and before invited signatories, a consul designate and the emperor's wife should have been joined together in formal marriage—for the purpose of rearing children'; that she should have listened to the diviners' words, assumed the wedding-veil, sacrificed to the gods; that the pair should have taken their places at a banquet, embraced, and finally spent the night as man and wife. But I am not inventing marvels. What I have told, and shall tell, is the truth. Older men heard and recorded it.

The imperial household shuddered—especially those in power, with everything to fear from a new emperor.

Tacitus *Annals* 11. 25-7
tr. Michael Grant (Penguin 1977)

K26   The Death of Claudius

Claudius was married for the fourth time to his niece, Agrippina the younger, daughter of Germanicus, who was an ambitious woman (cf. Tacitus Annals 12. 26, 37, 42). Her son, Lucius Domitius Ahenobarbus (the future Emperor Nero) was adopted by Claudius in AD 50 and given precedence over Britannicus, Claudius' own son, to ensure his succession.

(66)   Agrippina had long decided on murder. Now she saw her opportunity. Her agents were ready. But she needed advice about poisons. A sudden, drastic effect would give her away. A gradual, wasting recipe might make Claudius, confronted with death, love his son again. What was needed was something subtle that would upset the emperor's faculties but produce a deferred fatal effect. An expert in such matters was selected—a woman called Locusta, recently sentenced for poisoning but with a long career of imperial service ahead of her. By her talents, a preparation was supplied. It was administered by the eunuch Halotus who habitually served the emperor and tasted his food.

67   Later, the whole story became known. Contemporary writers stated that the poison was sprinkled on a particularly succulent mushroom. But because Claudius was torpid—or drunk—its effect was not at first apparent; and an evacuation of his bowels seemed to have saved him. Agrippina was horrified. But when the ultimate stakes are so alarmingly large, immediate disrepute is brushed aside. She had already secured the complicity of the emperor's doctor Xenophon; and now she called him in. The story is that, while pretending to help Claudius to vomit, he put

a feather dipped in a quick poison down his throat. Xenophon knew that major crimes, though hazardous to undertake, are profitable to achieve.

68   The senate was summoned. Consuls and priests offered prayers for the emperor's safety. But meanwhile his already lifeless body was being wrapped in blankets and poultices. Moreover, the appropriate steps were being taken to secure Nero's accession. First Agrippina, with heart-broken demeanour, held Britannicus to her as though to draw comfort from him. He was the very image of his father, she declared. By various devices she prevented him from leaving his room and like-wise detained his sisters, Claudia Antonia and Octavia. Blocking every approach with troops, Agrippina issued frequent encouraging announcements about the emperor's health, to maintain the Guard's morale and await the propitious moment forecast by the astrologers.

69   At last, at midday on October the thirteenth, the palace gates were suddenly thrown open. Attended by Sextus Afranius Burrus, commander of the Guard, out came Nero to the battalion which, in accordance with regulations, was on duty. At a word from its commander, he was cheered and put in a litter. Some of the men are said to have looked round hesitantly and asked where Britannicus was. However, as no counter-suggestion was made, they accepted the choice offered them. Nero was then conducted into the Guard's camp. There, after saying a few words appropriate to the occasion—and promising gifts on the generous standard set by his father—he was hailed as emperor. The army's decision was followed by senatorial decrees. The provinces, too, showed no hesitation.

Claudius was voted divine honours, and his funeral was modelled on that of the divine Augustus—Agrippina imitating the grandeur of her great-grandmother Livia, the first Augusta. But Claudius' will was not read, in case his preference of stepson to son should create a public impression of unfairness and injustice.

Tacitus *Annals* 12. 66–9
tr. Michael Grant (Penguin 1977)

L–O   THE PROVINCES

The study of Roman civilization cannot be confined to the study of Rome and Italy. Rome's relation with the provinces and client states (cf. C9–33) both cultural and economic, affected the political events in the Augustan Age. The sources in this section concentrate on four provinces Gaul (L), Germany (M), Britain (N), and Judaea (O). Each of these provinces illustrates different aspects of Roman foreign policy mainly from the Roman point of view. The exception is Judaea, with its own dominant and ancient culture, for which we have extensive Jewish sources. This section provides a dynamic picture of how Rome expanded her power and influence. Each of these provinces were at a different stage of their relations to Rome —and by looking at historical development of these relations we can gain some idea of how Rome conquered and ruled—or lost, and redefined her ambitions.

L ROME AND THE NORTHERN GAULS

L1 The division of Gaul

This division refers in effect only to the Northern Gauls, subjugated by Caesar between 58 and 50 BC. Gallia Transalpina had been under Roman rule for nearly a century, Gallia Cisalpina had been ruled as part of Italy before Sulla made it a province, and was enfranchised by the end of the Republic.

Gaul comprises three areas, inhabited respectively by the Belgae, the Aquitani, and a people who call themselves Celts, though we call them Gauls. All of these have different languages, customs, and laws. The Celts are separated from the Aquitani by the river Garonne, from the Belgae by the Marne and Seine. The Belgae are the bravest of the three peoples, being farthest removed from the highly developed civilization of the Roman Province, least often visited by merchants with enervating luxuries for sale, and nearest to the Germans across the Rhine, with whom they are continually at war. For the same reason the Helvetii are braver than the rest of the Celts; they are in almost daily conflict with the Germans, either trying to keep them out of Switzerland or themselves invading Germany. The region occupied by the Celts, which has one frontier facing north, is bounded by the Rhone, the Garonne, the Atlantic Ocean, and the country of the Belgae; the part of it inhabited by the Sequani and the Helvetii also touches the Rhine. The Belgic territory, facing north and east, runs from the northern frontier of the Celts to the lower Rhine. Aquitania is bounded by the Garonne, the Pyrenees, and the part of the Atlantic coast nearest Spain; it faces north-west.

Caesar *Gallic War* 1.1
tr. S. A. Handford (Penguin 1951)

L2 The social structure of the Gauls

The Celtic-speaking Gauls had begun to form unions of smaller tribal groups, ruled by an aristocratic warrior class called 'Knights' by Caesar.

In Gaul, not only every tribe, canton, and subdivision of a canton, but almost every family, is divided into rival factions. At the head of these factions are men who are regarded by their followers as having particularly great prestige, and these have the final say on all questions that come up for judgement and in all discussions of policy.

The object of this ancient custom seems to have been to ensure that all the common people should have protection against the strong; for each leader sees that no one gets the better of his supporters by force or by cunning—or, if he fails to do so, is utterly discredited. . . .

Everywhere in Gaul there are only two classes of men who are of any account or consideration. The common people are treated almost as slaves, never venture to act on their own initiative, and are not consulted on any subject. Most of them, crushed by debt or heavy taxation or the oppression of more powerful persons, bind themselves to serve men of rank, who exercise over them all the rights that masters have over slaves. The two privileged classes are the Druids and the Knights. The Druids officiate at the worship of the gods, regulate public and private sacrifices, and give rulings on all religious questions. Large numbers of young men flock to them for instruction, and they are held in great honour by the people. They act as judges in practically all disputes, whether between tribes or between individuals; when any crime is committed, or a murder takes place, or a dispute arises about an inheritance or a boundary, it is they who adjudicate the matter and appoint the compensation to be paid and received by the parties concerned. Any individual or tribe failing to accept their award is banned from taking part in sacrifice—the heaviest punishment that can be inflicted upon a Gaul. Those who are laid under such a ban are regarded as impious criminals. Everyone shuns them and avoids going near or speaking to them, for fear of taking some harm by contact with what is unclean; if they appear as plaintiffs, justice is denied them, and they are excluded from a share in any honour. All the Druids are under one head, whom they hold in the highest respect. On his death, if any one of the rest is of outstanding merit, he succeeds to the vacant place; if several have equal claims, the Druids usually decide the election by voting, though sometimes they actually fight it out. On a fixed date in each year they hold a session in a consecrated spot in the country of the Carnutes, which is supposed to be the centre of Gaul. Those who are involved in disputes assemble here from all parts, and accept the Druids' judgements and awards. The Druidic doctrine is believed to have been found existing in Britain and thence imported into Gaul; even to-day those who want to make a profound study of it generally go to Britain for the purpose. . . .

The second class is that of the Knights. When their services are required in some war that has broken out—and before Caesar's arrival in the country the Gallic states used to fight offensive or defensive wars almost every year—these all take the field, surrounded by their servants and retainers, of whom each Knight has a greater or smaller number according to his birth and fortune. The possession of such a following is the only criterion of position and power that they recognize.

Caesar *Gallic War* 6. 11; 13; 15
tr. S. A. Handford (Penguin 1951)

L3 Rome against the Helvetii

The Aedui were 'friends of Rome', and when they were threatened by a mass migration of the Helvetii they turned to Rome for help. Dumnorix, brother of Diviciacus, chief pro-Roman noble, had seen the Helvetian invasion as a chance to seize supreme power over the Aedui. Rome moved against the Helvetii after Caesar took command in Gaul in 58 BC.

(a)

On putting the same questions to others in private, Caesar found that his report was true. It was indeed Dumnorix that he had referred to, a man of boundless daring, extremely popular with the masses on account of his liberality, and an ardent revolutionary. For many years he had bought at a cheap price the right of collecting the river-tolls and other taxes of the Aedui, because when he made a bid at the auction not a soul dared bid against him. In this way he had made a fortune and amassed large resources to expend in bribery. He maintained at his own expense a considerable force of cavalry, which he kept in attendance upon him, and his power was not confined to his own country, but extended over the neighbouring tribes. To increase it he had arranged a marriage for his mother with a nobleman of very great influence among the Bituriges; his own wife was a Helvetian, and he had married his half-sister and other female relations to members of other tribes. On account of his matrimonial connection he was a keen partisan of the Helvetii, and he had his own reasons for hating Caesar and the Romans, because their arrival in Gaul had decreased his power and restored his brother Diviciacus to his former position of honour and influence. If disaster should befall the Romans, he felt sure that with the aid of the Helvetii the throne was within his grasp, whereas a Roman conquest of Gaul would mean that he could not hope even to retain his present standing, much less make himself king.

Caesar *Gallic War* 1. 18. 3-9
tr. S. A. Handford (Penguin 1951)

(b)

On the conclusion of the Helvetian campaign the leading men of tribes in almost every part of Gaul came to offer Caesar congratulations. They realized, they said, that although his motive in fighting the Helvetii was to punish them for their past injuries to Rome, what had happened was just as much to the advantage of Gaul as of the Romans. For the intention of the Helvetii, in abandoning their home at a time when they enjoyed great prosperity, was to make war on all Gaul and become masters of it, and so to have the whole country from which to select the district they thought most fertile and convenient for settlement, and to compel the other tribes to pay tribute. The deputies asked Caesar to let them fix a day for convening a pan-Gallic assembly, saying that there were certain requests they would like to submit to him when they were all agreed about them. With Caesar's consent they appointed a date for this assembly, and swore to one another not to disclose its proceedings without its express authority.

Caesar *Gallic War* 1 . 30
tr. S. A. Handford (Penguin 1951)

L4 Julius Caesar's policy

Lucius Domitius Ahenobarbus stood for the consulship of 55 BC. At that point the conquest of Gaul was not complete. Caesar's policy did eventually lead to the subjugation of Gaul; the dangers to which Suetonius refers were perhaps the revolts, such as that of 52 BC, resulting from a nationalistic reaction against a common enemy. Caesar created a ruling class loyal to him personally by placing his supporters in positions of power; his grants of citizenship to some troops reinforced ties with Rome.

At last Lucius Domitius Ahenobarbus stood for the consulship and openly threatened that, once elected, he would remove Caesar from his military command, having failed to do this while praetor. So Caesar called upon Pompey and Crassus to visit Lucca, which lay in his province, and there persuaded them to prolong his governorship of Gaul for another five years, and to oppose Domitius's candidature.

This success encouraged Caesar to expand his regular army with legions raised at his own expense: one even recruited in Transalpine Gaul and called *Alauda* (Gallic for 'The Crested Lark'), which he trained and equipped in Roman style. Later he made every Alauda legionary a full citizen.

He now lost no opportunity of picking quarrels—however flimsy the pretext—with allies as well as hostile and barbarous tribes, and marching against them; the danger of this policy never occurred to him. At first the Senate set up a commission of inquiry into the state of the Gallic provinces, and some speakers went so far as to recommend that Caesar should be handed over to the enemy. But the more successful his campaigns, the more frequent the public thanksgivings voted; and the holidays that went with them were longer than any general before him had ever earned.

Suetonius *Julius Caesar* 24
tr. R. Graves (Penguin 1957)

L5 Augustus' reorganization of Gaul

(a)
The reorganization of Gaul was roughly along the lines laid down by Caesar, and most probably occurred in connection with Augustus' visit to Gaul in 27 BC. There

553

may have been more than one version of the division, if Strabo is right in saying that Lugdunensis stretched to the upper Rhine. We know from later writers, such as Pliny and Ptolemy, also drawing on sources of the Augustan period, that this area (i.e. the civitates *of Helvetii, Sequani, and Lingones) was included in Belgica, and a rearrangement of this kind would make sense at the time of the Rhine offensive, since it kept the land next to the Rhine in one province.*

Augustus Caesar, however, divided Transalpine Celtica into four parts: the Celtae he designated as belonging to the province of Narbonitis; the Aquitani he designated as the former Caesar had already done, although he added to them fourteen tribes of the peoples who dwell between the Garumna and the Liger Rivers; the rest of the country he divided into two parts: one part he included within the boundaries of Lugdunum as far as the upper districts of the Rhenus, while the other he included within the boundaries of the Belgae. Now although the geographer should tell of all the physical and ethnic distinctions which have been made, whenever they are worth recording, yet, as for the diversified political divisions which are made by the rulers (for they suit their government to the particular times), it is sufficient if one state them merely in a summary way; and the scientific treatment of them should be left to others.

Now the whole of this country is watered by rivers: some of them flow down from the Alps, the others from the Cemmenus and the Pyrenees; and some of them are discharged into the ocean, the others into Our Sea. Further, the districts through which they flow are plains, for the most part, and hilly lands with navigable water-courses. The river-beds are by nature so well situated with reference to one another that there is transportation from either sea into the other; for the cargoes are transported only a short distance by land, with an easy transit through plains, but most of the way they are carried on the rivers—on some into the interior, on the others to the sea. The Rhodanus offers an advantage in this regard; for not only is it a stream of many tributaries, as has been stated, but it also connects with Our Sea, which is better than the outer sea, and traverses a country which is the most favoured of all in that part of the world. For example, the same fruits are produced by the whole of the province of Narbonitis as by Italy. As you proceed towards the north and the Cemmenus Mountain, the olive-planted and fig-bearing land indeed ceases, but the other things still grow. Also the vine, as you thus proceed, does not easily bring its fruit to maturity. All the rest of the country produces grain in large quantities, and millet, and nuts, and all kinds of live stock. And none of the country is untilled except parts where tilling is precluded by swamps and woods. Yet these parts too are thickly peopled—more because of the largeness of the population than because of the industry of the people; for the women are not only prolific, but good nurses as well, while the men are fighters rather than farmers. But at the present time they are compelled to till the soil, now that they have laid down their arms. However, although I am here speaking only in a general way of the whole of outer Celtica, let me now take each of the fourth parts separately and tell about them, describing them only in rough outline.

Strabo 4. 1. 1–4 tr. H. L. Jones (Loeb 1923)

(b)

Under Augustus each major community was encouraged to have a central admini-
strative capital, and these were often new cities, founded by Augustus. Lyon
(Lugdunum) was an administrative and cultural centre for the whole of Northern
Gaul, having been founded as a colony of Roman citizens under Munatius Plancus
in 43 BC.

Lugdunum itself, then, (a city founded at the foot of a hill at the confluence of the
River Arar and the Rhodanus), is occupied by the Romans. And it is the most
populous of all the cities of Celtica except Narbo; for not only do people use it as
an emporium, but the Roman governors coin their money there, both the silver
and the gold. Again, the temple that was dedicated to Caesar Augustus by all the
Galatae in common is situated in front of this city at the junction of the rivers. And
in it is a noteworthy altar, bearing an inscription of the names of the tribes, sixty in
number: and also images from these tribes, one from each tribe. . . .

Strabo 4. 3. 2
tr. H. L. Jones (Loeb 1923)

(c)

An inscription from Saintes. Lyon lay on the west bank of the Rhône, immediately
below its confluence with the Saône (Arar). At the Confluence itself (Condate)
between the two rivers, an altar to Rome and Augustus was dedicated by Drusus in
12 or 10 BC (see L. R. Taylor The Divinity of the Roman Emperor *(Connecticut*
1931) p. 209 for a discussion of the date). The Concilium Galliarum was set up, a
council consisting of representatives of sixty Gaulish tribes, whose main function
was to maintain the cult and elect a priest of Rome and Augustus each year. It is
possible that his Congonnetodubnus is the same as the one mentioned in Caesar BG
7. 3. For the continuity of Gaulish military traditions in Roman military service
cf. CIL *13. 1041.*

In honour of Gaius Julius Victor, son of Congonnetodubnus, of the tribe Voltinia,
grandson of Agedomopatis, *praefectus fabrum* (*staff officer*), military tribune
of the 1st cohort of Belgian (?) auxiliaries, priest of Rome and Augustus at the
Confluence, Gaius Julius Victor, of the tribe Voltinia, his son (dedicated this).

CIL 13. 1042–5
tr. K. Chisholm

L6 Licinus' Maladministration

Marcus Libo and Calpurnius Piso were consuls in 15 BC. Licinus was financial ad-
ministrator in Gaul at the beginning of Augustus' rule (schol. Juvenal 1. 106) and

became a byword for enriching himself at the expense of the Gauls (cf. Juvenal 14. 306).

For this reason Augustus had no need of arms, but in arranging other matters he consumed the whole of this year, as well as the next, in which Marcus Libo and Calpurnius Piso were consuls. For not only had the Gauls suffered much at the hands of the Germans, but much also at the hands of a certain Licinus. And of this, I think, the sea-monster had given them full warning beforehand; twenty feet broad and three times as long, and resembling a woman except for its head, it had come in from the ocean and become stranded on the shore. Now Licinus was originally a Gaul, but after being captured by the Romans and becoming a slave of Caesar's, he had been set free by him, and by Augustus had been made procurator of Gaul. This man, then, with his combination of barbarian avarice and Roman dignity, tried to overthrow every one who was ever counted superior to him and to destroy every one who was strong for the time being. He not only supplied himself with plenty of funds for the requirements of the office to which he had been assigned, but also incidentally collected plenty for himself and for his friends. His knavery went so far that in some cases where the people paid their tribute by the month he made the months fourteen in number, declaring that the month called December was really the tenth, and for that reason they must reckon two more (which he called the eleventh and the twelfth respectively) as the last, and contribute the money that was due for these months. It was these quibbles that brought him into danger; for the Gauls secured the ear of Augustus and protested indignantly, so that the emperor in some matters shared their vexation and in others tried to excuse Licinus. He claimed to be unaware of some of his extortions and affected not to believe others, while some matters he actually concealed, feeling ashamed to have employed such a procurator. Licinus, however, devised another scheme as follows, and laughed them all to scorn. When he perceived that Augustus was displeased with him and that he was likely to be punished, he brought the emperor into his house, and showing him many treasures of silver and gold and many other valuables piled up in heaps, he said: 'I have gathered all this purposely, master, for you and for the rest of the Romans, lest the natives, by having control of so much money, should revolt. At any rate, I have kept it all for you and now give it to you.'

Thus Licinus was saved, by pretending that he had sapped the strength of the barbarians in order to serve Augustus.

Dio Cassius 54. 21
tr. E. Cary (Loeb 1917)

L7 A funerary inscription

A number of prominent Gauls were enfranchised by Julius Caesar for their services to him. *Under Augustus it was also possible for provincials from communities with Latin rights, or those that had been granted the franchise by the Princeps, to become citizens by holding municipal office or joining the army. Since Gauls enfranchised by Caesar and Augustus normally took the names Julius, it is often impossible to determine by what route they reached the citizenship. The following passage is a funerary inscription found in Saintes, first restored by P. Grimal (REA 1947 pp. 130–4; AE 1948 no. 166). This is the first record of a municipal cursus from Mediolanum Santonum. The priesthood mentioned may be a local municipal one, not the one at the Altar. The text is in ILTG no. 149 and follows the emendation of A. Aymard (REA 1945 pp. 414–17); also in Ehrenberg and Jones[2] no. 340.*

In honour of Gaius Julius Marinus, son of Gaius Julius Ricoveriugus, of the tribe Voltinia, first to hold the priesthood of Augustus, head of the corporation of Roman citizens, quaestor, Vergobretus (*chief magistrate of his own town*); Julia Marina, his daughter, erected this.

CIL 13.1048
tr. K. Chisholm

L8 Gaul under Tiberius

Under Tiberius the Romanization of Northern Gaul progressed on Augustan lines, and the following passages are expressions of loyalty to the new head of the Imperial house.

(a) *A dedication found in Paris under the choir of Notre Dame*

With this inscription were found reliefs showing men in procession, some with armour, as well as deities which are more Gallic than Roman.

Under Tiberius Caesar Augustus this column sacred to Juppiter, Best and Greatest, was set up publicly by the shipping corporation of Paris.

ILTG 331 *Gallia* Suppl. 17 ed. P. Wuilleumier
tr. K. Chisholm

(b)
This inscription dates from AD 20 and comes from Herapel or Hiéraple, a hill-top village and sanctuary on a comparatively minor road south of Trier near the modern Saarbrucken. Merchants and craftsmen were often found in distinct areas or streets in Roman towns; here, their mere presence is noteworthy.

To Tiberius Caesar Augustus, son of the divine Augustus, grandson of the divine Julius, *pontifex maximus*, consul three times, acclaimed *imperator* eight times,

557

in the 22nd year of his tribunician power, the merchants resident in the village.

CIL 13.4481
tr. K. Chisholm

The Amphitheatre of the Three Gauls

(c) *A dedicatory inscription found in the Botanical Gardens at Lyon in 1958. This indicates that the Amphitheatre of the Three Gauls was built in the federal territory at Condate, at the confluence of the rivers Saône and Rhône, in the reign of Tiberius. The inscription was published in 1958 by J. Guey and M. Audin* CRAI *1958 pp. 106–10; for alternative readings and further articles see* Gallia Suppl. 17 *(1963) 80.*

[For the health] of Tiberius Caesar Augustus, Gaius Iulius Rufus, son of Gaius, priest of Rome and Augustus and [?Gaius Iulius, son of Gaius] his son [?and Gaius Iulius, son of Gaius] his grandson, of the community of the Santones, built (this) amphitheatre [with arena? and] parapet at their own expense.

ILTG 217 *Gallia* Suppl. 17 (1963) ed. P. Wuilleumier
tr. J. Reynolds

(d)
This inscription which dates from AD *18 or 19, comes from the triumphal arch at Saintes. The Julius Rufus responsible has been thought to be the same man as in (c). Whether or not this is the case, the inscription illustrates the manner in which notable Gallic aristocratic families adopted the Roman idea of making their wealth serve to beautify their city and show loyalty to the Imperial house.*

1a
In honour of Germanicus Caesar son of Tiberius Augustus, grandson of the divine Augustus, great-grandson of the divine Julius, augur, priest of Augustus, consul twice, acclaimed *imperator* twice.

1b
In honour of Tiberius Caesar Augustus, son of the divine Augustus, augur, *pontifex maximus*, consul three times (?) acclaimed *imperator* seven times, in the 21st (?) year of his tribunician power.

1c
In honour of Drusus Caesar son of Tiberius Augustus, grandson of the divine Augustus, great-grandson of the divine Julius, *pontifex*, augur, consul twice.

2
Gaius Julius Rufus, son of Gaius Julius Otuaneunus, grandson of Gaius Julius

Gedomon, great-grandson of Epotsorovidus, priest of Rome and Augustus at the altar beside the Confluence, *praefectus fabrum* (*staff officer*), donated this.

CIL 13.1036
tr. K. Chisholm

L9 The Revolt of Florus and Sacrovir

The rebellion of Julius Florus and Julius Sacrovir occurred in AD 21; its leaders were Romanized Gauls who focused the unrest caused by heavy taxes to finance Germanicus' campaigns as well as more local grievances. It did not spread very far and was suppressed by the Rhine legions under Gaius Silius and Visellius Varro.

(a)

40 In the same year heavy debts drove Gallic communities into rebellion. Its keenest instigators were Julius Florus among the Treviri and Julius Sacrovir among the Aedui—both noblemen, whose ancestors' services to Rome had earned them citizenship in days when this was scarce and conferred for merit. Secret conferences were attended by desperate characters and penniless, frightened men driven to crime by their evil records. It was agreed that Florus should raise the Belgae and Sacrovir the tribes farther south. There were treasonable gatherings and discussions about endless taxation, crushing rates of interest, and the brutality and arrogance of governors. 'Germanicus' death has demoralized the Roman army!' they cried. 'Besides, look at the contrast between your strength and Italy's weakness. Think of the unwarlike population of Rome. How the army needs us provincials! This is an ideal opportunity to regain independence.'

41 These seeds of rebellion were sown in almost every Gallic community. But the outbreak started among the Andecavi and Turoni. The imperial governor of Lugdunese Gaul, Acilius Aviola, suppressed both, the former with the city-police battalion which garrisoned Lugdunum, and the latter with regular troops sent by his colleague in Lower Germany, Gaius Visellius Varro. To hide their rebellious aims—for which the time was not yet ripe—certain Gallic chiefs supported the disciplinary measures. Sacrovir himself was to be seen encouraging the fighters—on the Roman side. He was bare-headed, ostensibly to attract attention to his valour; but prisoners said it was to show his identity and so avoid being aimed at. Tiberius received this information but disregarded it: his indecision did no good to the war.

42 Florus, pursuing his plans, tempted a cavalry regiment—raised among the Treviri but serving with us in Roman fashion—to begin hostilities by massacring our business-men. The majority remained loyal, but a few went over. A crowd of debtors and dependants also took up arms. Making for the Arduenna Forest, they were intercepted by brigades sent from opposite directions by the imperial governors

of Lower and Upper Germany. The Romans sent ahead a man of rebel nationality, Julius Indus by name, whose loyalty was stimulated by hatred for Florus. This man dispersed the still undisciplined crowd. But Florus escaped in the rout, and his hiding-place proved untraceable. Finally, however, seeing soldiers blocking every exit, he killed himself. So the rebellion among the Treviri ended.

43   The revolt of the Aedui was more formidable; for they were a richer nation, and less accessible to counter-measures. Sacrovir with an armed force occupied the capital, Augustodunum, and seized the youthful Gallic noblemen who were being educated there. Holding them as pledges to win over their parents and relations, he distributed among them secretly manufactured weapons. His army was forty thousand strong; one-fifth were equipped like Roman soldiers, the rest with hunters' spears, knives, and other such arms. There was also a party of slaves training to be gladiators. Completely encased in iron in the national fashion, these Crupellarii, as they were called, were too clumsy for offensive purposes but impregnable in defence. Reinforcements came in. The neighbouring communities had not yet openly joined, but supplied keen volunteers. And the Roman generals were quarrelling; both claimed to control operations. Finally the aged and infirm governor of Lower Germany yielded to his Upper German colleague of more active years, Gaius Silius.

(b)
45   Silius sent auxiliaries ahead to ravage villages of the Sequani (a frontier people who were allies and neighbours of the Aedui). Then he himself, with two brigades, moved rapidly against Augustodunum. There was much rivalry among Roman sergeant-majors to reach it first. Indeed, even the ordinary soldiers protested against the usual halts and rests at night. They felt that, once they and the enemy saw each other face to face, victory was as good as won. . . .   46   Our cavalry enveloped the enemy's flanks, while the infantry made a frontal attack. The Gallic flanks were driven in. The iron-clad contingent caused some delay as their casing resisted javelins and swords. However, the Romans used axes and mattocks, and struck at their plating and its wearers like men demolishing a wall. Others knocked down the immobile gladiators with poles or pitchforks, and, lacking the power to rise, they were left for dead. Sacrovir and his closest associates fled first to Augustodunum and then, fearing betrayal, to a house nearby. There he killed himself; and his companions killed each other. The house was set on fire, and the bodies burnt inside it.

Tacitus *Annals* 3. 40-3; 45-6 (abridged)
tr. M. Grant (Penguin 1977)

L10 Gaius' rule in Gaul

Gaius' famous nickname 'Caligula' dated from the time he accompanied his parents with the Rhine legions (see K6). His conduct in these anecdotes is probably exag-gerated but does indicate an interest in show and profit. (For Gaius see also K15-18).

(a)

20   Gaius gave several shows abroad—Athenian Games at Syracuse, and miscella-neous Games at Lyons, where he also held a competition in Greek and Latin oratory. The loser, it appears, had to present the winners with prizes and make speeches praising them; while those who failed miserably were forced to erase their entries with either sponges or their own tongues—at the threat of being thrashed and flung into the Rhône.

(b)

39   While in Gaul Gaius did so well by selling the furniture, jewellery, slaves, and even the freedmen of his condemned sisters at a ridiculous over-valuation that he decided to do the same with the furnishing of the Old Palace. So he sent to Rome, where his agents commandeered public conveyances, and even draught animals from the bakeries, to fetch the stuff north; which led to a bread shortage in the City, and to the loss of many law-suits, because litigants who lived at a distance were unable to appear in court and meet their bail. He then used all kinds of tricks for disposing of the furniture: scolding the bidders for their avarice, or for their shamelessness in being richer than he was, and pretending grief at this surrender of family property to commoners. Discovering that one wealthy provincial had paid the Imperial secretariat 2,000 gold pieces to be smuggled into a banquet, Caligula was delighted that the privilege of dining with him should be valued so highly and, when next day the same man turned up at the auction, made him pay 2,000 gold pieces for some trifling object—but also sent him a personal invitation to dinner.

Suetonius *Gaius* 20; 39
tr. R. Graves (Penguin 1957)

L11 The Rule of Claudius

In AD *48 Claudius gave Gaulish citizens the right to hold office at Rome and in-troduced into the Senate by* adlectio *a number of Gauls (see K23). He also ex-tended the number of provincial citizens, and gave whole communities the fran-chise. He may have given Latin rights to substantial areas of Gaul, though the evidence does not amount to proof. Seneca mocks him for this, but it was a policy which led to integration and stability.*

(a)

A dedicatory inscription, found at Senlis (Oise), dating from AD *48/9*

561

This is the first epigraphic evidence of the existence of the Silvanectes. It has been suggested that it was to thank Claudius for having founded their city, but the name Augusta Silvanectium points rather to Augustus. It was published by A. Piganiol CRAI (1959) 450-7. For notes and bibliography see ILTG p. 148.

In honour of Tiberius Claudius Caesar Augustus Germanicus *pontifex maximus*, in the 8th year of his tribunician power, consul four times, acclaimed *imperator* sixteen times, Father of his country, and censor; the community of the Sulbanectes (dedicate this) from public funds.

> *ILTG* 357 *Gallia* Suppl. 17 (1963) ed. P. Wuilleumier
> tr. K. Chisholm

(b)
Seneca's sarcastic comment is here put into the mouth of Clotho, one of the Three Fates, who has the task of ending Claudius' life.

Clotho replied: 'Upon my word, I did wish to give him another hour or two, until he should make Roman citizens of the half dozen who are still outsiders. (He made up his mind, you know, to see the whole world in the toga, Greeks, Gauls, Spaniards, Britons, and all.) But since it is your pleasure to leave a few foreigners for seed, and since you command me, so be it.'

> Seneca *Apocolocyntosis* 3
> tr. W. H. D. Rouse (Loeb 1969)

L12 Gallic Wealth

This inscription from Bordeaux cannot be closely dated but belongs to the first century AD. It again shows the enormous wealth which individual Gauls, often magistrates of their community, were prepared to spend on public amenities coupled with self-glorification. For a discussion see J. F. Drinkwater 'Gallic personal wealth' Chiron 9 (1979) 237-42.

Gaius Julius Secundus, praetor, gave (this) aqueduct, bequeathing 2,000,000 sesterces in his will for the purpose.

> *CIL* 13.596
> tr. K. Chisholm

M GERMANY

M1 Augustus' Foreign Policy

*The traditional view of Augustus' policy is that it was basically defensive; in effect that he was not concerned with expanding the territories ruled by Rome, only in ensuring the stability and security of those lands which Rome had already conquered. Based on an examination of the literary and archaeological evidence for Germany, C. M. Wells (*The German Policy of Augustus *(Oxford 1972)) argues that this was far from being the case, that Augustus' policy was imperialistic, and that his plans to conquer Germany were only shelved because of military defeat. This view of Augustus is supported indirectly by RG and by Suetonius (Augustus 21. 1-2–C3 (b)) who gives an impressive list of Augustus' conquests; in the following passage one can perhaps see an indication of Augustus' admiration for those who had added territory to the glory of Rome. See further E. N. Luttwak* The Grand Strategy of the Roman Empire *(Johns Hopkins 1976) ch. 1.*

Next to the Immortals, Augustus most honoured the memory of those citizens who had raised the Roman people from small beginnings to their present glory; which was why he restored many public buildings erected by men of this calibre, complete with their original dedicatory inscriptions, and raised statues to them, wearing triumphal dress, in the twin colonnades of his Forum. Then he proclaimed: 'This has been done to make my fellow-citizens insist that both I (while I live), and my successors, shall not fall below the standard set by those great men of old.' He also transferred Pompey's statue from the hall in which Julius Caesar had been assassinated to a marble arch facing the main entrance of the Theatre.

Suetonius *Augustus* 31. 5
tr. R. Graves (Penguin 1957)

M2 The Roman view of the Germans

The Germans were held to be a fierce warlike race, a threat to the newly conquered areas of Gaul, indeed a potential threat to Italy itself. In Book 1 of the Gallic War *Caesar emphasizes that the Germans lived beyond the Rhine (see L1) but in later passages he also speaks of Germans west of the Rhine. From the literary sources we gain an image of a barbarous race very different from the Gauls, but archaeological evidence of settlements in northern Gaul indicates that some of the tribes known as Germanic to the Romans may well have been Celtic, or a mixture of the two (see C. M. Wells,* The German Policy of Augustus *(Oxford 1972) ch. 2). Caesar's description of the Suebi provides an archetype for the Roman view of the Germans. His general description ((b) below) distinguishes the Germans as a whole by their savagery, nomadic life, religion, and language.*

(a)

The Usipetes and Tencteri invaded the Menapii, a Belgic tribe in the winter of 56/5 BC, because they themselves were under pressure from the Suebi.

In the following winter, in which the consulship of Pompey and Crassus began, the German tribes of the Usipetes and Tenctheri crossed the Rhine in large numbers not far from its mouth. They were forced to migrate because for several years they had been subjected to harassing attacks by the Suebi and prevented from tilling their land.

The Suebi are far the largest and most warlike of the German nations. It is said that they have a hundred cantons, each of which provides annually a thousand armed men for service in foreign wars. Those who are left at home have to support the men in the army as well as themselves, and the next year take their turn of service, while the others stay at home. Thus both agriculture, and military instruction and training, continue without interruption. No land, however, is the property of private individuals, and no one is allowed to cultivate the same plot for more than one year. They do not eat much cereal food, but live chiefly on milk and meat, and spend much time in hunting. Their diet, daily exercise, and the freedom from restraint that they enjoy—for from childhood they do not know what compulsion or discipline is, and do nothing against their inclination—combine to make them strong and as tall as giants. They inure themselves, in spite of the very cold climate in which they live, to wear no clothing but skins—and these so scanty that a large part of the body is uncovered—and to bathe in the rivers. Traders are admitted into their country more because they want to sell their booty than because they stand in any need of imports. Even horses, which the Gauls are inordinately fond of and purchase at big prices, are not imported by the Germans. They are content with their home-bred horses, which, although undersized and ugly, are rendered capable of very hard work by daily exercise. In cavalry battles they often dismount and fight on foot, training the horses to stand perfectly still, so that they can quickly get back to them in case of need. In their eyes it is the height of effeminacy and shame to use a saddle, and they do not hesitate to engage the largest force of cavalry riding saddled horses, however small their own numbers may be. They absolutely forbid the importation of wine, because they think that it makes men soft and incapable of enduring hard toil. They regard it as the proudest glory of a nation to keep the largest possible area round its frontiers uninhabited, because it shows that many other peoples are inferior to it in military might. It is said, for example, that on one side of the Suebic territory the country is uninhabited for a distance of more than five hundred and fifty miles. On the other side their nearest neighbours are the Ubii, who were once—by German standards—a considerable and

564

prosperous nation. They are somewhat more civilized than the rest of the Germans; for living on the Rhine close to the frontier of Gaul, where traders visit them regularly, they have adopted Gallic customs. The Suebi, after repeated attempts to oust them from their home by force of arms, found them too numerous and strong to be dispossessed, but compelled them to pay tribute and greatly reduced their pride and power.

The Usipetes and Tenctheri were in the same case. For many years they withstood the Suebi's pressure, but eventually were driven from their country, and after wandering for three years in many parts of Germany reached the Rhine in the territory of the Menapii, who had lands, farmhouses, and villages on both banks of the river. Terrified by the arrival of such a multitude, the Menapii abandoned their dwellings on the German bank and placed outposts on the Gallic bank to prevent the emigrants from crossing. The Germans tried every expedient; but not having boats with which to force a passage, and being unable to cross by stealth because of the Menapian pickets, they pretended to return to their home country, and marched in that direction for three days. Then they turned back again, and recovering the whole distance in a single night, their cavalry made a surprise attack on the unsuspecting Menapii, who, on being informed by their patrols of their enemy's departure, had fearlessly recrossed the Rhine and returned to their villages. The Germans slaughtered them, seized their boats, crossed the river before the Menapii on the Gallic side knew what was afoot, took possession of all their farmhouses, and lived on their provisions for the rest of the winter.

Caesar *Gallic War* 4. 1–4
tr. S. A. Handford (Penguin 1951)

(b)

Caesar emphasizes the warlike qualities of the Germans. However, from archaeological evidence of settlements of a traditionally Celtic type (La Tène culture) we can infer that although the tribes east of the Rhine may have been poorer and less advanced in culture, they did not all lead a nomadic life, preying on their richer neighbours.

The customs of the Germans are entirely different. They have no Druids to control religious observances, and are not much given to sacrifices. The only beings they recognize as gods are things that they can see, and by which they are obviously benefited, such as Sun, Moon, and Fire; the other gods they have never even heard of. They spend all their lives in hunting and warlike pursuits, and inure themselves from childhood to toil and hardship. Those who preserve their chastity longest are most highly commended by their friends; for they think that continence makes young men taller, stronger, and more muscular. To have had intercourse with a woman before the age of twenty is considered perfectly scandalous. They attempt no concealment, however, of the facts of sex: men and women bathe together in the rivers, and they wear nothing but hides or short garments of hairy skin, which leave most of the body bare.

The Germans are not agriculturalists, and live principally on milk, cheese, and meat. No one possesses any definite amount of land as private property; the magistrates and tribal chiefs annually assign a holding to clans and groups of kinsmen or others living together, fixing its size and position at their discretion, and the following year make them move on somewhere else. They give many reasons for this custom: for example, that their men may not get accustomed to living in one place, lose their warlike enthusiasm, and take up agriculture instead; that they may not be anxious to acquire large estates, and the strong be tempted to dispossess the weak; to prevent their paying too much attention to building houses that will protect them from cold and heat, or becoming too fond of money—a frequent cause of division and strife; and to keep the common people contented and quiet by letting every man see that even the most powerful are no better off than himself.

The various tribes regard it as their greatest glory to lay waste as much as possible of the land around them and to keep it uninhabited. They hold it a proof of a people's valour to drive their neighbours from their homes, so that no one dare settle near them, and also think that it gives them greater security by removing any fear of sudden invasion. When a tribe is attacked or intends to attack another, officers are chosen to conduct the campaign and invested with powers of life and death. In peace-time there is no central magistracy; the chiefs of the various districts and cantons administer justice and settle disputes among their own people. No discredit attaches to plundering-raids outside the tribal frontiers; the Germans say that they serve to keep the young men in training and prevent them from getting lazy. When a chief announces in an assembly his intention of leading a raid and calls for volunteers, those who like the proposal, and approve of the man who makes it, stand up and promise their assistance amid the applause of the whole gathering; anyone who backs out afterwards is looked on as a deserter and a traitor, and no one will ever trust him again. To wrong a guest is impious in their eyes. They shield from injury all who come to their houses for any purpose whatever, and treat their persons as sacred; guests are welcomed to every man's home and table.

There was a time when the Gauls were more warlike than the Germans, when they actually invaded German territory, and sent colonists across the Rhine because their own country was too small to support its large population. It was in this way that the most fertile district of Germany, in the neighbourhood of the Hercynian forest [which was known to Eratosthenes and other Greeks, who call it Orcynia] was seized and occupied by the Volcae Tectosages, who remain there to this day and have a high reputation for fair dealing and gallantry. Nowadays, while the Germans still endure the same life of poverty and privation as before, without any change in their diet or clothing, the Gauls, through living near the Roman Province and becoming acquainted with sea-borne products, are abundantly supplied with various commodities. Gradually accustomed to inferiority and defeated in many battles, they do not even pretend to compete with the Germans in bravery.

Caesar *Gallic War* 6. 21–4
tr. S. A. Handford (Penguin 1951)

(c)

By the mid-first century AD Gaul was a settled province and a frontier had been created, in effect the area beyond which the Romans could not maintain supremacy. Pliny distinguishes five different German races, or groups of tribes; these may represent successive waves of migration rather than specifically racial groups.

From this point more definite information begins to open up, beginning with the race of the Inguaeones, the first that we come to in Germany. Here there is an enormous mountain, the Saevo, as big as those of the Ripaean range, which forms an enormous bay reaching to the Cimbrian promontory; it is named the Codanian Gulf, and is studded with islands. The most famous of these is Scandinavia; its size has not been ascertained, and so far as is known, only part of it is inhabited, its natives being the Hilleviones, who dwell in 500 villages, and call their island a second world. Aeningia is thought to be equally big. Some authorities report that these regions as far as the river Vistula are inhabited by the Sarmati, Venedi, Sciri and Hirri, and that there is a gulf named Cylipenus, with the island of Latris at its mouth, and then another gulf, that of Lagnus, at which is the frontier of the Cimbri. The Cimbrian promontory projects a long way into the sea, forming a peninsula called Tastris. Then there are twenty-three islands known to the armed forces of Rome; the most noteworthy of these are Burcana, called by our people Bean Island from the quantity of wild beans growing there, and the island which by the soldiery is called Glass Island from its amber, but by the barbarians Austeravia, and also Actania.

The whole of the sea-coast as far as the German river Scheldt is inhabited by races the extent of whose territories it is impossible to state, so unlimited is the disagreement among the writers who report about them. The Greek writers and some of our own have given the coast of Germany as measuring 2500 miles, while Agrippa makes the length of Germany including Raetia and Noricum 686 miles and the breadth 248 miles, whereas the breadth of Raetia alone almost exceeds that figure; though to be sure it was only conquered about the time of Agrippa's death—for Germany was explored many years after, and that not fully. If one may be allowed to conjecture, the coast will be found to be not much shorter than the Greek idea of it and the length given by Agrippa.

There are five German races: the Vandals, who include the Burgodiones, Varinnae, Charini and Gutones; the second race the Inguaeones, including Cimbri, Teutoni and the tribes of the Chauci; nearest to the Rhine the Istiaeones, including the Sicambri; inland the Hermiones, including the Suebi, Hermunduri, Chatti and Cherusci; and the fifth section the Peucini, and the Basternae who march with the Dacians above mentioned. Notable rivers that flow into the Ocean are the Guthalus, the Visculus or Vistula, the Elbe, the Weser, the Ems, the Rhine and the Meuse. In the interior stretches the Hercinian range of mountains, which is inferior to none in grandeur.

Pliny *Natural History* 4. 96–100
tr. H. Rackham (Loeb 1952)

M3 Tacitus' Description of the Germans

The Germania *was written at the end of the first century* AD, *an informative treatise describing the Germans and their lands. Although Roman contacts with the peoples they called Germans had increased since the time of Caesar, Tacitus' work does not indicate detailed knowledge of German territories, customs or institutions. He did not have first-hand experience of Germany himself, but presumably he could draw on the knowledge of Roman soldiers and merchants, which appears to have been very limited.*

(a)
Tacitus' division of the German tribes into groups differs from that of Pliny (M2 (c)).

1   Germany as a whole is separated from the Gauls and from Raetians and Pannonians by the rivers Rhine and Danube: from the Sarmatians and Dacians by mutual misgivings or mountains: the rest of it is surrounded by the ocean, which enfolds wide peninsulas and islands of vast expanse, some of whose peoples and their kings have but recently become known to us: war has lifted the curtain.

The Rhine, rising from the inaccessible and precipitous crest of the Raetian Alps, after turning west for a reach of some length is lost in the North Sea. The Danube pours from the sloping and not very lofty ridge of Mount Abnoba, and visits more peoples on its course than the Rhine does, until at length it emerges by six of its outlets into the Pontic Sea: the seventh mouth is swallowed in marshes.

2   As for the Germans themselves, I should suppose them to be indigenous and very slightly blended with new arrivals from other races or alliances; for originally people who sought to migrate reached their destination in fleets and not by land; while, in the second place, the leagues of ocean on the farther side of Germany, at the opposite end of the world, so to speak, from us, are rarely visited by ships from our world. Besides, who, to say nothing about the perils of an awful and unknown sea, would have left Asia or Africa or Italy to look for Germany? With its wild scenery and harsh climate it is pleasant neither to live in nor look upon unless it be one's fatherland.

Their ancient hymns—the only style of record or history which they possess—celebrate a god Tuisto, a scion of the soil. To him they ascribe a son Mannus, the beginning of their race, and to Mannus three sons, its founders; from whose names the tribes nearest the Ocean are to be known as Ingaevones, the central tribes as Herminones, and the rest as Istaevones. Some authorities, using the licence which pertains to antiquity, pronounce for more sons to the god and a larger number of race names, Marsi, Gambrivii, Suebi, Vandilii; these are, they say, real and ancient names, while the name of 'Germany' is new and a recent application. The first tribes in fact to cross the Rhine and expel the Gauls, though now called Tungri, then bore the name Germans: so little by little the name—a tribal, not a national, name—prevailed, until the whole people were called by the artificial name of

'Germans,' first only by the victorious tribe Tungri in order to intimidate the Gauls, but afterwards by themselves also.

Tacitus *Germania* 1–2
tr. M. Hutton rev. E. H. Warmington (Loeb 1970)

(b)

This account reflects the traditional Roman view of the Germans.

28 That the fortunes of the Gaul were once higher than the German is recorded on the supreme authority of Julius of happy memory, and therefore it is easy to believe that the Gauls even crossed over into Germany: small chance there was of the river preventing each tribe, as it became powerful, from seizing and taking in exchange new land, still held in common, and not yet divided into powerful kingdoms: accordingly the country between the Hercynian forest and the rivers Rhine and Moenus [Main] was occupied by the Helvetii, and the country beyond by the Boii, both Gallic races: the name Boihaemum still subsists and testifies to the old traditions of the place, though there has been a change of occupants.

Whether, however, the Aravisci migrated into Pannonia from the Osi, or the Osi into Germany from the Aravisci, must remain uncertain, since their speech, habits, and type of character are still the same: originally, in fact, there was the same misery and the same freedom on either bank of the river, the same advantages and the same drawbacks.

The Treveri and Nervii conversely go out of their way in their ambition to claim a German origin, as though this illustrious ancestry delivers them from any affinity with the indolent Gaul.

On the river-bank itself are planted certain peoples indubitably German: Vangiones, Triboci, Nemetes. Not even the Ubii, though they have earned the right to be a Roman colony and prefer to be called 'Agrippinenses,' from the name of their founder, blush to own their German origin: they originally came from beyond the river, and were placed in charge of the bank itself, after they had given proof of their loyalty, in order to block the way to others, not in order to be under supervision.

29 Of all these races the most manly are the Batavi, who occupy only a short stretch of the river-bank, but with it the island in the stream: they were once a tribe of the Chatti, and on account of a rising at home they crossed the river for those lands which were to make them part of the Roman Empire. Their distinction persists and the emblem of their ancient alliance with us: they are not insulted, that is, with the exaction of tribute, and there is no tax-farmer to oppress them: immune from burdens and contributions, and set apart for fighting purposes only, they are reserved for war, to be, as it were, arms and weapons. In the same allegiance are the tribe of the Mattiaci; for the greatness of the Roman nation has projected the awe felt for our Empire beyond the Rhine, and beyond the long-established frontier. So by site and territory they belong to their own bank, but by sentiment and thought they act with us, and correspond in all respects with the

Batavi, except that among other things both the soil and climate of their land of themselves stimulate to greater animation.

I should not count among the people of Germany, though they have established themselves beyond the Rhine and Danube, the tribes who cultivate 'the ten-lands.' All the wastrels of Gaul, plucking courage from misery, took possession of that debatable land: latterly, since the frontier line has been driven and the garrisons pushed forward, these lands have been counted an outlying corner of the Empire and a part of a Roman province.

30   Beyond these people, the Chatti begin the front of their settlements with the Hercynian forest. The land is not so low and marshy as the other states of the level German plain; yet even where the hills cover a considerable territory they gradually fade away, and so the Hercynian forest, after escorting its Chatti to the full length of their settlement, drops them in the plain. This tribe has hardier bodies than the others, close-knit limbs, a forbidding expression, and more strength of intellect: there is much method in what they do, for Germans at least, and much shrewdness. They promote to office men of their own choice, and listen to the men so promoted; know their place in the ranks and recognise opportunities; reserve their attack; plan out their day; entrench at night; distrust luck, but rely on courage; and—the rarest thing of all, which only Roman discipline has been permitted to attain—depend on the initiative of the general rather than on that of the soldier. Their whole strength lies in their infantry, whom they load with iron tools and baggage, in addition to their arms: other Germans may be seen going to battle, but the Chatti go to war. Forays and casual fighting are rare with them: the latter method no doubt is part of the strength of cavalry—to win suddenly, that is, and as suddenly to retire; in infantry speed is near allied to panic, and deliberate action is more likely to be resolute.

Tacitus *Germania* 28–30
tr. M. Hutton, rev. E. H. Warmington (Loeb 1970)

M4   The defeat of Lollius

In 17 BC Marcus Lollius, then legate in Gaul, was defeated by a band of Germans on a raid. This has been seen as a major disaster (cf. Suetonius Augustus 23. 1, Velleius, 2. 97; Tac. Annals 1. 10. 3–B35), but the second part of this passage indicates that Lollius' defeat may have been exaggerated (see further Syme RR p. 429) Augustus' subsequent campaigns against the Germans were probably not a direct result of this incident as there is evidence of planning and preparations before 17 BC (see C. M. Wells The German Policy of Augustus p. 95).

The greatest, however, of the wars which at that time fell to the lot of the Romans, and the one presumably which drew Augustus away from the city, was that against the Germans. It seems that the Sugambri, Usipetes, and Tencteri had first seized in their own territory some of the Romans and had crucified them, after which they had crossed the Rhine and plundered Germania and Gaul. When the Roman cavalry approached, they surprised them from ambush; then, pursuing them as they fled, they fell in unexpectedly with Lollius, the governor of the province, and conquered him also. On learning of all this, Augustus hastened against them, but found no warfare to carry on; for the barbarians, learning that Lollius was making preparations and that the emperor was also taking the field, retired into their own territory and made peace, giving hostages.

Dio Cassius 54. 20. 4-6
tr. E. Cary (Loeb 1917)

M5 The new army regulations of 13 BC

Augustus was in Gaul between 16 and 13 BC and in 12 BC the Roman armies, under Drusus, invaded the lands of the Usipetes and Sugambri. On his return to Rome in 13 BC, Augustus promulgated changes in the army regulations (cf. C3) ensuring a professional standing army whose loyalty would be to the head of state rather than to individual commanders. The sum of money awarded to soldiers at the end of their term of service was paid out of Augustus's own private resources until AD 6 when the aerarium militare *was established (see C3 (c)); for a bibliography of the service conditions, pay, and recruitment of the Roman army see G. Webster* The Roman Imperial Army[2] *(A. & C. Black 1979).*

Now when Augustus had finished all the business which occupied him in the several provinces of Gaul, of Germany and of Spain, having spent large sums upon special districts and received large sums from others, having bestowed freedom and citizenship upon some and taken them away from others, he left Drusus in Germany and returned to Rome himself in the consulship of Tiberius and Quintilius Varus. . . .

After this he convened the senate, and though he made no address himself by reason of hoarseness, he gave his manuscript to the quaestor to read and thus enumerated his achievements and promulgated rules as to the number of years the citizens should serve in the army and as to the amount of money they should receive when discharged from service, in lieu of the land which they were always demanding. His object was that the soldiers, by being enlisted henceforth on certain definite terms, should find no excuse for revolt on this score. The number of years was twelve for the Pretorians and sixteen for the rest; and the money to be distributed was less in some cases and more in others. These measures caused the soldiers neither pleasure nor anger for the time being, because they neither obtained all they desired nor yet failed of all; but in the rest of the population the measures aroused confident hopes that they would not in future be robbed of their possessions.

Dio Cassius 54. 25. 1; 5-6 tr. E. Cary (Loeb 1917)

M6 The campaigns of Drusus

(a)

Drusus' campaigns of 12/11 BC against the German tribe of the Usipetes who lived in the area east of the Rhine and north of the Lippe were successful. The experience to which Dio refers in his first sentence is that Augustus denied Drusus a triumph, as he had denied one to Tiberius for victory over the Pannonians (Dio Cassius 54. 31. 4).

(a)

Drusus had this same experience. The Sugambri and their allies had resorted to war, owing to the absence of Augustus and the fact that the Gauls were restive under their slavery, and Drusus therefore seized the subject territory ahead of them, sending for the foremost men in it on the pretext of the festival which they celebrate even now around the altar of Augustus at Lugdunum. He also waited for the Germans to cross the Rhine, and then repulsed them. Next he crossed over to the country of the Usipetes, passing along the very island of the Batavians, and from there marched along the river to the Sugambrian territory, where he devastated much country. He sailed down the Rhine to the ocean, won over the Frisians, and crossing the lake, invaded the country of the Chauci, where he ran into danger, as his ships were left high and dry by the ebb of the ocean. He was saved on this occasion by the Frisians, who had joined his expedition with their infantry, and withdrew, since it was now winter. Upon arriving in Rome he was appointed praetor urbanus, in the consulship of Quintius Aelius and Paulus Fabius, although he already had the rank of praetor. At the beginning of spring he set out again for the war, crossed the Rhine, and subjugated the Usipetes. He bridged the Lupia, invaded the country of the Sugambri, and advanced through it into the country of the Cherusci, as far as the Visurgis. He was able to do this because the Sugambri, in anger at the Chatti, the only tribe among their neighbours that had refused to join their alliance, had made a campaign against them with all their population; and seizing this opportunity, he traversed their country unnoticed. He would have crossed the Visurgis also, had he not run short of provisions, and had not the winter set in and, besides, a swarm of bees been seen in his camp. Consequently he proceeded no farther, but retired to friendly territory, encountering great dangers on the way. For the enemy harassed him everywhere by ambuscades, and once they shut him up in a narrow pass and all but destroyed his army; indeed, they would have annihilated them, had they not conceived a contempt for them, as if they were already captured and needed only the finishing stroke, and so come to close quarters with them in disorder. This led to their being worsted, after which they were no longer so bold, but kept up a petty annoyance of his troops from a distance, while refusing to come nearer. Drusus accordingly conceived a scorn of them in his turn and fortified a stronghold against them at the point where the Lupia and the Eliso unite, and also another among the Chatti on the bank of the Rhine. For these successes he received the triumphal honours, the right to ride into the city on horseback, and to exercise the powers of a proconsul when he should finish his term as praetor. Indeed, the title of *imperator* was given him by the soldiers by acclamation as it had been given to Tiberius earlier; but it was not granted to him by Augustus, although the number of times the emperor himself gained this appellation was increased as the result of the exploits of these two men.

Dio Cassius 54. 32-3
tr. E. Cary (Loeb 1917)

(b)

Drusus continued campaigning in Germany until his death in 9 BC; he had reached the Weser without being opposed by the Sugambri, who were occupied in fighting the Chatti (11 BC; see Dio Cassius 54. 33 above), and the following year he turned against the Chatti. The closing of the temple of Janus would have been a premature indication of peace, or rather of the successful subjugation of the German tribes; Drusus continued the war against the Chatti in the following year, then turned north against the Cherusci (Dio Cassius 55. 1. 2 ff.) and reached the Elbe, but his death soon after prevented him from consolidating his military victories.

It was voted that the temple of Janus Geminus, which had been opened, should be closed, on the ground that the wars had ceased. It was not closed, however, for the Dacians, crossing the Ister on the ice, carried off booty from Pannonia, and the Dalmatians rebelled against the exactions of tribute. Against these people Tiberius was sent from Gaul, whither he had gone in company with Augustus; and he reduced them again to submission. The Germans, particularly the Chatti, were either harassed or subjugated by Drusus. The Chatti, it seems, had gone to join the Sugambri, having abandoned their own country, which the Romans had given them to dwell in. Afterwards Tiberius and Drusus returned to Rome with Augustus, who had been tarrying in Lugdunensis much of the time, keeping watch on the Germans from near at hand; and they carried out whatever decrees had been passed in honour of their victories or did whatever else devolved upon them.

Dio Cassius 54. 36. 2-4
tr. E. Cary (Loeb 1917)

M7 Tiberius' campaigns in Germany

(a)

Augustus's imperium was renewed in 8 BC; Tiberius took over the command of the German campaigns, and was awarded a triumph. This passage indicates that Augustus was not always ready to conclude peace treaties (cf. Suetonius Augustus 21. 1-2–C3 (b)); the treatment of the envoys indicates a determination to pursue the military defeat and subjugation of the German tribes.

After this, now that his second period of ten years had expired, Augustus once more accepted the supreme power,—though with a show of reluctance,—in spite of his oft-expressed desire to lay it down; and he made a campaign against the Germans. He himself remained behind in Roman territory, while Tiberius crossed the Rhine. Accordingly all the barbarians except the Sugambri, through fear of them, made overtures of peace; but they gained nothing either at this time,—for Augustus refused to conclude a truce with them without the Sugambri,—or, indeed, later. To be sure, the Sugambri also sent envoys, but so far were they from accomplishing anything that all these envoys, who were both many and distinguished, perished into the bargain. For Augustus arrested them and placed them in various cities; and they, being greatly distressed at this, took their own lives. The Sugambri were thereupon quiet for a time, but later they amply requited the Romans for their calamity.

Dio Cassius 55. 6. 1–3
tr. E. Cary (Loeb 1917)

(b)

Tiberius' exile in Rhodes lasted from 6 BC to AD 4; in his absence, L. Domitius Ahenobarbus, campaigning in Germany, crossed the Elbe and set up an altar to Augustus (Zonaras, Epitome of Dio Cassius *55. 10a). Ahenobarbus seems to have had unsuccessful relations with the Cherusci, which 'caused the other barbarians. . . to conceive a contempt for the Romans' (Zonaras loc. cit). War broke out and for three years was successfully conducted by M. Vinicius (Velleius Paterculus 2. 104. 2), but in AD 4 Augustus recalled Tiberius, adopted him (see B55) and sent him to Germany. Velleius' eulogistic account is certainly exaggerated, but in AD 6 Augustus was able to turn against the kingdom of Maroboduus in Bohemia, implying that Tiberius appeared to have successfully pacified Germany.*

It was at this time that I became a soldier in the camp of Tiberius Caesar, after having previously filled the duties of the tribunate. For, immediately after the adoption of Tiberius, I was sent with him to Germany as prefect of cavalry, succeeding my father in that position, and for nine continuous years as prefect of cavalry or as commander of a legion I was a spectator of his superhuman achievements, and further assisted in them to the extent of my modest ability. I do not think that mortal man will be permitted to behold again a sight like that which I enjoyed, when, throughout the most populous parts of Italy and the full extent of the provinces of Gaul, the people as they beheld once more their old commander, who by virtue of his services had long been a Caesar before he was such in name, congratulated themselves in even heartier terms than they congratulated him. Indeed, words cannot express the feelings of the soldiers at their meeting, and perhaps my account will scarcely be believed—the tears which sprang to their eyes in their joy at the sight of him, their eagerness, their strange transports in saluting him, their longing to touch his hand, and their inability to restrain such cries as 'Is it really you that we see, commander?' 'Have we received you safely back among us?' 'I served with you, general, in Armenia!' 'And I in Raetia!' 'I received my decoration from you in Vindelicia!' 'And I mine in Pannonia!' 'And I in Germany!'

He at once entered Germany. The Canninefates, the Attuarii, and Bructeri were subdued, the Cherusci (Arminius, a member of this race, was soon to become famous for the disaster inflicted upon us) were again subjugated, the Weser crossed, and the regions beyond it penetrated. Caesar claimed for himself every part of the war that was difficult or dangerous, placing Sentius Saturninus, who had already served as legate under his father in Germany, in charge of expeditions of a less dangerous character: a man many-sided in his virtues, a man of energy, of action, and of foresight, alike able to endure the duties of a soldier as he was well trained in them, but who, likewise, when his labours left room for leisure, made a liberal and elegant use of it, but with this reservation, that one would call him sumptuous and jovial rather than extravagant or indolent. About the distinguished ability of this illustrious man and his famous consulship I have already spoken. The prolonging of the campaign of that year into the month of December increased the benefits derived from the great victory. Caesar was drawn to the city by his filial affection, though the Alps were almost blocked by winter's snows; but the defence of the empire brought him at the beginning of spring back to Germany, where he had on his departure pitched his winter camp at the source of the river Lippe, in the very heart of the country, the first Roman to winter there.

Ye Heavens, how large a volume could be filled with the tale of our achievements in the following summer under the generalship of Tiberius Caesar! All Germany was traversed by our armies, races were conquered hitherto almost unknown, even by name; and the tribes of the Cauchi were again subjugated. All the flower of their youth, infinite in number though they were, huge of stature and protected by the ground they held, surrendered their arms, and, flanked by a gleaming line of our soldiers, fell with their generals upon their knees before the tribunal of the commander. The power of the Langobardi was broken, a race surpassing even the Germans in savagery; and finally—and this is something which had never before been entertained even as a hope, much less actually attempted—a Roman army with its standards was led four hundred miles beyond the Rhine as far as the river Elbe, which flows past the territories of the Semnones and the Hermunduri. And with the same wonderful combination of careful planning and good fortune on the part of the general, and a close watch upon the seasons, the fleet which had skirted the windings of the sea coast sailed up the Elbe from a sea hitherto unheard of and unknown, and after proving victorious over many tribes effected a junction with Caesar and the army, bringing with it a great abundance of supplies of all kinds.

Velleius Paterculus 2. 104. 3–106
tr. F. W. Shipley (Loeb 1924)

M8 The Varian Disaster

The Dalmatians rebelled in AD 6 when they were required to raise levies for the invasion of Bohemia, and the revolt spread throughout Illyria. Tiberius finally crushed the revolt in AD 9, but a great cost to Rome. The loss of Varus' three legions was a terrible blow to Augustus (see Suetonius Augustus *80). Velleius' account puts the blame completely on Varus, but see R. Syme (*CAH *vol. 10 p.374) for the view that Augustus' judgement was at fault.*

(a)
Arminius was leader of only a part of his own tribe but by annihilating Varus' army destroyed Roman prestige and her hold on Germany. Tiberius was dispatched with an impressive force but he did not venture far or for long beyond the Rhine (Velleius Paterculus 2. 121 ff.).

Scarcely had Caesar put the finishing touch upon the Pannonian and Dalmatian war, when, within five days of the completion of this task, dispatches from Germany brought the baleful news of the death of Varus, and of the slaughter of three legions, of as many divisions of cavalry, and of six cohorts—as though fortune were granting us this indulgence at least, that such a disaster should not be brought upon us when our commander was occupied by other wars. The cause of this defeat and the personality of the general require of me a brief digression.

Varus Quintilius, descended from a famous rather than a high-born family, was a man of mild character and of a quiet disposition, somewhat slow in mind as he was in body, and more accustomed to the leisure of the camp than to actual service in war. That he was no despiser of money is demonstrated by his governorship of Syria: he entered the rich province a poor man, but left it a rich man and the province poor. When placed in charge of the army in Germany, he entertained the notion that the Germans were a people who were men only in limbs and voice, and that they, who could not be subdued by the sword, could be soothed by the law. With this purpose in mind he entered the heart of Germany as though he were going among a people enjoying the blessings of peace, and sitting on his tribunal he wasted the time of a summer campaign in holding court and observing the proper details of legal procedure.

But the Germans, who with their great ferocity combine great craft, to an extent scarcely credible to one who has had no experience with them, and are a race to lying born, by trumping up a series of fictitious lawsuits, now provoking one another to disputes, and now expressing their gratitude that Roman justice was settling these disputes, that their own barbarous nature was being softened down by this new and hitherto unknown method, and that quarrels which were usually settled by arms were now being ended by law, brought Quintilius to such a complete degree of negligence, that he came to look upon himself as a city praetor administering justice in the forum, and not a general in command of an army in the heart of Germany. Thereupon appeared a young man of noble birth, brave in action and alert in mind, possessing an intelligence quite beyond the ordinary barbarian; he was, namely, Arminius, the son of Sigimer, a prince of that nation, and he showed in his countenance and in his eyes the fire of the mind within. He had been associated with us constantly on previous campaigns, had been granted the right of Roman citizenship, and had even attained the dignity of equestrian rank. This young man made use of the negligence of the general as an opportunity for treachery, sagaciously seeing that no one could be more quickly overpowered than the man who feared nothing, and that the most common beginning of disaster was a sense of security. At first, then, he admitted but a few, later a large number, to a share in his design; he told them, and convinced them too, that the Romans could be crushed, added execution to resolve, and named a day for carrying out the plot. This was disclosed to Varus through Segestes, a loyal man of that race and of illustrious name, who also demanded that the conspirators be put in chains. But fate now dominated the plans of Varus and had blindfolded the eyes of his mind. Indeed, it is usually the case that heaven perverts the judgement of the man whose fortune it means to reverse, and brings it to pass—and this is the wretched part of it—that that which happens by chance seems to be deserved, and accident passes over into culpability. And so Quintilius refused to believe the story, and insisted upon judging the apparent friendship of the Germans toward him by the standard of his merit. And, after this first warning, there was no time left for a second.

The details of this terrible calamity, the heaviest that had befallen the Romans on foreign soil since the disaster of Crassus in Parthia, I shall endeavour to set forth, as others have done, in my larger work. Here I can merely lament the disaster as a whole. An army unexcelled in bravery, the first of Roman armies in discipline, in energy, and in experience in the field, through the negligence of its general, the perfidy of the enemy, and the unkindness of fortune was surrounded, nor was as much opportunity as they had wished given to the soldiers either of fighting or of extricating themselves, except against heavy odds; nay, some were even heavily chastised for using the arms and showing the spirit of Romans. Hemmed in by forests and marshes and ambuscades, it was exterminated almost to a man by the very enemy whom it had always slaughtered like cattle, whose life or death had depended solely upon the wrath or the pity of the Romans. The general had more courage to die than to fight, for, following the example of his father and grandfather, he ran himself through with his sword. Of the two prefects of the camp, Lucius Eggius furnished a precedent as noble as that of Ceionius was base, who, after the greater part of the army had perished, proposed its surrender, preferring to die by torture at the hands of the enemy than in battle. Vala Numonius, lieutenant of Varus, who, in the rest of his life, had been an inoffensive and an honourable man, also set a fearful example in that he left the infantry unprotected by the cavalry and in flight tried to reach the Rhine with his squadrons of horse. But fortune avenged his act, for he did not survive those whom he had abandoned, but died in the act of deserting them. The body of Varus, partially burned, was mangled by the enemy in their barbarity; his head was cut off and taken to Maroboduus and was sent by him to Caesar; but in spite of the disaster it was honoured by burial in the tomb of his family.

On hearing of this disaster, Caesar flew to his father's side. The constant protector of the Roman empire again took up his accustomed part. Dispatched to Germany, he reassured the provinces of Gaul, distributed his armies, strengthened the garrison towns, and then, measuring himself by the standard of his own greatness, and not by the presumption of an enemy who threatened Italy with a war like that of the Cimbri and Teutones, he took the offensive and crossed the Rhine with his army. He thus made aggressive war upon the enemy when his father and his country would have been content to let him hold them in check, he penetrated into the heart of the country, opened up military roads, devastated fields, burned houses, routed those who came against him, and, without loss to the troops with which he had crossed, he returned, covered with glory, to winter quarters.

Due tribute should be paid to Lucius Asprenas, who was serving as lieutenant under Varus his uncle, and who, backed by the brave and energetic support of the two legions under his command, saved his army from this great disaster, and by a quick descent to the quarters of the army in Lower Germany strengthened the allegiance of the races even on the hither side of the Rhine who were beginning to waver. There are those, however, who believed that, though he had saved the lives of the living, he had appropriated to his own use the property of the dead who were slain with Varus, and that inheritances of the slaughtered army were claimed by him at pleasure. The valour of Lucius Caedicius, prefect of the camp, also deserves praise, and of those who, pent up with him at Aliso, were besieged by an immense force of Germans. For, overcoming all their difficulties which want rendered unendurable and the forces of the enemy almost insurmountable, following a design that was carefully considered, and using a vigilance that was ever on the alert, they watched their chance, and with the sword won their way back to their friends. From all this it is evident that Varus, who was, it must be confessed, a man of character and of good intentions, lost his life and his magnificent army more through lack of judgement in the commander than of valour in his soldiers. When the Germans were venting their rage upon their captives, an heroic act was performed by Caldus Caelius, a young man worthy in every way of his long line of ancestors, who, seizing a section of the chain with which he was bound, brought it down with such force upon his own head as to cause his instant death, both his brains and his blood gushing from the wound.

> Velleius Paterculus 2. 117–20
> tr. F. W. Shipley (Loeb 1924)

(b)

Dio's account is a more plausible description of the situation in Germany: Romanization had begun, markets and assemblies were set up. Varus was mistaken in trying to do too much too fast, in assuming too readily that military force was no longer needed in Germany to maintain Roman rule. C. M. Wells, The German Policy of Augustus *(Oxford 1972) p. 239, maintains that the mistake may well have been made at Rome by underestimating the force needed to keep Germany quiet and the time necessary for the Germans to adapt to Roman culture and civilization.*

Scarcely had these decrees been passed, when terrible news that arrived from the province of Germany prevented them from holding the festival. I shall now relate the events which had taken place in Germany during this period. The Romans were holding portions of it—not entire regions, but merely such districts as happened to have been subdued, so that no record has been made of the fact—and soldiers of theirs were wintering there and cities were being founded. The barbarians were adapting themselves to Roman ways, were becoming accustomed to hold markets, and were meeting in peaceful assemblages. They had not, however, forgotten their ancestral habits, their native manners, their old life of independence, or the power derived from arms. Hence, so long as they were unlearning these customs gradually and by the way, as one may say, under careful watching, they were not disturbed by the change in their manner of life, and were becoming different without knowing it. But when Quintilius Varus became governor of the province of Germany, and in the discharge of his official duties was administering the affairs of these peoples also, he strove to change them more rapidly. Besides issuing orders to them as if they were actually slaves of the Romans, he exacted money as he would from subject nations. To this they were in no mood to submit, for the leaders longed for their former ascendancy and the masses preferred their accustomed condition to foreign domination. Now they did not openly revolt, since they saw that there were many Roman troops near the Rhine and many within their own borders; instead, they received Varus, pretending that they would do all he demanded of them, and thus they drew him far away from the Rhine into the land of the Cherusci, toward the Visurgis, and there by behaving in a most peaceful and friendly manner led him to believe that they would live submissively without the presence of soldiers.

Consequently he did not keep his legions together, as was proper in a hostile country, but distributed many of the soldiers to helpless communities, which asked for them for the alleged purpose of guarding various points, arresting robbers, or escorting provision trains. Among those deepest in the conspiracy and leaders of the plot and of the war were Armenius and Segimerus, who were his constant companions and often shared his mess. He accordingly became confident, and expecting no harm, not only refused to believe all those who suspected what was going on and advised him to be on his guard, but actually rebuked them for being needlessly excited and slandering his friends. Then there came an uprising, first on the part of those who lived at a distance from him, deliberately so arranged, in order that Varus should march against them and so be more easily overpowered while proceeding through what was supposed to be friendly country, instead of putting himself on his guard as he would do in case all became hostile to him at once. And so it came to pass. They escorted him as he set out, and then begged to be excused from further attendance, in order, as they claimed, to assemble their allied forces, after which they would quickly come to his aid. Then they took charge of their troops, which were already in waiting somewhere, and after the men in each community had put to death the detachments of soldiers for which they had previously asked, they came upon Varus in the midst of forests by this time almost impenetrable.

And there, at the very moment of revealing themselves as enemies instead of subjects, they wrought great and dire havoc.

Dio Cassius 56. 18–19
tr. E. Cary (Loeb 1917)

M9 The mutiny on the Rhine (AD 14)

On the death of Augustus the legions on the Rhine mutinied. Germanicus used every means at his disposal to quell the rebellion, including emotional blackmail (Tacitus Annals 1. 31 ff. gives a full account—cf. K6), and finally diverted their energies and attentions by an attack across the Rhine, on the Marsi.

49   No civil war of any period has presented the features of this. Not in battle, not from opposing camps, but comrades from the same bed—men who had eaten together by day and rested together at dark—they took their sides and hurled their missiles. The yells, the wounds, and the blood were plain enough; the cause, invisible: chance ruled supreme. A number of the loyal troops perished as well: for, once it was clear who were the objects of attack, the malcontents also had caught up arms. No general or tribune was there to restrain: licence was granted to the mob, and it might glut its vengeance to the full. Before long, Germanicus marched into the camp. 'This is not a cure, but a calamity,' he said, with a burst of tears, and ordered the bodies to be cremated.

   Even yet the temper of the soldiers remained savage and a sudden desire came over them to advance against the enemy: it would be the expiation of their madness; nor could the ghosts of their companions be appeased till their own impious breasts had been marked with honourable wounds. Falling in with the enthusiasm of his troops, the Caesar laid a bridge over the Rhine, and threw across twelve thousand legionaries, with twenty-six cohorts of auxiliaries and eight divisions of cavalry, whose discipline had not been affected by the late mutiny.

   50   Throughout the pause, which the mourning for Augustus had begun and our discords prolonged, the Germans had been hovering gleefully in the neighbourhood. By a forced march, however, the Roman columns cut through the Caesian Forest and the line of delimitation commenced by Tiberius. By this line they pitched the camp, with their front and rear protected by embankments and the flanks by a barricade of felled trees. Then came a threading of gloomy forests and a consultation which of two roads to follow; the one short and usual, the other more difficult and unexplored, and therefore left unguarded by the enemy. The longer route was chosen, but otherwise all speed was made: for scouts had brought in news that the night was a German festival and would be celebrated with games and a solemn banquet. Caecina was ordered to move ahead with the unencumbered cohorts and clear a passage through the woods: the legions followed at a moderate

interval. The clear, starry night was in our favour; the Marsian villages were reached, and a ring of pickets was posted round the enemy, who were still lying, some in bed, others beside their tables, without misgivings and with no sentries advanced. All was disorder and improvidence: there was no apprehension of war, and even their peace was the nerveless lethargy of drunkards.

51   To extend the scope of the raid, the Caesar divided his eager legions into four bodies, and, for fifty miles around, wasted the country with sword and flame. Neither age nor sex inspired pity: places sacred and profane were razed indifferently to the ground; among them, the most noted religious centre of these tribes, known as the temple of Tanfana. The troops escaped without a wound: they had been cutting down men half-asleep, unarmed or dispersed.

The carnage brought the Bructeri, Tubantes, and Usipetes into the field; and they occupied the forest passes by which the army was bound to return. This came to the prince's ear, and he took the road prepared either to march or to fight. A detachment of cavalry and ten auxiliary cohorts led the way, then came the first legion; the baggage-train was in the centre; the twenty-first legion guarded the left flank; the fifth, the right; the twentieth held the rear, and the rest of the allies followed. The enemy, however, made no move, till the whole line was defiling through the wood: then instituting a half-serious attack on the front and flanks, they threw their full force on the rear. The light-armed cohorts were falling into disorder before the serried German masses, when the Caesar rode up to the men of the twenty-first, and, raising his voice, kept crying that now was their time to efface the stain of mutiny:—'Forward, and make speed to turn disgrace into glory!' In a flame of enthusiasm, they broke through their enemies at one charge, drove them into the open and cut them down. Simultaneously the forces in the van emerged from the forest and fortified a camp. From this point the march was un-molested, and the soldiers, emboldened by their late performances, and forgetful of the past, were stationed in winter quarters.

Tacitus *Annals* 1. 49–51
tr. J. Jackson (Loeb 1931)

M10   The further campaigns of Germanicus

Germanicus continued his campaigns in Germany in AD 15 and 16, Tacitus' account is biased as, contrasting Germanicus with Tiberius, he builds up an image of a successful, beloved, glorious commander (see also K6). For the topography of Germanicus' campaigns see Koestermann 'Die Feldzüge des Germanicus 14–16 n. Chr.' Historia 6 (1957) 429–79.

(a)
55   Drusus Caesar and Gaius Norbanus were now consuls, and a triumph was decreed to Germanicus with the war still in progress. He was preparing to prosecute

it with his utmost power in the summer; but in early spring he anticipated matters by a sudden raid against the Chatti. Hopes had arisen that the enemy was becoming divided between Arminius and Segestes: both famous names, one for perfidy towards us, the other for good faith. Arminius was the troubler of Germany: Segestes had repeatedly given warning of projected risings, especially at the last great banquet which preceded the appeal to arms; when he urged Varus to arrest Arminius himself, and the other chieftains, on the ground that, with their leaders out of the way, the mass of the people would venture nothing, while he would have time enough later to discriminate between guilt and innocence. Varus, however, succumbed to his fate and the sword of Arminius; Segestes, though forced into the war by the united will of the nation, continued to disapprove, and domestic episodes embittered the feud: for Arminius by carrying off his daughter, who was pledged to another, had made himself the hated son-in-law of a hostile father, and a relationship which cements the affection of friends now stimulated the fury of enemies.

56   Germanicus, then, after handing over to Caecina four legions, with five thousand auxiliaries and a few German bands drawn at summary notice from the west bank of the Rhine, took the field himself with as many legions and double the number of allies. Erecting a fort over the remains of his father's works on Mount Taunus, he swept his army at full speed against the Chatti: Lucius Apronius was left behind to construct roads and bridges. For owing to the drought—a rare event under those skies—and the consequent shallowness of the streams, Germanicus had pushed on without a check; and rains and floods were to be apprehended on the return journey. Actually, his descent was so complete a surprise to the Chatti that all who suffered from the disabilities of age or sex were immediately taken or slaughtered. The able-bodied males had swum the Eder, and, as the Romans began to bridge it, made an effort to force them back. Repelled by the engines and discharges of arrows, they tried, without effect, to negotiate terms of peace: a few then came over to Germanicus, while the rest abandoned their townships and villages, and scattered through the woods. First burning the tribal headquarters at Mattium, the Caesar laid waste the open country, and turned back to the Rhine, the enemy not daring to harass the rear of the withdrawing force—their favourite manœuvre in cases where strategy rather than panic has dictated their retreat. The Cherusci had been inclined to throw in their lot with the Chatti, but were deterred by a series of rapid movements on the part of Caecina: the Marsi, who hazarded an engagement, he checked in a successful action.

57   It was not long before envoys arrived from Segestes with a petition for aid against the violence of his countrymen, by whom he was besieged, Arminius being now the dominant figure, since he advocated war. For with barbarians the readier a man is to take a risk so much the more is he the man to trust, the leader to prefer when action is afoot. Segestes had included his son Segimundus in the embassy, though conscience gave the youth pause. For in the year when the Germanies revolted, priest though he was, consecrated at the Altar of the Ubians, he had torn off his fillets and fled to join the rebels. Once persuaded, however, that he could still hope in Roman clemency, he brought his father's message, and, after a kind

reception, was sent over with a guard to the Gallic bank. Germanicus thought it worth his while to turn back, engaged the blockading forces, and rescued Segestes with a large company of his relatives and dependants. They included some women of high birth, among them the wife of Arminius, who was at the same time the daughter of Segestes, though there was more of the husband than the father in that temper which sustained her, unconquered to a tear, without a word of entreaty, her hands clasped tightly in the folds of her robe and her gaze fixed on her heavy womb. Trophies even of the Varian disaster were brought in—booty allotted in many cases to the very men now surrendering. Segestes himself was present, a huge figure, dauntless in the recollection of treaties honourably kept.

Tacitus *Annals* 1.55-7
tr. J. Jackson (Loeb 1931)

(b)

While Segestes appealed for Roman aid, Arminius tried to spread the war.

60   His appeal roused, not the Cherusci only, but the bordering tribes as well; and it drew into the confederacy his uncle Inguiomerus, whose prestige had long stood high with the Romans. This deepened the alarm of Germanicus, and, to prevent the onslaught from breaking in one great wave, he despatched Caecina with forty Roman cohorts through the Bructeri to the Ems, so as to divide the enemy, while the prefect Pedo led the cavalry along the Frisian frontier.

He himself, with four legions on board, sailed through the lakes; and foot, horse, and fleet met simultaneously on the river mentioned. The Chauci promised a contingent, and were given a place in the ranks. The Bructeri began to fire their belongings, but were routed by Lucius Stertinius, who had been sent out by Germanicus with a detachment of light-armed troops; and while the killing and looting were in progress, he discovered the eagle of the nineteenth legion, which had been lost with Varus. Thence the column moved on to the extremity of the Bructeran possessions, wasting the whole stretch of country between the Ems and the Lippe. They were now not far from the Teutoburgian Forest, where, it was said, the remains of Varus and his legions lay unburied.

61   There came upon the Caesar, therefore, a passionate desire to pay the last tribute to the fallen and their leader, while the whole army present with him were stirred to pity at thought of their kindred, of their friends, ay! and of the chances of battle and of the lot of mankind. Sending Caecina forward to explore the secret forest passes and to throw bridges and causeways over the flooded marshes and treacherous levels they pursued their march over the dismal tract, hideous to sight and memory. Varus' first camp, with its broad sweep and measured spaces for officers and eagles, advertised the labours of three legions: then a half-ruined wall and shallow ditch showed that there the now broken remnant had taken cover. In the plain between were bleaching bones, scattered or in little heaps, as the men had fallen, fleeing or standing fast. Hard by lay splintered spears and limbs of horses,

while human skulls were nailed prominently on the tree-trunks. In the neighbouring groves stood the savage altars at which they had slaughtered the tribunes and chief centurions. Survivors of the disaster, who had escaped the battle or their chains, told how here the legates fell, where the eagles were taken, where the first wound was dealt upon Varus, and where he found death by the suicidal stroke of his own unhappy hand. They spoke of the tribunal from which Arminius made his harangue, all the gibbets and torture-pits for the prisoners, and the arrogance with which he insulted the standards and eagles.

62   And so, six years after the fatal field, a Roman army, present on the ground, buried the bones of the three legions; and no man knew whether he consigned to earth the remains of a stranger or a kinsman, but all thought of all as friends and members of one family, and, with anger rising against the enemy, mourned at once and hated.

At the erection of the funeral-mound the Caesar laid the first sod, paying a dear tribute to the departed, and associating himself with the grief of those around him. But Tiberius disapproved, possibly because he put an invidious construction on all acts of Germanicus, possibly because he held that the sight of the unburied dead must have given the army less alacrity for battle and more respect for the enemy, while a commander, invested with the augurate and administering the most venerable rites of religion, ought to have avoided all contact with a funeral ceremony.

63   Germanicus, however, followed Arminius as he fell back on the wilds, and at the earliest opportunity ordered the cavalry to ride out and clear the level ground in the occupation of the enemy. Arminius, who had directed his men to close up and retire on the woods, suddenly wheeled them round; then gave the signal for his ambush in the glades to break cover. The change of tactics threw our horse into confusion. Reserve cohorts were sent up; but, broken by the impact of the fugitive columns, they had only increased the panic, and the whole mass was being pushed towards swampy ground, familiar to the conquerors but fatal to strangers, when the Caesar came forward with the legions and drew them up in line of battle. This demonstration overawed the enemy and emboldened the troops, and they parted with the balance even.

Shortly afterwards, the prince led his army back to the Ems, and withdrew the legions as he had brought them, on shipboard: a section of the cavalry was ordered to make for the Rhine along the coast of the Northern Ocean. Caecina, who led his own force, was returning by a well-known route, but was none the less warned to cross the Long Bridges as rapidly as possible. These were simply a narrow causeway, running through a wilderness of marshes and thrown up, years before, by Lucius Domitius, the rest was a slough—foul, clinging mud intersected by a maze of rivulets. Round about, the woods sloped gently from the plain; but now they were occupied by Arminius, whose forced march along the shorter roads had been too quick for the Roman soldier, weighted with his baggage and accoutrements. Caecina, none too certain how to relay the old, broken-down bridges and at the same time hold off the enemy, decided to mark out a camp where he stood, so that part of the men could begin work while the others accepted battle.

Tacitus *Annals* 1.60-3 tr. J. Jackson (Loeb 1931)

(c)

Arminius reacted against the submission of Segestes to Germanicus by raising several tribes against the Romans. After pursuing him Germanicus withdrew without having fought a decisive battle. Caecina, who had joined Germanicus with four legions, managed to save his force from a disaster which would have been greater than that of Varus. It was less a victory than a withdrawal with honour only just intact. Tacitus' account of Tiberius' reaction does not take into consideration the inconclusive and wasteful nature of this expedition.

64   Skirmishing, enveloping, charging, the barbarians struggled to break the line of outposts and force their way to the working parties. Labourers and combatants mingled their cries. Everything alike was to the disadvantage of the Romans—the ground, deep in slime and ooze, too unstable for standing fast and too slippery for advancing—the weight of armour on their backs—their inability amid the water to balance the pilum for a throw. The Cherusci, on the other hand, were habituated to marsh-fighting, long of limb, and armed with huge lances to wound from a distance. In fact, the legions were already wavering when night at last released them from the unequal struggle.

Success had made the Germans indefatigable. Even now they took no rest, but proceeded to divert all streams, springing from the surrounding hills, into the plain below, flooding the ground, submerging the little work accomplished, and doubling the task of the soldiery. Still, it was Caecina's fortieth year of active service as commander or commanded, and he knew success and danger too well to be easily perturbed. On balancing the possibilities, he could see no other course than to hold the enemy to the woods until his wounded and the more heavily laden part of the column passed on: for extended between mountain and morass was a level patch which would just allow an attenuated line of battle. The fifth legion was selected for the right flank, the twenty-first for the left; the first was to lead the van, the twentieth to stem the inevitable pursuit.

65   It was a night of unrest, though in contrasted fashions. The barbarians, in high carousal, filled the low-lying valleys and echoing woods with chants of triumph or fierce vociferations: among the Romans were languid fires, broken challenges, and groups of men stretched beside the parapet or straying amid the tents, un-asleep but something less than awake. The general's night was disturbed by a sinister and alarming dream: for he imagined that he saw Quintilius Varus risen, blood-bedraggled, from the marsh, and heard him calling, though he refused to obey and pushed him back when he extended his hand. Day broke, and the legions sent to the wings, either through fear or wilfulness, abandoned their post, hurriedly occu-pying a level piece of ground beyond the morass. Arminius, however, though the way was clear for the attack, did not immediately deliver his onslaught. But when he saw the baggage-train caught in the mire and trenches; the troops around it in confusion; the order of the standards broken, and (as may be expected in a crisis) every man quick to obey his impulse and slow to hear the word of command, he ordered the Germans to break in. 'Varus and the legions,' he cried, 'enchained once

more in the old doom!' And, with the word, he cut through the column at the head of a picked band, their blows being directed primarily at the horses. Slipping in their own blood and the marsh-slime, the beasts threw their riders, scattered all they met, and trampled the fallen underfoot. The eagles caused the greatest difficulty of all, as it was impossible either to advance them against the storm of spears or to plant them in the water-logged soil. Caecina, while attempting to keep the front intact, fell with his horse stabbed under him, and was being rapidly surrounded when the first legion interposed. A point in our favour was the rapacity of the enemy, who left the carnage to pursue the spoils; and towards evening the legions struggled out on to open and solid ground. Nor was this the end of their miseries. A rampart had to be raised and material sought for the earthwork; and most of the tools for excavating soil or cutting turf had been lost. There were no tents for the companies, no dressings for the wounded, and as they divided their rations, foul with dirt or blood, they bewailed the deathlike gloom and that for so many thousands of men but a single day now remained.

66   As chance would have it, a stray horse which had broken its tethering and taken fright at the shouting, threw into confusion a number of men who ran to stop it. So great was the consequent panic (men believed the Germans had broken in) that there was a general rush for the gates, the principal objective being the decuman, which faced away from the enemy and opened the better prospects of escape. Caecina, who had satisfied himself that the fear was groundless, but found command, entreaty, and even physical force, alike powerless to arrest or detain the men, threw himself flat in the gateway; and pity in the last resort barred a road which led over the general's body. At the same time, the tribunes and centurions explained that it was a false alarm.

67   He now collected the troops in front of his quarters, and, first ordering them to listen in silence, warned them of the crisis and its urgency:—'Their one safety lay in the sword; but their resort to it should be tempered with discretion, and they must remain within the rampart till the enemy approached in the hope of carrying it by assault. Then, a sally from all sides—and so to the Rhine! If they fled, they might expect more forests, deeper swamps, and a savage enemy: win the day, and glory and honour were assured.' He reminded them of all they loved at home, all the honour they had gained in camp: of disaster, not a word. Then, with complete impartiality, he distributed the horses of the commanding officers and tribunes—he had begun with his own—to men of conspicuous gallantry; the recipients to charge first, while the infantry followed.

68   Hope, cupidity, and the divided counsels of the chieftains kept the Germans in equal agitation. Arminius proposed to allow the Romans to march out, and, when they had done so, to entrap them once more in wet and broken country; Inguiomerus advocated the more drastic measures dear to the barbarian:—'Let them encircle the rampart in arms. Storming would be easy, captives more plentiful, the booty intact!' So, at break of day, they began demolishing the fosses, threw in hurdles, and struggled to grasp the top of the rampart; on which were ranged a handful of soldiers apparently petrified with terror. But as they swarmed up the

fortifications, the signal sounded to the cohorts, and cornets and trumpets sang to arms. Then, with a shout and a rush, the Romans poured down on the German rear. 'Here were no trees,' they jeered, 'no swamps, but a fair field and an impartial Heaven.' Upon the enemy, whose thoughts were of a quick despatch and a few half-armed defenders, the blare of trumpets and the flash of weapons burst with an effect proportioned to the surprise, and they fell—as improvident in failure as they had been headstrong in success. Arminius and Inguiomerus abandoned the fray, the former unhurt, the latter after a serious wound; the rabble was slaughtered till passion and the daylight waned. It was dusk when the legions returned, weary enough—for wounds were in greater plenty than ever, and provisions in equal scarcity—but finding in victory strength, health, supplies, everything.

69   In the meantime a rumour had spread that the army had been trapped and the German columns were on the march for Gaul; and had not Agrippina prevented the demolition of the Rhine bridge, there were those who in their panic would have braved that infamy. But it was a great-hearted woman who assumed the duties of a general throughout those days; who, if a soldier was in need, clothed him, and if he was wounded, gave him dressings. Pliny, the historian of the German Wars, asserts that she stood at the head of the bridge, offering her praises and her thanks to the returning legions. The action sank deep into the soul of Tiberius. 'There was something behind this officiousness; nor was it the foreigner against whom her courtship of the army was directed. Commanding officers had a sinecure nowadays, when a woman visited the maniples, approached the standards and took in hand to bestow largesses—as though it were not enough to curry favour by parading the general's son in the habit of a common soldier, with the request that he should be called Caesar Caligula! Already Agrippina counted for more with the armies than any general or generalissimo, and a woman had suppressed a mutiny which the imperial name had failed to check.' Sejanus inflamed and exacerbated his jealousies; and, with his expert knowledge of the character of Tiberius, kept sowing the seed of future hatreds—grievances for the emperor to store away and produce some day with increase.

Tacitus *Annals* 1. 64–9
tr. J. Jackson (Loeb 1931)

(d)
The disturbances in the East were due to the struggle for the throne of Armenia after the death of Ariobarzanes in AD 16. Germanicus was preparing for the campaign of AD 16, designed to lead to a final victory in Germany.

5   For Tiberius the disturbances in the East were a not unwelcome accident, as they supplied him with a pretext for removing Germanicus from his familiar legions and appointing him to unknown provinces, where he would be vulnerable at once to treachery and chance. But the keener the devotion of his soldiers and the deeper the aversion of his uncle, the more anxious grew the prince to accelerate his victory;

and he began to consider the ways and means of battle in the light of the failures and successes which had fallen to his share during the past two years of campaigning. In a set engagement and on a fair field, the Germans, he reflected, were beaten—their advantage lay in the forests and swamps, the short summer and the premature winter. His own men were not so much affected by their wounds as by the dreary marches and the loss of their weapons. The Gallic provinces were weary of furnishing horses; and a lengthy baggage-train was easy to waylay and awkward to defend. But if they ventured on the sea, occupation would be easy for themselves and undetected by the enemy; while the campaign might begin at an earlier date, and the legions and supplies be conveyed together: the cavalry and horses would be taken up-stream through the river-mouths and landed fresh in the centre of Germany.

6   To this course, then, he bent his attention. Publius Vitellius and Gaius Antius were sent to assess the Gallic tribute: Silius and Caecina were made responsible for the construction of a fleet. A thousand vessels were considered enough, and these were built at speed. Some were short craft with very little poop or prow, and broad-bellied, the more easily to withstand a heavy sea: others had flat bottoms, enabling them to run aground without damage; while still more were fitted with rudders at each end, so as to head either way the moment the oarsmen reversed their stroke. Many had a deck-flooring to carry the military engines, though they were equally useful for transporting horses or supplies. The whole armada, equipped at once for sailing or propulsion by the oar, was a striking and formidable spectacle, rendered still more so by the enthusiasm of the soldiers. The Isle of Batavia was fixed for the meeting-place, since it afforded an easy landing and was convenient both as a rendezvous for the troops and as the base for a campaign across the water. For the Rhine, which so far has flowed in a single channel, save only where it circles some unimportant islet, branches at the Batavian frontier into what may be regarded as two rivers. On the German side, it runs unchanged in name and vehemence till its juncture with the North Sea: the Gallic bank it washes with a wider, gentler stream, known locally as the Waal, though before long it changes its style once more and becomes the river Meuse, through whose immense estuary it discharges, also into the North Sea.

7   However, while the ships were coming in, the Caesar ordered his lieutenant Silius to take a mobile force and raid the Chattan territory: he himself, hearing that the fort on the Lippe was invested, led six legions to its relief. But neither could Silius, in consequence of the sudden rains, effect anything beyond carrying off a modest quantity of booty, together with the wife and daughter of the Chattan chief, Arpus, nor did the besiegers allow the prince an opportunity of battle, but melted away at the rumour of his approach. Still, they had demolished the funeral mound just raised in memory of the Varian legions, as well as an old altar set up to Drusus. He restored the altar and himself headed the legions in the celebrations in honour of his father; the tumulus it was decided not to reconstruct. In addition, the whole stretch of country between Fort Aliso and the Rhine was thoroughly fortified with a fresh line of barriers and earthworks.

8   The fleet had now arrived. Supplies were sent forward, ships assigned to the legionaries and allies, and he entered the so-called Drusian Fosse. After a prayer to his father, beseeching him of his grace and indulgence to succour by the example and memory of his wisdom and prowess a son who had ventured in his footsteps, he pursued his voyage through the lakes and the high sea, and reached the Ems without misadventure. The fleet stayed in the mouth of the river on the left side, and an error was committed in not carrying the troops further up-stream or dis-embarking them on the right bank for which they were bound; the consequence being that several days were wasted in bridge-building. The estuaries immediately adjoining were crossed intrepidly enough by the cavalry and legions, before the tide had begun to flow: the auxiliaries in the extreme rear and the Batavians in the same part of the line, while dashing into the water and exhibiting their powers of swim-ming, were thrown into disorder, and a number of them drowned. As the Caesar was arranging his encampment, news came of an Angrivarian rising in his rear: Stertinius, who was instantly despatched with a body of horse and light-armed infantry, repaid the treachery with fire and bloodshed.

9   The river Weser ran between the Roman and Cheruscan forces. Arminius came to the bank and halted with his fellow-chieftains:—'Had the Caesar come?' he inquired. On receiving the reply that he was in presence, he asked to be allowed to speak with his brother. That brother, Flavus by name, was serving in the army, a conspicuous figure both from his loyalty and from the loss of an eye through a wound received some few years before during Tiberius' term of command. Leave was granted, (and Stertinius took him down to the river). Walking forward, he was greeted by Arminius; who, dismissing his own escort, demanded that the archers posted along our side of the stream should be also withdrawn. When these had retired, he asked his brother, whence the disfigurement of his face? On being told the place and battle, he inquired what reward he had received. Flavus mentioned his increased pay, the chain, the crown, and other military decorations; Arminius scoffed at the cheap rewards of servitude.

Tacitus *Annals* 2. 5-9
tr. J. Jackson (Loeb 1931)

(e)

After crossing the Weser, Germanicus met the forces of Arminius at a place called Idistaviso, and won a first engagement fought on unfavourable ground chosen by the Germans. Arminius escaped, the German forces regrouped and attacked from the north. The ensuing battle was claimed as a victory by Germanicus; he put up a trophy for conquering the German nations between the Rhine and the Elbe, but withdrew behind the Rhine. 'No attempt seems to have been made to re-occupy Germany in force' (C. M. Wells op. cit. p. 242), and Germanicus withdrew his armies by sea suffering great losses from bad weather. Tacitus' account of Germani-cus' recall has to be read bearing in mind the lack of any gains in territory, the enormous cost of the campaign, and his bias against Tiberius.

25   But though the rumoured loss of the fleet inspired the Germans to hope for war, it also inspired the Caesar to hold them in check. Gaius Silius he ordered to take the field against the Chatti with thirty thousand foot and three thousand horse: he himself with a larger force invaded the Marsi; whose chieftain, Mallovendus, had lately given in his submission, and now intimated that the eagle of one of Varus' legions was buried in an adjacent grove, with only a slender detachment on guard. One company was despatched immediately to draw the enemy by manœuvring on his front; another, to work round the rear and excavate. Both were attended by good fortune; and the Caesar pushed on to the interior with all the more energy, ravaging and destroying an enemy who either dared not engage or was immediately routed wherever he turned to bay. It was gathered from the prisoners that the Germans had never been more completely demoralized. Their cry was that 'the Romans were invincible—proof against every disaster! They had wrecked their fleet, lost their arms; the shores had been littered with the bodies of horses and men; yet they had broken in again, with the same courage, with equal fierceness, and apparently with increased numbers!'

26   The army was then marched back to winter quarters, elated at having balanced the maritime disaster by this fortunate expedition. Moreover, there was the liberality of the Caesar, who compensated every claimant in full for the loss he professed to have sustained. Nor was any doubt felt that the enemy was wavering and discussing an application for peace; and that with another effort in the coming summer, the war might see its close. But frequent letters from Tiberius counselled the prince 'to return for the triumph decreed him: there had been already enough successes, and enough mischances. He had fought auspicious and great fields: he should also remember the losses inflicted by wind and wave—losses not in any way due to his leadership, yet grave and deplorable. He himself had been sent nine times into Germany by the deified Augustus; and he had effected more by policy than by force. Policy had procured the Sugambrian surrender; policy had bound the Suebi and King Maroboduus to keep the peace. The Cherusci and the other rebel tribes, now that enough had been done for Roman vengeance, might similarly be left to their intestine strife.' When Germanicus asked for one year more in which to finish his work, he delivered a still shrewder attack on his modesty, and offered him a second consulate, the duties of which he would assume in person. A hint was appended that 'if the war must be continued, he might leave his brother, Drusus, the material for a reputation; since at present there was no other national enemy, and nowhere but in the Germanies could he acquire the style of *Imperator* and a title to the triumphal bays.'—Germanicus hesitated no longer, though he was aware that these civilities were a fiction, and that jealousy was the motive which withdrew him from a glory already within his grasp.

Tacitus *Annals* 2. 25–6
tr. J. Jackson (Loeb 1931)

N BRITAIN

N1 Caesar and Britain

Caesar's full account of his expeditions to Britain will be found in his Gallic War *4. 20-38 (expedition of 55 BC) and 5. 1-23 (expedition of 54 BC). The extracts below highlight the effects inside and outside Britain as he chose to record them.*

(a) *The second expedition united the Britons under Cassivellaunus of the Catuvellauni against Rome. Note that Catuvellaunian aggression against other British tribes had already become notorious.*

With the ships beached and the camp strongly fortified, I left the same troops as before to guard them and set off for the place from which I had returned. When I got there, I found that larger British forces had now assembled from all parts of the country. By general agreement the supreme command and direction of the campaign had been given to Cassivellaunus.

His territory lies about 80 miles from the sea and is separated from the maritime tribes by a river called the Thames. Previously Cassivellaunus had been in a continual state of war with the other tribes, but our arrival had frightened the Britons into appointing him commander-in-chief for the campaign.

Caesar *Gallic War* 5. 11
tr. Anne and Peter Wiseman

(b) *Caesar's settlement of Britain*

In the meantime the Trinobantes sent a deputation to me. They are perhaps the strongest tribe in the southeast of Britain and it was from them that young Mandubracius had come to me in Gaul to put himself under my protection, having had to flee for his life after his father, the king of the tribe, was killed by Cassivellaunus.

The envoys promised that the tribe would surrender and carry out my orders: they begged me to protect Mandubracius from Cassivellaunus and send him back to them to rule as king. I told them to send me 40 hostages and grain for my army, and then I sent Mandubracius back to them. They quickly carried out my instructions, sending me grain and the required number of hostages.

Now that the Trinobantes were under our protection and so in no danger of harm at the hands of our troops, other tribes sent embassies to me and surrendered. These included the Cenimagni, the Segontiaci, the Ancalites, the Bibroci, and the Cassi.

From these tribes I discovered that we were quite close to Cassivellaunus's *oppidum*. It was protected by forests and marshes, and a great number of men and cattle had been collected in it. I should mention that the Britons give the name 'oppidum' to *any* densely wooded place they have fortified with a rampart and trench and use as a refuge from the attacks of invaders.

I set off there with my legions and found that the site had excellent natural defences and was very well fortified. Nevertheless we proceeded to attack it on two sides. After putting up brief resistance, the enemy were unable to hold out against our men's onslaught, and they rushed out of their *oppidum* on the other side. Many of these fugitives were captured and killed. Inside the fortress we found a great quantity of cattle.

While these operations were going on there, Cassivellaunus sent messengers to Kent, an area by the sea as I have said above. There were four kings in that region, Cingetorix, Carvilius, Taximagulus, and Segovax, and Cassivellaunus ordered them to collect all their troops and make a surprise attack on our naval camp. When these forces reached the camp, our men made a sudden sortie, killing many of them and capturing one of their leaders, a nobleman called Lugotorix, before retiring again without loss.

When reports of this battle reached him, Cassivellaunus, alarmed by the many reverses he had suffered, the devastation of his country, and especially the defection of the other tribes, sent envoys to me to ask for terms of surrender, using Commius the Atrebatian as an intermediary.

I had decided to winter on the continent because of the danger that sudden risings might break out in Gaul. There was not much of the summer left and I realized that the Britons could easily hold out for that short time, so I accepted their surrender, ordering hostages to be given and fixing the tribute to be paid annually by Britain to Rome. I gave strict orders to Cassivellaunus not to molest Mandubracius or the Trinobantes.

When the hostages were delivered, I led the army back to the coast, where I found the ships had been repaired. We launched them, and because we had a great many prisoners and had lost some of our ships in the storm, I decided to make the return journey in two trips.

It happened that out of such a fleet of ships, making so many voyages both in that and the previous year, not a single one with troops on board was lost. But of those sent back to me empty from the continent (that is, those on their way back from Gaul after disembarking our first contingent, and the 60 that Labienus had had built after the start of the expedition), very few reached their destination, almost all the rest being driven back. I waited some time for these ships, but in vain. Then, because I was afraid that the approaching equinox would prevent us sailing, I was obliged to pack the men on board more tightly than usual on those ships that we had.

The sea then became very calm, so we set sail late in the evening and reached land at dawn. I had brought all the ships across in safety and we beached them.

Caesar *Gallic War* 5. 20-3
tr. Anne and Peter Wiseman

N2 Cicero's brother Quintus a senior officer serving with Caesar

(a) *Accurate news of the second campaign has not yet reached Rome.*

And now for the rest of my news. My brother in his letter gives me almost incredible news of Caesar's affection for me, and this is borne out by a very full letter from Caesar himself. We await the outcome of the war in Britain; it is known that the approaches to the island are 'fenced about with daunting cliffs'; and it has also become clear that there is not a scrap of silver on the island; there's no prospect of booty except slaves—and I don't imagine you are expecting any knowledge of literature or music among them!

Cicero *Letters to Atticus* 4. 16. 7
tr. LACT *Literary Sources*

(b) *Cicero is now able to report the completion of the campaign: the summary of the results is presumably his brother's. Note the continuing concentration on the profits—or lack of profits—from victory.*

On the 24th of October I received letters from my brother Quintus and Caesar; they were addressed on the 25th September from the nearest point on the British coast. The campaign in Britain is over; hostages have been taken and although there's no booty a tribute has been levied. They are bringing the army back from Britain.

Cicero *Letters to Atticus* 4. 18. 5
LACT *Literary Sources*

N3 Suetonius on Caesar's expeditions

Suetonius, writing a century and a half after Caesar, reveals what was chiefly remembered about the expeditions—that Caesar's invasion was the first, to an unknown island; that his motives were believed to be financial; that his loss of ships was considered important among the few faults in his military career and that he had extracted payments and hostages from the Britons.

(a)
He built a bridge across the Rhine and became the first Roman to attack and defeat heavily the Germans on the other side. He also attacked the Britons, a people unknown before, and after defeating them exacted sums of money and took hostages. Among so many successes he only suffered set-backs on three occasions: in Britain, when his fleet was almost destroyed by a violent storm; in Gaul, when a legion was

put to flight at Gergovia; and in German territory when his officers Titurius and Aurunculeius were killed in an ambush.

Suetonius *Julius* 25. 2
tr. LACT *Literary Sources*

(b)
They say that his attack on Britain was inspired by the prospect of pearls; sometimes he weighed them in his own hand when he was comparing their size.

Suetonius *Julius* 47
tr. LACT *Literary Sources*

N4 A British view?

Tacitus, writing in the same period as Suetonius, puts into the mouth of the British leader Caratacus a view of Caesar's expeditions that could be put out as propaganda for the British side in the war of AD 50.

Caratacus, as he hastened to one point and another, stressed that this was the day, this the battle, which would either win back their freedom or enslave them forever. He invoked their ancestors, who by routing Julius Caesar had valorously preserved their present descendants from Roman officials and taxes, and saved for them, undefiled, their wives and children.

Tacitus *Annals* 12. 34
tr. Michael Grant (Penguin 1956)

N5 The Panegyric of Constantius

At the very end of the third century AD a panegyric—a speech which it became conventional to address to the Emperor in praise of his achievements—was made after Constantius I (at that time Caesar, or junior Emperor under the new system introduced by Diocletian) had invaded and recovered Britain from the rival Emperor (or usurper) Allectus. Julius Caesar's expeditions are still the traditional yardstick against which success is measured. The orator is anxious to play up the success of his own hero: he is making the point that Constantius faced an island guarded by a fully trained and equipped army and fleet. Even so, he cannot deny Julius Caesar the glory of the 'Conquest of Ocean'.

When Caesar, the originator of your name, first of all the Romans entered Britain, he wrote that he had found another world. . . .

But at that time Britain was not prepared with ships for any kind of naval contest. . . In addition to this, the nation of the Britons was still at that time un-civilized and used to fighting only with the Picts and the Hibernians, both still half-naked enemies; and so they submitted to Roman arms so easily that the only thing that Caesar [i.e. Julius Caesar] ought to have boasted of was that he had navigated the Ocean.

Panegyric of Constantius Caesar 11. 2–4
tr. LACT *Literary Sources*

N6 Roman knowledge of Britain: literary sources

(a) *Caesar*

The interior of Britain is inhabited by people who claim, on the strength of their own tradition, to be indigenous. The coastal areas are inhabited by invaders who crossed from Belgium for the sake of plunder and then, when the fighting was over, settled there and began to work the land; these people have almost all kept the names of the tribes from which they originated. The population is extremely large, there are very many farm buildings, closely resembling those in Gaul, and the cattle are very numerous.

For money they use bronze or gold coins, or iron ingots of fixed standard weights. Tin is found there in the midland area, and iron near the coast, but not in large quantities. The bronze they use is imported. There is timber of every kind, as in Gaul, but no beech or fir. They think it wrong to eat hares, chickens, or geese, keeping these creatures only for pleasure and amusement. The climate is more temperate than in Gaul, the cold season being less severe.

The island is triangular in shape, with one side facing Gaul. One corner of this side points east and is on the coast of Kent, the landing point for almost all ships from Gaul; the lower corner points south. The length of this side is some 500 miles. The second side of the island faces westward, towards Spain. In this direction lies Ireland, which is thought to be half the size of Britain and is the same distance from Britain as Gaul is. Midway between Ireland and Britain is the Isle of Man, and it is believed that there are several smaller islands too, where, some writers say, there is continual darkness for 30 days in midwinter. We made numerous inquiries about this, but found out nothing. However, from accurate measurements with a water clock, we could tell that the nights were shorter than on the continent. This western side of Britain is, in the opinion of the natives, 700 miles long. The third side of the island faces north; there is no land opposite this side, but the eastern corner of it points roughly towards Germany. The length of this side is reckoned to be 800 miles, which means that the whole island is some 2,000 miles in circumference.

By far the most civilized of the Britons are those who live in Kent, which is an entirely maritime area; their way of life is very like that of the Gauls. Most of the tribes living in the interior do not grow grain; they live on milk and meat and wear skins. All the Britons dye their bodies with woad, which produces a blue colour and gives them a wild appearance in battle. They wear their hair long; every other part of the body, except for the upper lip, they shave. Wives are shared between groups of ten or twelve men, especially between brothers and between fathers and sons; but the children of such unions are counted as belonging to the man with whom the woman first cohabited.

Caesar *Gallic War* 5. 12-14
tr. Anne and Peter Wiseman

(b) *Strabo, writing in the Augustan period*

1   Britain is triangular in shape. Its longest side lies parallel to Gaul, and neither exceeds nor falls short of it in length. Each measures about 4,300 or 4,400 Stadia .... (The British shore) extends from Cantion (which is directly opposite the mouth of the Rhine), as far as the westerly end of the island which lies opposite Aquitania and the Pyrenees . . . .

2   There are four crossings in common use from the mainland to the island, those which start from the mouths of rivers—the Rhine, the Seine, the Loire and the Garonne. Those who cross from the Rhineland do not start from the river estuary, but from the territory of the Morini (who border on the Menapii) where Iction lies, which the deified Caesar used as a naval base when he crossed to the island . . . . Most of the island is low-lying and wooded, but there are many hilly areas. It produces corn, cattle, gold, silver and iron. These things are exported along with hides, slaves and dogs suitable for hunting. The Gauls however use both these and their own native dogs for warfare also. The men of Britain are taller than the Gauls and not so yellow-haired. Their bodies are more loosely built. This will give you an idea of their size: I myself in Rome saw youths standing half a foot taller than the tallest in the city although they were bandy-legged and ungainly in build. They live much like the Gauls but some of their customs are more primitive and barbarous. Thus for example some of them are well supplied with milk but do not know how to make cheese; they know nothing of planting crops or of farming in general. They are ruled by their own kings. For the most part they use chariots in war, like some of the Gauls. Their cities are the forests, for they fell trees and fence in large circular enclosures in which they build huts and pen in their cattle, but not for any great length of time. The weather tends to rain rather than snow. Mist is very common, so that for whole days at a stretch the sun is seen only for three or four hours around midday.

Strabo 4. 5. 1-2
tr. LACT *Literary Sources*

(c) *Pomponius Mela, writing under Claudius*

It will soon be possible to describe the nature of Britain and the character of the people she produces with greater certainty and knowledge gained from exploration; for indeed the closed book of Britain is being opened by the greatest of Emperors, victor over peoples not only unconquered, but before him absolutely unknown; as he sought to win credibility for the peculiar features [of Britain] by means of war, so he brings them back to display in his triumph.

Pomponius Mela 3.6.49
tr. K. Chisholm

(d) *Tacitus, probably writing in AD 98*

11 Be this as it may, the question who were the first inhabitants of Britain and whether they were indigenous or immigrant is one which, as one would expect among barbarous people, has never received attention. The physique of the people presents many varieties, whence inferences are drawn: the red hair and the large limbs of the inhabitants of Caledonia proclaim their German origin; the swarthy faces of the Silures, the curly quality, in general, of their hair, and the position of Spain opposite their shores, attest the passage of Iberians in old days and the occupation by them of these districts; those peoples, again, who adjoin Gaul are also like Gauls, whether because the influence of heredity persists, or because when two lands project in opposite directions till they face each other the climatic condition stamps a certain physique on the human body; but, taking a general view of the case, we can readily believe that the Gauls took possession of the adjacent island. You would find there Gallic ceremonies and Gallic religious beliefs; the language is not very different; there is the same recklessness in courting danger, and, when it comes, the same anxiety to escape it; but the Britons display a higher spirit, not having yet been emasculated by long years of peace. The Gauls also, according to history, once shone in war: afterwards indolence made its appearance hand in hand with peace, and courage and liberty have been lost together. This has happened to such of the Britons as were conquered long ago: the rest remain what the Gauls once were.

12 Their strength lies in their infantry; but certain tribes also fight from chariots: the driver has the place of honour, the combatants are mere retainers. Originally the people were subject to kings: now the quarrels and ambitions of petty chieftains divide them; nor indeed have we any weapons against the stronger races more effective than this, that they have no common purpose: rarely will two or three states confer to repulse a common danger; accordingly they fight individually and are collectively conquered. The sky is overcast with continual rain and cloud, but the cold is not severe. The length of the days is beyond the measure of our world: the nights are clear and, in the distant parts of Britain, short, so that there is but a brief space separating the evening and the morning twilight. If there be no clouds to hinder, the sun's brilliance—they maintain—is visible throughout the night: it does not set and then rise again, but simply passes over. That is to say,

the flat extremities of the earth with their low shadows do not project the darkness, and nightfall never reaches the sky and the stars.

The soil, except for the olive and the vine and the other fruits usual in warmer lands, is tolerant of crops and prolific of cattle: they ripen slowly, but are quick to sprout—in each case for the same reason, the abundant moisture of the soil and sky. Britain produces gold and silver and other metals: conquest is worth while. Their sea also produces pearls, but somewhat clouded and leaden-hued. Some people suppose that their pearl-fishers lack skill; in the Red Sea we are to imagine them torn alive and still breathing from the shell, while in Britain they are gathered only when thrown up on shore: for myself I could more readily believe that quality was lacking in the pearls than greed in Romans.

13 As for the people themselves, they discharge energetically the levies and tributes and obligations imposed by the government, provided always there are no abuses. They are restive under wrong: for their subjection, while complete enough to involve obedience, does not involve slavery. It was, in fact, Julius of happy memory who first of all Romans entered Britain with an army: he overawed the natives by a successful battle and made himself master of the coast; but it may be supposed that he rather discovered the island for his descendants than bequeathed it to them. Soon came the civil war, and the arms of Rome's leaders were turned against the state, and there was a long forgetfulness of Britain, even after peace came. Augustus of happy memory called this 'policy'; Tiberius called it 'precedent'.

That Gaius Caesar debated an invasion of Britain is well known; but his unstable mind was quick to repent: besides, his vast designs against Germany had failed. Claudius of happy memory was responsible for undertaking the great task: legions and auxiliary troops were transported across the Channel, and Vespasian was taken into partnership—the first step of the fame soon to come to him: tribes were conquered, kings captured, and destiny introduced Vespasian to the world.

Tacitus *Agricola* 11–13
tr. M. Hutton, rev. R. M. Ogilvie (Loeb 1970)

N7 Religion

(a) *The Druids*

Contrary to popular belief there is very little evidence to suggest that the Druids had great power among the Britons. The Romans took extreme measures to stamp out Druidism in Gaul: there is no mention of similar action in Britain. The best account is Stuart Piggott The Druids *(Thames & Hudson 1968). The tone of Caesar's reference here is that Britain was then regarded as the centre of Druidic lore. He says nothing about power, political influence, or even the practice of Druidic ritual in Britain in his day:*

It is thought that the doctrine of the Druids was invented in Britain and was brought from there into Gaul; even today those who want to study the doctrine in greater detail usually go to Britain to learn there.

Caesar *Gallic War* 6. 13
tr. Anne and Peter Wiseman

(b) *Holy islands*

Demetrius of Tarsus was in Britain in AD 83, which suggests that like so much of native religion these cults persisted strongly in the Roman period. Demetrius may here have been travelling beyond Roman-occupied territory, but an example (admittedly not remote but apparantly otherwise uninhabited) is Hayling Island on which recent excavation has revealed a pre-Roman temple rebuilt on an impressive scale early in the Roman period, with probable continuity of cult. It is not impossible that the inscription mentioning Cogidubnus came originally from this site. If so, it may well have been an important cult-centre of his kingdom (and possibly of those of Verica, Tincommius, and Commius before him.)

2   Nonetheless, shortly before the Pythian games celebrated when Callistratus held office, in our own day, two men travelling from opposite ends of the inhabited world met at Delphi. These were the scholar Demetrius, who was travelling home from Britain to Tarsus, and the Spartan Cleombrotus .... 18 Demetrius said that of the islands around Britain many were widely scattered and sparsely inhabited; several were called after deities or heroes. He himself had been commissioned by the emperor to sail to the nearest of these lonely islands to make enquiries and observations; it only had a few inhabitants, and they were all holy men who were considered sacrosanct by the Britons.

Plutarch *On the Disuse of Oracles* (extract)
tr. LACT *Literary Sources*

N8 Augustus and Britain

(a) *Before Actium*

Dio attributes this to 34 BC.

Augustus was also pressing ahead with a British expedition in emulation of his father; after the winter in which Antony (for a second time) and Lucius Libo held the consulship he had already reached Gaul when some newly conquered tribes rose in rebellion and were joined by the Dalmatians.

Dio Cassius 49. 38. 2

(b) *Early planning (31 BC)*

Wherever earth is bounded by Ocean, no part of it, Messalla, will raise arms against you. For you is left the Briton, whom Roman arms have not yet vanquished, and for you the other part of the world with the sun's path between.

Tibullus 3. 7. 147-50

(c) *This refers to 27 BC. See also Horace* Odes *3. 5. 1-4 (F22).*

Augustus also set out to campaign in Britain, but when he came to Gaul he lingered there. The Britons seemed likely to make terms, and affairs in Gaul were still unsettled, since the conquest of the country had been immediately followed by the civil war.

Dio Cassius 53. 22. 5

(d) *Dio attributes these events to 26 BC.*

Augustus was intending to campaign in Britain, where the people would not come to terms, but he was prevented because the Salassi were in revolt and the Cantabri and Astures had been antagonised.

Dio Cassius 53. 25. 2

(e) *This dates from c.26 BC.*

I pray that you may protect Caesar on his expedition against the Britons, the furthest nation of the world.

Horace *Odes* 1. 35. 29-30
tr. LACT *Literary Sources*

N9 Augustus' intentions

The dates of the books of Propertius are uncertain. However, the latest incident mentioned in Book 2, from which the passage below is quoted, is dated to 26 BC. The book is therefore likely to have been published in 26 itself or soon thereafter. However, unlike the last piece from Horace (N8(e)), it does not necessarily imply a current campaign. It may well indicate that an intention on the part of the Princeps to invade Britain was now an everyday assumption, a belief Augustus may have been happy to leave uncorrected, even if he had abandoned the project.

Mortals, you seek to know what none can say:
The hour when death will come, and by what way;
You seek Phoenician science in the sky;
Which planets man is blessed or blasted by.
Amid blind risks by sea or land we go
To chase the British or the Parthian foe;
And weep afresh that war besets our life,
When Mars throws dubious armies into strife.

Propertius 2. 27. 1–8
tr. A. E. Watts (Penguin 1961)

N10 Strabo's assessment of the worth of Britain

By comparing Strabo's argument against an occupation of Britain with Tacitus (N6(d)) the impression that Strabo reflects late Augustan policy is strengthened, since Tacitus there links Augustus' 'policy' not to invade Britain with Tiberius following 'precedent' (i.e. the Augustan decision not to extend the boundaries of the Empire, which C. M. Wells in The German Policy of Augustus *(Oxford 1972) argues was characteristic of Augustus only after the Varian disaster, in old age).*

(a)
And for the purposes of political power, there would be no advantage in knowing such [distant] countries and their inhabitants, particularly where the people live in islands which are such that they can neither injure or benefit us in any way, because of their isolation. For although the Romans could have possessed Britain, they scorned to do so, for they saw that there was nothing at all to fear from Britain, since they are not strong enough to cross over and attack us. No corresponding advantages would arise by taking over and holding the country. For at present more seems to accrue from the customs duties on their commerce than direct taxation could supply, if we deduct the cost of maintaining an army to garrison the island and collect the tribute. The unprofitableness of an occupation would be still more marked in the case of the other islands near Britain.

Strabo 2. 5. 8
tr. LACT *Literary Sources*

(b)
The deified Caesar crossed over twice to the island, but came back in haste, without accomplishing much or proceeding very far inland. This was not only because of trouble in Gaul involving both the barbarians and his own troops, but also because many of his ships were lost at full moon, when the tides are at their greatest. However,

he won two or three victories over the Britons, even though he took over only two legions, bringing back hostages, slaves and much other booty. At present however some of the kings have gained the friendship of Caesar Augustus by sending embassies and paying him deference. They have not only dedicated offerings in the Capitol, they have also more or less brought the whole island under Roman control. Furthermore they submit to heavy duties on the exports to Gaul, and on the imports from there (which include ivory bracelets and necklaces, amber and glassware and similar petty trifles), so that there is no need of a garrison for the island. It would require at least one legion and a force of cavalry to collect tribute from them, and the cost of such a force would offset the revenue gained. If tribute were imposed the customs duties would inevitably dwindle and at the same time the risks would be greater if force were employed.

Strabo 4. 5. 3
tr. LACT *Literary Sources*

N11 Relations with Britain under Tiberius and Gaius

(a) *An incident in AD 16*

After the storm which scattered Germanicus' ships some were sent back by the kings of that country.

Tacitus *Annals* 2. 24
tr. LACT *Literary Sources*

(b) *A prince of the Catuvellauni seeks the protection of the Emperor Gaius; for British kings as suppliants at the court of Augustus (Dumnovellaunus and Tincommius), see RG 32 (A1).*

He did nothing more than to receive the surrender (*deditio*) of Adminius, son of Cunobellinus king of the Britons, who had been exiled by his father and had fled to the Romans with a small force. But, as if the whole island had surrendered to him, he sent exaggerated letters to Rome, ordering the messengers to drive their vehicles right into the Forum and up to the Senate-house, and only to deliver the letters to the consuls before a full meeting of the Senate in the temple of Mars.

Suetonius *Gaius* 44. 2
tr. LACT *Literary Sources*

(c) *Gaius' preparations for invasion, AD 40; the conquest of Ocean is again an important theme: Gaius' propaganda clearly emphasized it. Various explanations have been advanced to suggest that Gaius' behaviour on the coast of Gaul was not as irrational as it would appear (see J. P. V. D. Balsdon,* The Emperor Gaius *(Oxford 1934) 91 ff.). It is, for example, possible that the sea-shells (which first appear in Suetonius as* conchae*) derive from a misunderstood report of the presence among the equipment assembled of* musculi, *a word with several meanings including mussels but also as being a technical military term for the mobile shelters used in siege-assaults. The Roman lighthouse at Boulogne survived till 1544.*

At length, as if about to go to war, he drew up a line of battle on the shore of the Ocean, deploying *ballistae* and other artillery. No-one knew or imagined what he could be going to do, when he suddenly ordered them to gather up shells to fill their helmets and the laps of their tunics. He called them 'spoils from the Ocean, dues to the Capitol and Palatine'. As a monument of his victory he erected a high tower, from which fires were to shine out at night as a guide to ships—just like the Pharos. Then, announcing a donation of 100 denarii to each soldier, as if he were showing unprecedented liberality, he said: 'Go on your way both happy and rich'.

Suetonius *Gaius* 46. 1
tr. LACT *Literary Sources*

(d) *Dio repeats the story, which has become the received account.*

1 When Gaius reached the Ocean, as if he were about to advance into Britain, he drew up his soldiers on the beach. 2 He then embarked on a trireme, putting out from the shore and then sailing back again. Then he took his seat on a lofty platform, and gave the soldiers the signal as for battle, ordering the trumpeters to urge them on. Then suddenly he ordered them to pick up sea-shells. 3 Having secured these spoils, for it was evident that he needed booty for his triumphal procession, he became greatly elated, as if he had subdued the Ocean itself. He gave many presents to his soldiers. He took back the shells to Rome, in order to exhibit his booty there as well.

Dio Cassius 59. 25. 1–3
tr. LACT *Literary Sources*

N12 Claudius and Britain

The invasion of AD 43 and the personal involvement of the Emperor

19. 1 . . . Aulus Plautius, a senator of great reputation, led an expedition to Britain, for a certain Berikos, who had been driven out of the island as a result of civil war, persuaded Claudius to send a force there. 2 Thus it came about that Plautius undertook the campaign, but he had difficulty in persuading his army to leave Gaul. The soldiers objected to the idea of campaigning outside the limits of the world

they knew, and would not obey Plautius until Narcissus, who had been sent out by Claudius, mounted Plautius's tribunal and attempted to address them. 3 At first they were angry at this and would not allow Narcissus to say anything. But suddenly they shouted in unison 'Io Saturnalia', for at the Saturnalia slaves don their masters' dress and hold festival, and returned to their obedience to Plautius. However, their mutiny had made their departure late in the season. 4 They were sent over in three divisions, so that their landing should not be hindered, as might have happened with a single force. On the way across, they were at first discouraged, because they were driven back on their course, but they recovered when they saw a flash of light shoot across the sky from east to west, the direction in which they were travelling. When they reached the island they found no-one to oppose them. 5 On the strength of the reports they received the Britons had concluded that they were not coming and had not assembled to meet them. Even when they did assemble, they refused to come to close quarters with the Romans, but fled to the swamps and forests, hoping to wear out the enemy and force him to sail away again, just as they had done in the time of Julius Caesar.

20. 1 So Plautius had a lot of trouble in finding them, but when at last he did, he first defeated Caratacus and then Togodumnus, the sons of Cunobelinus, who was now dead. (The Britons were not free and independent, but were ruled by various kings). 2 After these had fled, he won over a section of the Bodounni, who were subject to the Catuvellauni. Then, leaving behind a garrison, he continued his advance. He came to a river which the barbarians thought the Romans would be unable to cross without a bridge; in consequence they had camped in careless fashion on the far bank. But Plautius sent across a detachment of Germans, who were accustomed to swimming in full equipment across the strongest streams. 3 They fell unexpectedly on the enemy, but instead of attacking the men concentrated on their chariot-horses. In the ensuing confusion not even the enemy's mounted men escaped. Plautius thereupon sent across Flavius Vespasianus, who afterwards became emperor, and his brother Sabinus who was serving under him. 4 They managed to get across the river and surprised and killed many of the enemy. However the survivors did not take to flight. On the next day they joined battle again. The struggle was indecisive, until Gaius Hosidius Geta, after a narrow escape from capture, fell upon the Britons to such effect that he was later awarded the triumphal ornaments, even though he had not yet held the consulship.

5 The Britons now fell back on the river Thames, at a point near where it enters the sea, and at high tide forms a pool. They crossed over easily because they knew where to find firm ground and an easy passage. 6 But the Romans in trying to follow them were not so successful. However, the Germans again swam across, and other troops got over by a bridge a little upstream, after which they attacked the barbarians from several sides at once, and killed many of their number. But in pursuing the remainder incautiously some of the troops got into difficulties in the marshes, and a number were lost.

21. 1 Because of this, and because even though Togodumnus had perished, the Britons, far from yielding, had united all the more firmly to avenge him, Plautius

was afraid to advance further. He proceeded to consolidate what he had gained, and sent for Claudius. 2 He had been instructed to do this if he met any particularly strong opposition, and indeed considerable equipment, including elephants, had already been assembled as reinforcements. On receiving this message Claudius committed affairs in Rome, including the command of the troops, to his fellow-consul Lucius Vitellius, whom he had kept in office, like himself, for the full half-year, and set out for Britain. 3 Sailing down the river to Ostia, he followed the coast to Massilia. Thence he progressed, partly by road and partly by river, until he came to the Ocean. Crossing over to Britain he joined the troops that were waiting for him at the Thames. 4 Taking over the command of these troops he crossed the river and engaged the barbarians who had assembled to oppose him; he defeated them, and captured Camulodunum, the capital of Cunobelinus. After this he won over a number of tribes, some by diplomacy, some by force, and was saluted as Imperator several times, contrary to precedent, 5 for no-one may receive this title more than once for any one war. He deprived those who submitted of their arms, and putting these people under the control of Plautius, he ordered him to subdue the remaining areas. He himself now hastened back to Rome, sending on the news of his victory by his sons-in-law Magnus and Silanus.

Dio Cassius 60. 19. 1–21. 5
tr. LACT *Literary Sources*

N13 Claudius' celebration of victory

The following passages show how high a value Claudius placed on success in Britain.

(a)

22. 1 The Senate on hearing of this achievement voted him the title Britannicus, and gave him permission to hold a triumph. They also voted an annual festival to commemorate the event, and decreed that two triumphal arches should be erected, one in Rome and one in Gaul, since it was from Gaul that he had crossed over into Britain. 2 They bestowed upon his son the same title, and indeed in a way Britannicus came to be the boy's usual name. Messalina was granted the right of using a front seat at the theatre which Livia had enjoyed, and also the right of using a carriage (*carpentum*) in the city.

23. 1 Thus were parts of Britain conquered. Later, in the consulship of Gaius Crispus (for the second time) and Titus Statilius [AD 44], Claudius came back to Rome after an absence of six months, of which he spent only 16 days in Britain, and celebrated his triumph. In this he followed precedent, even ascending the steps of the Capitol on his knees, with his sons-in-law supporting him on either side. 2 He granted to the senators who had campaigned with him the triumphal orna-ments, and this not only to those who were of consular rank. . . . 4 After attend-ing to these matters, he celebrated his triumph . . . . 6 These things were done on

account of events in Britain, and in order that other tribes should the more readily come to terms, it was decreed that all agreements made by Claudius or his legates should be as binding as if they had been made by the Senate and People.

Dio Cassius 60. 22. 1–23. 6
tr. and abridged LACT *Literary Sources*

(b)   *The triumph of Claudius was held in AD 44.*

1   He undertook only one expedition, and that a modest one. The Senate had decreed him triumphal ornaments, but he regarded this as beneath his dignity as emperor. He sought the honour of a real triumph, and chose Britain as the best field in which to seek this, for no-one had attempted an invasion since the time of Julius Caesar and the island at this time was in a turmoil because certain refugees had not been returned to the island.
2   Voyaging from Ostia he was twice nearly drowned by north-westerly storms, once off Liguria and again off the Stoechades islands. So he finished the journey from Massilia to Gesoriacum by land. Crossing from there he received the submission of part of the island within a very few days without either battle or bloodshed. Within six months he had returned to Rome, where he celebrated his triumph with the greatest pomp.   3   To witness the spectacle he permitted not only provincial governors to come to Rome, but even certain exiles. And among the symbols of victory he fixed a Naval Crown next to the Civic Crown on the gable of the Palace, a token that he had crossed and as it were conquered the Ocean. His wife Messalina followed his triumphal chariot in a carriage (*carpentum*). Those who had won triumphal ornaments in the war also followed, but on foot, and in purple-bordered togas, except Marcus Crassus Frugi, who wore a tunic decorated with palms and rode on a horse decorated with *phalerae*, because this was the second time that he had won the honour.

Suetonius *Claudius* 17. 1–3
tr. LACT *Literary Sources*

(c)
He gave a show in the Campus Martius representing the siege and capture of a town (*oppidum*) in the manner of a real war, as well as of the surrender (*deditio*) of the kings of the Britons. He presided clad in a general's cloak. . . .
   . . . He also decreed an ovation to Aulus Plautius, going out to greet him when he entered the City, and 'giving him the wall' as he went to the Capitol and returned again.

Suetonius *Claudius* 21. 6; 24. 3
tr. LACT *Literary Sources*

(d)
His successor Claudius when celebrating a triumph after the conquest of Britain

advertised by placards that among the gold coronets there was one having a weight of 7000 pounds contributed by Hither Spain and one of 9000 from Gallia Comata.

Pliny *Natural History* 33. 54
tr. D. E. Eichholz (Loeb 1952)

(e) *A coin of Claudius*

Obverse: Head of Claudius wearing laurel-wreath. Around, TI(BERIVS) CLAVD-(IVS) CAESAR AVG(VSTVS) P(ONTIFEX) M(AXIMVS) TR(IBVNICIA) P(OTESTATE) VI IMP(ERATOR) XI = 'Tiberius Claudius Caesar Augustus, chief *pontifex*, in the sixth year of his possession of tribunician power, hailed *imperator* for the eleventh time.'

Reverse: Triumphal arch. Statue of the Emperor on horseback stands on the arch between two trophies. Arch is inscribed DE BRITANN(IS) = '(Erected in commemoration of victory) over the Britons.'

R I C Claudius 9
tr. LACT *Some Inscriptions*

N14 Extraordinary revivals of old customs

This passage re-emphasizes the importance placed on the conquest of Britain.

It was decided to re-introduce and perpetuate the 'Augury for the Welfare of Rome', suspended for the last seventy-five years. Claudius also extended the city boundary. Here he followed an ancient custom whereby those who have expanded the empire are entitled to enlarge the city boundary also. Yet no Roman commander except Sulla and the divine Augustus had ever exercised this right, however great their conquests.

Tacitus *Annals* 12. 23
tr. M. Grant (Penguin 1977)

N15 Two inscriptions relating to the conquest

(a) *The arch of Claudius in Rome was completed in AD 52; this dedicatory inscription partially survived and has been restored.*

To the Emperor Tiberius Claudius, son of Drusus, Caesar Augustus Germanicus, Pontifex Maximus, Tribunician power for the eleventh time, consul for the fifth time, saluted as Imperator twenty-two (?) times, Censor, Father of his country. Set up by the Senate and People of Rome because he received the formal submission of eleven Kings of the Britons, overcome without any loss, and because he was the first to bring barbarian peoples across the Ocean under the sway of the Roman people.

CIL 6. 920 (restored)
tr. Dudley *Urbs Roma*

(b) *In an inscription from an altar in Cyzicus in Asia Minor, the victory in Britain features as a major element in the Emperor's glory.*

In honour of the divine Augustus Caesar, of Tiberius Augustus, son of the divine Augustus, acclaimed *imperator*, and of Tiberius Claudius Caesar Augustus Germanicus, son of Drusus, *pontifex maximus*, in the 11th year of his tribunician power, father of his country, protector of freedom, conqueror of eleven British kings; the Roman citizens resident in Cyzicus together with the Cyzicans (erected this) arch under the supervision of . . . . .

ILS 217
tr. K. Chisholm

N16 Persistence of Claudius' reputation

Eutropius wrote in the second half of the fourth century AD. It is interesting to note what he thinks worth mentioning. He does not always get his facts exactly right when he deals with Britain. Gnaeus Sentius Saturninus was one of several Roman senators of consular rank known to have been in Britain with Claudius: it is possible, from the fact of this reference, that he had some specific job assigned to him. Particularly interesting is the claim that the Orkneys (Orcades) were acquired. If this is really true (Tacitus claims that Agricola's fleet was the first to discover and take those islands—in AD 83 and 84), then it must be that some chieftain from the far north was included in the eleven kings who made formal submission to Claudius, since it seems highly improbable that Roman warships ranged so far in Claudius' time.

Claudius waged war on Britain, where no Roman had set foot since the days of C. Caesar, and when the country had been vanquished by Cn. Sentius and A. Plautius, distinguished members of noble families, he held a magnificent triumph. He also added to the Roman empire certain islands in the Ocean beyond Britain, called the Orchades, and gave his son the name Brittanicus.

Eutropius *Breviarium* 7. 13. 2–3
tr. LACT *Literary Sources*

N17 The part played by Vespasian in Britain under Claudius

(a) *Josephus deliberately plays up the role of Vespasian in Britain (it is an obvious exaggeration, since Vespasian commanded only part of the expeditionary force: see also Tacitus Agricola 11–13–N6 d).*

Nero could find no one but Vespasian equal to the situation [i.e. in Judaea in AD 66], and capable of undertaking a campaign on such a scale. He had been a soldier from his youth, and had grown grey in the service. Earlier in his career he had pacified the west and rescued it from harassment by the Germans; with his troops he had added Britain, till then almost unknown, to the empire, and thus provided Claudius, the father of Nero, with a triumph which cost him no personal exertion.

> Josephus *BJ* 3. 1. 2 (4)
> tr. LACT *Literary Sources*

(b) *A more detailed account, including Vespasian's campaign in the West. Note the enormous power of the Imperial freedman Narcissus and the consequences both favourable and unfavourable, of being one of his protégés.*

On Claudius's accession, Vespasian was indebted to Narcissus for the command of a legion in Germany; and proceeded to Britain, where he fought thirty battles, subjugated two warlike tribes, and captured more than twenty towns, besides the entire Isle of Wight. In these campaigns he served at times under Aulus Plautius, the Consular commander, and at times directly under Claudius, earning triumphal decorations; and soon afterwards held a couple of priesthoods, as well as a consulship for the last two months of the year. While waiting for a proconsular appointment, however, he lived in retirement: for fear of Agrippina's power over Nero, and of the animosity which she continued to feel towards any friend of Narcissus's even after his death.

> Suetonius *Vespasian* 4. 1–2
> tr. R. Graves (Penguin 1957)

N18 A summary of events in Britain in the period from Claudius to Nero

Tacitus probably underplays the governorship of Aulus Didius Gallus. The situation left by Ostorius Scapula was difficult, and his successor's new forts, not yet certainly identified among the early sites known archaeologically on the Welsh border, at the very least consolidated and edged forward Roman-occupied territory and perhaps did more. It is even possible that the legionary fortress founded sometime in the mid-50s at Usk in Gwent, among the Silures, should be attributed to him. The next governor, Quintus Veranius, was able confidently to expect to smash British resistance finally; and it was on this programme that Suetonius Paulinus was in fact engaged when the Boudiccan revolt erupted behind him. The colony mentioned is Colchester. Cogidubnus (or Cogidumnus or Togidumnus—even the name is uncertain: see P. Salway Roman Britain and the Early Empire (A291 Unit 12 p. 66)) presents many problems. He is by no means certainly associated with the 'palace' at Fishbourne (though it is not improbable), and the only other written record (the inscription now at Chichester (RIB 91)) is fragmentary, imperfectly preserved and has been variously restored and differently interpreted. For some recent discussions see E. Birley Britannia 9 (1978) 244 f.; P. Salway Roman Britain (1981) Appendix IV; Anthony A. Barrett Britannia 10 (1979) 227 ff.; J. E. Bogaers Britannia 10 (1979) 243 ff.

The first consular governor to be placed in command of Britain was Aulus Plautius: soon after came Ostorius Scapula, both distinguished soldiers. The nearest portion of Britain was reduced little by little to the condition of a province: a colony of veterans was also planted. Certain states were handed over to King Cogidumnus—he has remained continuously loyal down to our own times—according to the old and long-received principle of Roman policy, which employs kings as tools of enslavement.

Next Didius Gallus maintained the ground gained by his predecessors, and pushed forward a few forts into remoter districts in order to gain credit for enlarging his province. Didius was followed by Veranius, who died within the year. Suetonius Paulinus after him had two successful years, reducing tribes and strengthening the garrisons: presuming upon which success, he attacked the island of Anglesey, a rallying-point of rebellion, and so left his rear open to surprise.

Tacitus *Agricola* 14
tr. M. Hutton, rev. R. M. Ogilvie, (Loeb 1970)

N19 The Claudian conquest in poetry

This dates from Nero's reign. Note that the conquest of Ocean and the Brigantes have entered Roman popular consciousness. Seneca, of course, had personal involvement with Britain and many have known reasonably accurately who the Brigantes were; but they made such an impression on the popular mind that their name sometimes seems to stand for the Britons as a whole.

> And the Britons beyond the sea-shores which one sees,
> Blue-shielded Brigantians too, all these
> He chained by the neck as the Roman's slaves.
> He spake, and the Ocean with trembling waves
> Accepted the axe of the Roman law.

Seneca *Apocolocyntosis* 12. 3
tr. W. H. D. Rouse (Loeb 1969)

N20 The second governor: Ostorius Scapula

Campaigns after AD 47

The disarming of the Britons, AD 47
In Britain the situation inherited by the imperial governor Publius Ostorius Scapula was chaotic. Convinced that a new commander, with an unfamiliar army and with winter begun, would not fight them, hostile tribes had broken violently into the Roman province. But Ostorius knew that initial results are what produce alarm or confidence. So he marched his light auxiliary battalions rapidly ahead, and stamped out resistance. The enemy were dispersed and hard pressed. To prevent a rally, or a bitter treacherous peace which would give neither general nor army any rest. Ostorius prepared to disarm all suspects and reduce the whole territory as far as the Trent and Severn.

The revolt of the Iceni
The first to revolt against this were the Iceni. We had not defeated this powerful tribe in battle, since they had voluntarily become our allies. Led by them, the neighbouring tribes now chose a battlefield at a place protected by a rustic earthwork, with an approach too narrow to give access to cavalry. The Roman commander, though his troops were auxiliaries without regular support, proposed to carry these defences. At the signal, Ostorius' infantry, placed at appropriate points and reinforced by dismounted cavalrymen, broke through the embankment. The enemy, imprisoned by their own barrier, were overwhelmed—though with rebellion on their consciences, and no way out, they performed prodigies of valour. During the battle the governor's son, Marcus Ostorius Scapula, won the Citizen's Oak-Wreath for the saving of a Roman's life.

Ostorius in North Wales
This defeat of the Iceni quieted others who were wavering between war and peace. The Roman army then struck against the Decangi, ravaging their territory and collecting extensive booty. The enemy did not venture upon an open engagement and, when they tried to ambush the column, suffered for their trickery.

First Roman intervention among the Brigantes
Ostorius had nearly reached the sea facing Ireland when a rising by the Brigantes recalled him. For, until his conquests were secured, he was determined to postpone further expansion. The Brigantes subsided; their few peace-breakers were killed, and the rest were pardoned.

Ostorius in South Wales: context of the foundation of the colony at Colchester, AD 49; probable movement of the 20th legion to Gloucester, Kingsholm (the 'brigade garrison')
But neither sternness nor leniency prevented the Silures from fighting. To suppress them, a brigade garrison had to be established. In order to facilitate the displacement

611

of troops westward to man it, a strong settlement of ex-soldiers was established on conquered land at Camulodunum. Its mission was to protect the country against revolt and familiarize the provincials with law-abiding government. Next Ostorius invaded Silurian territory.

Caratacus leads the Britons, first in South Wales, then in Central Wales
The natural ferocity of the inhabitants was intensified by their belief in the prowess of Caratacus, whose many undefeated battles—and even many victories—had made him pre-eminent among British chieftains. His deficiency in strength was compensated by superior cunning and topographical knowledge. Transferring the war to the country of the Ordovices, he was joined by everyone who found the prospect of a Roman peace alarming. Then Caratacus staked his fate on a battle.

Tacitus *Annals* 12. 31–3
tr. M. Grant (Penguin 1977)

N21 The defeat of Caratacus and the magnanimity of Claudius

Note again the importance placed on success in Britain.

35   It was a great victory. Caratacus' wife and daughter were captured: his brother surrendered. He himself sought sanctuary with Cartimandua, queen of the Brigantes. But the defeated have no refuge. He was arrested, and handed over to the conquerors.
36   The war in Britain was in its ninth year. The reputation of Caratacus had spread beyond the islands and through the neighbouring provinces to Italy itself. These people were curious to see the man who had defied our power for so many years. Even at Rome his name meant something. Besides, the emperor's attempts to glorify himself conferred additional glory on Caratacus in defeat. For the people were summoned as though for a fine spectacle, while the Guard stood in arms on the parade ground before their camp. Then there was a march past, with Caratacus' petty vassals, and the decorations and neck-chains and spoils of his foreign wars. Next were displayed his brothers, wife, and daughter. Last came the king himself. The others, frightened, degraded themselves by entreaties. But there were no downcast looks or appeals for mercy from Caratacus. On reaching the dais he spoke in these terms.
37   'Had my lineage and rank been accompanied by only moderate success, I should have come to this city as friend rather than prisoner, and you would not have disdained to ally yourself peacefully with one so nobly born, the ruler of so many nations. As it is, humiliation is my lot, glory yours. I had horses, men, arms, wealth. Are you surprised I am sorry to lose them? If you want to rule the world, does it follow that everyone else welcomes enslavement? If I had surrendered without a blow before being brought before you, neither my downfall nor your triumph

would have become famous. If you execute me, they will be forgotten. Spare me, and I shall be an everlasting token of your mercy!'

Claudius responded by pardoning him and his wife and brothers. Released from their chains, they offered to Agrippina, conspicuously seated on another dais nearby, the same homage and gratitude as they had given the emperor. That a woman should sit before Roman standards was an unprecedented novelty. She was asserting her partnership in the empire her ancestors had won.

38 Then the senate met. It devoted numerous complimentary speeches to the capture of Caratacus. This was hailed as equal in glory to any previous Roman general's exhibition of a captured king. They cited the display of Syphax by Publius Cornelius Scipio Africanus and of Perseus by Lucius Aemilius Paullus. Ostorius received an honorary Triumph. But now his success, hitherto unblemished, began to waver. Possibly the elimination of Caratacus had caused a slackening of energy, in the belief that the war was over. Or perhaps the enemy's sympathy with their great king had whetted their appetite for revenge.

Tacitus *Annals* 12. 35–8
tr. M. Grant (Penguin 1977)

N22 Events after Caratacus' defeat

The defeat of Caratacus was not the end of disturbances in Britain: there was further trouble with the Silures and the Brigantes.

(a)
On hearing of the governor's death the emperor, not wanting to leave the province masterless, appointed Aulus Didius Gallus to take over. Didius made for Britain rapidly. But he found a further deterioration. For in the interval a Roman brigade commanded by Manlius Valens had suffered a reverse. Reports were magnified— the enemy magnified them, to frighten the new general; and the new general magnified them to increase his glory if he won, and improve his excuse if resistance proved unbreakable. Again the damage was due to the Silures; until deterred by Didius' arrival, they plundered far and wide.

(b) *Venutius turns against Rome.*

However, since Caratacus' capture the best strategist was Venutius who as I mentioned earlier, was a Brigantian. While married to the tribal queen, Cartimandua, he had remained loyal and under Roman protection. But divorce had immediately been followed by hostilities against her and then against us. At first, the Brigantes had merely fought among themselves. Cartimandua had astutely trapped Venutius' brother and other relatives. But her enemies, infuriated and goaded by fears of humiliating feminine rule, invaded her kingdom with a powerful force of picked warriors. We had foreseen this, and sent auxiliary battalions to support her. The engagement that followed had no positive results at first but ended more favourably. A battle fought by a regular brigade under Caesius Nasica likewise had a satisfactory ending. Didius, of impressive seniority and incapacitated by age, was content to act through subordinates and on the defensive.

(These campaigns were conducted by two imperial governors over a period of years. But I have described them in one place since piecemeal description would cast a strain on the memory.) . . .

Tacitus *Annals* 12. 40
tr. M. Grant (Penguin 1977)

N23 The rebellion of Boudicca

The spelling Boudicca *has been adopted here. It is certain that the traditional* Boadicea *derives from corruption in the text of Tacitus, and that Tacitus spelt her name in the fashion now in general use in books on Roman Britain. However, there is philological evidence that to the Britons she was* Boudica, *pronounced* 'Bowdeekah' *(see Kenneth Jackson in* Britannia *10 (1979) 255). This form has been adopted by Graham Webster for his book* Boudica *(Batsford 1978) but is not yet in general use. (The date of the beginning of the Boudiccan rebellion has been much disputed, as between AD 60 and AD 61. See the discussion by Kevin K. Carroll in* Britannia *10 (1979) 197 ff.).*

(a) *The death of Prasutagus and its consequences for the Iceni*

Prasutagus. . . . king of the Iceni and famous for his long-standing display of wealth, had left as his heirs the emperor and his own two daughters, calculating by this act of subservience to preserve both his kingdom and his family from harm in the future. The very opposite occurred. As if they were spoils of war his kingdom was plundered by centurions of the Roman Army and his household by Roman slaves. At the beginning his widow was flogged and his daughters raped. Certain Icenian nobles were stripped of their ancestral estates, as if the Romans had been given the whole territory as an outright gift, and relatives of the king were treated as if they were slaves.

Tacitus *Annals* 14. 31
tr. Salway *Roman Britain and the Early Empire*

(b) *A duty of the provincial procurator*

1 Ulpian in the 16th book 'ad edictum':   2 This above all is the duty of the procurator of the emperor, that by his order a slave of Caesar's may take possession

of an inheritance in Caesar's name. If the emperor is designated heir, the procurator legally confirms this by personally assembling and taking possession of inherited property.

Ulpian in Justinian *Digest* 1. 19. 1–2
tr. LACT *Literary Sources*

(c) *The British view expressed*

Once they had had only one king to a tribe: now they had two. The governor oppressed their persons, the procurator their property. Whatever the quarrels between these two officials they were as one in ruining their subjects. From the one came centurions, from the other slaves, both to inflict violence and insult. No excess of greed or lust was omitted. In battle it was the strong who gained the spoils, but now it was at the hands of cowards and men totally unfit for war that they were being driven out of their homes and suffering both loss of their children and conscription of themselves into the Roman Army. Indeed that last indignity suggested that it was only for their own country that Britons did not know how to die.

Tacitus *Agricola* 15. 2–3
tr. Salway *Roman Britain and the Early Empire*

N24 The spread of the rebellion

The trouble spreads to the Trinovantes (note their particular grievances). The establishment of the Imperial cult was intended not only to impress the natives with the majesty of Rome and the Emperor, but also to act as a focus for loyalty. Involvement of the native aristocracy in Roman public life by enrolling them in its priesthood (in the same way that Roman nobles undertook ritual duties at Rome) should have encouraged the development of a loyal, Romanized governing class onto whom the responsibilities and burdens of running the local administration could eventually be shifted. The attempt has badly misfired. (For the arguments against believing that the temple at Colchester was dedicated to Claudius actually during his lifetime see D. Fishwick in Britannia *3 (1972) 164 ff.). The spelling of the tribal name varies in the ancient sources between Trinobantes and Trinovantes. Philology suggests the latter to be closer to the actual form current in Britain.*

These insults—and fear of even worse now that they had been reduced to provincial status—caused the Iceni to take up arms. The Trinobantes (of Essex) were stirred to revolt with them, together with some others who, not yet broken to servitude, had bound themselves by secret oaths to resume their independence. Hatred was greatest against the retired veterans from the Roman Army, since those who had been recently settled in the new colony of Colchester were in the process of driving the locals from their homes and land, calling them prisoners and slaves. In this intolerable behaviour the veterans were encouraged by serving soldiers who shared the same outlook and looked forward to similar lack of control when they themselves retired. In particular the Temple of the Divine Claudius was seen as a citadel and symbol of eternal slavery—and those who had been chosen as its priests found themselves obliged to pour out their whole fortunes in its service.

Tacitus *Annals* 14. 31
tr. Salway *Roman Britain and the Early Empire*

N25 Dio's version of the outbreak of the rebellion

2. 1   Claudius had given sums of money to the leading Britons, and according to Catus Decianus, the procurator of the island, this money had to be returned together with the rest. The confiscation of this money was the pretext for the war. In addition, Seneca, with a view to a good rate of interest, had lent the reluctant islanders 40,000,000 sesterces and had then called it all in at once, and not very gently. So rebellion broke out.   2   But above all the rousing of the Britons, the persuading of them to fight against the Romans, the winning of the leadership and the command throughout the war—this was the work of Buduica [Boudicca], a woman of the British royal family who had uncommon intelligence for a woman.   3   When she had collected an army about 120,000 strong, Buduica mounted a rostrum made in the Roman fashion of heaped-up earth. She was very tall and grim; her gaze was penetrating and her voice was harsh;   4   she grew her long auburn hair to the hips and wore a large golden torque and a voluminous patterned cloak with a thick plaid fastened over it. This was how she always dressed. Now, taking a spear too to add to her effect upon the entire audience, she made this speech...

7. 1   So Buduica harangued the people. She then led her army against the Romans, who happened to be without a leader because the general Paulinus was campaigning in Mona, (Anglesey) an island close to Britain. This gave her the chance to sack and plunder two Roman cities and perpetrate the indescribable slaughter to which I have already referred. Every kind of atrocity was inflicted upon their captives,   2   and the most fearful bestiality was when they hung up naked the noblest and best-looking women. They cut off their breasts and stitched them to their mouths, so that the women seemed to be eating them, and after this they impaled them on sharp stakes run right up the body.   3   While they were doing all this in the grove of Andate and other sacred places they performed sacrifices, feasted, and abandoned all restraint. (Andate was their name for victory, and she enjoyed their especial reverence.)

Dio Cassius 62. 2. 1-4; 7. 1-3
tr. LACT *Literary Sources*

N26 The fall of London and Verulamium

The governor, Suetonius Paulinus, ahead of the bulk of his army, decides to abandon London.

He decided to sacrifice the one town to save the general situation. Undeflected by the prayers and tears of those who begged for his help he gave the signal to move, taking into his column any who could join it. Those who were unfit for war because of their sex, or too aged to go or too fond of the place to leave, were butchered by the enemy. The same massacre occurred at the city of Verulamium, for the barbarian British, happiest when looting and unenthusiastic about real effort, bypassed the forts and garrisons and headed for where they knew lay the maximum of undefended booty. Something like 70,000 Roman citizens and other friends of Rome died in the places I have mentioned. The Britons took no prisoners, sold no captives as slaves and went in for none of the usual trading of war. They wasted no time in getting down to the bloody business of hanging, burning and crucifying. It was as if they feared that retribution might catch up with them while their vengeance was only half-complete.

Tacitus *Annals* 14. 33
tr. Salway *Roman Britain and the Early Empire*

N27 Britain after the defeat in battle of Boudicca and her allies

Wherever the British tribes had been hostile or neutral they were devastated by fire and the sword. Yet their worst tribulation was famine, for they had neglected to sow the crops, enlisting the men regardless of age and intending to capture our stores for their own. They were still slow to make peace because Julius Classicianus, posted out as successor to Catus as provincial procurator, and who, too, was at odds with Suetonius Paulinus, allowed private dislike to interfere with the public interest and put it about that they should wait for a new governor who would deal more mercifully with a surrendered enemy, being free from bitterness against a former enemy he had himself faced in war and not puffed up with the pride of personal victory. Classicianus also reported to Rome that there would be no end to hostilities till Suetonius was recalled and further attributed the reverses in Britain to Suetonius' own vices and the successes to luck.

The consequence was that Polyclitus, one of the emperor's freedmen, was sent to investigate the situation in Britain, Nero having great hopes that Polyclitus' personal authority would not only heal the rift between governor and procurator but also persuade the rebellious barbarians to accept the idea of peace. Nor did Polyclitus fail: burdening both Italy and Gaul on the way with his vast retinue he managed, after crossing the Channel, to strike terror even into our own army. The

617

enemy just thought him comic: themselves still imbued with notions of liberty they had not yet realized the power of degenerates. They were amazed that a general and his army who had successfully brought to a close such a great war should give obedience to mere servants. However everything was played down when reported to the emperor. Suetonius was retained in office, but a little later when a few ships had been wrecked on the shore and their crews lost he was retired as commander-in-chief in Britain as if he had been prolonging the war and replaced by Petronius Turpilianus who had just finished his consulship. The latter neither provoked the enemy nor was harassed by them and thus gained the honourable name of peace for what was disgraceful inactivity.

Tacitus *Annals* 14. 38–9
tr. Salway *Roman Britain and the Early Empire*

N28 The Emperor Nero's attitude to Britain

It is sometimes argued that this incident refers to the beginning of his reign (i.e. while Aulus Didius was governor). It does, however, seem more likely to have occurred during the Boudiccan rebellion or in the uncertain climate of its aftermath.

He was never at any time moved by any desire or hope of expanding the empire. He even contemplated withdrawing the army from Britain, and only desisted from his purpose because he did not wish to appear to belittle the glory of his father. . . .

Suetonius *Nero* 18
tr. LACT *Literary Sources*

N29 The fall of the client kingdoms

The revolt of Cartimandua and Venutius in AD 69

The background is the successive army revolts on the Continent, which led to the suicide of Nero and the Year of the Four Emperors.

As a result of this dissension and the frequent rumours of the Civil Wars, the Britons revived their ambitions. The leader in this was Venutius, a man of barbarous spirit who hated the Roman power. In addition he had motives of personal hostility against queen Cartimandua. On Cartimandua's high birth was based her rule over the Brigantes. Her power had grown when she captured king Caratacus by treachery and handed him over to embellish the triumph of the emperor Claudius. The result was riches, and the self-indulgence which flowers with prosperity. Venutius had been her husband. Spurning him, she made his armour-bearer Vellocatus her husband,

and her partner in government. The power of her house was shaken to its foundations by this outrage. The people of the tribe declared for Venutius: only the passion and the savage temper of the queen supported the adulterer. Venutius therefore summoned his supporters. The Brigantes rallied to him, reducing Cartimandua to the last extremity. She besought Roman protection. Our alae and cohorts fought indecisive battles, but at length rescued the queen from danger. The kingdom went to Venutius; we were left with a war to fight.

Tacitus *Histories* 3. 45
tr. LACT *Literary Sources*

N30 Britain after Nero

(a) *The Flavian governors*

This passage describes specifically actions taken by Tacitus' father-in-law, the governor Gnaeus Julius Agricola, in the winter of AD 79–80, but it is clear that under his predecessor, Julius Frontinus, the process had already begun. The difference between this and the support given earlier to client kings is that it is a deliberate attempt to create civitates *ruled by Romanized native aristocracy. The attempt to involve the locals in the Imperial Cult at Colchester had been bungled. This is a much more systematic and, apparently, widely extended policy. There is archaeological evidence to suggest it was not everywhere successful, and that it took Hadrian to revive it. But by the end of Hadrian's reign (AD 138), the initial development of the province as an integral part of the Empire was largely complete.*

The following winter was taken up with the soundest projects. In order to encourage rough men who lived in scattered settlements (and were thus only too ready to fall to fighting) to live in a peaceful and inactive manner by offering them the consequent pleasures of life, Agricola urged them privately and helped them officially to build temples, public squares with public buildings (*fora*), and houses (*domus*). He praised those who responded quickly and severely criticized the laggards. In this way competition for public recognition took the place of compulsion. Moreover he had the children of the leading Britons educated in the civilized arts and openly placed the natural ability of the Britons above that of the Gauls, however well trained. The result was that those who had once shunned the Latin language now sought fluency and eloquence in it. Roman dress, too, became popular and the toga was frequently seen. Little by little there was a slide towards the allurements of degeneracy: assembly-rooms (*porticus*), bathing establishments and smart dinner parties. In their inexperience the Britons called it civilization when it was really all part of their servitude.

Tacitus *Agricola* 21
tr. Salway *Roman Britain and the Early Empire*

(b) *The pattern of Roman Britain is finally established. Writing under Antoninus Pius (Emperor 138–61) Appian summarizes in a few words what must by now have become apparent, that Britain was always going to need a large garrison and administration which could hardly be balanced by what could be extracted from it.*

This is in the sharpest contrast to Strabo's underestimate of the army required (L10b). Yet failure to complete the conquest is, like Strabo's reason for Augustus' failure to launch it, still presented in terms of profit and loss. There is little evidence that Romans, except perhaps Hadrian himself, recognized limits to empire other than those imposed by current expediency which might change at any time.

The Romans have penetrated beyond the northern ocean to Britain, an island larger than a considerable continent. They rule the most important part of it—more than half—and have no need of the rest; in fact the part they have brings them in little money.

Appian *Preface to the Roman Wars* 5
tr. LACT *Literary Sources*

O JUDAEA

O1 Herod's interview with Octavian after Actium

[Herod then] hastened to Rhodes to meet Caesar. And when his ship arrived at the city, he removed his diadem but did not leave off anything else that belonged to his rank. And when, on meeting Caesar, he was permitted to converse with him, he showed still more fully the greatness of his spirit by neither turning to supplication, as would have been natural in the circumstances, nor offering a petition as if in acknowledgement of transgression; instead, he gave an account of what he had done, and this without making excuses for himself. For he told Caesar that he had had the greatest friendship for Antony and had done everything in his power to bring control of affairs into his hands. He had not, to be sure, taken part in his campaign because he had been distracted therefrom by the Arabs, but he had sent him money and grain, though these were more modest contributions than he ought to have made. . . . In this he had behaved less well than he ought but in one respect at least he was conscious of having done well, namely in not having abandoned Antony after his defeat in the battle of Actium and in not shifting his hopes when Antony's fortune was clearly changing. Instead, he had continued to show himself, if not a valuable fellow-fighter, at least a very skilful adviser to Antony, to whom he had suggested that the only way to save himself and not lose his power was to do away with Cleopatra. 'For', he said, 'if she had first been got out of the way, it would have been possible for him to keep his power, and he would have found it easier to come to an understanding with you. . . . But he paid no attention to any of these suggestions. . . . If now in your anger at Antony you also condemn my zeal in his cause, I will not deny that I have acted in this way nor will I be ashamed to speak openly of my loyalty to him. But if you disregard the outward appearance and examine how I behave towards my benefactors and what sort of friend I am, you can find out about me from what you learn concerning my past actions. For with merely a change in name the very ideal of firm friendship, as exemplified in me, will no less fully win approval.'

By such words and by his general behaviour he showed his freedom of soul, and greatly attracted Caesar, who was honourable and generous, so that the acts which had caused charges to be brought against Herod now served to form the basis of Caesar's goodwill towards him. He then restored his diadem to him, at the same time urging him to show himself no less a friend to him then he had formerly been to Antony.

Josephus *AJ* 15. 187–95 (abridged)
tr. R. Marcus and A. Wikgren (Loeb 1963)

O2 Antonia

Herod's new fortress in Jerusalem, Antonia, is here described by Josephus in con-nection with Titus' siege of Jerusalem in AD 70. The reference to a Roman infantry unit concerns Judaea as a Roman province; cf. the first paragraph of O37.

Antonia, situated at the junction of two colonnades of the first Temple court, the western and northern, was built on a rock 75 feet high and precipitous on every side. It was the work of king Herod and revealed in the highest degree the grandeur of his conceptions. In the first place, from the very bottom the rock was faced with polished stone slabs, both for ornament and to ensure that anyone who tried to climb up or down would slip off; next, before the actual tower was a $4\frac{1}{2}$ foot wall, and inside this the whole elevation of Antonia rose 60 feet into the air. The interior was like a palace in spaciousness and completeness; for it was divided into rooms of every kind to serve every need, colonnades, bathrooms, and wide courtyards where troops could encamp, so that in having all conveniences it was virtually a town, in its splendour a palace. In general design it was a tower with four other towers attached, one at each corner; of these three were 75 feet high, and the one at the south west corner 105 feet, so that from it the whole Temple could be viewed. Where it joined the Temple colonnades, stairs led down to both, and by these the guards descended; for a Roman infantry unit was always stationed there, and at the festivals they extended along the colonnades fully armed and watched for any sign of popular discontent. The city was dominated by the Temple, the Temple by Antonia, so that Antonia housed the guards of all three.

Josephus *BJ* 5. 238-45
tr. Williamson, rev. Smallwood

O3 Herod's three towers at the north-west angle of the city and his palace

Like Antonia (O2) these are described in connection with Titus' siege of Jerusalem in AD 70. The friend Hippicus is otherwise unknown. The tower named Phasael is still standing, under the misnomer of 'Tower of David'.

Opposite this tower was Hippicus and near to it two others, built by King Herod in the Old Wall, and superior in size, beauty, and strength to any in the whole world. For apart from his love of grandeur and his ambitions for the City, the king made the splendour of these works a means of expressing his own emotions, naming the towers after the three persons he cared for most, his brother, friend, and wife, to whose memory he dedicated them. His wife, as related already, he had himself killed through passionate love; the other two had fallen in battle, covered with glory. [*The tower named after Hippicus is then described.*]

The second tower, named Phasael after Herod's brother, was of equal length and width, 60 feet each way, the height of the solid part being also 60 feet. Round the top ran a colonnade 15 feet high, protected by breast-works and bulwarks. Rising from the middle of the colonnade was another tower, divided into splendid apartments which even included a bathroom, that the tower might lack nothing to make it seem a palace. The top was equipped with ramparts and turrets. The total height was about 135 feet, the general appearance like that of the tower at Pharos that shows the light of its fires to sailors approaching Alexandria; but the measurement round was much greater. [*The tower named after Herod's wife Mariamme is then described.*]

The great size of these three towers seemed much greater still because of their site. For the Old Wall in which they were placed was built on a high hill, and above the hill a sort of crest rose 45 feet higher. Erected on this the towers gained enormously in height. Another remarkable feature was the size of the stones: they did not consist of ordinary small stones or lumps that men might carry, but of white marble, cut into blocks, each 30 feet long, 15 wide, and $7\frac{1}{2}$ deep, so perfectly united that each tower looked like a single rock, sent up by mother earth and later cut and polished by artists' hands into shape and angles; so invisible from any viewpoint was the fitting of the joints.

A little way south of these towers and sheltered by them was the king's Palace, which no tongue could describe. Its magnificence and equipment were unsurpassable, surrounded as it was on every side by a wall 45 feet high, with ornamental towers evenly spaced along it, and containing huge banqueting halls and guest rooms with a hundred beds. Words cannot express the varied beauty of the stones, for kinds rare everywhere else were here brought together in quantity. There were ceilings remarkable for the length of the beams and the splendour of the ornamentation, and rooms without number, no two designed alike, and all luxuriously furnished, most of their contents being of gold or silver. On every side were numbers of intersecting colonnades, each differing in the design of its pillars. The open spaces between them were all green lawns, with coppices of different trees traversed by long walks, which were edged with deep canals and cisterns everywhere plentifully adorned with bronze statues through which the water poured out.

Josephus *BJ* 5. 161–81 (abridged)
tr. Williamson, rev. Smallwood

O4 Masada

Herod's refortification of Masada is here described in connection with the Roman siege of the fortress when the Jewish rebels made their last stand there in AD 73. The rock is not as high as Josephus implies—actually about 1,200 feet. (His remark that the bottom of the ravine is out of sight and similar remarks elsewhere suggest that he was short-sighted.) The path is not 3½ miles long, but about 2. Josephus seems unaware that there were two palaces on Masada; he describes the northern, private palace, though he is not clear about the three natural rock terraces descending in gigantic steps on which it was built, but places it 'on the western slope', where the larger administrative palace stood.

A rock with a very large perimeter and lofty all the way along is broken off on every side by deep ravines. Their bottom is out of sight, and from it rise sheer cliffs on which no animal can get a foothold except in two places where the rock can be climbed, though with difficulty. One of these paths comes from the Dead Sea to the east, the other from the west—an easier route. They call the first one the Snake, because of its narrowness and constant windings: it is broken as it rounds the projecting cliffs and often turns back on itself, then lengthening out again a little at a time, manages to make some trifling advance. Walking along it is like balancing on a tight-rope. The least slip means death; for on either side yawns an abyss so terrifying that it could make the boldest tremble. After an agonizing march of 3½ miles the summit is reached, which does not narrow to a sharp point but is a sort of elevated plateau. On this the high priest Jonathan first built a fortress and named it Masada: later King Herod devoted great care to the improvement of the place. The entire summit, measuring ¾ mile round, he enclosed within a limestone wall 18 feet high and 12 wide, in which he erected 37 towers 75 feet high: from these one could pass through a ring of chambers right round the inside of the wall. For the plateau was of rich soil more workable than any plain, and the king reserved it for cultivation, so that if ever there was a shortage of food from without, this should not injure those who had entrusted their safety to these ramparts. He built a palace, too, on the western slope, below the fortifications on the crest and sloping down northwards. The palace wall was of great height and strongly built, with 90 foot towers at the four corners. The design of the interior apartments, the colonnades, and the bathrooms was varied and magnificent, with supporting pillars cut from a single block in every case, and the walls and floors of the room tiled with stones of many hues. At every spot where people lived, whether on the plateau, round the palace, or before the wall, he had cut out in the rock numbers of great tanks to hold water, ensuring a supply as great as where spring water can be used. A sunken road led from the palace to the hill-top, invisible from outside. Even the visible roads were not easy for an enemy to use: the eastern one, as already explained, was by nature unusable; the western was guarded by a large fort at its narrowest point, at least 500 yards from the crest. To pass this was impossible, to capture it by no means easy, while it had been made difficult even for innocent travellers to get away. So strong had the fortress's defences against enemy attack been made both by nature and by human effort. [*The supplies of food and military equipment are then described.*] For these preparations, indeed, there were very strong reasons: it is believed that Herod equipped this fortress as a refuge for himself, suspecting a double danger—the danger from the Jewish masses, who might push him off his throne and restore to power the royal house that had preceded him, and the greater and more terrible danger from the Egyptian queen, Cleopatra.

Josephus *BJ* 7. 280–301 (abridged)
tr. Williamson, rev. Smallwood

O5 Herod's new port of Caesarea

(a) *The buildings*

When he observed that there was a place near the sea, formerly called Strato's Tower, which was very well suited to be the site of the city, he set about making a magnificent plan and put up buildings all over the city, not of ordinary material but of white stone. He also adorned it with a very costly palace, with civic halls and—what was greatest of all and required the most labour—with a well-protected harbour, of the size of the Piraeus, with landing-places and secondary anchorages inside. . . . Now this city is located in Phoenicia, on the sea-route to Egypt, between Joppa and Dora. These are small towns on the seashore and are poor harbours because the south-west wind beats on them and always dredges up sand from the sea upon the shore, and thus does not permit a smooth landing; instead, it is usually necessary for merchants to ride unsteadily at anchor off shore. To remedy this inconvenient feature of the land Herod laid out a circular harbour enclosing enough space for large fleets to lie at anchor near shore, and along this line he sank enormous rocks to a depth of twenty fathoms. Most of these rocks were fifty feet in length, and no less than eighteen in breadth, and nine in height, some of them being larger, some smaller than that. The structure which he set in the sea as a barrier was two hundred feet in width. Half of it was opposed to the surge of the waves and held off the flood of waters breaking there from all sides, and was therefore called a breakwater. The other half, supported on a stone wall, was divided at intervals by towers. . . . The entrance or mouth of the harbour was made to face north, for this wind always brings the clearest weather. The foundation of the whole circular wall on the left of those sailing into the harbour was a tower resting upon piled stones as a broad firm base to withstand pressure from the water, while on the right were two great stone blocks, larger than the tower on the other side, which were upright and joined together. In a circle round the harbour there was a continuous line of dwellings constructed of the most polished stone, and in their midst was a mound on which there stood a temple of Caesar, visible a great way off to those sailing into the harbour, which had a statue of Rome and also one of Caesar. The city itself is called Caesarea, and is most beautiful both in material and in construction. But below the city the underground passages and sewers cost no less effort than the structures built above them. Of these some led at equal distances from one another to the harbour and the sea, while one diagonal passage connected all of them, so that the rainwater and the refuse of the inhabitants were easily

625

carried off together. And whenever the sea was driven in from offshore, it would flow through the whole city and flush it from below. Herod also built a theatre of stone in the city, and on the south side of the harbour, farther back, an amphitheatre large enough to hold a great crowd of people and conveniently situated for a view of the sea.

Josephus *AJ* 15. 331–41 (abridged)
tr. R. Marcus and A. Wikgren (Loeb 1963)

(b) *The inauguration, between 12 and 9 BC*

The full name of Caesarea was 'Caesarea at the Augustan (Sebastos) Harbour'.

At about this time Caesarea Sebaste, which Herod had been building was completed. . . . And so there was to begin with a very great festival of dedication and most lavish arrangements. For he had announced a contest in music and athletic exercises, and had prepared a great number of gladiators and wild beasts and also horse races and the very lavish shows that are to be seen at Rome and in various other places. And this contest too he dedicated to Caesar, having arranged to celebrate it every fifth year. And Caesar, adding lustre to his love of glory, from his own resources sent all the equipment needed for such games. On her own account Caesar's wife Julia sent many of her greatest treasures from Rome, so that the entire sum was reckoned as no less than five hundred talents. When to see the sights there came to the city a great multitude as well as the envoys sent by communities because of the benefits that they had received, Herod welcomed them all and entertained them with lodgings and meals and continuous feasts.

Josephus *AJ* 16. 136–40
tr. R. Marcus and A. Wikgren (Loeb 1963)

O6 Herod's benefactions to places outside his kingdom

Herod's visit to Rome probably took place in 16 BC when he went to fetch Mariamme I's sons who had been educated at Augustus' court.

After this spate of building he extended his generosity to a great many cities outside his boundaries. For Tripolis, Damascus, and Ptolemais he provided gymnasia, for Byblus a wall, for Berytus and Tyre halls, colonnades, temples, and market-places, for Sidon and Damascus theatres, for the coastal Laodicea an aqueduct, and for Ascalon baths, magnificent fountains, and cloistered quadrangles remarkable for both scale and craftsmanship; in other places he dedicated woods and parks. Many towns, as if they belonged to his kingdom, received gifts of land; others he endowed with revenues to finance for all time the annual appointment of a gymnasiarch—Cos, for instance—that the office might never lapse. Corn he bestowed on all who needed it. To Rhodes he over and over again gave money for naval construction, and when the temple of Apollo was burnt down he rebuilt it with new spendour out of his own purse. . . . And the wide street in Syrian Antioch, once avoided because of the mud, did he not pave—two and a quarter miles of it—with polished marble, and to keep the rain off furnish it with a colonnade from end to end?

It may be suggested that all these benefits were enjoyed only by the particular community favoured; but his endowment of Elis was a gift not only to Greece in general but to every corner of the civilized world reached by the fame of the Olympic Games. Seeing that the games were declining for lack of funds and that the sole relic of ancient Greece was slipping away, he not only acted as president of the four-yearly meeting held when he happened to be on his way to Rome, but endowed them for all time with an income big enough to ensure that his presidency should never be forgotten.

Josephus *BJ* 1. 422-7
tr. Williamson, rev. Smallwood

O7 Herod's attempt at Hellenization in Jerusalem

The second of the Ten Commandments in Exodus 20 appears to prohibit all 'graven images', i.e. all representational art. It was, however, often interpreted as merely prohibiting representations of the human figure designed for worship.

Herod went still farther in departing from the native customs, and through foreign practices he gradually corrupted the ancient way of life, which had hitherto been inviolable. . . . For in the first place he established athletic contests every fifth year in honour of Caesar, and he built a theatre in Jerusalem, and after that a very large amphitheatre in the plain, both being spectacularly lavish but foreign to Jewish custom, for the use of such buildings and the exhibition of such spectacles have not been traditional with the Jews. Herod, however, celebrated the quinquennial festival in the most splendid way, sending notices of it to the neighbouring peoples and inviting participants from the whole nation. Athletes and other classes of contestants were invited from every land, being attracted by the hope of winning the prizes offered and by the glory of victory. . . . There was also a supply of wild beasts, a great many lions and other animals having been brought together for him, such as were of extraordinary strength or of very rare kinds. When the practice began of involving them in combat with one another or setting condemned men to fight against them, foreigners were astonished at the expense and at the same time entertained by the dangerous spectacle, but to the natives it meant an open break with the customs held in honour by them. For it seemed glaring impiety to throw men to wild beasts for the pleasure of other men as spectators, and it seemed a

627

further impiety to change their established ways for foreign practices. But more than all else it was the trophies that irked them, for in the belief that these were images surrounded by weapons, which it was against their national custom to worship, they were exceedingly angry.

That the Jews were highly disturbed did not escape Herod's notice, and since he thought it inopportune to use force against them, he spoke to some of them reassuringly in an attempt to remove their religious scruples. He did not, however, succeed, for in their displeasure at the offences of which they thought him guilty, they cried out with one voice that although everything else might be endured, they would not endure images of men being brought into the city—meaning the trophies,—for this was against their national custom. Herod, therefore, seeing how disturbed they were and that they could not easily be brought round if they did not get some reassurance, summoned the most eminent among them and, leading them to the theatre, showed them the trophies and asked just what they thought these things were. When they cried out 'Images of men', he gave orders for the removal of the ornaments which covered them and showed the people the bare wood.

Josephus *AJ* 15. 267-79 (abridged)
tr. R. Marcus and A. Wikgren (Loeb 1963)

O8 Herod's new Temple in Jerusalem, begun in 23/22 BC

(a) *The temple is described most fully by Josephus in connection with Titus' siege of Jerusalem in AD 70. He starts with some rather vague remarks about the enclosure and its substructures.*

Of such foundations the works above were entirely worthy. The colonnades were all double, the supporting pillars were $37\frac{1}{2}$ feet high, cut from single blocks of the whitest marble, and the ceiling was panelled with cedar. The natural magnificence of it all, the perfect polish, and the accurate jointing afforded a remarkable spectacle, without any superficial ornament either painted or carved. The colonnades were 45 feet wide and the complete circuit of them measures $\frac{3}{4}$ miles, Antonia being enclosed within them. The whole area open to the sky was paved with stones of every kind and colour. Anyone passing through this towards the second court found it enclosed within a stone balustrade $4\frac{1}{2}$ feet high, a perfect specimen of craftmanship. In this at equal intervals stood slabs announcing the law of purification, some in Greek and some in Roman characters. No foreigner was to enter the holy area— this was the name given to the second court. [*The courts and the flights of steps and gates between them are then described.*]

The Sanctuary itself, the Holy Temple, situated in the middle, was reached by a flight of twelve steps. Seen from the front it was of the same height and width, 150 feet each way, but behind it was 60 feet narrower, for the entrance was flanked by shoulders, as it were, projecting 30 feet on either side. The first gate was 105 feet high and $37\frac{1}{2}$ wide; it had no doors, thus revealing instead of excluding the vast expanse of heaven. The face was covered with gold all over, and through the arch the first chamber could all be seen from without, huge as it was, and the inner gate and its surrounding wall, all glistening with gold, struck the beholder's eye. The Sanctuary was divided into two chambers, but only the first was visible all the way up, as it rose 135 feet from the ground, its length being 75 and its width 30. The gate of this was, as I said, covered with gold all over, as was the entire wall surrounding it. Above it were the golden grape-vines, from which hung bunches as big as a man. . . . There were golden doors $82\frac{1}{2}$ feet high and 24 wide. In front of these was a curtain of the same length, Babylonian tapestry embroidered with blue, white linen thread, scarlet and purple, a marvellous example of the craftsman's art. . . . Worked in the tapestry was the whole vista of the heavens except for the signs of the Zodiac.

Passing through the gate one entered the ground-floor chamber of the Sanctuary, 90 feet high, 90 long, and 30 wide. But the length was again divided. In the first part, partitioned off at 60 feet, were three most wonderful, world-famous works of art, a lampstand, a table, and an altar of incense. The seven lamps branching off from the lampstand symbolized the planets. . . . The inmost chamber measures 30 feet and was similarly separated by a curtain from the outer part. Nothing at all was kept in it; it was unapproachable, inviolable, and invisible to all, and was called the Holy of Holies. . . .

Viewed from without the Sanctuary had everything that could amaze either mind or eyes. Overlaid all round with stout plates of gold, in the first rays of the sun it reflected so fierce a blaze of fire that those who endeavoured to look at it were forced to turn away as if they had looked straight at the sun. To strangers as they approached it seemed in the distance like a mountain covered with snow; for any part not covered with gold was dazzling white. . . . In front of the Sanctuary stood the Altar, $22\frac{1}{2}$ feet high and as much as 75 feet long and 75 wide, with the four corners jutting out like horns, and with a gentle slope leading up to it from the south. It was built without the use of iron, and no iron ever came in contact with it. Round the Sanctuary and the Altar ran a graceful parapet of beautiful stone about 18 inches high, separating the laity from the priests inside.

Josephus *BJ* 5. 190–226 (excerpts)
tr. Williamson, rev. Smallwood

(b) *The gates and the south colonnade*

The first arch of the viaduct 'over the ravine', i.e. leading across the Valley of the Cheese-makers to the Upper City, still stands; traces of the monumental staircase leading down into the south end of the Valley of the Cheese-makers also survive.

In the western part of the court of the temple there were four gates. The first led to the palace by a passage over the intervening ravine, two others led to the suburb, and the last led to the other part of the city, from which it was separated by many steps going down to the ravine and from here up again to the hill. For the City lay opposite the temple, being in the form of a theatre and being bordered by a deep ravine along its whole southern side. The fourth front of this court, facing south, also had gates in the middle, and had over it the Royal Portico, which had three aisles, extending in length from the eastern to the western ravine. It was not possible for it to extend farther. And it was a structure more noteworthy than any under the sun. . . . The columns of the portico stood in four rows, one opposite the other all along—the fourth row was attached to a wall built of stone—, and the thickness of each column was such that it would take three men with outstretched arms touching one another to envelop it; its height was 27 feet, and there was a double moulding running round its base. The number of all the columns was a hundred and sixty-two, and their capitals were ornamented in the Corinthian style of carving. . . . The ceilings of the porticoes were ornamented with deeply cut wood-carvings representing all sorts of different figures. The ceiling of the middle aisle was raised to a greater height, and the front wall was cut at either end into architraves with columns built into it, and all of it was polished, so that these structures seemed incredible to those who had not seen them, and were beheld with amazement by those who set eyes on them.

> Josephus *AJ* 15. 410–16 (abridged)
> tr. R. Marcus, and A. Wikgren (Loeb 1963)

O9 The Balustrade inscription

This inscription, in Latin and Greek, was set up at the gates in the balustrade round the inner court of the Temple. One complete Greek copy survives, in the Archaeological Museum in Istanbul. The wording is clumsy, as the translation shows. A passage in Josephus (BJ 6. 124–6) shows that even Roman citizens who trespassed could be executed.

No gentile is to pass inside the balustrade and wall round the Temple. Anyone who is caught is responsible to himself for the fact that death follows.

> W. Dittenberger *OGIS* 598 (Leipzig 1903–5)
> tr. E. M. Smallwood

O10 Herod's loss of Augustus' favour

(a) *The cause*

Soon after 12 BC border troubles arose between Herod and the Nabataeans, instigated by Syllaeus, the chief minister of the elderly Nabataean king Obadas and virtual ruler of the country. After failing to stop raids on his territory without recourse to arms, Herod got leave from the legate of Syria to take military action and won a victory.

Messengers hastened to Syllaeus in Rome and informed him of what had happened, and, as was natural, exaggerated each incident. Now Syllaeus had already managed to make himself known to Caesar, and at this particular time was in attendance at court. When he heard the news, he immediately changed into black dress and went in to Caesar and told him that Arabia had been ravaged by war and the whole kingdom devastated because Herod had plundered it with his army. . . . [He] added maliciously that he himself would not have left his country if he had not been sure that Caesar was concerned that they should all be at peace with one another, and that if he had been there, he would have made the war unprofitable for Herod. Irritated by these words, Caesar asked Herod's friends who were there and his own men who had come from Syria only this one question, whether Herod had led his army out of the country. Since they were compelled to answer that one question, and Caesar did not hear under what circumstances and how Herod had acted, he became still more angry and wrote to Herod in a harsh tone throughout and particularly in the main point of his letter, which was that whereas formerly he had treated him as a friend, he would now treat him as a subject.

> Josephus *AJ* 16. 286–90 (abridged)
> tr. R. Marcus and A. Wikgren (Loeb 1963)

(b) *The reconciliation*

A few years later Nicolas of Damascus, Herod's chief adviser, was allowed to put Herod's case, and persuaded Augustus that Syllaeus had been the villain of the piece. Aretas had seized the Nabataean throne on the death of Obadas a year or two earlier.

Finally, Caesar's attitude underwent such a change that he condemned Syllaeus to death and became reconciled with Herod, for he felt regret at having written to him so harshly as a result of the calumny. He said to Syllaeus something to the effect that he had compelled him by his false statements to act unfairly towards a man who was his friend. In sum, Syllaeus was sent back to pay the penalty and what he owed his creditors, and then to be punished accordingly. But Caesar was not well disposed to Aretas because he had seized the throne by himself and with no reference to him. He had also decided to give Arabia to Herod but was prevented from doing so by the letters which had been sent by the latter. [*These concerned the trial and execution of two of Herod's sons c.7 BC.*] When he read them Caesar did not think it would be well to add another kingdom to Herod now that he was old and having so much trouble with his sons.

> Josephus *AJ* 16. 352–5 (abridged)
> tr. R. Marcus and A. Wikgren (Loeb 1963)

O11 The Pharisees' opposition to Herod's increasingly secular rule

This incident is not dated but from its position in Josephus' narrative belongs late in his reign. Pheroras was Herod's youngest brother, by now on bad terms with him.

There was also a group of Jews priding itself on its adherence to ancestral custom and claiming to observe the laws of which the Deity approves, and by these men, called Pharisees, the women of the court were ruled. These men were able to help the king greatly because of their foresight, and yet they were obviously intent upon combating and injuring him. At least when the whole Jewish people affirmed by an oath that it would be loyal to Caesar and to the king's government, these men, over six thousand in number, refused to take this oath, and when the king punished them with a fine, Pheroras' wife paid the fine for them.

Josephus *AJ* 17. 41-2
tr. R. Marcus and A. Wikgren (Loeb 1963)

O12 Further opposition to Herod, 5 BC

Apparently the Pharisee rabbis were interpreting the Second Commandment strictly (cf. O7); there is no suggestion that the eagle was to be worshipped. Burning alive was not a normal Jewish method of execution.

There were two rabbis in the City with a great reputation as exponents of national tradition, and for that reason held in the highest esteem by the whole nation. . . . Many young students came to them for instruction in the laws; in fact they daily attracted a host of men in their prime. When they learnt that the king was succumbing to his sickness of body and mind, they dropped a hint to their acquaintances that here was a wonderful chance to strike a blow for God and to pull down the works erected contrary to the laws of their fathers. Although it was unlawful to have in the Sanctuary images or portrait-busts of the likeness of any living thing, the king had put up over the Great Gate a golden eagle. This the rabbis now urged them to cut down, saying that even if danger was involved, it was a glorious thing to die for the laws of their fathers; for those who came to such an end there was a sure hope of immortality and the eternal enjoyment of blessings . . .

While they were preaching thus, it was rumoured that the king was actually dying, so that the young men undertook the task with more confidence. At midday, when masses of people were walking about the Temple courts, they lowered themselves by stout ropes from the roof and began to cut down the golden eagle with axes. The news quickly reached the king's officer, who hurried to the spot with a large force, seized about forty young men and took them before the king. He began by asking them whether they had dared to cut down the golden eagle.

They said they had. Who told them to do it? The law of their fathers. What made them so cheerful when they were about to be executed? The knowledge that they would enjoy greater blessings after their death. At this the king exploded with rage, and forgetting his sickness went out to address a public meeting. He attacked the men at great length as temple-robbers, who pleading the Law as an excuse had some ulterior purpose, and demanded their punishment for sacrilege. The people, fearing punitive measures on a wide front, begged him to punish first those who had suggested the attempt, then those who had been caught in the act, and to take no action against the rest. The king reluctantly agreed: those who had lowered them-selves from the roof together with the rabbis he burnt alive; the rest of the men he handed over to his attendants for execution.

Josephus *BJ* 1. 648–58 (abridged)
tr. Williamson, rev. Smallwood

O13 Herod's last will

Auranitis, omitted here, also came under Philip.

Then because of the change of mind he had undergone, he once more altered his will and designated Antipas, to whom he had left his throne, to be tetrarch of Galilee and Peraea, while he bestowed the kingdom on Archelaus. Gaulanitis, Trachonitis, Batanaea and Paneas were to be given as a tetrarchy to his son Philip, who was a full brother of Archelaus, while Jamnia, Azotus and Phasaelis were given over to his sister Salome along with five hundred thousand pieces of coined silver. He also provided for all his other relatives and left them wealthy through gifts of money and the assignment of revenues. To Caesar he left ten million pieces of coined silver beside vessels of gold and silver and some very valuable garments, while to Caesar's wife Julia and some others he left five million pieces of silver. Having done this he died, on the fifth day after having his son Antipater killed.

Josephus *AJ* 17. 188–91
tr. R. Marcus and A. Wikgren (Loeb 1963)

O14 Archelaus' conduct immediately after Herod's death early in 4 BC

Archelaus continued to mourn for seven days out of respect for his father—the custom of the country prescribes this number of days—and then, after feasting the crowds and making an end of the mourning, he went up to the Temple. Wherever he passed there were acclamations and expressions of praise for him, and all the people vied with one another as to who should seem to acclaim him the most extravagantly. Then he went up to a high platform that had been built there, and taking his seat on a throne of gold, acknowledged the greetings of the crowd, being delighted by their acclamations and taking pleasure in their goodwill. He also expressed his gratitude that they did not bear him any ill-will for the injuries that his father had inflicted upon them, saying that he would try not to be remiss in repaying their devotion to him. For the present, however, he would refrain from taking the name of king, for he would not validly be honoured with this title until Caesar should confirm the will that had been made by his father. . . . Nevertheless, when the supreme power should come to him, he would not be lacking in the virtue of rewarding their goodwill, for he would make an effort to show himself kinder to them in every way than his father had been. The people believed, as is usual with a multitude, that the first days are likely to reveal the intentions of those who come into high office, and the more mildly and considerately Archelaus spoke to them, the more extravagant was the praise they gave him. Then they turned to him with requests for favours. Some cried out that he should lighten the yearly payments that they were making. Others demanded the release of the prisoners who had been put in chains by Herod—and there were many of these and they had been in prison for a long time. Still others demanded the removal of the taxes that had been levied upon public purchases and sales and had been ruthlessly exacted. To these demands Archelaus made no opposition, for he was eager to do anything to please the multitude, in the belief that the goodwill of the people would greatly help to preserve his power.

Josephus *AJ* 17. 200-8 (abridged)
tr. R. Marcus and A. Wikgren (Loeb 1963)

O15 Negotiations in Rome about Herod's kingdom

When the question of the succession was considered by Augustus and his consilium, *there was much family wrangling, and a delegation of Jews came to give their views.*

When permission to speak was given to the Jewish envoys who were waiting to ask for the dissolution of the kingdom, they applied themselves to accusing Herod of lawless acts. They argued that while he had been a king in name, he had brought together in his own person the most ruthless cruelties of all the various tyrants and had used their devices for the destruction of the Jews and had not been averse to adding many new forms of his own natural invention. Indeed, while many had perished through forms of destruction that had never been witnessed before, those who still lived were much more unfortunate in their suffering than these others because they were distressed not only by the wrongs that they witnessed and reflected upon, but also by the loss of their property. To be precise, he had not ceased to adorn neighbouring cities that were inhabited by foreigners, although this led to the ruin and disappearance of cities located in his own kingdom. He had indeed reduced the entire nation to helpless poverty after taking it over in as flourishing a condition as few had ever known, and he was wont to kill members of the nobility upon absurd pretexts and then take their property for himself; and if he did permit any of them to have the doubtful pleasure of living, he would condemn them to be stripped of their possessions. In addition to the collecting of the tribute that was imposed on everyone each year, lavish extra contributions had to be made to him and his household and friends and those of his slaves who were sent out to collect the tribute, because there was no immunity at all from outrage unless bribes were paid. . . . It was with good reason, therefore, that they had gladly welcomed Archelaus as their king, for they had thought that whoever should succeed to the throne would show himself to be more moderate than Herod. And they had joined in mourning his father out of consideration for him and had tried to conform to his wishes in other respects in the hope of being able to obtain reasonable treatment. But Archelaus, fearful that he might not be considered a legitimate son of Herod, without any delay and with great promptness showed the nation what his real intention was, and this he did before he obtained complete possession of the sovereignty, which only Caesar had the authority to give or to withhold. Archelaus had also given his future subjects an example of the kind of virtue to be expected of him in the way of moderation and respect for law to be used towards them, and did this in one of the first acts he performed in the sight of his fellow-citizens and of God, namely in causing the slaughter of three thousand of his countrymen in the Temple precinct. How could he then now fail to find good reason to hate them when to his other cruelties he could add the charge that they were opposed to his rule and were speaking against him? The sum and substance of their request was that they be delivered from kingship and such forms of rule, be joined to the province of Syria, and be made subject to the governors sent there.

Josephus *AJ* 17. 304-14 (abridged)
tr. R. Marcus and A. Wikgren (Loeb 1963)

O16 The reign of Archelaus, 4 BC-AD 6

A Jew was not allowed to marry the wife of his deceased brother if there was issue of the first marriage. Matthew 2: 19-23 bears out Josephus' picture of Archelaus: when the parents of Jesus heard that Archelaus had succeeded in Judaea, they were afraid to settle in Bethlehem, as they had apparently intended, and returned from Egypt to their original home in Galilee.

When Archelaus came to Judaea and took possession of his ethnarchy, he removed Joazar, the son of Boethus, from the High Priesthood, blaming him for having supported the rebels, and in his place appointed Joazar's brother Eleazar. He also rebuilt the royal palace in Jericho in splendid fashion, and diverted half the water that served to irrigate the village of Neara, leading it into a plain that had been planted by him with palm-trees. He also created a village and gave it the name of Archelais. And he transgressed ancestral law in marrying Glaphyra, who had been the wife of his brother Alexander and had borne him children, for it is abhorrent to the Jews to marry the wife of a brother. . . .

In the tenth year of Archelaus' rule the leading men among the Jews and Samaritans, finding his cruelty and tyranny intolerable, brought charges against him before Caesar the moment they learned that Archelaus had disobeyed his instructions to show moderation in dealing with them. Accordingly, when Caesar heard the charges, he became angry and summoning the man who looked after Archelaus' affairs at Rome—for he thought it beneath him to write to the ethnarch—he said to him, 'Go, sail at once and bring him here to us without delay.' So this man immediately set sail, and on arriving in Judaea and finding Archelaus feasting with his friends, he revealed to him the will of Caesar and speeded his departure. And when Archelaus arrived, Caesar gave a hearing to some of his accusers, and also let him speak, and then sent him into exile, assigning him a residence in Vienne, a city of Gaul, and confiscating his property.

> Josephus *AJ* 17. 339–44 (abridged)
> tr. R. Marcus and A. Wikgren (Loeb 1963)

O17 Philip's reign and his death in AD 33/4

The incorporation of Philip's territory into Syria lasted only until 37.

Now it was at this time that Philip, Herod's brother, died in the twentieth year of Tiberius' reign and after thirty seven years of his own rule over Trachonitis and Gaulanitis, as well as over the tribe called the Batanaeans. In his conduct of the government he showed a moderate and easy-going disposition. Indeed, he spent all his time in the territory subject to him. When he went on circuit he had only a few select companions. The throne on which he sat when he gave judgement accompanied him wherever he went. And so, whenever anyone appealed to him for redress along the route, at once without a moment's delay the throne was set up wherever it might be. He took his seat and gave the case a hearing. He fixed penalties for those who were convicted and released those who had been unjustly accused. He died in Julias. His body was carried to the tomb that he himself had had erected before he died and there was a costly funeral. Since he had died childless, Tiberius took over his territory and annexed it to the province of Syria.

> Josephus *AJ* 18. 106–8
> tr. L. H. Feldman (Loeb 1965)

O18 The foundation of Tiberias by Antipas (here called 'Herod') as the capital of his tetrarchy

The tetrarch Herod, inasmuch as he had gained a high place among the friends of Tiberius, had a city built, named after him Tiberias. . . . The new settlers were a promiscuous rabble, no small contingent being Galilaean, with such as were drafted from territory subject to him and brought forcibly to the new foundation. Some of these were magistrates. Herod accepted as participants even poor men who were brought in to join the others from any and all places of origin. It was a question whether some were even free beyond cavil. These latter he often and in large bodies liberated and benefited (imposing the condition that they should not quit the city), by equipping houses at his own expense and adding new gifts of land. For he knew that this settlement was contrary to the law and tradition of the Jews because Tiberias was built on the site of tombs that had been obliterated, of which there were many there. And our law declares that such settlers are unclean for seven days.

Josephus *AJ* 18. 36–8 (abridged)
tr. L. H. Feldman (Loeb 1965)

O19 The consequences of Antipas' second marriage

In the late 20s (the connection with John the Baptist gives the date) Antipas married Herodias—illegally, since her first husband, one of his half-brothers, was still alive— and Antipas' first wife fled to her father, Aretas king of Nabataea. He, however, did not seek vengeance till the mid 30s. Vitellius was legate of Syria.

Aretas made this the start of a quarrel. . . . Troops were mustered on each side and they were now at war, but they dispatched others as commanders instead of going themselves. In the ensuing battle, the whole army of Herod was destroyed when some refugees, who had come from the tetrarchy of Philip and had joined Herod's army, played him false. Herod sent an account of these events to Tiberius. The latter was incensed to think that Aretas had begun hostilities and wrote to Vitellius to declare war and either bring Aretas to him in chains, if he should be captured alive, or, if he should be slain, to send him his head. Such were the instructions of Tiberius to his governor in Syria.

But to some of the Jews the destruction of Herod's army seemed to be divine vengeance, and certainly a just vengeance, for his treatment of John, surnamed the Baptist. For Herod had put him to death, though he was a good man and had exhorted the Jews to lead righteous lives, to practise justice towards their fellows and piety towards God, and so doing to join in baptism. In his view this was a necessary preliminary if baptism was to be acceptable to God. They must not employ it to gain pardon for whatever sins they committed, but as a consecration

637

of the body implying that the soul was already thoroughly cleansed by right behaviour. When others too joined the crowds about him, because they were aroused to the highest degree by his sermons, Herod became alarmed. Eloquence that had so great an effect on mankind might lead to some form of sedition, for it looked as if they would be guided by John in everything that they did. Herod decided therefore that it would be much better to strike first and be rid of him before his work led to an uprising, than to wait for an upheaval, get involved in a difficult situation and see his mistake. Though John, because of Herod's suspicions, was brought in chains to Machaerus, the stronghold that we have previously mentioned, and there put to death, yet the verdict of the Jews was that the destruction visited upon Herod's army was a vindication of John, since God saw fit to inflict such a blow on Herod.

Vitellius got himself ready for war against Aretas with two legions of heavy-armed infantry and such light-armed infantry and cavalry as were attached to them as auxiliaries. Proceeding from the kingdoms that were under the Roman yoke, he pushed towards Petra and occupied Ptolemais. Since he had started to lead his army through the land of Judaea, the Jews of the highest standing went to meet him and entreated him not to march through their land. For, they said, it was contrary to their tradition to allow images, of which there were many attached to the military standards, to be brought upon their soil. Yielding to their entreaty, he abandoned his original plan and ordered his army to march through the Great Plain, while he himself, together with Herod the tetrarch and his friends, went up to Jerusalem to sacrifice to God during the traditional festival which the Jews were celebrating there. When he arrived there, he was greeted with special warmth by the Jewish multitude. He spent three days there, during which he deposed Jonathan from his office as High Priest and conferred it on Jonathan's brother Theophilus. On the fourth day, when he received a letter notifying him of the death of Tiberius, he administered to the people an oath of loyalty to Gaius. He now recalled his army, ordering each man to go to his own home for the winter, for he was no longer empowered as before to make war abroad now that the government had fallen into Gaius' hands. . . . Vitellius accordingly withdraw to Antioch.

Josephus *AJ* 18. 113–25 (abridged)
tr. L. R. Feldman (Loeb 1965)

O20 Antipas' proudest hour

In AD 36 news of trouble within the Parthian kingdom made Tiberius think that the king would be glad to get his hands free to deal with it by coming to terms with Rome.

At this news Tiberius took steps to make friends with Artabanus. When the offer was made, the Parthian was delighted to discuss the matter. He and Vitellius met on the Euphrates. The river was bridged and they met in the middle of the bridge, each with his bodyguard with him. After they had arrived at the terms of an agreement, Herod the tetrarch gave a feast for them in a luxurious pavilion which he constructed in the middle of the river. Artabanus sent as a hostage to Tiberius his son Darius, together with many gifts. . . . These terms having been arranged, Vitellius departed for Antioch and Artabanus for Babylonia. Meanwhile, Herod, in his desire to be the first to communicate the news to the emperor that hostages had been received, wrote and dispatched by couriers so precise and complete an account that he left nothing for the proconsul to report. When Vitellius had later sent his despatch and the emperor informed him that he knew the facts because Herod had been ahead of Vitellius in putting them at his disposal, Vitellius fell into a great fury.

> Josephus *AJ* 18. 101–5
> tr. L. H. Feldman (Loeb 1965)

O21 The start of Roman rule over the province of Judaea, AD 6

Luke 2: 1 dates the birth of Jesus, which the Nativity story in Matthew 2 puts before Herod's death in 4 BC, by a 'first census', conducted in Judaea by Quirinius. This implies a 'second census', presumably that of AD 6, and produces an extremely complicated and controversial problem. In brief, it seems very improbable that Quirinius was in the East shortly before 4 BC in any capacity in which he could have supervised a census in Herod's kingdom. Possibly Luke, aware of a census at the time of the Nativity, has confused it with the more famous one of AD 6 and attached Quirinius' name to it erroneously. Josephus' reference to Judas as a 'Gaulanite from Gamala' is probably a slip; in all other references (e.g. the second paragraph of this passage) he is a Galilean. In this passage Josephus drifts away from Judas' revolt to its long-term effects and events as far ahead as AD 66–70. For its suppression see Acts 5. 37. Joazar (cf. O16) had evidently been reappointed High Priest.

Quirinius, a Roman senator who had proceeded through all the magistracies to the consulship and a man who was extremely distinguished in other respects, arrived in Syria, dispatched by Caesar to be governor of the nation and to make an assessment of their property. Coponius, a man of equestrian rank, was sent along with him to rule over the Jews with full authority. Quirinius also visited Judaea, which had been annexed to Syria, in order to make an assessment of the property of the Jews and to liquidate the estate of Archelaus. Although the Jews were at first shocked to hear of the registration of property, they gradually condescended, yielding to the arguments of the High Priest Joazar, the son of Boethus, to go no further in opposition. So those who were convinced by him declared, without shilly-shallying, the value of their property. But a certain Judas, a Gaulanite from a city named Gamala, who had enlisted the aid of Saddok, a Pharisee, threw himself into the cause of rebellion. They said that the assessment carried with it a status amounting to downright slavery, no less, and appealed to the nation to make a bid for independence. They urged that in case of success the Jews would have laid the foundation of prosperity, while if they failed to obtain any such boon, they would win honour and renown for their lofty aim; and that Heaven would be their zealous helper to no lesser end than the furthering of their enterprise until it succeeded—all the more if with high devotion in their hearts they stood firm and did not shrink from the bloodshed that might be necessary. Since the populace, when they heard their appeals, responded gladly, the plot to strike boldly made serious progress; and so these men sowed the seed of every kind of misery, which so afflicted the nation that words are inadequate. When wars are set afoot that are bound to rage beyond control, and when friends are done away with who might have alleviated the suffering, when raids are made by great hordes of brigands and men of the highest standing are assassinated, it is supposed to be the common welfare that is upheld, but the truth is that in such cases the motive is private gain. They sowed the seed from which sprang strife between factions and the slaughter of fellow citizens. Some were slain in civil strife, for these men madly had recourse to butchery of each other and of themselves from a longing not to be outdone by their opponents; others were slain by the enemy in war. Then came famine, reserved to exhibit the last degree of shamelessness, followed by the storming and razing of cities until at last the very Temple of God was ravaged by the enemy's fire through this revolt. Here is a lesson that an innovation and reform in ancestral traditions weighs heavily in the scale in leading to the destruction of the congregation of the people. In this case certainly, Judas and Saddok started among us as an intrusive fourth school of philosophy; and when they had won an abundance of devotees, they filled the body politic immediately with tumult, also planting the seeds of those troubles which subsequently overtook it, all because of the novelty of this hitherto unknown philosophy.

[*Josephus now gives accounts of the Pharisees, the Sadducees, and the Essenes.*]

As for the fourth of the philosophies, Judas the Galilaean set himself up as leader of it. This school agrees in all other respects with the opinions of the Pharisees, except that they have a passion for liberty that is almost unconquerable, since they are convinced that God alone is their leader and master. They think little of submitting to death in unusual forms and permitting vengeance to fall on kinsmen and friends if only they may avoid calling any man master.

Josephus *AJ* 18. 1–10; 23
tr. L. H. Feldman (Loeb 1965)

O22 An inscription of Pontius Pilate

Pontius Pilate was governor of Judaea from AD 26 until the winter of 36–7. The following inscription was found in Caesarea c. 1960. The stone is broken and the verb is missing; alternatives to 'gave' are 'built' or 'dedicated'. A Tiberieum is a building in Tiberius' honour, but of unknown character.

Pontius Pilate, prefect of Judaea, gave a Tiberieum to the people of Caesarea.

A. Frova *Rendic. Istituto Lombardo* Cl. di Lettere etc. 95 (1961) 419–34
tr. E. M. Smallwood

O23 Pilate and the military standards

In the parallel account in the BJ *Pilate entered Jerusalem with the standards covered up. By an 'outrage to the Emperor' he meant an act of* maiestas *(on which see further D23).*

Now Pilate, the procurator of Judaea, when he brought his army from Caesarea and removed it to winter quarters in Jerusalem, took a bold step in subversion of the Jewish practices, by introducing into the city the busts of the emperor that were attached to the military standards, for our law forbids the making of images. It was for this reason that the previous procurators, when they entered the city, used standards that had no such ornaments. Pilate was the first to bring the images into Jerusalem and set them up, doing it without the knowledge of the people, for he entered at night. But when the people discovered it, they went in a throng to Caesarea and for many days entreated him to take away the images. He refused to yield, since to do so would be an outrage to the emperor; however, since they did not cease entreating him, on the sixth day he secretly armed and placed his troops in position, while he himself came to the speaker's stand. This had been constructed in the stadium, which provided concealment for the army that lay in wait. When the Jews again emerged in supplication, at a pre-arranged signal he surrounded them with his soldiers and threatened to punish them at once with death if they did not put an end to their tumult and return to their own places. But they, casting themselves prostrate and baring their throats, declared that they had gladly welcomed death rather than make bold to transgress the wise provisions of the laws. Pilate, astonished at the strength of their devotion to the laws, straightaway removed the images from Jerusalem and brought them back to Caesarea.

Josephus *AJ* 18. 55–9
tr. L. H. Feldman (Loeb 1965)

O24 Pilate and the aqueduct

Corban was the fund raised by the Temple tax. In the parallel account in the *AJ the aqueduct was only 25 miles long and even that may be an exaggeration. An aqueduct that has been traced for some 12 miles running towards Jerusalem from south-west of Bethlehem may be Pilate's.*

After this he stirred up further trouble by expending the sacred treasure known as Corban on an aqueduct fifty miles long. This roused the populace to fury, and when Pilate visited Jerusalem they surrounded the tribunal and shouted him down. But he had foreseen this disturbance, and had made the soldiers mix with the mob, wearing civilian clothing over their armour, and with orders not to draw their swords but to use clubs on the obstreperous. He now gave the signal from the tribunal and the Jews were cudgelled, so that many died from the blows, and many were trampled to death by their friends as they fled. The fate of those who perished horrified the crowd into silence.

Josephus *BJ* 2. 175-7
tr. Williamson, rev. Smallwood

O25 Pilate and the votive shields

On the context of this passage see O28.

With the intention of annoying the Jews rather than of honouring Tiberius, Pilate set up gilded shields in Herod's palace in the Holy City. They bore no figure and nothing else that was forbidden, but only the briefest possible inscription, which stated two things—the name of the dedicator and that of the person in whose honour the dedication was made. But when the Jews at large learnt of his action, which was indeed already widely known, they chose as their spokesmen the king's four sons, who enjoyed prestige and rank equal to that of kings, his other descendants, and their own officials, and besought Pilate to undo his innovation in the shape of the shields, and not to violate their native customs, which had hitherto been invariably preserved inviolate by kings and emperors alike. When Pilate, who was a man of inflexible, stubborn, and cruel disposition, obstinately refused, they shouted, 'Do not cause a revolt! Do not cause a war! Do not break the peace! Disrespect done to our ancient Laws brings no honour to the Emperor. Do not make Tiberius an excuse for insulting our nation. He does not want any of our traditions done away with. If you say that he does, show us some decree or letter or something of the sort, so that we may cease troubling you and appeal to our master by means of an embassy.' This last remark exasperated Pilate most of all, for he was afraid that if they really sent an embassy they would bring accusations against the rest of his administration as well, specifying in detail his venality, his violence, his thefts, his abusive behaviour, his frequent executions of untried prisoners, and his endless savage ferocity. So, as he was a spiteful and angry person, he was in a serious dilemma; for he had neither the courage to remove what he had once set up, nor the desire to do anything which would please his subjects, but at the same time he was well aware of Tiberius' firmness on these matters. When the Jewish officials saw this, and realised that Pilate was regretting what he had done, although he did not wish to show it, they wrote a letter to Tiberius, pleading their case as forcibly as they could. What words, what threats Tiberius uttered against Pilate when he read it! It would be superfluous to describe his anger, although he was not easily moved to anger, since his reaction speaks for itself. For immediately, without even waiting until the next day, he wrote to Pilate, reproaching and rebuking him a thousand times for his new-fangled audacity and telling him to remove the shields at once and have them taken from the capital to the coastal city of Caesarea . . . to be dedicated in the temple of Augustus.

Philo *Legatio* 299–305
tr. E. M. Smallwood (E. J. Brill 1970)

O26 The end of Pilate's governorship

On Antonia see O2; on Jonathan see O38b. For Vitellius' subsequent dealings with the Jews see O19, end.

The Samaritan nation too was not exempt from disturbances. For a man who made light of mendacity and in all his designs catered to the mob, rallied them, bidding them go in a body with him to Mount Gerizim, which in their belief is the most sacred of mountains. He assured them that on their arrival he would show them the sacred vessels which were buried there, where Moses had deposited them. His hearers, viewing this tale as plausible, appeared in arms. They posted themselves in a certain village named Tirithana, and, as they planned to climb the mountain in a great multitude, they welcomed to their ranks the new arrivals who kept coming. But before they could ascend, Pilate blocked their projected route up the mountain with a detachment of cavalry and heavy armed infantry, who in an encounter with the firstcomers in the village slew some in a pitched battle and put the others to flight. Many prisoners were taken, of whom Pilate put to death the principal leaders and those who were most influential among the fugitives.

When the uprising had been quelled, the council of the Samaritans went to Vitellius, a man of consular rank who was governor of Syria, and charged Pilate with the slaughter of the victims. For, they said, it was not as rebels against the Romans but as refugees from the persecution of Pilate that they had met in Tirithana. Vitellius thereupon dispatched Marcellus, one of his friends, to take charge of the administration of Judaea, and ordered Pilate to return to Rome to give the emperor his account of the matters with which he was charged by the Samaritans. And so Pilate, after having spent ten years in Judaea, hurried to Rome in obedience to the orders of Vitellius, since he could not refuse. But before he reached Rome Tiberius had already passed away.

Vitellius, on reaching Judaea, went up to Jerusalem, where the Jews were celebrating their traditional feast called the Passover. Having been received in magnificent fashion, Vitellius remitted to the inhabitants of the city all taxes on the sale of agricultural produce and agreed that the vestments of the High Priest and all his ornaments should be kept in the Temple in custody of the priests, as had been their privilege before. At that time the vestments were stored in Antonia—there is a stronghold of that name—for the following reason. One of the priests, Hyrcanus, the first of many by that name, had constructed a large house near the Temple and lived there most of the time. As custodian of the vestments—for to him alone was conceded the right to put them on—he kept them laid away there, whenever he put on his ordinary clothes in order to go down to the city. His sons and their children also followed the same practice. When Herod became king, he made lavish repairs to this building, which was conveniently situated, and, being a friend of Antony, he called it Antonia. He retained the vestments there just as he had found them, believing that for this reason the people would never rise in insurrection against him. Herod's successor as king, his son Archelaus, acted similarly. After him, when the Romans took over the government, they retained control of the High Priest's vestments and kept them in a stone building, where they were under the seal both of the priests and of the custodians of the treasury and where the warden of the guard lighted the lamp day by day. Seven days before each festival the vestments were delivered to the priests by the warden. After they had been purified, the High Priest wore them; then after the first day of the festival he put them back again in the building where they were laid away before. This was the procedure at the three festivals each year and on the Fast day. Vitellius was guided by our law in dealing with the vestments, and instructed the warden not to meddle with the question where they were to be stored or when they should be used. After he had bestowed these benefits upon the nation, he removed from his sacred office the high priest Joseph surnamed Caiaphas, and appointed in his stead Jonathan, son of Ananus the High Priest.

Josephus *AJ* 18. 85-95
tr. L. H. Feldman (Loeb 1965)

O27 Gaius' attempt to desecrate the Temple

Cereals ripen in April or May in Palestine, fruit trees not until the autumn; but Gaius was planning an Eastern tour then.

The letter about the dedication of the statue was written and did not just give a simple command but laid down all the precautions which were to be taken for safety's sake. For Gaius told Petronius, the legate of all Syria, to whom he had addressed the letter, to take half of the Euphrates army ... into Judaea to accompany the statue, not in order to lend dignity to the dedication, but in order to put to death at once anyone who opposed it. ... Now Petronius was gravely perplexed when he read his orders. He could not oppose Gaius because he was afraid—for he knew that he was ruthless not only to people who did not carry out his commands but even to those who failed to do so instantly; yet he could not set to work with an easy mind either, knowing as he did that the Jews would be prepared to undergo countless deaths, if it were possible, instead of a single death, rather than allow any forbidden action to be performed. [*Philo then expatiates on the Jews' devotion to their law.*]

Bearing all this in mind, Petronius was dilatory in setting to work, while he considered the magnitude and audacity of the undertaking. ... He also had in mind the vast numerical size of the Jewish nation, which is not confined, as every other nation is, within the borders of the one country assigned for its sole occupation, but occupies almost the whole world. For it has overflowed across every continent and island, so that it scarcely seems to be outnumbered by the native inhabitants. Would it not be highly dangerous to turn these vast hordes of enemies against himself? [*Philo then talks of the size and devotion of the Diaspora.*]

These were the arguments on which he based his delay. Then he was drawn in the other direction by the opposite arguments. [*He would endanger his life by disobedience to Gaius.*] The construction of the statue provided a breathing space for more detailed consideration. Gaius did not have one sent out from Rome ... So Petronius gave orders for the work to be carried out in one of the neighbouring countries. He sent for the most intelligent craftsmen in Phoenicia, and gave them the materials. They set to work in Sidon. He then sent for the Jewish religious and civil authorities also, intending to tell them about Gaius' letter and at the same time to advise them to submit to the orders of their master and to keep before their eyes the dangers facing them. For the pick of the military forces in Syria was ready and would deal death throughout the whole country. He thought that if he calmed them first, he would be able through them to induce the rest of the population also not to resist. But, as one might expect, he was mistaken. It is said that the Jewish leaders were aghast at his very first words and stood rooted to the ground at this story of unprecedented evil. Dumb with horror they let the fountains of their tears flow without restraint. Then they tore their beards and hair and commented thus:—'In the time of our great prosperity we have made many contributions towards a happy old age, only to behold now what none of our forefathers ever saw. But with what eyes shall we behold it? Our eyes shall be torn out together with our unhappy souls and our pain-filled lives, before they see such an evil, a sight not fit to be seen, which it would be wrong even to hear or think about.'

Such were their lamentations. But when the people in the Holy City and the rest of the country discovered what was afoot, they gathered as if at a single signal, the signal given by their common calamity, and came out in a body, abandoning their cities, villages and homes, and at a single impulse hurried to Phoenicia, where Petronius happened to be. When some of Petronius' staff saw a vast crowd sweeping towards them, they ran and warned him, so that he might take precautions, as they expected war. While they were still describing the scene, and Petronius was without a guard, the multitude of Jews suddenly descended like a cloud and covered the whole of Phoenicia, to the consternation of those who did not realize how numerous the nation was. At first there arose such a tremendous shout and such weeping and the beating of breasts, that the ears of bystanders could not take in its magnitude. For it did not cease when the Jews ceased, but echoed back even after they were silent. Then the Jews approached and made appeals such as the occasions suggested. [*A long speech follows, in which the Jews offer to make any sacrifice, even that of their lives, on behalf of the sanctity of the Temple, and then ask Petronius to let them send an embassy to plead with Gaius.*]

They made this appeal panting under the stress of intense and agonized emotion; their voices were choked, sweat poured over all their limbs, and their tears fell unceasingly. As a result their hearers began to sympathize, and Petronius, who was naturally kind and gentle, was carried away by the arguments and by the sight confronting him. For he considered that the arguments were entirely reasonable, and the intense emotion of those confronting him filled him with pity. He withdrew with his advisors and deliberated on the best course of action. . . . What, then, were his resolutions? Not to hurry the workmen but to tell them to bring the statue to a high state of artistic perfection by aiming, as far as possible, at reaching the standard of the famous sculptures which were their models, however long it took, since rough and ready things can be finished quickly, whereas things involving labour and skill need a long time. He also resolved not to authorize the embassy for which the Jews asked, as that would not be safe; not to oppose the party anxious to refer the matter to the *princeps* and master of the world; not to give a definite answer, Yes or No, to the multitude, as either would be dangerous; but to send Gaius a letter in which he would neither accuse the Jews of anything nor give an accurate description of their appeals and prayers, but would lay the blame for the delay over the dedication partly on the season of the year, which was providing serious and reasonable grounds for delay, which even Gaius himself could of necessity not fail to appreciate. For the harvest of wheat and other cereals was ripe, and he was afraid that the Jews, despairing of their traditions and despising life, would either ravage their fields or set fire to their corn-lands in the hills and on the plains; he needed a garrison to secure the safe gathering in of the harvests—the harvest from the fruit-trees as well as that from the fields. . . .

As Petronius' advisers approved of his plan, he had the letter written and chose some energetic men who were used to cutting down the time they spent on journeys to take it to Gaius. When they arrived they delivered the letter. Gaius got red in the face before he had finished reading, and was filled with anger as he noted each point. When he reached the end he clapped his hands and said, 'Excellent, Petronius; you have not learnt to obey the Emperor. Your successive magistracies have gone to your head. Up to now, apparently, you have not discovered even by hearsay what Gaius is like; before long you shall find out by experience. You are concerned about the laws of the Jews, a race which I detest, and yet you disregard the sovereign commands of your ruler. [*He then rants for a few lines about Petronius' arguments.*] But why am I talking instead of acting? Why do people know my decisions in advance? The man who is going to enjoy his wages, let him be the first to learn of it from his own experience. I will say no more, but I shall continue to think about the matter.' After a short pause he dictated his reply to Petronius to one of his secretaries. On the surface he complimented him for his forethought and detailed consideration for the future. For he was very much afraid of the provincial governors, since he saw that they held in their hands the means to rebel, especially the governors of large districts who commanded large armies, such as the Euphrates army in Syria. So he was polite to Petronius in the phrasing of his letter, and despite his anger he concealed his wrath until a suitable time. Then at the end of his letter he told him to put the speedy dedication of the statue before everything else, since the harvest, which had served as a pretext, whether true or false, could by that time have been gathered.

Philo *Legatio* 207-60 (excerpts)
tr. E. M. Smallwood (E. J. Brill 1970)

O28 Agrippa I's appeal to Gaius

He took a tablet and wrote the following letter: 'My lord, fear and modesty prevent me from pleading with you face to face. Fear seeks to avoid your threats, while modesty makes me alarmed at the magnitude of the dignity surrounding you. This letter will bring you my request, which I am presenting instead of the suppliant's olive branch.' [*The very long memorandum which follows discusses the situation of the Jews in the Roman Empire and the consideration shown towards them by Augustus and Tiberius, citing enactments in the Jews' favour; an excerpt from it appears above (O25). Finally Agrippa draws his conclusion:*]

'Therefore, my lord, since you have these striking precedents for a gentler policy than your own, all closely connected with the family from which you were descended and born and in which you have taken such pride, preserve what each of them has preserved. As Emperors they plead the cause of the laws to you as Emperor, as Augusti to you as Augustus, as your grandfathers and ancestors to you as their descendant, as many people to you who are but one, and they say in effect, "Do not abolish customs which have been maintained at our express wish up to the present day. For even if nothing sinister were to befall you as a result of their abolition, yet the uncertainty of the future is not entirely without terror even for the boldest, unless they despise the things of God."' [*Agrippa then speaks of the personal favours which he has received from Gaius, now valueless unless the Temple is spared.*]

Agrippa wrote this letter, sealed it, and sent it to Gaius. Then he shut himself up in his house and waited in an agony of confused feelings, wondering greatly how it would strike Gaius. . . . When Gaius received the letter and read it, he was angered at each of the points, since his purpose was not prospering; but at the same time he was moved by the mixture of arguments and plans. He partly approved of what Agrippa said, and partly disapproved. He objected to his excessive obsequiousness towards his compatriots, who were the only people to disobey him and to repudiate his deification, but he approved of the way in which he did not disguise or conceal any of his feeling, and said that this gave proof of a very independent and noble spirit. So he pretended to be appeased and decided to write Agrippa a fairly pleasant reply, granting him his first and most important request, that the dedication should not take place. He gave orders for a letter to be written to Publius Petronius, the legate of Syria, to the effect that he was to attempt no further innovations with regard to the Jewish Temple.

> Philo *Legatio* 276; 321–2; 330–3
> tr. E. M. Smallwood (E. J. Brill 1970)

O29 The deposition of Antipas and Agrippa I's acquisition of his territory, AD 40

Herodias, the sister of Agrippa and wife of Herod, tetrarch of Galilee and Peraea, begrudged her brother his rise to power far above the state that her husband enjoyed. . . . The spectacle of his royal visits in the customary regalia before the multitudes made her especially helpless to keep this unfortunate envy to herself. Instead she instigated her husband, urging him to embark for Rome and sue for equal status. . . .

For a while he resisted and tried to change her mind, for he was content with his tranquillity and was wary of the Roman bustle. The more, however, she saw him shying away, the more urgently she insisted, bidding him not to be remiss in seeking a throne at any cost. The upshot was that she never flagged till she carried the day. . . . And so, supplied as lavishly as possible and sparing no expense, he set sail for Rome, accompanied by Herodias. But Agrippa, when he learned of their plan and their preparations, made his own preparations. And when he heard that they had set sail, he himself also dispatched Fortunatus, one of his freedmen, to Rome, charged with presents for the emperor and letters against Herod, and ready to tell his story to Gaius himself as the opportunity presented itself. Fortunatus, putting out to sea in pursuit of Herod's party, had a favourable voyage and was so little behind Herod that while the latter had obtained an audience with Gaius, he landed and delivered his letters. Both of them had made port at Dicaearchia [Puteoli] and had found Gaius at Baiae. . . .

...At the very time that he was greeting Herod, whom he interviewed first, Gaius was perusing the letters of Agrippa which were composed as an indictment of him. The letters accused Herod of conspiring with Sejanus against the government of Tiberius and of being now in league with Artabanus the Parthian against the government of Gaius. As proof of this charge the letters stated that equipment sufficient for 70,000 heavy-armed foot-soldiers was stored in Herod's armouries. Spurred by these words, Gaius asked Herod whether the report about the arms was true. When Herod replied that the arms were there—for it was impossible for him to deny it in face of the truth—Gaius, regarding the accusations of revolt as confirmed, relieved him of his tetrarchy and added it to the kingdom of Agrippa. He likewise gave Herod's property to Agrippa and condemned Herod to perpetual exile, assigning him as his residence Lyons, a city in Gaul.

Josephus *AJ* 18. 240-5 (abridged)
tr. L. H. Feldman (Loeb 1965)

O30 Agrippa I as king of the whole of Palestine (AD 41-4)

(a) *His attitude to Judaism*

On Theophilus see O19.

Claudius sent Agrippa to take over his kingdom with more splendid honours than before, giving written instructions to the governors of the provinces and to the procurators to treat him as a special favourite. Agrippa naturally, since he was to go back with improved fortunes, turned quickly homewards. On entering Jerusalem, he offered sacrifices of thanksgiving, omitting none of the ritual enjoined by our law.... Accordingly he also arranged for a very considerable number of Nazarites to be shorn. Moreover, he hung up, within the sacred precincts, over the treasure-chamber, the golden chain which had been presented to him by Gaius, equal in weight to the one of iron with which his royal hands had been bound.... Having thus fully discharged his service to God, Agrippa removed Theophilus son of Ananus from the high priesthood and bestowed his high office on Simon son of Boethus.... Having in this way taken care of the high priesthood, the king recompensed the inhabitants of Jerusalem for their goodwill to him by remitting to them the tax on every house, holding it right to repay the affection of his subjects with a corresponding fatherly love.

Josephus *AJ* 19. 292-4; 297; 299 (abridged)
tr. L. H. Feldman (Loeb 1965)

(b) *His generosity and popularity*

Now king Agrippa was by nature generous in his gifts and made it a point of honour to be high-minded towards gentiles; and by expending massive sums he raised himself

649

to high fame. He took pleasure in conferring favours and rejoiced in popularity, thus being in no way similar in character to Herod, who was king before him. [*The next few lines denigrate Herod the Great.*] Agrippa had a gentle disposition and he was a benefactor to all alike. He was benevolent to those of other nations and exhibited his generosity to them also; but to his compatriots he was proportionately more generous and more compassionate. He enjoyed residing in Jerusalem and did so constantly; and he scrupulously observed the traditions of his people.

Josephus *AJ* 19. 328; 330-1 (abridged)
tr. L. H. Feldman (Loeb 1965)

O31 Agrippa I's new north wall of Jerusalem

Agrippa fortified the walls of Jerusalem on the side of the New City at the public expense, increasing both their breadth and height, and he would have made them too strong for any human force had not Marsus, the governor of Syria, reported by letter to Claudius Caesar what was being done. Claudius, suspecting that a revolution was on foot, earnestly charged Agrippa in a letter to desist from the building of the walls; and Agrippa thought it best not to disobey.

Josephus *AJ* 19. 326-7
tr. L. H. Feldman (Loeb 1965)

O32 Agrippa I's Hellenism and his conference of Eastern client kings

He erected many buildings in many other places but he conferred special favours on the people of Berytus. He built them a theatre surpassing many others in its costly beauty; he also built an amphitheatre at great expense, besides baths and porticoes; and in none of these works did he allow either the beauty or the size to suffer by stinting on the expenses. He was also magnificently lavish in his pro-vision at the dedication of them; in the theatre he exhibited spectacles, introducing every kind of music and all that made for a varied entertainment, while in the amphi-theatre he showed his noble generosity by the number of gladiators provided. . . .

Having completed the aforesaid ceremonies at Berytus, he went next to Tiberias, a city in Galilee. Now he was evidently admired by the other kings. At any rate, he was visited by Antiochus king of Commagene, Sampsigeramus king of Emesa, and Cotys king of Armenia Minor, as well as by Polemo, who held sway over Pontus, and Herod his [Agrippa's] brother who was ruler of Chalcis. His converse with all of them when he entertained and showed them courtesies was such as to demon-strate an elevation of sentiment that justified the honour done him by a visit of royalty. It so happened, however, that while he was still entertaining them, Marsus the governor of Syria arrived. The king therefore, to do honour to the Romans, advanced seven furlongs outside the city to meet him. Now this action, as events proved, was destined to be the beginning of a quarrel with Marsus; for Agrippa brought the other kings along with him and sat with them in his carriage; but Marsus was suspicious of such concord and intimate friendship among them. He took it for granted that a meeting of minds among so many chiefs of state was prejudicial to Roman interests. He therefore at once sent some of his associates with an order to each of the kings bidding him set off without delay to his own territory.

Josephus *AJ* 19. 335–42 (abridged)
tr. L. H. Feldman (Loeb 1965)

O33 The death of Agrippa I, AD 44

For another account of Agrippa's death see Acts 12: 20–3. For the festival see O5b.

After the completion of the third year of his reign over the whole of Judaea, Agrippa came to the city of Caesarea. . . . Here he celebrated spectacles in honour of Caesar, knowing that these had been instituted as a kind of festival on behalf of Caesar's well-being. For this occasion there were gathered a large number of men who held office or had advanced to some rank in the kingdom. On the second day of the spectacles, clad in a garment woven completely of silver so that its texture was indeed wondrous, he entered the theatre at daybreak. There the silver, illumined by the touch of the first rays of the sun, was wondrously radiant and by its glitter inspired fear and awe in those who gazed intently upon it. Straightway his flatterers raised their voices from various directions—though hardly for his good—addressing him as a god. . . . The king did not rebuke them nor did he reject their flattery as impious. [*He was then suddenly attacked by severe abdominal pain.*] Leaping up he said to his friends: 'I, a god in your eyes, am now bidden to lay down my life, for fate brings immediate refutation of the lying words lately addressed to me. I, who was called immortal by you, am now under sentence of death. But I must accept my lot as God wills it. In fact I have lived in no ordinary fashion but in the grand style that is hailed as true bliss.' Even as he was speaking these words, he was overcome by more intense pain. They hastened, therefore, to convey him to the palace; and the word flashed about to everyone that he was on the very verge of death. Straightway the populace, including the women and children, sat in sackcloth in accordance with their ancestral custom and made entreaty to God on behalf of the king. . . . The king, as he lay in his lofty bedchamber and looked down on the people as they fell prostrated, was not dry-eyed himself. Exhausted after five straight days by the pain in his abdomen, he departed this life in the fifty-fourth year of his life and the seventh of his reign. [*The stages of the acquisition of his kingdom are then recapitulated*.] He derived as much revenue as possible from these territories, amounting to twelve million drachmas, but he borrowed much, for, owing to his generosity, his expenditures were extravagant beyond his income, and his ambition knew no bounds of expense.

Josephus *AJ* 19. 343-52 (abridged)
tr. L. H. Feldman (Loeb 1965)

O34 The reconstitution of the province of Judaea, AD 44

Agrippa II was sixteen at this time. At Caesarea and Sebaste Agrippa I's death had been hailed with unseemly joy and his family had been insulted; hence Claudius' proposal to punish the troops recruited there.

Agrippa, the son of the deceased, was at Rome at this time, where he was being brought up at the court of Claudius Caesar. Caesar, on hearing of the death of Agrippa, . . . resolved to send the younger Agrippa at once to take over the kingdom, wishing at the same time to maintain the sworn treaty with him. He was, however, dissuaded by those of his freedmen and friends who had great influence with him, who said that it was hazardous to entrust so important a kingdom to one who was quite young and had not even passed out of boyhood and who would find it impossible to sustain the cares of administration. Even to a grown man, said they, a kingdom was a heavy responsibility. Caesar accordingly decided that their arguments were plausible. He therefore dispatched Cuspius Fadus as procurator of Judaea and of the whole kingdom. . . . Above all, he had resolved to instruct Fadus . . . to transfer to Pontus the squadron of cavalry composed of men from Caesarea and Sebaste, together with the five cohorts, in order to do their service there, and to enrol a proportionate number of soldiers from the Roman legions in Syria to fill their place. The troops were not, however, transferred as they had been ordered, for they sent a deputation which appeased Claudius and obtained leave to remain in Judaea. These men, in the period that followed, proved to be a source of the greatest disasters to the Jews by sowing the seed of the war in Florus' time.

Josephus *AJ* 19. 360-6 (abridged)
tr. L. H. Feldman (Loeb 1965)

O35 The question of the High Priest's vestments and Claudius' decree, AD 45

Cuspius Fadus was procurator of Judaea AD 44-6. On the vestments cf. O26, end. Cassius Longinus was legate of Syria. The authority to nominate the High Priest passed to Agrippa II on Herod's death in AD 48.

Fadus also at that time sent for the chief priests and the leaders of the people of Jerusalem and advised them to deposit the full-length tunic and the sacred robe, which it was the custom for the High Priest alone to wear, in Antonia, which is a fortress. There they were to be entrusted to the authority of the Romans, as in fact they had been in times past. They did not dare to gainsay him, but neverthe-less they petitioned Fadus and Longinus—for the latter, out of fear that Fadus' commands would force the Jewish people into rebellion, had himself come to Jerusalem with a large force—first to allow them to send a delegation to Caesar to ask him for permission to keep the sacred robe in their own hands, and secondly to wait until they knew what answer Claudius made to this petition. Fadus and Longinus replied that they would permit them to send a delegation if their children were delivered as hostages to them. To this they promptly agreed and delivered the hostages, whereupon the envoys were dispatched. On their arrival in Rome the younger Agrippa, son of the deceased king, who was at the court of Claudius Caesar . . . entreated Caesar to grant the Jews their petition . . . and to send a letter to Fadus to that effect.

Claudius, when he had summoned the envoys, informed them that he was grant-ing their petition, adding that they must thank Agrippa for it, since he was acting at Agrippa's request. To confirm his answer, he gave them a letter, which I quote: 'Claudius Caesar Germanicus, in the fifth year of tribunician power, designated consul for the fourth time, Imperator for the tenth time, Father of his Country, to the rulers, council, and people of Jerusalem and to the whole nation of the Jews, greeting. My friend Agrippa, whom I have brought up and now have with me, a man of the greatest piety, brought your envoys before me. They gave thanks for the tender care that I have shown your nation and earnestly and zealously requested that the holy vestments and the crown might be placed in your hands. I grant this request, in accordance with the precedent set by Vitellius, that excellent man for whom I have the greatest esteem. I have given my consent to this measure, first because I cherish religion myself and wish to see every nation maintain the religious practices that are traditional with it, and secondly because I know that in doing so I shall give great pleasure to King Herod himself and to Aristobulus the younger— excellent men for whom I have high regard, men of whose devotion to me and zeal for your interest I am aware and with whom I have very many ties of friendship. I am also writing on these matters to my procurator Cuspius Fadus. . . . Written on the fourth day before the Kalends of July [28 June], in the consulship of Rufus and Pompeius Silvanus.'

Herod, brother of the deceased Agrippa, who was at this time charged with the administration of Chalcis, also asked Claudius Caesar to give him authority over the Temple and the holy vessels and the selection of the high priests—all of which requests he obtained. This authority, derived from him, passed to his descendants alone until the end of the war.

Josephus AJ 20. 6-16 (abridged)
tr. L. H. Feldman (Loeb 1965)

O36 The first pseudo-messiah, between AD 44 and 46

Cf. Acts 5: 36, though there Theudas is inaccurately dated before the Judas of AD 6.

During the period when Fadus was procurator of Judaea, a certain imposter named Theudas persuaded the majority of the masses to take up their possessions and to follow him to the Jordan river. He stated that he was a prophet and that at his command the river would be parted and would provide them an easy passage. With this talk he deceived many. Fadus, however, did not permit them to reap the fruit of their folly, but sent against them a squadron of cavalry. These fell upon them unexpectedly, slew many of them and took many prisoners. Theudas himself was captured, whereupon they cut off his head and brought it to Jerusalem.

Josephus *AJ* 20. 97–8
tr. L. H. Feldman (Loeb 1965)

O37 The procuratorship of Ventidius Cumanus, AD 48–52

The parallel account of the incident at the Passover in the BJ *adds that stones as well as insults were hurled at Cumanus, and gives the even more improbable figure of 30,000 for the casualties. According to* BJ *the ex-High Priest Jonathan was included in the group sent to Rome, a point of importance in connection with O38b. The 'captain', i.e. of the Temple, was the High Priest's administrative deputy.*

While Cumanus was administering affairs in Judaea, an uprising occurred in the city of Jerusalem as a result of which many of the Jews lost their lives. . . . When the festival called Passover was at hand, . . . a large multitude from all quarters assembled for it. Cumanus, fearing that their presence might afford occasion for an uprising, ordered one company of soldiers to take up arms and stand guard on the porticoes of the temple so as to quell any uprising that might occur. This had been in fact the usual practice of previous procurators of Judaea at the festivals. On the fourth day of the festival, one of the soldiers uncovered his genitals and exhibited them to the multitude—an action which created anger and rage in the onlookers, who said that it was not they who had been insulted, but that it was a blasphemy against God. Some of the bolder ones also reviled Cumanus, asserting that the soldier had been prompted by him. Cumanus, when informed, was himself not a little provoked at the insulting remarks, but still merely admonished them to put an end to this lust for revolution and not to set disorders ablaze during the festival. Failing, however, to persuade them, for they only attacked him with more scurrilities, he ordered the whole army to take full armour and come to Antonia. . . . The crowd, seeing the arrival of the soldiers, was frightened and started to flee. But since the exits were narrow, they, supposing that they were being pursued by the enemy, pushed together in their flight and crushed to death many of their number who were caught in the narrow passages. Indeed, the number of those who perished in that disturbance was computed at twenty thousand. . . .

Their first mourning had not yet ceased when another calamity befell them. For some of the seditious revolutionaries robbed Stephen, a slave of Caesar, as he was travelling on the public highway at a distance of about one hundred furlongs from this city, and despoiled him of all his belongings. When Cumanus heard of this, he at once dispatched soldiers with orders to plunder the neighbouring villages and to bring before him their most eminent men in chains so that he might exact vengeance for their effrontery. After the sacking of the villages, one of the soldiers, who had found a copy of the laws of Moses that was kept in one of the villages, fetched it out where all could see and tore it in two while he uttered blasphemies and railed violently. The Jews, on learning of this, collected in large numbers, went down to Caesarea, where Cumanus happened to be, and besought him to avenge not them but God, whose laws had been subjected to outrage. For, they said, they could not endure to live, since their ancestral code was thus wantonly insulted. Cumanus, alarmed at the thought of a fresh revolution of the masses, after taking counsel with his friends, beheaded the soldier who had outraged the laws and thus prevented the uprising when it was on the verge of breaking out a second time.

Hatred also arose between the Samaritans and the Jews for the following reason. It was the custom of the Galilaeans at the time of a festival to pass through the Samaritan territory on their way to the Holy City. On one occasion, while they were passing through, certain of the inhabitants of a village called Ginae, which was situated on the border between Samaria and the Great Plain, joined battle with the Galilaeans and slew a great number of them. The leaders of the Galilaeans, hearing of the occurrence, came to Cumanus and besought him to seek out the murderers of those who had been slain. He, however, having been bribed by the Samaritans, neglected to avenge them. The Galilaeans, indignant at this, urged the Jewish masses to resort to arms and to assert their liberty; for, they said, slavery was in itself bitter, but when it involved insolent treatment, it was quite intolerable. Those in authority tried to mollify them and reduce the disorder, and offered to induce Cumanus to punish the murderers. The masses, however, paid no heed to them, but taking up arms and inviting the assistance of Eleazar son of Deinaeus— he was a brigand who for many years had had his home in the mountains—they fired and sacked certain villages of the Samaritans. When the affair came to Cumanus' ears, he took over the squadron of the Sebastenians and four units of infantry and armed the Samaritans. He then marched out against the Jews and, in an encounter, slew many, but took more alive. Thereupon those who were by rank and birth the leaders of the inhabitants of Jerusalem, when they saw to what depth of calamity they had come, changed their robes for sackcloth and defiled their heads with ashes and went to all lengths entreating the rebels. . . . The people dispersed and the brigands returned to their strongholds. From that time the whole of Judaea was infested with bands of brigands.

The leaders of the Samaritans met Ummidius Quadratus, the governor of Syria,

655

who at that time was at Tyre, and accused the Jews of firing and sacking their villages. [*Their complaints are then elaborated.*] The Jews, on the other hand, said that the Samaritans were responsible for the factional strife and the fighting, but in the highest degree Cumanus, who had been bribed by them to pass over in silence the murder of the Jewish victims. After the hearing, Quadratus deferred judgement, saying that he would announce his decision when he had reached Judaea and had gained a more accurate understanding of the case. . . . Not long afterwards Quadratus reached Samaria, where, after a full hearing, he came to the conclusion that the Samaritans had been responsible for the disorder. He then crucified those of the Samaritans and of the Jews who, he had learned, had taken part in the rebellion and whom Cumanus had taken prisoner. From there he came to Lydda . . . and sat on the judgement seat, where he gave a second thorough hearing to the case of the Samaritans. Here he was informed by a certain Samaritan that a leader of the Jews named Doëtus, together with four other revolutionaries, had instigated the mob to revolt against the Romans. These also Quadratus ordered to be put to death. As for the high priest Ananias and the captain Ananus and their followers, he put them in chains and sent them up to Rome to render an account of their actions to Claudius Caesar. He further ordered the leaders of the Samaritans, those of the Jews, and Cumanus the procurator . . . to set off to Italy to get a decision in the imperial court concerning the matters in dispute between them. He himself, fearing a fresh revolution on the part of the Jewish people, visited the city of Jerusalem, which he found at peace . . . and then returned to Antioch.

Cumanus and the leaders of the Samaritans with their companions who had been sent to Rome were assigned a day by the emperor on which they were to state their case in the matters at issue involving them. Caesar's freedmen and friends displayed the greatest partiality for Cumanus and the Samaritans, and they would have got the better of the Jews, had not Agrippa the Younger, who was in Rome and saw that the Jewish leaders were losing the race for influence, urgently entreated Agrippina, the wife of the emperor, to persuade her husband to give the case a thorough hearing in a manner befitting his respect for law and to punish the instigators of the revolt. Claudius was favourably impressed by this petition. He then heard the case through, and, on discovering that the Samaritans were the first to move in stirring up trouble, he ordered those of them who had come before him to be put to death, condemned Cumanus to exile.

Josephus *AJ* 20. 105–36 (abridged)
tr. L. H. Feldman (Loeb 1965)

O38 The Sicarii

(a) *Their origin*

Felix was procurator from AD 52 until 58 or 59. Sica is the Latin for dagger.

Felix captured the bandit chief Eleazar, who had been plundering the country for twenty years, with many of his men, and sent them as prisoners to Rome; the bandits whom he crucified, and the local inhabitants in league with them whom he caught and punished, were too many to count. When the countryside had been cleared of them, another type of bandit sprang up in Jerusalem, known as 'Sicarii'. These committed numerous murders in broad daylight and in the middle of the City. Their favourite trick was to mingle with festival crowds, concealing under their garments small daggers with which they stabbed their opponents. When their victims fell, the assassins melted into the indignant crowd.

Josephus *BJ* 2. 253–5
tr. Williamson, rev. Smallwood

(b)   *Their murder of the ex-High Priest Jonathan*

On Jonathan see also O26, end and O37, introduction.

Felix also bore a grudge against Jonathan the High Priest because of his frequent admonition to improve the administration of the affairs of Judaea. For Jonathan feared that he himself might incur the censure of the multitude in that he had requested Caesar to dispatch Felix as procurator of Judaea. Felix accordingly devised a pretext that would remove from his presence one who was a constant nuisance to him. . . . [He bribed] Jonathan's most trusted friend, a native of Jerusalem named Doras, with a promise to pay a great sum, to bring in brigands to attack Jonathan and kill him. Doras agreed and contrived to get him murdered by the brigands in the following way. Certain of these brigands went up to the city as if they intended to worship God. With daggers concealed under their clothes, they mingled with the people about Jonathan and assassinated him.

Josephus *AJ* 20. 162–4 (abridged)
tr. L. H. Feldman (Loeb 1965)

O39 Pseudo-messiahs during the procuratorship of Felix, AD 52–58/9

Cf. Acts 21: 37–8, where the prophet's followers are described as 4,000 Sicarii—a more credible number than the 30,000 of the BJ *version.*

Imposters and deceivers called upon the mob to follow them into the desert. For they said that they would show them unmistakable marvels and signs that would be wrought in harmony with God's design. Many were, in fact, persuaded and paid the penalty of their folly; for they were brought before Felix and he punished them. At this time there came to Jerusalem from Egypt a man who declared that he was a prophet and advised the masses of the common people to go out with him to the mountain called the Mount of Olives, which lies opposite the city at a distance of five furlongs. For he asserted that he wished to demonstrate from there that at his command Jerusalem's walls would fall down, through which he promised to provide them an entrance into the city. When Felix heard of this he ordered his soldiers to take up their arms. Setting out from Jerusalem with a large force of cavalry and infantry, he fell upon the Egyptian and his followers, slaying four hundred of them and taking two hundred prisoners. The Egyptian himself escaped from the battle and disappeared.

Josephus *AJ* 20. 167–71
tr. L. H. Feldman (Loeb 1965)

O40 The execution of James, bishop of Jerusalem

The date is AD 62. Festus was the successor of Felix (038). The elder Ananus had been appointed by Quirinius in AD 6; for his two older sons Jonathan and Theophilus see O26, 30(a), and 38(b). The words 'who was called the Christ' are probably a Christian interpolation; no Jewish writer would give Jesus this messianic title.

Upon learning of the death of Festus, Caesar sent Albinus to Judaea as procurator. The king removed Joseph from the high priesthood, and bestowed the succession to this office upon the son of Ananus, who was likewise called Ananus. It is said that the elder Ananus was extremely fortunate. For he had five sons, all of whom, after he himself had previously enjoyed the office for a very long time, became High Priests of God—a thing that had never happened to any other of our High Priests. The younger Ananus. . . was rash in his temper and unusually daring. He followed the school of the Sadducees, who are indeed more heartless than any of the other Jews, as I have already explained, when they sit in judgement. Possessed of such a character, Ananus thought that he had a favourable opportunity because Festus was dead and Albinus was still on the way. And so he convened the judges of the Sanhedrin and brought before them a man named James, the brother of Jesus who was called the Christ, and certain others. He accused them of having transgressed the law and delivered them up to be stoned. Those of the inhabitants of the city who were considered the most fair-minded and who were strict in observance of the law were offended at this. They therefore secretly sent to King Agrippa urging him, for Ananus had not even been correct in his first step, to order him to desist from any further such actions. Certain of them even went to meet Albinus, who was on his way from Alexandria, and informed him that Ananus had not authority to convene the Sanhedrin without his consent. Convinced by these words, Albinus angrily wrote to Ananus threatening to take vengeance upon him. King Agrippa, because of Ananus' action, deposed him from the high priesthood which he had held for three months.

Josephus *AJ* 20. 197–203 (abridged)
tr. L. H. Feldman (Loeb 1965)

O41 The corrupt administration of Lucceius Albinus, AD 62–4

Once more the Sicarii at the festival, for it was now going on, entered the city by night and kidnapped the secretary of the captain Eleazar—he was the son of Ananias the high priest—and led him off in bonds. They then sent to Ananias saying that they would release the secretary to him if he would induce Albinus to release ten of their number who had been taken prisoner. Ananias under this constraint persuaded Albinus and obtained this request. This was the beginning of greater troubles; for the brigands contrived by one means or another to kidnap some of Ananias' staff and would hold them in continuous confinement and refuse to release them until they had received in exchange some of the Sicarii. When they had once more become not inconsiderable in number, they grew bold again and proceeded to harass every part of the land. . . .

When Albinus heard that Gessius Florus was coming to succeed him, he sought to gain a name as one who had done some service to the inhabitants of Jerusalem. He therefore brought out those prisoners who clearly deserved to be put to death and sentenced them to execution, but released for a personal consideration those who had been cast into prison for a trifling and commonplace offence. Thus the prison was cleared of inmates and the land was infested with brigands.

Josephus *AJ* 20. 208-10; 215
tr. L. H Feldman, Loeb Classical Library (Heinemann 1965)

O42 Josephus' indictment of the last procurator

Gessius Florus was procurator from AD 64 until the revolt broke out in 66.

Gessius Florus, who had been sent by Nero as successor to Albinus, filled the cup of the Jews with many misfortunes. . . . So wicked and lawless was Florus in the exercise of his authority that the Jews, owing to the extremity of their misery, praised Albinus as a benefactor. For the latter used to conceal his villainy and took precautions not to be altogether detected; but Gessius Florus, as if he had been sent to give an exhibition of wickedness, ostentatiously paraded his lawless treatment of our nation and omitted no form of pillage or unjust punishment. Pity could not soften him, nor any amount of gain sate him; he was one who saw no difference between the greatest gains and the smallest, so that he even joined in partnership with brigands. In fact, the majority of people practised this occupation with no inhibitions, since they had no doubt that their lives would be insured by him in return for his quota of the spoils. There was no limit in sight. The ill-fated Jews, unable to endure the devastation by brigands that went on, were one and all forced to abandon their own country and flee, for they thought that it would be better to settle among gentiles, no matter where. What more need be said?

659

It was Florus who constrained us to take up war with the Romans, for we preferred to perish together rather than by degrees.

Josephus *AJ* 20. 252–7 (abridged)
tr. L. H. Feldman (Loeb 1965)

O 43 'The Sermon on the Mount' from the Gospel according to St. Matthew

5:3   'How blest are those who know that they are poor;
        the kingdom of Heaven is theirs.

4   How blest are the sorrowful;
        they shall find consolation.

5   How blest are those of a gentle spirit;
        they shall have the earth for their possession.

6   How blest are those who hunger and thirst to see right prevail;
        they shall be satisfied.

7   How blest are those who show mercy;
        mercy shall be shown to them.

8   How blest are those whose hearts are pure;
        they shall see God.

9   How blest are the peacemakers;
        God shall call them his sons.

10   How blest are those who have suffered persecution for the cause
        of right;
        the kingdom of Heaven is theirs.

11
12   'How blest you are, when you suffer insults and persecution and every kind of calumny for my sake. Accept it with gladness and exultation, for you have a rich reward in heaven; in the same way they persecuted the prophets before you.

13   'You are salt to the world. And if salt becomes tasteless, how is its saltness to be restored? It is now good for nothing but to be thrown away and trodden underfoot.

14
15
16   'You are light for all the world. A town that stands on a hill cannot be hidden. When a lamp is lit, it is not put under the meal-tub, but on the lamp-stand, where it gives light to everyone in the house. And you, like the lamp, must shed light among your fellows, so that, when they see the good you do, they may give praise to your Father in heaven.

17
18   'Do not suppose that I have come to abolish the Law and the prophets; I did not come to abolish, but to complete. I tell you this: so long as heaven and earth endure, not a letter, not a stroke, will disappear from the Law until all

that must happen has happened. If any man therefore sets aside even the 19
least of the Law's demands, and teaches others to do the same, he will have
the lowest place in the kingdom of Heaven, whereas anyone who keeps the
Law and teaches others so will stand high in the kingdom of Heaven. I tell 20
you, unless you show yourselves far better men than the Pharisees and the
doctors of the law, you can never enter the kingdom of Heaven.

'You have learned that our forefathers were told, "Do not commit murder; 21
anyone who commits murder must be brought to judgement." But what I tell 22
you is this: Anyone who nurses anger against his brother must be brought to
judgement. If he abuses his brother he must answer for it to the court; if he
sneers at him he will have to answer for it in the fires of hell.

'If, when you are bringing your gift to the altar, you suddenly remember 23
that your brother has a grievance against you, leave your gift where it is before 24
the altar. First go and make your peace with your brother, and only then
come back and offer your gift.

'If someone sues you, come to terms with him promptly while you are 25
both on your way to court; otherwise he may hand you over to the judge,
and the judge to the constable, and you will be put in jail. I tell you, once 26
you are there you will not be let out till you have paid the last farthing.

'You have learned that they were told, "Do not commit adultery." But 27,28
what I tell you is this: If a man looks on a woman with a lustful eye, He has
already committed adultery with her in his heart.

'If your right eye leads you astray, tear it out and fling it away; it is better 29
for you to lose one part of your body than for the whole of it to be thrown
into hell. And if your right hand is your undoing, cut it off and fling it away; 30
it is better for you to lose one part of your body than for the whole of it to
go to hell.

'They were told, "A man who divorces his wife must give her a note of 31
dismissal." But what I tell you is this: If a man divorces his wife for any cause 32
other than unchastity he involves her in adultery; and anyone who marries a
woman so divorced commits adultery.

'Again, you have learned that they were told, "Do not break your oath", 33
and, "Oaths sworn to the Lord must be kept." But what I tell you is this: 34
You are not to swear at all—not by heaven, for it is God's throne, nor by 35
earth, for it is his footstool, nor by Jerusalem, for it is the city of the great
King, nor by your own head, because you cannot turn one hair of it white 36
or black. Plain "Yes" or "No" is all you need to say; anything beyond that 37
comes from the devil.

'You have learned that they were told, "An eye for an eye, and a tooth 38
for a tooth." But what I tell you is this: Do not set yourself against the man 39
who wrongs you. If someone slaps you on the right cheek, turn and offer him
your left. If a man wants to sue you for your shirt, let him have your coat as 40
well. If a man in authority makes you go one mile, go with him two. Give 41,42
when you are asked to give; and do not turn your back on a man who wants
to borrow.

43 'You have learned that they were told, "Love your neighbour, hate your
44 enemy." But what I tell you is this: Love your enemies and pray for your
45 persecutors, only so can you be children of your heavenly Father, who makes
his sun rise on good and bad alike, and sends the rain on the honest and the
46 dishonest. If you love only those who love you, what reward can you expect?
47 Surely the tax-gatherers do as much as that. And if you greet only your
. brothers, what is there extraordinary about that? Even the heathen do as
48 much. You must therefore be all goodness, just as your heavenly Father is
all good.

6:1 'Be careful not to make a show of your religion before men; if you do, no
reward awaits you in your Father's house in heaven.
2 'Thus, when you do some act of charity, do not announce it with a flourish
of trumpets, as the hypocrites do in synagogue and in the streets to win
3 admiration from men. I tell you this: they have their reward already. No;
when you do some act of charity, do not let your left hand know what your
4 right is doing; your good deed must be secret, and your Father who sees what
is done in secret will reward you.
5 'Again, when you pray, do not be like the hypocrites; they love to say
their prayers standing up in synagogue and at the street-corners, for everyone
6 to see them. I tell you this: they have their reward already. But when you
pray, go into a room by yourself, shut the door, and pray to your Father who
is there in the secret place; and your Father who sees what is secret will
reward you.
7 'In your prayers do not go babbling on like the heathen, who imagine that
8 the more they say the more likely they are to be heard. Do not imitate them.
Your Father knows what your needs are before you ask him.
9 'This is how you should pray:

"Our Father in heaven,
Thy name be hallowed;
10 Thy kingdom come,
Thy will be done,
On earth as in heaven.
11 Give us today our daily bread.
12 Forgive us the wrong we have done.
As we have forgiven those who have wronged us.
13 And do not bring us to the test,
But save us from the evil one."

14 For if you forgive others the wrongs they have done, your heavenly Father
15 will also forgive you; but if you do not forgive others, then the wrongs you
have done will not be forgiven by your Father.
16 'So too when you fast, do not look gloomy like the hypocrites: they make
their faces unsightly so that other people may see that they are fasting. I tell

662

you this: they have their reward already. But when you fast, anoint your 17
head and wash your face, so that men may not see that you are fasting, but 18
only your Father who is in the secret place; and your Father who sees what is
secret will give you your reward.

'Do not store up for yourselves treasure on earth, where it grows rusty and 19
moth-eaten, and thieves break in to steal it. Store up treasure in heaven, where 20
there is no moth and no rust to spoil it, no thieves to break in and steal. For 21
where your wealth is, there will your heart be also. . . .

'Therefore I bid you put away anxious thoughts about food and drink to 25
keep you alive, and clothes to cover your body. Surely life is more than food,
the body more than clothes. Look at the birds of the air; they do not sow 26
and reap and store in barns, yet your heavenly Father feeds them. You are
worth more than the birds! Is there a man of you who by anxious thought 27
can add a foot to his height? And why be anxious about clothes? Consider 28
how the lilies grow in the fields; they do not work, they do not spin; and yet, 29
I tell you, even Solomon in all his splendour was not attired like one of these.
But if that is how God clothes the grass in the fields, which is there today, 30
and tomorrow is thrown on the stove, will he not all the more clothe you?
How little faith you have! No, do not ask anxiously, "What are we to eat? 31
What are we to drink? What shall we wear?" All these are things for the 32
heathen to run after, not for you, because your heavenly Father knows that
you need them all. Set your mind on God's kingdom and his justice before 33
everything else, and all the rest will come to you as well. So do not be anxious 34
about tomorrow; tomorrow will look after itself. Each day has troubles
enough of its own.

'Pass no judgement, and you will not be judged. For as you judge others, so 7:1,2
you will yourselves be judged, and whatever measure you deal out to others
will be dealt back to you. Why do you look at the speck of sawdust in your 3
brother's eye, with never a thought for the great plank in your own? Or how 4
can you say to your brother, "Let me take the speck out of your eye", when
all the time there is that plank in your own? You hypocrite! First take the 5
plank out of your own eye, and then you will see clearly to take the speck
out of your brother's. . . .

For everyone who asks receives, he who seeks finds, and to him who 8
knocks, the door will be opened.

'Is there a man among you who will offer his son a stone when he asks 9
for bread, or a snake when he asks for fish? If you, then, bad as you are, 10,11
know how to give your children what is good for them, how much more will
your heavenly Father give good things to those who ask him!

'Always treat others as you would like them to treat you: that is the Law 12
and the prophets. . . .

'Beware of false prophets, men who come to you dressed up as sheep while 15

16 underneath they are savage wolves. You will recognize them by the fruits they
17 bear. Can grapes be picked from briars, or figs from thistles? In the same way,
18 a good tree always yields good fruit, and a poor tree bad fruit. A good tree
19 cannot bear bad fruit, And when a tree does not yield good fruit it is cut
20 down and burnt. That is why I say you will recognize them by their fruits.

21 'Not everyone who calls me "Lord, Lord" will enter the kingdom of
22 Heaven, but only those who do the will of my heavenly Father. When that
day comes, many will say to me, "Lord, Lord, did we not prophesy in your
name, cast out devils in your name, and in your name perform many miracles?"
23 Then I will tell them to their face, "I never knew you: out of my sight, you
and your wicked ways!"

24 'What then of the man who hears these words of mine and acts upon them?
25 He is like a man who had the sense to build his house on rock. The rain came
down, the floods rose, the wind blew, and beat upon that house; but it did not
26 fall, because its foundations were on rock. But what of the man who hears
these words of mine and does not act upon them? He is like a man who was
27 foolish enough to build his house on sand. The rain came down, the floods
rose, the wind blew, and beat upon that house; down it fell with a great crash.'

28 When Jesus had finished this discourse the people were astounded at his
29 teaching; unlike their own teachers he taught with a note of authority.

O44 Excerpts from the Gospel according to St. Luke

(a) *The prelude*

[*The work opens with accounts of the births of John the Baptist and Jesus, and an
episode in Jesus' boyhood.*]

3:1 In the fifteenth year of the Emperor Tiberius, when Pontius Pilate was governor
of Judaea, when Herod was prince of Galilee, his brother Philip prince of
2 Ituraea and Trachonitis, and Lysanias prince of Abilene, during the high-
priesthood of Annas and Caiaphas, the word of God came to John son of
3 Zechariah in the wilderness. And he went all over the Jordan valley proclaim-
4 ing a baptism in token of repentance for the forgiveness of sins, as it is written
in the book of the prophecies of Isaiah:

> 'A voice crying aloud in the wilderness,
> "Prepare a way for the Lord;
> Clear a straight path for him.
5 > Every ravine shall be filled in,
> And every mountain and hill levelled;
> The corners shall be straightened,
> And the rough ways made smooth;
6 > And all mankind shall see God's deliverance."'

Crowds of people came out to be baptized by him, and he said to them: 7
'You vipers' brood! Who warned you to escape from the coming retribution?
Then prove your repentance by the fruit it bears; and do not begin saying to 8
yourselves, "We have Abraham for our father." I tell you that God can make
children for Abraham out of these stones here. Already the axe is laid to the 9
roots of the trees; and every tree that fails to produce good fruit is cut down
and thrown on the fire.'

The people asked him, 'Then what are we to do?' He replied, 'The man 10,11
with two shirts must share with him who has none, and anyone who has food
must do the same.' Among those who came to be baptized were tax-gatherers, 12
and they said to him, 'Master, what are we to do?' He told them, 'Exact no 13
more than the assessment.' Soldiers on service also asked him, 'And what of 14
us?' To them he said, 'No bullying; no blackmail; make do with your pay!'

The people were on the tiptoe of expectation, all wondering about John, 15
whether perhaps he was the Messiah, but he spoke out and said to them all, 16
'I baptize you with water; but there is one to come who is mightier than I.
I am not fit to unfasten his shoes. He will baptize you with the Holy Spirit
and with fire. His shovel is ready in his hand, to winnow his threshing-floor 17
and gather the wheat into his granary; but he will burn the chaff on a fire
that can never go out.'

(b) *The opening of Jesus' ministry*

During a general baptism of the people, when Jesus too had been baptized 21
and was praying, heaven opened and the Holy Spirit descended on him in 22
bodily form like a dove; and there came a voice from heaven, 'Thou art my
Son, my Beloved; on thee my favour rests.'

When Jesus began his work he was about thirty years old. . . . 23

Full of the Holy Spirit, Jesus returned from the Jordan, and for forty days 4:1,2
was led by the Spirit up and down the wilderness and tempted by the devil.

All that time he had nothing to eat, and at the end of it he was famished.
The devil said to him, 'If you are the Son of God, tell this stone to become 3
bread.' Jesus answered, 'Scripture says, "Man cannot live on bread alone."' 4

Next the devil led him up and showed him in a flash all the kingdoms of 5
the world. 'All this dominion will I give to you,' he said, 'and the glory that 6
goes with it; for it has been put in my hands and I can give it to anyone I
choose. You have only to do homage to me and it shall all be yours.' Jesus 7,8
answered him, 'Scripture says, "You shall do homage to the Lord your God
and worship him alone."'

The devil took him to Jerusalem and set him on the parapet of the temple. 9
'If you are the Son of God,' he said, 'throw yourself down; for Scripture says, 10
"He will give his angels orders to take care of you", and again, "They will sup- 11
port you in their arms for fear you should strike your foot against a stone."'
Jesus answered him, 'It has been said, "You are not to test the Lord your God."' 12

13   So, having come to the end of all his temptations, the devil departed, biding his time.

14   Then Jesus, armed with the power of the Spirit, returned to Galilee; and
15   reports about him spread through the whole countryside. He taught in their synagogues and all men sang his praises.
16   So he came to Nazareth, where he had been brought up, and went to synagogue on the Sabbath day as he regularly did. He stood up to read the
17   lesson and was handed the scroll of the prophet Isaiah. He opened the scroll and found the passage which says,

18   'The spirit of the Lord is upon me because he has anointed me;
        He has sent me to announce good news to the poor,
        To proclaim release for prisoners and recovery of sight for the blind;
        To let the broken victims go free,
19   To proclaim the year of the Lord's favour.'

20   He rolled up the scroll, gave it back to the attendant, and sat down; and all eyes in the synagogue were fixed on him.
21   He began to speak: 'Today', he said, 'in your very hearing this text has
22   come true.' There was a general stir of admiration; they were surprised that words of such grace should fall from his lips. 'Is not this Joseph's son?' they
23   asked. Then Jesus said, 'No doubt you will quote the proverb to me, "Physician, heal yourself!", and say, "We have heard of all your doings at Caper-
24   naum; do the same here in your own home town." I tell you this,' he went on:
25   'no prophet is recognized in his own country. There were many widows in Israel, you may be sure, in Elijah's time, when for three years and six months
26   the skies never opened, and famine lay hard over the whole country; yet it was to none of those that Elijah was sent, but to a widow at Sarepta in the
27   territory of Sidon. Again, in the time of the prophet Elisha there were many lepers in Israel, and not one of them was healed, but only Naaman, the
28,29 Syrian.' At these words the whole congregation were infuriated. They leapt up, threw him out of the town, and took him to the brow of the hill on
30   which it was built, meaning to hurl him over the edge. But he walked straight through them all, and went away.

(c)   *The Twelve Disciples*

5:1 One day as [Jesus] stood by the Lake of Gennesaret, and the people crowded
  2 upon him to listen to the word of God, he noticed two boats lying at the water's edge; the fishermen had come ashore and were washing their nets.
  3 He got into one of the boats, which belonged to Simon, and asked him to put out a little way from the shore; then he went on teaching the crowds
  4 from his seat in the boat. When he had finished speaking, he said to Simon,
  5 'Put out into deep water and let down your nets for a catch.' Simon answered, 'Master, we were hard at work all night and caught nothing at all; but if you

say so, I will let down the nets.' They did so and made a big haul of fish; and 6
their nets began to split. So they signalled to their partners in the other boat 7
to come and help them. This they did, and loaded both boats to the point of
sinking. When Simon saw what had happened he fell at Jesus's knees and said, 8
'Go, Lord, leave me, sinner that I am!' For he and all his companions were 9
amazed at the catch they had made; so too were his partners James and John, 10
Zebedee's sons. 'Do not be afraid,' said Jesus to Simon; 'from now on you
will be catching men.' As soon as they had brought the boats to land, they 11
left everything and followed him.

[*A healing miracle follows.*]

One day [Jesus] was teaching, and Pharisees and teachers of the law were 17
sitting round. People had come from every village of Galilee and from Judaea
and Jerusalem, and the power of God was with him to heal the sick. Some 18
men appeared carrying a paralysed man on a bed. They tried to bring him in
and set him down in front of Jesus, but found no way to do so because of 19
the crowd, they went up on to the roof and let him down through the tiling,
bed and all, into the middle of the company in front of Jesus. When Jesus 20
saw their faith, he said, 'Man, your sins are forgiven you.'

The lawyers and the Pharisees began saying to themselves, 'Who is this 21
fellow with his blasphemous talk? Who but God alone can forgive sins?' But 22
Jesus knew their thoughts and answered them: 'Why do you harbour thoughts
like these? Is it easier to say, "Your sins are forgiven you", or to say, "Stand 23
up and walk"? But to convince you that the Son of Man has the right on earth 24
to forgive sins'—he turned to the paralysed man—'I say to you, stand up, take
your bed, and go home.' And at once he rose to his feet before their eyes, 25
took up the bed he had been lying on, and went home praising God. They 26
were all lost in amazement and praised God; filled with awe they said, 'You
would never believe the things we have seen today.'

Later, when he went out, he saw a tax-gatherer, Levi by name, at his seat 27
in the custom-house. He said to him, 'Follow me'; and he rose to his feet, left 28
everything behind, and followed him.

Afterwards Levi held a big reception in his house for Jesus; among the 29
guests was a large party of tax-gatherers and others. The Pharisees and the 30
lawyers of their sect complained to his disciples: 'Why do you eat and drink',
they said, 'with tax-gatherers and sinners?' Jesus answered them: 'It is not 31
the healthy that need a doctor, but the sick; I have not come to invite virtuous 32
people, but to call sinners to repentance.' . . .

One Sabbath [Jesus] was going through the cornfields, and his disciples were 6:1
plucking the ears of corn, rubbing them in their hands, and eating them.
Some of the Pharisees said, 'Why are you doing what is forbidden on the 2
Sabbath?' Jesus answered, 'So you have not read what David did when he and 3
his men were hungry? He went into the House of God and took the conse- 4
crated loaves to eat and gave them to his men, though priests alone are allowed

5 to eat them, and no one else.' He also said, 'The Son of Man is sovereign even over the Sabbath.'

6 On another Sabbath he had gone to synagogue and was teaching. There
7 happened to be a man in the congregation whose right arm was withered; and the lawyers and the Pharisees were on the watch to see whether Jesus would cure him on the Sabbath, so that they could find a charge to bring against
8 him. But he knew what was in their minds and said to the man with the withered arm, 'Get up and stand out here.' So he got up and stood there.
9 Then Jesus said to them, 'I put the question to you: is it permitted to do
10 good or to do evil on the Sabbath, to save life or to destroy it?' He looked round at them all and then said to the man, 'Stretch out your arm.' He did so,
11 and his arm was restored. But they were beside themselves with anger, and began to discuss among themselves what they could do to Jesus.

12 During this time he went out one day into the hills to pray, and spent the
13 night in prayer to God. When day broke he called his disciples to him, and
14 from among them he chose twelve and named them Apostles: Simon, to whom he gave the name of Peter, and Andrew his brother, James and John, Philip
15 and Bartholomew, Matthew and Thomas, James son of Alphaeus, and Simon
16 who was called the Zealot, Judas son of James, and Judas Iscariot who turned traitor.

(d) *Jesus' work as teacher and healer*

[*Chapter 6 ends with a long discourse which has much material in common with Matt. 5-7. Chapter 7 opens with two healing miracles.*]

7:18,19 John too was informed of all this by his disciples. Summoning two of their number he sent them to the Lord with this message: 'Are you the one who is
20 to come, or are we to expect some other?' The messengers made their way to Jesus and said, 'John the Baptist has sent us to you: he asks, "Are you the
21 one who is to come, or are we to expect some other?"' There and then he cured many sufferers from diseases, plagues, and evil spirits; and on many
22 blind people he bestowed sight. Then he gave them his answer: 'Go', he said, 'and tell John what you have seen and heard: how the blind recover their sight, the lame walk, the lepers are clean, the deaf hear, the dead are raised to
23 life, the poor are hearing the good news—and happy is the man who does not find me a stumbling-block.'

24 After John's messengers had left, Jesus began to speak about him to the crowds: 'What was the spectacle that drew you to the wilderness? A reed-bed
25 swept by the wind? No? Then what did you go out to see? A man dressed in silks and satins? Surely you must look in palaces for grand clothes and luxury.
26 But what did you go out to see? A prophet? Yes indeed, and far more than a
27 prophet. He is the man of whom Scripture says,

"Here is my herald, whom I send on ahead of you,
And he will prepare your way before you."

I tell you, there is not a mother's son greater than John, and yet the least in 28
the kingdom of God is greater than he.'

When they heard him, all the people, including the tax-gatherers, praised 29
God, for they had accepted John's baptism; but the Pharisees and lawyers, 30
who refused his baptism, had rejected God's purpose for themselves.

[*Jesus then discusses John the Baptist and his work.*]

One of the Pharisees invited [Jesus] to dinner; he went to the Pharisee's 36
house and took his place at table. A woman who was living an immoral life 37
in the town had learned that Jesus was dining in the Pharisee's house and had
brought oil of myrrh in a small flask. She took her place behind him, by his 38
feet, weeping. His feet were wetted with her tears and she wiped them with
her hair, kissing them and anointing them with the myrrh. When his host the 39
Pharisee saw this he said to himself, 'If this fellow were a real prophet, he
would know who this woman is that touches him, and what sort of woman
she is, a sinner.' Jesus took him up and said, 'Simon, I have something to say 40
to you.' 'Speak on, Master', said he. 'Two men were in debt to a money- 41
lender: one owed him five hundred silver pieces, the other fifty. As neither 42
had anything to pay with he let them both off. Now, which will love him
most?' Simon replied, 'I should think the one that was let off most.' 'You 43
are right', said Jesus. Then turning to the woman, he said to Simon, 'You see 44
this woman? I came to your house: you provided no water for my feet; but
this woman has made my feet wet with her tears and wiped them with her
hair. You gave me no kiss; but she has been kissing my feet ever since I came 45
in. You did not anoint my head with oil; but she has anointed my feet with 46
myrrh. And so, I tell you, her great love proves that her many sins have been 47
forgiven; where little has been forgiven, little love is shown.' Then he said to 48
her, 'Your sins are forgiven.' The other guests began to ask themselves, 'Who 49
is this, that he can forgive sins?' But he said to the woman, 'Your faith has 50
saved you; go in peace.' ...

People were now gathering in large numbers, and as they made their way to 8:4
him from one town after another, [Jesus] said in a parable: 'A sower went 5
out to sow his seed. And as he sowed, some seed fell along the footpath, where
it was trampled on, and the birds ate it up. Some seed fell on rock and, after 6
coming up, withered for lack of moisture. Some seed fell in among thistles, 7
and the thistles grew up with it and choked it. And some of the seed fell into 8
good soil, and grew, and yielded a hundredfold.' As he said this he called out,
'If you have ears to hear, then hear.'

His disciples asked him what this parable meant, and he said, 'It has been 9,10
granted to you to know the secrets of the kingdom of God; but the others
have only parables, in order that they may look but see nothing, hear but
understand nothing.

'This is what the parable means. The seed is the word of God. Those along 11,12
the footpath are the men who hear it, and then the devil comes and carries

13 off the word from their hearts for fear they should believe and be saved. The seed sown on rock stands for those who receive the word with joy when they hear it, but have no root; they are believers for a while, but in the time of
14 testing they desert. That which fell among thistles represents those who hear, but their further growth is choked by cares and wealth and the pleasures of
15 life, and they bring nothing to maturity. But the seed in good soil represents those who bring a good and honest heart to the hearing of the word, hold it fast, and by their perseverance yield a harvest. . . .'
22 One day [Jesus] got into a boat with his disciples and said to them, 'Let us
23 cross over to the other side of the lake.' So they put out; and as they sailed along he went to sleep. Then a heavy squall struck the lake; they began to
24 ship water and were in grave danger. They went to him, and roused him, crying, 'Master, Master, we are sinking!' He awoke, and rebuked the wind and
25 the turbulent waters. The storm subsided and all was calm. 'Where is your faith?' he asked. In fear and astonishment they said to one another, 'Who can this be? He gives his orders to wind and waves, and they obey him.'
[*Other miracles follow—a case of serious mental derangement and a chronic haemorrhage are healed and a dead child is restored to life.*]

9:1 [Jesus] now called the Twelve together and gave them power and authority
2 to overcome all the devils and to cure diseases, and sent them to proclaim the
3 kingdom of God and to heal. 'Take nothing for the journey,' he told them, neither stick nor pack, neither bread nor money; nor are you each to have a
4 second coat. When you are admitted to a house, stay there, and go on from
5 there. As for those who will not receive you, when you leave their town shake
6 the dust off your feet as a warning to them.' So they set out and travelled from village to village, and everywhere they told the good news and healed the sick. . . .
10 On their return the apostles told Jesus all they had done; and he took them
11 with him and withdrew privately to a town called Bethsaida. But the crowds found out and followed him. He welcomed them, and spoke to them about
12 the kingdom of God, and cured those who were in need of healing. When evening was drawing on, the Twelve approached him and said, 'Send these people away; then they can go into the villages and farms round about to find
13 food and lodging; for we are in a lonely place here.' 'Give them something to eat yourselves', he replied. But they said, 'All we have is five loaves and two fishes, nothing more—unless perhaps we ourselves are to go and buy provisions
14 for all this company.' (There were about five thousand men.) He said to his
15 disciples, 'Make them sit down in groups of fifty or so.' They did so and got
16 them all seated. Then, taking the five loaves and the two fishes, he looked up to heaven, said the blessing over them, broke them, and gave them to the
17 disciples to distribute to the people. They all ate to their hearts' content; and when the scraps they left were picked up, they filled twelve great baskets.
18 One day when he was praying alone in the presence of his disciples, he

asked them, 'Who do the people say I am?' They answered, 'Some say John 19 the Baptist, others Elijah, others that one of the old prophets has come back to life.' 'And you,' he said, 'who do you say I am?' Peter answered, 'God's 20 Messiah.' Then he gave them strict orders not to tell this to anyone. And he 21,22 said, 'The Son of Man has to undergo great sufferings, and to be rejected by the elders, chief priests, and doctors of the law, to be put to death and to be raised again on the third day.'. . .

About eight days after this conversation [Jesus] took Peter, John, and James 28 with him and went up into the hills to pray. And while he was praying the 29 appearance of his face changed and his clothes became dazzling white. Sud- 30 denly there were two men talking with him; these were Moses and Elijah, who appeared in glory and spoke of his departure, the destiny he was to 31 fulfil in Jerusalem. Meanwhile Peter and his companions had been in a deep 32 sleep; but when they awoke, they saw his glory and the two men who stood beside him. And as these were moving away from Jesus, Peter said to him, 33 'Master, how good it is that we are here! Shall we make three shelters, one for you, one for Moses, and one for Elijah?'; but he spoke without knowing what he was saying. The words were still on his lips, when there came a cloud 34 which cast a shadow over them; they were afraid as they entered the cloud, and from it came a voice: 'This is my Son, my Chosen; listen to him.' When 35,36 the voice had spoken, Jesus was seen to be alone. The disciples kept silence and at that time told nobody anything of what they had seen. . . .

As the time approached when [Jesus] was to be taken up to heaven, he set 51 his face resolutely towards Jerusalem, and sent messengers ahead. . . . 52

As they were going along the road a man said to him, 'I will follow you 57 wherever you go.' Jesus answered, 'Foxes have their holes, the birds their 58 roosts; but the Son of Man has nowhere to lay his head.' To another he said, 59 'Follow me', but the man replied, 'Let me go and bury my father first.' Jesus 60 said, 'Leave the dead to bury their dead; you must go and announce the kingdom of God.'. . .

[*A successful preaching and healing mission by seventy followers is then related.*]

On one occasion a lawyer came forward to put this test question to [Jesus]: 10:25 'Master, what must I do to inherit eternal life?' Jesus said, 'What is written 26 in the Law? What is your reading of it?' He replied, 'Love the Lord your God 27 with all your heart, with all your soul, with all your strength, and with all your mind; and your neighbour as yourself.' That is the right answer,' said 28 Jesus; 'do that and you will live.'

But he wanted to vindicate himself, so he said to Jesus, 'And who is my 29 neighbour?' Jesus replied, 'A man was on his way from Jerusalem down to 30 Jericho when he fell in with robbers, who stripped him, beat him, and went off leaving him half dead. It so happened that a priest was going down by the 31

32 same road; but when he saw him, he went past on the other side. So too a
Levite came to the place, and when he saw him went past on the other side.
33 But a Samaritan who was making the journey came upon him, and when he
34 saw him was moved to pity. He went up and bandaged his wounds, bathing
them with oil and wine. Then he lifted him on to his own beast, brought him
35 to an inn, and looked after him there. Next day he produced two silver pieces
and gave them to the inn-keeper, and said, "Look after him; and if you spend
36 any more, I will repay you on my way back." Which of these three do you
37 think was neighbour to the man who fell into the hands of the robbers?' He
answered, 'The one who showed him kindness.' Jesus said, 'Go and do as he
did.'

*[Chapter 11 opens with a short passage of teaching, which includes the prayer
given in Matt. 6.]*

11:14 [Jesus] was driving out a devil which was dumb; and when the devil had come
15 out, the dumb man began to speak. The people were astonished, but some of
them said, 'It is by Beelzebub prince of devils that he drives the devils out.'
16,17 Others, by way of a test, demanded of him a sign from heaven. But he knew
what was in their minds, and said, 'Every kingdom divided against itself goes
18 to ruin, and a divided household falls. Equally if Satan is divided against himself, how can his kingdom stand?—since, as you would have it, I drive out the
19 devils by Beelzebub. If it is by Beelzebub that I cast out devils, by whom do
your own people drive them out? If this is your argument, they themselves
20 will refute you. But if it is by the finger of God that I drive out the devils,
then be sure the kingdom of God has already come upon you. . . .' *[Further
teaching follows.]*

37 When [Jesus] had finished speaking, a Pharisee invited him to dinner. He
38 came in and sat down. The Pharisee noticed with surprise that he had not
39 begun by washing before the meal. But the Lord said to him, 'You Pharisees!
You clean the outside of cup and plate; but inside you is nothing but greed and
40 wickedness. You fools! Did not he who made the outside make the inside
41 too? But let what is in the cup be given in charity, and all is clean.

42 'Alas for you Pharisees! You pay tithes of mint and rue and every garden-
herb, but have no care for justice and the love of God. It is these you should
have practised, without neglecting the others. . . .' *[Further criticism of the
Pharisees follows.]*

53 After he had left the house, the lawyers and Pharisees began to assail him
54 fiercely and to ply him with a host of questions, laying snares to catch him
with his own words.

12:1 Meanwhile, when a crowd of many thousands had gathered, packed so close
that they were treading on one another, [Jesus] began to speak first to his
disciples: 'Beware of the leaven of the Pharisees; I mean their hypocrisy. . . .'

[A long passage of teaching follows, dealing first with God's care for man and then with the need to prepare for God's kingdom—]

'Be ready for action, with belts fastened and lamps alight. Be like men who wait for their master's return from a wedding-party, ready to let him in the moment he arrives and knocks. Happy are those servants whom the master finds on the alert when he comes. I tell you this: he will buckle his belt, seat them at table, and come and wait on them. Even if it is the middle of the night or before dawn when he comes, happy they if he finds them alert. And remember, if the householder had known what time the burglar was coming he would not have let his house be broken into. Hold yourselves ready, then, because the Son of Man is coming at the time you least expect him.' 35,36 37 38 39 40

Peter said, 'Lord, do you intend this parable specially for us or is it for everyone?' The Lord said, 'Well, who is the trusty and sensible man whom his master will appoint as his steward, to manage his servants and issue their rations at the proper time? Happy that servant who is found at his task when his master comes! I tell you this: he will be put in charge of all his master's property. But if that servant says to himself, "The master is a long time coming", and begins to bully the menservants and maids, and eat and drink and get drunk; then the master will arrive on a day that servant does not expect, at a time he does not know, and will cut him in pieces. Thus he will find his place among the faithless. 41 42 43 44 45 46

'The servant who knew his master's wishes, yet made no attempt to carry them out, will be flogged severely. But one who did not know them and earned a beating will be flogged less severely. Where a man has been given much, much will be expected of him; and the more a man has had entrusted to him the more he will be required to repay. 47 48

'I have come to set fire to the earth, and how I wish it were already kindled! I have a baptism to undergo, and how hampered I am until the ordeal is over! Do you suppose I came to establish peace on earth? No indeed, I have come to bring division. For from now on, five members of a family will be divided, three against two and two against three; father against son and son against father, mother against daughter and daughter against mother, mother against son's wife and son's wife against her mother-in-law.' . . . 49 50 51 52 53

[Chapter 13 opens with a healing miracle on a Sabbath.]

'What is the kingdom of God like?' he continued. 'What shall I compare it with? It is like a mustard-seed which a man took and sowed in his garden; and it grew to be a tree and the birds came to roost among its branches.' 13:18 19

Again he said, 'What shall I compare the kingdom of God with? It is like yeast which a woman took and mixed with half a hundred-weight of flour till it was all leavened.' 20 21

[More teaching about the Kingdom follows. Chapter 14 contains another healing miracle on a Sabbath followed by parables.]

15:1 Another time the tax-gatherers and other bad characters were all crowding in
2 to listen to [Jesus]; and the Pharisees and the doctors of the law began
grumbling among themselves: 'This fellow', they said, 'welcomes sinners and
3,4 eats with them.' He answered them with this parable; 'If one of you has a
hundred sheep and loses one of them, does he not leave the ninety-nine in
5 the open pasture and go after the missing one until he has found it? How
6 delighted he is then! He lifts it on to his shoulders, and home he goes to call
his friends and neighbours together. "Rejoice with me!" he cries. "I have
7 found my lost sheep." In the same way, I tell you, there will be greater joy in
heaven over one sinner who repents than over ninety-nine righteous people
who do not need to repent. . . .'
11,12 Again he said: 'There was once a man who had two sons; and the younger
said to his father, "Father, give me my share of the property." So he divided
13 his estate between them. A few days later the younger son turned the whole
of his share into cash and left home for a distant country, where he squandered
14 it in reckless living. He had spent it all, when a severe famine fell upon that
15 country and he began to feel the pinch. So he went and attached himself to
one of the local landowners, who sent him on to his farm to mind the pigs.
16 He would have been glad to fill his belly with the pods that the pigs were
17 eating; and no one gave him anything. Then he came to his senses and said,
"How many of my father's paid servants have more food than they can eat,
18 and here am I, starving to death! I will set off and go to my father, and say
19 to him, 'Father, I have sinned, against God and against you; I am no longer
20 fit to be called your son; treat me as one of your paid servants.'" So he set
out for his father's house. But while he was still a long way off his father saw
him, and his heart went out to him. He ran to meet him, flung his arms
21 round him, and kissed him. The son said, "Father, I have sinned, against God
22 and against you; I am no longer fit to be called your son." But the father said
to his servants, "Quick! fetch a robe, my best one, and put it on him; put a
23 ring on his finger and shoes on his feet. Bring the fatted calf and kill it, and
24 let us have a feast to celebrate the day. For this son of mine was dead and has
come back to life; he was lost and is found." And the festivities began. . . .
[*Further teaching and parables follow.*]

18:9 And here is another parable that [Jesus] told. It was aimed at those who were
10 sure of their own goodness and looked down on everyone else. 'Two men
went up to the temple to pray, one a Pharisee and the other a tax-gatherer.
11 The Pharisee stood up and prayed thus: "I thank thee, O God, that I am not
like the rest of men, greedy, dishonest, adulterous; or, for that matter, like
12,13 this tax-gatherer. I fast twice a week; I pay tithes on all that I get." But the
other kept his distance and would not even raise his eyes to heaven, but beat
14 upon his breast, saying, "O God, have mercy on me, sinner that I am." It was
this man, I tell you, and not the other, who went home acquitted of his sins.

For everyone who exalts himself will be humbled; and whoever humbles himself will be exalted.'

They even brought babies for him to touch; but when the disciples saw them they scolded them for it. But Jesus called for the children and said, 'Let the little ones come to me; do not try to stop them; for the kingdom of God belongs to such as these. I tell you that whoever does not accept the kingdom of God like a child will never enter it.' 15 16 17

A man of the ruling class put this question to him: 'Good Master, what must I do to win eternal life?' Jesus said to him, 'Why do you call me good? No one is good except God alone. You know the commandments: "Do not commit adultery; do not murder; do not steal; do not give false evidence; honour your father and mother."' The man answered, 'I have kept all these since I was a boy.' On hearing this Jesus said, 'There is still one thing lacking: sell everything you have and distribute to the poor, and you will have riches in heaven; and come, follow me.' At these words his heart sank; for he was a very rich man. When Jesus saw it he said, 'How hard it is for the wealthy to enter the kingdom of God! It is easier for a camel to go through the eye of a needle than for a rich man to enter the kingdom of God.' Those who heard asked, 'Then who can be saved?' He answered, 'What is impossible for men is possible for God.' 18 19 20 21 22 23 24 25 26 27

Peter said, 'Here are we who gave up our belongings to become your followers.' Jesus said, 'I tell you this: there is no one who has given up home, or wife, brothers, parents, or children, for the sake of the kingdom of God, who will not be repaid many times over in this age, and in the age to come have eternal life.' 28 29 30

(e) *The end of Jesus' life*

[Jesus] took the Twelve aside and said, 'We are now going up to Jerusalem; and all that was written by the prophets will come true for the Son of Man. He will be handed over to the foreign power. He will be mocked, maltreated, and spat upon. They will flog him and kill him. And on the third day he will rise again.' But they understood nothing of all this. [*Episodes on the journey via Jericho follow.*] 18:31 32 33 34

With that Jesus went forward and began the ascent to Jerusalem. As he approached Bethphage and Bethany at the hill called Olivet, he sent two of the disciples with these instructions: 'Go to the village opposite; as you enter it you will find tethered there a colt which no one has yet ridden. Untie it and bring it here. If anyone asks why you are untying it, say, "Our Master needs it."' The two went on their errand and found it as he had told them; and while they were untying the colt, its owners asked, 'Why are you untying that colt?' They answered, 'The Master needs it.' So they brought the colt to Jesus. 19:28,29 30 31 32,33 34,35

Then they threw their cloaks on the colt, for Jesus to mount, and they carpeted the road with them as he went on his way. And now, as he approached 36 37

the descent from the Mount of Olives, the whole company of his disciples in
their joy began to sing aloud the praises of God for all the things they had seen:

38   'Blessings on him who comes as king in the name of the Lord!
        Peace in heaven, glory in highest heaven!'

39   Some Pharisees who were in the crowd said to him, 'Master, reprimand
40 your disciples.' He answered, 'I tell you, if my disciples keep silence the stones
    will shout aloud.'

41,42   When he came in sight of the city, he wept over it and said, 'If only you
    had known, on this great day, the way that leads to peace! But no; it is
43 hidden from your sight. For a time will come upon you, when your enemies
    will set up siege-works against you; they will encircle you and hem you in at
44 every point; they will bring you to the ground, you and your children within
    your walls, and not leave you one stone standing on another, because you did
    not recognize God's moment when it came.'

45,46   Then he went into the temple and began driving out the traders, with these
    words: 'Scripture says, "My house shall be a house of prayer", but you have
    made it a robbers' cave.'

47   Day by day he taught in the temple. And the chief priests and lawyers
    were bent on making an end of him, with the support of the leading citizens,
48 but found they were helpless, because the people all hung upon his words.

20:1   One day, as he was teaching the people in the temple and telling them the
    good news, the priests and lawyers, and the elders with them, came upon
2 him and accosted him. 'Tell us', they said, 'by what authority you are acting
3 like this; who gave you this authority?' He answered them, 'I have a question
4 to ask you too: tell me, was the baptism of John from God or from men?'
5 This set them arguing among themselves: 'If we say, "from God", he will
6 say, "Why did you not believe him?" And if we say, "from men", the people
7 will all stone us, for they are convinced that John was a prophet.' So they
8 replied that they could not tell. And Jesus said to them, 'Neither will I tell
    you by what authority I act.'

9   He went on to tell the people this parable: 'A man planted a vineyard, let
10 it out to vine-growers, and went abroad for a long time. When the season
    came, he sent a servant to the tenants to collect from them his share of the
11 produce; but the tenants thrashed him and sent him away empty-handed. He
    tried again and sent a second servant; but he also was thrashed, outrageously
12 treated, and sent away empty-handed. He tried once more with a third; this
13 one too they wounded and flung out. Then the owner of the vineyard said,
    'What am I to do? I will send my own dear son; perhaps they will respect
14 him." But when the tenants saw him they talked it over together. "This is
    the heir," they said; "let us kill him so that the property may come to us."
15 So they flung him out of the vineyard and killed him. What then will the
16 owner of the vineyard do to them? He will come and put these tenants to
    death and let the vineyard to others.'

When they heard this, they said, 'God forbid!' But he looked straight at 17
them and said, 'Then what does this text of Scripture mean: "The stone
which the builders rejected has become the main corner-stone"? Any man 18
who falls on that stone will be dashed to pieces; and if it falls on a man he
will be crushed by it.'

The lawyers and chief priests wanted to lay hands on him there and then, 19
for they saw that this parable was aimed at them; but they were afraid of the
people. So they watched their opportunity and sent secret agents in the guise 20
of honest men, to seize upon some word of his as a pretext for handing him
over to the authority and jurisdiction of the Governor. They put a question 21
to him: 'Master,' they said, 'we know that what you speak and teach is sound;
you pay deference to no one, but teach in all honesty the way of life that
God requires. Are we or are we not permitted to pay taxes to the Roman 22
Emperor?' He saw through their trick and said, 'Show me a silver piece. Whose 23,24
head does it bear, and whose inscription?' 'Caesar's', they replied. 'Very well 25
then,' he said, 'pay Caesar what is due Caesar, and pay God what is due to
God.' Thus their attempt to catch him out in public failed, and, astonished 26
by his reply, they fell silent.

Then some Sadducees came forward. They are the people who deny that 27
there is a resurrection. Their question was this: 'Master, Moses laid it down 28
for us that if there are brothers, and one dies leaving a wife but no child, then
the next should marry the widow and carry on his brother's family. Now, 29
there were seven brothers: the first took a wife and died childless; then the 30
second married her, then the third. In this way the seven of them died leaving 31
no children. Afterwards, the woman also died. At the resurrection whose wife 32,33
is she to be, since all seven had married her?' Jesus said to them, 'The men 34
and women of this world marry; but those who have been judged worthy of 35
a place in the other world and of the resurrection from the dead, do not
marry, for they are not subject to death any longer. They are like angels; 36
they are sons of God, because they share in the resurrection. That the dead 37
are raised to life again is shown by Moses himself in the story of the burning
bush, when he calls the Lord, "the God of Abraham, Isaac, and Jacob". God 38
is not God of the dead but of the living; for him all are alive.'

At this some of the lawyers said, 'Well spoken, Master.' For there was no 39,40
further question that they ventured to put to him.

[*In the Temple Jesus prophesied war and the destruction of the city.*]

Now the festival of Unleavened Bread, known as Passover, was approaching, 22:1
and the chief priests and the doctors of the law were trying to devise some 2
means of doing away with [Jesus]; for they were afraid of the people.

Then Satan entered into Judas Iscariot, who was one of the Twelve; and 3,4
Judas went to the chief priests and officers of the temple police to discuss
ways and means of putting Jesus into their power. They were greatly pleased 5
and undertook to pay him a sum of money. He agreed, and began to look 6
for an opportunity to betray him to them without collecting a crowd.

677

7 Then came the day of Unleavened Bread, on which the Passover victim
8 had to be slaughtered, and Jesus sent Peter and John with these instructions:
9 'Go and prepare for our Passover supper.' 'Where would you like us to make
10 the preparations?' they asked. He replied, 'As soon as you set foot in the city
a man will meet you carrying a jar of water. Follow him into the house that
11 he enters and give this message to the householder: "The Master says, 'Where
12 is the room in which I may eat the Passover with my disciples?'" He will
show you a large room upstairs all set out: make the preparations there.'
13 They went and found everything as he had said. So they prepared for Passover.
14 When the time came he took his place at table, and the apostles with him;
15 and he said to them, 'How I have longed to eat this Passover with you before
16 my death! For I tell you, never again shall I eat it until the time when it finds
its fulfilment in the kingdom of God.'
17 Then he took a cup, and after giving thanks he said, 'Take this and share
18 it among yourselves; for I tell you, from this moment I shall drink from the
fruit of the vine no more until the time when the kingdom of God comes.'
19 And he took bread, gave thanks, and broke it; and he gave it to them, with
the words: 'This is my body.'
21 'But mark this—my betrayer is here, his hand with mine on the table.
22 For the Son of Man is going his appointed way; but alas for that man by
23 whom he is betrayed!' At this they began to ask among themselves which of
them it could possibly be who was to do this thing. . . .

39 Then [Jesus] went out and made his way as usual to the Mount of Olives,
40 accompanied by the disciples. When he reached the place he said to them,
41 'Pray that you may be spared the hour of testing.' He himself withdrew from
42 them about a stone's throw, knelt down, and began to pray: 'Father, if it be
thy will, take this cup away from me. Yet not my will but thine be done.'
43 And now there appeared to him an angel from heaven bringing him strength,
44 and in anguish of spirit he prayed the more urgently; and his sweat was like
clots of blood falling to the ground.
45 When he rose from prayer and came to the disciples he found them asleep,
46 worn out by grief. 'Why are you sleeping?' he said. 'Rise and pray that you
may be spared the test.'
47 While he was still speaking a crowd appeared with the man called Judas,
48 one of the Twelve, at their head. He came up to Jesus to kiss him; but Jesus
said, 'Judas, would you betray the Son of Man with a kiss?' . . .

52 Turning to the chief priests, the officers of the temple police, and the elders,
who had come to seize him, [Jesus] said, 'Do you take me for a bandit, that
53 you have come out with swords and cudgels to arrest me? Day after day,
when I was in the temple with you, you kept your hands off me. But this is
54 your moment—the hour when darkness reigns.' [*Then they arrested him and
led him away.*]

When day broke, the elders of the nation, chief priests, and doctors of the 66
law assembled, and [Jesus] was brought before their Council. 'Tell us,' they 67
said, 'are you the Messiah?' 'If I tell you,' he replied, 'you will not believe me;
and if I ask questions, you will not answer. But from now on, the Son of Man 68,69
will be seated at the right hand of Almighty God.' 'You are the Son of God, 70
then?' they all said, and he replied, 'It is you who say I am.' They said, 'Need 71
we call further witnesses? We have heard it ourselves from his own lips.'

With that the whole assembly rose, and they brought him before Pilate. 23:1
They opened the case against him by saying, 'We found this man subverting 2
our nation, opposing the payment of taxes to Caesar, and claiming to be
Messiah, a king.' Pilate asked him, 'Are you the king of the Jews?' He replied, 3
'The words are yours.' Pilate then said to the chief priests and the crowd, 'I 4
find no case for this man to answer.' But they insisted: 'His teaching is causing 5
disaffection among the people all through Judaea. It started from Galilee and
has spread as far as this city.'

When Pilate heard this, he asked if the man was a Galilean, and on learning 6,7
that he belonged to Herod's jurisdiction he remitted the case to him, for
Herod was also in Jerusalem at that time. When Herod saw Jesus he was 8
greatly pleased; having heard about him, he had long been wanting to see
him, and had been hoping to see some miracle performed by him. He ques- 9
tioned him at some length without getting any reply; but the chief priests 10
and lawyers appeared and pressed the case against him vigorously. Then 11
Herod and his troops treated him with contempt and ridicule, and sent him
back to Pilate dressed in a gorgeous robe. That same day Herod and Pilate 12
became friends: till then there had been a standing feud between them.

Pilate now called together the chief priests, councillors, and people, 13
and said to them, 'You brought this man before me on a charge of subversion. 14
But, as you see, I have myself examined him in your presence and found
nothing in him to support your charges. No more did Herod, for he has 15
referred him back to us. Clearly he has done nothing to deserve death. I there- 16
fore propose to let him off with a flogging.' But there was a general outcry, 18
'Away with him! Give us Barabbas.' (This man had been put in prison for a 19
rising that had taken place in the city, and for murder.) Pilate addressed them 20
again, in his desire to release Jesus, but they shouted back, 'Crucify him, 21
crucify him!' For the third time he spoke to them: 'Why, what wrong has he 22
done? I have not found him guilty of any capital offence. I will therefore let
him off with a flogging.' But they insisted on their demand, shouting that 23
Jesus should be crucified. Their shouts prevailed and Pilate decided that they 24
should have their way. He released the man they asked for, the man who had 25
been put in prison for insurrection and murder, and gave Jesus up to their
will. . . .

There were two others with [Jesus], criminals who were being led away to 32
execution; and when they reached the place called The Skull, they crucified 33

679

34 him there, and the criminals with him, one on his right and the other on his left. Jesus said, 'Father, forgive them; they do not know what they are doing.'

35 They divided his clothes among them by casting lots. The people stood looking on, and their rulers jeered at him: 'He saved others: now let him save

36 himself, if this is God's Anointed, his Chosen.' The soldiers joined in the

37 mockery and came forward offering him their sour wine. 'If you are the king

38 of the Jews,' they said, 'save yourself.' There was an inscription above his head which ran: 'This is the king of the Jews.' . . .

44 By now it was about midday and there came a darkness over the whole land,

45 which lasted until three in the afternoon; the sun was in eclipse. And the

46 curtain of the temple was torn in two. Then Jesus gave a loud cry and said, 'Father, into thy hands I commit my spirit'; and with these words he died.

47 The centurion saw it all, and gave praise to God. 'Beyond all doubt', he said, 'this man was innocent.'

48 The crowd who had assembled for the spectacle, when they saw what had happened, went home beating their breasts.

49 His friends had all been standing at a distance; the women who had accompanied him from Galilee stood with them and watched it all.

50 Now there was a man called Joseph, a member of the Council, a good,

51 upright man, who had dissented from their policy and the action they had taken. He came from the Jewish town of Arimathaea, and he was one who

52 looked forward to the kingdom of God. This man now approached Pilate

53 and asked for the body of Jesus. Taking it down from the cross, he wrapped it in a linen sheet, and laid it in a tomb cut out of the rock, in which no one had

54 been laid before. It was Friday, and the Sabbath was about to begin.

55 The women who had accompanied him from Galilee followed; they took

56 note of the tomb and observed how his body was laid. Then they went home and prepared spices and perfumes; and on the Sabbath they rested in obedi-

24:1 ence to the commandment. But on the Sunday morning very early they came

2 to the tomb bringing the spices they had prepared. Finding that the stone had

3 been rolled away from the tomb, they went inside; but the body was not to

4 be found. While they stood utterly at a loss, all of a sudden two men in

5 dazzling garments were at their side. They were terrified, and stood with eyes cast down, but the men said, 'Why search among the dead for one who lives?

6 Remember what he told you while he was still in Galilee, about the Son of

7 Man: how he must be given up into the power of sinful men and be crucified,

8,9 and must rise again on the third day.' Then they recalled his words and, returning from the tomb, they reported all this to the Eleven and all the others. [*That evening Jesus appeared to two followers, who immediately reported their experience to the disciples.*]

36 As they were talking about all this, there [Jesus] was, standing among

37,38 them. Startled and terrified, they thought they were seeing a ghost. But he said, 'Why are you so perturbed? Why do questionings arise in your minds?

Look at my hands and feet. It is I myself. Touch me and see; no ghost has 39
flesh and bones as you can see that I have.' They were still unconvinced, still 41
wondering, for it seemed too good to be true. So he asked them, 'Have you
anything here to eat?' They offered him a piece of fish they had cooked, 42
which he took and ate before their eyes. 43

And he said to them, 'This is what I meant by saying, while I was still with 44
you, that everything written about me in the Law of Moses and in the prophets
and psalms was bound to be fulfilled.' Then he opened their minds to under- 45
stand the scriptures. 'This', he said, 'is what is written: that the Messiah is to 46
suffer death and to rise from the dead on the third day, and that in his name 47
repentance bringing the forgiveness of sins is to be proclaimed to all nations.
Begin from Jerusalem: it is you who are the witnesses to all this. And mark 48,49
this: I am sending upon you my Father's promised gift; so stay here in this
city until you are armed with the power from above.'

[*A brief reference to the Ascension, given fully in Acts 1, ends the work.*]

tr. New English Bible
(Oxford–Cambridge 1961, 1970)

O45 An Excerpt from The Gospel according to St. John

From Caiaphas Jesus was led into the Governor's headquarters. It was now 18:28
early morning, and the Jews themselves stayed outside the headquarters to
avoid defilement, so that they could eat the Passover meal. So Pilate went out 29
to them and asked, 'What charge do you bring against this man?' 'If he were 30
not a criminal,' they replied, 'we should not have brought him before you.'
Pilate said, 'Take him away and try him by your own law.' The Jews answered, 31
'We are not allowed to put any man to death.' Thus they ensured the fulfil- 32
ment of the words by which Jesus had indicated the manner of his death.

Pilate then went back into his headquarters and summoned Jesus. 'Are 33
you the king of the Jews?' he asked. Jesus said, 'Is that your own idea, or 34
have others suggested it to you?' 'What! am I a Jew?' said Pilate. 'Your own 35
nation and their chief priests have brought you before me. What have you
done?' Jesus replied, 'My kingdom does not belong to this world. If it did, 36
my followers would be fighting to save me from arrest by the Jews. My
kingly authority comes from elsewhere.' 'You are a king, then?' said Pilate. 37
Jesus answered, '"King" is your word. My task is to bear witness to the
truth. For this was I born; for this I came into the world, and all who are not
deaf to truth listen to my voice.' Pilate said, 'What is truth?', and with those 38
words went out again to the Jews. 'For my part,' he said, 'I find no case
against him. But you have a custom that I release one prisoner for you at 39
Passover. Would you like me to release the king of the Jews?' Again the 40

clamour rose: 'Not him; we want Barabbas!' (Barabbas was a bandit.)

19:1,2   Pilate now took Jesus and had him flogged; and the soldiers plaited a crown of thorns and placed it on his head, and robed him in a purple cloak.

3   Then time after time they came up to him, crying, 'Hail, King of the Jews!', and struck him on the face.

4   Once more Pilate came out and said to the Jews, 'Here he is; I am bringing

5   him out to let you know that I find no case against him'; and Jesus came out,

6   wearing the crown of thorns and the purple cloak. 'Behold the Man!' said Pilate. The chief priests and their henchmen saw him and shouted, 'Crucify! crucify!' 'Take him and crucify him yourselves,' said Pilate; 'for my part I

7   find no case against him.' The Jews answered, 'We have a law; and by that law he ought to die, because he has claimed to be Son of God.'

8,9   When Pilate heard that, he was more afraid than ever, and going back into his headquarters he asked Jesus, 'Where have you come from?' But Jesus gave

10   him no answer. 'Do you refuse to speak to me?' said Pilate. 'Surely you know that I have authority to release you, and I have authority to crucify you?'

11   'You would have no authority at all over me', Jesus replied, 'if it had not been granted you from above; and therefore the deeper guilt lies with the man who handed me over to you.'

12   From that moment Pilate tried hard to release him; but the Jews kept shouting, 'If you let this man go, you are no friend to Caesar; any man who

13   claims to be a king is defying Caesar.' When Pilate heard what they were saying, he brought Jesus out and took his seat on the tribunal at the place

14   known as 'The Pavement' ('Gabbatha' in the language of the Jews). It was the eve of Passover, about noon. Pilate said to the Jews, 'Here is your king.'

15   They shouted, 'Away with him! Away with him! Crucify him!' 'Crucify your

16   king?' said Pilate. 'We have no king but Caesar', the Jews replied. Then at last, to satisfy them, he handed Jesus over to be crucified.

tr. New English Bible
(Oxford-Cambridge 1961, 1970)

O46 Excerpts from the Acts of the Apostles

(a)   *The foundation of the Church*

[*Jesus' appearances to his disciples continued for forty days after his resurrection.*]

1:4   While he was in their company he told them not to leave Jerusalem. 'You must wait', he said, 'for the promise made by my Father, about which you

5   have heard me speak: John, as you know, baptized with water, but you will be baptized with the Holy Spirit, and within the next few days.'

6   So, when they were all together, they asked him, 'Lord, is this the time

when you are to establish once again the sovereignty of Israel?' He answered, 7
'It is not for you to know about dates or times, which the Father has set
within his own control. But you will receive power when the Holy Spirit 8
comes upon you; and you will bear witness for me in Jerusalem, and all over
Judaea and Samaria, and away to the ends of the earth.'

When he had said this, as they watched, he was lifted up, and a cloud 9
removed him from their sight. As he was going, and as they were gazing 10
intently into the sky, all at once there stood beside them two men in white
who said, 'Men of Galilee, why stand there looking up into the sky? This 11
Jesus, who has been taken away from you up to heaven, will come in the
same way as you have seen him go.'

Then they returned to Jerusalem . . . 12

While the day of Pentecost was running its course they were all together in 2:1
one place, when suddenly there came from the sky a noise like that of a strong 2
driving wind, which filled the whole house where they were sitting. And 3
there appeared to them tongues like flames of fire, dispersed among them and
resting on each one. And they were all filled with the Holy Spirit and began 4
to talk in other tongues, as the Spirit gave them power of utterance.

Now there were living in Jerusalem devout Jews drawn from every nation 5
under heaven; and at this sound the crowd gathered, all bewildered because 6
each one heard the apostles talking in his own language. They were amazed 7
and in their astonishment exclaimed, 'Why, they are all Galileans, are they
not, these men who are speaking? How is it then that we hear them, each of 8
us in his own native language? Parthians, Medes, Elamites; inhabitants of 9
Mesopotamia, of Judaea and Cappadocia, of Pontus and Asia, of Phrygia and 10
Pamphylia, of Egypt and the districts of Libya around Cyrene; visitors from
Rome, both Jews and proselytes, Cretans and Arabs, we hear them telling in 11
our own tongues the great things God has done.' And they were all amazed 12
and perplexed, saying to one another, 'What can this mean?' Others said 13
contemptuously, 'They have been drinking!'

But Peter stood up with the Eleven, raised his voice, and addressed them: 14
'Fellow Jews, and all you who live in Jerusalem, mark this and give me a
hearing. These men are not drunk, as you imagine; for it is only nine in the 15
morning. [*This phenomenon is a fulfilment of Old Testament prophecies.*]

'Men of Israel, listen to me: I speak of Jesus of Nazareth, a man singled 22
out by God and made known to you through miracles, portents, and signs,
which God worked among you through him, as you well know. When he had 23
been given up to you, by the deliberate will and plan of God, you used
heathen men to crucify and kill him. But God raised him to life again, setting 24
him free from the pangs of death, because it could not be that death should
keep him in its grip.

'For David says of him: 25

"I forsaw that the presence of the Lord would be with me always,
For he is at my right hand so that I may not be shaken;
26 Therefore my heart was glad and my tongue spoke my joy;

> Moreover, my flesh shall dwell in hope,
> 27 For thou wilt not abandon my soul to Hades,
> Nor let thy loyal servant suffer corruption.
> 28 Thou hast shown me the ways of life,
> Thou wilt fill me with gladness by thy presence."

29 'Let me tell you plainly, my friends, that the patriarch David died and was
30 buried, and his tomb is here to this very day. It is clear therefore that he
spoke as a prophet who knew that God had sworn to him that one of his own
31 direct descendants should sit on his throne; and when he said he was not
abandoned to Hades, and his flesh never suffered corruption, he spoke with
32 foreknowledge of the resurrection of the Messiah. The Jesus we speak of has
33 been raised by God, as we can all bear witness. Exalted thus with God's right
hand, he received the Holy Spirit from the Father, as was promised, and all that
36 you now see and hear flows from him. . . . Let all Israel then accept as certain
that God has made this Jesus, whom you crucified, both Lord and Messiah.'
37 When they heard this they were cut to the heart, and said to Peter and the
38 apostles, 'Friends, what are we to do?' 'Repent,' said Peter, 'repent and be
baptized, every one of you, in the name of Jesus the Messiah for the forgive-
41 ness of your sins; and you will receive the gift of the Holy Spirit.'. . . Then
those who accepted his word were baptized, and some three thousand were
added to their number that day.
42 They met constantly to hear the apostles teach, and to share the common
43 life, to break bread, and to pray. A sense of awe was everywhere, and many
44 marvels and signs were brought about through the apostles. All whose faith
45 had drawn them together held everything in common: they would sell their
property and possessions and make a general distribution as the need of each
46 required. With one mind they kept up their daily attendance at the temple,
and, breaking bread in private houses, shared their meals with unaffected joy,
47 as they praised God and enjoyed the favour of the whole people. And day by
day the Lord added to their number those whom he was saving.

(b) The Church in Jerusalem

3:1 One day at three in the afternoon, the hour of prayer, Peter and John were
2 on their way up to the temple. Now a man who had been a cripple from birth
used to be carried there and laid every day by the gate of the temple called
3 'Beautiful Gate', to beg from people as they went in. When he saw Peter and
4 John on their way into the temple he asked for charity. But Peter fixed his
5 eyes on him, as John did also, and said, 'Look at us.' Expecting a gift from
6 them, the man was all attention. And Peter said, 'I have no silver or gold; but
7 what I have I give you: in the name of Jesus Christ of Nazareth, walk.' Then

he grasped him by the right hand and pulled him up; and at once his feet and ankles grew strong; he sprang up, stood on his feet, and started to walk. He 8 entered the temple with them, leaping and praising God as he went. . . .

And as he was clutching Peter and John all the people came running in 11 astonishment towards them in Solomon's Cloister, as it is called. Peter saw 12 them coming and met them with these words: 'Men of Israel, why be surprised at this? Why stare at us as if we had made this man walk by some power or godliness of our own? The God of Abraham, Isaac, and Jacob, the 13 God of our fathers, has given the highest honour to his servant Jesus, whom you committed for trial and repudiated in Pilate's court. . . . But God raised 15 him from the dead; of that we are witnesses. And the name of Jesus, by awak- 16 ening faith, has strengthened this man, whom you see and know, and this faith has made him completely well, as you can all see for yourselves.

'And now, my friends, I know quite well that you acted in ignorance, and 17 so did your rulers; but this is how God fulfilled what he had foretold in the 18 utterances of all the prophets: that his Messiah should suffer. Repent then 19 and turn to God, so that your sins may be wiped out. Then the Lord may grant you a time of recovery and send you the Messiah he has already ap- 20 pointed, that is, Jesus. He must be received into heaven until the time of 21 universal restoration comes, of which God spoke by his holy prophets. Moses 22 said, "The Lord God will raise up a prophet for you from among yourselves as he raised me; you shall listen to everything he says to you, and anyone who 23 refuses to listen to that prophet must be extirpated from Israel." And so said 24 all the prophets, from Samuel onwards; with one voice they all predicted this present time. . . .

They were still addressing the people when the chief priests came upon 4:1 them, together with the Controller of the Temple and the Sadducees, exas- 2 perated at their teaching the people and proclaiming the resurrection from the dead—the resurrection of Jesus. They were arrested and put in prison for 3 the night, as it was already evening. But many of those who had heard the 4 message became believers. The number of men now reached about five thousand.

Next day the Jewish rulers, elders, and doctors of the law met in Jerusa- 5 lem. . . . They brought the apostles before the court and began the exam- 7 ination. 'By what power', they asked, 'or by what name have such men as you done this?' Then Peter, filled with the Holy Spirit, answered, 'Rulers of the 8 people and elders, if the question put to us today is about help given to a sick 9 man, and we are asked by what means he was cured, here is the answer, for all 10 of you and for all the people of Israel: it was by the name of Jesus Christ of Nazareth, whom you crucified, whom God raised from the dead. . . . This 11 Jesus is the stone rejected by the builders which has become the keystone— and you are the builders. There is no salvation in anyone else at all, for there 12 is no other name under heaven granted to men, by which we may receive salvation.'

13   Now as they observed the boldness of Peter and John, and noted that they were untrained laymen, they began to wonder, then recognized them as
14 former companions of Jesus. And when they saw the man who had been
15 cured standing with them, they had nothing to say in reply. So they ordered them to leave the court, and then discussed the matter among themselves. . . .
18 They then called them in and ordered them to refrain from all public speaking and teaching in the name of Jesus.
19   But Peter and John said to them in reply: 'Is it right in God's eyes for us
20 to obey you rather than God? Judge for yourselves. We cannot possibly give up speaking of things we have seen and heard.'
21   The court repeated the caution and discharged them. They could not see how they were to punish them, because the people were all giving glory to God for what had happened.

5:17 [*As a result of the continued growth of the new movement—*] the High Priest and his colleagues, the Sadducean party as it then was, were goaded
18 into action by jealousy. They proceeded to arrest the apostles, and put them
19 in official custody. But an angel of the Lord opened the prison doors during
20 the night, brought them out, and said, 'Go, take your place in the temple and speak to the people, and tell them about this new life and all it means.'
21 Accordingly they entered the temple at daybreak and went on with their
27 teaching. [*They were then arrested again. The police*] brought them and stood
28 before the Council; and the High Priest began his examination. 'We expressly ordered you', he said, 'to desist from teaching in that name; and what has happened? You have filled Jerusalem with your teaching, and you are trying
29 to make us responsible for that man's death.' Peter replied for himself and
30 the apostles: 'We must obey God rather than men. The God of our fathers raised up Jesus whom you had done to death by hanging him on a gibbet.
31 He it is whom God has exalted with his own right hand as leader and saviour,
32 to grant Israel repentance and forgiveness of sins. And we are witnesses to all this, and so is the Holy Spirit given by God to those who are obedient to him.'
33   This touched them on the raw, and they wanted to put them to death.
34 But a member of the Council rose to his feet, a Pharisee called Gamaliel, a teacher of the law held in high regard by all the people. He moved that the
35 men be put outside for a while. Then he said, 'Men of Israel, be cautious in deciding what to do with these men. [*The pseudo-messianic movements of
38 Theudas and Judas of Galilee failed.*] And so now: keep clear of these men, I tell you; leave them alone. For if this idea of theirs or its execution is of
39 human origin, it will collapse; but if it is from God, you will never be able to put them down, and you risk finding yourselves at war with God.'
40   They took his advice. They sent for the apostles and had them flogged; then they ordered them to give up speaking in the name of Jesus, and dis-
41 charged them. So the apostles went out from the Council rejoicing that they

had been found worthy to suffer indignity for the sake of the Name. And 42
every day they went steadily on with their teaching in the temple and in
private houses, telling the good news of Jesus the Messiah.

[*A paragraph on the organization of the community follows: some lay
officials were appointed, including Stephen.*]

The word of God now spread more and more widely; the number of 6:7
disciples in Jerusalem went on increasing rapidly, and very many of the
priests adhered to the Faith.

Stephen, who was full of grace and power, began to work great miracles 8
and signs among the people. But some members of the synagogue called the 9
Synagogue of Freedmen, comprising Cyrenians and Alexandrians and people
from Cilicia and Asia, came forward and argued with Stephen, but could not 10
hold their own against the inspired wisdom with which he spoke. They then 11
put up men who alleged that they had heard him make blasphemous statements
against Moses and against God. They stirred up the people and the elders and 12
doctors of the law, set upon him and seized him, and brought him before the
Council. They produced false witnesses who said, 'This man is for ever saying 13
things against this holy place and against the Law. For we have heard him say 14
that Jesus of Nazareth will destroy this place and alter the customs handed
down to us by Moses.' And all who were sitting in the Council fixed their 15
eyes on him, and his face appeared to them like the face of an angel.

Then the High Priest asked, 'Is this so?' And he said, 'My brothers, fathers 7:1,2
of this nation, listen to me. [*Stephen then gave a survey of Jewish history
from Abraham to Solomon, arguing that God's self-revelation to man had not
been confined to the land of Israel and that the Jews had often misunderstood it. He then spoke about Jesus—*]

'How stubborn you are, heathen still at heart and deaf to the truth! You 51
always fight against the Holy Spirit. Like fathers, like sons. Was there ever a 52
prophet whom your fathers did not persecute? They killed those who foretold the coming of the Righteous One; and now you have betrayed him and
murdered him, you who received the Law as God's angels gave it to you, and 53
yet you have not kept it.' [*This infuriated the Sanhedrin, and Stephen was
executed by stoning.*]

(c) *The expansion of the Church*

This was the beginning of a time of violent persecution for the church in 8:1
Jerusalem; and all except the apostles were scattered over the country districts of Judaea and Samaria. . . . Saul, meanwhile, was harrying the church; 3
he entered house after house, seizing men and women, and sending them to
prison.

As for those who had been scattered, they went through the country 4
preaching the Word. Philip came down to a city in Samaria and began pro- 5
claiming the Messiah to them. The crowds, to a man, listened eagerly to what 6

Philip said, when they heard him and saw the miracles [of healing] that he performed. [*Many were converted by his preaching and were baptized.*]

14 The apostles in Jerusalem now heard that Samaria had accepted the word 15 of God. They sent off Peter and John, who went down there and prayed for 16 converts, asking that they might receive the Holy Spirit. For until then the Spirit had not come upon any of them. They had been baptized into the 17 name of the Lord Jesus, that and nothing more. So Peter and John laid their hands on them and they received the Holy spirit. . . .

26 Then the angel of the Lord said to Philip, 'Start out and go south to the road 27 that leads down from Jerusalem to Gaza.' (This is the desert road.) So he set out and was on his way when he caught sight of an Ethiopian. This man was a eunuch, a high official of the Kandake, or Queen, of Ethiopia, in charge of 28 all her treasure. He had been to Jerusalem on a pilgrimage and was now on his 29 way home, sitting in his carriage and reading aloud the prophet Isaiah. The 30 Spirit said to Philip, 'Go and join the carriage.' When Philip ran up he heard him reading the prophet Isaiah and said, 'Do you understand what you are 31 reading?' He said, 'How can I understand unless someone will give me the clue?' So he asked Philip to get in and sit beside him. . . .

34 'Now', said the eunuch to Philip, 'tell me, please, who it is that the prophet 35 is speaking about here: himself or someone else?' Then Philip began. Starting 36 from this passage, he told him the good news of Jesus. As they were going along the road, they came to some water. 'Look,' said the eunuch, 'here is 38 water: what is there to prevent my being baptized?', and he ordered the carriage to stop. Then they both went down into the water, Philip and the eunuch; and he baptized him. . . .

9:1 Meanwhile Saul was still breathing murderous threats against the disciples of 2 the Lord. He went to the High Priest and applied for letters to the synagogues at Damascus authorizing him to arrest anyone he found, men or women, who 3 followed the new way, and bring them to Jerusalem. While he was still on the road and nearing Damascus, suddenly a light flashed from the sky all around 4 him. He fell to the ground and heard a voice saying, 'Saul, Saul, why do you 5 persecute me?' 'Tell me, Lord,' he said, 'who you are.' The voice answered, 6 'I am Jesus, whom you are persecuting. But get up and go into the city, and 7 you will be told what you have to do.' Meanwhile the men who were travelling with him stood speechless; they heard the voice but could see no one. 8 Saul got up from the ground, but when he opened his eyes he could not see; 9 so they led him by the hand and brought him into Damascus. He was blind for three days, and took no food or drink.

10 There was a disciple in Damascus named Ananias. He had a vision in which he heard the voice of the Lord: 'Ananias!' 'Here I am, Lord', he answered. 11 The Lord said to him, 'Go at once to Straight Street, to the house of Judas, 12 and ask for a man from Tarsus named Saul. You will find him at prayer; he has a vision of a man named Ananias coming in and laying his hands on him

to restore his sight.' [*With some reluctance, Ananias carried out his instruc-*
tions.] And immediately it seemed that scales fell from [Saul's] eyes, and he 18
regained his sight. Thereupon he was baptized, and afterwards he took food 19
and his strength returned.

He stayed some time with the disciples in Damascus. Soon he was pro- 20
claiming Jesus publicly in the synagogues: 'This', he said, 'is the Son of God.'
All who heard were astounded. 'Is not this the man', they said, 'who was in 21
Jerusalem trying to destroy those who invoke this name? Did he not come
here for the sole purpose of arresting them and taking them to the chief
priests?' But Saul grew more and more forceful, and silenced the Jews of 22
Damascus with his cogent proofs that Jesus was the Messiah. [*He then had
to leave because of a plot against his life.*]

When he reached Jerusalem he tried to join the body of disciples there; 26
but they were all afraid of him, because they did not believe that he was
really a convert. Barnabas, however, took him by the hand and introduced 27
him to the apostles. . . . Saul now stayed with them, moving about freely in 28
Jerusalem. He spoke out boldly and openly in the name of the Lord, talking 29
and debating with the Greek-speaking Jews. But they planned to murder
him, and when the brethren learned of this they escorted him to Caesarea 30
and saw him off to Tarsus.

Meanwhile the church, throughout Judaea, Galilee, and Samaria, was left in 31
peace to build up its strength. In the fear of the Lord, upheld by the Holy
Spirit, it held on its way and grew in numbers. [*Two healing miracles by
Peter are then related.*]

At Caesarea there was a man named Cornelius, a centurion in the Italian 10:1
Cohort, as it was called. He was a religious man, and he and his whole family 2
joined in the worship of God. He gave generously to help the Jewish people,
and was regular in his prayers to God. One day about three in the afternoon 3
he had a vision in which he clearly saw an angel of God, who came into his
room and said, 'Cornelius!' He stared at him in terror. 'What is it, my lord?' 4
he asked. The angel said, 'Your prayers and acts of charity have gone up to
heaven to speak for you before God. And now send to Joppa for a man 5
named Simon, also called Peter: he is lodging with another Simon, a tanner, 6
whose house is by the sea.' So . . . he summoned two of his servants and a 7
military orderly who was a religious man, told them the whole story, and 8
sent them to Joppa.

Next day, while they were still on their way and approaching the city, 9
about noon Peter went up on the roof to pray. He grew hungry and wanted 10
something to eat. While they were getting it ready, he fell into a trance. He 11
saw a rift in the sky, and a thing coming down that looked like a great sheet
of sail-cloth. It was slung by the four corners, and was being lowered to the
ground. In it he saw creatures of every kind, whatever walks or crawls or flies. 12
Then there was a voice which said to him, 'Up, Peter, kill and eat.' But Peter 13,14

15 said, 'No, Lord, no: I have never eaten anything profane or unclean.' The voice came again a second time: 'It is not for you to call profane what God
16 counts clean.' This happened three times; and then the thing was taken up again into the sky.
17 While Peter was still puzzling over the meaning of the vision he had seen, the messengers of Cornelius had been asking the way to Simon's house, and
18 now arrived at the entrance. They called out and asked if Simon Peter was
19 lodging there. But Peter was thinking over the vision, when the Spirit said to
20 him, 'Some men are here looking for you; make haste and go downstairs. You may go with them without any misgiving, for it was I who sent them.' . . .
24 The day after that, he arrived at Caesarea. Cornelius was expecting them and
25 had called together his relatives and close friends. When Peter arrived, Cornelius
26 came to meet him, and bowed to the ground in deep reverence. But Peter
27 raised him to his feet and said, 'Stand up; I am a man like anyone else.' Still
28 talking with him he went in and found a large gathering. He said to them, 'I need not tell you that a Jew is forbidden by his religion to visit or associate with a man of another race; yet God has shown me clearly that I must not call
29 any man profane or unclean. That is why I came here without demur when you sent for me. May I ask what was your reason for sending?' [*Cornelius then related his vision.*]
34,35 Peter began: 'I now see how true it is that God has no favourites, but that in every nation the man who is godfearing and does what is right is acceptable
36 to him. He sent his word to the Israelites and gave the good news of peace
37 through Jesus Christ, who is Lord of all. I need not tell you what happened lately all over the land of the Jews, starting from Galilee after the baptism
38 proclaimed by John. You know about Jesus of Nazareth, how God anointed him with the Holy Spirit and with power. He went about doing good and
39 healing all who were oppressed by the devil, for God was with him. And we can bear witness to all that he did in the Jewish country-side and in Jerusalem.
40 He was put to death by hanging on a gibbet; but God raised him to life on the
41 third day, and allowed him to appear, not to the whole people, but to witnesses whom God had chosen in advance—to us, who ate and drank with him after
42 he rose from the dead. He commanded us to proclaim him to the people, and affirm that he is the one who has been designated by God as judge of the
43 living and the dead. It is to him that all the prophets testify, declaring that everyone who trusts in him receives forgiveness of sins through his name.'
44 Peter was still speaking when the Holy Spirit came upon all who were
45 listening to the message. The believers who had come with Peter, men of Jewish birth, were astonished that the gift of the Holy Spirit should have
46,47 been poured out even on Gentiles. . . . Then Peter spoke: 'Is anyone prepared to withhold the water for baptism from these persons, who have received the
48 Holy Spirit just as we did ourselves?' Then he ordered them to be baptized in the name of Jesus Christ. . . .

News came to the apostles and the members of the church in Judaea that 11:1
Gentiles too had accepted the word of God; and when Peter came up to 2
Jerusalem those who were of Jewish birth raised the question with him. 'You 3
have been visiting men who are uncircumcised,' they said, 'and sitting at table
with them!' Peter began laying before them the facts as they had happened. 4
[*His account of the episode at Caesarea ends*–] 'God gave them no less a gift 17
than he gave us when we put our trust in the Lord Jesus Christ; then how
could I possibly stand in God's way?'

When they heard this their doubts were silenced. They gave praise to 18
God and said, 'This means that God has granted life-giving repentance to the
Gentiles also.'

Meanwhile those who had been scattered after the persecution that arose over 19
Stephen made their way to Phoenicia, Cyprus, and Antioch, bringing the
message to Jews only and to no others. But there were some natives of 20
Cyprus and Cyrene among them, and these, when they arrived at Antioch,
began to speak to pagans as well, telling them the good news of the Lord
Jesus. The power of the Lord was with them, and a great many became 21
believers, and turned to the Lord.

The news reached the ears of the church in Jerusalem; and they sent 22
Barnabas to Antioch. When he arrived and saw the divine grace at work, he 23
rejoiced, and encouraged them all to hold fast to the Lord with resolute
hearts. . . . And large numbers were won over to the Lord. 24

He then went off to Tarsus to look for Saul; and when he had found him, 25,26
he brought him to Antioch. For a whole year the two of them lived in fellowship with the congregation there, and gave instruction to large numbers. It
was in Antioch that the disciples first got the name of Christians. . . .

It was about this time that King Herod attacked certain members of the 12:1
church. He beheaded James, the brother of John, and then, when he saw that 2,3
the Jews approved, proceeded to arrest Peter also. This happened during the
festival of Unleavened Bread. Having secured him, he put him in prison under 4
a military guard, four squads of four men each, meaning to produce him in
public after Passover. So Peter was kept in prison under constant watch, while 5
the church kept praying fervently for him to God. [*Peter, however, was
miraculously released. The death of Herod Agrippa I is then related.*]

(d) *Paul's missionary work*

While [the Christians in Antioch] were keeping a fast and offering worship to 13:2
the Lord, the Holy Spirit said, 'Set Barnabas and Saul apart for me, to do the
work to which I have called them.' Then, after further fasting and prayer, they 3
laid their hands on them and let them go.

So these two, sent out on their mission by the Holy Spirit, [*went to Cyprus* 4
and on to southern Asia Minor. In Pisidian Antioch–] On the Sabbath they 14

15 went to synagogue and took their seats; and after the readings from the Law and the prophets, the officials of the synagogue sent this message to them: 'Friends, if you have anything to say to the people by way of exhortation,
16 let us hear it.' Paul rose, made a gesture with his hand, and began:
17 'Men of Israel and you who worship our God, listen to me! The God of this people of Israel chose our fathers. [*He then summarizes Jewish history*
23 *from the Exodus to David.*] This is the man from whose posterity God, as he
24 promised, has brought Israel a saviour, Jesus. John made ready for his coming by proclaiming baptism as a token of repentance to the whole people of Israel.
25 And when John was nearing the end of his course, he said, "I am not what you think I am. No, after me comes one whose shoes I am not fit to unfasten."
26 'My brothers, you who come of the stock of Abraham, and others among you who revere our God, we are the people to whom the message of this
27 salvation has been sent. The people of Jerusalem and their rulers did not recognize him, or understand the words of the prophets which are read
28 Sabbath by Sabbath; indeed they fulfilled them by condemning him. Though they failed to find grounds for the sentence of death, they asked Pilate to
29 have him executed. And when they had carried out all that the scriptures said
30 about him, they took him down from the gibbet and laid him in a tomb. But
31 God raised him from the dead; and there was a period of many days during which he appeared to those who had come up with him from Galillee to Jerusalem.
32 'They are now his witnesses before our nation; and we are here to give you
33 the good news that God, who made the promise to the fathers, has fulfilled it for the children by raising Jesus from the dead, as indeed it stands written. . .'
[*He then adduces evidence from the Old Testament.*]
42 As they were leaving the synagogue they were asked to come again and
43 speak on these subjects next Sabbath; and after the congregation had dispersed, many Jews and gentile worshippers went along with Paul and Barnabas, who spoke to them and urged them to hold fast to the grace of God.
44 On the following Sabbath almost the whole city gathered to hear the word
45 of God. When the Jews saw the crowds, they were filled with jealous resent-
46 ment, and contradicted what Paul and Barnabas said, with violent abuse. But Paul and Barnabas were outspoken in their reply. 'It was necessary', they said, 'that the word of God should be declared to you first. But since you reject it and thus condemn yourselves as unworthy of eternal life, we now turn to the
47 Gentiles. For these are our instructions from the Lord: "I have appointed you to be a light for the Gentiles, and a means of salvation to earth's farthest
48 bounds."' When the Gentiles heard this, they were overjoyed and thankfully acclaimed the word of the Lord, and those who were marked out for eternal
49 life became believers. So the word of the Lord spread far and wide through
50 the region. But the Jews stirred up feeling among the women of standing who were worshippers, and among the leading men of the city; a persecution was
51 started against Paul and Barnabas, and they were expelled from the district. So

692

they shook the dust off their feet in protest against them and went to Iconium.

[*At Iconium the same thing happened. The rest of their evangelistic campaign in Asia Minor is then summarized.*]

Now certain persons who had come down from Judaea began to teach the 15:1
brotherhood that those who were not circumcised in accordance with Mosaic
practice could not be saved. That brought them into fierce dissension and 2
controversy with Paul and Barnabas. And so it was arranged that these two
and some others from Antioch should go up to Jerusalem to see the apostles
and elders about this question. . . .

When they reached Jerusalem they were welcomed by the church and the 4
apostles and elders, and reported all that God had helped them to do. Then 5
some of the Pharisaic party who had become believers came forward and said,
'They must be circumcised and told to keep the Law of Moses.'

The apostles and elders held a meeting to look into this matter; and, after 6,7
a long debate, Peter rose and addressed them. 'My friends,' he said, 'in the
early days, as you yourselves know, God made his choice among you and
ordained that from my lips the Gentiles should hear and believe the message
of the Gospel. And God, who can read men's minds, showed his approval of 8
them by giving the Holy Spirit to them, as he did to us. He made no difference 9
between them and us; for he purified their hearts by faith. Then why do you 10
now provoke God by laying on the shoulders of these converts a yoke which
neither we nor our fathers were able to bear? No, we believe that it is by the 11
grace of the Lord Jesus that we are saved, and so are they.'

At that the whole company fell silent and listened to Barnabas and Paul as 12
they told of all the signs and miracles that God had worked among the Gentiles
through them. [*James then summed up and concluded–*]

'My judgement therefore is that we should impose no irksome restrictions 19
on those of the Gentiles who are turning to God, but instruct them by letter 20
to abstain from things polluted by contact with idols, from fornication, from
anything that has been strangled, and from blood. Moses, after all, has never 21
lacked spokesmen in every town for generations past; he is read in the synagogues Sabbath by Sabbath.'

Then the apostles and elders, with the agreement of the whole church, 22
resolved to choose representatives and send them to Antioch with Paul and
Barnabas. [*A letter conveying the above ruling to the churches outside
Palestine follows. Chapters 16–20 then describe Paul's further missionary
work in Greece and Asia Minor and his return to Jerusalem with his sights
set on going on to Rome.*]

(e)   *Paul's arrest and trial*

At the end of our stay we packed our baggage and took the road up to 21:15
Jerusalem. . . . where the brotherhood welcomed us gladly.   17

18   Next day Paul paid a visit to James; we were with him, and all the elders
19 attended. He greeted them, and then described in detail all that God had done
20 among the Gentiles through his ministry. When they heard this, they gave
praise to God. Then they said to Paul: 'You see, brother, how many thousands
of converts we have among the Jews, all of them staunch upholders of the
21 Law. Now they have been given certain information about you: it is said that
you teach all the Jews in the gentile world to turn their backs on Moses, telling
them to give up circumcising their children and following our way of life. [*At
their request Paul proved his orthodoxy by performing a Jewish ritual. But*
27 *shortly after that*—] the Jews from the province of Asia saw him in the temple.
28 They stirred up the whole crowd, and seized him, shouting, 'Men of Israel,
help, help! This is the fellow who spreads his doctrine all over the world,
attacking our people, our law, and this sanctuary. On top of all this he has
29 brought Greeks into the temple and profaned this holy place.' For they had
previously seen Trophimus the Ephesian with him in the city, and assumed
that Paul had brought him into the temple.

30   The whole city was in a turmoil, and people came running from all directions. They seized Paul and dragged him out of the temple; and at once the
31 doors were shut. While they were clamouring for his death, a report reached
32 the officer commanding the cohort, that all Jerusalem was in an uproar. He
immediately took a force of soldiers with their centurions and came down on
the rioters at the double. As soon as they saw the commandant and his troops,
33 they stopped beating Paul. The commandant stepped forward, arrested him,
and ordered him to be shackled with two chains; he then asked who the man
34 was and what he had been doing. Some in the crowd shouted one thing, some
another. As he could not get at the truth because of the hubbub, he ordered
35 him to be taken into barracks. When Paul reached the steps, he had to be
36 carried by the soldiers because of the violence of the mob. For the whole
crowd were at their heels yelling, 'Kill him!'

37   Just before Paul was taken into the barracks he said to the commandant,
'May I say something to you?' The commandant said, 'So you speak Greek,
38 do you? Then you are not the Egyptian who started a revolt some time ago
39 and led a force of four thousand terrorists out into the wilds?' Paul replied,
'I am a Jew, a Tarsian from Cilicia, a citizen of no mean city. I ask your per-
40 mission to speak to the people.' When permission had been given, Paul stood
on the steps and with a gesture called for the attention of the people. As soon
as quiet was restored, he addressed them in the Jewish language: [*Paul's
speech ignores his supposed offence, and gives an account of his persecution
of the Christians, his conversion, and his commission as an apostle to the
gentiles.*]

22:22   Up to this point they had given him a hearing; but now they began shout-
23 ing, 'Down with him! A scoundrel like that is better dead!' And as they were
24 yelling and waving their cloaks and flinging dust in the air, the commandant
ordered him to be brought into the barracks and gave instructions to examine

694

him by flogging, and find out what reason there was for such an outcry against
him. But when they tied him up for the lash, Paul said to the centurion who 25
was standing there, 'Can you legally flog a man who is a Roman citizen, and
moreover has not been found guilty?' When the centurion heard this, he went 26
and reported it to the commandant. 'What do you mean to do?' he said. 'This
man is a Roman citizen.' The commandant came to Paul. 'Tell me, are you a 27
Roman citizen?' he asked. 'Yes', said he. The commandant rejoined, 'It cost 28
me a large sum to acquire this citizenship.' Paul said, 'But it was mine by
birth.' Then those who were about to examine him withdrew hastily, and the 29
commandant himself was alarmed when he realized that Paul was a Roman
citizen and that he had put him in irons.

The following day, wishing to be quite sure what charge the Jews were bringing 30
against Paul, he released him and ordered the chief priests and the entire
Council to assemble. He then took Paul down and stood him before them.
[*No charge was established, because Paul's deliberate introduction of the
question of resurrection caused uproar between the Pharisees on the Sanhedrin
who accepted it and the Sadducees who did not.*] The dissension was mount- 23:10
ing, and the commandant was afraid that Paul would be torn in pieces, so he
ordered the troops to go down, pull him out of the crowd, and bring him into
the barracks.

The following night the Lord appeared to him and said, 'Keep up your 11
courage; you have affirmed the truth about me in Jerusalem, and you must
do the same in Rome.' [*A plot was then made to ambush and kill Paul. It
was betrayed to the commandant who sent Paul, for his own safety, to
Caesarea with a large armed guard and a letter to Felix the procurator.*]

Five days later the High Priest Ananias came down, accompanied by some 24:1
of the elders and an advocate named Tertullus, and they laid an information
against Paul before the Governor. When the prisoner was called, Tertullus 2
opened the case.

'Your Excellency,' he said, 'we owe it to you that we enjoy unbroken
peace. It is due to your provident care that, in all kinds of ways and in all
sorts of places, improvements are being made for the good of this province.
We welcome this, sir, most gratefully. And now, not to take up too much of 3,4
your time, I crave your indulgence for a brief statement of our case. We have 5
found this man to be a perfect pest, a fomenter of discord among the Jews
all over the world, a ringleader of the sect of the Nazarenes. He even made an 6
attempt to profane the temple; and then we arrested him. If you will examine 8
him yourself you can ascertain from him the truth of all the charges we bring.'
The Jews supported the attack, alleging that the facts were as he stated. 9

Then the Governor motioned to Paul to speak, and he began his reply: 10
'Knowing as I do that for many years you have administered justice in this
province, I make my defence with confidence. You can ascertain the facts for 11

yourself. It is not more than twelve days since I went up to Jerusalem on a
12 pilgrimage. They did not find me arguing with anyone, or collecting a crowd,
13 either in the temple or in the synagogues or up and down the city; and they
14 cannot make good the charges they bring against me. But this much I will
admit: I am a follower of the new way (the "sect" they speak of), and it is
in that manner that I worship the God of our fathers; for I believe all that is
15 written in the Law and the prophets, and in reliance on God I hold the hope,
which my accusers too accept, that there is to be a resurrection of good and
wicked alike. [*Since the charge of causing a disturbance is not being*
20 *pressed*—] it is for these persons here present to say what crime they discovered
21 when I was brought before the Council, apart from this one open assertion
which I made as I stood there: "The true issue in my trial before you today
is the resurrection of the dead."'

22   Then Felix, who happened to be well informed about the Christian movement, adjourned the hearing. 'When Lysias the commanding officer comes
23 down', he said, 'I will go into your case.' He gave orders to the centurion to
keep Paul under open arrest and not to prevent any of his friends from making
26 themselves useful to him. . . . At the same time he had hopes of a bribe from
Paul; and for this reason he sent for him very often and talked with him.
27 When two years had passed, Felix was succeeded by Porcius Festus. Wishing
to curry favour with the Jews, Felix left Paul in custody.

25:1   Three days after taking up his appointment Festus went up from Caesarea to
2 Jerusalem, where the chief priests and the Jewish leaders brought before him
3 the case against Paul. They asked Festus to favour them against him, and
pressed for him to be brought up to Jerusalem, for they were planning an
4 ambush to kill him on the way. Festus, however, replied, 'Paul is in safe
5 custody at Caesarea, and I shall be leaving Jerusalem shortly myself; so let
your leading men come down with me, and if there is anything wrong, let
them prosecute him.'

6   After spending eight or ten days at most in Jerusalem, he went down to
Caesarea, and next day he took his seat in court and ordered Paul to be
7 brought up. When he appeared, the Jews who had come down from Jerusalem
stood round bringing many grave charges, which they were unable to prove.
8 Paul's plea was: 'I have committed no offence, either against the Jewish law,
9 or against the temple, or against the Emperor.' Festus, anxious to ingratiate
himself with the Jews, turned to Paul and asked, 'Are you willing to go up to
10 Jerusalem and stand trial on these charges before me there?' But Paul said,
'I am now standing before the Emperor's tribunal, and that is where I must be
tried. Against the Jews I have committed no offence, as you very well know.
11 If I am guilty of any capital crime, I do not ask to escape the death penalty;
but if there is no substance in the charges which these men bring against me,
it is not open to anyone to hand me over as a sop to them. I appeal to Caesar!'

Then Festus, after conferring with his advisers, replied, 'You have appealed to 12
Caesar: to Caesar you shall go.'
[*Agrippa II then visited Festus, who told him about the case of Paul, which
to him was completely baffling, and readily granted the king's request to hear
the prisoner himself. The hearing ended in a certain amount of acrimony but
in agreement that Paul could be released but for his appeal to the Emperor.
The last two chapters relate Paul's adventurous voyage to Italy and his reception by the Church already established in Rome, and the work ends—*]
He stayed there two full years at his own expense, with a welcome for all who 28:30
came to him, proclaiming the kingdom of God and teaching the facts about 31
the Lord Jesus Christ quite openly and without hindrance.

tr. New English Bible (Oxford-Cambridge 1961, 1970)

O47 Excerpts from Paul's letter to the Church in Rome

*This church was well established some years before Paul's arrival there to
stand trial.*

(a)
What, then, are we to say about Abraham, our ancestor in the natural line? If
Abraham was justified by anything he had done, then he has a ground for pride.
But he has no such ground before God; for what does Scripture say? 'Abraham put
his faith in God, and that faith was counted to him as righteousness.' Now if a man
does a piece of work, his wages are not 'counted' as a favour; they are paid as debt.
But if without any work to his credit he simply puts his faith in him who acquits
the guilty, then his faith is indeed 'counted as righteousness'. . . . Consider: we say,
'Abraham's faith was counted as righteousness'; in what circumstances was it so
counted? Was he circumcised at the time, or not? He was not yet circumcised, but
uncircumcised; and he later received the symbolic rite of circumcision as the hall-
mark of the righteousness which faith had given him when he was still uncircumcised.
Consequently, he is the father of all who have faith when uncircumcised, so that
righteousness is 'counted' to them; and at the same time he is the father of such of
the circumcised as do not rely upon their circumcision alone, but also walk in the
footprints of the faith which our father Abraham had while he was yet uncircumcised.

(b)
For at the very time when we were still powerless, then Christ died for the wicked.
Even for a just man one of us would hardly die, though perhaps for a good man one
might actually brave death; but Christ died for us while we were yet sinners, and
that is God's own proof of his love towards us. And so, since we have now been
justified by Christ's sacrificial death, we shall all the more certainly be saved through

697

him from final retribution. For if, when we were God's enemies, we were reconciled to him through the death of his Son, much more, now that we are reconciled, shall we be saved by his life.

Romans 4. 1-5 9-12; 5. 6-10
tr. New English Bible (Oxford–Cambridge 1961, 1970)

O48 Two excerpts from a letter to the Church at Corinth

(a)

In giving you these injunctions I [Paul] must mention a practice which I cannot commend: your meetings tend to do more harm than good. To begin with, I am told that when you meet as a congregation you fall into sharply divided groups; and I believe there is some truth in it (for dissensions are necessary if only to show which of your members are sound). The result is that when you meet as a congregation, it is impossible for you to eat the Lord's Supper, because each of you is in such a hurry to eat his own, and while one goes hungry another has too much to drink. Have you no homes of your own to eat and drink in? Or are you so contemptuous of the church of God that you shame its poorer members? What am I to say? Can I commend you? On this point, certainly not!

For the tradition which I handed on to you came to me from the Lord himself: that the Lord Jesus, on the night of his arrest, took bread and, after giving thanks to God, broke it and said: 'This is my body, which is for you; do this as a memorial of me.' In the same way, he took the cup after supper, and said: 'This cup is the new covenant sealed by my blood. Whenever you drink it, do this as a memorial of me.' For every time you eat this bread and drink the cup, you proclaim the death of the Lord, until he comes.

It follows that anyone who eats the bread or drinks the cup of the Lord unworthily will be guilty of desecrating the body and blood of the Lord. A man must test himself before eating his share of the bread and drinking from the cup. For he who eats and drinks eats and drinks judgement on himself if he does not discern the Body. . . .

Therefore, my brothers, when you meet for a meal, wait for one another. If you are hungry, eat at home, so that in meeting together you may not fall under judgement. The other matters I will arrange when I come.

(b)

First and foremost, I [Paul] handed on to you the facts which had been imparted to me: that Christ died for our sins, in accordance with the scriptures; that he was buried; that he was raised to life on the third day, according to the scriptures; and that he appeared to Cephas [Peter], and afterwards to the Twelve.

1 *Corinthians* 11. 17–34; 15. 3–5
tr. New English Bible (Oxford–Cambridge 1961, 1970)

049 Pliny on the Christians

In AD 112 as governor of Bithynia Pliny had to hold an investigation into the sect known as Christians, in order to establish whether their practices were criminal or not. Some renegades gave him the following account of their weekly gatherings. (The word translated 'oath' is sacramentum, *and Pliny may well have misunderstood its Christian connotation as 'sacrament'.)*

They had met regularly before dawn on a fixed day to chant verses alternately amongst themselves in honour of Christ as if to a god, and also to bind themselves by oath, not for any criminal purpose, but to abstain from theft, robbery, and adultery, to commit no breach of trust and not to deny a deposit when called upon to restore it. After this ceremony it had been their custom to disperse and reassemble later to take food of an ordinary, harmless kind.

Pliny *Letters* 10. 96. 7
tr. Betty Radice (Penguin 1963)

INDEX OF SOURCES

ANONYMOUS
  On Famous Men 22.1.1–3   393
APPIAN
  Civil Wars
    1.1.7   420
    3.2.11   24–5
    3.6.40   31
    3.7.43   31
    3.7.47–8   32
    3.12.87–8   32–3
    4.1.2   33–4
    4.1.3   420–1
    4.2.8–11   35–6
    4.4.4   160
    5.2.12–15   41–2
    5.7.64–5   40
    5.8.67–8   43–4
    5.10.92–4   44–5
    5.13.132   45–6
  Preface to the Roman Wars 5   620
APULEIUS
  The Golden Ass (Metamorphoses)
    11.9–11; 16–17   394–5
AUGUSTUS
  Res Gestae   3–10
AULUS GELLIUS
  Attic Nights 2.24.13–14   170
AURELIUS VICTOR
  The Caesars 1.4   70
CAESAR
  Gallic War
    1.1   550
    1.18.3–9   552
    1.30   552–3
    4.1–4   563–5
    5.11   591
    5.12–14   595–6
    5.20–3   591–2
    6.11;13;15   550–1
    6.13   598–9
    6.21–4   565–6
CATO
  On Agriculture
    (extracts)   414–15
    1.1   414
CICERO
  Against Verres
    2.5.48.127;4.59.132   406
  Brutus 89–91   400–2
  De Divinatione 2.33.70   387–8
  De Finibus 1.18–20   375

De Natura Deorum
  1.43–4   376
  1.105–7   376–7
De Officiis
  1.4b; 5–7   312–13
  1.8–10   313–14
  1.36   384–5
  1.51–2   321–2
  1.150–1   413–14
  1.153–5   315–16
  1.157–60   320–1
  2.2–3;5   311
  2.7–8   314–15
  2.30–1   316–17
  2.55–7   317–18
  2.59–60   318–19
  2.73–4;78   319–20
  3   322–49
Laws
  1.5–7   402–3
  2.8.19ff.   385
  2.14.36   163
Letter to his brother Quintus 2.10.3   374
Letters to Atticus
  4.16.7   593
  4.18.5   593
  5.21.7   391
  14.5   26
  14.6   27
  14.10   27
  14.12   27
  15.2   27
  16.8   27
  16.9   28
  16.11   28
  16.11.4;6   309–10
  16.14.1;3   310
Letters to Friends
  7.1   426
  11.20   29
To M. Brutus
  1.3   28
  1.17   28
Philippics
  3.6.15   29
  5.16–17   29–30
  13.11.24–5   30
Pro Archia Poeta 10.23   402
Pro Sestio
  104   308
  139   307–8

[Q. CICERO]
A Short Guide to Electioneering 2–3
  308–9
COLUMELLA
On Agriculture 1.6–9; 3.3   417–18
CORNELIUS NEPOS
Atticus 20   194
CRINAGORAS
(*Greek Anthology* 16.61)   105
DIO CASSIUS
Roman History
  38.12   306
  45.3.2   25
  49.38.2   599
  49.43 1–4   426
  51.21.2–5   50
  51.22.1–3   193–4
  53.1.5   51
  53.2.4   389–90
  53.11–16.4,16.6–17.1   52–5
  53.13.2–3   179
  53.21.1–22.1   108
  53.22.2   209
  53.22.5   600
  53.25.2   600
  53.27.2–3   198–9
  53.32   57
  54.1–4   59–61
  54.8.4   143
  54.10   61–2
  54.16.1–2   179
  54.16.3–5   177–8
  54.20.4–6   570–1
  54.21   555–6
  54.24   199–200
  54.25.1;5–6   571
  54.32–3   572–3
  54.36.2–4   573
  55.2.5–6   179
  55.6.1–3   573–4
  56.10   180
  56.18–19   578–80
  56.28.2–3   111
  56.46.1–47.1   91
  57.1–4   497–9
  57.7–8.4;9;13.6   505–7
  58.2.4–5   95–6
  58.5.1–2   518–19
  58.6.2–5;7.4–12.4   520–4
  59.25.1–3   603
  60.8.1–3   410
  60.19.1–21.5   603–5
  60.22.1–23.6   605–6
  62.2.1–4;7.1–3   616
  63.1.2–5.4   411–12
DIODORUS SICULUS
Historical Library
  1.8.1–9   377–8

  5.13.1–2   424–5
DIONYSIUS OF HALICARNASSUS
Roman Antiquities
  4.24.4–6   171–2
  4.62   391–2
EUTROPIUS
Breviarium
  7.13.2–3   608
  8.5   70
FRONTINUS
The Water Supply of Rome 100, 104,
    106, 108, 125, 127, 129   144–7
GAIUS
Institutes
  1.13;18–20;28–9;36–41   172–4
  1.32c   409–10
  1.42–6   175
  1.145   183–4
  1.194   184
  2.111   186
  2.144   184
  2.206–8   184
  2.225–7   185
  2.239   175
  2.286   186
  3.42–54   181–3
HORACE
The Centennial Hymn   155–7
Epistles
  1.13   250–1
  2.1.156–67;245–59   251–2
Epodes 9   49
Odes
  1.1   252–3
  1.4   253–4
  1.5   254
  1.9   255
  1.14   255–6
  1.27   256–7
  1.35.29–30   600
  1.37   257–8
  2.1   258–9
  2.7   260
  2.11   382–3
  2.15   260–1; 421
  2.16   261–2
  2.18   422
  3.5   263–4
  3.6   388–9
  3.9   264–5
  3.29   265–7
  3.30   267
  4.4   267–9
  4.5   86–8
  4.7   270
Satires 1.6.45–88   249–50
INSCRIPTIONS
  CIL 1².32 Marius   189

INSCRIPTIONS: *CIL* (*cont.*)

1².581 Letter of the consuls concerning
   Bacchic associations   392–3

3.6286–8;6843 Sepulchral inscriptions
         118

3.14147 The first prefect of Egypt 126

4.202;429;787;581; 1904 Election
   notices   427–8

5.7231 Client states   123

6.457 The Volcanal   201

6.826 Dedicatory inscriptions   448

6.912 The Lupercal   201

6.920 Relating to the conquest 607–8

6.930 Law on Vespasian's *imperium*
       58–9

6.1244 Augustus repairs the aqueducts
       147

6.2305 An agricultural calendar 418–9

6.32323 lines 50–63 Two decrees of
   the Senate on the Secular Games
       151–2

6.32323 lines 64–end Record of the
   Secular Games   152–5

10.817 Ministri Fortunae Augustae
       442

10.846 Rebuilding of the Temple of
   Isis   442

10.908 Ministri Augusti   442

12.4333 Religious honours to Augustus
       164–6

13.596 Gallic wealth   562

13.1036 Gaul under Tiberius 558–9

13.1042–5 Augustus' re-organization
   of Gaul   555

13.1048 Funerary inscription 556–7

13.1668 Senators from Gaul 542–3

13.4481 Gaul under Tiberius 557–8

14.2112 A burial society 440–1

14.85 Aqueducts   448

CRAI 1910 Egyptian mines   127

Ehrenberg and Jones

II The Calendars   16–20

   The Fasti   11–16

   303 Letter to Mylasa   138

Frova, A., *Rendiconti dell'Istituto Lombardo* Cl.di Lettere etc.
   95(1961) 419–34

Inscription of Pontius Pilate   641

IGRR 4.33 Treaty with Mytilene   133

4.1031b Letter to Cnidos 134–5

4.1756 lines 6–27 Resolution on the
   coming of age of Gaius Caesar
       99–100

ILS 81 Dedicatory inscriptions   447

84 Public works   142

92,99 Dedicatory inscriptions   447

102 Public works   143

103 Dedicatory inscription   447

139,140 Resolutions of the town
   council of Pisa on the deaths of
   Augustus' grandsons   101–3

217 Inscription relating to the conquest   608

886, 932, 938 Senatorial careers under
   Augustus   115–16

1314 Equestrian careers under Augustus
       117

2237–8 Sepulchral inscriptions   118

2683, 2698, 2700 Equestrian careers
   under Augustus   116–17

3090 Dedicatory inscriptions   447

5828 Public works   143

6579 Honours from the city of Veii
   to a freedman of Augustus   441

8784 Honours to Augustus' family
       167–8

9370, 9371 Public works   142

ILTG 217, 331 *Gallia* Suppl. 17 (1963)
   Gaul under Tiberius   557–8

357 *Gallia* Suppl. 17 The rule of
   Claudius   561–2

IRT 319 Dedication of the Augustan
   market at Lepcis Magna   131–2

324a Dedications to Augustus   166

I SYR 3.1 (1950) no. 718 Grant of
   privileges to the Admiral Seleucos
       135–8

L'Année épigraphique 1928 no. 2 The
   mausoleum of Augustus   198

Mnemosyne 47 (1919) W. Vollgraff
   Agrippa's letter to the Gerusia of
   Argos   133–4

OGIS 458 Letter of the proconsul and
   decrees of the provincial assembly
   of Asia   139–40

532 Paphlagonian oath of allegiance
       140–1

598 The Balustrade inscription   630

659 Dedications to Augustus   166

Pleket, H.W., *The Greek Inscriptions in
   the 'Rijksmuseum van Oudheden'
   at Leiden* no. 57 A Decree of 27 BC
       132

RIC Claudius 9   607

SEG 9.8 The Cyrene Edicts 128–31

SIG 781 Religious administration 166–7

785 Letter of a Proconsul to Chios
       134

797 An oath of allegiance   530

JOSEPHUS

Antiquitates Judaicae

15.187–95   621

15.267–79   627–8

15.331–41   625–6

15.410–16   629–30

16.136–40   626

JOSEPHUS *Antiquitates Judaicae (cont.)*

16.162–5	398–9
16.286–90	630–1
16.352–5	631
17.41–2	632
17.188–91	633
17.200–8	633–4
17.304–14	634–5
17.339–44	635–6
18.1–10;23	639–40
18.36–8	637
18.55–9	641
18.85–95	643–4
18.101–5	638–9
18.106–8	636
18.113–25	637–8
18.240–5	648–9
19.212–67	536–9
19.292–4; 297; 299	649
19.326–7	650
19.328;330–1	649–50
19.335–42	650–1
19.343–52	651–2
19.360–6	652
20.6–16	652–3
20.97–8	654
20.105–36	654–6
20.162–4	657
20.167–71	657–8
20.197–203	658
20.208–10; 215	659
20.252–7	659–60

Bellum Judaicum

1.422–7	626–7
1.648–58	632–3
2.175–7	642
2.253–5	656–7
3.1.2(4)	609
5.161–81	622–3
5.190–226	628–9
5.238–45	622
7.5.122–56	429–30
7.280–301	623–5

JUSTINIAN

Digest

1.17 (from Ulpian *On the Edict* 15)	
	127
1.19.1–2 (Ulpian)	614–15
4.4.37	180

Institutes

4.18.2–3	176–7
4.18.8–11	175–6

JUVENAL

Satires

3.59–67	397
6.512–58	395–7
10.56–81	524–5

LIVY

Ab Urbe Condita

1.19.1–3	202
3.20.5	388
4.20.7	194–5
5.51.4–10;52;54.7	383–4
7.25.8–9	169

LUCRETIUS

De Rerum Natura

1.1–57;62–115;127–45	350–2
1.146–66;215–31;250–97;311–69; 483–510	352–5
2.1–52	356
2.216–93	357–8
3.1–86	362–3
3.425–44;459–75;558–94	363–4
3.830–42;862–911;1024–8; 1042–end	364–7
4.1–25	358–9
4.29–97	359–60
4.353–86;426–31;436–42; 462–8; 478–510	360–2
5.146–80;195–234;1161–1217;1226– 40	367–9
5.783–836;855–77;925–1027;1091– 1160	369–74

MACROBIUS

Saturnalia

1.24	225
2.4	73–6

MARTIAL

Spectacula 1.2	451

NEW TESTAMENT

Matthew 5 The Sermon on the Mount

	660–4
Luke 3–13; 15; 18–20; 22–4	664–81
John 18–19	681–2
Acts of the Apostles (excerpts)	682–97
I Corinthians 11.17–34;15.3–5	698–9
Romans 4.1–5;9–12;5.6–10	697–8

NICOLAUS OF DAMASCUS

Life of Augustus 18	24

OROSIUS

Historiae adversum Paganos 6.22.1;7.3.7	
	[202

OVID

Amores

1.1	282–3
1.2	284–5
1.4	285–7
1.5	287–8
1.11	288–90
1.13	290–1
2.5	291–3
2.7	293–4
2.10	295–6
3.2	296–8

OVID *Amores* (*cont.*)
    3.11 — 298–9
    3.14 — 300–1
  Ars Amatoria
    1.35–52 — 279
    1.67–162 — 279
    1.177–84 — 100–1
    2.273–86 — 282
    2.359–72 — 282
    3.121–8 — 169–70
  Fasti
    1.709–22 — 200–1
    2.127–44 — 88
    2.639–62 — 162
    3.419–28 — 89
    4.905–42 — 157–8
    4.951–4 — 203
    5.147–59 — 204
    5.419–44 — 158–9
    5.549–98 — 192–3
    6.637–49 — 204
  From Pontus 2.1.19–48 — 106
  Metamorphoses 15.745–879 — 274–8
  Tristia
    2.353–70 — 274
    4.10 — 270–4
[OVID]
  Consolation to Livia 67–74 — 99
PANEGYRIC OF CONSTANTIUS CAESAR
  11.2–4 — 595
PAPYRI
  Berlin Papyrus no. 628 (*FIRA* 1.56) Edict of Octavian on the privileges of veterans — 115
  British Museum Papyrus no. 1912 Letter to the Alexandrians — 539–41
  Ehrenberg and Jones no. 366 P. Colon, inv. nr. 4701 — 94
  Papyri Osloenses (Academy of Science and Letters of Oslo 1925–31) — 119
  Wilcken *Chrestomathie* 112 — 167
  Yale Classical Studies 7 (1940) The Feriale Duranum — 159
PETRONIUS
  Satyricon 83 — 211
PHILO
  Legatio ad Gaium
    143–51 — 69–70
    155–8 — 398
    207–60 — 644–7
    276;321–2;330–3 — 647–8
    299–305 — 642–3
    349–67 — 530–1
PHAEDRUS 4.16 — 96
PLINY
  Natural History
    2.18.19 — 390
    3.136–8 — 124

    4.96–100 — 567
    7.147–50 — 68
    11.54.143 — 73
    12.41.84 — 407
    14.1.5–6 — 177
    18.21 — 410
    19.1.3–4 — 409
    31.10 — 212
    33.54 — 607
    33.148–9 — 169
    34.13 — 199
    34.18 — 210
    34.62 — 512–13
    35.4–6;12–13 — 208–9
    35.17–18 — 206
    35.26–8 — 204–5
    35.91 — 193
    35.116–17 — 205–6
    35.118 — 205–6
    35.120 — 451
    35.125 — 205
    36.13 — 207
    36.28 — 206–7
    36.33 — 211
    36.35–6 — 207
    36.38 — 199
    36.102 — 190
    36.121–2 — 448–9
    36.189 — 210
    36.196 — 207–8
    37.8 — 211–12
    37.11 — 210
PLINY THE YOUNGER
  Epistles
    2.17 — 423
    3.9 — 412–13
    4.19 — 423–4
    10.33–4;92–3 — 439–40
    10.96.7 — 699
PLUTARCH
  Antony
    16–17 — 25–6
    21–2 — 34
    26 — 39
    54–5 — 46–7
    58 — 47–8
  Cato the Elder 22–23b — 399–400
  Cicero
    45.4–46.4 — 36
    49 — 37
  Lucullus 39.1–41.2 — 406–7
  Pompey 42; 50.5 — 189
  Moralia 508A–B — 104
  On the Disuse of Oracles — 599
POLYBIUS
  Histories 6.56 — 386–7
POMPONIUS MELA
  De Chorographia 3.6.49 — 597

PROPERTIUS
Elegies
1.21	380
1.22	379
2.7	178–9
2.15.41–9	380
2.27.1–8	601
2.31	195
3.4	380–1
3.9.48–end	381
4.6	196–8
4.10.27–37	380

ST. AUGUSTINE
City of God 4.32	385–6

ST. JEROME
Chronicle	374–5

SCHOLIAST TO JUVENAL
6.158	99

SENECA
Apocolocyntosis 3
Apocolocyntosis 3	562
12.3	610

Moral Epistles
7.3–5	428–30
47	444–5

On Anger
2.5.5	141
3.23.4–8	76–7
3.40.1–4	77

On Benefits
1.15.5	70
3.27.1–4	80
6.32.1–4	98

On Mercy
1.9.1–1.11.2	71–3
1.10.1	111
1.15.3–1.16.1	77–8
1.24.1	444

To Marcia On Consolation
4.1	96–7
15.2	93

SENECA THE ELDER
Suasoriae and *Controversiae* (extracts)
	404–5

SIBYLLINE ORACLES 3.367–80   39–40
See also under Zosimus

STRABO
Geography
2.5.8	601
3.2.5	148
3.2.6	408–9
3.4.20	124
4.1.1–4	553–4
4.3.2	555
4.5.1–2	596
4.5.3	601–2
4.192	207
4.6.6	122
5.236	190–1

6.4.2	70
12.8.14;16	409
17.1.7	148
17.1.12–13	125–6
17.3.24–5	119–20

SUETONIUS
Augustus
1–2; 3–4	22–3
8	23–4
12–13;15	38
19	79–80
20–1	113–14
22	51
24–5	112–13
27	58
28	56
28–30	187–9
29	191
31	149–50
31	195–6
31.5	563
33–4	168–9
35–40	108–11
40.3	170–1
43	190
45	81
46	121
47–8	120–1
49	114
50	212
52	81
56	191
57–8	78–9
63–5	92
71	104–5
72.1–2	203
75–6	81
76	105
85–6; 89	83
90–2	162–3
93	390
99.1	91
100–1	89–90

Claudius
2–4	533–5
6–7	535
10	535–6
17.1–3	606
18–19	425
21	427
21.6; 24.3	606
25.2	443
28–9	545–6
41	433–4

Gaius
13–17; 19; 22	528–9
20	560–1
23.2	97

39	561	4.9	209
44.2	602	4.20	431–2
46.1	602–3	4.32–3	489–90
56; 58–60	532–3	4.34	432–3
Julius Caesar		4.37–8	513–14
24	553	4.57–9; 67	519–20
25.2	593–4	4.71	97
44	189	5.1–2	95
47	594	6.13.1–2	425
56.7	83	6.45–51	525–7
83	23	11.23–5	542–5
88	164	11.25–7	546–7
Nero		12.22–3	411
18	618	12.23	607
31	450–1	12.31–3	611–12
Tiberius		12.34	594
7	427	12.35–8	612–13
7–13	491–3	12.40	613–14
21	493–4	12.66–9	547–8
23	94	13.42	434
63	433	14.31	614
68	494–5	14.31	615–16
73; 75–6	527	14.33	617
Vespasian 4.1–2	609	14.38–9	617–18
[SUETONIUS]		14.42–5	443–4
Life of Horace	247–8	15.38–41	449–50
Life of Virgil	213–17	15.42	451
TACITUS		16.19–end	434–9
Agricola		*Dialogue on Oratory* 30–2	405–6
11–13	597–8	*Germania*	
14	609–10	1–2	568–9
15.2–3	615	28–30	569–70
21	619	*Histories*	
42	430	3.45	618–9
Annals		4.53	452
1–10	62–7	TIBULLUS	
1.11–13	496–7	*Poems* 2.1.1–26	161
1.33–49	500–5	[TIBULLUS]	
1.49–51	580–1	3.7.147–50	600
1.55–7	581–3	ULPIAN IN JUSTINIAN	
1.60–3	583–4	*Digest* 1.19.1–2	614–15
1.64–9	585–7	ULPIAN	
1.72–6	507–9	*Epitome*	
2.3–4	141–2	1.10–15	174
2.5–9	587–9	13–14	180–1
2.24	602	16.1–3	185–6
2.25–6	589–90	29.3–7	183
2.27–31	509–10	*On the Edict* 15 see Justinian *Digest* 1.17	
2.32	430–1	VALERIUS MAXIMUS	
2.50	511	*Preface*	164
2.87	512	7.7.3	185
3.24	98	VARRO	
3.40–3; 45–6	559–60	*On Landed Estates*	
3.49–51	511–12	1.1.4–6	160–1
3.53–4	407–8	(extracts)	415–17
3.65	490	VELLEIUS PATERCULUS	
3.72	200	*Historiae Romanae*	
4.1–15	514–18	2.39	408

VELLEIUS PATERCULUS
Historiae Romanae (cont.)
2.45.1–3 — 306–7
2.81.3 — 203
2.84–7 — 48
2.89 — 50
2.93 — 93
2.104.3–106 — 574–5
2.117–20 — 576–8
2.124.2–125 — 495–6
2.127.3–128.4 — 518

VIRGIL
Aeneid
1.257–96 — 221–2
6 — 225–47
8.626–731 — 222–5
Eclogues
1 — 84–6
4 — 217–19
Georgics
1.24–35 — 219
1.489–514 — 220
2.165–76 — 382
3.40–8 — 220

VITRUVIUS
On Architecture
Preface — 453–4
1.1.1–11 — 454–6

1.2.1–9 — 457–8
1.3.1–2 — 459
1.5.1–5 — 459
1.6.1;3;6–8 — 460–2
1.7.1 — 462
2.1.1–5 — 462–3
2.3.1–4 — 463–4
2.4.1–3 — 464–5
2.6.1–6 — 465–6
2.7.1–5 — 467–8
2.8.1–2;7–9;16–18;20 — 468–70
5.1.1–10 — 470–2
5.3.3–5 — 472–3
5.9.1–3;5;7–9 — 472–4
5.10.1–5 — 474–5
5.12.1–4;5–7 — 475–7
6.3.1–9;11 — 477–9
6.5.1–3 — 479–80
6.8.1–5;8–10 — 480–2
7.3.1–8 — 482–4
7.4.4–5 — 484
7.5.1–4 — 484–5
7.6.1 — 485–6
7.9.1–4 — 486
8.6.1–10 — 487–8
9.1–3 — 403–4

ZOSIMUS
2.6 (Sibylline Oracle in) — 150–1